FINANCIAL INSTITUTION MANAGEMENT

Text and Cases

Third Edition

Fred C. Yeager
Neil E. Seitz

St. Louis University

Prentice-Hall International, Inc.

18 FEB 1994

To Helen, Mary Colleen, Tim,
Tom, and Margie
To Bente, Laura, and Kirsten

This edition may be sold only in those countries to which
it is consigned by Prentice-Hall International. It is not to
be re-exported and it is not for sale in the U.S.A., Mexico,
or Canada.

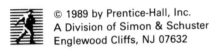 © 1989 by Prentice-Hall, Inc.
A Division of Simon & Schuster
Englewood Cliffs, NJ 07632

All rights reserved. No part of this book may be
reproduced, in any form or by any means,
without permission in writing from the publisher.

Printed in the United States of America

10 9 8 7 6 5 4 3 2 1

1671347

ISBN 0-13-317686-X

Prentice-Hall International (UK) Limited, *London*
Prentice-Hall of Australia Pty. Limited, *Sydney*
Prentice-Hall Canada Inc., *Toronto*
Prentice-Hall Hispanoamericana, S.A., *Mexico*
Prentice-Hall of India Private Limited, *New Delhi*
Prentice-Hall of Japan, Inc., *Tokyo*
Simon & Schuster Asia Pte. Ltd., *Singapore*
Editora Prentice-Hall do Brasil, Ltda., *Rio de Janeiro*
Prentice-Hall, Inc., *Englewood Cliffs, New Jersey*

Contents
In Brief

Contents

Preface

This book differs from most other financial institutions texts in that it focuses on the management, rather than the description, of financial institutions. The concentration is primarily on policy questions, such as the appropriate loan portfolio mix, rather than operating questions such as credit evaluation for a specific loan. The focus was chosen for several reasons:

1. Many students taking financial institution courses will eventually seek employment with financial institutions. Thus, a knowledge of the principles guiding their management will help the students to understand the management policies and decisions, and eventually participate in them.
2. Deregulation of the financial sector has proceeded in the 1980s with roller-coaster speed, producing new challenges and new opportunities for financial institution managers. Legislative and financial market developments in the 1980s have resulted in heightened needs for financial skills. Technological developments, together with an increased tendency on the part of the financial sector to test the limit of profitable activities permitted by regulators, has resulted in large scale interstate and interindustry competition. Managerial tools and techniques such as *gap management, financial futures hedging,* and *option pricing models* have suddenly come of age. Never has the need for financial management skills within our nations financial institutions been greater.

A book which describes without a theme leaves its reader with many facts, but with no conceptual framework within which the facts may be analyzed. Thus this book has a theme—management. Because this book focuses on policy level management decisions, it should help to provide readers with a framework for understanding the material presented. Even the nonmanagement reader will better understand why particular institutions choose to do what they do and, therefore, why the financial system behaves as it does.

This book differs from other financial institution texts in that it includes both text and cases. The cases serve a number of purposes. First, they reinforce learning by illustrating that techniques discussed in the text have application to real-life problems. Second, they have proved useful in helping the student transfer learning from sterile problems to complex real-life situations. Finally, the cases contain substantial information about the financial institutions involved, thereby helping the students to further understand their operations. Some cases were contributed by professors and practitioners around the country who took the time to describe actual decision problems being faced by specific financial institutions.

This third edition of our book reflects updating to recognize changes in our understanding of the financial environment since the second edition was completed. We have benefited immensely from reviews and from comments by college and university professors from across the nation. As a result of this input and our own experiences and observations of a financial sector in evolution, this current edition contains a number of improvements:

1. This edition contains four additional chapters. One new chapter is on the analysis of financial statements of financial intermediaries and another new chapter is on financial futures and options. The other two added chapters are in an expanded four-chapter section on asset and liability management, liquidity and interest rate risk management, capital adequacy, required returns, and loan management.
2. Eight of the cases are new, and two are updated.
3. Cases have been moved to the ends of chapters, so that it is easier to assign a case that focuses on concepts introduced in a particular chapter.
4. This edition contains approximately 100 more end-of-chapter problems than the second edition.

We are indebted to the many academic colleagues who have generously shared their comments and suggestions. At the risk of omitting important contributions, we would like to thank Elliott L. Attamian, Thomas A. Bankston, Mark Bayless, Mona J. Gardner, B. E. Lee, Edward D. Marting, Patricia Matthews, and Walter D. Rogers. Our colleagues in practice have also been extremely helpful in conversations too numerous to mention. We would like to give special thanks to Michael Summers, Robert Schmitz, Craig Chandler, Tom Harvey, John Ream, John Nelke, Charles Papp, and George Poland, all of Citicorp. We would also like to thank Harry Gallagher and Tom Robinson of the Missouri Financial Services Association. Considerable assistance was also provided by many members of the staff of the Federal Reserve Bank of St. Louis. We recognize, of course, the contributions of colleagues who have written many of the cases contained within this book. Each of these contributors is identified on the first page of the respective cases.

This book is designed for a one-semester course at the graduate or advanced undergraduate level. Prior coursework in elementary economics and statistics would be helpful in understanding the material; the student who has not had these courses, however, should still be able to understand the text and analyze the cases (with a little more work).

Our debts start with our parents and end with our students whose candid comments on earlier drafts and on this edition helped to improve the final product.

We, and the users of this book, owe a particular debt of gratitude to the case writers who took the time to research real business problems and share their information with us. We stand ready to receive and to consider for publication additional cases that users of this book might wish to offer as well as to share new cases and other materials that we at Saint Louis University have developed. Finally, we thank our colleagues at Saint Louis University for their support during this task. Bouquets will be shared with those who have helped in the development of this book. Brickbats should be aimed only at us.

Fred C. Yeager
Neil E. Seitz

1

Functions and Goals of
Financial Institutions

In a primitive economy each household produces what it needs and fulfillment of personal economic needs does not depend on communication between households. A complex modern economy, with its specialized producers and diverse products, requires a vast amount of communication between units. The great depression of the 1930s bears stark witness to what happens when this communication system fails or is inadequate. The smooth functioning of a modern economy is dependent on intermediaries who act as go-betweens, matching the needs of one unit with the output of another. Financial institutions are among the vital intermediaries contributing to economic health.

Financial intermediation is the process of acquiring surplus funds from economic units—business firms, governmental agencies, and individuals—for the purpose of making available such funds to other economic units. Financial institutions exist for the primary purpose of facilitating the intermediation process. Examples of financial intermediaries in the United States include:

Commercial banks
Savings and loan associations
Mutual savings banks
Commercial and consumer finance companies
Leasing companies
Insurance companies
Credit unions
Pension funds

Certain governmental units
Trust companies
Securities dealers
Investment trusts

Financial intermediaries play an important role in society. They issue *securities*[1] to those from whom funds have been entrusted and accept securities from those to whom funds have been loaned or invested. Thus, intermediaries act as a buffer between suppliers and users of funds, gathering funds in quantities and on terms that are acceptable to savers, and supplying funds in quantities and on terms agreeable to the users. Intermediaries assist society in innumerable ways. Savers and investors benefit in that funds may be left in relative safety, and to the extent securities issued by intermediaries bear interest or dividends, the value of entrusted funds is enhanced. Ultimate users of funds benefit by the availability of capital to purchase homes, acquire durable consumer goods, and finance business operations. In performing these functions, financial intermediaries contribute to a high standard of living for those countries with well-developed financial systems.

THE CIRCULAR FLOW OF INCOME AND MONEY

The Circular Flow of Income

Consider a society without financial intermediaries and with no medium of exchange—a barter economy. Income earned in a barter economy is paid in the form of goods and services. Income may be earned by the recipient for any of three basic reasons. First, income may be received in return for the provision of labor. Second, income may be received if the recipient allows others to use his physical property—land, tools, or other goods. Third, income may accumulate if the recipient has provided services of an entrepreneurial nature. The circular flow of income for a barter economy is described in figure 1-1.

Those who are willing and able to do so provide physical property, labor, and entrepreneurial ability for production purposes (figure 1-1). Note that either products or services may be produced. In return for contributions of property, labor, and entrepreneurial skills, providers of these resource inputs are entitled to receive production outputs, i.e., income. Thus for each round of resource provision, production output is generated.

It should be pointed out that with the barter economy of figure 1-1, all transactions are "real": For each unit of resource input, a certain amount of production output is immediately acquired. Thus, "financial assets" such as cash, demand deposits, savings accounts, accounts receivable, and other securities are nonexistent. It should also be noted that the barter economy will not function smoothly unless there is a complete willingness on the part of providers of resources to accept production outputs regard-

---

[1]Any form of evidence representing debt or equity is a security.

Figure 1-1:   Circular flow of income for a barter economy.

less of the nature of such outputs. For the circular flow to continue, resource providers must continue to happily swap their services for the output that streams forth.

A complex economy simply could not operate smoothly based on barter. First, the model assumes a comprehensive and complete *coincidence of wants*. In other words, it assumes that producers of products and services will require the precise quantities of physical property, labor, and entrepreneurial ability offered, and these resources will be utilized without delay. The model further assumes that production of goods and services is instantaneous and that suppliers of resources will happily accept all production generated, without regard to the nature of such production, as compensation for the use of their resources. In practice, the automobile worker may be reluctant to accept a transmission as compensation for his week's labor. A complex industrial society could not function in this way.

The barter model does, however, illustrate the important point that resources must be supplied if production is to occur. In addition, the model illustrates the fact that in one way or another, those who provide the resources are compensated, ultimately at least, in terms of goods and services.

We will now begin to expand the model with the introduction of money into the circular flow.

The Circular Flow and Money

An important distinction exists between figure 1-2 and figure 1-1. The providers of resources are now receiving money as compensation. Note that money so received may now be used to acquire goods and services that are produced as a result of resource provision.

Introduction of money into the circular flow means that "real" transactions (the direct exchange of resource inputs for production outputs) are not the only type of transactions that may occur. Since money exists, resource inputs, products, and services

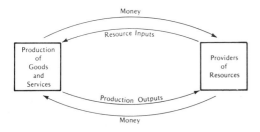

Figure 1-2:   Circular flow of income for a money economy.

may now be exchanged for money. Thus money is functioning as a *standard of value* and *a store of value*.[2] The value of resource inputs or production outputs is defined in terms of money and is stored in money. Since money is accepted in exchange for resources or production, the transactions may be defined as "monetary" transactions.

The introduction of money permits certain other changes to occur (figure 1-2). It is no longer necessary to have a comprehensive and complete coincidence of wants. Since money may now be received in exchange for resources or products, the seller has converted these resources or products into "generalized purchasing power." No longer must the seller accept only those goods or services which the buyer can offer. The introduction of money has made transactions easier and more realistic, thereby making the circular flow function more conveniently. Money can be exchanged for goods and services instead of goods and services being exchanged for other goods and services.

Discussion of the circular flow, to this point, implicitly assumed that all who were willing and able to provide resources would do so. In exchange for resources provided, production outputs in the form of products and services would be provided. As we shall see, a major advantage of money is that it provides a means of accommodating providers of resources who may wish to defer their spending of at least some income derived from their provision of land, labor, and physical property.

To the extent that income recipients defer spending, producers of products and services will find that demand for their production declines and that lower levels of production are thus appropriate. Fewer resources are required to produce the smaller levels of production, and resource unemployment will logically develop; national income will decline. On the other hand, certain of those who defer from spending may find a coincidence of wants with producers or other resource providers who wish to engage in current spending in excess of current income. Should such a coincidence of wants develop, those with excess spending power will find others with whom such spending power may be invested. It is reasonable, of course, that lenders or investors should expect to be compensated for providing such spending power. To the extent that comprehensive and complete coincidence of wants exists between those with excess spending power and those to whom such spending power is transferred, a happy situation prevails. All who are able and wish to refrain from current spending may do so, and receive compensation to boot. Production and national income may continue at high levels.

But once again our model must be reevaluated. The assumption of comprehensive and complete coincidence of wants on the part of those with surplus funds and those who wish to acquire such spending power is unrealistic. For example, the borrower may need funds for a long time to build a factory while the lender is willing to commit funds for only a short time. The need is evident for financial intermediaries whose purpose is to gather funds in quantities and on terms acceptable to savers and investors, as well as to supply funds in quantities and on terms agreeable to users.

[2]Anything that functions as money is money, and money functions as a medium of exchange, a standard of value, and a store of value.

THE ROLE OF FINANCIAL INTERMEDIARIES

In order to analyze the full benefits of intermediation, it is useful to identify those services that are performed as a result of the intermediation process. These services may be summarized in terms of the following four categories:

Asset transmutation
Liquidity
Income reallocation over time
Transactions aid

Asset Transmutation[3]

Financial institutions hold assets in the form of promises to pay, with terms set to meet the needs of the borrowers. They finance these assets by accepting funds from savers on terms set to meet savers' needs. Thus they convert the borrower's obligation to an asset with a maturity to meet the needs of the saver. This process is known as asset transmutation.

Economic units in need of funds issue *primary securities*. Primary securities include all securities issued by nonfinancial economic units for the purpose of acquiring funds. Examples of primary securities are mortgages executed by individuals or businesses, stocks and bonds sold by corporations, and U.S. Treasury bills. In each case, primary securities were issued for the purpose of acquiring funds. They may be either debt or equity (part ownership). The form and maturity of the security is selected to satisfy the needs of the unit acquiring funds.

The securities issued by those acquiring funds may differ in size, maturity, and form from the needs of those with funds. Financial intermediaries solve this problem by acquiring primary securities with funds they have raised through the issuance of *secondary securities*. Secondary securities include all securities issued by financial intermediaries. Examples of secondary securities include demand and time deposits, credit union shares, and cash value of life insurance policies. For selected examples of primary and secondary securities held by economic units as a result of the intermediation process, see table 1-1. Households are net suppliers of funds and nonfinancial businesses are net users; yet some individual households are net users and some individual businesses are net suppliers.

By issuing secondary securities in exchange for financial resources of surplus units and in turn exchanging these resources for primary securities issued by deficit units, intermediaries transmute or convert the securities of business units to obligations desired by households. Through this transmutation process, intermediaries both facilitate the production of real wealth and provide households with the financial rewards associated with such production. In the process, intermediaries generate economies of scale by combining funds received at times and in quantities suitable for producer units.

[3]The term is that of Basil J. Moore, *An Introduction to the Theory of Finance* (New York: The Free Press, 1968).

Table 1-1:

Selected Primary and Secondary Securities

NET DEFICIT ECONOMIC UNITS (Nonfinancial Business Units)		FINANCIAL INTERMEDIARIES		NET SURPLUS ECONOMIC UNITS (Households)	
Assets	Liabilities	Assets	Liabilities	Assets	Liabilities
Secondary securities	Primary securities	Primary securities	Secondary securities	Secondary securities	Primary securities
		Loans	Demand deposits		
		Leases	Time deposits		
		Investments	Life ins. reserves		
		Stocks	Pension fund reserves		
		Bonds	Investment co. shares		
		Mortgages			

Intermediaries also provide economies of scale by generating knowledge of various alternative investments in producer units, thereby reducing or eliminating the need for individual surplus units to generate independent knowledge of such alternatives. And because intermediaries acquire funds from large numbers of surplus units and provide funds to large numbers of deficit units, substantial diversity is effected and the risk of financial loss is reduced.

Liquidity

Liquidity refers to the ability to generate cash quickly. Some secondary securities are acquired by businesses and households primarily for purposes of liquidity. Secondary securities such as savings and time deposits provide a high degree of liquidity, safety, and income as well. Such instruments are essential to the normal conduct of financial affairs. To the extent economic units acquire secondary securities for purposes of liquidity, intermediaries perform an important financial service.

Income Reallocation Over Time

Many individuals earn satisfactory incomes today, but realize they will eventually face retirement and curtailment of income. They wish to reallocate some of their present income to that future time. They could do this by storing goods, but the acquisition of secondary securities such as savings accounts, pension fund reserves, or investment company share is more convenient and provides the opportunity to earn a return on these savings. On the other hand, many young individuals and households issue primary securities, thereby allocating future income to the present or making it possible to pay for assets as they are being used. Primary examples of this latter activity are loans for home or automobile purchases.

Business units are also influenced to acquire or issue securities for purposes of income reallocation over time. However, net income reallocation effects on the part of business units differ from those of households in terms of the direction in which income is shifted. Households consist of individuals, many of whom are engaged in the systematic acquisition of secondary securities for no other reason than the expectation of reduced earnings beyond retirement. Business units as a group have no automatic expectation of reduced future earnings. Life expectancy of the typical business corporation is perpetual, and future income under normal economic circumstances is not expected to decline.

Business units also differ from the household sector in terms of the purpose for which primary securities are issued. Households normally issue primary securities so as to acquire goods or services for consumption, and not for the purpose of generating future income. Business units normally issue primary securities for the purpose of investment in assets which are expected to increase future income. Secondary securities acquired by business units are obtained primarily to facilitate transactions and to provide liquidity. In contrast to households, business units seek to issue large quantities of primary securities relative to secondary securities acquired, thereby shifting future income to the present.

Transactions

Certain secondary securities issued by financial intermediaries represent *money* and constitute a part of the payments system. Traditional demand deposits and certain other deposit accounts function as money and are acquired by households and business units to facilitate the exchange of goods and services. To the extent that economic units acquire secondary securities in order to accommodate day-to-day settlement of financial claims, intermediaries serve a major purpose in facilitating monetary transactions.

AN OVERVIEW OF THE SAVINGS MARKET

The supply and use of savings in the economy of the United States is summarized in figure 1-3. As shown in the figure, households are net surplus units with holdings of financial assets exceeding their financial liabilities. The financial institutions, as intermediaries, have financial assets approximately equal to their financial liabilities. Business and government are the primary users of these funds.

It is evident that households hold substantial quantities of both primary and secondary securities. The proportion of each type varies over time due to a complex variety of economic and social conditions. Fluctuations in the market value of corporate stock, for example, have a heavy impact on year-to-year changes in household wealth.

Another major factor influencing household decisions in their acquisition of debt securities is the relative interest rates prevailing for different classes of securities. For example, generally high market interest rates prevailed for many securities in the early 1980s. However, maximum rates for most secondary securities were fixed by law,[4] and such maximums or ceilings were less than rates generally available on primary securities. Many households switched from secondary to primary securities during these years.[5]

An overview of the savings market can be completed with a brief look at the relative roles of the various financial institutions. Commercial banks continue to be the most important financial institutions (figure 1-4). However, banks can be considered a mature industry with a growth rate limited by the growth rate of the economy. Credit unions and pension funds in particular have shown rapid growth in the last decade. This growth is a result of a favorable cost structure for the credit unions and new laws requiring a higher level of funding of pension fund liabilities. Each of these institutions is examined in depth in later chapters.

GOALS OF FINANCIAL INSTITUTIONS

Students and the general public are sometimes confused as to the objectives that guide financial institution managers in their decision making. Because they hold other people's money, financial institutions are probably more closely regulated than any other industry. Furthermore, statements by many critics of the industry seem to reflect the view that

[4]These regulations were phased out over a number of years due to the Financial Institution Deregulation and Monetary Control Act of 1980.

[5]This process of shifting from secondary securities issued by financial intermediaries to primary securities is known as *disintermediation*.

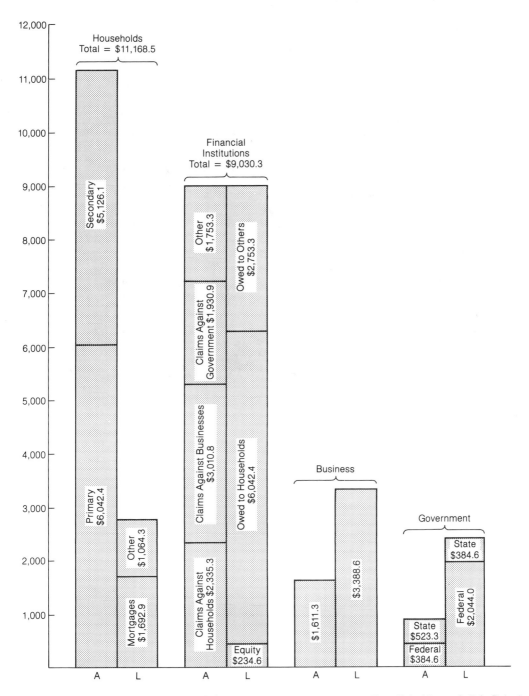

Figure 1-3: Financial assets, liabilities, and equity by sector, in $ billions, January 1, 1987. (From *Federal Reserve Bulletin,* Federal Reserve *Flow of Funds accounts, Treasury Bulletin,* and other estimates.)

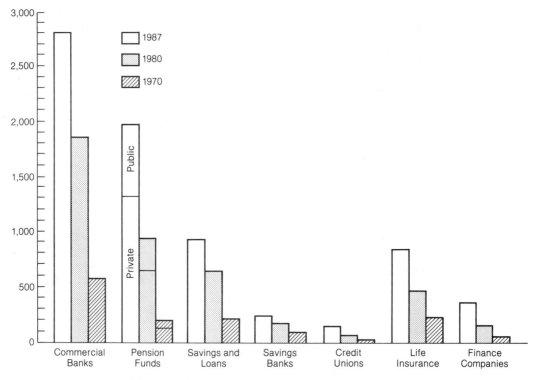

Figure 1-4:   Total assets by type of financial institution (in $ billions).

financial institutions are quasi-government agencies that should be guided primarily by social objectives. Interviews with executives of financial institutions yield an entirely different viewpoint. For the most part, financial institutions are owned by shareholders who invest their own funds as equity in the institution. They make these investments for the purpose of earning a profit. The management is selected by the board of directors elected by these shareholders. Because they answer to a board of directors elected by shareholders interested in making a profit, financial institution managers view making a profit as their first obligation.

The conflict between the profit objective and the desire to provide services may not be as great as first appears. Like any business, a financial institution can only earn a profit by providing a desired service to some group capable of paying for that service. Thus serving the needs of some sector of society is a prerequisite to profitability. In addition, there are many things that managers, as good citizens, can do to help the community without hurting profits. The conflict arises when a critic feels financial institutions should take actions that would decrease profitability but would contribute to some objective deemed desirable by that particular critic. Legislation has occasionally been passed leading institutions to take actions that would not be taken in simple pursuit of profit. However, general government policy suggests that, within the limits of the law, financial institutions should behave like other businesses in pursuing their profit objective.

The primary focus of this book is on the management of financial institutions as opposed to a pure description of what they do. A primary interest in profitability and efficient usage of funds is assumed. The book begins with a discussion of the environment in which institutions operate and some general principles used in managerial decision making in financial institutions. Attention is then turned to the principles followed in the management of each major type of financial institution. Because of the growing importance of international finance, the final chapter deals with a discussion and analysis of a number of important issues associated with financial institution management on an international scale.

SUMMARY

Financial intermediation is the process of acquiring surplus funds from economic units and of making such funds available to other economic units. In a complex industrial society, a great deal of financial communication and funds transfer is necessary if the economy is to function efficiently. Although surplus units invest directly in securities issued by deficit units, financial institutions accommodate the majority of funds transfers by acting as a buffer between suppliers and users of funds, issuing secondary securities to funds suppliers and accepting primary securities from funds users. In their role as financial middlemen, intermediaries facilitate the circular flow of income. Services relating to transactions, liquidity, income reallocation, and asset transmutation are among the most important of those performed by intermediaries in facilitating this flow.

Growth and development of any society and the well-being of its citizens is clearly influenced by the efficiency and capability of its financial institutions.

QUESTIONS

1-1.   How does financial intermediation facilitate the circular flow of income?

1-2.   Distinguish between primary and secondary securities.

1-3.   In what way or ways does the motivation of households differ from that of business firms in their desire to hold secondary securities?

1-4.   What might be the possible economic consequences of disintermediation? Comment on possible means by which the problem of disintermediation may be resolved.

1-5.   Comment on benefits of financial intermediation in terms of the income reallocation and asset transmutation effects.

SELECTED REFERENCES

AMERICAN BANKERS ASSOCIATION. *Statistical Information on the Financial Services Industry,* Washington, D.C. (published annually).

BOARD OF GOVERNORS OF THE FEDERAL RESERVE SYSTEM. *Annual Statistical Digest,* Washington, D.C.

BOARD OF GOVERNORS OF THE FEDERAL RESERVE SYSTEM. *Federal Reserve Bulletin,* Washington D.C. (published monthly)

COOPER, KERRY, AND FRASER, DONALD R. *Banking Deregulation and the New Competition in Financial Services* (Cambridge, Massachusetts: Ballinger Publishing Company, 1984).

HEMPEL, GEORGE, II, AND YAWITZ, JESS B. *Financial Management of Financial Institutions* (Englewood Cliffs, N.J.: Prentice-Hall, Inc.) 1977.

WRISTON, WALTER B. *You Can't Tell the Players With a Scorecard* (New York: Public Affairs Department, Citicorp) 1981.

CASE 1

IDENTIFYING FINANCIAL INSTITUTIONS

In general, the financial statements of financial institutions are similar in appearance to those of nonfinancial, manufacturing, and retailing corporations. Both types of business firms have assets, liabilities, revenues, expenses, etc. However, for the most part the assets and liabilities differ significantly. For many financial institutions, the primary profit-making assets are financial in nature and are normally held in the form of loans and/or investment securities. Revenue is generated from these assets in the form of interest income. The financing of these assets (liabilities) often occurs in part in the form of customer deposits, some of which may receive interest (or dividends). The interest expense from these deposits and other liabilities often is a major expense item to the firm.

All financial institutions are playing an increasingly important role in the ever-changing economy. In addition, regulation is slowly reducing the distinctive differences between financial institutions. For example, commercial banks may now pay interest on demand deposits, savings and loan associations may issue drafts similar to checks, credit unions may issue credit cards, etc. Although the expectation of a further reduction in distinguishable characteristics is not unreasonable, some differences remain.

Table 1 summarizes financial assets and liabilities for commercial banks and is taken from the *Flow of Funds Accounts* published by the Board of Governors of the Federal Reserve System.

This case was originally prepared by Professor Ernest W. Swift of Georgia State University. With Professor Swift's permission, it has been modified and updated by the text authors.

Table 1

Commercial Banking Financial Assets and Liabilities
December 31, 1986
(in $ billions)

TRANSACTIONS CATEGORY	ASSETS	LIABILITIES
Total assets	$2,573.8	
Total liabilities		$2,530.8
Checkable deposits and currency	2.5	559.0
Small time and savings deposits		965.7
Large time deposits		334.8
Federal funds and security RPs		210.3
Corporate equities	.1	
Credit market instruments	2,181.7	178.1
U.S. Treasury securities	205.1	
Federal agency securities	114.8	
Tax-exempt securities	211.3	
Corporate and foreign bonds	38.5	75.0
Mortgages	500.2	
Consumer credit	315.4	
Bank loans	729.1	
Open market paper	10.4	103.1
Other loans	56.8	
Security credit	36.2	
Miscellaneous	353.4	282.6

Table 2 is also taken from the Federal Reserve's *Flow of Funds Accounts* and contains data for the twelve financial institutions listed below in alphabetical order. See if you can match the balance sheet data in Table 2 with the appropriate financial institution. Figure 1-4 in chapter one may provide some help in the matching process.

1. Credit unions
2. Finance companies
3. Life insurance companies
4. Money market funds
5. Mutual savings banks
6. Open-end investment companies
7. Other insurance companies
8. Private pension funds
9. Real estate investment trusts
10. Savings and loan associations
11. Security brokers and dealers
12. State and local government retirement funds.

Table 2

Private Nonbank Financial Institutions Financial Assets and Liabilities
December 31, 1986
(in $ billions)

Transaction category	TOTAL		A		B		C		D		E		Line
	Assets	Liabilities	Assets	Liabilities	Assets	Liabilities	Assets	Liabilities	Assets	Liabilities	Assets	Liabilities	
1 Total assets	5,307.5	—	1,158.5	—	239.2	—	164.9	—	880.9	—	827.9	—	1
2 Total liabilities	—	5,123.9	—	1,130.9	—	218.4	—	164.9	—	853.6	—	827.9	2
3 Checkable deposits	58.0	75.1	13.7	40.7	6.4	21.3	4.7	13.1	5.4	—	4.5	—	3
4 Small time and savings deposits	13.0	994.5	—	717.4	—	139.7	13.0	137.4	—	—	—	—	4
5 Money market fund shares	—	228.4	—	—	—	—	—	—	—	—	—	—	5
6 Large time deposits	99.2	161.3	9.5	128.4	.1	31.2	14.4	1.7	35.8	—	35.8	—	6
7 Federal funds and security RPs	108.4	55.5	34.6	55.5	6.3	—	9.9	—	—	—	—	—	7
8 Deposit abroad	22.2	—	—	—	—	—	—	—	—	—	—	—	8
9 Life insurance reserves	—	256.5	—	—	—	—	—	—	—	256.5	—	—	9
10 Pension fund reserves	—	1,800.7	—	—	—	—	—	—	—	471.0	—	827.9	10
11 Corporate equities	949.5	485.1	—	—	7.0	—	—	—	89.1	—	437.4	—	11
12 Credit market instruments	3,671.0	447.3	968.5	146.6	205.3	—	112.2	—	719.0	—	272.9	—	12
13 U.S. Treasury securities	496.5	—	38.9	—	9.7	—	7.6	—	59.8	—	61.9	—	13
14 Federal agency securities	387.3	—	165.4	—	29.7	—	8.7	—	56.0	—	51.1	—	14
15 Tax-exempt securities	245.5	—	.9	—	2.2	—	—	—	11.0	—	—	—	15
16 Corporate and foreign bonds	680.5	117.8	665.7	12.0	16.1	—	11.3	—	312.1	—	122.9	—	16
17 Mortgages	1,081.1	2.7	50.1	—	118.9	—	84.6	—	190.9	—	4.8	—	17
18 Consumer credit	327.0	—	—	—	19.8	—	—	—	—	—	—	—	18
19 Bank loans	—	35.7	—	26.0	—	—	—	—	—	—	—	—	19
20 Open market paper	211.6	182.5	25.4	—	8.9	—	—	—	34.9	—	32.1	—	20
21 Other loans	241.5	108.6	22.2	108.6	—	—	—	—	54.3	—	—	—	21
22 Security credit	46.5	64.5	—	—	—	—	—	—	—	—	—	—	22
23 Trade credit	29.7	—	—	—	—	—	—	—	—	—	—	—	23
24 Taxes payable	—	1.5	—	*	—	—	—	—	—	.4	—	—	24
25 Miscellaneous	310.0	553.6	132.2	42.3	14.1	26.2	10.8	12.7	67.5	125.7	77.2	—	25

Transaction category	F Assets	F Liabilities	G Assets	G Liabilities	H Assets	H Liabilities	I Assets	I Liabilities	J Assets	J Liabilities	K Assets	K Liabilities	L Assets	L Liabilities	Line
1 Total assets	501.8	—	330.3	—	409.7	—	8.6	—	485.1	—	228.4	—	72.3	—	1
2 Total liabilities	—	501.8	—	230.0	—	411.0	—	6.7	—	485.1	—	228.4	—	65.4	2
3 Checkable deposits	2.5	—	3.6	—	7.0	—	—	—	6.5	—	*	—	3.7	—	3
4 Small time and savings deposits	—	—	—	—	—	—	—	—	—	—	—	228.4	—	—	4
5 Money market fund shares	—	—	—	—	—	—	—	—	—	—	—	—	—	—	5
6 Large time deposits	20.3	—	25.4	—	—	—	—	—	—	—	19.1	—	—	—	6
7 Federal funds and security RPs	—	—	—	—	—	—	—	—	—	—	32.2	—	—	—	7
8 Deposit abroad	—	—	—	—	—	—	—	—	—	—	22.2	—	—	—	8
9 Life insurance reserves	—	—	—	—	—	—	—	—	—	—	—	—	—	—	9
10 Pension fund reserves	—	501.8	—	—	—	—	—	—	—	—	—	—	—	—	10
11 Corporate equities	180.3	—	68.4	—	—	—	—	—	157.9	485.1	—	—	9.5	—	11
12 Credit market instruments	298.7	—	203.2	—	402.7	294.6	6.8	6.1	320.7	—	148.5	—	12.6	—	12
13 U.S. Treasury securities	98.3	—	43.2	—	—	—	—	—	135.0	—	43.2	—	-1.2	—	13
14 Federal agency securities	50.0	—	26.4	—	—	—	—	—	—	—	—	—	—	—	14
15 Tax exempt securities	.7	—	88.9	—	—	—	—	—	139.4	—	—	—	2.5	—	15
16 Corporate and foreign bonds	134.6	—	42.3	—	—	104.0	6.8	1.8	41.2	—	—	—	11.2	—	16
17 Mortgages	15.1	—	2.4	—	65.2	—	—	2.7	—	—	—	—	—	—	17
18 Consumer credit	—	—	—	—	172.5	—	—	—	—	—	—	—	—	—	18
19 Bank loans	—	—	—	—	—	9.0	—	.7	—	—	—	—	—	—	19
20 Open market paper	—	—	—	—	165.0	181.6	—	.9	—	—	105.3	—	—	—	20
21 Other loans	—	—	—	—	—	—	1.8	—	5.1	—	—	—	—	—	21
22 Security credit	—	—	—	—	—	—	—	—	—	—	—	—	46.5	64.5	22
23 Trade credit	—	—	29.7	.1	—	.1	—	—	—	—	—	—	—	—	23
24 Taxes payable	—	—	—	—	—	—	—	—	—	—	—	—	—	.8	24
25 Miscellaneous	—	—	—	229.9	—	116.3	—	.6	—	—	6.5	—	—	—	25

2

Financial Systems, the Federal Reserve, and Money Creation

A financial system can be described as a mechanism or framework in which economic exchange is accommodated. The college student who pays tuition with funds earned through a summer job is engaging in economic exchange. The householder who completes the weekly shopping trip after depositing the family paycheck is engaged in economic exchange, as is the office worker who systematically buys shares in a mutual fund in anticipation of a retirement nest egg.

Financial systems can be simple or complex. They can be free of regulation or heavily regulated. They can be technologically efficient or inefficient. In a modern society, the financial system plays a particularly important role in influencing the level of economic activity.

TYPES OF FINANCIAL SYSTEMS

Several basic types of financial systems can be identified. These include:

Direct barter
Indirect barter
Warehouse receipt systems
Reserve banking systems
Fiat systems
Electronic systems

Direct Barter

Direct barter was discussed in chapter 1 and is the most fundamental financial system. In a direct barter system, money does not exist, and economic resources (goods or services) are directly traded for other economic resources. Direct barter is an inefficient system because, in the absence of money, there must be a *coincidence of wants* for an exchange of goods or services to occur, e.g., the plumber must find a barber whose pipes need to be fixed. A complex economy could not function with a direct barter system.

Indirect Barter (Commodity Money)

A logical extension and improvement over a direct barter system is the use of one or more commodities as money. Throughout history, gold and silver have been the most widely used commodities for indirect barter; however, almost any commodity can be used. During the colonial period in American history, tobacco leaves were a commonly accepted medium of exchange and for a time served as the cornerstone of the domestic financial system. During World War II, cigarettes were widely used as the medium of exchange (money) by American soldiers held in prisoner of war (POW) camps. The major advantage of such indirect barter over direct barter is that a coincidence of wants is not a condition for trade. The value of goods and services are expressed instead in terms of the commodity. For example, one candy bar (contained in POW Red Cross rations) may have been worth two cigarettes, while one can of peaches may have "sold" for one cigarette.

Warehouse Receipt System

Although indirect barter—the use of commodity money—is an improvement over direct barter, storage and transportation of the commodity can be a problem. Efficiency of the system can be improved by simply storing the commodity in a warehouse provided for that purpose. Receipts issued by the warehouse owner or operator can then be exchanged for goods or services. For example, gold receipts from goldsmiths were widely used as a medium of exchange.

Fractional Reserve Banking System

In the warehouse receipt system discussed above, the warehouse owner or operator, if not restricted from doing so, might decide to function as a lender: by lending the commodity under his care, or more likely, by simply issuing warehouse receipts to borrowers who are expected to repay the loan with interest. In making such loans, the warehouse owner would be operating as a fractional reserve banker because the amount of warehouse receipts would exceed the amount of the commodity. Fractional reserve banking systems have been widely used, but they require careful regulation to avoid abuses such as excessive and risky lending. Typically, the government will specify the maximum ratio of reserves (commodity) to receipts (money).

Fiat Systems

Fiat systems exist when government issues nonconvertible paper notes and defines these notes as money. Typically, the notes are issued initially as payment for goods or services, e.g., payment to members of the military service. Acceptance of these notes within the state or community is typically enhanced by government declaration that the notes are *legal tender*. They *must* be accepted in payment of all debts, public and private. A fractional reserve banking system with fiat money requires financial intermediaries to hold fiat money (or its equivalent) equal to some specified portion of the outstanding deposit receipts it has issued. The United States financial system has evolved from direct and indirect barter, to warehouse receipts, and finally to fractional reserve banking combined with a fiat system. The receipts issued by banks are in the form of checking account and savings account deposit balances.

Electronic Systems

A financial system is useful because it facilitates resource transfer by functioning as the payment mechanism. The financial system is also useful in that it provides the framework within which individuals and institutions keep track of financial assets and liabilities. On payday, an employee might receive either cash or a paycheck for services rendered. Alternatively, computerized electronic impulses could simply reduce the employer's account and increase the employee's account at the local bank. In either case, payment is made and assets are transferred. In the first case, the transfer was accommodated through use of cash or check (a paper-based financial system). In the second case, the same result was achieved electronically. The financial system is evolving toward increased use of electronic funds transfers.

Full Faith and Credit

Figure 2-1 provides an overview of selected financial assets held within the financial system. The public held almost $1.7 trillion in savings and time deposits and $554 billion in demand and checkable deposits by 1987 (figure 2-1). Interestingly, most

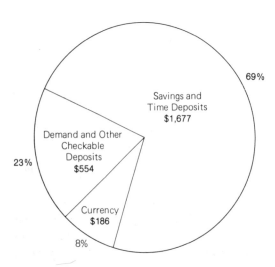

Figure 2-1: Currency, checking-type deposits, and savings held by the nonbank public in banks and thrift institutions. Data are approximate for early 1987 (in $ billions). (From *Federal Reserve Bulletin.*)

of these deposits are merely bookkeeping entries. Since only a small fraction of these accounts are backed up by currency in the financial system, banks and thrift institutions could not begin to repay depositors should large numbers of persons demand cash repayment at any given time. An indispensible ingredient in the financial system then, is the widespread belief on the part of the public that the financial system is sound. As long as this confidence in the system is maintained, the system will, in fact, be sound. The Federal Reserve System plays a key role in the maintenance of public confidence.

THE FEDERAL RESERVE SYSTEM

The Federal Reserve System was created by Congress in 1913 to address four major needs faced by the country:

1. *Payments system.* Federal Reserve banks act as banks for bankers. Payments between banks can be handled by additions and subtractions to their account balances with Federal Reserve banks.
2. *Unexpected withdrawal demand.* As banks for banks, Federal Reserve banks are expected to curtail bank runs arising from loss of confidence by loaning banks money to meet unexpected deposit withdrawal demand.
3. *Supervision and Examination.* To ensure sound banking practices, to increase public confidence, and to curtail bank runs, Federal Reserve banks play a major role in bank supervision and examination.
4. *Control of the money supply.* It is well recognized that too much money can cause inflation and too little money can cause unemployment. A major role of the Federal Reserve System is to regulate the flow of money and credit to promote economic stability and growth.

Over the years, the role of the Federal Reserve System has been expanded and today includes the direct provision of certain financial services to nonbank financial institutions.

STRUCTURE OF THE FEDERAL RESERVE SYSTEM

Board of Governors

The Federal Reserve System is under the control of a seven-member board of governors appointed by the President and confirmed by the Senate. Their staggered fourteen-year terms are designed to insulate them from political pressure. The chairman and vice-chairman are selected from this seven-person board by the President of the United States for four-year terms and may be redesignated. The operating structure of the system is summarized in figure 2-2.

Federal Open Market Committee

Day-to-day actions to control the money supply fall under the jurisdiction of the open market committee. Under the supervision of the open market committee is the buying and selling of securities for the Federal Reserve System's account, effectively

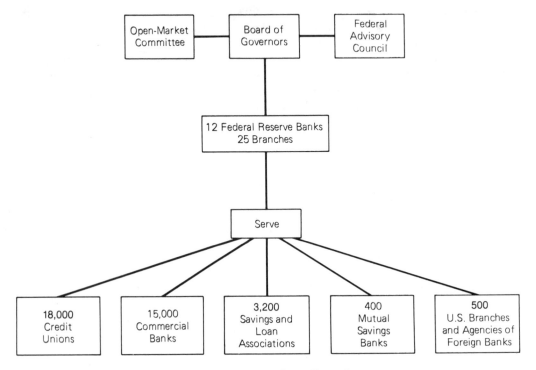

Figure 2-2:   Structure of the Federal Reserve System.

paying for securities by creating money. This activity, carried out by the trading desk of the Federal Reserve Bank of New York, is quite important to the economy. Its importance is discussed at length later in this chapter.

Federal Advisory Council

The Federal Advisory Council is composed of bankers and consists of twelve members, one from each of the Federal Reserve districts. Each of the twelve representatives is elected by directors of the Federal Reserve bank of the district which he represents. A major purpose of the advisory council is to advise the board of governors concerning current developments.

Federal Reserve Banks

When the Federal Reserve System was created in 1913, the United States was (in a financial sense) a group of economic sections rather than a cohesive union of states. There also existed in 1913 a fear of excessive concentration of the nation's financial resources in one geographic locale. Consequently, the Federal Reserve Act of 1913 divided the nation into twelve financial districts and provided that a Federal Reserve bank be located in the principal banking city of each district (figure 2-3).

Figure 2-3: The Federal Reserve System—boundaries of Federal Reserve districts and their branch territories. Note: Alaska and Hawaii are included in Federal Reserve District 12.

21

Each of the twelve Federal Reserve banks is a distinct corporation with its own board of directors. The district banks are viewed as *quasi*-private institutions in that each is owned by the member banks which purchase stock in the district Federal Reserve bank. Each Federal Reserve bank has nine directors, six of whom are elected by member banks. The remaining three directors—one of whom is designated as chairman and another as deputy chairman—are appointed by the board of governors. Although overall system policy is the responsibility of the board of governors, individual Federal Reserve Banks provide input into the policy setting process. In particular, Federal Reserve banks perform a number of functions designed to maintain day-to-day operations of the financial system.

FUNCTIONS OF THE FEDERAL RESERVE SYSTEM

The major current purposes and functions of the Federal Reserve System can be summarized as follows:

Maintenance of an effective monetary policy
Supervision and examination
Financial system services
Fiscal agent for the government

Maintenance of an Effective Monetary Policy

Monetary conditions favorable to high levels of employment, economic growth, price stability, and a sound international balance of payments are objectives shared by all modern economies. Although elusive, such goals are none the less pursued by governments through appropriate fiscal and monetary policies. In general, *monetary policy* refers to the extent to which the volume of money is allowed to grow within the economy over some designated time period.

Supervision and Examination

Financial institutions—particularly depository institutions such as commercial banks and thrifts—are closely regulated and supervised so as to maintain a high degree of public trust and confidence in the financial system. A major responsibility of the Federal Reserve System is to examine the books and operations of certain banks and other institutions on an ongoing basis. In this regard, the Federal Reserve System examines all bank holding companies,[1] Edge Act corporations,[2] and certain commercial banks.

The body examining a particular bank depends on certain choices made by that

[1] A bank holding company is simply a corporation which owns one or more banks, and possibly other subsidiary (nonbanking) corporations.
[2] An Edge Act corporation is a subsidiary of a bank and is engaged in foreign activities (e.g., loans to foreign governments).

Table 2-1

Examination Responsibility for Commercial Banks, Bank Holding Companies, and Edge Act Corporations

FINANCIAL INSTITUTION	EXAMINATION RESPONSIBILITY
State-chartered commercial bank, Federal Reserve System member	Federal Reserve System or state*
State-chartered commercial bank, Federal Reserve System nonmember	FDIC
Nationally chartered bank	Comptroller of the Currency
Edge Act corporation	Federal Reserve System
Bank holding companies	Federal Reserve System

*Frequently on a rotating basis, with the state examining one year and the Federal Reserve System examining the next.

bank. First, the bank faces a choice of whether to be chartered by the state or federal government. If the bank is chartered by the federal government, it must be a member bank of the Federal Reserve System[3] and its deposits must be insured by the Federal Deposit Insurance Corporation (FDIC). If the bank has a state charter, it may choose to become a member of the Federal Reserve System, in which case it must also have its deposits insured by the FDIC. If a state bank does not choose to join the Federal Reserve System, it still has the option of having its deposits insured by the FDIC.[4] The assignment of examining duties in light of these choices is spelled out in table 2-1.

Financial System Services[5]

The Federal Reserve System provides a variety of services to the financial community. Prior to passage of the *Monetary Control Act of 1980*,[6] these services were provided only to member banks. With passage of the Monetary Control Act, these same services were made more widely available and are now offered to all depository institutions represented in figure 2-2. Services may be categorized as follows:

Coin and currency
Check clearing and funds transfer
Loans
Fiscal agent for the government

[3]A member bank is a bank that owns stock of the Federal Reserve bank in its particular district. A member bank is *not* one of the twelve district banks of the system.

[4]As a practical matter, as a condition for awarding a bank charter, the various states require that FDIC insurance be obtained by the proposed bank.

[5]Discussion in this section relies heavily on materials provided by the Federal Reserve Bank of St. Louis. The authors are grateful to the Federal Reserve Bank of St. Louis for permission to summarize and/or reproduce these materials.

[6]For a detailed discussion of the Monetary Control Act of 1980, see chapter 3.

Coin and Currency   One responsibility of the Federal Reserve System is to meet the cash requirements of our nation's economy. On behalf of the U.S. Treasury, the Federal Reserve System circulates coin and currency using depository institutions as a channel of distribution. The cash flows through these institutions for use by the public.

Federal Reserve banks send out new and reusable coin and Federal Reserve notes (currency) to depository institutions and accept for credit, redemption, exchange, or replacement currency and coin that are unfit for further circulation. The volume of currency held by the public is subject to seasonal influences. The volume tends to increase, for example, over the Christmas holidays. The amount of currency held by the public has increased over the years and stood at $186 billion by 1987 (figure 2-1).

Check Clearing and Funds Transfer   A major function of the Federal Reserve System involves check clearing and funds transfer. While the mechanics of this process will be discussed in the next section, noted here is the fact that the U.S. payments system is largely a paper-based system with more than forty billion checks processed each year. Checks are simply negotiable orders directing that funds be taken from the account of the drawer (payor) and be given to the drawee (payee).

The paper checks are cleared through the financial system when the payor's account is reduced and the payee's account is increased by the amount of the check. If the drawer and drawee maintain accounts at the same bank and the check is originally presented to that bank, the transaction may be handled by the bank itself, and there is no need for the Federal Reserve System to participate in the transfer. Similarly, if the drawer's bank and the drawee's bank are located in the same town (or trading region), the checks could be cleared through a local clearing house established by community financial institutions for that purpose. Yet, many of these are cleared through the Federal Reserve System.[7] Large numbers of checks, however, are drawn on financial institutions which are geographically remote from the institution into which the check is first deposited. Through its nationwide system of Federal Reserve banks, the Federal Reserve System has the capability to provide for nationwide check clearing.

By the early 1970s, it was believed that funds transfer could be accommodated more efficiently through electronic debit and credit entries between financial institutions for customer accounts. Thus, the financial community established *automated clearing houses* (ACHs) in the early 1970s to clear items locally. By the mid-1980s, thirty-two ACHs were in operation in the United States, with all but one operated by Federal Reserve banks. These systems were eventually interconnected and were capable of transferring funds electronically, thus replacing large numbers of paper checks. Currently, the ACH services accommodate a large number of transactions, including payroll deposits, recurring government payments such as social security and veterans' payments, and other routine types of expenditures not only of government but of the private sector as well. The historical and expected growth in check volume and in the number of ACH items processed is illustrated in figure 2-4.

[7]Traditionally, checks were processed by the Federal Reserve System without charge. As a consequence of the Monetary Control Act of 1980, service charges were imposed on various services provided by the Federal Reserve System including check processing. Consequently, the volume of checks processed by the Federal Reserve System declined.

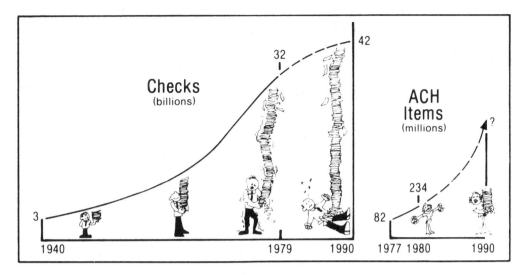

Figure 2-4: National volume trends. 1940–1990. (Source: Federal Reserve Bank of St. Louis.)

Loans   Traditionally, the Federal Reserve System has been a source of liquidity to member banks through its *discount window.* As a consequence of the Monetary Control Act of 1980, the discount window is now accessible by any depository institution, regardless of Federal Reserve membership, so long as the institution holds *transaction accounts* or *nonpersonal time deposits.*[8]

The principal purpose of the Federal Reserve discount window is to make loans to depository institutions so as to provide help for short-term liquidity needs. For example, an institution may experience an unexpected loss of deposits or the need to satisfy an unexpected loan demand in its trading area.

On the other hand, the discount window is not intended as a source of funds to assist financial institutions in maximizing profit. For example, it would be inappropriate for a depository financial institution to borrow from the Federal Reserve System and purchase securities for the purpose of investing in securities paying a higher interest rate than the discount rate.

Although the major purpose of the Federal Reserve discount window is to accommodate short-term liquidity needs (typically from one to a few days) extended credit may be provided for specific credit needs. For example, smaller institutions serving communities dependent upon farming or resort businesses may qualify for longer term credit under seasonal, or other extended-credit programs.

[8]Transaction accounts include demand deposits, negotiable order of withdrawal (NOW) accounts, automatic transfer service (ATS) accounts, share draft accounts, and accounts permitting telephone or similar transfers for payments to third parties. Nonpersonal time deposits are defined as time deposits which are transferable *or* as time deposits held by corporations or by other institutions.

Fiscal Agent for the Government   The Federal Reserve System performs a large number of financial services on behalf of the U.S. government. The process of collecting large sums in taxes and spending equally large sums requires substantial banking services. Each year the U.S. Treasury sells new and retires old securities valued in the billions of dollars. These sales and redemptions are administered by the Federal Reserve. The Federal Reserve, therefore, functions as a bank for financial institutions and as a bank for the United States government.

Monetary Operations of the Federal Reserve System

As previously noted, the Federal Reserve System issues currency, buys and sells U.S. government securities, and serves depository financial institutions by making loans and clearing payments between institutions. These activities are illustrated below with sample balance sheets. As the first sample balance sheet shows, the primary assets are loans to financial institutions and U.S. government securities. The primary liabilities are currency that has been issued and deposits received from financial institutions.

SIMPLIFIED COMPOSITE FEDERAL RESERVE BANK BALANCE SHEET
(in $ billions)

Loans to fin. inst.	$ 10	Currency	$100
U.S. government securities	140	Deposits from fin. inst.	50
Other assets	3	Equity	3
Total assets	$153	Total liabilities and net worth	$153

Suppose the Federal Reserve System wishes to expand the volume of loanable funds within the financial system. Such an expansion may be commenced through the purchase of government securities. The securities would likely be purchased directly from a financial institution; but if securities were purchased from an individual, the individual would deposit the check used for payment with a financial institution, achieving the same results. In this example, the Federal Reserve banks purchase $10 billion worth of U.S. government securities directly from commercial banks. The balance sheet below reflects the changes that occurred. The arrows highlight accounts that have changed. As can be seen, the Federal Reserve pays for these securities by crediting the selling commercial bank's deposit account. Notice that the Federal Reserve banks do not need money to purchase securities. The transaction merely involves a series of accounting entries.

FEDERAL RESERVE BANK BALANCE SHEET

Loans to fin. inst.	$ 10	Currency	$100
U.S. government securities	150←	Deposits from fin. inst.	60←
Other assets	3	Equity	3
Total assets	$163	Total liabilities and net worth	$163

The selling commercial bank has now replaced U.S. government securities with liquid funds in the form of a deposit with a Federal Reserve bank. Because financial institutions can settle accounts with each other by transferring ownership of deposits with the Federal Reserve, the commercial bank can view these Federal Reserve deposits as loanable funds. The commercial bank can take advantage of these new funds by making a loan, which is normally accomplished by increasing the borrower's transaction deposit balance. If the borrower then writes a check that is deposited elsewhere and is later presented by another bank for payment, the lending bank can use its Federal Reserve bank deposit to make payment. Thus, an increase in its Federal Reserve bank deposits represents funds that a bank can loan. The Federal Reserve System can increase or decrease the amount of loanable funds by purchasing or selling U.S. government securities.

Continuing with this example, we can observe the process of currency creation. Suppose commercial banks do decide to loan more money and some borrower requests cash. Suppose that the $10 billion Federal Reserve System's purchase of U.S. government securities eventually results in a demand for an additional $2 billion of currency. Since the cash is being withdrawn from commercial banks, these banks will request $2 billion in currency. The Federal Reserve banks forward the $2 billion in currency to the individual commercial banks, deducting the amounts from the commercial banks' deposit accounts. Thus, deposits from banks decrease by $2 billion and currency liability increases by $2 billion.

FEDERAL RESERVE BANK BALANCE SHEET
(in $ billions)

Loans to fin. inst.	$ 10	Currency	$102←
U.S. government securities	150	Deposits from fin. inst.	58←
Other assets	3	Equity	3
Total assets	$163	Total liabilities and net worth	$163

From the perspective of the Federal Reserve banks' accounts, currency in circulation and deposits from financial institutions are similar, interchangeable liabilities. Currency is simply physical evidence of a Federal Reserve bank liability. From the public's point of view, there is little difference between currency and a transactions account deposit since either can be used for payment and one can be readily exchanged for the other. The form in which money is held is based mainly on convenience factors.

A loan to a financial institution is also a matter of offsetting transactions. If commercial banks were to borrow $5 billion from Federal Reserve banks, the "loans to financial institutions" account would be increased by $5 billion and the deposits from financial institutions would be increased by $5 billion. Thus, Federal Reserve banks do not need a source of funds in order to make loans.

The final type of transaction involves clearing accounts between financial institutions. Financial institutions may pay each other by transferring ownership of part of their Federal Reserve bank deposit balances. A member bank receives a check written on another bank. The member bank deposits the check with the Federal Reserve bank, receiving credit to its deposit account for the amount of the check. This amount is then deducted from the balance sheet of the bank on which it was drawn. Of course, each commercial bank may deposit thousands of checks per day, with its deposit balance with the Federal Reserve bank reflecting the net effect of all checks.

The following example shows the accounts of a Federal Reserve bank and two member banks before and after a series of checks are cleared. In this example, Bank A deposits checks worth a total of $2 less than checks that are deposited by other banks and written against it. Bank B deposits checks worth $2 more than checks that are deposited against it.

The individual commercial banks show changes in deposit liabilities owed to their customers which offset changes in their accounts with the Federal Reserve bank. However, total deposit liabilities of commercial banks and Federal Reserve banks have not changed.

Most of the functions of the Federal Reserve System could be easily handled by other institutions. In many countries, currency is issued as an obligation of the treasury department of the government rather than by the central bank.

FEDERAL RESERVE BANK	BEFORE CHECKS ARE CLEARED	AFTER CHECKS ARE CLEARED
Total assets	$163	$163
Liabilities and equity		
Currency	$100	$100
Deposits from financial institutions		
Bank A	6	4←
Bank B	5	7←
All other financial institutions	49	49
Equity	3	3
	$163	$163
Bank A		
Currency	$ 3	$ 3
Deposits with the Fed	6	4←
U.S. gov. securities	70	70
Other assets	1	1
Total assets	$ 80	$ 78
Deposits	$ 70	$ 68←
Equity	10	10
	$ 80	$ 78
Bank B		
Currency	$ 2	$ 2
Deposits with the Fed	5	7←
U.S. gov. securities	60	60
Other assets	1	1
Total assets	$ 68	$ 70
Deposits	$ 60	$ 62←
Equity	8	8
Total liabilities	$ 68	$ 70

Checks can be cleared through clearing house associations. In fact, private clearing houses are used for stock and commodity trading as well as for a good deal of check processing. Deposit insurance, not Federal Reserve credit, brought an end to banking

Table 2-2:

Major Components of Money Stock Measures

M1	Private demand deposits at commercial banks plus balances in NOW accounts, share draft accounts, and other transaction accounts at financial institutions plus currency held by the nonbank public.
M2	M1 plus savings and small-denomination time deposit accounts, plus money market mutual fund shares.
M3	M2 plus large-denomination time deposits.
L	M3 plus other liquid assets such as commercial paper, U.S. Treasury bills, etc.

panics. There is, however, one function the Federal Reserve System is uniquely qualified to provide: The Federal Reserve System is the primary agency responsible for controlling the money supply.

CREATING AND CONTROLLING THE MONEY SUPPLY

Recall that a major purpose of the Federal Reserve System is to regulate the flow of money and credit in order to promote economic stability and growth. In the United States, as in many other countries, history has aptly demonstrated the severe economic consequences of overly restrictive or overly expansive rates of growth in the money supply.

In the United States we learned that loss of faith in the value of money[9] can lead to a collapse of the economic system, with a depression following. In other countries, we have seen that failure to control the supply of money can lead to revolution. If money were still primarily in the form of currency, the supply could be controlled by controlling the printing press. With most money being in the form of deposits in financial institutions, controlling the supply is a more complex problem. Various money stock measures are defined in table 2-2.

Our discussion will now center on the way money is created and controlled, and more specifically on ways in which the Federal Reserve and the financial system influence the narrow money supply, specifically M1. Recall that M1 is defined as currency and transaction accounts held by the nonbank public (table 2-2). We begin with some rather elementary accounting transactions.

Step 1: $100 in Currency Is Deposited in Centerre Bank

CHANGES IN CENTERRE BANK'S BALANCE SHEET

Currency	+$100	Demand deposits	+$100

In Step 1 above, $100 in currency, formerly owned by the nonbank public is now owned by Centerre Bank.[10] In return for the currency, the customer's demand deposit account was credited, and the customer now owns a $100 deposit. Note that the money supply did not change. Only the *composition* of the money supply changed in that the currency

[9]Checking account money in the 1930s and currency in some earlier crises.
[10]It is important to recall that only currency *outside* depository financial institutions counts as a part of the money supply.

Table 2-3:

Reserve Requirements for Financial Institutions 1987

NET TRANSACTION ACCOUNT BALANCES

$0-$36.7 million	3%
Over $36.7 million	12%

NONPERSONAL TIME DEPOSITS
By original maturity

Less than 1½ years	3%
1½ years or more	0

EUROCURRENCY LIABILITIES

All types	3%

Notes:

The amount of transaction accounts against which the 3 percent reserve requirement applies is increased annually in accordance with an index established by the Monetary Control Act of 1980.

Nonpersonal time deposits are time deposits which are transferable *or* as time deposits held by corporations or by other institutions.

component of M1 declined and the demand deposit component of M1 increased by exactly the same amount. It is useful to note at this point that while the Step 1 transaction involved a bank, the financial institution could just as easily have been a credit union, savings and loan, mutual savings bank, i.e., any institution offering transaction (check-type) accounts.

To continue our discussion of creating and controlling the money supply, it is useful at this point to note the importance of *reserve requirements*. All depository financial institutions are required to hold reserves in the form of cash or deposits with the Federal Reserve bank equal to some percentage of its deposit liabilities (table 2-3.)[11] To simplify the calculations, the *required reserve ratio* in our example is assumed to be 10 percent. Thus, $10 ($100 × 0.10) must be held by Centerre Bank either as currency in the vault or as a deposit with the Federal Reserve. The remaining $90 ($100 − $10) are *excess* reserves and may be loaned or otherwise invested. We note here that any single bank can loan *dollar for dollar of excess reserves*.

Step 2: Excess Reserves Are Loaned

*IMPACT ON CENTERRE BANK'S BALANCE
SHEET (CASH LOAN)*

Currency	$10	Demand deposits	$100
Loans	90		

[11]Prior to passage of the Monetary Control Act of 1980, only member banks held reserves with the Federal Reserve. Today, all depository financial institutions must hold reserves with the Federal Reserve.

In Step 2, Centerre Bank has loaned its excess reserves and in the process has created $90 in new money. To simplify our illustration, we will initially assume that loan customers borrowed $90 in cash. Since M1 is defined as currency and transaction accounts held by the nonbank public, and since no change occurred in demand deposits held by the public, it is clear that the money supply increased by $90 as a result of the bank loan. Suppose though that Centerre Bank had loaned the $90 by increasing the borrower's demand account (a common means of dispersing loan proceeds), rather than by dispersing cash. In that case, Centerre's balance sheet immediately after making the loan would have changed as follows:

IMPACT ON CENTERRE BANK'S BALANCE
SHEET
(DEMAND DEPOSIT CREDIT)

Currency	$100	Demand deposits	$190
Loans	90		

It is recognized, however, that in a short time the borrower would likely spend the loan proceeds by drawing checks against his demands deposit. If we assume that these $90 in loan proceeds are spent and that the recipients of these spent funds deposit them in some second bank (or second generation of banks), the result for Centerre Bank is the same as our original Step 2 balance sheet where a cash loan transaction was assumed.

Step 3: $90 in Step 2 Loan Proceeds Are Deposited

IMPACT ON BALANCE SHEET FOR SECOND-GENERATION BANKS

Cash (reserves)	$90	Demand deposits	$90

In Step 3, the $90 loan proceeds have been deposited in a second set (generation) of banks. Note that the Step 3 transaction does not change the money supply, since the public gave up $90 in money to acquire $90 in deposits (which are also money).

Step 4: Excess Reserves Are Loaned

CHANGE IN BALANCE SHEETS FOR SECOND-GENERATION BANKS

Reserves	$9	Demand deposits	$90
Loans	81		

In Step 4, loans of $81 ($90 − 9) have been made; if this *expansion of depository institution credit* is continued to the maximum possible, the $81 will be deposited in some third set of banks. Once again, we note that these additional loans are now part of the money supply and that the money supply has been increased by an additional $81 by virtue of the Step 4 transactions. The initial deposit of $100 in currency can expand

Table 2-4:

Maximum Expansion of Depository Institution Credit

DEPOSITORY FINANCIAL INSTITUTION	ACQUIRED RESERVES AND DEPOSITS	REQUIRED RESERVES (10%)	EXCESS RESERVES	AMOUNT WHICH CAN BE LOANED
A	$100	$10.00	$90.00	$90.00
B	90	9.00	81.00	81.00
C	81	8.10	72.90	72.90
.	.	.	.	.
.	.	.	.	.
.	.	.	.	.
Other Institutions	629	72.90		656.10
		Total amount loaned		$900.00

the money supply by $900, given a 10 percent reserve requirement, the assumption of no *leakage*,[12] and maximum expansion (table 2-4).

The expansion potential can be formalized in the formula:

$P = E/r$

where $P =$ Potential expansion in the money supply (or expansion of credit)
$E =$ excess reserves
$r =$ percentage reserve requirement.

In our example, the original deposit of $100 with Centerre Bank resulted in excess reserves of $90 ($100 − 10). Thus, total new money created was $900 ($90/0.10).

The actual expansion of credit is likely to be less than this potential figure because of "leakage" to cash. If the first borrower of $90 chose to hold the cash, expansion would be stopped with the first $90. In practice, the creation of $1 of excess reserves appears to increase the money supply by only $2 to $3.

The money supply is controlled by the Federal Reserve System through activities that influence the volume of reserves within the financial system. One way for the Federal Reserve System to influence reserves is to change the legal reserve requirement. An increase in reserve requirements leads to a curtailment of lending activity and, therefore, diminishes the creation of money. Likewise, a decrease in reserve requirements gives banks the authority to make additional loans and create more money.

Reserve requirements are actually changed infrequently because a small change in reserve requirements leads to a large change in the money supply. On the other hand, the money supply is adjusted on a day-to-day basis using *open market operations*—the buying and selling of U.S. government securities by the Federal Reserve banks.

A situation whereby the Federal Reserve is seeking to increase the money supply through open market operations is illustrated in figure 2-5. The Federal Reserve

---

[12]"Leakage" would occur if some borrowers chose to hold loan proceeds in cash.

FEDERAL RESERVE BANK OF NEW YORK

U.S. government securities	+$10		Demand deposits (Citibank)	+$10

CITIBANK

Reserves	+$10	
U.S. government securities	−$10	

Figure 2-5: Federal open market operations resulting in increased reserves (in $ millions).

Bank of New York, by offering a price acceptable to Citibank, a large New York bank, has acquired $10 million in U.S. Treasury securities (figure 2-5). The Federal Reserve System pays for these by increasing Citibank's reserves by $10 million. Note that the open market transaction has caused no change in deposit liabilities on Citibank's balance sheet. Thus, the entire $10 million is now excess reserves. If all of the $10 million is loaned by Citibank, and assuming reserve requirements of 10 percent, new money equal to $100 million ($10/0.10) can potentially be created through the expansion process.

By selling U.S. government securities, Federal Reserve banks can reverse the process and decrease the money supply.

The *discount rate* is another method used in controlling the money supply. The discount rate is the rate charged by the Federal Reserve on loans to member banks. The importance of the discount rate is limited by the fact that commercial banks are discouraged from regular borrowing from the Federal Reserve. However, the discount rate is frequently used as a signaling device. An increase in the discount rate would lead banks to begin curtailing their lending activity in anticipation of monetary restriction.

In addition to control of the money supply, the Federal Reserve System has available several other tools for use in attempting to control economic activity. *Margin requirements* determine the percentage of value that purchasers of stocks and bonds are allowed to borrow. If there is evidence of excessive-speculative pressure in the securities markets, effective demand can be decreased through an increase in margin requirements. The present 50 percent requirement was set in 1974. Finally, the Federal Reserve System operates in the *foreign exchange markets,* buying and selling dollars to smooth out movements in exchange rates.

An important objective of Federal Reserve policy is economic growth. The Federal Reserve System shares with the U.S. government a statutory obligation to work toward healthy economic conditions. The Federal Reserve System attempts to draw a reasonable balance between the objectives of encouraging economic growth through the provision of adequate credit and of avoiding inflation brought on by excessive money growth.

As noted earlier, the governing body of the Federal Reserve System is the Federal Reserve Board. Each member is appointed by the President of the United States with the consent of the Senate for a period of fourteen years. This structure was designed to create an "independent" Federal Reserve that would pursue appropriate policy objectives without undue short-term political pressure. However, the chairman only serves a four-year term and is appointed by the President from among the members. Thus, the President generally has an opportunity to appoint someone of his choosing to the board and then appoint that person chairman sometime during his term. The record of the Federal Reserve System with regard to following the economic leadership of the President or striking its own course is mixed, as is opinion on the degree of independence it should have.

SUMMARY

Financial systems change over time in response to changing technology and the needs of society. In the United States, the financial system is a combination of reserve banking, fiat, and electronic systems. Since money is no longer backed directly by anything of value, its supply must be controlled by some agency enjoying a high level of public confidence. In the United States, the Federal Reserve System was structured as an agency free from day-to-day pressures of election politics for this purpose. The Federal Reserve System, which acts as the central bank, controls the supply of money primarily through reserve requirements and open market operations. Its control of the money supply is carried out with the dual (and frequently conflicting) objectives of stable prices and full employment.

The rate of growth in the money supply is a function of excess reserves generated by depository financial institutions, which in turn is dependent upon federal reserve policy. The volume of reserves so held influences the amount of new lending and thus the volume of new money created.

QUESTIONS

2-1.   Identify several different types of financial systems. Of the several types, which would best describe the U.S. financial system?

2-2.   If there exists in the United States only $186 billion in currency, how is it possible for deposits in U.S. financial institutions to exceed $1.6 trillion?

2-3.   Describe the structure and operating characteristics of the Federal Reserve System.

2-4.   To whom does the chairman of the Federal Reserve System report? To what extent does the structure of the system ensure independence?

2-5.   What determines the value of money? Is it important to have money backed by precious metals such as gold and silver or by other commodities?

2-6.   Identify and define the various money supply measures.

2-7.   Why are depository financial institutions required to hold reserves?

2-8.   Distinguish between required reserves and excess reserves.

2-9.   Whenever currency is deposited in a commercial bank, the money supply decreases. Do you agree?

2-10.   Discuss how the tools of monetary policy may be used by the Federal Reserve to influence the money supply.

PROBLEMS

2-1.   Suppose $1,000 in currency is deposited in a transaction account at Home Federal Savings and Loan Association.
      a. Has the money supply changed?
      b. If the required reserve ratio is 10 percent, how much could Home Federal lend as a result of the $1,000 deposit?
      c. Assuming maximum expansion and no leakage, how much new money could the financial system create as a result of the initial deposit?
      d. Answer parts b and c given a reserve requirement of 12 percent.

2-2.   The following is a hypothetical balance sheet for the Boatmen's National Bank. The reserve ratio is 15 percent.

ASSETS		LIABILITIES	
Reserves	$ 60	Transaction	
Investments	140	accounts	$400
Loans	200		

      a. How much excess reserves does the bank now have?
      b. If customers deposit $10 in currency in transaction accounts, would the money supply change?
      c. As a result of the $10 deposit, can Boatmen's Bank create money? If so, how and by how much?
      d. Assuming maximum expansion and no leakage, how much new money could be created as the result of the initial $10 deposit?

2-3.   Below are T accounts for the Federal Reserve and for a commercial bank. Show how a $10 million sale of U.S. government securities to that commercial bank would change the accounts.

FEDERAL RESERVE BANK BALANCE SHEET
(in $ millions)

Loans to banks	$ 10,000	Currency	$100,000
U.S. government securities	150,000	Deposits from banks	60,000
Other assets	3,000	Equity	3,000
Total assets	163,000	Total liabilities	$163,000

FIRST NATIONAL BANK OF JOHNSTOWN
(in $ millions)

Currency	$ 3	Deposits	$70
Deposits with Fed	16	Equity	10
U.S. government securities	10		$80
Other assets	51		
	$80		

2-4.   Banks are fully loaned up and face 10 percent reserve requirements. The Federal Reserve System purchases $10 million of U.S. government bonds from a commercial bank. Assume any loans by that bank will be made by increasing the borrowers' transaction accounts and will result in the borrowers immediately writing checks against their accounts.
      a. By how much can that bank increase loans?
      b. Ignoring leakage to cash, by how much can all banks in the system increase loans?

2-5.   The Heritage National Bank has reserves of $40,000 and deposits of $200,000. The required reserve ratio is 20 percent. Customers deposit an additional $10,000 in currency. How much excess reserves does the bank now have?

2-6.   The Heritage National Bank (problem 2-5) again has reserves of $40,000 and deposits of $200,000. The reserve ratio continues at 20 percent. Heritage now sells $10,000 in securities to the Federal Reserve bank in its district. How much excess reserves does the bank now have?

2-7.   Craig Feldt deposits $1,000 in currency to his checking account at the Chesterfield Bank. Several hours later, Tom McCormack negotiates a loan for $1,250 and receives the loan proceeds in cash. By how much and in what direction did the money supply change?

SELECTED REFERENCES

BOARD OF GOVERNORS OF THE FEDERAL RESERVE SYSTEM. *The Federal Reserve System Purposes and Functions,* Washington, D.C., 1984.

BRADLEY, MICHAEL D., AND JANSEN, DENNIS W. "Federal Reserve Operating Procedure in the Eighties," *Journal of Money, Credit and Banking* (August 1986): 323–335.

BURDEKIN, RICHARD. "Fiscal Pressure and Central Bank Policy Objectives," *Federal Reserve Bank of Dallas Economic Review* (May 1986), 1–9.

CUKIERMAN, ALEX. "Central Bank Behavior and Credibility," *Federal Reserve Bank of St. Louis Review* (May 1986): 5–17.

MORRIS, FRANK E. "Rules Plus Discretion in Monetary Policy—An Appraisal of Our Experience Since October 1979," *Federal Reserve Bank of Boston New England Economic Review* (September/October 1985): 3–8.

SIMPSON, THOMAS D. "Developments in the U.S. Financial System Since the Mid-1970s," *Federal Reserve Bulletin* (January 1988): 1–13.

SPRINKEL, BERYL W. "Confronting Monetary Policy Dilemmas: The Legacy of Homer Jones," *Federal Reserve Bank of St. Louis Review* (March 1987): 5–8.

WENNINGER, JOHN, AND KLITGAARD, THOMAS. "Exploring the Effects of Capital Movements on M1 and the Economy," *Federal Reserve Bank of New York Quarterly Review* (Summer 1986): 21–31.

3

Regulation of Financial Institutions

INAUGURATION DAY 1933

> The White House, midnight, Friday, March 3, 1933. Across the country the banks of the nation had gradually shuttered their windows and locked their doors. The very machinery of the American economy seemed to be coming to a stop. The rich and fertile nation, overflowing with natural wealth in its fields and forests and mines, equipped with unsurpassed technology, endowed with boundless resources in its men and women, lay stricken. "We are at the end of our rope," a weary President Hoover at last said, as the striking clock announced the day of his retirement. "There is nothing more we can do."[1]

The United States financial system is built on trust and confidence. Central to its well-being is the belief that funds placed on deposit with banks (or other depository institutions) will be available on demand or when due and will be payable to the depositor. Currency represents only a small fraction of the money supply, and most "money" on deposit with financial institutions is represented simply by accounting entries (chapter 2). Clearly, our financial system is backed only by the confidence of the public. As Schlesinger so eloquently describes, the nation was in a state of despair in 1933; financial markets had collapsed; the banking system was on the verge of disintegration; unemployment was rampant; and calls for financial reform were heard throughout the nation. On 4 March 1933, President Franklin D. Roosevelt was installed

[1]Arthur J. Schlesinger, Jr., "The Valley of Darkness," *The Crisis of the Old Older, 1919– 1933* (Boston: Houghton-Mifflin Company, 1957), summarized in *Economic Issues* (McGraw-Hill Book Company, 1963): 35–36.

as President. On 5 March, Congress was called into special session and the President declared a banking holiday. Over the next 100 days, Congress passed sweeping legislative measures, and from the financial anguish of the 1930s evolved a strengthened American financial system.

THE AMERICAN FINANCIAL SYSTEM

To develop insight into the American financial system, we will examine its evolution; and to understand where we are today, it is useful to analyze financial and regulatory developments within four major historical periods of American history: before 1913, 1913–1933, 1933–1980, and 1980 and beyond.

Regulatory Environment Before 1913

In contrast with many European economies, characterized by large central banks, controlled—if not owned—by the central government, the American banking system functioned as a decentralized, privately owned and largely privately controlled banking system before 1913. As late as the 1890s, a South Dakota court held banking a strictly private business in which the proprietor had an absolute right to own and operate his bank without supervision or control by any government authority.[2]

As far back as the eighteenth century, the federal government had sought to exert at least some control over banking. The first bank to receive a federal charter was the First Bank of the United States. This first federally chartered bank was given a twenty-year charter (1791–1811). In some ways, the First Bank performed a role similar to that of a Federal Reserve bank today. In addition to its role as a regular commercial bank, it functioned as a "banker's bank," receiving deposits from and transferring funds on behalf of state-chartered banks. It also functioned as a fiscal agent for the federal government by receiving government deposits and transferring these around the country and by lending to the government. This first federally chartered bank served as a regulator of the state banks. It did so by collecting the notes issued by individual state banks and then presenting these to the issuing bank. It asked for immediate redemption in specie (precious metal which backed the notes), thus encouraging state banks to refrain from excessive issue of bank notes. At the end of the twenty-year period, however, the bank's charter was not renewed. Some argued that the issuance of a federal bank charter violated the Constitution, although the Constitution did give government the right to "coin money and regulate the value thereof." Others objected to the bank's practice of issuing paper notes, arguing that the only "good" money was "hard" money (gold or silver). Also, a number of state-chartered banks objected to its regulatory role. Finally, the issue of "states" rights" and the resentment caused by central government interference in private business ensured the demise of the First Bank of the United States.

[2]Susan Estabrook Kennedy, *The Banking Crisis of 1933* (University Press of Kentucky, 1973): 6.

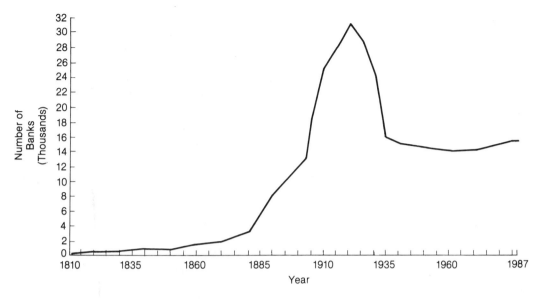

Figure 3-1: Number of banks in operation. (From *Historical Statistics of the United States*. U.S. Department of Commerce.)

Following the charter expiration of the First Bank, the nation entered into a period of *state banking* for the next five years (1811–1816). During this period, the number of state banks approximately tripled; the number increased from 88 in 1811 to 246 in 1816 (figure 3-1). Poor bank management, the lack of a central fiscal agent for the government, rapid expansion of the volume of bank notes, and other abuses resulted in efforts to again charter a national bank. Five years following the demise of the first federally chartered bank, the Second Bank of the United States was given a twenty-year charter (1816–1836). The second bank performed in ways that were similar to that of the first bank; thus it too succumbed to political bickering and its charter was not renewed.

The period 1836–1863 witnessed a return to state banking in the United States. While some states sought to effectively regulate and control banking, others were lax. Banking abuses, overissue of bank notes, counterfeiting, and other such practices were rampant. By 1863, it was widely believed that something must be done to "clean up" American banking. The National Bank Act of 1864 (which superseded legislation passed the previous year) provided for the chartering of banks by the federal government. Unlike the First and Second Banks of the United States which were partially owned by the federal government and which functioned with nationwide branches, the banks provided for in the 1864 act were privately owned banks with powers similar to those enjoyed by *state-chartered* banks. The National Banking System was established to provide a national uniform paper currency, to counteract chaotic local banking, and to help finance the Union war effort.

A major objective of the National Bank Act of 1864 was to encourage *state-chartered* banks to join the National Bank System. To provide that encouragement, Congress imposed a tax on bank notes issued by banks outside the system. Most state banks joined the system, since it would not be profitable to make loans through note issue when the 10 percent tax frequently exceeded interest charged on the loan. Unfortunately, deficiencies still remained in the nation's banking system. Banks joining the National Bank System were required to purchase U.S. bonds, against which bank notes could be issued. The dependence upon government bonds for note issuance caused bank note shortages. Also, capital requirements for members of the National Bank System were high ($50,000 for population areas of less than 6,000). Thus rural areas were not well served by the system.[3] Finally, a banking panic in 1907 confirmed the inadequacy of the National Banking System and a National Monetary Commission was formed by Congress in 1908. The commission was charged with the responsibility of studying banking systems at home and abroad and of recommending a new system to the U.S. Congress. Finally, in 1913, the Federal Reserve System was established.

Regulatory Environment 1913–1933

While the National Monetary Commission recommended the establishment of a strong central bank, the Wilson administration was determined that, in correcting weaknesses of the National Bank Act, it would not add to centralized financial power. Rather than one central bank, the Federal Reserve Act of 1913 provided for a system of regional Federal Reserve banks.

In the early years of the Federal Reserve System, the authority and effectiveness of the Federal Reserve System was limited. Only national banks were required to join, and the system did not act as a powerful force to promote monetary stability. While the Federal Reserve System could influence bank reserves through the discount window and through open market operations, these activities were uncoordinated in that each of the twelve banks set its own discount rate, and open market operations were effectively controlled by the Federal Reserve Bank of New York rather than by the system. Rather than stabilize the economy through the explosive growth of the 1920s, for example, the Federal Reserve System contributed to the expansion in the late 1920s by lowering the discount rate and by engaging in open market purchases, thereby inflating credit. Much of this credit was used for real estate and stock market speculation which contributed to inflated markets and their collapse in October 1929. Critics charged that the Federal Reserve Bank of New York was effectively "under the control of Wall Street." Indeed in February 1929, the Federal Reserve System asked the Federal Reserve banks to provide "direct pressure" and ask member banks not to make speculative loans. But the New York Federal Reserve Bank opposed this move and did not comply. From a practical point of view, the Federal Reserve System was powerless. If financial institutions met membership and reserve requirements of the Federal Reserve Act of 1913, they needed pay no further deference to the system.[4]

The Hoover administration tried to deal with the deteriorating situation in the early 1930s. In 1932, it created the Reconstruction Finance Corporation which provided

---

[3]Some banks began to make loans by increasing checking account balances rather than note issue, thus avoiding the tax and avoiding the necessity of joining the National Banking System.

[4]For an excellent historical analysis of this period, see Susan Estabrook Kennedy, *The Banking Crisis of 1933* (University Press of Kentucky, 1973).

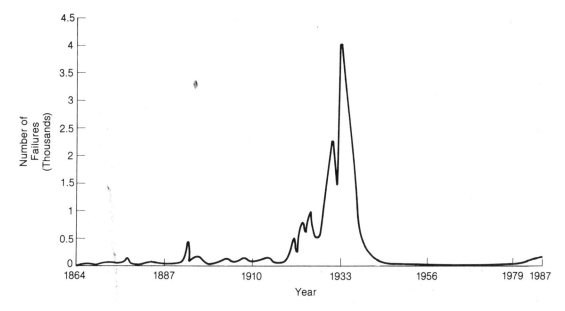

Figure 3-2: Bank suspensions: 1864–1987. (From *Historical Statistics of the United States,* U.S. Department of Commerce and FDIC annual reports.)

loans to financial and other institutions. In that same year, it also created the Federal Home Loan Bank System which was modeled after the Federal Reserve System and designed to provide a central credit facility for home financing institutions—principally savings and loan associations.

Unfortunately these actions were too few and too late. From the end of 1929 to the beginning of 1933, over five thousand banks—20 percent of the banks in the United States—failed. The situation continued to deteriorate through the spring of 1933, until Hoover's term as President ended in early March (figure 3-2).

Regulatory Environment 1933–1980

On 5 March 1933, one day after taking office. President Roosevelt declared a four-day bank holiday, which was later extended indefinitely. Within days of this bank holiday announcement, Congress enacted emergency banking legislation, approving the President's authority to proclaim a national banking holiday and providing a framework for reopening closed banks. In effect, the reopening procedure signaled a more active regulatory role for the Federal Reserve System. The procedure called for the secretary of the treasury to license (and thus authorize the reopening) of any member bank whose financial condition was judged to be sound by the district Federal Reserve bank.[5] State banking authorities could reopen sound nonmember banks at their discretion.

[5]In his first "fireside chat" with the American public (Sunday evening, 12 March 1933), President Roosevelt stated that those banks "found to be all right" by Treasury examination would be reopened; the remaining banks would resume business eventually. Many of the remaining banks never reopened.

While much financial legislation was enacted during the Roosevelt administration, perhaps the most significant in terms of its effect on the financial system, and particularly depository financial institutions, was the Banking Act of 1933.

The Banking Act of 1933, also known as the *Glass–Steagall Act*, introduced broad reform into the U.S. financial system. The important provisions of the Glass–Steagall Act were that it:

1. *Created the Federal Reserve Open Market Committee* and brought open market operations under formal control of the statutory body of the Federal Reserve System for the first time.
2. *Created the Federal Deposit Insurance Corporation (FDIC)* and provided for a temporary deposit insurance fund, initially insuring deposits to $2,500.
3. *Prohibited the payment of interest on demand deposits and authorized the Federal Reserve Board to regulate interest rates payable on savings and time deposits.*
4. *Prohibited member banks and the affiliates of member banks to engage in investment banking activities.*
5. *Provided for greater regulation of the operations of member banks.*

Thus the Banking Act of 1933 restricted bank operations, centralized banking control, and introduced federal deposit insurance, setting the stage for a tightly controlled regulatory environment which would continue for the next several decades.

Banks were not treated differently from other business in being subjected to these rules. It was felt that recovery would be encouraged if businesses could be protected from competition. Industries as diverse as interstate trucking and stock brokerage were brought under regulatory control. An important aspect of such control was the elimination of price competition.

A fundamental result of legislation enacted in the 1930s was the division of permissable activities among the various financial institutions and the division into compartments of the financial sector. Neither banks nor affiliates of banks could engage in brokerage and other security market activities. Of course, securities firms could not engage in banking. Savings and loan associations could not offer demand deposits, nor could they make commercial or most other types of loans. They were restricted almost totally to the making of home mortgage loans in their local market. Credit unions, established in 1934, could not accept demand deposits and were largely limited to the provision of credit to people "of small means" (according to the 1934 Federal Credit Union Act). In later years, the owners of some banks sought to engage in activities prohibited to commercial banks by forming holding companies to which the bank could be sold. The holding company might acquire other nonbank subsidiaries; and since the holding company managers controlled both the bank and nonbank subsidiaries, there existed the possibility that bank resources could be used to favor such nonbank subsidiaries or that other conflict-of-interest situations might arise.

To close the possible loophole in banking regulation that the holding company structure posed, Congress passed the Bank Holding Company Act of 1956 which required holding companies owning one-fourth or more of the voting stock of *two or more* banks to register with the Federal Reserve Board. In subsequent amendments (1966 and

Table 3-1

Permissible Nonbank Activities for Bank Holding Companies That Require Prior Approval

1. Making and servicing loans—consumer finance, credit card, mortgage, commercial, factoring
2. Industrial banking
3. Trust company functions
4. Investment or financial advice
5. Leasing personal or real property
6. Community development
7. Data processing
8. Insurance sales
9. Underwriting credit, life, accident, and health insurance
10. Courier services
11. Management consulting to depository institutions
12. Money orders, savings bonds, and traveler's checks
13. Real estate appraising
14. Arranging commercial real estate financing
15. Securities brokerage
16. Underwriting and dealing in government obligations and money market instruments
17. Foreign exchange advisory and transactional services
18. Futures commission merchant
19. Tax planning and preparation
20. Check guarranty services
21. Operating collection agency
22. Operating credit bureau

Source: *Federal Reserve Bulletin,* February 1984, pp. 134–137, and *Federal Reserve Bulletin,* December 1986, pp. 833–834.

1970), Congress revised and extended the Bank Holding Company Act to cover holding companies owning just one bank. These revisions further provided that nonbank companies owned by bank holding companies must be engaged in activities "closely related to banking." Such "closely related" activities were to be decided and defined by the Federal Reserve System (table 3-1).

Since 1956, the number of bank holding companies and the volume of deposits held by them has increased dramatically (table 3-2).

By the 1970s, depression era conditions had faded from the minds of the American public. Federal deposit insurance and financial regulation had accomplished the objective of restoring confidence and of reducing bank and other depository institution failures to a fraction of their former numbers.[6] Indeed, the regulatory authorities followed the practice of merging failed institutions with stronger ones, so that deposit and other creditor losses were virtually eliminated. While safety was the primary focus of earlier legislation, quality and price of financial services became the principal issue by the 1970s. The division into compartments of the financial sector was questioned, and a number of government-mandated studies were released.

[6]In 1934, the number of bank failures declined to sixty one. Beginning in 1943 and for the next three decades the number of bank failures was less than ten per year.

Table 3-2

Offices and Deposits of Banks Affiliated With Bank Holding Companies by Year

Year	1956	1970	1971	1980	1986
Number of companies	53	121	1567	3056	6489
Banks	429	895	2420	4954	9415
Branches	783	3260	10382	24970	39716
Total offices	1211	4155	13252	29924	49131
Offices as a percentage of all bank offices	5.7%	11.8%	36.1%	56.2%	82.9%
Domestic deposits (in $ billions)	$14.8	$78.0	$297.0	$840.6	$2,069.0
Domestic deposits as a percentage of all bank deposits	7.5%	16.2%	55.1%	71.0%	91.2%

Source: *Bank Holding Company Facts,* Spring 1983; Association of Bank Holding Companies, *Statistical Abstract of the United States;* Board of Governors of the Federal Reserve System, *Annual Statistical Digest,* 1986.

WINDS OF CHANGE

Recent decades have witnessed the completion of several studies of the structure and regulation of financial institutions by special government commissions. Many of the recommendations of these commissions have become law and represent an important departure from the limited competition philosophy developed in the 1930s. While safety was the primary focus of earlier legislation, quality and price of services have been the focus of this recent legislation.

Hunt Commission

In 1971, the Hunt Commission (formally, the President's Commission on Financial Structure and Regulation) completed a sweeping study of financial institutions and the supply and demand for credit. The commission concluded that attempts to regulate the flow of funds had led to market inefficiency and had generally failed to achieve stated objectives. In general, the commission recommended that competition be increased. The major specific recommendations of the commission were as follows:

1. *Elimination of interest rate ceilings on deposits.* Deposit rate ceilings were supposed to protect the savings of individuals by protecting financial institutions from expensive competition for savings. In addition, they were supposed to ensure the availability of funds to the housing industry.[7] This latter objective was pursued by allowing thrift institutions to pay a higher rate (first unrestricted, then 0.25 percent) than banks for deposits. This advantage to thrift institutions had been negated in recent years by disintermediation—investors took their money out of financial institutions and invested directly. Rather than securing a stable,

[7]An unspoken "advantage" of regulating interest rates on small savings deposits was that it allowed the federal government to finance part of its debt by selling savings bonds to small investors at an interest rate well below that paid on large-denomination U.S. government bonds.

low-cost supply of funds, the interest rate ceilings may have contributed to the lack of stability in the supply of funds.

2. *Allow all depository financial institutions to offer a full range of time deposits.* This is consistent with the first recommendation. With the ability to bid at prevailing rates for funds of any maturity, institutions should be in a position to manage the maturity structure of their liabilities. By bidding for longer-term deposits, they would also gain in ability to develop more stable sources of funds.

3. *Allow all depository institutions to offer checking account services.* This recommendation followed the general philosophy that the best way to ensure low-cost services was to allow as many competitors as possible to offer the service.

4. *Broaden lending powers of all institutions.* The commission felt that the public would be better served if more competitors existed for each type of loan. It was also believed that institutions would gain from greater diversity if they were not forced to concentrate on one segment of the market.

Institutional Investor Study

The Institutional Investor Study, sponsored by the Securities and Exchange Commission, was also completed in 1971. The study was undertaken against a background of complaints that certain institutions, particularly insurance companies, mutual funds, pension funds, and bank trust departments, were distorting the equity capital markets through a tendency to trade large quantities of securities and to buy or sell the same security at the same time. The commission did not find evidence of sheeplike behavior by financial institutions, but it did find that the trading of large blocks of stock caused some distortions in reported prices, primarily because market structure did not lead to an efficient reporting of these prices. Commissions on stock traded on an exchange were fixed at levels that discouraged institutions from using the exchanges. Thus a great deal of trading occurred between institutions not using an exchange. The elimination of fixed commissions and reliance on the market to set commissions was recommended.

National Commission on Consumer Finance

The National Commission on Consumer Finance was created by Congress and completed its work in 1972. An important part of this commission's work was a study of the impact of state usury laws. The commission concluded that attempts to regulate interest rates charged to individuals had failed to achieve the desired results. Usury laws had led to problems such as circuitous methods of charging higher interest rates. For example, if restrictive state usury ceilings result in reduced credit availability, consumers may go to a so-called credit retailer who sells virtually all of his merchandise on credit and in effect builds interest costs into the price of the product. The effect of the usury ceiling in this case is to restrict the consumer's opportunity to shop for the best interest rate and the best price for the product.

As with other studies, this commission concluded that problems could best be dealt with through encouraging competition. This required consumer lending authority to be extended to as many lenders as possible and interest charges to be fully disclosed so that now people can effectively shop for the best interest cost.

The general thrust of the recommendations from all of these studies was that competition should be relied on to allocate funds to their best use, and to provide the best prices to both consumers and institutions. These recommendations stood in sharp contrast to the regulatory philosophy developed in the 1930s. Then it was felt that elimination of competition was the most effective approach to achieving national goals.[8]

What accounted for the change in attitude about the way in which financial institutions should set prices and allocate resources? In a broad sense, this change was part of a general shift in public attitude in recent years. Reliance on competition relative to government control had grown in popularity as a means of achieving the goals of individuals and society. Suggestions for financial institution deregulation paralleled movement toward deregulation in airlines, trucking, and other fields.

Some legislation of the 1970s generally followed the thrust of the recommendations for greater reliance on the marketplace. Brokerage commission regulations were repealed, and the result has been the development of a wider variety of services and costs available to individual investors. The brokerage houses previously charged identical commissions and competed by offering other services such as security analysis. Today, conventional brokerage houses compete with discount houses that offer no services other than purchase and sale of securities at the lowest commission possible. The result of freedom from rate regulation has been lower commission rates for many investors and a wider range of available services. However, the advent of the 1980s witnessed a dramatic change in the regulatory environment as Congress moved to further deregulate the financial sector.

REGULATORY ENVIRONMENT 1980 AND BEYOND

Although the Hunt Commission and other studies had called for deregulation and greater reliance on market forces, history has shown that significant and substantial financial legislation, particularly legislation that signals shifts in the direction of regulation, is likely to occur when major disruptions have occurred in financial markets. The 1970s and particularly the late 1970s witnessed severe inflation, interest rate increases, and financial market chaos that threatened the solvency of sizable components of the financial sector. Substantial disintermediation occurred as depositors transferred funds from savings and time deposits in financial institutions to newly created *money market funds*. Money market funds merely combined sums received from savers and invested those funds into money market instruments[9] which were not subject to regulatory imposed interest rate ceilings. Fund managers deducted fees from the funds' assets in return for services and were able to pass along high market returns to investors in the fund. Subject to interest rate restrictions on their deposits, depository financial institutions were unable to compete on a price basis with interest rates generated by the

---

[8]A continued resistance to the competition-based philosophy is represented by a dissenting statement from Lane Kirkland, then Secretary/Treasurer of the AFL-CIO: "I cannot believe that a financial institution should be encouraged to lend money for only the most profitable purposes." *Report of the President's Commission on Financial Structure and Regulation*, U.S. Government Printing Office, 1972. Stock #4000-0272.

[9]Money market instruments are covered in detail in chapter 7.

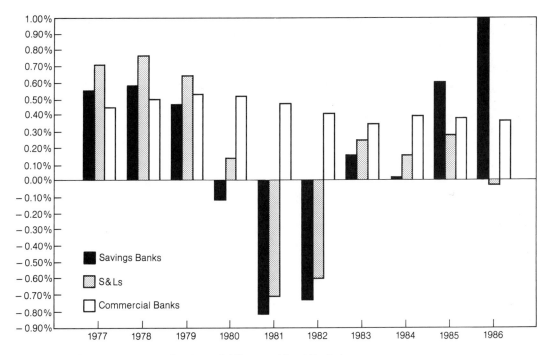

Figure 3-3: Net income as percent of total assets held by types of financial institutions.
Source: *National Fact Book of Savings Institutions,* 1987.

money market funds. Additionally, market interest rates for mortgages and other loans made by depository institutions had exceeded legal usury ceilings in many states. Depository institutions and particularly the thrifts, were thus faced with regulatory restrictions detrimentally affecting both sides of the balance sheet. By 1980, the impact on thrift institutions, particularly savings and loans and mutual savings banks was severe. Saddled with long-term, fixed-rate, low-yielding mortgages made in former years and with the partial deregulation of the liability side of their balance sheet[10], profitability of the industry diminished. By the early 1980s, the industry was generating negative returns (figures 3-3 and 3-4) and by some definitions was insolvent. The market value of savings and loan assets (though not the book value) had fallen below the market value of the industry's liabilities.

The Financial Institution Deregulation and Monetary Control Act of 1980

The 1980 Financial Institution Deregulation and Monetary Control Act, commonly referred to as *The Monetary Control Act,* was undoubtedly the most sweeping piece of financial legislation since the Banking Act of 1933 and was signed into law on

[10]Beginning in mid-1978, in response to deposit drains attributed largely to the money market funds, depository institutions were permitted to offer money market certificates on $10,000 minimum deposits. Interest rates were tied to the six-month Treasury bill rate.

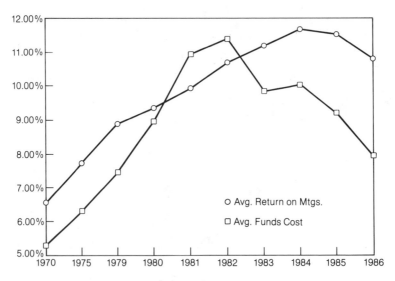

Figure 3-4: Return on mortgage portfolio and cost of funds for insured savings and loans associations. (From *Statistical Abstract of the United States* and *1987 National Fact Book of Savings Institutions.*)

30 March 1980. The act contained nine titles, each of which addressed major financial issues. Important provisions contained within this 1980 act included:

1. *Reserve requirements were imposed on all depository financial institutions.*
2. *Interest rate ceilings on savings and time deposits were to be phased out over a six-year period ending March 1986.*
3. *Federal deposit insurance limit (FDIC, FSLIC, and NCUA Share Insurance Fund) was immediately increased from $40,000 to $100,000.*
4. *State usury ceilings were overridden for home mortgage and mobile home loans.* The override was to be permanent unless reimposed by individual states within three years. Rate ceilings on business and agricultural loans were temporarily suspended for three years unless reimposed earlier by the individual state. Federal usury ceilings were scaled by a certain number of percentage points above the discount rate. Usury ceilings for federal credit unions were raised from 12 percent to 15 percent, and the National Credit Union Administration was authorized to raise the ceiling even further.
5. *Access to the Federal Reserve's discount windows was provided for all depository financial institutions having transaction accounts and nonpersonal time deposits.*
6. *Thrift institutions were given expanded lending powers and were authorized to invest 20 percent of their assets in consumer loans, commercial paper, and corporate debt securities.*
7. *Federal Reserve services were to be explicitly priced.* Among others, such services include check clearing and collection, wire transfer, and automated clearing house operations.

The thrust of this deregulation and the Monetary Control Act was thus to establish a "more level playing field" within the financial sector, to reduce the compart-

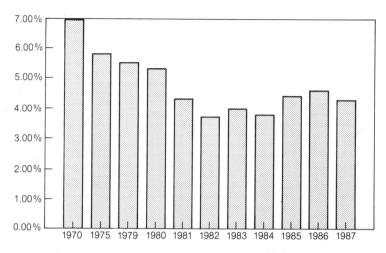

Figure 3-5: Ratio of net worth to total assets, FSLIC-insured savings institutions.
Source: *Statistical Abstract of the United States* and *1987 National Fact Book of Savings Institutions.*

mentalization of depository financial institutions, to allow the monetary authority more control over bank and thrift reserves, and to generally allow greater flexibility within the financial sector.

In accordance with provisions of the act and with decisions of the Depository Institutions Deregulation Committee (DIDC), deregulation commenced. In January 1981, negotiable order of withdrawal (NOW) accounts (transaction accounts which pay interest) became available nationwide, and by mid-1982 rate ceilings were removed on certain long-term deposit accounts. But because of continued high market rates, disintermediation continued and money market funds held some $230 billion (about 10 percent of M2) of the nation's funds by early fall 1982. Sizable portions of the financial sector, particularly savings and loan associations and mutual savings banks, remained in jeopardy. Net worth of the savings and loan industry fell by 22 percent between 1980 and 1982, and hundreds of savings and loans were merged. In the face of this continuing crisis, Congress enacted (October 1982) major legislation to "shore up" savings and loan associations and mutual savings banks. This 1982 act also speeded up deregulation initiated by the Monetary Control Act of 1980 and generally expanded the deregulatory environment.

The Garn–St. Germain Depository Institutions Act of 1982[11]

The Garn–St. Germain Act, passed in October 1982, amended certain sections of the Monetary Control Act of 1980 and provided certain additional powers to depository financial institutions. Important provisions included within this 1982 act were as follows:

[11]Discussion in this section relies heavily on Gillian Garcia, et. al., "The Garn–St. Germain Depository Institutions Act of 1982," *Federal Reserve Bank of Chicago Economic Perspectives* (March/April, 1983).

1. *Authorized money market deposit accounts (MMDAs) for depository financial institutions.* These accounts would be directly competitive with money market mutual funds, were federally insured, were free of interest rate ceilings (with initial and average maintained balances of $2,500 or more), and became available 14 December 1982.
2. *Federal, state, and local governments were authorized to hold NOW accounts.* (Previously these accounts were limited to persons and to nongovernment, nonprofit organizations).
3. *Federally chartered savings and loan associations were permitted to offer demand deposits to business and agricultural customers.* (Previously only commercial and mutual savings banks were permitted to accept demand deposits).
4. *Regulation Q rate differentials were phased out effective 1 January 1984.* (Previously thrifts could pay 0.25 percent above that of commercial banks on most types of deposits.
5. *Federally chartered S&Ls and SBs may make overdraft loans, and importantly, commercial loans.* Authority to make certain other loans and investments was expanded.
6. *Thrifts were given wide powers to alter their charters for state to federal and conversely (where state law permits).* They may switch between mutual and stock form and between savings and loan association and savings bank charters.
7. *State banks and thrifts were empowered to offer variable rate mortgages.* (Federally chartered institutions had been granted this authority previously.)
8. *Regulatory authorities including the FDIC, FSLIC, and NCUA were given emergency powers to aid troubled banks and thrifts.* Included in this provision is the authority for regulatory agencies to approve both interstate and interindustry acquisitions and mergers under certain conditions. For example, a banking institution located in New York could acquire a savings and loan association located in Florida.

SUBSEQUENT EVENTS AND THE COMPETITIVE EQUALITY BANKING ACT OF 1987

Passage of the Deregulation and Monetary Control Act in 1980, and of the Garn–St. Germain Act, commenced the process of dismantling the compartmentalization of the financial sector. Savings banks and savings and loans took advantage of their expanded powers and began to restructure their portfolios. The volume of mortgage loans held in the industry's portfolio declined, and other types of loans and investments increased. By the late 1980s, some had begun emphasizing commercial lending and many had become active in consumer lending programs. Also, the nature of ownership of thrift institutions was rapidly evolving. In 1980, only 2 of the 424 savings banks that then existed were stockholder-owned. By early 1987, about one-third of all savings banks had converted to stock form. A similar picture was emerging with regard to savings and loans. But problems of the times continued to plague large numbers of thrift institutions. By the late 1980s, the combination of a depressed energy industry and problems in the agricultural sector had resulted in enormous losses for large numbers of banks and thrifts in the southwestern portion of the United States. By September 1987 the volume of bank failures was double the previous year's pace, and almost one-third of all bank failures had occurred in the state of Texas. While deposits at banks and S&L's were generally rising, they had declined by several billion dollars in Texas.[12] Also, while savings banks located principally in the northeastern United States enjoyed record earnings, and while the majority of savings and loans had a remarkably profitable year, 20 percent of all S&L's had such severe asset quality problems that they managed to lose more than the profitable institutions earned.[13] By 1987, the problem of failing thrifts had become so acute that public confidence in the industry was declining. The Federal Savings and Loan Insurance Corporation (FSLIC) had virtually depleted its assets and had reached the point where it could no longer afford to close down insolvent S&L's. Funds were no longer sufficient to reimburse depositors and incur other expenses frequently associated with closing and/or merging failed institutions. Consequently, Congress, in August 1987, enacted the *Competitive Equality Banking Act of 1987,* a key feature of which was the reaffirmation that insurance by the FSLIC or by the FDIC represents the "full faith and credit" of the United States. This restated Congress' commitment to back FSLIC's own resources and reserves with general (taxpayer) funds—if need be, to reimburse any FSLIC-insured depositor up to $100,000. More specifically, the act authorized FSLIC to borrow, through a newly created financing corporation, up to $10.8 billion through bond issues. Clearly, as the nation approached the final decade of the twentieth century, the financial system was continuing to evolve, and more than ever its institutions depended on the trust and confidence of the public.

SUMMARY

The United States financial system and its institutions depend on the trust and confidence of the public. As technology, information, and communication systems change, the financial structure must change to meet new needs. Blind adherence to a system based on yesterday's technology and customs will not efficiently and effectively meet today's requirements.

For purposes of analyzing the American financial system, four major historical periods may be identified. The first such period, pre-1913, identifies a time frame where banking functioned as a privately owned, ineffectively regulated industry. The period 1913–1933 witnessed major changes in U.S. technology and industrial development. Although the Federal Reserve System had been formed in 1913, the system was largely ineffectual and is believed to have contributed to the financial collapse which occurred in late 1929. The third period, 1933–1980, was one of greater financial stability and of restored confidence in the nation's financial system. Because the financial sector was divided into compartments, it was not sufficiently flexible to respond to innovations brought about by increasingly sophisticated systems of communication and information processing. Also, the system could not satisfactorily respond to high levels of inflation and interest rates. Consequently, a new era was ushered in. This new era was sparked

[12]"Problems of Banks, S&Ls in Texas Worry Some Depositors There," *The Wall Street Journal,* September 1, 1987.
[13]National Council of Savings Institutions, *National Fact Book of Savings Institutions,* 1987, p. 4.

by technological developments and communication improvements, by the increased sophistication of savers in money matters, and by a changing philosophy in government concerning competition within and among industries. Laws were passed in 1980 and 1982 which fundamentally affected the financial sector of the United States, principally through deregulation. Vestiges of the former lack of diversification and regional disparities, though, continued to plague large numbers of depository institutions, and legislation to shore up public confidence was again passed in late 1987. Such changes in the 1980s promise new challenges as the managers of today's financial institutions prepare for the final decade of the twentieth century.

QUESTIONS

3-1.   Throughout history, precious metals such as gold and silver have served as money and retained value, while paper money frequently declined in value. Why has this been true?

3-2.   In what way or ways did the First Bank and Second Bank of the United States perform functions similar to that of the Federal Reserve System today? In what way or ways was the performance dissimilar?

3-3.   The United States financial system is based on the trust and confidence of the public. Is it possible for modern economics to have financial systems which are not so based?

3-4.   Identify several defects in the structure of the U.S. financial system that may have contributed to the economic collapse of 1929.

3-5.   By the mid-1930s, some semblance of stability had returned to the United States financial system. How do you explain this return to stability?

3-6.   For the past several decades, the American financial system has been "compartmentalized." Give examples of such compartmentalization and comment on current trends with regard to compartmentalization of the financial system.

3-7.   Although relatively stable from the mid-1930s to the late 1970s, the American financial system was again threatened as the 1970s drew to a close. How do you account for this condition?

3-8.   Summarize the main features of the major financial legislation discussed in this chapter.

3-9.   From your reading of current newspapers and periodicals, identify new trends or examples of evolutionary change within our financial system today.

SELECTED REFERENCES

BENSTON, GEORGE J. "Why Continue to Regulate Banks?: An Historical Assessment of Federal Banking Regulation," *Midland Corporate Finance Journal* (Fall 1987): 67–82.

"Bill is Signed to Restore Faith in Ailing S&L Insurance Fund," *Congressional Quarterly Weekly Report*, 45 (33) (August 15, 1987): 1905–1907.
CORRIGAN, GERALD E., "A Perspective on the Globali-

zation of Financial Markets and Institutions," *Federal Reserve Bank of New York Quarterly Review* (Spring 1987): 1–9.

"Depository Institutions Deregulation and Monetary Control Act of 1980," *Federal Reserve Bank of Chicago Economic Perspectives* (September/October 1980).

GART, ALEN. *The Insider's Guide to the Financial Services Revolution* (New York: McGraw-Hill Book Company, 1984).

FORTIER, DIANA, AND PHILLIS, DAVE. "Bank and Thrift Performance since DIDMCA," *Federal Reserve Bank of Chicago Economic Perspectives* (September/October 1985): 58–68.

FRASER, DONALD R., AND ROSE, PETER S. *Financial Institutions and Markets in a Changing World* (Plano, Texas: Business Publications, Inc., 1987).

GOLEMBE, CARTER H., AND HOLLAND, DAVID S. *Federal Regulation of Banking: 1983–84* (Washington, D.C.: Golembe Associates Inc., 1983).

SIMPSON, THOMAS D. "Developments in the U.S. Financial System since the Mid-1970s," *Federal Reserve Bulletin* (January 1988): 1–13.

"The Garn–St. Germain Depository Institutions Act of 1982," *Federal Reserve Bank of Chicago Economic Perspectives* (March/April 1983).

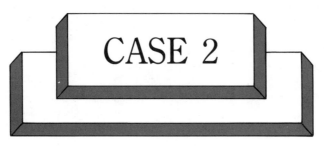

CASE 2

THE MISSOURI FINANCIAL SERVICES ASSOCIATION

In January 1978, a major concern of the Missouri Financial Services Association was the restrictive interest rate structure applicable to direct cash loans imposed on lenders through the Missouri usury statutes. Consequently, representatives of the consumer finance industry had gathered in Jefferson City to analyze the political climate and to discuss strategy in an effort to seek rate relief through the Missouri legislature. The discussion focused on a bill, recently introduced in the Missouri state legislature and endorsed by the Missouri Financial Services Association, which would increase the small-loan base from $500 to $1200.

THE MISSOURI FINANCIAL SERVICES ASSOCIATION

The Missouri Financial Services Association is an industry trade group consisting of member finance companies operating within Missouri. Members firms varied in size from small companies with only one office to large national companies such as Household Finance, CIT, Commercial Credit, Associates Corporation, and others with branch operations throughout the United States. In terms of structure, state consumer financial services associations are similar to state banking associations, savings and loan

This case was prepared by Fred C. Yeager and Neil Seitz, Department of Finance, Saint Louis University.

The authors are grateful to the Missouri Financial Services Association, and particularly to Tom Harvey, former chairman of the Association's Executive Committee, for invaluable assistance in developing the necessary data for this case.

leagues, and credit union associations. Their purpose is to pursue objectives common to the industry; objectives which frequently involve state legislation.

Day-to-day operations of the Missouri Financial Services Association were guided by Harry Gallagher, the executive vice-president of the association; policy matters were determined by an executive committee drawn from the ranks of member finance companies. In 1978, 111 firms were members of the consumer financial services association in Missouri. Although most of the members were small companies with one or only a few offices, about 15 percent of them were large finance companies that operated two-thirds of all consumer finance offices in the state and about one-half of all consumer finance offices in the nation. The main operating expenses of the state association included salaries for the executive director and the small staff, rent, newsletter printing, and other office-related expenditures. These operating expenses were paid through membership fees and through assessments against member finance companies.

RATE REGULATION OF CONSUMER CREDIT

Early interest rate theory, dating back to Aristotle, held that interest was primarily a means of exploiting those who were forced by temporary hardship to resort to borrowing. It was this view of interest that led to legal and religious restrictions on interest charges that existed through much of the history of our Western culture.

In the United States, the first general usury statute (essentially being inherited from England) was enacted by Massachusetts in 1641 and fixed maximum interest rates at 8 percent. Usury statutes quickly spread throughout the American colonies. Because the mandated rate ceilings were set at artificially low levels, a legal installment loan market was effectively outlawed.

By 1900, almost every large city in the United States had loan companies. All the companies were operating illegally, many were charging annual rates of 200 percent or more, and some were employing collection tactics which could at best be described as unbusiness like.[1]

The Russell Sage Foundation, established in 1907, sponsored studies of consumer lending activities. Disclosures of illegal lending practices and related activities led to development of the first Uniform Small Loan Law which initially set maximum interest rates for small loans (up to $300) at 42 percent per year. In subsequent years this law, or a modification thereof, had been adopted by all states except Arkansas, thus creating an exception to the general usury ceiling.

RATE REGULATION IN MISSOURI

Missouri usury law in 1978 specified a maximum annual interest rate of 6 percent when no other rate had been agreed upon by the parties. For written contracts, the maximum agreed rate was 10 percent. Over the years, however, the state legislature had pro-

---

[1]One collection procedure was known as the "bawlerout" technique, whereby female loan company employees would visit the delinquent borrower at his place of employment and bawl him out in front of his colleagues.

vided for a number of "exceptions" to the general usury ceiling. Higher rates were allowed for various types of credit including credit card balances, time sales financing, and certain other consumer-related receivables. Most business loans were exempt from rate regulation, as were loans above $5,000 secured by specified securities. Unlike many states, where usury exceptions pertain to certain types of lenders, e.g., finance companies but not banks, the Missouri state constitution provided that the usury statute and exceptions pertain to the type of loan. The maximum contract rate for residential real estate loans, for example, was 10 percent regardless of the lender class (bank, savings and loan, finance company, etc.).

Of particular interest to the Missouri Financial Services Association was the exception in the statute that dealt with direct cash loans of up to $500 to consumers. That particular exception, unchanged since 1959, permitted negotiated rates of up to 15 percent add-on, or at the equivalent simple interest rate of 2.218 percent per month (26.616 percent per annum assuming a one year maturity) for loans of up to $500.[2] Under the statute, direct cash loans of any amount could be made to consumers. However, interest charges on loan balances in excess of $500 were subject to maximum rates of 0.833 per month (10 percent per annum).[3]

THE PROBLEM

Statistical data concerning the consumer finance industry in Missouri is provided in tables 1 through 6 and charts 1 through 6. There was a relatively stable level of APR from 1961 through 1976 (tables 1 and 2 and chart 1). However, debt cost for the industry almost doubled over the same time span. Also, consumer income and inflation more than doubled over the time periods contained in the tables and charts. Between 1965 and 1976, for example, the national average loan made by a consumer finance company increased from $558 to $1,384.

As a result of financial constraints faced by the industry, and beginning in the early 1970s, many firms began to curtail business operations in Missouri. Also, the legislature had recently enacted legislation reducing maximum premiums for credit life insurance, commissions from which had kept a number of finance company offices afloat (table 3 and chart 2). By 1978, the effect of inadequate profitability had begun to threaten the continued existence of the consumer finance industry in Missouri. While the number of loan offices in the United States remained relatively constant, the number in Missouri declined by 40 percent between the late 1960s and 1978. From 1973 through early 1978, 300 loan offices closed. Per capita loans by consumer finance companies had declined (chart 3) and a consumer credit gap had developed (table 4 and chart 4). A recent study of the industry concluded that "had Missouri per capita cash loan (from all lenders) and bank credit card receivables grown at the national rate, such receivables would have been greater in 1976 by approximately $151 million."

---

[2] See chapter 4 of this text for a discussion of add-on and simple interest rates.

[3] In 1976, the maximum contract rate was increased from 8 percent to 10 percent. While this change provided significant rate relief for residential real estate lenders, the impact on finance companies was inconsequential.

Table 1

Average Net APR Earned by Licensed Lenders in Missouri

(000s omitted for all dollar figures)

YEAR (1)	AVERAGE LOANS OUTSTANDING[1] (2)	INTEREST COLLECTED (3)	RECOVERIES OF CHARGED OFF LOANS (4)	LOANS CHARGED OFF (5)	RESERVE FOR BAD DEBTS (6)	NET INTEREST (3) + (4) − (5) − (6) (7)	NET APR (2) ÷ (7) (8)
1976	360,828	59,401.72	879.73	6,080.06	5,723.92	48,477.47	13.44
1975	358,409	59,631.65	812.88	5,397.82	5,634.10	49,394.61	13.78
1974	356,913	57,984.04	755.14	3,890.40	5,737.32	49,111.46	13.76
1973	360,079	53,860.14	924.51	5,203.68	4,024.40	45,556.57	12.65
1972	342,476	53,013.54	842.82	4,482.71	4,501.47	44,872.18	13.10
1971	323,985	50,162.05	801.83	4,161.77	4,191.40	42,610.71	13.15
1970	331,998	52,246.46	766.39	4,996.30	3,814.06	44,202.49	13.31
1969	337,888	52,847.28	766.80	3,940.14	3,772.89	45,901.05	13.58
1968	325,215	51,098.41	833.31	3,095.44	4,264.96	44,571.32	13.71
1967	312,085	50,929.88	734.53	3,358.73	3,868.78	44,436.90	14.24
1966	296,259	47,691.24	1,100.33	3,165.23	4,679.99	40,946.35	13.82
1965	271,278	45,307.41	753.48	2,641.56	5,007.10	38,412.23	14.16
1964	252,274	40,459.92	550.97	3,162.94	4,218.56	33,629.39	13.33
1963	267,069	37,812.22	391.11	3,308.87	3,613.71	31,280.75	11.71
1962	251,507	35,728.95	406.91	1,942.60	3,281.95	30,911.31	12.29
1961	204,422	33,041.25	401.35	1,657.97	2,970.22	28,814.81	14.10

Source: Division of Finance, State of Missouri.

[1](Beginning net loans + ending net loans) ÷ 2.

Table 2

Cost of Debt—Finance Co.

YEAR	S & P HIGH GRADE CORP. BOND INDEX[1]	FIN. CO. COMM. PAPER RATE[2]	EST. COST OF FIN. CO. DEBT[3]
1976	8.36%	5.22%	7.81%[4]
1975	8.63	6.16	8.24[3]
1974	8.25	8.62	8.31
1973	7.56	7.40	7.53
1972	7.26	4.52	6.79
1971	7.38	4.91	6.96
1970	7.84	7.23	7.74
1969	6.93	7.16	6.97
1968	6.05	5.69	5.99
1967	5.53	4.89	5.42
1966	5.13	5.36	5.17
1965	4.47	4.22	4.43
1964	4.37	3.77	4.27
1963	4.24	3.40	4.10
1962	4.29	3.07	4.08
1961	4.36	2.68	4.07

[1]S & P trade and security statistics.
[2]*Federal Reserve Bulletin.*
[3]*NCFA Research Report on Finance Companies in 1976.* National Consumer Finance Association: Washington, D.C., 1977.
[4]P(8.36) + (1 − P)5.22 = 7.81; P = 0.82
P(8.63) + (1 − P)6.16 = 8.24; P = 0.84.
Average P = (0.84 + 0.82) + 2 = .83.
Cost of fin. co. debt = 0.83 (High grade corp. bond rate) + 0.17 (fin. co. commercial paper rate).

THE PROPOSED SOLUTION

Maximum permissible cash loan rate data for Missouri, contiguous states, and the nation are contained in table 5 and chart 5. The data (table 5 and chart 5) reveal that maximum allowable APRs were lower for Missouri finance companies relative to the national average and relative to the average for contiguous states at all loan sizes. Legislation which was recently introduced in the state legislature would increase the small-loan base to which the rate of 2.218 percent per month (26.616 percent per annum) could be applied from $500 to $1200. If approved by the legislature (and signed by the governor), interest rate ceilings would be as shown by table 6 and chart 6.

As the executive committee of the Missouri Consumer Financial Services Association pondered these matters, they were keenly aware that attempts to gain rate relief had failed in previous years. They knew that critics of their industry would fight every move to seek higher interest rates for small loans. The rate relief bill had been assigned to committees in the state house of representatives and in the state senate. The executive committee knew that a strategy to ensure passage of the legislation must be developed.

Chart 1

Average Annual Percentage Rate Earned and Cost of Debt for Missouri Finance Companies

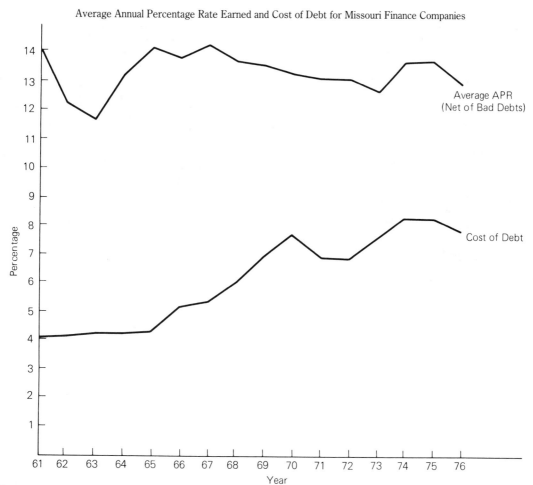

Source: Tables 1 and 2.

Table 3

Return on Asset Analysis of Licensed Lenders in Missouri: Total Missouri Business

YEAR (1)	TOTAL ASSETS (000) (2)	NET OPERATING INCOME EXCL. INS. COMM.[1] (000) (3)	ROA EXCL. INSURANCE (3) ÷ (2) (4)	INSURANCE COMMISSION (000) (5)	NET OPERATING INCOME INCL. INS. COMM. (000) (6)	ROA INCL. INSURANCE (6) ÷ (2) (7)
1976	414,290	20,353	4.91%	14,985	35,338	8.53%
1975	429,235	17,147	3.99	15,139	32,286	7.52
1974	407,886	19,273	4.73	14,783	34,056	8.35
1973	455,963	19,264	4.22	15,014	34,278	7.52
1972	446,058	18,821	4.22	15,047	33,868	7.59
1971	394,793	16,761	4.25	13,543	30,304	7.68
1970	386,797	21,220	5.49	13,504	34,724	8.98
1969	399,247	18,522	4.64	14,212	32,734	8.20
1968	396,010	17,604	4.44	13,995	31,599	7.98
1967	372,600	16,376	4.93	13,155	29,531	7.93
1966	368,238	15,300	4.15	12,899	28,199	7.66
1965	329,337	15,708	4.76	11,834	27,542	8.36
1964[2]						
1963	288,600	11,801	4.09	10,248	22,049	7.64
1962	272,954	13,201	4.84	9,545	22,746	8.33
1961	256,597	13,124	5.11	8,948	22,072	8.60
1960	232,685	5,838	2.51	9,118	13,955	6.00

[1]From annual report to Missouri Finance Division.
[2]The 1964 data are not compatible.

Chart 2

Return on Assets for Missouri Finance Companies

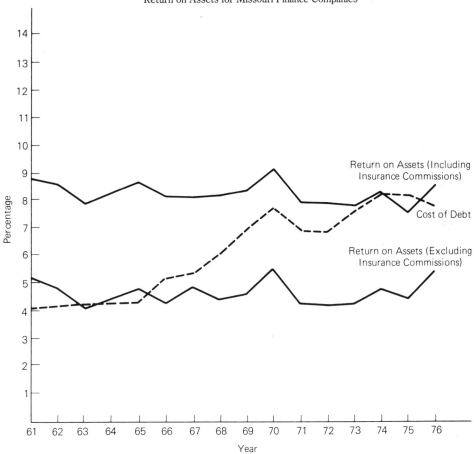

Source: Tables 2 and 3.

Chart 3

Per Capita Loans by Consumer Finance Companies (1967 $)

Source: Missouri data based on consolidated annual reports, Division of Finance, State of Missouri. U.S. data furnished by Research and Law Departments, Household Finance Company.

Table 4

Per Capita Cash Loan Balances and Credit Card Balances in Missouri and the United States

Year	MISSOURI			UNITED STATES		
	Cash Loans	Bank Credit Cards	Total	Cash Loans	Bank Credit Cards	Total
1965	127.93	NA	NA	144.06	NA	144.06
1970	260.96	15.59	276.55	283.84	17.22	301.06
1971	284.66	18.65	303.31	319.20	20.10	339.30
1972	319.40	24.17	343.57	350.21	22.32	372.53
1973	334.43	31.27	365.70	381.35	29.73	411. 08
1974	358.96	39.51	398.47	420.48	36.13	456.61
1975	374.66	43.25	417.91	436.98	38.90	475.88
1976	402.86	50.59	453.45	490.56	46.39	536.95

Source: Research and Law Departments, Household Finance Company.

Note: Cash loan data includes cash loans made by all lenders.

Chart 4

Per Capita and Bank Credit Card Credit for Missouri and the United States

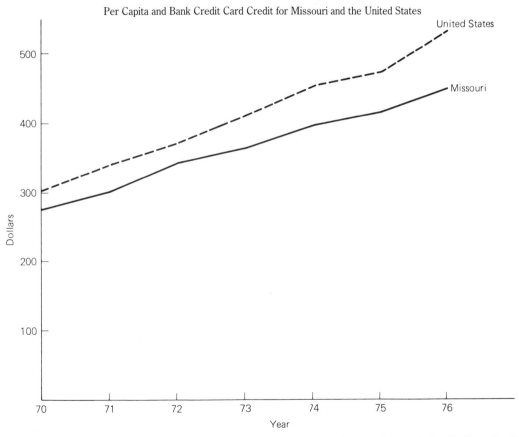

Source: Missouri data based on consolidated annual reports, Division of Finance, State of Missouri. U.S. data furnished by Research and Law Departments, Household Finance Company.

Table 5

Distribution of Maximum Permissible Interest Rates (APRs) for
Loans Subject to State Consumer Loan Laws
(Existing Median Rates—January 1978)

LOAN SIZE	MISSOURI	CONTIGUOUS STATES[1]	ALL STATES
$ 100	26.62	33.00	35.08
300	26.62	32.71	34.22
500	26.62	30.45	30.00
1,000	21.89	26.03	26.23
1,500	18.70	24.30	24.33
2,500	15.58	20.02	21.67
5,000	12.93	18.83	18.58
10,000	11.50	18.79	18.00

Source: Internal files of a national consumer finance company.

[1]States contiguous to Missouri included Arkansas, Oklahoma, Illinois, Iowa, Kansas, Nebraska, Kentucky, and Tennessee. Above data excludes Arkansas and Tennessee. Arkansas has no consumer loan law, and consumer finance companies do not maintain loan offices within the state. Tennessee's Industrial Loan and Thrift Act was declared unconstitutional 22 August 1977, and a constitutional referendum was then pending. Inclusion of Tennessee's rates as they existed prior to 22 August would raise the median slightly for loan categories of $1,500 and more. Median rates for loan categories of $300 through $1,000 would be reduced slightly. It is further noted that state small-loan ceilings of $3,000 and $7,500 exist in Nebraska and Kentucky, respectively. Thus, Nebraska is excluded in the above computations for loan sizes of $5,000 and $10,000, while Kentucky is excluded at the $10,000 loan size level.

Table 6

Distribution of Maximum Permissible Interest Rates (APRs) for
Loans Subject to State Consumer Loan Laws
(Proposed—January 1978)

LOAN SIZE	PROPOSED MISSOURI	CONTIGUOUS STATES*	ALL STATES
$ 100	26.62	33.00	35.08
300	26.62	32.71	34.22
500	26.62	30.45	30.00
1,000	26.62	26.03	26.23
1,500	25.64	24.30	24.33
2,500	21.54	20.02	21.67
5,000	16.57	18.83	18.58
10,000	13.47	18.79	18.00

*See note—table 5.

Chart 5

Existing Interest Rate Ceilings for Missouri and Average Ceilings for Other States (excluding Arkansas and Tennessee which do not have consumer loan laws in effect)

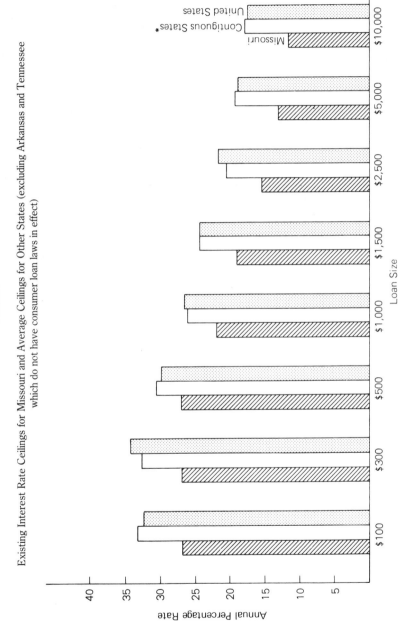

Source: Table 5.

Chart 6

Proposed Interest Rate Ceilings for Missouri and Average Ceilings for Other States (excluding Arkansas and Tennessee which do not have consumer loan laws in effect)

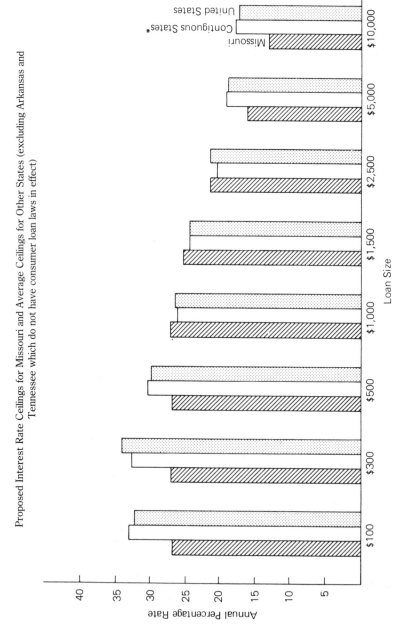

QUESTIONS

1. Should ceiling interest rates be set by law for the various categories of credit to consumers?
2. From the point of view of the Missouri Financial Services Association, develop a strategy designed to maximize prospects for passage of the legislation proposed in the case.
3. If you were a member of the Missouri state legislature, would you vote for the proposed legislation?

4

Interest Analysis

Interest plays the same role in financial markets that price plays in the market for goods. Funds are allocated to the uses that can pay the highest rent; thus interest is rent for money. A financial institution manager must have a thorough understanding of its meaning and computation.

Lenders are required to notify borrowers what interest rate they are charging and are sometimes restricted by law as to the interest rate they can charge. Therefore they must understand the impact of such things as service charges on the effective interest rate. Portfolio managers must be able to do such things as determine the interest rate earned on a bond that is purchased for less than its face value. Pension fund and life insurance company managers must be able to determine the amount of money they will have if funds are invested for a set number of years at a particular interest rate. And these are but a few examples of the ways in which managers must use interest analysis. This chapter, then deals with interest definitions, principles, and practices.

INTEREST RATE COMPARISONS

Both actual interest rates and methods of computation vary between markets. It is necessary to distinguish between the various ways in which interest rates are quoted or implied and to develop a methodology by which explicit or implicit interest charges may be calculated and directly compared. The difficulties in comparing the true cost of money over time are illustrated by the following situations:

1. A department store charges 1.5 percent per month on the average outstanding account balance.
2. A commercial bank offers to lease industrial equipment. Monthly lease payments are 3.38 percent of the equipment purchase price on a thirty-six month financial lease.
3. An automobile dealer offers to finance $3,000 of the cost of a new car for three years at an annual add-on interest rate of 6 percent. Repayment terms call for monthly payments. In other words, the dealer charges total interest of 0.06 × 3 × 3,000 = $540 and the monthly payment is (3,000 + 540)/36 = $98.33.
4. A mortgage payable monthly over thirty years is negotiated. Although the stated annual interest rate is 8 percent, terms of the mortgage call for payment of a service charge equal to three points (3 percent of the mortgage) at the time loan proceeds are disbursed.
5. A bank negotiates a $1,000 commercial loan with the interest rate stated as 7 percent discount. Loan terms call for repayment of the total loan one year hence. With this arrangement, the borrower receives $1,000 less 7 percent interest, or $930, and pays back $1,000.
6. A security originally issued several years ago may be purchased for $918.90. The holder of the security will receive $30 interest twice each year for the next five years. In addition, par value of the security ($1,000) is payable at the end of year five.

Common to the above situations is the fact that each involves the extension of credit and charging of interest, either explicitly or implicitly. Frequently, the decision maker must calculate the true interest rate inherent in such transactions. Once the rate is known, the creditor or debtor is in a position to compare credit alternatives.

TIME VALUE OF MONEY: THE MATHEMATICS OF INTEREST

To develop an understanding of the techniques used to compare interest rates, it is first necessary to develop the theory of compound interest. That development is completed in this section.

Compound Value of a Single Payment

The first step in understanding interest rates relates to the concept of compound value. Suppose that $1,000 is deposited in a savings account paying 6 percent interest compounded annually. Interest of $60 will be earned during the first year, and the account balance at the end of the first year will be $1,060. If the account is left undisturbed for two years, interest for the second year is $1,060 × 0.06 = $63.60. The account balance at the end of the second year is $1,060 + 63.60 = $1,123.60. This process by which interest is computed against both the original principal and previously accumulated interest is known as compound interest. If a financial institution credited interest on the original deposit but did not compound it, the saver could simply remove and reinvest funds once interest had been credited, achieving the same result. Thus compound interest, or interest on interest, is a normal practice in the case of savings accounts and other investment instruments.

If the funds were to be left for a large number of years in the account described above, it would be possible to find the amount to which the account would grow by continuing a series of calculations like those completed for the first two years. However, it is convenient to take a more systematic approach. The amount in the account at the end of the first year is

$$\$1,000 + 0.06(\$1,000) = \$1,000(1.06)$$
$$= \$1,060.$$

The amount in the account at the end of the second year equals

$$\$1,060(1.06) = \$1,000(1.06)^2 = 1,123.60$$

and the amount in the account at the end of the third year is

$$\$1,000(1.06)^2(1.06) = \$1,000(1.06)^3$$
$$= \$1,191.02.$$

This process can be generalized for the future value (FV_n) of an investment of P dollars at i percent interest per period for n periods:

$$FV_n = P(I + i)^n. \tag{4-1}$$

If the previous investment were allowed to continue growing for ten years, the value at the end of ten years would be

$$FV_{10} = \$1,000(1.06)^{10}.$$

While the procedure is the same for ten years as for two, the calculations can be tedious if done manually. To alleviate this problem, financial calculators or time value tables are used. Table 4-1 contains values of $(1 + i)^n$ for various combinations of i and n. Table A-1 in the appendix to this book is a continuation of table 4-1, containing compound values for additional combinations of i and n. The value of the account at the end of ten years is found by locating the intersection of the ten-year row and the 6 percent column in table 4-1. A value of 1.7908 is found, and the solution to the problem is

$$FV_{10} = \$1,000(1.06)^{10}$$
$$= \$1,000(1.7908) = \$1,790.80.$$

In the above examples, interest was calculated and added to the account at the end of each year. This is referred to as *annual compounding*. In some cases interest is compounded, or added to the principal, more than once a year. The result of compounding more than once a year is to raise the growth rate slightly. The future value formula when interest is compounded k times per year is

Table 4-1

Compound Value of a Dollar (Annual Compounding)

YEAR	3%	4%	5%	6%	7%	8%	9%	10%
1	1.0300	1.0400	1.0500	1.0600	1.0700	1.0800	1.0900	1.1000
2	1.0609	1.0816	1.1025	1.1236	1.1449	1.1664	1.1881	1.2100
3	1.0927	1.1249	1.1576	1.1910	1.2250	1.2597	1.2950	1.3310
4	1.1255	1.1699	1.2155	1.2625	1.3108	1.3605	1.4116	1.4641
5	1.1593	1.2167	1.2763	1.3382	1.4026	1.4693	1.5386	1.6105
6	1.1941	1.2653	1.3401	1.4185	1.5007	1.5869	1.6771	1.7716
7	1.2299	1.3159	1.4071	1.5036	1.6058	1.7138	1.8280	1.9487
8	1.2668	1.3686	1.4775	1.5938	1.7182	1.8509	1.9926	2.1436
9	1.3048	1.4233	1.5513	1.6895	1.8385	1.9990	2.1719	2.3579
10	1.3439	1.4802	1.6289	1.7908	1.9672	2.1589	2.3674	2.5937

$$FV_n = P\left(1 + \frac{i}{k}\right)^{kn}$$

$$(4\text{-}2)$$

Thus investing funds for three years at 12 percent per year with semiannual compounding provides the same growth as investing the funds for six years at 6 percent with annual compounding. If $1,000 is invested for three years at a 12 percent annual rate with interest compounded two times per year, the future value is

$$FV_3 = \$1,000\left(1 + \frac{0.12}{2}\right)^{2\cdot3}$$

$$= \$1,000(1.06)^6 = \$1,418.50.$$

Among compounding periods other than annual, monthly compounding is the most important for understanding interest practices. A $100 investment pays interest of 7 percent per year, compounded monthly. By the end of one year the investment will grow to

$$FV_1 = \$100\left(1 + \frac{0.07}{12}\right)^{12\cdot1}$$

$$= \$100(1.0723) = \$107.23.$$

Thus 7 percent compounded monthly would provide the same growth as 7.23 percent compounded annually. Due to the wide use of monthly compounding in such areas as mortgage loan analysis, special tables for monthly compounding are provided. Table 4-2 contains values of $[1 + (i/12)]^{12n}$ for various combinations of i and n. (Table A-2 in the appendix contains compound values for additional combinations of i and n.)

A $5,000 investment has a three-year maturity, a 7 percent interest rate, and monthly compounding. Principal and interest are payable at the end of the three-year

Table 4-2

Compound Value of a Dollar (Monthly Compounding)

YEA	3%	4%	5%	6%	7%	8%	9%	10%
1	1.0304	1.0407	1.0512	1.0617	1.0723	1.0830	1.0938	1.1047
2	1.0618	1.0831	1.1049	1.1272	1.1498	1.1729	1.1964	1.2204
3	1.0941	1.1273	1.1615	1.1967	1.2329	1.2702	1.3086	1.3482
4	1.1273	1.1732	1.2209	1.2705	1.3221	1.3757	1.4314	1.4894
5	1.1616	1.2210	1.2834	1.3489	1.4176	1.4898	1.5657	1.6453
6	1.1969	1.2707	1.3490	1.4320	1.5201	1.6135	1.7126	1.8176
7	1.2334	1.3225	1.4180	1.5204	1.6300	1.7474	1.8732	2.0079
8	1.2709	1.3764	1.4906	1.6141	1.7478	1.8925	2.0489	2.2182
9	1.3095	1.4325	1.5668	1.7137	1.8742	2.0495	2.2411	2.4504
10	1.3494	1.4908	1.6470	1.8194	2.0097	2.2196	2.4514	2.7070

period. To find the amount to which $1 would grow at the end of three years, we locate the intersection of the three-year row and 7 percent column in table 4-2. The value found there is 1.2329, and in three years the investment will grow to

$$FV_3 = \$5,000\left(1 + \frac{0.07}{12}\right)^{12\cdot3}$$

$$= \$5,000(1.2329) = \$6,164.50.$$

Frequently, the tables will not contain the precise interest rate desired. A decision maker wishing to find the compound value of a dollar for ten years at 6.4 percent with monthly compounding is faced with the fact that table 4-2 contains compound value factors for 6 percent and 7 percent, but not for 6.4 percent. The compound value factor for 6.4 percent can be estimated using *linear interpolation*. The linear interpolation formula, which is imposing to look at but easy to use, is

$$TVF_I = TVF_b + (TVF_a - TVF_b)\frac{I - I_b}{I_a - I_b} \tag{4-3}$$

where TVF_I = time value factor for desired interest rate
TVF_b = time value factor for interest rate below desired rate
TVF_a = time value factor for interest rate above desired rate
I = interest rate for which time value factor is desired
I_b = interest rate below rate for which time value factor is desired
I_a = interest rate above rate for which time value factor is desired.

Applying the interpolation formula to the above problem, the compound value factor for an annual interest rate of 6.4 percent for ten years with monthly compounding is

$$CVF_{6.4\%} = 1.8194 + (2.0097 - 1.8194)\frac{0.064 - 0.06}{0.07 - 0.06} = 1.8955.$$

The same interpolation approach can be used with table 4-1 when appropriate.[1]

Compound Value of an Annuity (Stream of Payments)

The decision maker is frequently interested in the amount to which a single payment or investment will grow; other problems of interest involve the growth of a series of payments. Such problems may be found in areas such as retirement planning, pension fund management, insurance portfolio management, and loan analysis. The procedure used is an extension of that used in the previous section.

A savings program calls for depositing $100 at the *end* of each year for the next three years in an account which pays 6 percent interest compounded annually. The amount in the account at the end of three years can be found as follows:

Value at the end of Year 1:	$100.
Value at the end of Year 2:	$100(1.06) + $100 = $206.
Value at the end of Year 3:	$206(1.06) + $100 + $318.36.

While this approach provides the correct answer, the calculations would be quite tedious if a large number of years were involved. Again, a table has been provided which contains compound values of $1 per year for selected combinations of years (n) and interest rates (i) with annual compounding (table 4-3). The formula for table 4-3 is[2]

$$CVA(i,n) = 1 + (1 + i)^1 + (1 + i)^2 + \ldots + (1 + i)^{n-1}. \qquad (4\text{-}4)$$

The intersection of the three-year row and 6 percent column in table 4-3 yields a compound value factor of 3.1836 which, when multiplied by $100 yields the $318.36 found above. If $100 were to be deposited at the end of each year for ten years, the value at the end of 10 years, based on the ten-year, 6 percent factor from table 4-3, would be:

$100 × 13.181 = $1,318.10

A number of lending and investment situations involve monthly payments with monthly compounding. Table 4-4 (and table A-4 in the appendix) contains compound

[1] A pocket calculator with a power function makes possible an exact solution:

$$\left(1 + \frac{0.064}{12}\right)^{10 \cdot 12} = 1.8933.$$

[2] With some rearrangement of terms, this formula can be reduced to

$$CVA(i,n) = [(1 + i)^n - 1]/i.$$

Table 4-3

Compound Value of an Annuity of $1 (Annual Payments, Annual Compounding)

YEAR	3%	4%	5%	6%	7%	8%	9%	10%
1	1.0000	1.0000	1.0000	1.0000	1.0000	1.0000	1.0000	1.0000
2	2.0300	2.0400	2.0500	2.0600	2.0700	2.0800	2.0900	2.1000
3	3.0909	3.1216	3.1525	3.1836	3.2149	3.2464	3.2781	3.3100
4	4.1836	4.2465	4.3101	4.3746	4.4399	4.5061	4.5731	4.6410
5	5.3091	5.4163	5.5256	5.6371	5.7507	5.8666	5.9847	6.1051
6	6.4684	6.6330	6.8019	6.9753	7.1533	7.3359	7.5233	7.7156
7	7.6625	7.8983	8.1420	8.3938	8.6540	8.9228	9.2004	9.4872
8	8.8923	9.2142	9.5491	9.8975	10.260	10.637	11.028	11.436
9	10.159	10.583	11.027	11.491	11.978	12.488	13.021	13.579
10	11.464	12.006	12.578	13.181	13.816	14.487	15.193	15.937

Table 4-4

Compound Value of an Annuity of $1 (Monthly Payments, Monthly Compounding)

YEAR	3%	4%	5%	6%	7%	8%	9%	10%
1	12.166	12.222	12.279	12.336	12.393	12.450	12.508	12.566
2	24.703	24.943	25.186	25.432	25.681	25.933	26.188	26.447
3	37.621	38.182	38.753	39.336	39.930	40.536	41.153	41.782
4	50.931	51.960	53.015	54.098	55.209	56.350	57.521	58.722
5	64.647	66.299	68.006	69.770	71.593	73.477	75.424	77.437
6	78.779	81.223	83.764	86.409	89.161	92.025	95.007	98.111
7	93.342	96.754	100.33	104.07	108.00	112.11	116.43	120.95
8	108.35	112.92	117.74	122.83	128.20	133.87	139.86	146.18
9	123.81	129.74	136.04	142.74	149.86	157.43	165.48	174.05
10	139.74	147.25	155.28	163.88	173.08	182.95	193.51	204.84

values of $1 per month for n years at an annual percentage rate of i with monthly compounding. The formula for table 4-4 is[3]

$$CVA_m(i,n) = 1 + \left(1 + \frac{i}{12}\right)^1 + \left(1 + \frac{i}{12}\right)^2 + \cdots + \left(1 + \frac{i}{12}\right)^{12n-1} \tag{4-5}$$

A savings program involves investing $100 at the end of each month for the next ten years at a 6 percent annual interest rate with monthly compounding. The amount in

[3]With some rearrangment of terms, this formula can be reduced to

$$CVA_m(i,n) = \left[\left(1 + \frac{i}{12}\right)^{12n} - 1\right] \Big/ (i/12).$$

the account at the end of ten years, based on the ten-year, 6 percent figure from table 4-4, is the following:

$$\$100 \times 163.88 = \$16,388$$

As with compounding of a single payment, interpolation can be used when the desired interest rate is not available. One hundred dollars is to be deposited the end of each month for the next ten years in an account paying 7.30 percent interest per year with monthly compounding. The compound value factor can be estimated by using equation (4-3) to interpolate between the 7 percent, ten-year factor and the 8 percent, twenty-year factor in table 4-4:

$$173.08 + (182.95 - 173.08) \, \frac{.073 - 07}{.08 - .07} = \$176.04.$$

The same interpolation procedure can be used with table 4-3 for appropriate problems.

Present Value of a Future Sum: Reverse Compounding

If a dollar invested today will grow to an amount greater than a dollar at some future date, a dollar received at some future date is less valuable than a dollar received today. Financial institutions acquire and issue securities which provide the holder with one or more future cash payments. Sometimes securities will have a provision whereby a certain cash payment is to be given the holder at the end of a designated period, with no intervening payments prior to maturity. For example, the prospective purchaser of a certificate of deposit issued by a savings institution may wish to know how much he must invest today in order to have a certain sum two years hence. Similarly, a corporate treasurer may be charged with the responsibility of investing sufficient funds from current earnings to ensure the firm's ability to meet construction progress payments due several years hence. Numerous other examples could be cited where the investor knew the amount to be realized in the future and would wish to know what that amount is worth today. Today's value depends, of course, on the interest rate implied in the investment and on the frequency with which interest is compounded.

Suppose an investment will pay $5,000 two years from today. If the investor has alternate opportunities paying 6 percent interest, the amount required to have $5,000 two years from today can be found by restating equation (4-1):

$$P = FV_n \times \frac{1}{(1 + i)^n}$$

$$P = \$5,000 \, \frac{1}{(1.06)^2} \tag{4-6}$$

$$= \$5,000 \times 0.8900 = \$4,450.$$

Thus the *present value* of $5,000 received two years from today, given an annual interest or growth rate of 6 percent compounded annually, is $4,450. The present value of $5,000 received five years from today, *discounted*[4] at 7 percent per annum, would be

$$P = \$5,000 \, \frac{1}{(1.07)^5}$$
$$= \$5,000 \times 0.7130 = \$3,565.$$

This value can be verified by showing that $3,565 invested today at 7 percent compounded annually will grow to $5,000 by the end of five years.

Table 4-5 (and table A-5 in the appendix) contains values of $1/(1 + i)^n$ for selected combinations of i and n. The intersection of the five-year row and 7 percent column in table 4-5 yields the present value factor 0.7130 used above. A payment of $10,000 is to be received ten years from today. An investor who wishes to earn a return of 7 percent compounded annually can find the amount she must pay for the investment by referring to the 7 percent, ten-year interest factor in table 4-5.

$$\$10,000 \times 0.5083 = \$5,083$$

Table 4-6 (and table A-6 in the appendix) is used for problems of the same type when monthly compounding is involved. If alternate investments pay a 6 percent annual interest rate with monthly compounding, the present value of $1,000 received ten years from today, based on the ten-year, 6 percent factor from table 4-6 is

$$\$1,000 \times 0.5496 = \$549.60.$$

As with future value of a single payment, interpolation using equation (4-3) can be used if the desired interest rate is not available.

Present Value of an Annuity

If a security is to provide a *stream* of future payments, the present value of that stream and thus the market value of the security, can be found in a manner similar to that discussed for a single payment. At a required return of 6 percent, a security which is to provide cash flow or payment of $500 at the end of each year for the next two years would have a present value (*PV*) of

$$PV = 500 \times \frac{1}{1.06} + 500 \times \frac{1}{(1.06)^2}$$
$$= \$916.70.$$

[4]The term "discounted" as used in this section should not be confused with the term "discount rate." The latter is a rate applied to original loan principal as a method of calculating interest charges. The former relates to the use of a simple interest rate so as to reduce the value of future cash payments in order to determine their present value.

Table 4-5

Present Value of a Dollar (Annual Compounding)

YEAR	3%	4%	5%	6%	7%	8%	9%	10%
1	0.9709	0.9615	0.9524	0.9434	0.9346	0.9259	0.9174	0.9091
2	0.9426	0.9246	0.9070	0.8900	0.8734	0.8573	0.8417	0.8264
3	0.9151	0.8890	0.8638	0.8396	0.8163	0.7938	0.7722	0.7513
4	0.8885	0.8548	0.8227	0.7921	0.7629	0.7350	0.7084	0.6830
5	0.8626	0.8219	0.7835	0.7473	0.7130	0.6806	0.6499	0.6209
6	0.8375	0.7903	0.7462	0.7050	0.6663	0.6302	0.5963	0.5645
7	0.8131	0.7599	0.7107	0.6651	0.6227	0.5835	0.5470	0.5132
8	0.7894	0.7304	0.6768	0.6274	0.5820	0.5403	0.5019	0.4665
9	0.7664	0.7026	0.6446	0.5919	0.5439	0.5002	0.4604	0.4241
10	0.7441	0.6756	0.6139	0.5584	0.5083	0.4632	0.4224	0.3855

Table 4-6

Present Value of a Dollar (Monthly Compounding)

YEAR	3%	4%	5%	6%	7%	8%	9%	10%
1	0.9705	0.9609	0.9513	0.9419	0.9326	0.9234	0.9142	0.9052
2	0.9418	0.9232	0.9050	0.8872	0.8697	0.8526	0.8358	0.8194
3	0.9140	0.8871	0.8610	0.8356	0.8111	0.7873	0.7641	0.7417
4	0.8871	0.8524	0.8 191	0.7871	0.7564	0.7269	0.6986	0.6714
5	0.8609	0.8190	0.7792	0.7414	0.7054	0.6712	0.6387	0.6078
6	0.8355	0.7869	0.7413	0.6983	0.6578	0.6198	0.5839	0.5502
7	0.8108	0.7561	0.7052	0.6577	0.6135	0.5723	0.5338	0.4980
8	0.7869	0.7265	0.6709	0.6195	0.5721	0.5284	0.4881	0.4508
9	0.7636	0.6981	0.6382	0.5835	0.5336	0.4879	0.4462	0.4081
10	0.7411	0.6708	0.6072	0.5496	0.4976	0.4505	0.4079	0.3694

If the investment were to provide the same cash flow each year for twenty years instead of two, the procedure would be the same but the calculations would become quite tedious. Calculations can be aided by generalizing the approach as follows:[5]

$$PV = CF \times \frac{1}{1 + i} + CF \times \frac{1}{(1 + i)^2} + \cdots + CF \times \frac{1}{(1 + i)^n}$$
$$= CF \left[\frac{1}{1 + i} + \frac{1}{(1 + i)^2} + \cdots + \frac{1}{(1 + i)^n} \right]$$

(4-7)

[5]With some rearrangement of terms, this formula can be reduced to

$$PV = CF[1 - 1/(1 + i)^n]/i.$$

Table 4-7

Present Value of an Annuity of $1 (Annual Payments, Annual Compounding)

YEAR	3%	4%	5%	6%	7%	8%	9%	10%
1	0.9709	0.9615	0.9524	0.9434	0.9346	0.9259	0.9174	0.9091
2	1.9135	1.8861	1.8594	1.8334	1.8080	1.7833	1.7591	1.7355
3	2.8286	2.7751	2.7232	2.6730	2.6243	2.5771	2.5313	2.4869
4	3.7171	3.6299	3.5460	3.4651	3.3872	3.3121	3.2397	3.1699
5	4.5797	4.4518	4.3295	4.2124	4.1002	3.9927	3.8897	3.7908
6	5.4172	5.2421	5.0757	4.9173	4.7665	4.6229	4.4859	4.3553
7	6.2303	6.0021	5.7864	5.5824	5.3893	5.2064	5.0330	4.8684
8	7.0197	6.7327	6.4632	6.2098	5.9713	5.7466	5.5348	5.3349
9	7.7861	7.4353	7.1078	6.8017	6.5152	6.2469	5.9952	5.7590
10	8.5302	8.1109	7.7217	7.3601	7.0236	6.7101	6.4177	6.1446

where PV = present value (of the security)
CF = amount to be received at the end of each year
i = required rate of return
n = number of years the cash flows are to continue.

Table 4-7 contains values of this function for selected combinations of i and n. (Table A-7 in the appendix contains values for additional combinations.) The use of the table eliminates a good deal of tedious calculation. A security will provide cash flows of $5,000 a year for ten years. If the required return is 7 percent, the value associated with ten years and 7 percent in table 4-7 is 7.0236 and the present value of the cash flows or value of the security is

$$PV = \$5,000 \times 7.0236 = \$35,118.$$

If payments are to be received monthly, with interest compounded monthly, the present value is[6]

$$PV = CF\left[1 \Big/ \left(1 + \frac{i}{12}\right) + 1 \Big/ \left(1 + \frac{i}{12}\right)^2 + \cdots + 1 \Big/ \left(1 + \frac{i}{12}\right)^{12n} \right] \quad (4\text{-}8)$$

Table 4-8 and table A-8 in the appendix contain values of this function for various combinations of i and n.

Suppose a lender wished to grant a loan with monthly payments and an annual interest rate of 7 percent. By referring to table 4-8, the lender could determine that the present value of $1 received each month for ten years, discounted at 7 percent per

[6]With some rearrangement of terms, this formula can be reduced to

$$PV = CF\left[1 - 1 \Big/ \left(1 + \frac{i}{12}\right)^{12n} \right] \Big/ (i/12).$$

Table 4-8

Present Value of an Annuity of $1 (Monthly Payments, Monthly Compounding)

YEAR	3%	4%	5%	6%	7%	8%	9%	10%
1	11.807	11.744	11.681	11.619	11.557	11.496	11.435	11.375
2	23.266	23.028	22.794	22.563	22.335	22.111	21.889	21.671
3	34.386	33.871	33.366	32.871	32.386	31.912	31.447	30.991
4	45.179	44.289	43.423	42.580	41.760	40.962	40.185	39.428
5	55.652	54.299	52.991	51.726	50.502	49.318	48.173	47.065
6	65.817	63.917	62.093	60.340	58.654	57.035	55.477	53.979
7	75.681	73.159	70.752	68.453	66.257	64.159	62.154	60.237
8	85.255	82.039	78.989	76.095	73.348	70.738	68.258	65.901
9	94.545	90.572	86.826	83.293	79.960	76.812	73.839	71.029
10	103.56	98.770	94.281	90.073	86.126	82.421	78.942	75.671

annum and compounded monthly, is $86.126. Thus a loan of $86.126 repaid in monthly payments of $1 per month over ten years yields an annual return on investment of 7 percent compounded monthly. If the loan were to be for a larger amount, say $30,000, we would divide the loan amount by 86.126 to find the monthly payment:

$30,000/86.126 = $348.33

DETERMINING INTEREST RATES

Analysis of loan and investment alternatives frequently requires that the decision maker determine the true interest rate associated with a given loan or investment. Insurance companies for example, are often asked to invest in major projects such as proposed shopping centers. In a project of this type, the investor may receive future cash flows based at least in part on rental income derived from shopping center tenants. In this illustration, the decision maker will know the amount of investment required, and a reasonable estimate of future cash inflows may be projected. It remains then, to determine the interest rate or return inherent in the transaction. Alternatively, suppose that a security which offers a certain series of future cash flows is available for purchase at a specified price. Such a security could be a new or existing bond, a new or existing mortgage, a negotiable certificate of deposit, or one of a variety of other financial instruments. The decision to purchase or reject such securities is influenced by the interest rate inherent in the transaction. It is important therefore, that the decision maker be at least conceptually familiar with the process by which the rate is determined. This process involves use of equations and tables previously discussed.

Assume that a particular investment requires $5,000 and will grow in value to $7,000 at the end of five years. The problem can be restated as a simple compound value problem using equation (4-1):

$$\$5,000(1 + i)^5 = \$7,000$$
$$(1 + i)^5 = \$7,000/5,000 = 1.4.$$

Previous use of table 4-1 involved searching for the compound value factor associated with a particular interest rate. Our objective now is to refer to table 4-1 and find the interest rate associated with a particular compound value factor. If we proceed to the five-year row in that table, and look for the interest factor 1.4, a value of 1.4026 is found in the 7 percent column. We conclude that the effective interest rate on the investment is approximately 7 percent compounded annually.

This same procedure can be used when a stream of future payments is involved. An investment requires payments of $100 per month and will grow to $9,000 in six years. The ratio of future value to monthly cash flow is 9000/100 = 90.00. In table 4-4 an examination of the six-year row reveals a compound value factor of 89.161 at 7 percent and 92.025 at 8 percent. The effective interest rate lies between 7 percent and 8 percent.

Interpolation can be used to prepare an estimate of the exact interest rate in a manner similar to that used with equation (4-3) when an estimate of exact compound value is desired:

$$I = I_b + (I_a - I_b)\frac{TV_I - TV_b}{TV_a - TV_b} \tag{4-9}$$

$$= .07 + (.08 - .07)\frac{90 - 89.161}{92.025 - 89.161} = 7.3\%.$$

Many times the effective interest rate will be desired for an uneven stream of cash flows. An investment which costs $1,130 today will provide $90 at the end of each year for the next ten years and then $1,000 at the end of ten years. The effective interest rate is the rate which will make the present value of the cash inflows equal to the cost. This rate is found by a trial-and-error process. We decide to start the search with 7 percent. Referring to tables 4-5 and 4-7, we find the present value factors for 7 percent, ten years, and apply these to determine the present value of the cash flows:

DATES	CASH FLOW	×	PV FACTOR (7%)	PRESENT VALUE
Year 1—10 (annual)	90		7.0236	$632.12
Year 10	$1,000		0.5083	508.30
			Total present value:	$1,140.42

We are seeking an interest rate which would result in a total present value of $1,130. Since a higher interest rate results in a lower present value, we try a higher rate. We decide to try 8%:

DATES	CASH FLOW	×	PV FACTOR (8%)	=	PRESENT VALUE
Year 1–10 (annual)	90		6.7101		$603.91
Year 10	$1,000		0.4632		463.20
			Total present value:		$1,067.11

Since we are looking for a present value of $1,130, we know the effective interest rate is between 7 percent and 8 percent. We can estimate the exact interest rate by interpolation, using equation (4-9):

$$I = 0.07 + (0.08 - 0.07)\frac{1130 - 1140.42}{1067.11 - 1140.42} = 7.14\%.$$

INTEREST PRACTICES AND EFFECTIVE INTEREST RATES

Having developed the general mathematics of interest, we are now ready to examine specific interest practices. This section has two major objectives. The first is to develop an understanding of interest terminology and payment practices which are commonly used. The second is to develop a methodology for comparing interest charges which are quoted or computed in different ways.

Annual Percentage Rate

Early in this chapter it was noted that different computational methods sometimes result in different interest charges even though stated interest rates are identical. The annual percentage rate (also referred to as the simple interest rate) is normally used as the standard of comparison. Indeed, truth in lending legislation of recent years requires disclosure of the effective annual percentage rate (APR) in virtually all types of consumer lending.

When we identified or computed effective interest rates in the previous section, we were dealing with the annual percentage rate. As an example, take a $1,200 note with a 6 percent annual percentage rate, a one-year maturity, and a lump sum payment. Interest on the note will be $72 ($1,200 × 0.06), and the amount due at maturity will be $1,272.00. If this same loan were to be paid in equal installments at the end of each month, interest charged each month would be 0.005 (0.06/12) of the balance due at the beginning of the month. The amount required to retire the loan in twelve monthly payments can be found by referring to table A-8 in the appendix. The present value of $1 per month for one year at 6 percent is found to be 11.619. The monthly payment required is $103.28 ($1,200/11.619). The allocation of the payment between principal and interest is shown in table 4-9.

The same approach to finding the payment and constructing an amortization schedule can be used when the life of the security is greater than one year. To find the

Table 4-9

Amortization Schedule for a $1,200, 6 Percent, One-Year, Simple Interest Note with Equal Installments Payable at the End of Each Month

MONTH	BEGINNING LOAN BALANCE	MONTHLY PAYMENT	INTEREST PAYMENT*	PRINCIPAL REDUCTION	ENDING BALANCE
1	$1,200.00	$ 103.28	$ 6.00	$ 97.28	$1,102.72
2	1,102.72	103.28	5.51	97.77	1,004.95
3	1,004.95	103.28	5.02	98.26	906.69
•	•	•	•	•	•
•	•	•	•	•	•
•	•	•	•	•	•
12	102.77	103.28	0.51	102.77	0.00
Total		$1,239.36	$39.36		

*Sample interest calculations:

	P	×	R	×	t	=	Interest
1st month	1,200.00	×	0.06	×	$\frac{1}{12}$	=	6.00
2nd month	1,102.72	×	0.06	×	$\frac{1}{12}$	=	5.51
3rd month	1,004.95	×	0.06	×	$\frac{1}{12}$	=	5.02

monthly payment necessary to amortize an 8 percent, ten-year mortgage, the present value factor for 8 percent, ten years (82.421) is first located in table A-8. The amount of the loan is then divided by this present value factor. If the mortgage loan were for $50,000, the monthly payment would be $606.64 ($50,000/82.421). Alternatively, if the loan were to be repaid in *annual* installments, we would find the 8 percent, ten-year figure of 6.7101 in table A-7 and the annual payment would be $7,451.45 ($50,000/ 6.7101).

Frequently one wants to know the amount still owed after some number of payments without constructing a complete amortization schedule. Suppose, for example, an individual who took out a 12 percent APR $6,000 three-year automobile loan wants to repay the loan after one year. Using table A-8, the monthly payment would be $6,000 ÷ 30.108 = $199.29. The balance owed after one year is the present value of the remaining payments. Since there are two years of remaining monthly payments and the loan carries a 12 percent interest rate, the 12 percent, two-year figure from table A-8 is used:

Balance due = $199.29 × 21.243 = $4,234.

This is the same answer that would have been achieved by constructing an amortization table like table 4-9.

Rule of 78s   When a loan is repaid before maturity, some consumer lenders use a method called the rule of 78s rather than the approach described in the previous paragraph (which is called the straight amortization method). When the rule of 78s is used, the finance charge is reduced by

$$\frac{m(m + 1)}{n(n + 1)} \times \text{total finance charge}$$

where m is the number of payments remaining when the loan is repaid and n is the number of payments called for in the original loan agreement.

For the 12 percent, three-year, $6,000 automobile loan described in the paragraph before last, the monthly payment is $199.29 and the total finance charge is 36 × $199.29 − $6,000 = $1,174.44. If the loan is repaid when twenty-four payments are still to be made, the rule of 78s reduction of the finance charge is

$$\frac{24(24 + 1)}{36(36 + 1)} \times \$1,174.44 = \$529.03.$$

The balance due is therefore 24 × $199.29 − $529.03 = $4,254, compared to $4,234 that was still owed with straight amortization.

When a loan is repaid before maturity, the amount still due is always higher with the rule of 78s than with straight amortization. This increases the effective APR when the loan is repaid early. The differences between the two methods are small for loans with short maturities, but can be quite large for loans with long maturities, such as mortgage loans. The rule of 78s is seldom if ever used for these longer maturity loans.

Add-on and Discount Rates

Add-on interest rates are frequently used in consumer installment transactions and, to a lesser extent, in business and other commercial loans. Discount rates are also common to both consumer and business transactions. A key distinction between both add-on and discount rates as opposed to annual percentage rates is that calculation of interest charges is based upon the original loan principal and ignores the fact that the principal balance may decline over time as periodic payment of principal and interest is made. The method by which interest charges are calculated can have a dramatic effect on total loan charges (table 4-10).

Suppose someone wishes to borrow $1,200 and is told that the loan is available at an annual interest rate of 6 percent add-on with repayment in equal installments, one at the end of each month. With the add-on method, the total interest charge will be 0.06 × $1,200 = $72.00 (compared to $39.36 when the rate was 6 percent simple) and monthly payments will be $106 ($1272/12). The effective annual percentage rate for this loan can be found using table A-8. We know that the time is one year and the ratio of loan value to payment is 11.321 ($1,200/106). Scanning across the one-year row of table A-8, we find the value of 11.375 at 10 percent and 11.315 at 11.0 percent. By interpolation, the annual percentage rate is approximately 10.90 percent. Note that this is close to twice the quoted add-on rate.

If the discount method is used, the interest charge of $72 (0.06 × $1,200) is immediately deducted from the amount loaned. In this case, the borrower has initial use of only $1,128. If monthly payments are to be made, they will be $100 per month over twelve months. Interest charges total $72. Obviously, the discount method involves a higher annual percentage rate than the add-on method. With the discount method, the borrower receives $1,128 and pays monthly installments of $100. The ratio of loan to

Table 4-10

Comparison of Interest Charges and True Annual Interest Rates Applicable to Three Loans, Each Bearing Stated
Interest of 6 Percent

	ADD-ON METHOD	DISCOUNT METHOD	SIMPLE INTEREST METHOD
Stated annual rate	6%	6%	6%
Amount loaned	$1,200.00	$1,200.00	$1,200.00
Loan maturity	1 year	1 year	1 year
Repayment terms	Monthly	Monthly	Monthly
Interest charges	$ 72.00	$ 72.00	$39.36
Loan proceeds	1,200.00	1,128.00	1,200.00
Time balance	1,272.00	1,200.00	1,239.36
Monthly payments	106.00	100.00	103.28*
Annual simple interest rate	10.89%	11.58%	6.00%

*Using table A-8, $1.200 ÷ 11.6189 = $103.28

payment is 1128/100 = 11.28. Again, the effective annual percentage rate can be found using table A-8. Present value factors of 11.315 and 11.255 are found at 11 percent and 12 percent, respectively. Thus the annual percentage rate lies between 11 percent and 12 percent. By interpolation, the effective simple interest rate is approximately 11.6 percent.

Financial Leases

A specific type of financial instrument and one which has received increased use in recent years is the financial lease. Frequently, financial institutions act in the capacity of a lessor, purchasing assets on behalf of a customer (lessee) and, in turn, leasing the assets under terms of a lease agreement. Terms of a pure financial lease differ from those typically associated with an operating or service lease. In the case of the latter, the lessor provides maintenance and other services. Furthermore, operating or service leases are often cancelable on short notice. Financial leases, on the other hand, are simply an alternative method of financing assets. In a financial lease, the lessee assumes all obligations normally associated with ownership. The lessor merely provides the capital necessary for acquisition of the asset, holds title to the asset, and enters into an agreement whereby the lessee promises to make a series of payments sufficient to provide a return of all costs as well as a profit to the lessor.

Since a lease is not a loan, interest charges are technically nonexistent and are thus unspecified in the lease agreement. However, an interest rate is *implied* in the transaction, and a financial lease is frequently an alternative to a loan. Thus, the decision maker should evaluate the lease agreement in terms of the annual percentage rate implied in the agreement.

The information in table 4-11 was drawn from the files of a leasing corporation and provides information relating to one method of quoting lease payments. Specific rates vary over time, and the quotations contained in table 4-11 happened to be in effect for that company in the spring of 1973. Suppose that a prospective lessee wished to lease equipment priced at $30,000 from the company whose rates are represented in table 4-11. If the term of the lease were three years, monthly lease payments would be (3.38% × $30,000) = $1,014.00. Thus, $1,014 represents an annuity to be paid (or received) over a thirty-six-month period. The present value of that annuity is $30,000. Expressed in terms of a dollar, the present value factor is

$30,000/$1,014 = 29.586.

Referring to table A-8 and looking across the three-year row, we find the factor 29.679 associated with 13 percent and 29.259 associated with 14 percent. We conclude that the interest rate inherent in the lease is between 13 percent and 14 percent. Linear interpolation results in an estimate of 13.22 percent. Thus an annual percentage rate of 13.22 percent is implied in the lease agreement.

Table 4-11

Financial Lease Terms Quoted by a Leasing Corporation

ASSET COST (INCLUDING ALL TAXES AND CHARGES)	TERM (NUMBER OF YEARS)	MONTHLY RENTAL (% OF TOTAL COST)
Less than $1,000	1	9.28
	2	5.11
1,000 to 5,000	3	3.53
5,000 to 10,000	3	3.47
	4	2.79
	5	2.44
10,000 to 25,000	3	3.42
	5	2.38
25,000 to 50,000	3	3.38
	5	2.33
50,000 to 100,000	3	3.36
	5	2.30
Over 100,000	3	3.33
	5	2.28

Source: Internal files of a leasing corporation.

Points and Service Charges

The collection of a charge payable at the time a loan is granted is a common practice that has the effect of increasing the annual percentage rate. Points will be used as an example, although discounts and other service charges have a similar impact. A point, normally used in connection with a mortgage loan, is a service charge or discount equal to 1 percent of the value of the loan. Thus a $20,000 mortgage with a three-point charge would require a fee of $600 (0.03 × $20,000). The financial institution would advance a net $19,400 ($20,000 − $600) but would receive payments and calculate interest charges as if the investment had been $20,000. This procedure obviously raises the true rate above that which is stated.

A $20,000 mortgage loan with a thirty-year maturity and an 8 percent stated interest rate would require monthly payments of $20,000/136.28 = $146.75 (from table A-8). Since the net investment is only $19,400, the ratio of loan to payment is $19,400/146.75 = 132.198. In the thirty-year row of table A-8, an interest factor of 136.28 is found at 8 percent, and a factor of 124.28 is found at 9 percent. The annual percentage rate is between 8 percent and 9 percent. By interpolation, it is approximately 8.3 percent.

While points are of some significance if the loan is carried to maturity, they are of much greater significance if the loan is retired early. In general, the sooner a loan is retired, the greater the true annual percentage rate when points or similar charges had been levied against the original loan.

Frequency of Compounding and Effective Interest Rates

In quoting interest rates on certificates of deposit and other savings instruments, it is common practice to advertise that the use of frequent compounding periods increases the effective interest rate. For example, a bank might advertise that its 10 percent certificate of deposit provides daily compounding for an effective interest rate of 10.515 percent. If interest is compounded k times per year, formula (4-2) shows that the future value is

$$FV_n = P\left(1 + \frac{i}{k}\right)^{kn}$$

where i is the interest rate and n is the number of years. If interest is compounded annually ($k = 1$) and the annual interest rate is 10 percent, the amount a dollar will grow to by the end of the year is

$$FV_1 = 1\left(1 + \frac{.10}{1}\right) = \$1.10.$$

If interest is compounded daily, the value at the end of one year will be

$$FV_1 = 1\left(1 + \frac{0.10}{365}\right)^{365} = \$1.10515.$$

Since $1 grows to $1.10515 in one year, this is equivalent to an interest rate of 10.515 percent with annual compounding.

Occasionally, the concept of continuous compounding is used. This means that the compounding periods are infinitely short. Using a proof available in most college algebra texts, it can be shown that:

$$\lim_{k \to \infty}\left(1 + \frac{i}{k}\right)^{nk} = e^{in}$$

where $e = 2.71828\ldots$, the base of the common logarithm. Thus, $1 invested for one year at 10 percent per year, compounded continuously, would grow to $1 \cdot e^{0.10} = \$1.10517$. This is equivalent to an interest rate of 10.517 percent a year with annual compounding.

The continuous compounding approach can also be used to find the present value of a future amount. For example, the present value of $20,000 to be received ten years from today, discounted at an annual interest rate of 12 percent with continuous compounding would be

$$PV = \$20,000 \div 2.71828^{0.12 \cdot 10} = \$6,023.89.$$

Bonds: Value and Yield to Maturity

Bonds are frequently bought and sold by financial institutions and by other investors long after they are issued. Although interest payments and the terminal value of the bond are fixed, the market value of the security may fluctuate depending on shifts in the market interest rate for that type of security. The relationship between par or face value of the bond and the periodic interest payments paid to the holder is called the *stated* or *coupon* interest rate and does not change. The ratio of annual interest payment to current market value is called the *current yield*. However, the current yield is not the true interest rate earned, because it does not include the capital gain or loss—the difference between the current market value and the amount that will be repaid at maturity. The *yield to maturity* is the true interest rate earned and is identical with the annual percentage rate. It recognizes both the interest payment received and any capital gain or loss that will occur if the bond is held to maturity. The yield to maturity is thus defined as the interest rate that equates the present value of the future cash flows (interest payments and terminal value) to the current market price of the bond.

A typical bond has a face or par value of $1,000 and pays interest twice a year. Thus a $1,000, 6 percent bond pays $30 each six months and $1,000 at maturity. As previously suggested, bonds frequently trade above or below their face value, making the true interest rate or yield to maturity different than the stated or coupon rate. Market quotations are stated as a percentage of face value: a price quote of 91.89 would mean that a $1,000 bond is being traded at $918.90.

Suppose the above 6 percent bond is five years from maturity and interest rates have risen such that bonds of this type are selling to provide a yield of 8 percent. What is this existing bond worth? We can answer this question by turning to tables A-5 and A-7, assuming semiannual compounding. The 91.89 figure for the above bond is derived using the present value of $1 per year for ten years at 4 percent and the present value of a single payment of $1 in ten years at 4 percent.[7]

$$\$30 \times 8.1109 = \$243.33$$
$$1,000 \times 0.6756 = \underline{675.60}$$
$$\$918.93$$
or 91.893 percent
of face value

A borrower who received $918.93 from a lender and agreed to the series of payments described above would have agreed to a loan with an annual percentage rate (APR) of 8 percent. $918.93 will earn an APR of 8 percent. However, the bond trader will not use the term APR: A yield to maturity of 8 percent will be quoted instead.

In practice, the yield to maturity on a bond is often found using a set of bond

[7]Tables A-5 and A-7 assume annual cash flows and thus annual compounding. When flows are received semiannually, these same tables may be used in their evaluation. It is necessary only to divide the interest rate by two and to double the time periods. Thus, cash inflows discounted at 8 percent per annum over five years, when received semiannually, may be evaluated at 4 percent per time period over 10 six-month periods, as in the above illustration.

Table 4-12

Relationship between Bond Yield to Maturity and Price Face or Coupon Rate: 6 Percent

YIELD	1 YR	2 YR	3 YR	4 YR	5 YR	6 YR	7 YR	8 YR
5.00%	100.96	101.88	102.75	103.59	104.38	105.13	105.85	106.53
5.10	100.87	101.69	102.47	103.22	103.93	104.60	105.24	105.85
5.20	100.77	101.50	102.20	102.86	103.48	104.08	104.64	105.18
5.30	100.67	101.31	101.92	102.49	103.04	103.56	104.05	104.52
5.40	100.58	101.12	101.64	102.13	102.60	103.04	103.46	103.86
5.50	100.48	100.93	101.37	101.77	102.16	102.53	102.87	103.20
5.60	100.38	100.75	101.09	101.42	101.72	102.01	102.29	102.55
5.70	100.29	100.56	100.82	101.06	101.29	101.51	101.71	101.91
5.80	100.19	100.37	100.54	100.70	100.86	101.00	101.14	101.27
5.90	100.10	100.19	100.27	100.35	100.43	100.50	100.57	100.63
6.00	100.00	100.00	100.00	100.00	100.00	100.00	100.00	100.00
6.10	99.90	99.81	99.73	99.65	99.57	99.50	99.44	99.37
6.20	99.81	99.63	99.46	99.30	99.15	99.01	98.88	98.75
6.30	99.71	99.44	99.19	98.95	98.73	98.52	98.32	98.14
6.40	99.62	99.26	98.92	98.61	98.31	98.03	97.77	97.53
6.50	99.52	99.08	98.66	98.26	97.89	97.55	97.22	96.92
6.60	99.43	98.89	98.39	97.92	97.48	97.07	96.68	96.32
6.70	99.33	98.71	98.13	97.58	97.07	96.59	96.14	95.72
6.80	99.24	98.53	97.86	97.24	96.66	96.11	95.60	95.13
6.90	99.14	98.35	97.60	96.90	96.25	95.64	95.07	94.54
7.00	99.05	98.16	97.34	96.56	95.84	95.17	94.54	93.95
7.10	98.96	97.98	97.07	96.23	95.44	94.70	94.01	93.37
7.20	98.86	97.80	96.81	95.89	95.04	94.24	93.49	92.80
7.30	98.77	97.62	96.55	95.56	94.63	93.77	92.97	92.23
7.40	98.67	97.44	96.29	95.23	94.24	93.31	92.46	91.66
7.50	98.58	97.26	96.04	94.90	93.84	92.86	91.95	91.10
7.60	98.49	97.08	95.78	94.57	93.45	92.40	91.44	90.54
7.70	98.39	96.90	95.52	94.24	93.05	91.95	90.93	89.99
7.80	98.30	96.73	95.27	93.92	92.66	91.50	90.43	89.44
7.90	98.21	96.55	95.01	93.59	92.28	91.06	89.93	88.89
8.00	98.11	96.37	94.76	93.27	91.89	90.61	89.44	88.35

yield tables, a sample of which is contained in table 4-12. The bond yield tables contain the sum of the combined values from tables A-5 and A-7. The price of 91.89 is found at the intersection of the 8 percent row and the five-year column. Conversely, the yield to maturity can be determined if the market price is known. If we knew that the market price was 91.89, we could scan down the five-year column until 91.89 was found and observe that the value is associated with an 8 percent interest rate.

Anyone who deals in bonds will have a calculator or a book-length set of bond yield tables readily at hand. If a bond yield table is not readily available, the yield to maturity can be estimated using the approximation formula:

$$Y = \frac{Int + (F - M)/N}{(F + M)/2} \qquad (4\text{-}10)$$

where Int = dollar interest payments per year
M = market value of the bond
F = face value of the bond
N = number of years until maturity.

Applying this formula to the above bond, the yield to maturity is approximately

$$Y = \frac{60 + (1{,}000.00 - 918.90)/5}{(1{,}000.00 + 918.90)/2} = 7.9\%.$$

SUMMARY

Interest is basic to the operation of the fianancial system. It is defined as rent paid for the use of money. The general structure of interest rates is a function of the quantity and quality of investment alternatives, future expectations of consumers and businessmen, financial and nonfinancial habits which shift over time, and the level of inflation.

Time Value of Money

Compound Value is the amount to which an investment will grow over a particular time horizon at a given interest rate. The amount to which an investment (P) will grow in n periods with an interest rate of i per period is

$$FV_n = P(1 + i)^n.$$

If interest is compounded or added on k times per year, the amount to which a sum (P) will grow is

$$FV_n = P\left(1 + \frac{i}{K}\right)^{nk}$$

Compound Value of an Annuity or stream of payments is the sum of the compound values of individual payments. The compound value of an annuity of $1 per year for n years at i percent is as follows:

$$CVA(i,n) = 1 + (1 + i) + (1 + i)^2 + \ldots + (1 + i)^{n-1}.$$

Present Value of a Single Payment is the inverse of the compound value of a single payment. With annual compounding, the present value of $1 received n years from today at interest rate i, is

$$P = \frac{1}{(1 + i)^n}$$

Present Value of an Annuity is the sum of the present values of the individual payments. The present value of $1 per year of n years at i percent is

$$PV = \frac{1}{1+i} + \frac{1}{(1+i)^2} + \ldots + \frac{1}{(1+i)^n}$$

Annual Percentage Rate

Many problems faced by financial institutions involve cases where the cash flows are known and the interest rate is desired. For such problems, the annual percentage rate is the discount rate which makes the present value of the cash inflows equal to the present value of the cash outflows.

QUESTIONS

4-1. Why is it important to convert all methods of computing interest to some common basis?

4-2. In competing for deposits, financial institutions have taken to compounding interest more than once a year. Why would they do this instead of simply raising the annual compounding rate directly?

4-3. Why do lenders charge points on mortgage loans rather than just increasing the stated interest rate?

4-4. Other things being equal, a long-term investment will carry a higher interest rate than one with a short maturity. Why then do automobile loans frequently carry higher effective interest rates than mortgage loans?

4-5. Determine the interest rate and points being charged on mortgage loans at a local financial institution. Convert this to an effective interest rate, if necessary, and compare it to the prime rate that is being charged the best business customers. (The prime rate is published in the *Federal Reserve Bulletin*.) How do you account for the difference?

PROBLEMS

4-1. A five-year certificate of deposit pays 8 percent compounded annually. A $5,000 deposit will grow to what amount in five years?

4-2. A competing certificate of deposit pays 6 percent interest with semiannual compounding. Which provides the higher return?

4-3. An investment plan calls for depositing $1,200 at the end of each year for the next twenty years in an account which pays 8 percent interest compounded annually. What will be the value at the end of twenty-years?

4-4. Another investment plan calls for depositing $1,000 at the end of each month for the next twenty years in an account which pays 8 percent compounded monthly. What will be the value at the end of twenty years?

4-5. A non-interest-bearing second mortgage for $10,000 has a maturity of five years. The holder of the mortgage needs cash for another investment and wishes to sell it today. If similar mortgages yield 10 percent annual compound return, how much could the holder expect to sell the mortgage for?

4-6. A $1,000 lump sum payment is to be received in one year. What is the present value at 8 percent discounted monthly?

4-7. A $1,000 bond pays $40 interest at the end of each six-month period and will mature in five years. At 6 percent required return, with semiannual compounding, what is the value of the bond?

4-8. Three alternate loan policies involve simple interest of 8 percent, add-on interest of 7.5 percent, or discount interest of 7.25 percent. In any case, retirement will be through thirty-six equal monthly installments. A $10,000 note is signed. Compute the net proceeds of the loan, the monthly payments, and the effective annual percentage rate for each method using the procedure shown in table 4-10.

4-9. A bond, which pays a face or coupon rate of 6 percent and will mature in eight years, is quoted at 96.32. What is the yield to maturity?

4-10. What would happen to the price of the above bond if the yield to maturity were to increase to 8 percent?

4-11. What size equal monthly payments would be required to retire a $30,000, 8 percent mortgage in twenty years? In thirty years?

4-12. If the above mortgage required a four-point service charge and was to be retired in twenty years, what would be the annual percentage rate?

4-13. A $50,000 piece of machinery has a five-year life and zero salvage value. A lease with equal annual payments at the end of each year for five years and a 14 percent annual percentage rate is desired. What will be the size of the annual lease payments?

4-14. A certificate of deposit pays an annual interest rate of 12 percent with continuous compounding. What is the effective annual interest rate?

SELECTED REFERENCES

BONKER, DICK. "The 'Rule of 78,'" *Journal of Finance* 31 (June 1976): 877–888.

FLEISHER, D. A. "Discounting an Intraperiod Cash Flow," *The Engineering Economist* 32 (Fall 1986): 56–58.

HORVATH, PHILIP A. "A Pedagoic Note on Intraperiod Compounding and Discounting," *The Financial Review* 20 (February 1985): 116–118.

KALAY, AVNER, AND RABINOVITCH, RAMON. "On Individual Loans Pricing, Credit Rationing, and Interest Rate Regulation," *Journal of Finance* 33 (September 1978): 1071–1085.

KAU, JAMES B., AND KEENAN, DONALD. "The Theory of Housing and Interest Rates," *Journal of Financial and Quantitative Analysis* 14 (November 1980): 833–847.

CASE 3

THE UNIVERSAL ACCOUNT

Like other thrift institutions, Community Savings had suffered through low profitability due to fluctuating interest rates in the 1970s and early 1980s. While interest rates had stabilized somewhat in the later years of the 1980s, Community faced new challenges from competitors. Checking and savings accounts were being offered by a wide variety of institutions, and increased competition had decreased spreads in the mortgage market. Price competition in all areas of the business had cut profits to unacceptably low levels.

Community Savings had the most extensive branch network in its market area. This branch network had been an asset in earlier years when interest rates paid on deposits were set by regulators, and the convenience was a major advantage in attracting deposits. With deregulation, though, price competition had become the order of the day, and the branch network gave Community Savings the highest fixed costs in its market. Community's overall strategy was to develop a set of financial products that depended on an extensive branch network and therefore could not be readily duplicated by competitors.

The first product developed was the Universal account. The Universal account would serve as a regular checking account but would also do much more. It would serve as a money market account in that balances above a specified minimum would be automatically moved into an account paying rates competitive with money market accounts. In addition, minimum balances and fees would be adjusted automatically for usage rates so the customer would not need to guess usage and balances in order to choose an account. Furthermore, a line of credit would be available so that a loan would be automatically granted if the customer wrote a check in excess of the balance. The account would also be universal in that it could be accessed from any branch. This was important because many people lived in the suburbs and worked in the city.

The Universal account would require an extensive investment in software and system design, so it could not be easily duplicated by smaller institutions. Furthermore, the ability to access the account from almost anywhere in the city would be unique to Community. Therefore, management was optimistic about the opportunity for profitability.

System design, market research, and other development costs were estimated to be $300,000. Initial advertising expenses would be $600,000. Monthly operating costs would be approximately $7.13 per account per month, and monthly fee income would average $4.50 per account. It was estimated that 90 percent of the accounts would have positive balances at any given time, and that the average balance for these accounts would be $2,000. The interest paid on these accounts would average 2 percent a year less than it would cost to attract this same money by bidding for large-denomination certificates of deposit. The other 10 percent of accounts would have loan balances averaging $1,500. The loans would earn an interest rate 5 percent above the cost of money acquired by bidding for large-denomination certificates of deposit.

Community Savings paid taxes equal to 34 percent of net income. Both development costs and initial advertising costs would be expensed immediately for tax purposes. Management required a 16 percent return on the cash flows generated for the owners by an investment of this type, and Community had adequate capital.

The marketing department estimated that 20,000 accounts could be attracted initially, and that the number of accounts would grow 10 percent a year thereafter. The chief financial officer was less optimistic and assumed that profits from any new product would be squeezed down to only a fair return within a few years. The chief financial officer wanted to base the analysis on 16,000 accounts, a five-year life for the product, and no growth in the number of accounts.

QUESTIONS

1. Identify the owner's cash outflows and cash flows for the first year of operation under the assumption of 20,000 accounts.
2. Assuming cash flows will grow 10 percent a year thereafter, compute the present value of all benefits over a five year life.
3. Identify the initial cash flows and cash flows for the first year of operation under the assumption of 16,000 accounts.
4. Compute the net present value of all benefits assuming 16,000 accounts, a five-year life, and no growth.
5. Should Community Savings invest in this new product?

5

Required Return and Value

In the previous chapter we developed the general principles of interest, frequently referred to as the mathematics of finance. For the manager to apply these principles it is frequently necessary to have an understanding of the factors determining the required interest rate on a particular investment. It is also necessary to have an understanding of the relationship between required return and value. Both topics are developed in this chapter.

These are two related questions in the determination of interest rates. First, there is the question of how the genereal level of interest rates is established. Second, there is the question of how time until maturity and risk cause interest rate differentials between different securities. In this chapter, we begin with a discussion of factors affecting the general level of interest rates.[1] We then consider certain variables that influence interest rate differentials between securities. Finally, we discuss the relationship between required return and value.

DETERMINANTS OF THE GENERAL LEVEL OF INTEREST RATES

Modern theory recognizes that interest has a role similar to the role of price in determining the supply and demand for other goods. There is a supply curve for money to

[1]While the "general level of interest rates" refers to a spectrum of rates which tend to move in the same direction over time, it is convenient to speak as if there were a single rate during the early part of our analysis.

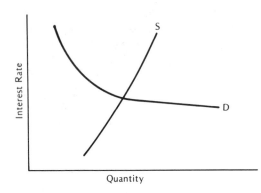

Figure 5-1:   Supply and demand for loanable funds.

loan:[2] The higher the interest rate, the more funds will be available for lending. Likewise, there is a demand curve for funds: The lower the interest rate, the more credit will be desired (figure 5-1). In this section, the various factors affecting these supply and demand curves will be examined.

Supply of Funds

The supply of loanable funds available within the economy may be viewed as a schedule relating the various quantities of dollars available for loan at different interest rates, given existing economic conditions. Determinants of the supply schedule include the following:

Time preference for consumption
Expectations concerning future income
Desire for money balances
Actions of monetary authorities

Time Preference for Consumption   This was the first component of the supply schedule to be recognized by economists. It was assumed that consumers were impatient, thus preferred present to future consumption. One person could consume in excess of his current income only if another consumed less. Compensation in the form of interest would thus encourage one to forgo consumption today in return for the prospect of even greater consumption at some future date.

The existence of a multibillion dollar consumer finance industry bears adequate witness to the fact that there are those willing to pay a premium for the privilege of consuming now rather than later. However, it does not necessarily follow that savers are motivated to save primarily by a desire to earn interest. For example, people continue to save even when the real interest rate—the interest rate after adjustment for changes in buying power—is negative. While high interest rates may serve to encourage some savings, interest is clearly not the only motivation for savings.

[2]For convenience, we limit the present discussion to borrowing and lending. A company may choose to sell stock instead of borrow, and some savers may choose to buy stock instead of lend. For purposes of studying the overall supply and demand for funds, stock may be viewed as synonymous with debt instruments.

Expectations Concerning Future Income Another important determinant of the amount of savings is one's income. If it is expected to fall at a future time, savings today assure some level of consumption at that future time. A significant portion of saving is in the form of contributions to various retirement funds to provide income in the retirement years. Uncertainty about future income, caused by factors such as the possibility of a layoff or ill health, also encourages savings. This effect is most frequently seen in terms of increased savings in response to concern about the possibility of a recession. Thus expectations of falling future income or uncertainty about future income may lead to an increased supply of savings.

Desire for Money Balances Sometimes a dollar of savings can result in less than a dollar in loans. Savings may be held in the form of money balances—currency and bank demand deposits—or they may be invested in direct loans and securities. One important reason for holding money balances is transactions demand. A person who is paid on a weekly basis will hold money at the beginning of the week to handle transactions later in the week. Likewise, businesses hold money for transaction purposes.

In addition to transactions balances, money is held because of uncertainty. Investment in securities, even U.S. government securities, can result in a loss if the interest rate rises sharply. Thus uncertainty about future interest rates will lead to increased desire for money balances. Uncertainty about future income and future investment opportunities are other factors that may lead to increased desire to hold money balances.

The holding of money balances reduces the availability of credit. Money balances held in the form of currency are obviously not available for lending. More importantly, the requirement that financial institutions hold reserves equal to some portion of transaction account balances means that the decision to hold money balances in any form reduces the supply of credit.

Monetary Authorities Government officials have an impact on the supply of credit. Control of credit availability is an important part of government action to stabilize the economy. One form of control is to change the reserve requirements for commercial banks, thus influencing the proportion of bank deposits available in lending markets. Another, more frequently used approach is for the Federal Reserve System to buy or sell U.S. government securities. When the Federal Reserve System purchases securities, it creates money, thereby increasing funds available to loan in credit markets. Of course, the sale of securities owned by the Federal Reserve System has the opposite effect. Thus the Federal Reserve System acts to increase or decrease the availability of credit in response to current economic conditions.

In summary, the supply of credit is affected by the time preference for consumption, expectations concerning future income, the form in which savings are held, and Federal Reserve actions to control credit. Line S in figure 5-1 represents the amount of credit that will be made available at each interest rate under a particular set of economic conditions. The higher the interest rate, the more credit will be made available. A change in conditions can cause S to shift. For example, Federal Reserve policy to decrease credit through a change in reserve requirements would cause less credit to be available at each interest rate and would cause the supply curve to shift to the left.

Interest rates are not determined by the supply curve acting alone; they are determined by the interaction of supply and demand. We now turn our attention to the other half of the credit market—demand.

Demand for Funds

The demand for loanable funds within the economy may be viewed as a schedule relating the dollar volume of credit desired at each interest rate, given existing economic conditions. Components of the demand for credit include the following:

Demand for consumer credit
Government borrowing
Acquisition of capital

Demand for Consumer Credit This is generally thought to be relatively insensitive to the interest rate; a rise in interest rates would cause only a small decline in the desire of consumers to borrow. Factors relating to income are believed to have a greater impact. Debt capacity is determined by the ability to make payments. An actual or anticipated increase in income increases the willingness of consumers to borrow so they can enjoy the benefits of that future income today. Stability of income is another factor. If income is viewed as stable, consumers feel more confident of their ability to handle additional debt. Age and family characteristics of the population are also important determinants of the demand for consumer credit. Young people at the family formation age normally demand more consumer credit than older members of the population. While the interest rate had some impact on the demand for consumer credit, these other considerations are of major importance.

Government Borrowing Like consumer borrowing, government borrowing is affected more by revenue expectations and perceived needs than by interest rates. The size of the government deficit is the major determinant of the extent to which government enters credit markets on the demand side. The demand for credit by government is thus insensitive to the rate of interest.

Acquisition of Capital The component of demand which exhibits the greatest sensitivity to interest rates is acquiring capital. Capital goods, such as machinery and factories, make greater production possible. For a capital investment to be attractive, its anticipated return must be at least as great as the interest rate that will be charged. At any time there will be a series of capital investment opportunities, some with higher returns than others. Thus the quantity of credit demanded for the purpose of acquiring capital goods depends on the level of interest rates.

In addition to factories and machinery, another important type of capital good is the residential structure. The quantity of funds demanded for first mortgage loans—characterized by long-term maturities—displays some sensitivity to interest rate movements because the interest rate has a major impact on the monthly cost of owning a home. A small shift in interest rates typically results in a relatively large shift in monthly payments for loans of this type. From 1966 to 1984 the monthly payment per $1,000 of principal value of a mortgage loan nearly doubled, solely because of an increase in the interest rate. Thus interest represents a major portion of the cost of residential real estate.

The shape of the demand curve in figure 5-1 illustrates the shape of a demand curve when some components of demand are sensitive to interest rate levels while other components are relatively insensitive. As interest rates rise to higher levels, demand becomes relatively insensitive to changes in the interest rate, resulting in a near vertical demand curve at these higher levels.

Inflation and Interest Rates

The impact of inflation on interest rates has been a matter of growing concern. To understand the impact of inflation, it is first necessary to differentiate between real and nominal interest rates. The nominal interest rate is the contract interest rate paid, while the real rate reflects changes in buying power. If the nominal interest rate is 7 percent and you have $1.00, the dollar will grow by 7 percent to $1.07 over a year if invested. Suppose that some commodity (basket of goods) costs $1.00 per unit at the beginning of the year. If the inflation rate is 5 percent, the commodity will cost $1.05 at the end of the year. If you purchase today, your dollar will purchase one unit. If you invest the dollar for a year, you can buy $1.07/$1.05 = 1.019 units. The real interest rate is therefore 1.9 percent because you can purchase 1.9 percent more units than you could at the beginning of the year. This definition of the real interest rate can be summarized in a simple formula:

$$\text{Real int. rate} = \frac{1 + \text{nominal int. rate}}{1 + \text{inflation rate}} - 1.0$$

Applied to the above situation, the real interest rate is computed as $(1.07/1.05) - 1 = 0.019$. As a quick approximation, it is sometimes said that the real interest rate is approximately the difference between the nominal interest rate and the inflation rate, approximately 2 percent for this example.

Traditional theory has held that the real interest rate will not be affected by inflation and that the nominal rate will increase by the expected inflation rate because savers must be compensated in the form of real returns if they are to be encouraged to lend out their money.

INTEREST RATE DIFFERENTIALS

Up to this point we have treated interest rates as if there were one rate applicable to all securities and loans rather than the array of rates that actually exists at any one time. The rates on securities vary with regard to both risk and maturity. Understanding these differentials is vital for dealing with many financial institution management problems. The two types of differentials are taken up in this section.

Term Structure of Interest Rates

The term structure of interest rates represents the relationship between yield and maturity. U.S. government securities can be used to illustrate the impact of maturity as they differ with regard to maturity but not with regard to safety of principal. Figure 5-2 is a yield curve, showing the interest rates on U.S. government securities of various maturities. It represents a more-or-less typical yield curve, with the interest rate increasing as maturity increases. The three main approaches to explanation of the shape of the yield curve are liquidity premium theory, expectation theory, and market segmentation theory. Each of these is discussed in the following paragraphs.

Liquidity Premium   Even though U.S. government securities are considered virtually risk-free with regard to payment at maturity, there is still a risk associated with an early need for funds. If a holder of long-term bonds should need the funds before maturity, the bonds must be sold in the secondary securities market. If the general level of interest rates has risen in the meantime, the price of outstanding bonds will have fallen. The longer the maturity of a bond, the greater will be the change in the price resulting from a change in interest rates.[3] Thus, even among securities that are risk-free with regard to payment at maturity, longer maturities result in greater risk. Under normal conditions, higher return is necessary to encourage people to accept the greater liquidity risk associated with long-term securities.

Expectation Theory   Another factor affecting the shape of the yield curve is the set of expectations with regard to future interest rates. In the absence of liquidity risk or market restrictions, the yield curve would represent an average of short-term rates expected over each maturity. Thus the yield curve reflects both liquidity risks and expected changes in the general level of interest rates. Figure 5-3 illustrates a yield curve in which short-term rates are higher than long-term rates. This cannot be accounted for with liquidity premium theory. Expectation theory would argue that the difference in shape between figures 5-2 and 5-3 is explained if 30 September 1983 was a time when investors were expecting a rise in the level of interest rates and 26 February 1982 was a time when they felt interest rates would decline after about a year. If interest rates were expected to fall, borrowers would tend to avoid long-term borrowing and temporarily borrow short-term with the hope of refinancing through issuance of long-term securities when rates fall. Lenders, on the other hand, would be attempting to acquire long-term securities before rates fell. This combination of actions would tend to drive short-term rates up and long-term rates down until each rate equals the average of expected short-term rates over its maturity.

As an example of how expectation theory explains interest rates, assume that the interest rate on one-year investments is presently 5 percent, and that the interest rate

[3]A review of bond yield computations in chapter 4 will confirm this.

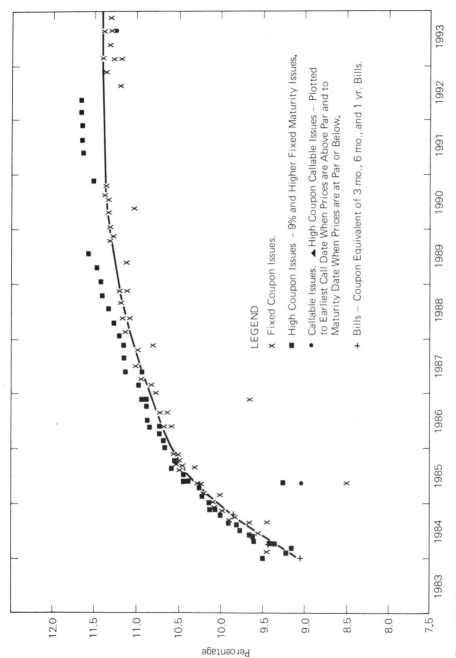

Figure 5-2: Yields of Treasury Securities, June 30, 1987 (Source: *Treasury Bulletin*.)

LEGEND

x   Fixed Coupon Issues.

■   High Coupon Issues – 9% and Higher Fixed Maturity Issues.

●   Callable Issues. ▲ High Coupon Callable Issues — Plotted to Earliest Call Date When Prices are Above Par and to Maturity Date When Prices are at Par or Below.

+   Bills — Coupon Equivalent of 3 mo., 6 mo., and 1 yr. Bills.

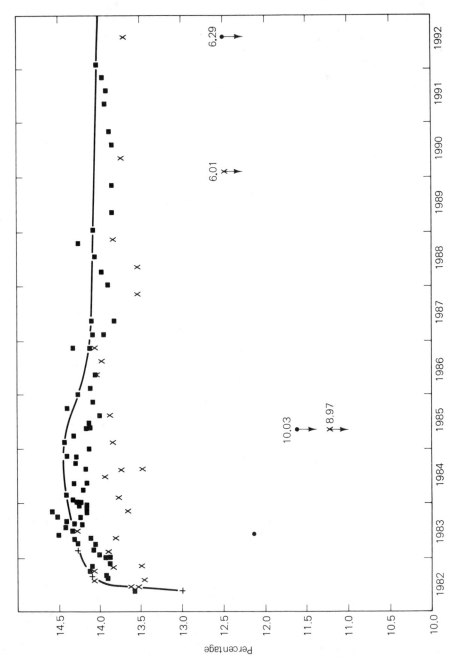

Figure 5-3: Yields of Treasury Securities, February 26, 1982. (Source: *Treasury Bulletin.*)

on two-year investments is presently 10 percent. With the two-year asset, a dollar will grow to $1.21 in two years. With a one-year asset, a dollar will grow to $1.05 in one year. To end up with $1.21 in two years, the rate that must be earned in the second year (r_2) is found as follows:

$$1.05 (1 + r_2) = 1.21; \quad r_2 = 15.24\%.$$

Suppose three-year securities carry an interest rate of 11 percent. A dollar invested for 3 years at 11 percent would grow to 1.3676, so the implied one-year interest rate expected in Year 3 is found as follows:

$$1.21 (1 + r_3) = 1.3676; \quad r_3 = 13.02\%.$$

Market Segmentation Theory   A third method is used to explain interest rate differentials. With this approach, the market for funds is looked at as a set of markets, not a single market. For example, the short-term maturity market can be viewed as a liquidity adjustment market, while the long-term market can be viewed as a market for capital investment funds. To the extent maturity needs rather than interest rate consider-ations determine maturity, there are separate markets for each maturity, and interest rate differentials are determined by supply and demand conditions in the various matu-rity markets. Using this approach, the inverted yield curve of figure 5-3 would be explained by heavy demand in the liquidity adjustment end of the markets.

It is probably most helpful to look at these three approaches to the shape of the yield curve as complementary rather than competing models. First, it is reasonable to expect some compensation for holding longer maturities and giving up some liquidity. Second, it is reasonable for expectations to be reflected in the term structure, because some borrowers and lenders can adjust their maturity structure in response to expected interest rate changes. Third, there is some segmentation in the markets. An example of the impact of this is a federal funds rate well above the rate on maturing Treasury bills. Thus all three reasons should be considered when studying term structure.

Adjusting positions in response to existing and anticipated yield curve shapes can have a substantial impact on profitability. Many borrowers and lenders, particu-larly portfolio managers of large institutions, study the shape of the yield curves, pre-pare their own interest rate forecasts, and attempt to pattern their activities in the credit markets in response to these factors.

Duration   In studying the term structure of interest rates and the sensitivity of security prices to interest rates, one is frequently confronted by differences between average life and absolute maturity. Consider, for example, a thirty-year mortgage and a thirty-year pure discount bond—a bond that provides no annual interest payments, but promises only one payment at the end of thirty years to cover both principal and accrued interest. Both of these are thirty-year instruments, but half of the mortgage payments are received before the fifteenth year. Thus, the average time to receipt of cash flow from the mortgage is much less, and the mortgage will be less sensitive to interest rate changes.

Duration is a measure of the average maturity of a security. Its computation is

$$
D = \frac{\left[\dfrac{P_1}{(1+r)^1}\right]1 + \left[\dfrac{P_2}{(1+r)^2}\right]2 + \cdots + \left[\dfrac{P_n}{(1+r)^n}\right]n}{\dfrac{P_1}{(1+r)^1} + \dfrac{P_2}{(1+r)^2} + \cdots + \dfrac{P_n}{(1+r)^n}}
$$

where P_1 is the cash flow in Year 1, P_2 is the cash flow in Year 2, etc., with no distinction made between principal and interest payments, and r is the required return. If the security is publicly traded, the denominator in the equation equals the market price of the security.

Example   A $1,000, 10 percent bond calls for three annual interest payments of $100 each and then a $1,000 principal payment at the end of three years. Interest rates have risen so that the required return is 14 percent. The duration is

$$
D = \frac{[100/(1.14)]1 + [100/(1.14^2)]2 + [(100 + 1000)/(1.14^3)]3}{[100/(1.14)] + [100/(1.14^2)] + [(100 + 1000)/(1.14^3)]}
$$

$$
= 2469.03/907.14 = 2.72 \text{ years.}
$$

Items with the same absolute maturity can have substantially different durations. At a 14 percent required return, for example, a twenty-year bond with a 6 percent coupon rate has a duration of 8.65 years, while a twenty-year bond with a 16 percent coupon rate has a duration of 7.44 years. At a 14 percent required return a twenty-year mortgage calling for equal annual payments to cover principal and interest would have a duration of 6.57 years (regardless of the face interest rate on the mortgage). Some of the variations around the yield curves (figures 5-2 and 5-3) are probably accounted for by differences between maturity and duration.

Risk and Required Rates of Return

Another major factor which leads to interest rate differentials is risk[4] with regard to the actual stream of income emanating from a particular security. The value of a share of stock or a bond is a function of the anticipated future cash flows to be derived therefrom and is equal to the discounted present value of these flows. For a debt instrument, the returns are in the form of principal and interest payments, while for stock the return is in the form of dividends. The present value of this stream of returns and thus the price of the security can change because the general level of interest rates (and therefore the required rate of return) changes. The value of the security will also change if there is a change in the stream of cash flow expected, normally caused by a change in

[4]Risk in this context can be thought of as the probability that the stream of anticipated returns will not be realized. More generally, risk can be thought of as the probability of a financial loss.

actual or anticipated profitability of the firm. When risk increases, the required return also increases. The bond issuers are rated as to the quality of the issue. The most widely known of these rating agencies are Moody's and Standard and Poor (for Moody's rating, see table 8-3).

The rating is one standard measure of the risk level. Figure 5-4 shows average yields of bonds by rating over the past fifty years. The interest rates are higher for more risky bonds, and the size of the spread increases as the general level of interest rates increases (figure 5-4). It is also known that the spread increases with increased uncertainty about the economic outlook.

The data on bond yields do not provide any specific information about the relationship between risk and required return. Studies of the specific relationship between risk and required rate of return have, for the most part, been based on common stock returns, although the results can be generalized to investments of any kind. A major result of these studies—the mean-variance capital asset pricing model—is summarized in appendix 5-A.

FORECASTING INTEREST RATES

Future interest rate movements are of vital concern to institutions. Profits can be favorably influenced through accurate projection of interest rates followed by appropriate policy decisions. The savings and loan industry has at times found its profits severely eroded by being on the wrong side of a change in interest rates, granting long-term loans while relying on short-term deposits in periods of rising interest rates. The industry has responded to these losses by increasing its efforts to acquire long-term funds, such as long-term certificates of deposit. If this action had been taken earlier in anticipation of rising interest rates, substantial losses could have been avoided.

Most efforts to forecast interest rates concentrate on what is considered the intermediate term by forecasters: from one-quarter to several years in the future. Over the intermediate term, interest rates respond primarily to a set of economic variables discussed in this section. Short-term forecasts of a few days to a few weeks are normally prepared by forecasting the recent trend of interest rates. Long-term forecasts involve such factors as changing age characteristics of the population.[5] Both because of the type of factors involved and because of the importance to institutions, this section will concentrate on intermediate-term forecasting.

Methods of preparing forecasts of the general level of interest rates range from application of judgment to mathematical models. Regardless of the method used, the major factors studied in preparing interest rate forecasts are:

1. Federal Reserve policy
2. Changes in gross national product
3. The liquidity of the economy

[5]See, for example, John S. Burton and John R. Toth, "Forecasting Secular Trends in Long-Term Interest Rates." *Financial Analysts Journal* (September/October 1974): 73—87, or the series of papers on long-term trends in interest rates published in the January 1970 issue of *Business Economics*.

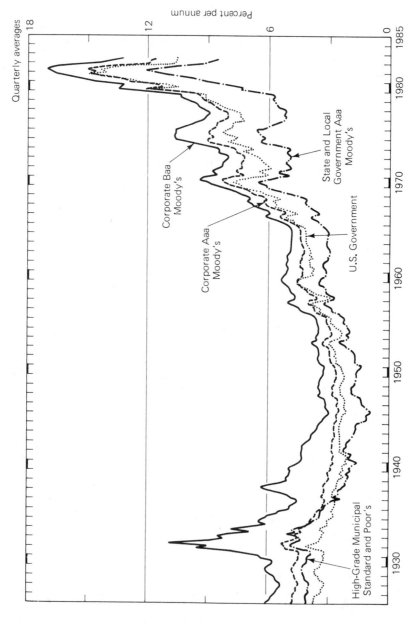

Figure 5-4: Bond yields by type of bond. (Source: *Federal Reserve Board Historical Chartbook.*)

4. The outlook for the supply and demand for funds
5. The inflation rate[6]

Federal Reserve Policy   This factor can be measured primarily in terms of the money supply. Target rates of growth are announced by the Federal Reserve and are widely published in the general press. Target growth rates are compared to actual growth rates in preparing forecasts of the money supply. Money supply figures are published monthly in the *Federal Reserve Bulletin,* as well as in the business press generally.

Gross National Product   Increases in the growth rate of gross national product (GNP) generally cause increased demand for funds for both consumer credit and capital acquisition. Thus increases in the growth rate of gross national product cause interest rates to rise, while declines in the growth rates typically have a downward impact. Individuals can prepare their own GNP forecasts or obtain them from publicly available sources.

The Liquidity Position of the Economy   As was mentioned earlier, savings do not automatically result in a direct increase in the supply of credit. The amount of credit supply increase actually achieved depends on the desires of people and business to hold money balances. For example, if there is a general desire for increased money balances, an effort by the Federal Reserve to increase the money supply may be offset by increased liquid balances, not increased economic activity.

Obviously, the trick here is to forecast the demand for money balances in comparison to present measures of the money supply and to adjust the credit supply forecast accordingly. This is easier said than done. As was discussed earlier in this chapter, desired money balances depend on various factors such as transactions needs and uncertainty about future conditions. A good deal of experienced judgment is required, and errors in this area are frequent.

Outlook for the Supply and Demand for Credit   A major part of the interest forecasting problem, the outlook is usually prepared by using the sources and uses of credit data published monthly in the *Federal Reserve Bulletin.* A condensed version appears in table 5-1. The individual components of the supply and demand for credit can be forecast using the outlook for GNP growth, government budgets, capital spending plan surveys, housing construction forecasts, etc. It is then possible to make a prediction as to whether supply or demand will increase more rapidly, thus whether the pressure on interest rates will be upward or downward.

Expected Inflation   As indicated previously, the interest rate includes a real return and some compensation for expected inflation; the interest rate will be expected to rise with an increase in the expected rate of inflation. Many forecasting models use

[6]Francis H. Schott, "Interest Rate Forecasting in Theory and Practice," *Business Economics* 102 (September 1977): 55–60.

Table 5-1

Sources and Uses of Funds to Nonfinancial Sectors in U.S. Credit Markets (in $ billions)

	1984	1985	1986
Users of credit funds			
Total credit funds raised	762.2	856.0	842.4
Foreign uses	8.3	1.2	9.0
Total domestic uses	753.9	854.8	833.4
U.S. government uses	198.8	223.6	214.3
Total private domestic use	555.1	631.2	619.1
State and local governments	27.4	91.8	46.4
Households	234.6	293.4	279.9
Farms	−0.1	−13.9	−15.1
Corporate	196.0	166.7	192.0
Noncorporate	97.0	93.1	115.9
Sources of credit funds			
Total credit funds raised	762.2	856.0	842.4
Noninstitutional sources			
Lending by U.S. government	91.4	118.3	185.0
Monetary authorities	8.4	21.6	30.2
Foreign lenders	57.9	62.3	102.1
From domestic financial institutions	559.8	579.5	726.1
Commercial banks	168.9	186.3	194.7
Savings institutions	150.2	83.0	105.8
Insurance and pension funds	121.8	156.0	175.9
Other financial institutions	118.9	154.2	249.6
Sources of domestic fin. inst. funds			
Private domestic deposits	316.9	213.2	272.8
Credit market borrowing	77.0	97.4	116.8
Foreign funds	5.4	17.7	12.4
Insurance and pension fund reserves	118.6	141.0	152.5
Treasury balances	4.0	10.3	1.7
Other	37.9	99.9	169.9
Direct lending in credit markets	196.7	273.2	90.1
U.S. government securities	123.6	145.3	43.4
State and local obligations	30.4	47.6	−0.8
Corporate and foreign bonds	5.2	11.8	34.4
Open market paper	9.3	43.9	−4.8
Other	28.1	24.6	17.9

Çlassification of state and local government as "private" is the work of the Federal Reserve statisticians, not the authors.

Source: Condensed from *Federal Reserve Bulletin.*

an average of inflation rates for previous years to forecast interest rates for the coming period; others use surveys of economists.

The various factors can be weighed in the mind of the interest rate forecaster, who relies on his judgment and past experience to develop actual forecasts, or they can be combined using mathematical models.

VALUE

The pursuit of the profitability objective normally involves two steps: the selection of assets with the highest value relative to their cost, and the management of liabilities to achieve the lowest cost of funds. Valuation principles are used to determine what a financial asset is worth, to determine the quality of collateral, and to determine the vulnerability of an asset's price to interest rate changes. Thus valuation is important for both profitability and risk analysis. It is particularly important for financial institutions, because most of their assets are financial instruments.

The valuation principles discussed here are limited to revenue-producing assets. We do not deal with approaches such as replacement value (sometimes used in the case of residential property) or aesthetic value (which may have some application in the world of art). We do concern ourselves with market value to the extent that we are discussing the market value of a revenue-producing asset.

Valuation principles are primarily an application of interest and required return principles discussed in this and the previous chapter. A financial asset has three primary characteristics for this type of analysis: a stream of expected cash flows, a required rate of return, and a value. If two of these variables are known, the third can be inferred from the other two. Thus valuation is the topic that brings interest and required return analysis together in a useful form.

Fixed-Income Assets

To begin the analysis of value, an asset having no maturity and paying a constant stream of cash flows provides a good illustration. An example of this type of asset is the British Consul, a bond issued to finance the Napoleonic wars. It carries no maturity date but pays a fixed amount of interest each year. Preferred stock, of course, has similar characteristics. For such an instrument, the value (V) is based on the annual cash flows (CF) and the required rate of return (r):

$$V = CF/r. \tag{5-1}$$

For an instrument with a $80 per year cash flow and a 6 percent required return, the value is

$$V = 80/0.06 = \$1,333.$$

This basic valuation principle can be readily verified from common observation. If a savings account pays 6 percent interest, a $1,333 deposit would yield interest of $80 ($0.06 \times \$1,333$) per year. Thus a promise to pay $80 per year would not be worth more than the amount that you would need to deposit in a savings account to achieve the same result.[7]

---

[7]This comparison ignores the fact that the savings account would normally carry a lower required return because it is more liquid. Unless the yield curve were perfectly flat, there would be some differences between the required return on the Consul and the savings account interest rate.

The simple problem above can be used to illustrate the relationship among the three characteristics. For example, if we know that the value is $1,333 and the annual cash flow is $80, then the rate of return is found by solving for r (equation 5-1). In this case, the answer would be 6 percent.

The value of an asset with no maturity is particularly sensitive to interest rate changes. If we wanted to test the sensitivity of value to interest rate changes, we could simply solve equation 5-1 for various levels of required return as is done below:

$$V = 80/0.02 = \$4,000$$
$$V = 80/0.06 = \$1,333$$
$$V = 80/0.7 \ = \$1,143$$
$$V = 80/0.15 = \ \ \$533.$$

Even a one percentage point change in interest rate leads to a 14 percent change in value. Interest rates of such obligations have risen from the 2 percent range to the 15 percent range, resulting in a loss of nearly 90 percent of the previous value with no decline in the credit worthiness of the borrower.

The same general principles apply to the valuation of all financial assets. The value equals the present value of all cash flows, discounted at the required rate of return. However, the existence of a maturity increases the difficulty of computation, requiring the use of the present value tables. A bond with a maturity of ten years, an $80 annual interest paid in semiannual installments, and a $1,000 maturity value will be used as an example. If the required return is 6 percent, the twenty-year, 3 percent tables are used instead of the ten-year, 6 percent tables because payment is semiannual. The value of the bond would be[8]

$$14.877 \times 40 + 0.5537 \times 1,000 = \$1,148.78$$

To test the sensitivity of the value of this bond to various interest rates, we can simply repeat the calculation at other rates:

8%: $13.590 \times 40 + 0.4564 \times 1,000 = \$1,000$
10%: $12.462 \times 40 + 0.3769 \times 1,000 = \$875.38$
12%: $11.470 \times 40 + 0.3118 \times 1,000 = \$770.60$
14%: $10.594 \times 40 + 0.2584 \times 1,000 = \$682.16$

The existence of a fairly limited maturity decreases the sensitivity of value to interest rate changes. In this case one percentage point increase in the interest rate causes the value of the bond to decline by less than 7 percent as opposed to over 14 percent for the perpetual bond.

Sensitivity of the market values of mortgages can be treated in a similar manner. Using table A-8, we find that the monthly payment for a thirty-year, 9 percent, $50,000 mortgage would be $402.32 ($50,000/124.28). If the interest rate were to rise to

---

[8]Based on tables A-5 and A-7. Review the present value methods in chapter 4 if the reasons for this are not clear.

12 percent, the value of such a mortgage would decline to $39,112 ($402.32 × 97.218) (again using table A-8), a loss in value of 22 percent. By way of contrast, a fifteen-year mortgage would have suffered only a 15 percent decline in value under the same circumstances.

Any fixed-income security can be converted to a stream of cash flows, and its value can be determined by discounting this stream at the appropriate required return. Alternately, the rate of return can be found if the value and the stream of cash flows are known. This was illustrated for bonds in chapter 4.

Certain nonfinancial assets, such as rental property, can be valued in a similar manner. The value of rental property, for example, equals the present value of the cash flows generated. These include rental income, net of expenses, and terminal value. An income property will cost $25,000 in cash and will require the assumption of an $80,000 mortgage. Annual cash flow, net of all cash expenses including tax and mortgage repayment, would be $3,000 per year, and the value of the property at the end of the twenty-year period would be $20,000. At a 12 percent required return, the value would be

$$3,000 \times 7.4694 + 20,000 \times 0.1037 = \$24,482.$$

The value of the cash flows is less than the amount required to purchase the building. Thus it provides a return below 12 percent and would not be an attractive investment.[9]

Equity Securities

While the same principles apply to equity securities, the problem is complicated by the fact that equity securities do not provide a contractual payment, but provide returns based on profits of the firm whose ownership they represent. It is necessary to develop some indirect method of determining value. Two frequently used approaches are discussed here.

The *price-earnings ratio* approach provides one such method of valuation. The price-earnings ratio is simply the ratio of market price to earnings per share for a company's common stock. It can be used as a multiplier like a present value factor. Its use is based on the argument that the earnings, whether paid out or reinvested to provide future dividends, are the return to shareholders. The multiplier applied to these earnings depends on the stability and expected growth of the earnings, as well as other opportunities for investment. While the average price-earnings ratio is presently about 10, the range is so broad that ratios of 50 or more are not unheard of.

As an example of the use of this approach, suppose the stock of a company that is not publicly owned is to be given an estimated value. Earnings per share for the

[9]The same approach could be applied to speculative real estate providing no current income. If the required return is 12 percent, the property is expected to be worth $100,000 in five years, and annual holding expense (tax and insurance) is $2,000, the value of the property today is

$$-\$2,000 \times 3.6048 + \$100,000 \times 0.5674 = \$49,530.$$

company are $3.20. We would begin by looking at the price-earnings ratios for companies in similar business lines whose stock was publicly traded. Suppose that we find a range of 12 to 15. We would then multiply $3.20 by each of these numbers and establish a value range between $38.40 and $48.00. The location of the value within this range would depend on the prospects for this company versus the others in the same business area, as well as factors such as marketability of shares.

The *dividend growth model* is another method of valuing common stock. It is most likely to be applied in a case such as a utility where the dividend level is stable and the growth rate is moderate. In this case, the value of a share of stock equals the present value of the dividends directly:

$$V = \frac{d}{r - g} \tag{5-2}$$

where d = expected dividends over the next year
r = required rate of return
g = anticipated growth rate of dividends.

For example, a company is expected to pay dividends of $2.38 over the next year and dividends are expected to grow at the rate of 4 percent a year. At a required return of 14 percent, the value would be

$$V = \frac{2.38}{0.14 - 0.04} = \$23.80.$$

The use of this approach involves two problems. First, there is the problem of a growth rate. The model assumes a stable, continuous growth rate. Since growth rates greater than the overall economy are not sustainable, it can only be used with low, stable growth rates. Second, there is the problem of determining the appropriate rate of return. The mean-variance capital market model, discussed in appendix 8-A, is frequently used to determine the required rate of return.

The valuation of common stock is made difficult by the fact that there is no accurate way to predict the stream of cash flow. Sometimes these estimating problems are avoided by assuming that the book value per share represents the actual value. This approach ignores the fact that the earnings stream, not historical cost, determines value.

SUMMARY

We have examined both the factors affecting the general level of interest rates and the factors affecting interest rate differentials. The general level of interest rates is determined by supply and demand. The primary factors affecting the supply of credit are

1. Time preference for consumption
2. Expectations concerning future income
3. Desire for money balances

The primary components of demand for credit are

1. Demand for consumer credit
2. Government borrowing
3. Acquisition of capital

The general level of interest rates is also affected by the anticipated rate of inflation. Although the adjustment appears to be less than complete, with the nominal interest rising by less than the anticipated increase in inflation, the interest rate will nevertheless increase in response to an increase in expected inflation.

Interest rate differentials between securities are attributed to risk and time until maturity. The yield curve shows the relationship between interest rate and time until maturity. The shape of the yield curve depends primarily on liquidity preference, expectations concerning future interest rates, and conditions in various sectors of the market for funds.

Interest rate forecasters study the factors leading to changes in interest rates discussed in the first part of the chapter. The five major factors studied are

1. Federal Reserve policy
2. Changes in gross national product
3. The liquidity of the economy
4. The outlook for supply and demand for funds
5. The inflation rate

These factors are combined using either the judgment and experience of the forecaster or mathematical models.

Valuation is an application of interest and required return analysis. The value of a financial asset equals the present value of the cash flows discounted at the required rate of return. For fixed-income securities, the calculation is relatively straightforward. For equity securities, the problem is complicated by the fact that cash flows are not known and must be estimated.

Required return and valuation principles are useful to institution managers in gauging profitability and risk exposure. Thus they play a vital role in asset management. As we will see in the following chapter, they also play an important role in management of sources of funds.

QUESTIONS

5-1.   Why does a yield curve generally slope upward? What factors would lead to other shapes?

5-2.   As a library project, trace the volume of demand for funds. Which use—government, consumer, capital investment—appears to be the most volatile?

5-3.   Locate at least two recent articles discussing the expected trend in interest rates. Compare and contrast the conclusions and the reasoning.

5-4.   What are the primary sources and uses of credit in the United States?

5-5.   We rely on the rate of return as the method of allocating funds in a free economy. Does this method lead to any problems? What other methods are possible?

PROBLEMS

5-1.   Construct a figure illustrating the downward sloping demand curve and upward sloping supply curve for funds. Illustrate, by showing shifts in the curve, the impact of
        a. An increase in government deficit spending.
        b. A decrease in the savings rate.

5-2.   Construct a yield curve for the most recent date available using information from the *Federal Reserve Bulletin*. Do you find evidence of any anticipated changes in interest rates?

5-3.   The nominal interest rate for a particular year was 8 percent and the inflation rate was 5 percent. What was the real rate of interest?

5-4.   Dividends for American Dynamics are expected to be $4 a share next year. The required rate of return is 18 percent. Compute the value of a share of stock for expected dividend growth rates of 8 percent, 4 percent, and 0 percent a year.

5-5.   Two five-year bonds are available. Either will provide a 14 percent yield to maturity. Bond A is selling for its par value of $1,000 and pays $140 a year. Bond B pays no interest and simply pays its par value of $1,000 at maturity. The second bond is selling for $519.36. Compute the duration of each bond. Which bond would show the greatest price change with a change in interest rates?

5-6.   You have $1 million to invest. You want to divide your money between one-year, 10 percent Treasury securities and one of the bonds in problem 5-5. You want to be sure that if the interest rate rises to 16 percent, your wealth (market value plus interest received) will increase at least 8 percent during the first year.
        a. What allocation between Asset A and the one-year Treasury securities will ensure this rate of return?
        b. What allocation between Asset B and the one-year Treasury securities will ensure this rate of return?
        c. Given the minimum acceptable income standard for Year 1, would you recommend the combination identified in part a or the combination identified in part b?

5-7.   The interest rate on one-year and two-year securities (which make both principal and interest payments at maturity) are 8 percent and 10 percent, respectively. If you invest in a one-year security now, what interest rate must you earn in Year 2 to be as well off as if you had invested in a two-year, 10 percent security? If expectation theory explains the shape of the yield curve, what is the expected interest rate on one-year securities in Year 2?

5-8. Given the conditions in problem 5-7 and an interest rate of 11 percent on three-year securities, what is the expected interest rate on one-year securities in Year 3?

5-9. A thirty-year mortgage is fully amortized through monthly payments over its life. A thirty-year bond is paid off at maturity, with only the interest paid annually during its life. Each instrument carries a 10 percent interest rate. A 1 percent increase in market interest rates will lead to a decline of what percent in the value of each asset?

5-10. Information about two common stocks is shown below. Assume the required return for either stock is 14 percent. Compute the value of each stock. If the required return decreases by 1 percent, by how much will the price of each stock increase? Which stock would you buy if you were expecting an increase in interest rates? A decrease in interest rates?

STOCK	A	B
Expected dividend	$3.60	$2.70
Dividend growth rate	2%	5%

5-11. Using the *Federal Reserve Bulletin* or a similar source, find the most recent inflation rate and the interest rate on one-year Treasury securities. What is the real interest rate?

5-12. Shown below are inflation rates and interest rate on short-term Treasury securities for recent years. What can you conclude about the relationship between interest rates and inflation rates? Does the real interest rate appear to be stable?

Year	77	78	79	80	81	82	83	84	85	86
Int.	5.5	7.6	10.0	11.4	13.8	11.1	8.8	9.8	7.7	6.0
Infl.	6.8	9.0	13.3	12.4	8.9	3.9	3.8	4.0	3.8	1.1

CASE 4

OLD FORTRESS

Specialization reached new heights in the mortgage business in the middle 1980s, as financial institutions sought ways to increase profitability and decrease risk in a deregulated marketplace. In the traditional market, a bank or savings and loan sought applicants, made the credit decision, provided the loan money, and handled collections. The new practice was for institutions to specialize in only one of these activities. The loans that made this specialization possible were those qualifying for guarantees of credit quality by agencies of the U.S. government. With credit risk re- •
moved, mortgage loans could be readily sold by the original lender. For example, one institution might focus on loan origination, seeking applicants, handling the paperwork process of qualifying for guarantees, granting the loan, packaging it with a portfolio of other guaranteed loans, and then selling the portfolio to some other investor, typically another financial institution. Another institution might focus on warehousing: buying and holding portfolios of loans. Still another institution might focus on servicing, processing payments for the holder, managing escrow accounts[1], and handling the collection effort on delinquent accounts. While a collection effort was involved, there were no credit losses, as loans deemed uncollectible were sold back to the guaranteeing agency. Banks, savings and loans, and private mortgage companies acted as originators and servicers, while life insurance companies and pension funds often acted as warehouses.

Pat Carson managed the mortgage loan portfolio for Old Fortress Insurance

[1]Borrowers are generally required to make a payment each month to cover their insurance and tax payment. These balances are held in an account called an escrow account until the insurance and tax payments are made.

Company. Like most life insurance companies, Old Fortress held substantial reserves, and its profitability was heavily affected by the returns earned on these reserves. Old Fortress had made a major commitment to mortgage portfolios in an effort to increase returns without taking substantial risks. In January 1986 Carson was preparing a bid for a $20 million portfolio of mortgages. Developing a proper bid was critical to profitability. An error on the low side would mean that Old Fortress would be outbid. An error on the high side would almost ensure that Old Fortress would get a portfolio it did not want. Thus, the bidding process tended to bias acquisitions toward overvalued portfolios, eliminating the extra returns Old Fortress was trying to achieve.

Bidding for a portfolio of fixed-income securities might seem simple enough on the surface, but there were complications. This particular portfolio consisted of $20 million of recently packaged, thirty-year insured home mortgages paying an interest rate of 10 percent. Interest rates on new mortgages were presently 10.85 percent, but it was common practice to achieve part of that interest rate through the use of points. Thus, the originator had actually advanced less than $20 million and expected to receive less than $20 million.

Government guarantees made the loans risk-free with regard to principal but hardly made them a risk-free investment. The actual rate of return earned depended on how long the loans remained outstanding, and very few thirty-year mortgage loans remained outstanding for thirty-years. Loans were repaid early for one of three reasons. Borrowers would repay their loans early if they decided to sell their home. Borrowers would also repay early if interest rates fell enough so that they could reduce their costs by refinancing the loan. Finally, a loan would be repaid early if the borrower defaulted and the loan was sold to the guaranteeing agency.

Defaults are low enough in early years that they can be ignored for simplicity. Historically, the average mortgage loans had remained outstanding an average of seven years before the borrower sold the property and repaid the loan. The default rate would increase during the recession, and the rate of property sale would decline if interest rates rose sharply, but the greatest source of uncertainty was the amount of refinancing. Fees associated with refinancing would cost the borrower approximately one percent of the amount borrowed. Furthermore, refinancing was time-consuming and inconvenient for the borrower. This, associated with the fact that the loans carried rates below the going market interest rate as a result of points, gave some protection from refinancing. However, a sharp decline in interest rates could lead to as much as half of the portfolio being repaid over a period of a few months.

Repayment of a loan may not seem like bad news to a lender, but it is bad news when interest rates are low; the lender must then reinvest the funds at lower interest rates. U.S. government bonds, which were free of default risk and could not be called before maturity, were selling to yield 9.3 percent. The interest rate on three-month Treasury bills was 7.04 percent. Aaa-rated corporate bonds, which had little default risk, but which also had call risk, were currently selling to yield 10.05 percent.

As was often the case, the interest rate outlook was uncertain in early 1986. Mortgage rates had been declining fairly steadily since 1981, when they had peaked at over 16 percent, and were still high by historical standards. But a continued decline was not at all certain. If inflation heated up or the value of the dollar declined in international markets, the Federal Reserve might act to tighten the money supply, thereby increasing interest rates. The history of interest rates, shown in figure 5-4 illustrates their potential volatility.

QUESTIONS

1. Assume that some years have gone by and the loans are now twenty-five years from maturity. By how much must interest rates fall before refinancing would reduce the borrower's payments. Assume the new loan will be large enough to repay the old loan and cover refinancing costs.

2. As a borrower, would you refinance as soon as the interest rate was at the level indicated in your answer to question 1?

3. Assume that the interest rate has fallen 1 percent below the rate needed to justify refinancing and the entire portfolio is paid off. What price for the portfolio would provide a 10.5 percent return under these circumstances?

4. Use the assumptions from question 3 and assume that funds are then reinvested in Treasury bonds, which have declined in yield by the same amount as mortgage loans. Would the company be better off purchasing mortgages now and Treasury bonds in five years, or would it be better off buying Treasury bonds now?

5. Of course, it is possible that interest rates will not fall and that Old Fortress will earn a substantially higher return with mortgages than with Treasury bonds. Considering the risk-return trade-offs involved, prepare a bid for the mortgage portfolio.

SELECTED REFERENCES

BOND, BICHAEL T., AND SMOLEN, GERALD E. "Nominal Interest Rates and Marginal Tax Rates," *Quarterly Journal of Business and Economics* 26 (Spring 1987): 104–109.

CORNELL, BRADFORD. "Inflation Measurement, Inflation Risk, and the Pricing of T-bills," *Journal of Financial Research* 9 (Fall 1986): 193–202.

COX, JOHN C., INGERSOLL, JONATHAN E., JR., AND ROSS, STEPHEN A. "A Reexamination of Traditional Hypotheses About the Term Structure of Interest Rates," *Journal of Finance* 36 (September 1981): 769–799.

HARDOUVELIS, GIKAS A. "Reserves Announcements and Interest Rates: Does Monetary Policy Matter?" *Journal of Finance* 42 (June 1987): 407–422.

HO, THOMAS S. Y., AND LEE, SANG-BIN. "Term Structure Movements and Pricing Interest Rate Contingent Claims," *Journal of Finance* 41 (December 1986): 1011–1030.

LEONARD, DAVID C., AND SOLT, MICHAEL E. "Recent Evidence on the Accuracy and Rationality of Popular Inflation Forecasts," *Journal of Financial Research* 9 (Winter 1986): 281–290.

LIVINGSTON, MILES. "Flattening of Bond Yield Curve," *Journal of Financial Research* 10 (Spring 1987): 17–24.

LOMBRA, RAYMOND E. "The Changing Role of Real and Nominal Interest Rates," *Federal Reserve Bank of Kansas City Economic Review* (February 1984): 12–25.

OOGDEN, JOSEPH P. "An Analysis of Yield Curve Notes," *Journal of Finance* 42 (March 1987): 99–110.

ROLEY, VANCE V. "The Determinants of the Treasury Security Yield Curve," *Journal of Finance* 36 (December 1981): 1103–1126.

THIES, CLIFFORD F. "New Estimates of the Term Structure of Interest Rates 1920–1937," *Journal of Financial Research* 8 (Winter 1985): 297–306.

6

Analyzing Financial Statements of Financial Intermediaries

If you had turned to the business section of any local newspaper as this chapter was being written, you would have found daily discussions of the importance of balance sheet strength for banks. This daily press coverage of bank balance sheets, precipitated by Citicorp's decision to add $3 billion to its loan loss reserves, highlights the importance of being able to read and interpret the financial statements of financial institutions. The ability to understand and interpret these statements is important for a wide variety of people concerned with financial institutions, including regulators, lenders, equity investors, and managers. Interpretation and analysis of income statements and balance sheets, the principal financial statements, are covered in this chapter.

Financial statement analysis is carried out with the objectives of measuring profitability, liquidity, and safety. *Profitability* is the ability to earn a rate of return on the owners' investment. *Liquidity* is the ability to meet anticipated and unanticipated demands for funds. *Safety* of the organization is ultimately interpreted in terms of ability to cover all costs and meet all obligations. When studying financial statements, safety is evaluated by looking at *credit quality* and *capital adequacy.*

Financial statements often do not tell us everything we want to know about profitability, liquidity, and safety, but they provide important insights. A person analyzing financial statements is like a doctor conducting diagnostic tests. The analysis is helpful in ruling out problems and identifying potential sources of problems. The results of the analysis must be interpreted in light of knowledge about the meaning of a particular measure and the overall conditions at the time. Financial statement analysis is particularly useful in calling attention to potential problem areas that need further examination.

Financial statement analysis goes beyond simply reading financial statements to measuring key relationships. One way to measure relationships is to put financial statements on a common size basis, with all income statement and balance sheet items restated as a percentage of total assets. The common size approach is illustrated in table 6-1. Another approach is to compute key ratios, such as the ratio of net income to owners' equity. Once common size statements and key ratios have been computed, the results must be interpreted. As part of the interpretation, the company's performance can be compared to that of other companies, or trends for the same company can be analyzed. These methods of analysis and interpretation are illustrated in this chapter using the financial statements of Citicorp, as shown in table 6-1.

The financial statements of Citicorp are self-explanatory for the most part and follow generally accepted accounting principles. Some items peculiar to financial insititutions should be pointed out though. Methods of dealing with bad debt losses and methods of valuing assets are of particular interest.

Bad Debts.   If 1,000 new loans are made today, the lender knows that some of them will not be repaid. The lender does not, of course, know which loans will go bad, but some almost assuredly will. Default rates tend to rise with the passage of time after the granting of a group of loans, at least for a while. Financial institutions recognize this by creating a *credit loss reserve* on the balance sheet. Additions to this reserve are considered an expense, called *provision for credit losses,* and treated as expenses on the income statement. When a loan goes bad and is written off, the amount owed is subtracted from the gross loan amount and from the credit loss reserve. The amount written off is not subtracted from income because the estimated losses were subtracted from income when the reserve was established.

If the company changes its estimates of future losses and decides to increase its credit loss reserves, the amount of increase is an expense and reduces income. In May 1987, Citicorp's management announced its decision to add $3 billion to credit loss reserves because of concern about the quality of its loans in foreign countries. This resulted in a sharp increase in the expense item *provision for credit losses* and caused the company to show a net loss for the year 1987.

Valuation of Assets: The primary assets of financial institutions are loans and investment securities. In preparing financial statements, values for these assets must be determined. Loans and investment securities held by financial institutions are generally shown on the financial reports at cost. This differs from the practice of nonfinancial businesses, most of which show the values of securities at the lower of cost or market value. This distinction is important because many financial institutions would be declared insolvent in periods of high interest rates if they were required to adjust their assets to market value.

Having briefly looked at accounting conventions of particular importance to financial institutions, we turn our attention to financial statement analysis. Common size statements are discussed first, followed by ratio analysis.

Table 6-1

Citicorp Financial Statements

Year	IN $ MILLIONS		PERCENT OF AVERAGE ASSETS	
	1985	1986	1985	1986
Interest and loan fee income	$19,474	$19,224	12.13	10.45
Interest expense	14,028	13,096	8.74	7.12
Net interest revenue	5,446	6,128	3.39	3.33
Other revenue	3,030	4,272	1.89	2.32
Provision for loan losses	1,243	1,825	0.77	0.99
Other operating costs	5,517	6,875	3.44	3.74
Income before tax	1,716	1,700	1.07	0.92
Income tax	718	642	0.45	0.35
Net income	$ 998	$ 1,058	0.62	0.57
Earnings per share	7.12	7.14		
Fully diluted	7.11	7.13		

			PERCENT OF YEAR-END ASSETS	
Cash and due from banks	5,218	5,181	3.01	2.64
Investments	35,086	43,156	20.21	22.00
Loans—Gross	116,499	130,904	67.11	66.75
Credit loss reserves	1,235	1,698	0.71	0.87
Loans (net)	115,264	129,206	66.40	65.88
Premises and equipment	2,544	3,177	1.47	1.62
Other assets	15,575	15,404	8.91	7.86
Total assets	173,597	196,124	100.00	100.00
Deposits	104,959	114,689	60.46	58.48
Purchased funds and other borrowings	26,616	33,731	15.33	17.20
Long-term debt	16,316	20,695	9.40	10.55
Subordinated capital notes	1,899	2,648	1.09	1.35
Other liabilities	16,002	15,261	9.22	7.78
Redeemable preferred stock	40	40	0.02	0.02
Nonredeemable preferred stock	1,215	1,365	0.70	0.70
Common equity	6,550	7,695	3.77	3.92
Total liab. and net worth	173,597	196,124	100.00	100.00
Average total assets	160,505	184,013		
Average stockholders' equity*	7,024	8,394		
Net credit losses**	962	1,371		
Investments due within one year	2,501	2,291		

*Including both common equity and nonredeemable preferred stock.
**Defined as amounts actually written off during the year, minus any previously written off loans that were collected during the year.

COMMON SIZE FINANCIAL STATEMENTS

It is usually difficult to decide whether $34 million of profit is good or bad. For this number to be meaningful, it must be compared to something. One way to make the numbers comparable is to adjust them for the size of the institution by restating them as a percentage of total assets. Income statement items are expressed as a percentage of average assets when information on average assets is available. Average assets are used because the income statement represents flows over the year, while the balance sheet represents assets on a particular day. Using average assets gives an indication of what the company achieved with the assets it had to use over the year.

The income statements of Citicorp give some indication of the usefulness of the common size approach in gaining insights. Looking at the dollar amounts, for example, we note that net income increased almost $60 million from 1985 to 1986. As a percent of average assets, though, net income declined. Earnings before tax, as a percentage of average assets, declined 5 basis points (a basis point is one one-hundredth of 1 percent) from 1985 to 1986. Net interest revenue declined six basis points, and other revenue rose forty-three basis points, so profitability before operating costs, per dollar of assets, increased. The decline in profit per dollar of assets largely resulted from increased operating expenses and an increased allowance for bad debts. These two items received extensive discussion in the press. The increased allowance for bad debts was based on a reassessment of the riskiness of foreign loans and was viewed as sound policy by most analysts. Rising operating expenses were viewed with concern by security analysts as evidence that Citicorp was not operating efficiently and was not benefiting from economies of scale.

The common size balance sheets are year-end amounts divided by year-end total assets. It is not necessary to use average balance sheet accounts as was done when looking at the income statement, because we are not comparing activity over the year to balance sheet items. We are simply trying to get snapshots of the company's asset and liability structure on two different dates. It is fortunate that the snapshots provide insights, because average amounts are not reported for most balance sheet categories.

Looking at the balance sheet in dollar amounts, we note that every asset and liability category has increased. The common size statements show how the company has changed proportions in its asset and liability structure, though. Loans as a percentage of assets have decreased, credit loss reserves have increased, investments have increased, and investment in premises and equipment has increased. The increase in loan loss reserves as a percentage of assets reflects a growing consumer loan portfolio and increased concern about foreign loans. A high ratio of loans to total assets is generally thought of as contributing to profitability, while a high ratio of investments to total assets, particularly investments with maturities of less than one year to total assets, is thought of as contributing to liquidity.

On the liability side, deposits have decreased as a percentage of assets, while purchased funds have increased. Purchased funds are loans, often for periods as short as overnight, usually arranged by telecommunications contact in highly impersonal markets. Deposits are generally thought of as a more stable source of money, while purchased funds increase liquidity risk.

Long-term debt, subordinated capital notes[1], and equity have increased. Each of these sources of funds is included in at least one measure of the company's capital, so the company has increased the relative amount of capital. This may decrease return on equity by decreasing financial leverage, but it also increases the safety of the institution by providing a larger cushion to cover possible losses.

As illustrated in the previous discussion, common size financial statements are useful in identifying trends in both profitability and balance sheet structure. Additional insights can be gained by supplementing these data with certain key ratios. Ratios are discussed and the use of ratio analysis is demonstrated in the following paragraphs.

RATIO ANALYSIS

The major areas of performance examined with ratio analysis are profitability, liquidity, credit quality, and capital adequacy. Ratios for each area of analysis are discussed and illustrated in the following paragraphs.

Profitability

Profitability is ultimately measured in terms of the rate of return earned by equity investors, who are the owners of the business. Over time, profitability can be measured as the discount rate that makes the present value of all future cash benefits equal to the amount invested. This rate of return does not reflect the performance of the company, though; it reflects the discount rate investors apply to future cash flows in determining a price for the company's stock. Income in relation to resources committed is used to measure profitability from the financial statement.

Return on Equity

Return on equity, defined as net income divided by equity[2], is the most direct measure of profitability. It is the measure of income earned per dollar of the owners' money that was committed. When this measure is applied to the 1985 and 1986 performances of Citicorp, using average equity, the results are as follows:

$$\text{Return on equity (ROE)} = \text{net income} \div \text{equity}$$
$$1985: \text{ROE} = 998 \div 7{,}024 = 14.21\%$$
$$1986: \text{ROE} = 1{,}058 \div 8{,}394 = 12.60\%.$$

[1] Subordinated capital notes are repaid in bankruptcy only after all other creditors have been repaid. Citicorp has the option of deferring interest payments on some of the capital notes if dividends have not been paid on Citicorp stock for at least six months.

[2] Total equity included preferred stock. Return on common equity is net income, minus preferred dividends, divided by common equity. Citicorp excludes *redeemable* preferred stock from equity because redeemable preferred stock can be retired at the option of the holder.

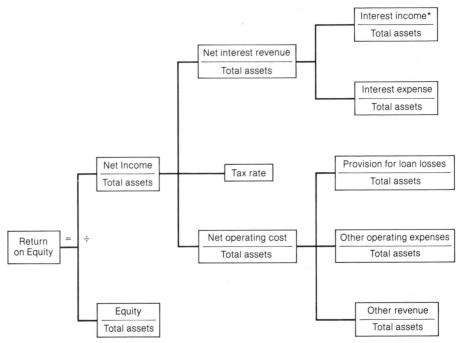

*Loan fees are included with interest income.

Figure 6-1: Profitability model for financial intermediaries.

1986 was a record profit year, with net income exceeding $1 billion for the first time. But return on equity declined. Managers and investment analysts would want to look more deeply to find out why profitability declined.

Figure 6-1 contains a profitability analysis model showing the primary relationships that affect profitability in a financial intermediary. This model will be used to analyze the profitability of Citicorp as each of the ratios is discussed. First, it is important to note the relationship between return on equity, net income to total assets, and equity to total assets:

$$\frac{\text{Net income}}{\text{Equity}} = \frac{\text{net income}}{\text{total assets}} \div \frac{\text{equity}}{\text{total assets}}$$

or

$$\frac{\text{Net income}}{\text{Equity}} = \frac{\text{net income}}{\text{total assets}} \times \frac{\text{total assets}}{\text{equity}}.$$

The ratio of equity to total assets is often determined by regulation, so the ratio of net income to total assets, also called *return on total assets*, is a key ratio for the evaluation of financial institution profitability.

Return on Total Assets

Return on total assets (ROTA) equals net income divided by total assets. Return on total assets for Citicorp in each year, using average assets, was as follows:

Return on total assets (ROTA) = net income ÷ total assets
1985: ROTA =   998 ÷ 160,505 = 0.62%
1986: ROTA =   1,058 ÷ 184,013 = 0.57%.

Return on assets did decline. In other words, Citicorp achieved less profit per dollar of assets in 1986 than in 1985. If financial leverage had remained unchanged, this would have resulted in a decrease in return on equity. The equity-capital ratio tells us what actually happened to financial leverage.

Equity-Capital Ratio

The equity-capital ratio is defined as equity divided by total assets. Other things being equal, a lower equity-capital ratio leads to a higher return on equity. The equity-capital ratios for Citicorp, using average equity and average total assets, are as follows:

Equity capital ratio = equity ÷ total assets
1985 Equity-capital ratio = 7,024 ÷ 160,505 = 4.38%
1986 Equity-capital ratio = 8,394 ÷ 184,013 = 4.56%.

The equity-capital ratio rose, which would have resulted in a *decline* in return on equity even if ROTA had remained constant. The decline in ROTA combined with the increased equity-capital ratio to decrease return on equity. The increased equity was a response to changing regulatory requirements.

Income tax, as a percentage of income before tax, declined from 42 percent to 38 percent. Other things being equal, a lower tax rate would have increased ROTA. Therefore, the decline in ROTA must be attributed to net interest revenue or net operating expenses.

Spread (Net Interest Revenue ÷ Total Assets)

Spread is net interest revenue divided by total assets. Net interest revenue is interest, plus loan fee income, minus interest expense. Spread is followed more closely than either interest income or interest expense as a percentage of total assets because interest income and interest expense both change with changes in the general level of interest rates. The profitability question of interest is the spread between interest income and interest expense. The spreads for Citicorp, using average assets, were as follows:

$$\text{Spread} = \frac{\text{interest and loan fee income}}{\text{total assets}} - \frac{\text{interest expense}}{\text{total assets}}$$

1985: Spread = 12.13% − 8.74% = 3.39%
1986: Spread = 10.45% − 7.12% = 3.33%.

Falling general interest rates brought down both interest income and interest expense, but interest income as a percentage of total assets declined slightly faster. As a result, spread declined six basis points in 1986.

Net Operating Cost Ratio

The net operating cost ratio is net operating costs divided by total assets. Net operating costs consist of operating costs, plus provision for loan losses, minus other income. For Citicorp, the operating cost ratios, using average assets, were as follows:

Net operating cost ratio = net operating costs   ÷ total assets
1985: Net operating cost ratio = (5,517 + 1,243 − 3,030) ÷ 160,505 = 2.32%
1986: Net operating cost ratio = (6,875 + 1,825 − 4,272) ÷ 184,013 = 2.41%.

The net operating cost ratio increased in 1986. This, along with the decline in spread, lead to the drop in ROTA and in turn the drop in return on equity. It is worthwhile to also look at the components of net operating cost:

	1985	1986
Other expense ÷ total assets	3.44%	3.74%
− Other revenue ÷ total assets	1.89	2.32
Difference	1.55	1.42
+ Credit provision ÷ total assets	0.77	0.99
Net operating cost ratio	2.32%	2.41%

This breakdown of the components of net operating cost is revealing. When other revenue and other expense both increase, this may be the result of increased emphasis on fee-based businesses such as transaction services as opposed to asset-based business such as loans. In fact, other expense minus other revenue declined, which is good news. However, the provision for credit losses increased by twenty-two basis points, enough to offset the other gains and increase the net operating cost ratio by eleven basis points.

It is often handy to place all the ratio information on a graphic profitability model, as illustrated in figure 6-2. Figure 6-2 makes a useful diagnostic tool. The change in return on equity is noted first. In this case, we noted a decline and turned our attention to two possible causes: ROTA and leverage. We discovered that leverage declined a bit because of regulatory requirements, and ROTA declined five basis points. Relatively small changes in ROTA and leverage combined to drive return on equity down sharply. This illustrates the extreme sensitivity of financial institution profitability, and therefore the level of skill required by managers.

Looking at the factors affecting ROTA, we note that the tax rate declined, which would result in an increase in ROTA if there were no other changes. However, spread

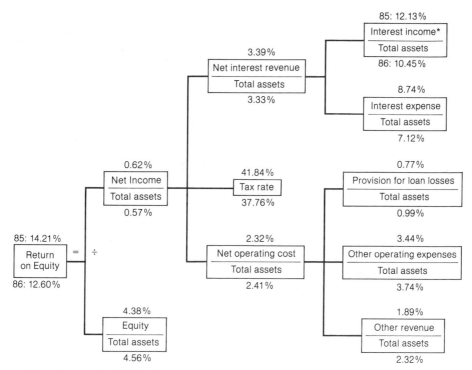

*Loan fees are included with interest income.

Figure 6-2: Profitability model applied to Citicorp.

declined six basis points and the net operating cost ratio increased by nine basis points. The increase in the net operating cost ratio arises from increased operating expenses and a twenty-one basis point increase in the provision for loan losses.

Security analysts responded negatively to the thirty basis point increase in operating expenses other than provision for loan losses. Managers cannot do much about leverage or tax rates, but they can attempt to improve spread by seeking more profitable loans and by seeking market imperfections that allow them to raise funds at lower costs. Managers probably cannot reduce the provision for loan losses in the immediate future because of overseas loan exposure. They will, however, probably focus on automation and other methods of controlling operating costs.

If improvements in all categories of performance were to total twenty-six basis points with no change in leverage or tax rates, return on equity would increase from 12.6 percent to over 16 percent. Likewise, a cumulative change of twenty-six basis points in the wrong direction would decrease return on equity to 9 percent. Again, the profitability of a financial institution is highly sensitive to small changes in costs and revenues; the details matter.

We have focused on comparing Citicorp's 1986 performance to its 1985 performance. It would also be useful to look at trends over longer periods. Analysts concerned about operating costs, for example, studied the trend in operating cost ratios over a period of ten years. It is also helpful to compare probitability between companies. Industry average ratios for the banking industry are available from several sources, as discussed later in this chapter.

Liquidity

Liquidity refers to the ability to meet cash obligations as they come due. Liquidity is probably the most difficult aspect of the financial performances of a financial institution to measure from the published financial statements. Although liquidity analysis requires a detailed comparison of the maturities of assets and liabilities, several ratios can be used to give an indication of liquidity.

Investments Maturing in Less Than One Year to Total Assets

Investments maturing in less than one year can generally be sold quickly with little or no loss in value if additional funds are needed. Thus, the quantity of these assets is one source of liquidity. The year-end ratios of these assets to total assets were as follows:

YEAR	INVESTMENTS MATURING IN LESS THAN ONE YEAR TO TOTAL ASSETS
1985	$2,501 \div 173,597 = 1.44\%$
1986	$2,291 \div 196,124 = 1.17\%$

This compares to approximately 1.35 percent for other major money center banks, indicating that Citicorp was slightly less liquid.

Loans to Total Assets

Loans are nonliquid assets. Most loans cannot be sold and must be held until maturity. Thus, a high ratio of loans to total assets means low liquidity. On the other hand, loans are generally the most profitable assets, so a high ratio of loans to total assets generally contributes to profitability. The ratios of year-end loans to year-end total assets for Citicorp were as follows:

YEAR	RATIO OF LOANS TO TOTAL ASSETS
1985	66.40%
1986	65.88%

The slight decrease in loans as a percent of total assets would indicate an improvement in liquidity at the cost of profitability.

Purchased Liabilities to Total Assets

Purchased liabilities are short-term funds raised in the highly impersonal money markets. Purchased liabilities, also called *hot money*, are considered to be a major demand on liquidity. Purchased liabilities mature quickly, and financial institutions generally plan on selling new short-term securities to replace maturing securities. Unstable money market conditions or questions about the strength of the institution can make it virtually impossible to roll over the purchased liabilities. The ratios of year-end purchased liabilities to year-end total assets for Citicorp were as follows:

YEAR	PURCHASED LIABILITIES TO TOTAL ASSETS
1985	15.33%
1986	17.20%

Citicorp has increased the proportion of assets financed with hot money, which is an indication of a decrease in liquidity.

A complete picture of liquidity depends on an assessment of the maturity structures of assets and liabilities, as explained in chapter 11. In addition, factors such as the company's reputation in the financial markets are important. Citicorp relies heavily on its ability to raise funds to meet its liquidity needs, and market confidence is therefore a major consideration in liquidity analysis. Market confidence depends on as assessment of safety, which in turn depends to a large extent on credit quality and capital adequacy.

Credit Quality

Defaults on loans are one of the major risks faced by financial institutions. Profits are generally less than 1 percent of total loans, so the cushion with which to absorb loan losses is small. Furthermore, equity is often as low as a few percent of assets, providing little cushion from that source.

Financial institutions can afford to make loans that are individually risky as long as the default rate for the group of loans is predictable. For example, a 2 percent loss rate on a group of consumer loans will not cause difficulty as long as the loss rate is anticipated and the interest rate on the loans is high enough to provide a profit after deducting loan losses. A problem arises when loss rates are higher than anticipated. With consumer loans, for example, a recession may lead to unemployment and a 4 percent default rate, wiping out credit loss reserves and moving the company from a profit to a loss.

It is difficult to measure credit quality using financial statement information, but some insights can be gained through ratio analysis.

Credit Loss Provisions to Total Assets

The ratio of *credit loss provisions to total assets* is one such measure. The ratios of credit loss provisions to average total assets for Citicorp were as follows:

YEAR	RATIO OF PROVISION FOR CREDIT LOSSES TO TOTAL ASSETS
1985	0.77%
1986	0.99%

This ratio must be interpreted in light of other information about the company. Citicorp's provision for credit loan losses as a percentage of total assets increased sharply from 1985 to 1986. This could be the result of the company moving into more risky loans, the realization that existing loans are more risky than previously thought, or a change toward a more conservative management approach. The ratio does not tell us which reason dominated, but the public press tells us that Citicorp switched to a more conservative approach to its international loans. In light of discussions in the press, we know that one reason for the increased credit loss provision is an attempt to take a more conservative approach to the risks associated with overseas debt. In addition, Citicorp has increased the proportion of total assets represented by consumer loans, and defaults on these loans tend to be higher than for commercial loans.

Credit Loss Coverage

The credit loss coverage measures the margin for error provided by income. The credit loss coverage ratio definition and credit loss coverage ratios for Citicorp appear below.

$$\text{Credit loss coverage} = \frac{\text{earnings before tax} + \text{provision for credit losses}}{\text{provision for credit losses}}$$

1985: $(1,716 + 1,243) \div 1,243 = 2.38$
1986: $(1,700 + 1,825) \div 1,825 = 1.93.$

A high credit loss coverage ratio means a greater margin for error and therefore more safety, other things being equal. However, the decline in the coverage ratio in this particular case must be interpreted in light of that fact that a more conservative approach to loan loss provisions has been adopted. An examination of credit loss reserves complements the examination of credit loss coverage.

Credit Loss Reserves to Total Assets

Recall that, when the bank decides it will not be able to collect a loan, the loan is written off and the amount deducted from the credit loss reserve. The ratio of credit loss reserves to total assets is a measure of the percent of assets that can be declared uncollectable without having to reduce income. This is another measure of the cushion for covering loan losses. The credit loss reserve ratios for Citicorp, using average assets, were as follows:

YEAR	CREDIT LOSS RESERVES TO TOTAL ASSETS
1985	0.71%
1986	0.87%

The credit loss reserve ratio must be interpreted in light of the quality of assets and the credit loss reserves established by institutions with similar assets. Citicorp's increasing credit loss reserve ratio reflects the more conservative approach to overseas loans previously discussed, and increased consumer lending. Note, however, that the reserve is still less than 1 percent of total assets, which does not leave a large cushion for losses. The average major bank had a credit loss reserve of over 1.5 percent of total assets. Citicorp subsequently responded to this low ratio by adding an extra $3 billion to reserves in 1987.

Net Credit Losses to Total Assets

Net credit losses are the amounts actually written off during the year as uncollectable, minus any previously written-off loans that were collected during the year. Net credit losses as a percentage of average total assets were as follows:

YEAR	NET CREDIT LOSSES TO TOTAL ASSETS
1985	$962 \div 160{,}505 = 0.60\%$
1986	$1{,}371 \div 184{,}013 = 0.75\%$

Net credit losses increased, which would indicate decreasing quality of the loan portfolio. A detailed examination of the footnotes to the financial statement would have revealed that the growth in net credit losses was primarily a result of a growing portfolio of consumer loans, which have a higher default rate than commercial loans. According to the footnotes to the financial statement, commercial loans increased 1 percent from 1984 to 1986, while consumer loans increased 60 percent. The loan loss provision was growing faster than net loan losses, resulting in an increase in loan loss reserve. This is an indication that the company is recognizing the higher default rates in consumer lending and is building its reserves accordingly.

To summarize, the company is experiencing increased loan losses. However, additional reserves for consumer loan losses are being established. It is, of course, possible that management has underestimated future loan losses in the consumer loan portfolio and should be increasing the loan loss reserve even faster. Of more concern in this case, though, is the portfolio of foreign debt. Loans in this group do not tend to go bad in isolation; when trouble hits, an entire country defaults. Thus, foreign debt cannot be evaluated using past net credit losses. The possibility of a major default must be assessed. Citicorp had established smaller reserves than a number of other banks, and this fact caused concern among investment analysts, many of whom shied away from Citicorp as an investment. This is why the stock price jumped sharply in May 1987 when a $3 billion addition to loan loss reserves was announced.

Capital Adequacy

Capital provides protection for depositors and other creditors in the event that assets decline in value or the financial institution suffers losses. There are several definitions of capital, depending on the regulatory agency involved. Some of these measures include loan loss reserves, redeemable preferred stock, and certain qualified debt instruments. A more detailed analysis of capital adequacy is covered in chapter 12. In this chapter, we focus on equity capital.

Equity-Capital Ratio

Equity capital is defined as the book value of common stock, plus the book value of nonredeemable preferred stock. The ratios of year-end equity capital to year-end total assets for Citicorp were:

YEAR	RATIO OF EQUITY CAPITAL TO TOTAL ASSETS
1985	$(1,215 + 6,550) \div 173,597 = 4.47\%$
1986	$(1,365 + 7,695) \div 196,124 = 4.62\%$

Citicorp has been gradually increasing its equity base for a number of years, as reflected in the increase in the equity-capital ratio from 1985 to 1986. This was not entirely by choice, though. Regulators required the banks to increase their capital because of concerns about safety of individual banks and the banking system.

FINANCIAL INSTITUTIONS OTHER THAN FINANCIAL INTERMEDIARIES

The measures developed in this chapter are directly applicable to financial intermediaries: banks, savings and loans, mutual savings banks, credit unions, and finance companies. Each of these institutions concentrates on making loans financed by deposits or borrowed money. Specialized performance measures are used for insurance companies and pension funds. These measures will be discussed in the chapters focusing on these institutions.

SUMMARY

The ability to understand and interpret financial statements is important for a wide variety of people concerned with financial institutions, including regulators, lenders, equity investors, and managers. Financial statement analysis is carried out with the objectives of measuring profitability, liquidity, and safety. *Profitability* is the ability to earn a rate of return on the owners' investment. *Liqudity* is the ability to meet anticipated and unanticipated demands for funds. *Safety* of the organization is ultimately interpreted in terms of ability to cover all costs and meet all obligations. When studying financial statements, safety is evaluated by looking at *credit quality* and *capital adequacy*.

One way to measure relationships is to put the financial statements on a common size basis, with all income statement and balance sheet items restated as a percent-

Table 6-2

Key Financial Ratios

PROFITABILITY

Return on equity (ROE)   = net income ÷ equity
Return on total assets (ROTA) = net income ÷ total assets
Equity capital ratio   = equity ÷ total assets

$$\text{Spread} = \frac{\text{interest and loan fee income}}{\text{Total assets}} - \frac{\text{interest expense}}{\text{total assets}}$$

Net operating cost ratio   = net operating costs ÷ total assets

LIQUIDITY

Investments maturing in less than one year to total assets
Loans to total assets
Purchased liabilities to total assets

CREDIT QUALITY

Provision for credit losses to average total assets

$$\text{Credit loss coverage} = \frac{\text{earnings before tax} + \text{provision for credit losses}}{\text{provision for credit losses}}$$

Credit loss reserves to total assets
Net credit losses to average total assets

CAPITAL ADEQUACY

Equity-capital ratio = equity capital ÷ total assets

---

age of total assets. Another approach is to compute key ratios. Trends for a single company can be studied, and the performance for one company can be compared to that of others. Some of the more commonly used ratios are summarized in table 6-2.

QUESTIONS

6-1.   What are the main categories of performance studied through financial statement analysis?

6-2.   What are the two main methods of analyzing financial statements?

6-3.   Explain the meaning of provision for credit losses, credit loss reserves, and net credit losses.

6-4.   Explain the difference between the accounting treatment of investment securities on the books of financial institutions and of other corporations.

6-5.   Once a ratio is computed, how does the analyst decide if the level is good or bad?

6-6.   What is ROTA and why is it watched closely by managers of financial intermediaries?

6-7.   Why is spread often considered more important than the ratio of either interest income or interest expense to total assets?

PROBLEMS

6-1.   Giant National Bank has an equity capital ratio of 0.08 and a ROTA of 0.01. What is Giant's return on equity?

6-2.   Giant National Bank has interest income of 9 percent of assets and interest expense of 6 percent of assets. What is the spread?

6-3.   Giant National Bank had a provision for credit losses of $1 million in 1987. Credit loss reserves were $3 million at the start of 1987, and net credit losses were $1.2 million in 1987. What were credit loss reserves at the end of 1987?

6-4.   American Savings and Loan has a spread of three percentage points, a net operating cost ratio of 2 percent, and a tax rate of 34 percent. What is the ROTA for American Savings?

6-5.   American Savings (problem 6-4) has an equity capital ratio of 0.05. What is the return on equity for American?

6-6.   Partially completed financial statements for Delta Savings and Loan appear below. The spread is 2 percent, the income tax rate is 33.33 percent, return on equity is 16 percent, and ROTA is 0.8 percent. Fill in the missing information.

Interest and loan fee income	$100,000
Interest expense	
Net interest revenue	
Net operating expense	8,000
Earnings before tax	
Income tax	
Net income	
Total assets	$1,000,000
Equity	

6-7.   The 1984 financial statements of Citicorp appear below (in $ millions). Compute the key financial ratios for 1984 and compare the financial performances for 1985 and 1986 with the financial performance for 1984. Comment on any trends you observe.

Interest and loan fee income	$18,194
Interest expense	13,875
Net interest revenue	4,319
Other revenue	2,300
Provision for loan losses	619
Other operating costs	4,456
Income before taxes	1,544
Income tax	654
Net income	$ 890

		Deposits	$ 90,349
Cash and due from banks	$ 3,528	Purchased funds and other borrowings	24,390
Investments	27,565	Long-term debt	12,993
Loans—gross	103,624	Subord. capital notes	1,649
Credit loss reserves	917	Other liabilities	14,739
Loans (net)	102,707	Redeemable pref. stock	40
Premises and equipment	2,140	Nonredeemable pref. stock	640
Other assets	14,646	Common equity	5,786
Total assets	$150,586	Total liabilities and net worth	$150,586

Average total assets	142, 631
Average stockholders' equity	6,159
Net credit losses	507

6-8. Given the 1984 Citicorp financial statements in problem 6-7, what would the return on equity have been if the equity-capital ratio had been
        a. 3 percent?
        b. 6 percent?

6-9. Given the 1984 Citicorp financial statement in problem 6-7, what would the return on equity have been if interest expense had been 9.2 percent of average total assets instead of 9.7 percent of average total assets?

6-10. Shown below are key financial ratios for money center banks for 1985.[3] Compare the performance of Citicorp (table 6-1) to that of the average money center bank. Compared to the average money center bank, what are Citicorp's strengths and weaknesses?

RATIO	*MONEY CENTER AVERAGE*
Gross interest income ÷ TA	10.30%
Interest expense ÷ TA	7.16
Net interest revenue ÷ TA	3.14
Noninterest income ÷ TA	1.56
Noninterest expense ÷ TA	2.79
Loan loss provision ÷ TA	0.64
Pretax income ÷ TA	1.27
Income tax ÷ TA[4]	0.59
Net income ÷ TA	0.68
Return on equity	13.87

[4]Including tax-equivalent adjustment for tax-free bonds.

[3]*A Review of Bank Performance: 1986 Edition* (New York: Salomon Brothers, Inc., 1986).

6-11. Shown below are financial statement summaries for Ford Motor Credit Company. Examine the performance of Ford Motor Credit and identify any favorable or unfavorable trends.

YEAR	1980	1981	1982	1983	1984	1985	1986
Total financial revenue	$2,172	$2,624	$2,468	$2,481	$3,004	$3,739	$4,540
Interest expense	1,623	2,039	1,695	1,502	1,932	2,199	2,539
Net interest income	550	585	773	979	1,072	1,541	2,000
Other income	230	226	167	146	179	254	433
Operating expenses	390	422	446	462	538	651	859
Prov. for credit losses	131	79	82	117	178	372	509
Earnings before tax	258	310	412	545	535	772	1,066
Prov. for income tax	99	124	183	253	225	332	455
Net income	159	186	229	292	310	441	611
Net receivables	16,095	17,069	15,312	18,434	23,092	30,192	38,061
Other assets	589	651	850	674	943	1,121	1,842
Total assets	16,684	17,720	16,162	19,108	24,035	31,313	39,902
Short-term debt	8,302	8,585	7,279	8,804	11,950	14,578	17,341
Other liabilities	6,845	7,514	7,041	8,401	10,003	14,171	19,583
Stockholders' equity	1,537	1,620	1,842	1,903	2,082	2,565	2,978

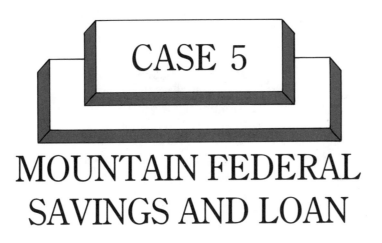

CASE 5

MOUNTAIN FEDERAL SAVINGS AND LOAN

Mountain Federal Savings and Loan demonstrated impressive growth in both assets and profits during the first seven years of the 1980s. In 1980, Mountain had assets of $726 million and suffered a loss of slightly over $1 million. The company earned a profit every year after 1982, including income of over $16 million in 1986. At the same time, assets reached a 1986 level of over $5,208 billion, an annual growth rate of 39 percent. In this period, Mountain Federal converted itself from a local company, operating in one part of one state, to a holding company with savings and loans in over a dozen states from Virginia to California.

Mountain Federal's performance was particularly impressive in light of the performance of other savings and loans during the period. Asset growth for the industry was less that 10 percent, and the industry suffered substantial losses. In fact, the industry suffered a record number of bankruptcies during the period.

Mountain had achieved the bulk of its growth through the acquisition of other savings and loans, primarily savings and loans that were in financial difficulty. These acquisitions were often negotiated with the Federal Savings and Loan Insurance Corporation (FSLIC), with FSLIC often purchasing some questionable assets of the failed savings and loan.

A number of savings and loans had chosen a strategy of rapid expansion through acquisition, like the strategy of Mountain Financial. Some of these institutions had been forced into bankruptcy, causing concern about the strategy. Many of the agressive savings and loans in oil patch states like Texas had gotten into difficulty, for example. In this environment, both investors and regulators were concerned about the safety of these new giants of the savings and loan industry.

1. Compare Mountain with the savings and loan industry with regard to both profitability and safety. What signs of strength and weakness do you see?
2. Study past trends in the performance of Mountain Financial. What favorable and unfavorable trends do you see?
3. If you were a regulator primarily interested in the safety of the system, would you allow Mountain to continue on the path of rapid expansion?
4. If you were an investor primarily interested in profitable investments, would you be interested in acquiring the stock of Mountain?

Table 1

Composite Financial Performance of Savings and Loans, as a Percent of Total Assets

YEAR	1980	1981	1982	1983	1984	1985	1986
Gross operating income	9.49	10.30	10.69	10.66	11.23	10.80	9.93
Interest expense	8.02	10.00	10.51	9.02	9.42	8.55	7.51
Cust. net revenue	1.47	0.30	0.18	1.64	1.81	2.25	2.43
Operating expense	1.34	1.42	1.51	1.64	1.71	1.91	2.06
Earning before tax	0.20	−0.98	−0.88	0.36	0.16	0.59	0.38
Tax	0.07	−0.25	−0.24	0.09	0.03	0.21	0.29
Net income	0.14	−0.73	−0.64	0.27	0.12	0.37	0.10
Loans	87.47	86.16	84.01	83.02	81.67	81.23	80.31
Deposits	74.61	71.40	72.06	72.11	68.65	68.77	66.28
Net worth	5.27	4.27	3.69	4.03	3.81	4.38	4.56
Return on average net worth	2.50	−15.28	−16.20	6.88	3.14	9.05	2.20

Table 2

Financial Statements for Mountain Federal

YEAR	1980	1981	1982	1983	1984	1985	1986
Int. and div. income	$62,044	$67,474	$121,217	$157,853	$267,745	$391,095	$488,139
Interest expense	56,591	70,713	120,756	140,219	235,075	343,996	395,098
Net int. income	5,453	−3,239	461	17,634	32,670	47,099	93,041
Other income		4,321	75,144	15,683	36,801	63,700	49,814
Other expense		11,434	24,320	33,311	61,629	87,773	110,924
Provision for loan losses		198	2,150	362	1,412	8,016	15,156
Income before tax		−10,550	49,135	644	6,430	15,010	16,775
Federal income tax		−18,459	−1,437	0	9	2,139	322
Net income	−1,068	−7,909	50,572	644	6,421	12,871	16,453
Loans	656,093	669,035	1,174,061	1,408,374	2,591,579	3,157,442	4,158,606
Other assets	70,025	70,776	861,984	852,742	800,036	952,049	1,049,540
Total assets	726,118	739,811	2,036,045	2,261,116	3,391,615	4,109,491	5,208,146
Savings deposits	596,664	598,295	1,814,052	1,995,676	2,657,805	3,242,692	3,842,627
Other liabilities	89,325	109,296	139,201	155,290	611,767	666,836	1,139,636
Pfd. stock (subsidiary)						38,959	39,288
Stockholder equity	40,129	32,220	82,792	110,150	122,043	161,004	186,595
Liab. and net worth	726,118	739,811	2,036,045	2,261,116	3,391,615	4,109,491	5,208,146

SELECTED REFERENCES

BELONGIA, MICHAEL T., AND GILBERT, R. ALTON. "Agricultural Banks: Causes of Failures and Conditions of Survivors," *Federal Reserve Bank of St. Louis Review* 69 (May 1987): 30–37.

PATTEN, JAMES A. *Fundamentals of Bank Accounting* (Reston, Va.: Reston Publishing Company, 1983).

SHOME, DILIP K., SMITH, STEPHEN, AND HEGGESTAD, ARNOLD. "Do Banks Have Adequate Capital?" *The Bankers Magazine* 170 (July/August, 1987): 21–23.

SINKEY, JOSEPH F., JR., TERZA, JOSEPH V., AND DINCE, ROBERT. "A Zeta Analysis of Failed Commercial Banks," *Quarterly Journal of Business and Economics* 26 (Autumn 1987): 35–49.

SMIRLOCK, MICHAEL, AND KAUFOLD, HOWARD. "Bank Lending, Mandatory Disclosure Rules, and Reactions of Bank Stock Prices to the Mexican Debt Crisis," *Journal of Business* 60 (July 1987): 347–364.

SPECIAL REPORT: "Bank Profitability" (five separate articles), *ABA Banking Journal* 79 (August 1987).

WEST, R. C. "A Factor-Analytic Approach to Bank Condition," *Journal of Banking and Finance* 9 (June 1985): 253–266.

7

Money Markets

The money and capital markets are similar in that they provide an investment outlet for those with excess funds and a source for those in need of funds. The markets differ with regard to the type of funds involved. As the capital markets deal in long-term securities, they provide a permanent or semi-permanent outlet for funds. The money markets, on the other hand, provide an outlet and source of short-term borrowing; they are primarily liquidity markets.

The money markets are a group of markets in which short-term, generally high-quality credit instruments are bought and sold; money market instruments normally mature in one year or less. Because it is necessary to quickly establish the safety of such an instrument, borrowing within this market is limited to large, safe, well-recognized organizations. Financial institutions, major corporations, and governmental units are the major issuers of money market instruments.

The major securities bought and sold in the money markets include:

1. *Treasury bills*—obligations of the U.S. Treasury with maturities of one year or less.
2. *Agency securities*—obligations of agencies of the U.S. government.
3. *Commercial paper*—obligations of large, stable corporations and financial institutions. Maturities normally range from a few days to a maximum of 270 days.
4. *Negotiable certificates of deposit*—marketable deposit receipts issued by commercial banks and bearing specified rates of interest for a specified period of time.

5. *Banker's acceptances*—obligations of a firm, guaranteed by a bank. The instruments normally arise through international commerce and carry an average maturity of ninety days.
6. *Federal funds*—loans between commercial banks, typically on an overnight basis.
7. *Repurchase agreement*—sales of securities, normally by a securities dealer, in which the seller agrees to repurchase the same securities within a specified time at a specified price.
8. *Eurodollars*—U.S. dollar-denominated deposits held by banks outside the United States, including foreign branches of U.S. banks.

Each of these instruments, as well as other money market instruments, will be discussed in greater depth in this chapter.

There is no central physical location which serves as the money market. Separate market structures have developed for each type of instrument, and none of these markets have central meeting places. The primary machinery for bringing together borrower and lender (or buyer and seller) consists of approximately forty-six "money market banks" and a handful of specialized dealers and brokers. These "money market banks" include the largest New York banks and banks in other financial centers around the country. There are about twenty government securities dealers, some of which are banks, and about twelve commercial paper dealers. There are also a few banker's acceptances dealers and a number of brokers, such as federal funds brokers. The money markets operate by telephone with brokers and dealers functioning to match supply and demand. The market for each instrument will be discussed in more detail in later parts of this chapter.

The money markets are important because of their volume. In 1987, the volume of outstanding Treasury bills alone totaled nearly $1800 for every person in the United States. Also, the money markets are important because they are a major medium through which the Federal Reserve implements monetary policy. The Federal Reserve increases the money supply by purchasing U.S. government securities and decreases the money supply by reselling these securities.

Many money market instruments do not pay interest directly, but are sold at a *discount*. That is, the instruments are sold at less than their face value with the buyer receiving face value at maturity. Therefore, prices and available returns on money market instruments vary with market conditions and the general level of interest rates. The higher the general level of interest rates, the greater will be the yield necessary for a money market instrument to provide its buyer a competitive rate of return.

Most purchasers of money market instruments are large corporations, institutions, or governmental units. Since most money market transactions involve large volumes of money for short time periods, few individuals have the financial capacity to participate in these markets. The main exception to this generalization involves Treasury bills which are presently sold in denominations as small as $10,000. Even in this market, individual participation is quite small relative to total volume.

The bulk of this chapter is devoted to a discussion of the various money market instruments—issuers, holders, market, and volume. Final sections of the chapter are devoted to the determinants of interest rates in the money markets and the impact of Federal Reserve policy decisions on these markets.

TREASURY BILLS

The Treasury bill market is the largest single segment of the money market. From the time of their first issue in 1929 until 1987 the volume of Treasury bills outstanding has increased from $100 million to $427 billion. Thus Treasury bills provide an important outlet for temporarily idle funds and an important source of borrowed funds for the U.S. government. In addition, the trading of Treasury bills in secondary markets is a major tool in the implementation of monetary policy.

A Treasury bill is an obligation of the U.S. government to pay the bearer a fixed sum at a specified date. Treasury bills are regularly issued in maturities of 91 days, 182 days, and 365 days, with the 182-day or six-month bill representing the largest volume. Treasury bills range in denomination from $10,000 to $1,000,000.

Treasury bills are sold in an auction market with the Federal Reserve System handling the sale on behalf of the Treasury. Treasury bills do not pay interest directly but are sold at a discount, with the amount of discount being determined by the auction process. The actual interest rate earned depends on the amount of the discount. Suppose, for example, that an average accepted bid for 182-day bills is $94.130 per $100 of face value. The published interest rate is based on the amount of discount and on an assumed 360-day year. The quoted rate (often called the discount interest rate) is

$$\frac{100 - 94.130}{100} \times \frac{360}{182} = 11.611\%.$$

While this method of computing and reporting interest on Treasury bills has become commonplace, it is not comparable to the manner in which the rate is computed for many other instruments. In calculating the yield to maturity on direct interest-bearing issues such as bonds, the denominator is the amount invested rather than the maturity value, and the number of days per year is 365 rather than the 360 used in the above computation. A more accurate measure, called bond-equivalent yield, is

$$\frac{100 - 94.130}{94.130} \times \frac{365}{182} = 12.506\%.$$

Since the former rate is one that is frequently quoted and the latter procedure represents the method of quotation for interest-bearing issues, this difference must be remembered when comparing interest rates.

Treasury bills are auctioned each week by the Treasury Department, with bids being collected and tabulated by the Federal Reserve System. Bids for the weekly offering are accepted at Federal Reserve banks and their branches until 1:30 P.M. (New York time) on Monday. Bids for amounts less than $500,000 may be submitted on a noncompetitive basis. Treasury bills are first allocated to noncompetitive bids. Competitive bids are then accepted in descending order until the week's issue has been fully allocated. Successful bidders pay their bid price, and bills are awarded to noncompetitive bidders at a price equal to the weighted average of accepted bids. Delivery then occurs on Thursday. The average weekly issue is several billion dollars; most of the proceeds go to retire existing issues.

Treasury bills provide an excellent temporary outlet for funds held to meet possible liquidity needs. First, they are considered risk-free because they are obligations of the U.S. government. Second, there is an active secondary market. Government security dealers continually stand ready with bid and ask prices—prices at which they will buy or sell—for all outstanding issues. The typical spread is four basis points[1] or about 1¢ per $100 of a three-month bill. Third, there is no risk of a large shrinkage if the holder needs to sell Treasury bills quickly to meet liquidity needs. Because of the short maturity, even a large interest rate movement will result in only a relatively small change in the price of a Treasury bill.

As an example of how little value loss is risked, we look at the 182-day Treasury bill used above to see how the interest rate is computed. At the time of issue, that particular bill had a discount interest rate of 11.611 percent and a price of $94.130 per $100 of face value. Normally we would expect the price to rise steadily as the issue gets closer to maturity. However, a rise in the required rate of return or general level of interest rates might prevent this from happening. By the end of thirty days from time of issue, with no change in the quoted interest rate, the price of this issue would rise to 95.098.[2] Suppose, however, that interest rates rise over the thirty-day period to the point that the discount rate is 13 percent, a quite rapid rise in interest rates. The market value would then be 94.511. While this is a small gain over the 94.130 price one month earlier, this price is still above the price originally paid. Thus the chance of a significant loss in market value is quite small.

Holders of Treasury bills include Federal Reserve banks, commercial banks, money market mutual funds, state and local governments, nonfinancial corporations, and individuals. U.S. government trust funds are also substantial holders from time to time. A substantial volume of holdings is also in the hands of foreign holders, both central banks and others.

The Role of Treasury Bills in Economic Policy

In addition to being the largest of the money markets, the Treasury bill market is important because it is the market through which much of the Federal Reserve's monetary policy is implemented. Increases in the supply of money will generally stimulate economic activity if the economy is operating below capacity. Conversely, decreases in the money supply will decrease the ability of financial institutions to lend money, thus

---

[1]The term "basis point" is a short-hand method of describing small fluctuations in interest rates. One hundred basis points represents 1 percent.

[2] $$\frac{100 - P}{100} \times \frac{360}{152} = 0.1161; P = 95.098.$$

decreasing overall demand for goods and services. Through the impact on demand, changes in the money supply also affect the rate of inflation. When the economy is at or near full capacity, an increase in the money supply and a resultant increase in demand will result in an increase in prices. The Federal Reserve System attempts to control the money supply to create a balance that will encourage a healthy, steady rate of economic growth without encouraging inflation.

While there are several ways that the money supply can be controlled, day-to-day control is primarily maintained through the open market operations of the Federal Reserve. Open market operations consist of buying or selling U.S. government securities—primarily Treasury bills. When the Federal Reserve buys Treasury bills, the seller receives payment through credit to his demand deposit account. If the seller is a commercial bank, the payment is in the form of a credit to its account with the Federal Reserve. This is an increase in the bank's reserves and an increase in its ability to loan money. For a nonbank seller, the seller ends up with credit to his demand deposit with his bank; the bank ends up with an increase in its deposit account with the Federal Reserve, again resulting in an increase in its ability to make loans. Conversely, the selling of Treasury bills by the Federal Reserve serves to decrease the money supply. The Federal Reserve buys or sells Treasury bills on a daily basis to change the money supply as needed to encourage stable economic growth and avoid encouraging more inflation. In recent years, the Federal Reserve has held between 20 and 25 percent of outstanding Treasury bills.

U.S. GOVERNMENT AGENCY SECURITIES

The debt of U.S. government agencies has become increasingly important in the money and capital markets. Debt instruments issued by government agencies can be divided into two groups: those directly guaranteed by the U.S. government and those sponsored but not guaranteed by the government. The principal government-guaranteed agency issues include obligations of the Federal Housing Administration (FHA), the Government National Mortgage Association (GNMA or "Ginnie Mae"), the Tennessee Valley Authority (TVA), the Export-Import Bank, and certain obligations of the U.S. Postal Service. The Tennessee Valley Authority and the Export-Import Bank owed $17 billion and $14 billion, respectively, by 1987.

The other guaranteed agencies owed a combined total of only $6 billion, a small volume when compared with the outstanding volume of Treasury bills.

The claims of the federally sponsored agencies represent a larger volume of liabilities. These agencies act primarily as financial intermediaries, raising funds for the purpose of loaning to others. Typically, these agencies were originally owned by the U.S. government, with their stock being later sold to private holders. For example, all of the shares of the Federal Home Loan banks are now owned by members, primarily savings and loan associations. While most of these agency issues are not directly guaranteed by the U.S. government, many observers believe that the government would come to the rescue of any agency facing default. Thus issues of sponsored agencies are generally considered to be almost as safe as those of guaranteed agencies. Because of their importance, the major sponsored agencies are discussed in more detail in the paragraphs below.

THE FEDERAL NATIONAL MORTGAGE ASSOCIATION   (FNMA or "Fannie Mae") currently represents the largest issuer of nonguaranteed debt. This agency was formed to provide a secondary market for mortgages and issues both short-term and long-term obligations. Thus some of its liabilities qualify as money market instruments. By 1987, debt obligations of this agency had expanded to $93 billion.

THE FEDERAL HOME LOAN BANK (FHLB) SYSTEM   was created in part to enhance the flow of credit to the residential housing market. The banks which constitute the system were patterned somewhat after the Federal Reserve System and were designed to provide a source of liquidity for mortgage lenders (principally savings and loan associations). Funds raised in security markets by the Federal Home Loan Bank System are, in turn, loaned out to member institutions to support mortgage lending activities. The FHLB varies its mixture of long-term and short-term issues in response to market conditions. At the beginning of 1987, FHLB debt outstanding totalled $90 billion.

THE FARM CREDIT BANKS   began issuing bonds on a regular basis in 1979 to replace the separate financing operations of the Federal Land Banks, the Federal Intermediate-Term Credit Banks, and the Banks for Cooperatives. The Federal Land Banks make mortgage credit available to farmers, while the Federal Intermediate-Term Credit Banks make credit available by purchasing notes from production credit associations. The Banks for Cooperatives were established to encourage the development of farmers' cooperatives for marketing and related purposes. The total debt of these four agencies was $60 billion by 1987.

In addition to these agencies, a number of smaller agencies also have several billion dollars in outstanding debt.

Agencies market three specific types of securities: short-term notes (generally discount notes), unsecured bonds, and participation certificates. A participation certificate represents an interest in a pooled group of loans. Rather than selling mortgages to investors, the issuing agency continues to hold the loans and collect payments. The payments are then used to service the participation certificates. Certificates such as these are guaranteed by the federal government and paid from the Treasury if collections from the assets are not sufficient to meet the contractual interest and repayment terms of the certificates.

While agency securities are negotiable and relatively easy to sell, the secondary market for these securities is not as well developed as that for Treasury bills. Thus Treasury bills are more likely to be used for primary liquidity needs. Because of their limited marketability, market interest rates on agency issues are normally a fraction of a percent higher than those for Treasury bills with similar maturities.

Holdings of agency securities are not concentrated in any particular sector. They are fairly well distributed among financial institutions, nonfinancial corporations, state and local governments, and individuals.

To complete this overview, table 7-1 presents a summary of the outstanding U.S. government debt.

Table 7-1

Summary of U.S. Government Debt, January 1987 (in $ billions)

	SHORT TERM	INTERMEDIATE AND LONG-TERM	TOTAL
Treasury obligations	$427	$1,788	$2,215
Federal National Mortgage Association			93
Federal Home Loan Bank			90
Farm Credit Banks (and related agencies)			60
Tennessee Valley Authority			17
Export-Import Bank			14
Other			31

Source: *Federal Reserve Bulletin.*

COMMERCIAL PAPER

The commercial paper market is a uniquely American institution. Canada is the only other country with a commercial paper market of any significance, and its market is relatively small. Commercial paper is a short-term unsecured promissory note issued by a corporation with a well-known, impeccable credit rating. Maturities range from a few days to 270 days. Most issuers back their commercial paper by maintaining unused bank lines of credit equal to or approaching the amount of commercial paper outstanding.

Commercial paper has advantages for both issuer and purchaser. For the issuer, the commercial paper rate is normally below the prime rate—the interest rate charged by banks to their best commercial customers. In some recent years, the commercial paper rate has been more than a full percentage point below the prime rate. From the buyer's point of view, commercial paper offers a return above the rate earned on alternate securities such as Treasury bills with only a small amount of additional risk.

Because of its advantages to both buyer and seller, the commercial paper market has grown rapidly since its inception by General Motors Acceptance Corporation in 1920. The amount of commercial paper outstanding reached $5 billion in 1960, $40 billion in 1970, and $350 billion by 1987.

Like Treasury bills, the vast majority of commercial paper is sold at a discount and redeemed at face value. The computation used in publishing interest rates is the same as that used for Treasury bills.

Only about 600 firms issue commercial paper, with about two dozen finance companies accounting for approximately half the total. In addition to finance companies, other issuers are bank affiliates and large nonfinancial corporations, especially utilities. This limited number of issuers reflects the nature of the security involved. Purchase of a short-term unsecured obligation cannot realistically be preceded by a lengthy credit investigation if the transaction is to be profitable. This makes it essential that companies issuing commercial paper have well-known, impeccable credit ratings.[3]

[3]This is not to say that commercial paper has been default-free. The commercial paper market was taken by surprise when Penn Central defaulted on its commercial paper in 1970.

Commercial paper is sold either directly to lenders (direct placement) or through commercial paper dealers. About 55 percent of the commercial paper is placed directly with almost all directly placed paper being issued by finance companies. The remainder of the commercial paper is sold through dealers. There are about six major dealers in the United States with all but one being New York investment banking houses. The dealers earn their fee in the form of a spread between the price they pay and the price they sell the issue for. The minimum spread amounts to one-eighth of 1 percent per annum.

The secondary market for commercial paper is quite restricted. Most commercial paper is held to maturity by its original purchaser. However, many direct issuers have "gentlemen's agreements" that they will buy back the paper before maturity (and adjust the interest rate) if the lender suffers severe liquidity problems. The borrowers can do this because they are continually in the commercial paper market in the same way banks continually accept deposits and because they have back-up lines of credit with commerical banks.

Of the $350 billion of commercial paper outstanding in 1987, 78 percent was issued by financial institutions and the remainder was issued by nonfinancial corporations. Primary holders are banks, nonfinancial corporations, insurance companies, trust funds, and pension funds.

Despite the fact that commercial paper markets have generally not developed in other countries, this type of market has been very useful in meeting the needs of United States borrowers and lenders as attested by the significant growth and development of this instrument. With the volume in this market more than doubling in the last five years, it appears to be a stable factor in the country's financial structure.

NEGOTIABLE CERTIFICATES OF DEPOSIT

The market for negotiable certificates of deposit (CDs) is the newest of the large money markets. It began in 1961 when First National City Bank of New York issued the first negotiable certificates of deposit and a government securities dealer agreed to make a second market in them. The outstanding amount was $50 billion in 1987.

A certificate of deposit is a receipt for a bank deposit with a specified maturity and bearing a specified interest rate. This type of deposit has been around since at least the beginning of this century. It was the conversion to a negotiable (salable) form and the development of a secondary market that made these instruments important ones in money markets. Negotiable CDs can be sold with a fixed maturity which guarantees the issuing institution funds for that period of time; they can be sold in the secondary market if necessary, which provides liquidity to the holders.

Negotiable CDs differ from Treasury bills and commercial paper in that they bear interest payable at maturity rather than being issued at a discount. Further, interest is based on a 365-day year rather than a 360-day year, as is the case with Treasury bills and commercial paper. Because of these computational differences, quoted rates are not strictly comparable. For purposes of rate comparability, the Treasury bill or commercial paper rate discount interest rate must be recomputed to a bond equivalent yield.

Negotiable CDs are insured only up to Federal Deposit Insurance Corporation limits (currently $100,000). Thus the quality of the bank issuing the CDs is a matter of concern. The largest money market banks are normally able to issue their CDs at one-eighth to one-half percentage point below those issued by smaller regional banks. In addition, secondary markets for CDs issued by smaller banks tend to be less active than those for the large, well-known banks. Some corporations divide temporarily idle funds among several different types of money market instruments—Treasury bills, negotiable CDs of major money market banks, and negotiable CDs of smaller banks—thereby providing different levels of liquidity.

When banks first began issuing negotiable CDs, maximum interest rates were established by regulation. The result was that during periods of tight money (such as those which existed in 1966 and 1969) banks could not offer CD rates competitive with those available on competing money market instruments. The volume of outstanding CDs declined, and the ability of commercial banks to compete for funds was threatened. In 1970 regulations were removed for shorter-term large-denomination CDs, and in 1973 they were removed for all CDs of $100,000 or more. Today, of course, interest rate ceilings for CDs no longer exist, regardless of size. Thus today's rates are set entirely by market conditions. The removal of rate ceilings has resulted in greater stability in terms of the ability of banks to issue new CDs. However, wide swings in CD volume and rates may be observed as banks' needs for funds and lending opportunities change.

The buyers of negotiable CDs are primarily nonfinancial corporations. Indeed, negotiable CDs came into existence as a means of competing for corporate deposits that were leaving the banks in search of more attractive outlets for temporarily idle funds. CD holders frequently meet day-to-day liquidity needs by adjusting Treasury bill balances while holding negotiable CDs as a secondary reserve asset. Thus secondary market volume in CDs is considerably less than that for Treasury bills.

As previously indicated, the main issuers of negotiable CDs are large money market banks. The majority of the issues are by banks with assets in excess of $1 billion. Approximately 40 percent of the total volume originates with large New York banks. These banks tend to have substantial loan commitments and enjoy the credit and reputation which facilitate sale of large CDs.

The negotiable CD market is an excellent example of the manner in which financial institutions and instruments evolve to meet economic needs. Negotiable CDs were originated in response to a need to compete for corporate deposits that were being lost to other money market instruments. Legislation and regulation gradually changed in response to market needs. Within a relatively few years, this new instrument rose to challenge commercial paper as the second largest volume money market instrument.

BANKER'S ACCEPTANCES

One of the oldest of money market instruments, banker's acceptances, came into existence primarily through foreign trade. These acceptances provide an alternate to open account credit, primarily when goods are to be shipped across national borders. As banker's acceptances are negotiable, they are money market instruments. They have grown in importance with the growth in foreign trade; their volume outstanding was $70 billion in 1987.

To understand this somewhat confusing credit instrument, we begin with an example of an American firm wishing to purchase overseas goods for import. The buyer secures a letter of credit for the order from a well-known American bank, authorizing the seller of the goods to write a draft on the buyer's bank upon shipment of the goods. The draft instructs the bank to pay a specified amount on a specific date.

The seller has two alternatives: One is holding the draft until the date specified for payment; the second, attaching the shipping documents to the draft as evidence of shipment and selling the draft to his bank at a discount from face value. If the second alternative is taken, the seller's bank then forwards the draft and shipping documents to its American correspondent, which in turn presents them to the buyer's bank. The buyer's bank examines and removes the shipping documents and stamps the draft "I accept," making it a negotiable instrument guaranteed by the buyer's bank. The draft is now the obligations of both the buyer's bank and the seller. Because of these obligations, they are considered nearly as safe as Treasury bills.

Once the draft has been accepted, a number of things can happen to it. Since the seller's bank bought the draft at a discount, it may simply instruct its correspondent to hold the draft until maturity as an investment, or it may instruct the correspondent to sell the draft immediately. In this case, it may be sold to the buyer's bank or in the market. Thus this accepted draft or banker's acceptance serves as a money market instrument.

This example involves a foreign seller and a U.S. buyer. Of course, the whole process can be reversed, with the foreign buyer's bank acceptance or guarantee of the draft. Although the greatest growth has been in support of foreign trade, banker's acceptances can also be used as a method of financing domestic trade.

Maturities of banker's acceptances range from 30 to 180 days, with 90 being the most common. From the accepting bank's point of view, this procedure represents an attractive means of helping customers with their short-term credit needs. If the accepting bank does not hold the acceptance itself, it is making credit available by lending its name rather than its money. If the accepting bank holds the acceptance itself, it is effectively lending the buyer the amount of the acceptance. However, the acceptance is recorded on the bank's financial statements as a secondary reserve asset rather than as a loan.

Banker's acceptances have not experienced as active a secondary market as have most of the other money market instruments previously discussed. Accepting banks hold about one-fourth of all outstanding banker's acceptances, and foreign financial institutions hold some 60 percent. The remainder are held by domestic owners and by Federal Reserve banks. The secondary market is made up mostly of a few government security dealers that make a market in these securities. One reason acceptances are attractive short-term dollar investments for foreigners is that they are not subject to American income taxes as is the interest on Treasury bills.

FEDERAL FUNDS

The federal funds market arises from the requirement that commercial banks[4] hold certain levels of liquid reserves, primarily in the form of deposits with their Federal Reserve banks. A bank with excess reserves can lend these reserves to a bank with insufficient reserves. The lending bank instructs its Federal Reserve bank via check or wire to transfer ownership of part of its deposit to the borrowing bank. As these loans are almost entirely overnight,[5] the borrowing bank sends an order the next day transferring ownership back to the lending bank.

Although the federal funds market is almost entirely restricted to overnight loans, it is still profitable for a bank with excess reserves to make such loans. The denominations are large: Transactions are normally in multiples of $1 million. At an effective annual interest rate of 12 percent, the interest on an overnight loan of $5 million would be in excess of $1,600. Thus it is worth the bank's trouble to make an overnight loan if it has excess reserves. From the borrower's point of view, borrowing in the federal funds market avoids the necessity of less desirable alternatives such as turning down loan applications or selling marketable securities.

Growth of the federal funds market was stimulated over the past two decades by general increases in the level of interest rates and the resultant opportunity cost associated with idle bank funds. While any particular bank could be a net seller (lender) of funds or a net buyer (borrower), large banks as a group tend to be net buyers; small banks generally, net sellers. While the fed funds market has traditionally served as a means for participating banks to balance reserve requirements, many of the nation's larger banks have been involved as consistent net borrowers and on a daily basis rely on this source of funds.

Federal funds transactions occur primarily on an unsecured basis, because collateral is troublesome for such short-term loans. When security is required, the borrower is typically a smaller bank and U.S. government securities are placed in a special custody account for the one-day period.

The federal funds market, like all markets, depends on some method of bringing buyer and seller together. The role of market maker falls primarily on certain large New York banks because they tend to be net buyers (borrowers) of funds and because most banks throughout the nation maintain a correspondent relationship with a New York bank. Normally the New York banks are willing to borrow the funds themselves and have knowledge of who needs funds. Other banks, a few stock exchange firms, and some institutional money brokers also act as brokers, collecting information on who has excess federal funds and who needs funds. The federal funds market differs from the money markets previously discussed in that the market makers primarily act as brokers, bringing borrower and lender together. For the other money market instru-

---

[4]With the Depository Institutions Deregulation and Monetary Control Act of 1980, other institutions having transaction accounts were brought under these reserve requirements over a period of several years. Thus they have become participants in this market.

[5]Federal funds transactions occurring on Friday are "three-day" transactions because transactions are not conducted on weekends.

ments, market makers act as dealers, actually purchasing and reselling securities. The federal funds market also differs from other money markets in that direct participation is limited to banks and financial institutions with deposits at Federal Reserve banks.

Market rates for federal funds are particularly volatile; they react to short-term shifts in supply and demand conditions. Banks must adjust their position quickly to meet reserve requirements. In periods of tight money, these adjustments can result in rapid shifts in federal funds rates. Furthermore, a tendency for some banks to look to the federal funds market as a more-or-less permanent method of meeting funds requirements has caused demand to be heavy and rates to be high during periods of tight money. Conversely, demand and interest rates can fall sharply in recessionary periods. The federal funds rate is closely watched by the monetary authorities as a barometer of supply and demand for bank credit.

Volume in the federal funds market is a bit difficult to measure because banks report federal funds and repurchase agreements in combined form. In 1987 the sum of these two types of borrowing outstanding on the books of commercial banks was $243 billion.

Repurchase Agreements

Repurchase agreements (RPs) are defined as the sale of securities concurrent with an agreement to repurchase them at a later date. The arrangement may call for repurchase at a specific date for a specific price, or it may be open-ended with either party able to end the arrangements at any time. In the latter case, the lender would be guaranteed a fixed return per day over the time the agreement remained in effect. Maturities of repurchase agreements range from one day to several months.

While any two parties may enter into a repurchase agreement, this arrangement has served primarily as a method of financing for U.S. government securities dealers. With the growth in U.S. government debt, dealers in U.S. government securities require extremely large sums of money to finance their inventories of securities. These dealers rely primarily on credit, maintaining debt to total asset ratios of 98 percent or more. They meet their financing needs through borrowing and repurchase agreements.

Because U.S. government securities dealers hold billions of dollars in inventories, their need for funds is quite large, and a major part of their daily activity consists of arranging financing at the lowest possible cost. Financing is achieved through direct borrowing, with the securities serving as collateral and through repurchase agreements.

Lenders (purchasers) include New York banks, regional banks, and other institutions, including nonfinancial corporations. Most dealers begin their day by seeking funds from sources located outside New York, as New York rates tend to be slightly higher. Later in the day they complete the financing of their daily needs through the New York banks. Several New York banks post daily rates at which they will meet the dealer financing of any desired volume of government securities. This posted rate varies from one New York bank to another, depending on how eager each bank is to make additional loans.

Since the dealers are in permanent need of funds, they can tailor maturities to the needs of a particular supplier of funds. Thus corporations view dealer loans and RPs as a flexible method of placing temporarily excess funds. Some funds suppliers prefer direct loans; others prefer repurchase agreements. Repurchase agreements are most likely to be employed when funds are to be advanced for more than a few days. The expense of transferring title for very short periods does not make such transfer economical.

The repurchase agreement market is also an important medium for exercise of short-term money supply control by the Federal Reserve. When there is a temporary need for additional funds in the system, the Federal Reserve can buy U.S. government securities under repurchase agreement. The Federal Reserve is assured that there is a specific date when this agreement will end and the supply of funds to the market can be withdrawn. A reverse RP is also used on occasion. In this case, the Federal Reserve sells securities under repurchase agreements to temporarily decrease the money supply.

EURODOLLARS

The Eurodollar market is another relatively young market whose development as an active market can be traced to the late 1950s. Eurodollars are U.S. dollar-denominated deposits held by banks outside the United States, including foreign branches of domestic banks. They represent an important source of funds for businesses and an important market in which banks adjust liquidity.

To come to grips with the operations of the Eurodollar market, we will follow an example of the development and transfer of Eurodollars.

A German exporting company has received payment in U.S. dollars and presently holds a demand deposit with Citibank in New York. Because the company expects to need dollars in the future, it converts its asset by making a dollar-denominated time deposit with a German bank; the German bank receives ownership of the Citibank demand deposit as an offsetting asset. Thus, Eurodollars have been created.

The German bank has received a number of other dollar-denominated time deposits as well and is paying interest on these time deposits while receiving no interest on its offsetting dollar-denominated demand deposit assets. It will wish to turn these demand deposits to some profitable use.

The German bank may have a customer in need of a dollar-denominated loan. If not, it will lend the demand deposit to another bank, which in turn lends it to a customer. A U.S. bank continues to have the same demand deposit liability, but ownership of this deposit may change many times.

Like the other money markets, the Eurodollar market has no physical location; it is based on wire communications. However, the center of activity is London, and the London interbank loan rate (LIBOR) is considered the primary "market" rate. Like the federal funds market, the Eurodollar market is primarily an interbank market; banks have deposits from and loans to their customers. Similar markets exist for other major currencies; London is the center for all currencies except the pound.

A particularly important aspect of the Eurodollar market with regard to the domestic money market is the practice by American banks of borrowing from their foreign affiliates in periods of tight money. The foreign affiliates can borrow Eurodollars in the same way that federal funds or some other short-term credit instrument can be used. The affiliate then deposits the funds with the parent American bank, thereby increasing the parent's reserves of loanable funds. As a foreign borrower, the affiliate (foreign branch) is free of restrictions on the interest rate paid for the Eurodollar deposit; thus, the affiliate is provided an avenue for circumventing interest rate regulation.

Reliable statistics on the Eurodollar market are extremely limited. However, it appears that total volume is probably in the neighborhood of $2.5 trillion. The Eurodollar market is discussed in more detail in chapter 19.

INTEREST RATES IN THE MONEY MARKETS

The general level of interest rates in the money markets moves with the overall credit markets.[6] Interest rate differentials between money market instruments depend on risk, marketability, and supply or demand conditions in particular submarkets. Among generally available instruments, Treasury bills display the greatest marketability and the lowest risk. Thus, they normally carry the lowest interest rates. Agency securities normally follow, with similar risk but less marketability. Following U.S. government obligations, commercial paper, negotiable certificates of deposit, and banker's acceptances fall close together and are typcially grouped at a rate $\frac{1}{4}$ to $\frac{1}{2}$ percent above Treasury bill rates. Their individual rankings change from time to time because they are close together in yield and because market conditions continually change.

Federal funds represent a special submarket. While rates are not divorced from those in other markets, they do respond to a special set of supply and demand conditions, since they represent the method banks use to adjust their overnight reserve positions. In a recession the federal funds rate will normally lie below all other domestic money market rates. Toward the end of the expansion phase of the business cycle, federal funds typically carry rates above those associated with other domestic money market instruments.

The Eurodollar market represents another special case. Eurodollar rates depend on a host of factors: perceived strength of the dollar, financial conditions in other countries, and balance of payment considerations. In recent years the Eurodollar rate has been consistently above domestic interest rates.

A history of interest rate movements for money market instruments and an illustration of the factors discussed in the above paragraphs is provided in figure 7-1. This figure illustrates the long-term trend toward higher interest rates and increased interest rate volatility.

SUMMARY

The money markets are actually a series of distinct markets in which specific financial instruments are traded. In addition to being regular sources of funds for certain sectors, the money markets provide a medium for liquidity adjustment. The major money market instruments are summarized in table 7-2.

[6]See chapter 5 for a discussion of general levels of interest rates.

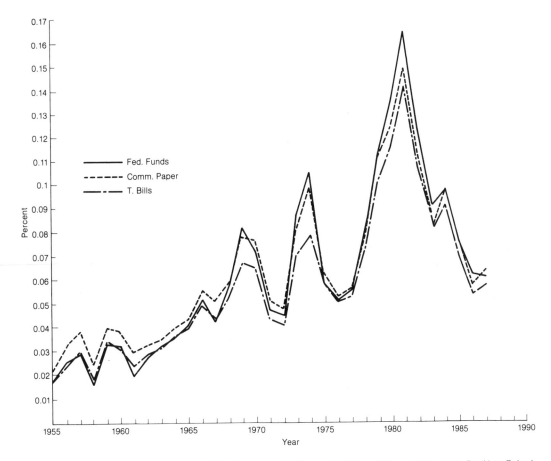

Figure 7-1: Average annual interest rates on selected money market instruments. (Source: *Economic Report of the President, Federal Reserve Bulletin.*)

QUESTIONS

7-1.   How could an individual with $10,000 to invest go about purchasing a Treasury bill?

7-2.   Using the *Federal Reserve Bulletin,* find the yields for various money market instruments of three-month and six-month maturity. How do you explain the differences between rates?

7-3.   Why does the Federal Reserve System itself hold large quantities of Treasury bills?

7-4.   Where is the secondary market for Treasury bills located?

7-5.   If a decision is made to increase the money supply, what agency acts? How does the agency act with regard to Treasury bills?

Table 7-2

Major Money Market Instruments

INSTRUMENT	ISSUER (BORROWER)	VOLUME*
Treasury bills	U.S. government	$427 bil
Agency securities	U.S. government agencies	305 bil**
Commercial paper	Large finance companies and nonfinancial corporations	350 bil
Negotiable CDs	Large commercial banks	50 bil
Banker's acceptances	Corporations, normally importers (with the guarantee of a bank)	70 bil
Repurchase agreements } Federal funds }	U.S. government security dealers } Commercial banks }	243 bil
Eurodollars	They represent liabilities of major banks	2,534 bil

*Volumes change substantially with economic and money market conditions.

**Including long-term issues.

Source: Negotiable CD volume data from Board of Governors of the Federal Reserve System, *Statistical Release G.9* (410) released June 23, 1987. Eurodollar volume data from Morgan Guaranty Trust Company, *World Financial Markets*. All other volume data from *Federal Reserve Bulletin*.

7-6.   What is the primary purpose for which federally sponsored agencies borrow and relend money?

7-7.   Why would a company issue commercial paper instead of using bank borrowing?

7-8.   Why would issuers of commercial paper maintain back-up lines of credit with banks?

7-9.   What types of companies are the primary borrowers of funds through the commercial paper market?

7-10.   Why did the regulatory authorities remove interest rate restrictions on large bank deposits (in the form of large-denomination certificates of deposit) while maintaining regulation Q ceilings for smaller deposits in the early 1970s?

7-11.   For a bank that is "loaned up" and still wants to help a loan customer, what is the advantage of a banker's acceptance?

7-12.   Why are Federal funds rates among the most volatile of money market rates?

PROBLEMS

7-1.   A bid of 97.270 is accepted on three-month Treasury bills. What discount interest rate would be published?

7-2.   For the above Treasury bill, restate the annual interest rate in a way that would make it comparable to rates quoted on bonds (bond equivalent yield).

7-3.   For the Treasury bill in problem 7-1, assume that the discount interest rate has risen to 12 percent thirty days after issue. What price will the Treasury bills be selling at? What annual rate would the holder have earned if he had bought the Treasury bill when it was first issued and then resold it after thirty days?

7-4. At a 14 percent federal funds rate, what would be the dollar interest on a three-day (week-end) loan of $10 million in the federal funds market?

7-5. A 91-day negotiable certificate of deposit is quoted at an annual interest rate of 13.8 percent and 91-day Treasury bills are quoted at a 14.2 percent discount interest rate. Restate these rates on a (coupon equivalent) comparable basis.

7-6. A money fund manager notes that ninety-day commercial paper currently yields 7.19 percent on a discounted basis and a ninety-day CD yields 7.26 percent. Which is the more attractive investment?

7-7. The manager of a utility company needs to acquire $100 million for 270 days. One alternative is to borrow at the bank prime lending rate, currently 8.75 percent. Alternatively, he could directly sell $100 million in commercial paper at a discount interest rate of 7 percent. If the commercial paper alternative is chosen, the manager would be required to arrange for a back-up line of credit. Fees charged by the bank to provide the back-up line would total $250,000 payable up front.
   a. To acquire net proceeds of $100 million, calculate the face value of commercial paper that must be sold.
   b. Which alternative is the most cost effective?

7-8. An investor notes that Fannie Mae has announced plans to market six-month notes maturing in 182 days that will bear interest equal to the bond equivalent yield on six-month Treasury bills plus seventy-five basis points. The current discount rate on 182-day T. Bills is 6.51 percent. Compute interest earnings on a $1 million investment in the Fannie Mae notes.

7-9. A large commercial bank enters into a repurchase agreement with Anheuser Busch. The agreement provides that Anheuser Busch will buy Treasury bills valued at $10 million. The securities will be repurchased by the bank in 15 days for $10,040,000. What rate of return did Anheuser Busch earn on this transaction?

7-10. St. Louis University has $10 million available for investment purposes but will need the funds in order to meet a hospital construction progress payment which will be due in three months (91 days). The university administration plans to invest the funds on a short-term basis and is considering investment alternatives. GMAC currently quotes a discount interest rate of 6.925 percent on three-month commercial paper, a major bank current quotes a rate of 7.25 percent on three-month CDs, and three-month Treasury bills bear interest at the discounted rate of 5.74 percent. The university administration plans to invest in Treasury bills unless one of the alternatives produces interest earnings of at least $25,000 greater than the Treasury bill return in order to justify the increased risk. What should the university do?

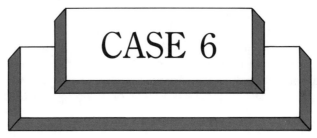

CASE 6

JACKSON BANK AND TRUST COMPANY

STARTING A NEW BANK

Bill Rivers, president and chief executive officer of the newly organized (but not yet open) Jackson Bank and Trust Company, was reviewing the accomplishments of his first month on the job. The challenge of starting a new bank and being the president had lured him from the number two position at a larger bank in another part of the state. Bill had already put in more working hours and been involved in more decision making in the previous four weeks than he had realized would be necessary.

Final regulatory approval for the new bank had been received ninety days earlier when the Federal Deposit Insurance Corporation granted insurance of accounts. The directors rapidly signed a contract for the construction of a building. Completion was on schedule, and full possession of the facility had been accepted ten days ago. A grand opening was set for next week. Earlier, Bill had prepared a checklist of major tasks to be accomplished prior to opening for business:

- Notification to the subscribers of the success of the organization effort and a call for the subscription price of the stock.
- Selection and supervision of the installation of banking equipment.
- Design of logos and signs.
- Design and selection of forms, contracts, and stationery.
- Design and establishment of records systems and control procedures.

This case was prepared by G. K. Rakes, O'Bleness Professor of Finance and Banking, College of Business Administration, Ohio University, Athens, Ohio.

- Recruiting of bank employees
- Training of new employees
- Planning an opening advertising campaign
- Selection of the various banking services to be offered
- Establishment of the loan policies of the bank
- Establishment of the investment policies of the bank
- Determination of the initial asset distribution and investment of cash assets

Everything on the list had been accomplished except the last two items. The directors had issued a call for the balance of the subscription money as soon as they had received the regulatory approvals. This provided $1 million for capital and related equity accounts. Organization and preopening expenses amounted to approximately $35,000. The remaining funds had been deposited with the primary correspondent, United Central Bank, in a nearby city. Exhibit 1 provides a current balance sheet for the Jackson Banking and Trust Company.

Since most of his time and attention would be devoted to the day-to-day operations of the bank until after the "opening rush" slowed down, Bill planned to attend to the investment position within the next couple of days. A meeting with the investment committee of the board of directors and representatives of the correspondent bank's investment group was scheduled for the Monday preceding the grand opening on the following Friday. As a typical rural institution, Jackson Bank and Trust would probably rely on the investment advice from the correspondent. A new bank with only two officers could not expect to devote sufficient resources for staying current in the money market to do a really first-rate job. However, it seemed important to impress the visitors from the "big" bank that Bill was knowledgeable in the field. The more sophisticated the management of a customer bank appeared, the more time and consideration the corre-

Exhibit 1.

Jackson Bank and Trust Company

PREOPENING BALANCE SHEET

Assets	
Cash and due from banks	$ 715,000
Bank premises (building)	$ 190,000
Furniture, fixtures, and equipment	$ 60,000
Net organization and preopening expenses*	35,000
Total assets	$1,000,000
Liabilities and capital	
Capital	$ 500,000
Surplus	$ 300,000
Reserves	200,000
Total liabilities and capital	$1,000,000

*Net loss for the first 12 months of operations is expected to be around $25,000, based on current interest rates and operating plans.

Exhibit 2.

Jackson Bank and Trust Company

ESTIMATED DEPOSITS

Type of Deposit	Estimated Volume at End of:		
	First Year	Second Year	Third Year
Individuals, partnerships, and corporations			
Demand deposits	$ 573,600	$ 834,000	1,296,000
Savings deposits	913,200	1,266,000	1,902,000
Time deposits	1,191,600	1,774,800	2,852,400
Public funds			
Demand deposits	50,000	60,000	100,000
Time deposits	60,000	75,000	100,000
Total demand deposits	$ 623,600	$ 894,000	$1,396,000
Total time and savings deposits	2,164,800	3,115,800	4,854,400
	$2,788,400	$4,009,800	$6,250,400

ESTIMATED LOAN DIVERSIFICATION

Commercial	$ 120,000	$ 240,000	$ 360,000
Installment	120,000	300,000	600,000
Real estate	240,000	600,000	960,000
Term	120,000	300,000	600,000
Purchased loan participants	240,000	240,000	
	$ 840,000	$1,680,000	$2,520,000

spondent people were likely to provide. Their advice was a "free" service. At least it would be provided as long as Bill used United Central Bank as the primary depository for a large portion of his bank's funds.

Bill decided to develop his own investment program based on the current balance sheet and expected loan and deposit activity in the new bank (Exhibit 2). This information was drawn from application for a bank charter and insurance of accounts that were filed with state and federal regulatory agencies. The estimates were over a year old and involved conservative loan demand expectations. The investment plan should include an initial investment portfolio which considered the liquidity requirements, reserve position, and the income needs of the bank. Bill also decided that he needed a pro forma balance sheet for the bank at the end of the first year of operation.

A review of the files produced a "model investment policy"[1] outline that he decided to use to establish a policy for approval by the bank directors. The elements of the suggested policy were as follows:

1. Basic policy objectives.
2. Responsibility.
3. Composition of investments.
4. Acceptable securities.
5. Maturities.
6. Quality and diversification.
7. Making portfolio adjustments.
8. Pledging.
9. Safekeeping.
10. Deliveries.
11. Computer program.
12. Gains and losses on securities sales.
13. Swapping of securities.
14. Trading activity.
15. Credit files.
16. Exceptions to this policy.

A quick review of the regulations affecting state-chartered banks revealed few recent changes. An amount equal to 10 percent of the demand deposits and 4 percent of the time and savings deposits must be maintained in acceptable liquidity items. Cash, deposits in other banks, and certain debt obligations qualified as liquidity items. U.S. Treasury, agency, corporate (AAA-rated), and most municipal obligations were acceptable. Up to 10% of the assets of the bank could be invested in Grade A corporate bonds and as much as 5 percent of the assets could be invested in the bonds of domestic corporations without regard to their rating.

Bill decided to wait until today's *Wall Street Journal* arrived and set up his own investment program, pro formas, and purchase schedule for securities.

[1]David L. Hoffland. "Bank Funds Management," *Financial Analysis Journal* (May/June 1978): 64–67.

QUESTIONS

1. What policy decisions should be made with regard to the investment account of Jackson Bank and Trust Company?
2. How does the current economic outlook and pattern of interest rates affect the bank's investment policy?

3.   What types of securities should the bank invest in and in approximately what proportions?

SELECTED REFERENCES

COOK, TIMOTHY, A. AND SUMMERS, BRUCE J. *Instruments of the Money Market,* 5th ed., (Richmond: Va: Federal Reserve Bank of Richmond, 1981).

GENDREAU, BRIAN C. "When Is the Prime Rate Second Choice?" *Federal Reserve Bank of Philadelphia Business Review* (May/June 1983): 13–23.

HAMBURGER, MICHAEL J., AND PLATT, E.N. "The Expectations Hypothesis and the Efficiency of the Treasury Bill Market," *Review of Economics and Statistics* (May 1975): 190–199.

JENSON, FREDERICK H., AND PARKINSON, PATRICK M. "Recent Developments in the Banker's Acceptance Market," *Federal Reserve Bulletin* (January 1986): 1–12.

MAEROWITZ, SETH P. "The Market for Federal Funds," *Federal Reserve Bank of Richmond Economic Review* (July/August 1981): 3–7.

MORGAN GUARANTY TRUST COMPANY OF NEW YORK. *World Financial Markets* (published monthly).

SYRON, RICHARD, AND TSCHINKEL, SHEILA L. "The Government Securities Market: Playing Field for Repos," *Federal Reserve Bank of Atlanta Economic Review* (September 1985): 10–19.

8

Capital Markets

The capital markets are normally thought of as the markets in which long-term securities, both debt and equity, are bought and sold. The securities involved are corporate stock and bonds; federal, state, and local government bonds and notes; and mortgage-backed securities; among others. A broader definition would include direct loans, but such a definition is not used here as those aspects of the financial system are covered in other parts of this book. While the money markets are primarily liquidity adjustment markets, the capital markets are primarily markets for long-term funds to meet permanent or semipermanent needs.

Risk is an important factor in the capital markets. Money market instruments are nearly risk-free with regard to default; they involve minimal risks of price fluctuation due to their short-term maturities; yet, both types of risk are frequently present in capital market securities. With the exception of U.S. government securities, all capital market instruments involve some risk of default. Even among those with no risk of default, there is still a substantial risk of price fluctuation with changes in the general level of interest rates. For example, a $1,000 bond with a 6 percent annual interest payment and twenty years to maturity would decline in market value to $657 if the level of required interest rate for this type of security rose to 10 percent.[1]

Because corporations and government units meet a major portion of their external financing needs in the capital markets, the smooth functioning of these markets is important for both. Because financial institutions hold the majority of all capital market securities, the financial institution manager should have a good understanding of the

[1]The mathematics of value are discussed in chapters 4 and 5.

capital markets. In this chapter, we discuss significant aspects of the capital markets: types of securities, the markets in which they are bought and sold, the users of funds, and the suppliers of funds.

CORPORATE SECURITIES

In addition to private sources of credit such as trade credit and bank loans, corporations rely heavily on the capital markets to meet their needs for capital. They acquire funds by selling bonds and shares in ownership of their business (stock). For larger firms, both bonds and stock enjoy active primary and secondary markets. Financial institutions furnish a significant amount of funds to corporations through the purchase of these securities, particularly bonds.

Stock

Stock represents ownership of a corporation. It is sold by corporations at the time of formation and when they need additional equity capital for expansion. It is also regularly resold by investors who need funds or who wish to adjust their investment portfolios. Stock comes in two primary varieties, common and preferred; common stock represents the largest volume.

Common Stock   represents residual ownership. The common shareholders own the corporation similar to the way a group of partners would own a business not organized as a corporation. Unlike most other securities, common stock does not promise any particular return to its purchaser. All earnings not specifically owed to others are used for the benefit of the common shareholders, either paid out as dividends or reinvested with the hope of achieving even greater dividends in the future.

Since common shareholders are not promised a specific return, they must have some method of exercising control over the company to enforce their claim. The primary method of exercising control is through the election of a board of directors, who in turn elect the top management of the corporation. In a sense the common shareholders exercise control over the corporation in the same manner citizens of a democracy exercise control over government. In addition to the right to vote for a board of directors, the common shareholders have certain other rights:

1. The right to receive dividends, when voted by the directors
2. The right to examine the books of the corporation[2]
3. The right to vote on mergers
4. The preemptive right—the right to be given the opportunity to buy a proportion of any new equity issue equal to the proportion of existing equity presently held
5. The right to a list of fellow shareholders.

[2]The courts have normally ruled that a copy of the annual report satisfies this right.

Table 8-1

Primary Market Volume, 1986 (in $ billions)

	VOLUME OF ISSUES	NET INCREASE IN AMOUNT OUTSTANDING
Corporate securities		
Bonds	$356	$109
Stocks	68	687*
U.S. government securities		
Bills	411	26.8
Bonds and notes	709	153.7
State and municipal	147	46
Mortgages	n.a.	298

*Valued at market. All other table values at par.

Source: Board of Governors of the Federal Reserve System, *Annual Statistical Digest,* 1986.

Thus the common shareholders, unlike creditors, are promised no fixed return but enjoy residual claims and exercise control over the corporation.

Preferred Stock is an intermediate security with some features of debt and some features of common stock. Typically, preferred stock carries a stated dividend rate, but this dividend is not a legal requirement and is paid only if voted each period by the board of directors. Thus preferred shareholders expect a fixed return but cannot force the company to pay the dividend. Usually their interest is protected in two ways. First, most preferred stock is cumulative, meaning that dividends cannot be paid on common stock until dividends not paid to preferred stockholders during previous periods are paid. Second, preferred stockholders generally have the right to elect a minority of the board of directors if dividends have not been paid for a specific number of quarters. While the pressure that can be applied by preferred shareholders is less than that which can be brought by creditors, it is usually sufficient to ensure dividends except in times of hardship. Insurance companies are major purchasers of preferred stock because 80 percent of the dividends received by a corporation are normally excluded from taxable income.[3]

The value of new stock sold is much smaller than the value of new bonds (table 8-1). However, the total amount of stock outstanding, whether valued at par or market, is several times the amount of bonds. The smaller value of new equity occurs because retained earnings are an important source of equity and because stock does not have a maturity date at which it must be refunded. Furthermore, some debt is convertible to common stock, resulting in a further decrease in the amount of new stock that must be sold to increase the equity base.

Stock is primarily held by individuals (table 8-2). More than two-thirds of all common stock is held by individuals. About 5 percent of corporate stock is held by foreigners, while insurance companies and pension funds hold most of the rest. Most

[3]Prior to the Tax Reform Act of 1986, 85 percent of such dividends were excluded.

Table 8-2:

Amounts of Outstanding Securities by Type and Owner, 1986 (in $ billions)

	ISSUER				
Holder	*Corporate and Foreign Bonds*	*Corporate Stock**	*U.S. Government Securities*	*State and Local Government Securities*	*Mortgages***
Total	919.8	3,464.5	2612.7	723.0	2555.1
Households	63.9	2,351.5	589.6	251.2	156.6
Nonfinancial business	—	—	44.5	7.0	—
State and local governments	—	—	276.1	7.9	84.9
Monetary authority	—	—	221.4	—	—
Commercial banks	38.5	0.1	319.9	211.3	500.2
Nonbank finance	680.5	949.5	883.8	245.5	1081.1
Foreign	136.1	163.4	271.6	—	—
Other	—	—	5.8	—	732.3

*Valued at market. All other table values are at par.

**Mortgages classified as "other" includes those held by federal and related agencies and by mortgage pools.

Source: Board of Governors of the Federal Reserve System, *Flow of Fund Accounts.*

depository financial institutions hold little or no stock because the residual ownership nature causes it to be excessively risky for their portifolios.

Corporate Bonds

Bonds are marketable debt instruments of corporations. They are long-term promissory notes, normally with maturities between five years and thirty years, normally issued in denominations of $1,000. Bonds represent a major source of external capital to American corporations.

There are two primary documents involved with a bond: the *bond certificate* and the *indenture*. The bond certificate is the evidence of ownership of the particular claim and states a limited amount of information. For example, the bond certificate states when and how interest and principal are to be paid. The certificate may be in either registered or coupon form; the registered form is more common. With the registered form, the corporation has a record of who owns each bond and mails interest payments to the bondholder at the times specified, typically semiannually. Whereas, with the coupon form, a coupon must be cut from the bond and then turned in to the corporation or a financial institution such as a commercial bank that handles coupons as a customer service. Of course, the risk of loss is greater with the coupon form, since interest is paid to whoever has the coupon.

The indenture is a lengthy document which often runs to hundreds of pages. It not only specifies the details of the agreement between borrower and lender, but also covers provisions for retiring the issue. Moreover, it contains a detailed description of pledged assets, identifies the trustees, and enumerates the responsibilities of the trustee.

In addition to other related matters, it contains a set of restrictive covenants. Examples of such restrictive convenants include restrictions on the issuance of additional debt, restrictions on the sale of assets, and requirements that a particular level of liquidity be maintained. While the indenture represents an agreement between the company and the lenders, it is not an agreement reached through negotiations with them. The indenture is prepared before the bonds are issued and contains the provisions that are felt to be necessary to successfully sell the issue. The trustee, normally a bank or trust company, acts as the representative of the bondholders in enforcing the provisions of the indenture.

Bonds differ with regard to a number of features. One such feature is *callability*. The company frequently retains the right to retire the bonds before maturity by repurchasing them from the holders. Such a provision is usually seen as important to the issuing company because it gives the flexibility to change the financial structure as necessary. If a bond is callable, the call price that must be paid by the company is normally higher than the face value of the bond by a premium equal to between six months' interest and one year's interest. Thus, bondholders receive some compensation in the event of early retirement.

Bonds also differ with regard to security offered. A *debenture* is a bond that is secured only by the general good name of the company. Because many debentures are issued by the more credit-worthy companies, the default rate is frequently lower than on bonds secured by the pledge of specific assets. Pledging generally takes one of two forms. The mortgage bond is based on the pledge of specific real assets—land and buildings—as collateral. Equipment trust certificates are based on the pledge of equipment such as railroad cars rather than on land or buildings.

Convertibility is another important feature of many bond issues. A convertible bond can be exchanged for a fixed number of shares of common stock at the option of the bondholder. This feature gives the bondholder the potential for a capital gain if the value of the company's stock rises, while still offering the contractual payment of a bond. It is used either as a "sweetener" to sell a risky bond issue or as a sequential method of financing for a company constantly in need of funds. As one issue is converted, it provides the equity base for a new debt issue.

Repayment of bonds can take one of several forms; a sinking fund is a common method. With a sinking fund provision, the indenture calls for annual payments to a sinking fund managed by the trustee. Depending on the conditions specified in the indenture, payments are invested in safe securities to accumulate funds for repayment at maturity or used to purchase a certain amount of the issue each year and retire it. If part of the issue is to be retired each year, it will be purchased in the open market if the market price is below the call price; it will be called if the market price is over the call price.

Alternatives to the sinking fund arrangement include a balloon arrangement and serial bonds. Under a *balloon arrangement,* a large portion or all of the issue is repaid at maturity. In such cases, the company frequently issues new debt to retire existing debt. In the case of a *serial issue,* different bonds in the issue have different maturity dates so that the issue is systematically retired over its life. This has an advantage over the use of the call provision in that the buyer knows how long the bonds will be outstanding.

Bonds also differ with regard to risk, which in turn depends on the credit-worthiness of the company issuing them and the quality of collateral provided. Investment advisory services (Moody's Corporation and Standard and Poor's Corporation are the best known) rate them according to risk (table 8-3). Interest rates are affected by rating; the lower ratings carry higher interest rates as compensation for risk. A bond with a Moody's Baa rating will typically carry an interest rate from one to two percentage points above that for a bond with an Aaa rating. (A detailed discussion of these interest rate differentials can be found in chapter 5.)

When a company borrows by selling its bonds, the bonds are normally sold through an investment banker. Purchasers of the bonds who later wish to sell them turn to the secondary markets consisting of both the organized exchanges and the over-the-counter market. The operations of both of these markets are covered in some detail in the following sections of this chapter.

Corporations in virtually every industry category finance part of their operations through bonds. However, the market is restricted to relatively large companies. Fixed administrative costs are such as to rule out small bond issues. On a small bond issue of under $1 million, the cost of issuance can run as high as 20 percent, while issue costs can fall to 1 percent or less for an issue of several hundred million dollars.

While individuals do hold corporate bonds as investments, the majority of bonds are held as investments by financial institutions. Only 7 percent of all corporate bonds are held by individuals. The majority of all outstanding bonds are held by either pension funds or insurance companies, and a growing proportion is held by foreigners.

Primary Markets for Stocks and Bonds

Companies normally employ the services of an investment banker for selling both stock and bond issues to private investors and financial institutions. A major exception is private placement stocks or bonds, which involves an entire issue being sold to one or a few financial institutions. Investment banking services are provided by companies that specialize only in investment banking and by many of the larger brokerage houses.

Investment bankers normally act as dealers; they purchase an entire issue from the issuing corporation and resell it in smaller quantities to investors interested in holding it. Occasionally a best-efforts arrangement will be used, wherein the investment banker does not buy the entire issue but merely sells as much of it as possible for the issuing company. The steps followed in the issuance of securities through an investment banker are discussed on the following pages. Essentially the same approach applies to the issue of stocks and corporate bonds.

Preunderwriting Conference   The company meets with the investment banker to determine if the investment banker is interested in underwriting an issue for it and what type of issue—debt or equity—would be salable. Investment bankers wish to maintain their reputation and will not sell an issue unless they have carefully evaluated the company and found it to be sound and with good prospects for success. In addition, different investment bankers specialize in different types of issues, and a particular

Table 8-3

Key to Moody's Corporate Ratings

Aaa

Bonds which are rated Aaa are judged to be of the best quality. They carry the smallest degree of investment risk and are generally referred to as "gilt edge." Interest payments are protected by a large or by an exceptionally stable margin and principal is secure. While the various protective elements are likely to change, such changes as can be visualized are most unlikely to impair the fundamentally strong position of such issues.

Aa

Bonds which are rated Aa are judged to be of high quality by all standards. Together with the Aaa group they comprise what are generally known as high grade bonds. They are rated lower than the best bonds because margins of protection may not be as large as in Aaa securities or fluctuation of protective elements may be of greater amplitude or there may be other elements present which make the long term risks appear somewhat larger than in Aaa securities.

A

Bonds which are rated A possess many favorable investment attributes and are to be considered as upper medium grade obligations. Factors giving security to principal and interest are considered adequate but elements may be present which suggest a susceptibility to impairment sometime in the future.

Baa

Bonds which are rated Baa are considered as medium grade obligations, i.e., they are neither highly protected nor poorly secured. Interest payments and principal security appear adequate for the present but certain protective elements may be lacking or may be characteristically unreliable over any great length of time. Such bonds lack outstanding investment characteristics and in fact have speculative characteristics as well.

Ba

Bonds which are rated Ba are judged to have speculative elements: their future cannot be considered as well assured. Often the protection of interest and principal payments may be very moderate and thereby not well safeguarded during both good and bad times over the future. Uncertainty of position characterizes bonds in this class.

B

Bonds which are rated B generally lack characteristics of the desirable investment. Assurance of interest and principal payments or of maintenance of other terms of the contract over any long period of time may be small.

Caa

Bonds which are rated Caa are of poor standing. Such issues may be in default or there may be present elements of danger with respect to principal or
interest.

Ca

Bonds which are rated Ca represent obligations which are speculative in a high degree. Such issues are often in default or have other marked
shortcomings.

C

Bonds which are rated C are the lowest rated class of bonds and issues so rated can be regarded as having extremely poor prospects of ever attaining any real investment standing.

Note: Moody's applies numerical modifiers, 1, 2 and 3 in each generic rating classification from Aa through B in its corporate bond rating system. The modifier 1 indicates that the security ranks in the higher end of its generic rating category; the modifier 2 indicates a mid-range ranking; and the modifier 3 indicates that the issue ranks in the lower end of its generic rating category.

Source: *Moody's Bond Record*

investment banking house may not be interested in the issue even though a number of others are. If a general agreement is reached, an *underwriting agreement* is signed between the company and the investment banker.

Registration Statement   Once an underwriting agreement has been reached, the issue must be registered with the Securities and Exchange Commission (SEC). The issue cannot be sold until the registration becomes effective—twenty days after the registration statement is filed unless the SEC objects or asks for more time. The SEC uses this period to study the registration statement and determine if the appropriate information is being furnished. The SEC does not rule on the quality of the investment, but on whether appropriate information about the investment is properly disclosed. Although, the investment banker cannot sell any of the issue during this period, the banker can circulate a preliminary prospectus (also called a "red herring") giving all the information in the regular prospectus except the price at which the issue will be sold.

The prospectus is a statement designed to be helpful to a potential investor in deciding whether to purchase some of the securities being offered. It contains a detailed description of the company, detailed financial statements, and a discussion of the way in which the funds will be used. In the case of a debt issue, it also contains the various provisions of the debt instruments such as restrictions on further borrowing or when and how interest is to be paid.

Underwriting Syndicate and Selling Group   Issues worth hundreds of millions of dollars are not uncommon, and issues worth several billion dollars are not unheard of. Since the investment banker normally buys the issue and then attempts to resell it, capital is being put at risk. Very seldom can a single investment banker absorb the entire issue. Normally an underwriting syndicate is formed by the originating investment banker. With this arrangement, each of a number of investment bankers buys part of the issue and resells it. Each investment banker has its own selling group—typically a group of brokerage firms—acting as a group of retailers, while the investment bankers act as wholesalers. While the selling group handles the actual sale, the underwriters accept the risk of the issue not being sold.

Price Setting and Sale   After the registration becomes effective, the price at which the issue is to be sold is set. Typically this is just before issue time because of market volatility. The selling group then proceeds to sell the issue through public advertisements or contact with investors who may be interested. Since potentially interested investors are notified before the offering via a preliminary prospectus, the entire issue is frequently sold in a matter of hours once the registration becomes effective. In any event, the investment bankers hope to sell the entire issue within a few days because they cannot accept the capital commitment and risk of a long-term holding.

Market Stabilization   This is the last act of the managing underwriter. The underwriter stands ready to buy at the offering price any part of the issue that investors attempt to resell before the entire issue is sold. Thus there is no risk of a decline in market price before the entire issue is sold. However, this price pegging is limited to a maximum of thirty days. If all the issue is not sold by that time, the investment banker must simply face losses or hold the remainder of the issue and hope the price will rise.

Costs of flotation depend on the size of the issue, the quality of the issuer, and whether it is debt or equity. One study found that the average flotation cost as a percentage of net proceeds was 13.4 percent for equity issues of one-half to one million dollars. For equity issues over one hundred million dollars, the average cost was 3.95 percent.[4] As indicated earlier, the issue costs can fall to less than 1 percent for a large bond issue. The problem for small issues is that because many costs are fixed, they are very high as a percentage of the issue.

Secondary Markets for Corporate Stocks and Bonds

The secondary markets for corporate securities consist of the organized exchanges, such as the New York Stock Exchange, and the over-the-counter market. The greatest volume of stock transactions in the secondary markets occurs in the organized exchanges, although the vast majority of stocks (eligible for sale and purchase) are not listed on organized exchanges. Stocks of large corporations, particularly those that are frequently bought and sold, are normally listed on an exchange. The majority of corporate bond volume, on the other hand, occurs in the over-the-counter markets.

The secondary market for stock is much more active than the primary market, with annual trading volume equal to many times the volume of new issues. Bonds tend to change hands less frequently and are often held to maturity by the original purchaser.

While funds are not furnished directly to users through the secondary markets, these markets are important because they provide liquidity and a continuous test of value. The owner of a security can find the current value by checking yesterday's market price in the newspaper and can sell the securities quickly if funds are needed. Thus the existence of an active secondary market makes corporate securities more attractive and makes it easier for the corporation to raise funds. In this section, the secondary markets are discussed in detail.

Organized Exchanges Most resale of stocks occurs on the organized exchanges. The two major organized exchanges are the New York Stock Exchange and the American Stock Exchange, both located in New York City. The New York Stock Exchange accounts for approximately 80 percent of total stock exchange volume and the American Stock Exchange accounts for less than 10 percent. The concentration of this business on one street in southern Manhattan has led to Wall Street being synonymous with finance. Large regional exchanges include the Midwest, the West Coast, and the Baltimore-Philadelphia-Washington exchanges.

The primary purpose of an organized exchange is to provide a physical meeting place for the buying and selling of securities; exchange members buy and sell either for themselves or for those they represent. Additionally, the exchanges provide communication and bookkeeping systems for recording and reporting transactions. Finally, the

[4]Clifford W. Smith, Jr., "Substitute Methods for Raising Additional Capital: Rights Offerings Versus Underwritten Issues," *Journal of Financial Economics* 5 (December 1977).

exchanges provide sets of rules and enforcement procedures to ensure an orderly market place.

The organized exchanges are *continuous auction* markets. The floor of the exchange consists of a number of different posts—meeting places for transactions in a particular group of securities. For example, the New York Stock Exchange provides a market for approximately 2000 different securities and divides them among twenty-seven trading posts.

Transactions are based on bid and ask prices. For example, a broker carrying an order for a client who would like to purchase 100 shares of IBM at $70 per share would go to the trading post for IBM and call out the bid. If someone accepted the bid, a transaction would occur. Someone wishing to sell would call out his asking price in the same fashion. These orders are described as limit orders because the investor wishes to buy or sell only if a certain price can be obtained. A *market order* would instruct the broker to buy or sell at the best price available. The broker would then take the best price available from those at the trading post. Once a sale has been agreed on, the price and quantity are recorded and reported to the public. Thus there is a continuous test of value.

Anyone who visits an exchange, particularly on a brisk trading day, would question the use of the word "organized." To the casual observer, it more closely resembles a melee. People are rushing to and from the various posts to communicate with or join other people there. Trading consists of a group of people shouting at each other in what appears to be a totally unorganized manner. However, to the trained, quick-witted participant, it provides a swift, efficient way of buying and selling securities at the best price currently available in the marketplace.

The people trading in a security at a particular post are of several types. First, there are the brokers trading on behalf of clients around the country who have placed an order to buy or sell through their local brokerage house. Second, there are members who buy and sell for their own accounts, speculating on short-term movements in prices. Third, there are specialists, a group of members who have available to them special information about supply and demand as reflected in unfilled *limit orders*.[5] In exchange for this information, they are required to "make a market" by continually posting both a bid and an ask price. There is only one specialist for each security, although each specialist is responsible for more than one security. The specialist normally quotes an ask price of $0.125 to $0.25 above his bid price. He thus guarantees that a continuous market will exist.[6] In exchange for this service he makes a profit through information about supply and demand, and through selling at an asking price above his bid price.

Volume of sales on the organized exchanges far exceeds the volume of new

[5]A limit order is one for which the price is specified. The alternative is a market order which instructs the broker to buy or sell at the best price presently available.

[6]A notable exception to this "guarantee" occurred on "Black Monday," 19 October, 1987. On that day, the Dow Jones industrial average plunged 508 points and a major decline in stock values commenced. While reasons for the decline were still not fully understood by market researchers at this writing, a presidential task force assigned to investigate the matter concluded that large numbers of specialists did not perform as the system expected them to. See, for example, "Phelan Defends Specialists in Market's October Plunge," *The New York Times*, January 26, 1988.

stock sold. The stock of a company, once issued, typically remains outstanding for the life of the company. However, the typical owner of stock may hold it for a few years or less, with some purchasers (called floor traders) holding the stock for no more than a few hours. Volume on the New York Stock Exchange alone in 1986, averaged 141 million shares a day. More than one-fifth of the shares listed on the New York Stock Exchange are sold each year.

Over-the-Counter Markets   A membership in an organized exchange is referred to as a *seat,* though its owner will find no place to sit on the exchange floor. Likewise, the over-the-counter (OTC) market does not involve a counter. The OTC consists of a group of investment houses acting as market makers in certain securities and a communication network to tie them together. The stocks of large, well-known corporations are generally listed on one of the organized stock exchanges. Stocks of lesser known companies and most bonds are bought and sold on the OTC.

In the OTC, one or more investment houses act as market makers which stand ready to buy and sell like the specialist on an organized exchange. Instead of a physical meeting place, market makers and brokers are tied together through the National Association of Security Dealers Automated Quotation (NASDAQ) system. A central computer system and telecommunication lines tie this market together. It has been argued that modern technology has rendered physical meeting places obsolete. Indeed, the present NASDAQ system was designed with enough capacity to handle all organized exchange volume.

Eurobonds

Eurobonds are a specialized type of corporate debt issue designed to increase salability by decreasing the risk of loss from currency devaluation. A Eurobond is defined as a bond denominated in a currency other than that of the country in which it is being sold. Thus an American company doing business in Europe might decide to finance its European operations by selling bonds in Europe but denominating them in dollars.

Eurobonds can be denominated in any currency, and some have even given the holder a choice of currencies. Dollars have traditionally been the most popular currency.

Like domestic bonds, Eurobonds are issued through investment bankers. The main difference is that they are not advertised to the public; they are sold entirely through direct contact with potential buyers. They are rarely sold through private placement, as is frequently done in the case of domestic bonds.

U.S. GOVERNMENT DEBT

Beginning with borrowing to finance wars and expanding with increases in social programs, the U.S. government has become a major borrower in the capital markets, accounting for $2.3 trillion in debt outstanding at mid-1987. U.S. government securities are unique in that they are the only securities in the U.S. capital markets considered risk-free with regard to default. Another factor leading to particular importance of U.S. government debt is its use as part of economic stabilization policy.

U.S. government debt is issued in different forms. First, there are the regular Treasury issues: bills, notes, and bonds. Bills have maturities of one year or less, notes have maturities of one to five years, and bonds have maturities of longer than five years. In 1987, 17 percent of the U.S. Treasury debt was in the form of bills, 43 percent was in the form of notes, and the remaining 40 percent was in the form of bonds and nonmarketable debt.

In addition to the regular Treasury issues, several U.S. government agencies issue debt. These agencies were discussed individually in chapter 7. Most of the agencies act primarily as financial institutions, selling securities and using the proceeds to provide funds to the mortgage markets. The proportion of their debts financed by bonds depends on market conditions. In general, though, the bulk of their financing is long-term.

While interest is earned on Treasury bills only through the discount from face value at which they are sold, other securities pay interest based on the face value, normally on a semiannual basis.

Approximately 28 percent of U.S. Treasury debt is held by U.S. government trust funds and by Federal Reserve banks. The remaining 72 percent is in private hands, with only a small proportion of the total held by individuals. A small amount is held by nonfinancial corporations, and the rest is held by financial institutions; commercial banks are particularly large holders.

Primary Markets

Unlike corporations, the federal government does not use underwriting. The Federal Reserve acts as fiscal agent, handling the mechanics of sale, but neither underwrites nor markets the issues. Thus it is important that the yield be set so as to make the issues attractive to investors. The yields are usually set with the objective of achieving a slight increase in price following initial issue. If this is done, a type of unofficial underwriting occurs, with U.S. government security dealers and commercial banks acquiring part of a new issue as a short-term holding, thus easing its absorption into the market.

The issue procedure differs from the auction market for Treasury bills. The yield of the issue is set so that the Treasury is relatively sure the bonds or notes will sell. Press releases are given out, and descriptive circulars are sent to potential buyers. The issues are then allocated to those wishing to purchase. On average, approximately two-thirds of the dollar value of new issues goes to commercial banks and U.S. government securities dealers.

Obviously, a large proportion of U.S. government bond sales occur merely to refund maturing issues. Sometimes, because of a desire to increase average maturity of outstanding debt, advance refunding is used. With this technique, new long-term securities of longer maturity are offered in exchange for issues that are close to their maturity date. Yields of the new securities must be higher than those of the existing maturities, since conversion is voluntary and there must be some incentive to convert.

Secondary Markets

While it was once common practice to buy and sell U.S. government bonds and notes in the organized exchanges, the market has shifted to the U.S. government securities dealers. For each issue, the dealers continually post prices at which they will buy and prices at which they will sell. Thus they provide a continuous market for those wishing to buy or sell U.S. government securities.

STATE AND LOCAL GOVERNMENT BONDS

Bonds issued by state and local governments are called *municipal bonds*. They provide a distinct investment opportunity because the interest received from such bonds is exempt from federal income tax.

Municipals may be guaranteed by the *full faith and credit* of the government unit involved or they may be guaranteed only by *revenue* from a specific investment such as a water system or toll bridge. In recent years, approximately 70 percent of the newly issued municipal bonds have been revenue bonds. The building of schools, roads, and other capital projects has traditionally been financed through the issuance of bonds, although some cities—New York is the most notable example—have used debt to finance current spending.

Because of their tax status, municipal bonds can be sold at yields below those for other securities, with high-grade municipal bonds normally selling to yield several percentage points below U.S. government bonds.[7]

Municipal bonds are attractive only to investors facing relatively high tax rates. At a municipal bond rate of 7.59 percent and a corporate bond rate of 10.25 percent, the tax rate necessary to make municipals an attractive investment is found as follows:

$$10.25 \, (1 - T) = 7.59.$$

In the above example, municipal bonds would be an attractive alternative to corporate bonds if the investor faced a marginal federal income tax rate of 26 percent or greater. The primary holders of municipal bonds are wealthy individuals, banks, and property and casualty insurance companies.

Municipal bonds are sold through underwriting in a manner similar to corporate bonds. An important difference is that banks, which do not underwrite corporate securities, participate in the underwriting of municipals. The underwriter of the original issue also normally makes a second market by acting as a dealer.

Municipal bonds are not risk-free, as illustrated by a number of defaults. The rating services that rate corporate bonds also rate municipal bonds, with yields varying according to rating (table 8-3).

---

[7]Effective 1 July, 1987, the top corporate tax rate was reduced from 46 percent to 34 percent. This reduction together with certain other changes contained in the Tax Reform Act of 1986 was expected to reduce the relative attractiveness and thus reduce the rate differentials between municipals and other bonds.

Table 8-4

Sample Bond Rating

State of New Mexico Highway Debentures Rate "AAA"

RATING RATIONALE: The Highway Debentures are special obligations of the State, payable from gasoline excise taxes, motor vehicle registration fees, and a limited $1.5 million general property tax which has never been levied or used. This issue is part of a $20 million authorization, of which $5.7 million has been issued and retired. The State may not issue any parity debentures beyond the initial authorization. Presently, there are no plans to issue the remaining authorized debentures. Motor fuel taxes and registration fees covered estimated maximum debt service 44.20 times in 1978. Total pledged revenues, including the $1.5 million tax levy, would have covered estimated maximum debt service fifty times during this period. The state has enacted legislation which, effective in 1980, will provide for the escalation of the gasoline tax. The tax rate, which will use $0.07 a gallon as a base, is determined by reference to the average wholesale price of gasoline plus federal excise taxes. The annual incremental increase/decrease may not exceed $0.01 per gallon for each twelve-month period.

Based upon the overwhelming debt service coverage, the limited general property tax pledge and the short maturity schedule, we are rating these bonds "AAA."

PROPOSED ISSUE: $5,000,000 Highway Denbentures, Series 1979, selling 26 June 1979.

Dated: 15 July 1979.

Due: Serially 1980–1984; the debentures are not subject to redemption prior to their respective maturities.

Source: Standard and Poor's *Fixed Income Investor*

State and local government debt grew rapidly during the 1970s to reach one-third of the federal debt by the beginning of the 1980s. That growth has abated somewhat in recent years. State and local debt levels have approximated one-fourth of federal debt levels in recent years.

EMERGING TRENDS: SECURITIZATION AND THE GROWTH OF SECONDARY SECURITY MARKETS

Loan sales by financial institutions have increased dramatically in recent years. More and more banks and other depository financial institutions are selling loans. This practice takes many forms. One form involves the pooling of mortage loans by such agencies as the Government National Mortgage Association and the subsequent sale of securities representing undivided interest in these mortgage pools. More recently, banks and other depository financial institutions have begun pooling other kinds of loans—automobile loans, credit card and lease receivables, agricultural loans, and even pools of charged-off loans. In addition to pooling loans, some banks are selling whole, short-term commercial, and industrial loans. This entire range of activities, from the sale of shares in a pool of loans to the sale of whole loans, is called *securitization*.[8]

While mortgage pools and other forms of loan sales are not new, their growth appears to have been one result of deregulation of the financial sector. In 1984, com-

---

[8]Sean Becketti and Charles S. Morris, "Loan Sales: Another Step in the Evolution of the Short-Term Credit Market, *Federal Reserve Bank of Kansas City Economic Review*, (November 1987): 22.

mercial banks sold roughly $148 billion of loans. By 1985, loan sales by commercial banks jumped nearly 75 percent to $258 billion. Sales of other types of loans are also picking up. The market for mortgage-backed securities has mushroomed from a $500 billion industry in 1981 to a $2 trillion industry in 1985. Also, packages of auto loans and credit card receivables are increasingly being sold to third-party investors. In 1985, for example, only about $1 billion of auto loans were securitized, but in 1986, $10 billion were sold under this method.[9]

Several reasons are likely to be behind the rapid increase in securitization and thus the growth in secondary market activity.

- A financial institution may wish to alter the diversification of its loan portfolio, selling certain types of loans in order to buy or originate other types of assets.
- Loans may be sold in order to fund other activities rather than attempting to raise more deposits for that purpose.
- The financial institution manager may believe it has a comparative advantage in originating and servicing loans relative to funding the loan.
- Interest rate risk may be reduced by a policy of, say, selling all newly made fixed-rate mortgage loans and retaining all variable-rate loans.
- The shift in recent years toward higher and more stringent capital requirements for depository financial institutions has the effect of making certain types of loans more costly to fund. By early 1988, for example, Federal Reserve capital proposals which were expected to be enacted required that banks hold $8 in capital for every $100 in loans to the private sector and to foreign governments and their businesses. In contrast, other loans or investments deemed to be less risky, U.S. government securities for example, would require less than $8 in capital for every $100 of the asset.[10]

While these developments of the 1980s need further study to determine their ultimate impact on financial market stability, they appear to be a natural outgrowth of the transition from a highly regulated financial system to one where free market forces play a greater role in determining the manner in which economic activity is ultimately financed.

SUMMARY

Capital markets are the markets for long-term securities, both debt and equity. The primary instruments bought and sold in these markets are corporate stock and bonds, U.S. government bonds, state and local government bonds, and marketable mortgages. Companies and government units wishing to raise funds turn to a system of primary markets made up mostly of investment bankers who purchase the issue and resell it. Original purchasers of securities may hold them until maturity or resell them in a secondary market system composed of organized security exchanges, the over-the-

[9]Christine Pavel and David Phillis, "Why Commercial Banks Sell Loans: An Empirical Analysis," *Federal Reserve Bank of Chicago Economic Perspectives*, (May/June 1987).

[10]"Capital Plan is Based on Risks Involved in Bank Assets," *The New York Times*, February 1, 1988. (Capital structure and the cost of funds for financial institutions will be discussed in chapter 12.)

counter security market, and a number of dealers who buy and sell for their own inventory.

A review of tables 8-1 and 8-2 is helpful in developing a perspective on the participants in this market and on the importance of various instruments. With regard to new issues, U.S. government securities dominate in the primary markets. With reference to newly issued corporate securities, debt instruments clearly dominate equity securities (table 8-1).

A somewhat different picture is seen when we look at total holdings as opposed to new issues and increases in amount outstanding. Corporations are dominant in terms of the value of total securities outstanding, followed by mortgages, U.S. government securities, and state and local government securities. Within the corporate securities, equity dominates debt in terms of total amount outstanding. Households are the primary suppliers of funds. They hold the majority of equity securities directly. While financial institutions hold the majority of debt securities, they are largely using the funds of households.

The financial system of the 1980s has been characterized by rapid growth in securitization and the sale of both short- and long-term loans by financial institutions; thus secondary markets have grown rapidly. This growth appears to represent a normal outgrowth of financial market deregulation and appears to be a response to increased interest rate risk in the 1980s and to the need for profit improvement within a more competitive environment.

QUESTIONS

8-1. What are the primary types of risk involved in the ownership of capital market instruments?

8-2. What are the rights of a common stockholder?

8-3. Explain the differences between common stock and preferred stock.

8-4. Why are lengthy indentures required for corporate bonds when a similar document is not required for commercial paper issued by the same corporation?

8-5. Select a bond issue listed in the *Wall Street Journal*. Find the bond's Moody's rating. Would you recommend this bond to an investor looking for a safe investment?

8-6. Summarize the process by which a new stock or bond issue is sold.

8-7. Leading stocks are traded at a physical location (New York Stock Exchange or American Stock Exchange), while there is no central physical location for the purchase and sale of money market instruments. How do you account for this difference in trading arrangements?

8-8. Why would a company use underwriting for a stock or bond issue? Why does the U.S. government not use underwriting?

8-9. U.S. government issues are considered risk-free with regard to default. Is there any way an investor can lose money on an investment in U.S. government bonds?

8-10.   Explain the difference between a full faith and credit bond and a revenue bond. Which type is likely to be more risky?

8-11.   Since municipal bonds are generally considered more risky than U.S. government bonds, why do they sell at lower yields?

8-12.   Why might a financial institution manager believe that the institution has a comparative advantage in making and servicing loans but not in funding certain types of loans?

8-13.   Explain the growth in securitization in the 1980s. Is it likely that such growth will continue to diminish in the future?

PROBLEMS

8-1.   In early 1988, the yield to maturity on high-grade corporate bonds was 9.5 percent, while yields on similarly rated municipal bonds were 7.51 percent. For an investor facing a 28 percent federal income tax rate, would corporate or municipal bonds provide a higher after-tax return?

8-2.   If municipal securities of a given grade are yielding 8.23 percent, calculate the equivalent before-tax yield of corporate securities of the same grade for an investor subject to a marginal tax rate of 28 percent.

8-3.   Effective in mid-1987, the top corporate tax rate was reduced from 46 percent to 34 percent. Springfield Municipal Hospital plans to issue $10 million in tax-exempt bonds during 1988. Springfield's bonds are unrated and not widely traded. Previous issues have been issued through local banks and purchased by a consortium of large local corporations in support of the hospital. Such corporations have traditionally relied on a formula whereby the hospital bond interest rate was 70 percent of the yield on A-rated corporate bonds (currently 10 percent). If Springfield's bonds are viewed as having the same risk/return characteristics as before and if A-rated corporate bonds are currently yielding 10 percent, what interest rate can Springfield expect to pay on the new bond issue?

8-4.   Given your answer to problem 8-3 above, calculate the dollar impact on the hospitals first year's interest expense as the result of the change in corporate income tax rates.

Appendix 8-A
Mean-Variance Capital Asset Pricing Model

Students of finance have long recognized that the required returns are higher for risky assets. However, conversion from this general observation to a specific relationship between risk and required return proved to be an elusive goal. Mean-variance portfolio theory, developed by Harry Markowitz in the early 1950s,[1] provided the foundation for a more precise approach to risk. The work of Sharpe,[2] Treynor,[3] and Jensen[4] in the 1960s was largely responsible for building from the foundation provided by Markowitz to a specific model of the relationship between risk and the required rate of return.

The model has proved to have numerous uses in practice. First, it provided a method of adjusting for risk in evaluating returns from investment portfolios. Second, it has been used in determining required returns for investments by profit-seeking corporations. Additional uses have been in areas such as public utility rate case hearings.

The model begins with the observation that investors are, in general, risk-averse. Therefore, at any given level of expected return, the typical investor prefers less risk to more. Figure 8A-1 represents the spectrum of all portfolios available to investors at a particular time. Each point in figure 8A-1 represents a given combination of securities (a portfolio) identified as to risk and expected return. Portfolios represented by points B and C, for example, are expected to produce the same return, but portfolio B is more risky. Because investors prefer less risk and more expected return, a particular portfolio will be preferred to any portfolio directly above it or above it and to the left. Portfolio M will be preferred over portfolio B by all investors. However, the choice between M and C is not so obvious. C involves less risk and less expected return. The choice would depend on how risk-averse a particular investor is, i.e., his *risk preference function*. A portfolio like M or C, for which there exists no portfolio providing less risk without less return or more return without more risk, is referred to as an *efficient portfolio*. The set of all such portfolios is referred to as the efficient frontier.

Thus far we have spoken of risk only in general terms. In practice, standard deviation, a widely used statistical measure, is normally used as a risk measure. The standard deviation of the probability distribution of expected returns (σ_p) is normally used as a measure of risk. The formula for the standard deviation is

$$\sigma_p = \sqrt{\sum_{i=1}^{n} p_i(R_i - E_p)^2}$$

(8A-1)

where R = return for the portfolio if outcome i occurs
   p_i = probability of outcome i occurring
   n = number of different possible outcomes
   E_p = expected return for the portfolio.[5]

[1] Harry Markowitz, "Portfolio Selection," *Journal of Finance* (March 1952): 77–91.

[2] William Sharpe, "Capital Asset Prices: A Theory of Market Equilibrium Under Conditions of Risk," *The Journal of Finance* (September 1964): 425–442.

[3] Jack Treynor, "How to Rate Management of Mutual Funds," *Harvard Business Review* (January–February 1965): 63–75.

[4] Michael Jensen, "Risk, the Pricing of Capital Assets, and the Evaluation of Investment Portfolios," *Journal of Business* (April 1969): 167–247.

[5] The expected return for the portfolio is computed as follows:

$$E_p = \sum_{i=1}^{n} p_i R_i.$$

Figure 8A-1: Investment opportunity set.

We now introduce a very important type of investment—a risk-free security such as a Treasury bill. Line F in figure 8A-2 represents the efficient frontier shown in Figure 8A-1. The efficient frontier can be drawn as a line rather than a series of points because a near-infinite number of different portfolios is possible. By investing a portion of his funds in risky portfolio M and the remainder in a risk-free asset, an investor can create a new portfolio on the straight line connecting M (referred to as the *tangent portfolio*) and point R_f. By varying the proportion of his funds invested in M and putting the remainder in the risk-free asset, the investor can achieve a portfolio anywhere on the line connecting M and R_f. Furthermore, he can achieve points on this line above M if he can borrow at a similar interest rate. Thus, these various combinations of M and the risk-free security provide portfolios superior to all other portfolios on the efficient frontier, such as C. M would be preferred by all investors, and they would adjust for their individual degree of risk aversion by varying the proportion of funds invested in M and the proportion invested at the risk-free rate.

As an example, suppose the risk-free rate is 6 percent, the expected return for portfolio M is 10 percent, and the standard deviation of expected returns for portfolio M is 4 percent. Portfolio C' consists of two-thirds of the investor's funds invested in portfolio M and one-third invested in the risk-free asset. The expected return and standard deviation for portfolio C' are

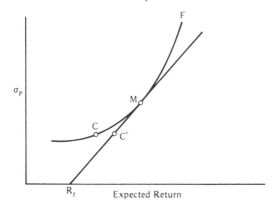

Figure 8A-2: Efficient frontier analysis.

$$\text{Expected return} = \frac{2}{3} \times 0.10 + \frac{1}{3} \times 0.06 = 8.6\%$$

$$\text{Standard deviation} = \frac{2}{3} \times 0.04 = 2.67\%.$$

Portfolio C' would be preferred over portfolio C by all investors; C' has the same standard deviation but has a higher expected return. Thus an investor wishing to accept a different amount of risk than M would move to a portfolio such as C' rather than a portfolio such as C.

If investors are in agreement about the prospects for particular securities, M must eventually contain all risky securities. The prices of individual securities will rise or fall so that demand for each, as a component of M, is neither greater nor less than the supply available. M is referred to as the *market* portfolio.

From the foregoing analysis it follows that the important aspect of risk for an individual security is its contribution to the risk of the market portfolio. The total risk of a security can be divided into two parts: diversifiable and nondiversifiable risk. For example, the purchaser of stock in one automobile company faces the risk that that company's new model will be unpopular. That risk can be diversified away by dividing funds among all automobile companies. Likewise, the possibility of a change in taste or technology resulting in a shift from products produced by one industry to those of another can be diversified away by including in the portfolio securities issued by firms in different industries. Eventually though, there are risks that cannot be diversified away. The possibility of a recession or restrictive monetary policy leading to a decreased return on all security investments can be avoided only by choosing the risk-free security instead. Aggregate risks of the type that tend to affect the economy in general cannot be diversified away.

If a group of stocks had only diversifiable risk, they could be combined in a portfolio and the portfolio would be risk-free. If this risk-free portfolio had a higher return than the risk-free rate, all investors wishing to hold a risk-free investment would choose the portfolio rather than the single risk-free asset. Thus it is necessary for market equilibrium that the return on such a portfolio be the same as the risk-free rate. Therefore, risky portfolios and risky securities pay a higher return than the risk-free rate as compensation for accepting *nondiversifiable* risk.

Nondiversifiable risk is caused by the tendency of certain factors to affect all securities in the same way. An increase in the general level of interest rates, for example, will cause an increase in required returns for all securities and will drive the prices of all securities down. Likewise, a recession will decrease the profitability and increase the riskiness of most business enterprises. The degree of nondiversifiable risk for a particular security is measured in terms of the tendency of returns for the security to move in the same direction as other securities.

The most widely used method of measuring nondiversifiable risk is *beta*. Beta is a measure of the sensitivity of return for a particular investment to returns for investments in general. The beta can best be explained using a graph illustrating the common stock of a particular company (figure 8A-3). Over a period of time, we observe that when returns on securities in general rise, returns for this particular security rise, and when returns for securities in general decline, returns for this particular security decline.

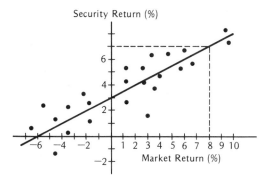

Figure 8A-3: Relation of security to market.

We observed the returns (dividends and price appreciation) a holder of this security would have received during each of a number of periods and observed the return that an investor would have received during each of these periods if he had held some broad-based portfolio representing all common stocks. Each dot in figure 8A-3 represents one such pair of observations. The line is drawn to fit the dots as closely as possible and represents the return we might expect from the security at each possible level of return for stocks in general. The greater the slope of this line, the greater the sensitivity of the investment to overall conditions and the greater the nondiversifiable risk.

Beta provides a measure of the slope of this line, and therefore of nondiversifiable risk. Beta is defined as

$$\text{Beta} = \frac{\text{change in expected return for the security}}{\text{change in expected return for all stocks}} \quad (8A-2)$$

Expected return for the security is 3 percent if expected return for stocks in general is 0 percent (from figure 8A-3). Expected return for the security is 7 percent if expected return for stocks in general is 8 percent. The beta for the security is then

$$\text{Beta} = \frac{0.07 - 0.03}{0.08 - 0.00} = 0.5.$$

Obviously, for any particular security during any particular time period, these relationships will not hold precisely. Factors affecting a particular security may cause actual return to be above or below what would be expected based on overall market conditions. For example, return to investors holding the stock of a particular company will depend on acceptance of that company's products as well as on overall market conditions. Once again, a well-diversified portfolio will cancel out the risks associated only with a particular security. However, the expected relationship between the security and securities in general cannot be offset through diversification.

The higher the beta, the greater is the nondiversifiable risk. A beta of two indicates that if returns for stocks in general increase, return for the particular security will be expected to increase twice as much, and if returns for stocks in general decrease, return for the particular security will be expected to decrease twice as much. Betas for publicly traded common stocks are regularly reported by investment advisory services such as Value Line.

As stated earlier, the required return for a particular investment is a function of the general level of interest rates and the nondiversifiable risk associated with that particular investment. The interest rate on risk-free investments, such as U.S. government securities, is normally used as a measure of the general level of interest rates, and beta is used as the measure of nondiversifiable risk. Thus, an individual security's beta measures its contribution to portfolio risk. The required rate of return is a function of the interest rate on risk-free assets, return for other risky assets, and the security's beta. It can be shown[6] that the required return, or interest rate necessary to attract investors to a risky asset is

$$K_e = R_f + \beta(E_m - R_f)$$

where K_e = required rate of return
R_f = rate of risk-free securities
β = beta
E_m = expected average return for common stocks in general.

The term $E_m - R_f$ is the difference between expected average return for all stocks and the risk-free interest rate. It is the average compensation for risk in the security market, or the risk premium. As the formula shows, the risk premium for a particular security is a function of its beta and the risk premium for stocks in general.

Thus we have a concise measure of security risk as well as a concise statement of the relationship between risk and the required return. The model has proved to be quite useful for evaluating portfolio managers and determining the required returns for specific assets.

An Example

First National Bank is considering a new equity issue to expand its capital base. To decide if this action is in the best interest of the present stockholders, the bank must determine whether the return required by equity investors is above or below the return it can earn with additional funds. The required return on equity cannot be observed directly in the market place as can the return on Treasury bills or corporate bonds. The returns expected from investments of the latter type can be determined because they

---

[6] A proof and detailed discussion can be found in any advanced investment text. For example, see Jack Clark Francis, *Investments: Analysis and Management* (New York: McGraw-Hill, 1980).

carry a fixed, contractual obligation and have an observable market price. Common stock has an observable market price, but does not carry a fixed obligation. Therefore, the return required by investors is not directly observable. It must be estimated using available information about general levels of return and risk premiums.

To estimate the required return, the bank must first develop measures of the risk-free interest rate, the average risk premium for the market in general, and the beta for the bank's stock. Studies covering extensive time periods (up to fifty years) have shown that the difference between the interest rates on long-term U.S. government bonds and the realized return on common stock (the realized risk premium) has averaged approximately 5.4 percent. According to the *Value Line Investment Survey*, the beta for the average commercial bank listed there is approximately 0.90. Assume that the Treasury bond rate is presently 8.6 percent. Thus, the estimate of the required return for common stock in general is

$$E_m = 0.086 + 0.054 = 14\%.$$

The required return for the bank's stock would then be

$$K_c = 0.086 + 0.90(0.14 - 0.086) = 13.5\%.$$

Therefore, according to this model, the equity issue would be in the long-run best interest of investors if the bank is successful in producing a return in excess of 13.5 percent for its equity investors.

QUESTIONS

8A-1. Explain the difference between diversifiable and nondiversifiable risk.

8A-2. What are the characteristics of an efficient portfolio?

PROBLEMS

8A-1. Returns for ABC common stock and the market in general for each of the last ten years appear below. What is the beta?

Year	1	2	3	4	5	6	7	8	9	10
Mkt.	0.10	0.15	−0.05	0.05	0.00	0.20	0.12	0.06	0.07	0.10
ABC	0.13	0.20	−0.10	0.05	−0.05	0.25	0.15	0.06	0.10	0.12

8A-2. Returns for stocks in general are expected to be 12 percent, and the risk-free rate is 6 percent. Middle American Finance has a beta of 1.3. Compute the required return for Middle American common stock.

8A-3. Over a particular five-year-period, common stock in general provided an average return of 12 percent per year and the risk-free rate averaged 6 percent. A pension fund managed by Southwest Trust had a return of 15 percent over the same period. It was managed aggressively and had a relatively high beta of 2.0. Evaluate Southwest's performance.

SELECTED REFERENCES

DUNN, K.B., AND McCONNELL, J.J. "Valuation of GNMA Mortage-Backed Securities," *Journal of Finance* (June 1981): 599–616.

LIVINGSTON, MILES. "Measuring the Benefit of a Bond Refunding: The Problem of Nonmarketable Call Options," *Financial Management* (Spring, 1987): 38–40.

McCORMICK, JAMES M. "The Role of Securitization in Transforming Banks Into More Efficient Financial Intermediaries," *Midland Corporate Finance Journal* (Fall 1987): 50–61.

MELTON, CARROLL R., AND PUKULA, TERRY V. *Financial Futures: Practical Applications for Financial Institutions* (Reston, Va.: Reston Publishing Company, 1984).

MIKKELSON, W. H., AND PARTCH, M. M. "Valuation Effects of Security Offerings and the Insurance Process," *Journal of Financial Economics* (January–February 1986): 31–60.

OGDEN, JOSEPH P. "Determinants of the Relative Interest Rate Sensitivities of Corporate Bonds," *Financial Management* (Spring 1987): 22–30.

ROSE, SANFORD. "Rethinking Securitization," *Midland Corporate Finance Journal* (Fall 1987): 62–63.

ROSE, SANFORD. "Extending the Loan Sales Revolution," *Midland Corporate Finance Journal* (Fall 1987): 64–66.

9

Financial Futures and Options

In days remembered but gone, neighborhood lending institutions collected deposits, made loans and investments at favorable interest rate spreads, and lived happily thereafter. Unlike the price of commodities such as wheat or corn or soybeans, the price of money changed very little. Interest rate levels were highly predictable. Everyone knew that long term interest rates were always higher than short term rates, and neither ever changed by much. Then came the 1960's; the Vietnam War, deficit spending, and inflation, followed by higher and more volatile interest rates. Somehow the rules had changed.

The volatility and the high level of interest rates have become major influencing factors in the management of financial institutions (figure 9-1). The prime rate hit 12 percent in 1974, dropped to 6 percent in 1976, headed back up to $15\frac{3}{4}$ percent in 1979, and reached an unprecedented 20 percent in April 1980—only to begin a precipitous decline a month later. By December 1980, the prime reached a record-breaking $21\frac{1}{2}$ percent. It changed 42 times in 1980 and 29 times in 1981.[1] While interest rate volatility slowed somewhat during the 1980s, the prime did not again drop to a single-digit level until the second half of the 1980s. The rules of the game had changed. Interest rate stability of previous decades was but a fond and fading memory.[2]

[1] *A Guide to Financial Futures at the Chicago Board of Trade,* Chicago Board of Trade.

[2] The prime rate changed only about twice per year during the decades of the 1950s and 1960s, in sharp contrast to the 1970s, when the prime interest rate changed over 100 times. See James V. Baker, Jr., "Why You Need a Formal Asset/Liability Management Policy," *Banking* (June 1978): 33.

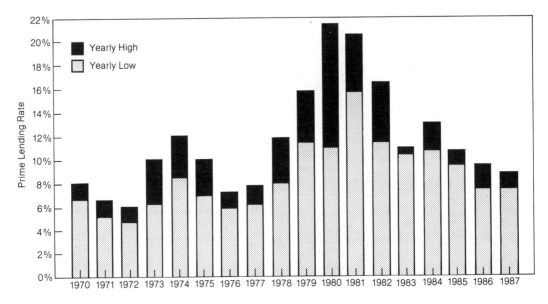

Figure 9-1:   Prime lending rate by year, 1970–1987.
Source: *A Guide to Financial Futures at the Chicago Board of Trade, Economic Report of the President,* and *Federal Reserve Bulletin.*

Such rate volatility poses significant managerial problems for financial institution managers. Because of the inverse relationship between interest rates and security prices (figure 9-2), managers face substantial risk if methods for guarding against such risk are not in place. Consider the following examples:

- Six months from now, a pension fund portfolio manager will receive $1 million. She plans to invest in Treasury bonds and wishes to guard against the possibility of falling interest rates.
- A mortgage banker plans to accumulate a large inventory of fixed-rate mortgages over the next several months. He plans to make mortgage loans at current market rates and to sell the portfolio to a large insurance company nine months from now. If market rates fall, the mortgage portfolio value will rise; but if rates rise, the portfolio value will decline.
- A savings and loan manager plans to issue subordinated debentures to improve the institution's capital ratio. Because interest rates have been rising, he is concerned that rates will be higher when the time arrives to market the bonds, thus decreasing the price received and effectively increasing the financing costs.

This chapter is about ways to hedge against the risk of financial loss caused by interest rate fluctuations. It concerns financial futures and options, some of the most exciting financial products to be developed in this century. To develop a conceptual understanding of these products, we begin with a discussion of *forward* contracts.

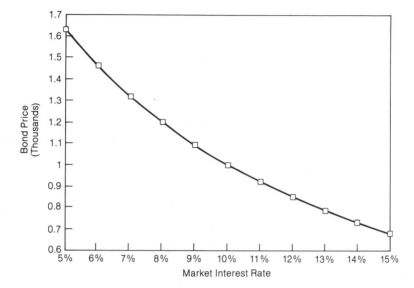

Figure 9-2:   Bond prices and interest rates.

FORWARD CONTRACTS

Consider the college student who plans the purchase of a new car following graduation next spring. The car could be purchased today for $12,000, but proposed import restrictions might increase the price substantially by the time the student is in a position to acquire it. Suppose, however, that the student found someone who agreed to contract for delivery of the car to the student next spring for $12,000. An agreement of this type is referred to as a *forward* contract. Forward contracts are simply written or verbal agreements that call for the exchange of money and commodities at some future date. Agreements to rent apartments, to acquire real estate, or to purchase a textbook from a friend at the semester's end at a price agreed on today are examples of forward contracts.

    Well over a century ago, Chicago was rapidly becoming a center for agricultural products. Wagonloads of grain arrived in Chicago from throughout the Midwest in the fall. Transportation networks were developing that could carry the grain to distant markets by rail and by water. But few storage facilities existed, and grain prices, cheap in the fall, increased dramatically by spring. There was a need to improve the organization of grain markets and to explore ways to raise the capital needed to construct storage facilities, thus ensuring a dependable supply of grain. In response to this need, in 1848, 82 merchants formed the Board of Trade for the City of Chicago and oversaw the organization of a commercial exchange.[3]

---

[3] Edward W. Schwarz, *How to Use Interest Rate Futures Contracts* (Homewood, Ill.: Dow Jones-Irwin, 1979), ch. 1.

As Chicago continued to grow as a grain marketplace, and with improvements in market organization and storage facilities, forward contracting began to appear. The grain farmer could contract in the spring to sell his product in the fall at a price sufficient to cover production costs and allow a reasonable profit. In so doing, the farmer *hedged*, thus reducing the risk of loss. If by fall the cash or *spot* price was less than the price specified in the forward contract, the farmer could deliver his product to the buyer (called a *speculator*) at the specified price. By forward contracting, the farmer could effectively shift the risk of price fluctuation to the speculator. If by fall harvests were large and spot prices low, the speculator was committed to purchase the product at the (higher) contractual price. If by fall spot prices were high, the farmer was committed to sell his product at the (lower) agreed-upon price.

While forward contracting represented some improvement over the chaos produced by widely fluctuating prices, default by either the buyer or seller was common. In addressing this problem, a practice developed whereby earnest money (called *margin*) was deposited with a third party. Also, contracts began to be traded and the last buyer took delivery from the first seller. Eventually, however, a third-party practice developed and the exchange began to clear transactions. In so doing, the exchange recorded the various buy and sell transactions. Also, rather than take physical possession of the product, the last buyer received a warehouse receipt, issued by the exchange, which documented delivery of the commodity. Finally, as trading volume increased, contracts were standardized as to future delivery dates and as to the amount and quality of product represented by one contract. Contracts were traded daily on the exchange, and prices were set through a system of *open outcry* whereby floor traders gathered in some specified section of the trading floor (called a trading *pit*) and traded contracts in an auction-type environment. This more formal market arrangement resulted in additional advantages to both sellers and buyers of contracts. Although two parties were a necessary part of each transaction, the exchange assumed responsibility for contract performance, thus placing itself between the two parties.

To ensure against loss through default, the exchange required a daily margin adjustment (called *marked to market*), meaning that if a contract changed in value, benefiting one party at the expense of the other, the benefited party would receive funds from the margin account while the other was required to deposit funds. By virtue of this daily margin adjustment, all profits or losses have been incurred when the delivery date arrives and the incentive to default is effectively eliminated.

As commodity contracts became more formalized, they were referred to as *futures* contracts. A forward contract designed for a specific need has certain advantages. The precise delivery date can be specified, and the product can be anything on which the parties agree. But such a contract has disadvantages too. The lack of standardization, the lack of a secondary market, the difficulty in locating a buyer or seller for the contract, and the risk of default are but a few of the disadvantages. A futures contract however, is a standardized instrument traded on an exchange where the type, quantity, and grade of the commodity or product is specified and where effective trading rules are in place. To minimize default risk, daily settlement is generally required.

With the formalization of commodity markets and the standardization of procedures and contracts, greater participation on the part of speculators was induced. This larger participation brought increased liquidity to the market. Also, farmers no longer found it necessary to deliver their product to the contract holder or to some specified warehouse. Rather, the farmer could *offset* his contract or contracts, each of which required that he deliver a specified quantity of his product at a specified date. Rather than deliver the commodity, he could offset his position by acquiring contracts (equal in number to those he currently held) on the opposite side, i.e., contracts that gave him the right to receive the product he was currently committed to provide. By offsetting his position, the farmer's overall position was canceled and any remaining funds in the margin account returned to him. Since cash and futures prices tend to move in parallel fashion, any gain or loss on the cash sale of the farmer's product is at least partially offset by a corresponding loss or gain on the futures transactions.

EXAMPLE.   To illustrate the use of commodity futures contracts in hedging, consider a grain farmer who knows in May that the price received in August for his wheat harvest might not cover production costs. The farmer knows that if he can realize at least $2.75 per bushel, his production costs will be covered and a satisfactory profit will be realized. Through his broker, the farmer is able to sell, in May, wheat futures for September delivery at a price of $2.77 per bushel. Consequently the farmer "locks in" his price.

Table 9-1

Short Hedge in Wheat Futures

MAY: A farmer expects to harvest wheat in August with a price objective of $2.75 per bushel. He sells September wheat futures at a price of $2.77 per bushel.			
(1) August price turns out to be	$2.50	$3.00	$3.50
(2) Gain or loss from offsetting future contract [$2.77 − row (1)]	0.27	−0.23	−0.73
(3) Sales price of wheat in cash market [row (1)]	2.50	3.00	3.50
(4) Total earnings per bushel [rows (1)+(2)]	2.77	2.77	2.77

The foregoing example illustrates a *short* or selling hedge and the basic features of a futures contract. By selling futures contracts in May, the farmer knew his total earnings per bushel and effectively locked in his earnings at $2.77 per bushel. The speculator, as the other party to the transaction, suffered an economic loss if the spot price turned out to be less than $2.77 or realized a profit if the spot price exceeded $2.77.

In addition to short or selling hedges, *long* or buying hedges are often employed as a risk reduction technique by users of basic commodities produced by farmers and others. As an example, consider the New York coffee importer and dealer who is called upon, in May, to quote selling prices for coffee beans that will be delivered several months hence. Through experience, the importer knows that unpredictable events, such as volcanic activity in certain coffee-producing regions, can result in large price swings. By "going long" or buying coffee futures, the importer locks in the price which must be paid for the necessary quantity of coffee beans. The importer is thus able to cover his anticipated operating costs and to ensure a satisfactory level of profit.

EXAMPLE.   To illustrate the use of commodity futures contracts in hedging, consider the coffee importer who knows in May that the price received in December for coffee he is committed to provide might not cover operating costs.

Table 9-2

Long Hedge in Coffee Futures

MAY: A New York coffee importer contracts to sell coffee beans to a food processor in December. He buys December coffee futures at a price of $1.18 per pound.

(1) December price turns out to be	$0.90	$1.20	$1.50
(2) Gain or loss from offsetting future contract [$1.18 − row (1)].	0.28	−0.02	−0.32
(3) Purchase price of coffee in cash market [row (1)]	0.90	1.20	1.50
(4) Total cost per bushel [row (2) + row (3)]	1.18	1.18	1.18

FINANCIAL FUTURES

Before 1975, interest rate or financial instrument futures contracts did not exist. But by the mid-1970s, the interest rate stability of the previous decades was gone. The Chicago Board of Trade, relying on a basic premise that money, or more precisely the cost of money, can be viewed the same as any other commodity, introduced the first financial futures contract. The first contract was in Government National Mortgage Association (GNMA) mortgage-backed certificates. In subsequent years, trading in several additional financial instruments including Treasury bond and Treasury note futures, among others, was introduced.

Financial futures, or interest rate futures are futures contracts based on financial instruments whose price fluctuates with changes in interest rates. As with commodity futures previously discussed, financial futures represent a firm contract to buy or sell a specified financial instrument during a specified month, at a price established by open outcry in a central, regulated marketplace. With the introduction of financial futures, financial institution managers and others were provided with a way to decrease risks arising from fluctuating interest rates, and they provided speculators with a new market in which fortunes could be won or lost in hours.

The basic problem (and opportunity) addressed in the financial futures markets is the sensitivity of values of existing fixed-income securities to changes in interest rates. The relationship between interest and value can be briefly illustrated with a perpetual bond, one that provides an interest payment each year forever with the principal never being repaid. A $1,000, 10 percent bond, for example, pays $100 (0.10 × $1,000) a year forever. Suppose the owner of the bond wants to sell it. The yield to a buyer is

$$\text{Yield} = \frac{\text{annual interest payment}}{\text{price}}.$$

If interest rates have risen such that investors will not buy unless they can earn a yield of 14 percent, the (current market) price of a $1,000 face value perpetual bond that pays interest at the rate of 10 percent of its face value can be determined using the above equation:

$$0.14 = \frac{\$100}{\text{price}}.$$

Solving, price equals $714. Thus, the investor who originally bought the bond for $1,000 would suffer a loss of $286 on resale. Similar price movements occur for financial instruments with finite lives. For example, a change in interest rates from 10 percent to 14 percent would cause a thirty-year, 10 percent mortgage to decline in value by 26 percent. The financial futures market provides a way to protect the value of one's portfolio from such risks or to attempt to profit by predicting interest rate movements.

EXAMPLE.   Citizens Savings and Loan illustrates why and how financial futures markets are used to reduce risk. Citizens has agreed with a builder to provide $1 million of mortgages with an interest rate of 12 percent. Citizens intends to sell the package of mortgages rather than hold them. The package will be assembled and ready for sale in six months, and Citizens is concerned about interest rate movements in the meantime. If interest rates rise to 13 percent by that time, a $1 million package of 9 percent mortgages could be sold for approximately $930,000, which would result in a $70,000 loss. The futures market provides a way for Citizens to eliminate this risk.

Citizens Savings and Loan can reduce the risk arising from interest rate uncertainty by entering into a futures contract. Because all financial instruments respond in similar ways to changes in interest rates, Citizens can hedge its risk by acquiring futures contracts that will provide gains approximately equal to any losses in the value of its own portfolio. As futures contracts are regularly traded for U.S. Treasury bills, Treasury bonds, and Treasury notes, as well as certificates of deposit and mortgages (actually GNMA collateralized deposit certificates, called GNMA CDRs), there are enough choices available to make a good—though not perfect— match.

Another factor allowing Citizens to hedge with similar rather than identical securities is the infrequency of actual delivery of financial instruments in this market. Suppose, for example, Citizens entered into a contract to sell, in six months, U.S. Treasury bonds with a $1 million face value and an 8 percent interest rate. Further suppose that the agreed-upon future price was the same as the face value: $1 million. If, at the end of the six-month period these bonds are actually selling for $930,000 because of a rise in interest rates, it is not necessary for Citizens to actually own bonds for delivery. Also, the investor who entered into the futures contract to buy will most likely not actually wish to purchase the bonds for $1 million. Instead, the investor and Citizens will simply offset their positions. In effect, the investor will pay the $70,000 difference and Citizens will receive the $70,000 difference. Citizens could then proceed to sell the mortgages in the cash market for $930,000. Had the bonds increased in value because of falling interest rates, Citizens would have paid the amount by which the bonds increased in value and the investor would have received this amount. Futures contracts are regularly arranged for several securities with price movements similar to the price movements of Citizens' mortgages.

Organized futures markets incorporate the use of clearing corporations, thus ensuring the integrity of contracts. The use of a clearing corporation ensures Citizens that it is contracting with a party willing and able to complete its contract. Although Citizens' broker and the investor's broker strike an agreement with each other, Citizens technically contracts to deliver the package of securities to the clearing corporation, and the investor technically contracts to purchase securities from the clearing corporation. Therefore, the clearing corporation has agreed to complete the contract with Citizens even if the investor should default.

MECHANICS OF THE FUTURES MARKETS

One of the more widely traded financial futures, U.S. Treasury bond futures, are used to explain the technical details of financial futures trading. The standard Treasury bond futures contract calls for delivery of $100,000 face value of 8 percent coupon rate U.S. Treasury bonds with a maturity of fifteen years or more. Treasury bond contracts are traded for delivery in March, June, September, and December going out two and a half years into the future—a total of ten different contracts.

As an example, we will use the March 1988 Treasury bond contract as traded on 1 October 1987. Financial futures are traded in face-to-face meetings of the floor of an exchange whose membership includes speculators as well as brokers representing clients such as Citizens Savings and Loan. The 1 October 1987 daily trading summary for March 1988 Treasury bond futures is published in the financial press:

OPEN	HIGH	LOW	SETTLE	CHANGE
80–31	81–12	80–21	80–29	+1

	YIELD	CHANGE	OPEN INTEREST	
	10.266	−0.005	36,723	

Prices are stated as a percentage of the $100,000 face value, and trading is in increments of $1/32$ of one percent. Thus, the opening contract for the day was for delivery of $100,000 face value of 8 percent Treasury bonds in March 1988 for $80^{31}/_{32}$ percent (80.96875), or $80,968.75. The highest contract of the day was for $81^{12}/_{32}$ percent of face value. The lowest price was $80^{21}/_{32}$ percent of face value, and the price settled at $80^{29}/_{32}$ percent of face value. The price was up $1/32$ of a percent of face value from the price at the end of the previous day. The yield to maturity that would be earned by someone buying the bonds at that price is 10.266 percent, which is down 0.005 percent from the yield at the end of the previous day's trading. Open interest is the number of contracts outstanding. Thus at the end of the day's trading, there were outstanding contracts for $3.6723 billion ($100,000 × 36,723) of face value of Treasury bonds for March 1988 delivery.

Once the contract is agreed to on the floor of the exchange, both parties must post a deposit (margin). The minimum allowable margin for a $100,000 Treasury bond contract is $2,000, but brokerage houses commonly require margins larger than this minimum. If the March 1988 delivery price begins to rise, the buyer will be required to put up more money; and if it falls, the seller will be required to put up more money.

Offsetting the Futures Position

Either party can cancel out its position by acquiring an offsetting contract. Suppose, for example, that several months have passed. In the interim, bond interest rates have increased and bond prices have decreased. Suppose further that the March delivery price has decreased from 80–29 to 79–27. The person who contracted to sell at 80–29 can place a new order with his or her broker to buy at 79–27. When that transaction is completed, the investor will have two contracts wtih the clearing corporation—one to sell at 80–29 and one to buy at 79–27. These two contracts cancel each other out and the person receives $1062.50 ($100,000 × 80^{29}/$_{32}$% − $100,000 × 79^{27}/$_{32}$%) plus the initial margin. Most contracts are settled through the acquisition of an offsetting contract rather than through the actual delivery of the underlying financial instrument.

HEDGING WITH FINANCIAL FUTURES[4]

Long Hedge

As previously discussed with reference to commodity futures, there are two types of hedges—long (or buying) hedges and short (or selling) hedges. The long hedge involves the purchase of futures contracts today as a temporary substitute for the purchase of the actual commodity in the future. The *long* hedge therefore, and with reference to *financial* futures, involves a condition whereby the hedger has contracted to *buy* securities at some specified future time at a price fixed today.

EXAMPLE. On April 1, a pension fund portfolio manager anticipates the receipt of $1 million three months hence. She plans to invest in Treasury bonds and wishes to guard against the possibility of falling interest rates.

Twenty-year $8\frac{1}{4}$ percent Treasury bonds are currently yielding 12.26 percent in the open market. The manager, fearing the prospect of falling rates and the concurrent prospect of bond price increases, decides to "go long" in Treasury bond futures. She purchases ten September bond futures contracts at the current price of 68–10. By July 2, interest rates have dropped as she anticipated and the price of bonds has increased.

---

[4]. Discussion and examples contained in this section rely heavily on *A Guide to Financial Futures at the Chicago Board of Trade,* Chicago Board of Trade.

Because cash and futures prices tend to move in the same direction, in a rough (but rarely precise) parallel fashion,[5] September bond futures contracts have also increased and by July 2 stand at 80-07. She offsets her position by selling ten September bond futures contracts—each for 80-07. These two positions cancel each other out, and the manager receives a profit of $119,062.50 [($100,000 × 80$^{7}\!/\!_{32}$% − $100,000 × 68$^{19}\!/\!_{32}$%) × 10 contracts].

By the time the cash is available for the anticipated purchase, the price of Treasury bonds has increased from 68-14 to 82-13. This translates into an opportunity loss of $139,687.50 for the portfolio—but this loss is offset by a gain in the futures market. On July 2, the manager pays $824,062.50 ($1,000,000 × 82 $^{13}\!/\!_{32}$%) for $1 million face value twenty-year, 8$\frac{1}{4}$ percent U.S. Treasury bonds with a yield of 10.14 percent, her effective cost is only $705,000.00, since she had a $119,062.50 gain in the futures market. Consequently, she was able to purchase the securities at a net cost which approximated (but which did not precisely match) the lower price which existed on April 1.

Table 9-3

Long Hedge in Treasury Bond Futures

CASH MARKET	FUTURES MARKET
April 1: Wants to take advantage of today's higher yield level on 20-year, 8$\frac{1}{4}$% Treasury bonds at 68-14	*April 1:* Buys 10 September bond futures contracts at 68-10
July 2: Buys $1 million of 20-year, 8$\frac{1}{4}$% Treasury bonds at 82-13 (yielding 10.14%)	*July 2:* Sells 10 September bond futures contracts at 80-07
Loss: $139, 687.50	Gain: $119,062.50

Short Hedge

In contrast to the long hedge, the *short* hedge involves a condition whereby the hedger contracts to *sell* financial futures at some specified future time at a price fixed today.

EXAMPLE.   On January 15, Midtown Savings and Loan Association holds $5 million of GNMA 10s priced at 89-00 on that day. Midtown anticipates that interest rates will continue their upward climb and wants to protect its GNMA portfolio from a drop in value. On January 15, Midtown sells 50 June GNMA futures contracts at 78-04. By March 20, interest rates have risen still further, and the price of GNMAs in Midtown's portfolio has declined to 78-22. The association offsets its position in the futures market by buying 50 GNMA contracts at 69-00.

---

[5] Cash and futures prices tend to be influenced in the same direction by the same economic forces. The difference between the cash and futures price for any given financial instrument is called the *basis*. While the basis for financial instruments can change over time, such changes tend to be much less dramatic (more stable) than changes in the cash and futures price for the underlying instrument.

Table 9-4

Short Hedge: GNMAs

CASH MARKET	FUTURES MARKET
January 15: Wants to protect the value of $5 million GNMA portfolio at 89-00	*January 15:* Sells 50 June GNMA futures contracts at 78-04
March 20: Value of GNMAs in portfolio declines to 78-22	*March 20:* Buys 50 GNMA futures contracts at 69-00
Loss: $515,625.00	Gain: $456,250.00

In this example, the loss of $515,625.00 to Midtown in its holdings of GNMAs is at least partially offset by the gain of $456,250.00 in the futures market.

Designing a Financial Futures Hedge

A financial futures hedge is designed to decrease the risk of security price fluctuation due to changes in interest rates. A portfolio manager holding U.S. Treasury bonds might, for example, wish to hedge his position by entering into a contract for the future sale of Treasury bonds at a price set today. In a perfect hedge, the profit or loss on the financial futures contract will exactly offset the profit or loss from some other activity. Any gain or loss in the value of the Treasury bonds held by the portfolio manager would, for example, be almost exactly offset by gains or losses in the value of the futures contract. The portfolio manager is not betting on interest rate predictions; with a perfect hedge, profit will be the same regardless of the direction in which interest rates move.

Because there are futures contracts going out to two and a half years in three-month intervals, a hedger's first choice is the appropriate delivery date. A mortgage banker assembling a package of mortgages for sale in three months would have little difficulty in deciding that three months forward was the appropriate delivery date for a futures contract to sell. For others, the decision is not quite so easy. Almost all depository institutions accept an average maturity of liabilities that is shorter than the average maturity of assets. However, a well-managed institution will have a policy concerning the amount of mismatch it is willing to tolerate. When the mismatch begins to exceed the policy limit, action is taken. A savings and loan may, for example, effectively increase the maturity of its six-month certificates of deposit (CDs) to one year by entering into a futures contract to sell CDs at the end of six months at a price (and therefore interest rate) determined today. Likewise, it could enter into CD futures contracts for delivery in one year, one and a half years, etc., to effectively increase the maturity of its six-month CDs up to three years. The exact maturity chosen is a tactical decision to implement the firm's policy with regard to exposure to maturity mismatches; it is not determined exactly by the maturity of any asset.

The second problem faced by a hedger is the choice of the security on which to place a futures contract. If a portfolio manager is holding U.S. Treasury bonds, the fairly obvious hedge choice is a futures contract in U.S. Treasury bonds. However, Treasury bond futures contracts are based on an assumed 8 percent coupon rate, while most bonds carry coupon rates other than 8 percent; a perfect match is impossible. Furthermore, many hedgers find that their risk is related to price movements of securities for which there are no futures contracts. They must therefore use a *cross-hedge,* a future delivery contract in some instrument with price movements similar to the movements of the security they are actually interested in. A consequence of these differences between the instrument being held and the instrument involved in the hedge contract is that the best hedge may be for a futures contract of a different amount than the value of the securities being hedged. The determination of the appropriate hedge size is explained in the following paragraphs.

Equivalent Principal Balance

With the use of futures contracts for GNMA collateralized depository receipts (CDRs) as an example, the standard contract is for delivery of $100,000 of face value of 8 percent coupon certificates or the equivalent. The equivalent face values for some other coupon rates follow.(Similar tables are available for other instruments on which financial futures are traded.)

GNMA COUPON INTEREST RATE	FACE AMOUNT TO BE DELIVERED
7%	$107,816.70
8	$100,000.00
10	87,146.00
12	76,792.40
14	68,823.10
16	62,208.40
18	56,737.60

For example, a person who enters into a futures contract for delivery of $100,000 of 8 percent certificates is allowed to substitute $62,208.40 face value of 16 percent certificates. Stated another way, $1.00 of 16 percent GNMA CDRs can be delivered in place of $1.608 (100,000/62,208.4) of 8 percent GNMA CDRs. Thus a portfolio manager who wants to hedge $100 million of 16 percent GNMA CDRs will enter into future delivery contracts for $160.8 million of 8 percent GNMA CDRs. Since the standard contract is for $100,000 face value, the hedger will need 1,608 contracts.

Cross-Hedges

A cross-hedge is used when there is no futures contract for the instrument the manager wants to hedge. In this case, the hedger enters into a similar futures contract for delivery of an instrument with similar price movement behavior. For example, there are no traded futures contracts for corporate bonds, and a manager who wants to hedge corporate bonds may choose a futures contract in U.S. Treasury bonds.

When a cross-hedge is used, it is necessary to determine the relative sensitivity of the security being hedged and the futures contract price. One way to do this is with regression analysis. For example, we might determine that

$$P_t = 0.10 + 0.8\, P_c$$

Where P_t is the price of Treasury bond futures as a percent of face value and P_c is the price of the corporate bond (or portfolio of corporate bonds) as a percentage of face value. Because Treasury bond futures prices (for the particular delivery period) move in price only by 0.8 as much as the corporate bonds, a cross-hedge will require a Treasury bond contract in an amount greater than that of the corporate bonds being held. If the manager has $10.0 million face value of corporate bonds, a good cross-hedge will require futures contracts to sell $12.5 million ($10 million/0.8) face value of Treasury bonds.

To illustrate how a hedge of this type works, consider a portfolio manager who has developed the above estimation equation and holds corporate bonds with a face value of $10 million and a market value of $8 million. The portfolio manager enters into futures contracts to sell $12.5 million face value of 8 percent coupon treasury bonds at a price of 74-0, or 0.74 × $12.5 million = $9.25 million. Subsequently, the value of the corporate bonds falls to $7 million. If the relationship holds as expected, the Treasury bond futures price will fall to 0.10 + 0.8(0.7) = 0.66 times face value, or $8.25 million. The portfolio manager loses $1 million on the corporate bonds and gains $1 million on the futures contract because he first contracted to sell at $9.25 million and then later offset that contract with a contract to buy at $8.25 million.

It is only fair to point out that things never work out this neatly. While a cross-hedge uses securities with highly correlated price movements, one will never find two securities with perfectly correlated price movements. Consequently, the cross-hedge is a risk reduction tool rather than a risk elimination tool.

OPTIONS

An option is the right to buy or sell something at a specified price within a specified time. Unlike a futures contract which requires the buyer and seller to complete the contract according to its terms, an option provides that one party, the option *holder* or *buyer,* has the right to require or forgo contract compliance. The original option seller (called the *writer*) must comply with the terms of the option contract if the holder chooses to complete the contract (*exercise* the option). An option to *buy* something is called a *call* option, while an option to *sell* is termed a *put* option.

While option contracts have existed for centuries, many such agreements (as was true with futures contracts) have long dealt with agricultural commodities and included items such as coffee, cocoa, platinum, silver, and copper. As was the case with financial futures, growth in trading of financial options coincided with the deregulation of financial markets and with the increased volatility of interest rates and security prices in the 1970s and 1980s. Indeed, it was not until 1973 that puts and calls were traded on an organized exchange. With the advent of the *Chicago Board Options Exchange* created in that year, an organized clearinghouse with established rules that enhanced and facilitated the growth of option trading was born. In subsequent years, growth in option trading, particularly for financial instruments, was dramatic.

EXAMPLE.   Suppose an investor holds an option to buy (a call option) 100 shares of IBM stock over the next six months at a *strike* or *exercise* price of $100. If IBM currently sells for $110, the option price (called the *premium*) must be at least $10 because the option holder has the right to buy IBM from the option writer at a price of $100. Similarly, if an investor holds an option to sell IBM (a put option) at a strike price of, say, $125, and again assuming that IBM stock is currently selling for $110, the premium must be at least $15. Of course, under the above assumptions, the call might sell for more than $10 and the put might sell for more than $15, depending on certain factors including the time until *expiration* (option *maturity*) and volatility of the underlying stock, among others.[6] Following its expiration, the option has no value.[7]

The difference between the option striking price and the market price of the underlying security is called the *intrinsic* value of the option. Of course, the intrinsic value cannot fall below zero. If in the above example, IBM currently sells for $110 and the call option strike price is $100, the intrinsic value of the option is $10 (although the market value may exceed $10). Of course, for a put option to have intrinsic value, the option strike price must be *greater* than the market value of the underlying security.

In addition to the terminology defined thus far, there are three terms used extensively by those who deal in options. They are defined here with reference to a call option. An *in-the-money option* is one where *the underlying security's price exceeds the exercise price.* In this case, the security has positive intrinsic value. An *out-of-the-money option* is one where *the underlying security's price is less than the exercise price.* Finally, an option is said to be *at the money* when the market price of the underlying security *equals the strike price.* For put options, the definitions are reversed.

Since they were first traded on the CBOE in 1973, trading in options has been expanded to a number of other exchanges. The trading procedure is similar to that for financial futures. Contracts are standardized to aid trading, and their prices are determined in open auction. Technically, the buyers and sellers contract with the clearing corporation to eliminate the risk of default. Most contracts are allowed to expire without being exercised or are offset by opposite contracts rather than by exercise. An option writer who sells an IBM call option for 100 shares and is thus obligated to buy IBM at the stated strike price can get out of the market by buying a 100-share IBM call option which has the same strike price. The option writer in this example will gain or lose, depending on whether the option price decreased or increased in the interim.

Options may be used by speculators, by hedgers, and by those simply looking to improve return on a common stock portfolio. A speculator buys or writes put or call

---

[6] A model for determining the value of an option is explained in the appendix to this chapter.

[7] Options which may be exercised at any time prior to or at maturity are called *American* options. Those which may be exercised only at maturity are called *European* options. Most options which are traded in the United States and elsewhere and which are discussed in this chapter are American options.

options on stock he does not own in order to profit if his predictions of future prices are correct. An investor who simply wants to improve portfolio return month in and month out in exchange for sacrificing the chance to make really large profits may write call options at striking prices well above the current stock price. Chances are that the stock will not reach the striking price, the option will simply be allowed to expire, and the seller will keep the amount for which he sold the option. If prices do rise rapidly, the option seller can sell the stock for the striking price and also retain proceeds from the original option sale—a good profit but not as large as the profit that would have been realized had an option not been written.

EXAMPLE.   Citizens Savings and Loan has committed to a builder funds sufficient to provide mortgage loans to support the sale of new homes at a fixed interest rate. Because the builder has not yet finalized construction and marketing plans, Citizens cannot be certain that the loans will actually be made. If Citizens uses a futures contract for hedging purposes, the loans were not actually made, and if rates fall, a substantial loss will be incurred. Alternatively however, Citizens could purchase a put option rather than enter into a futures contract. There is no traded put option for mortgages, but there is a market for put options on U.S. Treasury bonds. Citizens could purchase a put option on U.S. Treasury bonds, possibly charging the builder a commitment fee equal to the cost of the option. If the loans are made and interest rates rise, the loss in loan value will be offset by a profit on the put option. If the loans are not made and interest rates rise, the option will provide a windfall profit, as its price will rise. If the loans are made but interest rates remain stable or fall, the option will simply be allowed to expire and its cost will have been an insurance cost. Thus the option can provide a more effective hedge than can a futures contract under certain conditions.

OPTIONS ON FUTURES

Before leaving our discussion of options, we note the fact that exchange-traded *options on futures* in financial instruments have developed rapidly over the past dozen years or so. Options on certain stock index futures and options on debt instrument futures such as U.S. Treasury bond futures are now regularly traded. The availability of such options provides financial institution managers with an even greater capability to manage large portfolios. By purchasing the appropriate number of "options on futures," it is possible to achieve protection "insurance" against an adverse change in interest rates while still retaining the opportunity to benefit from a favorable interest rate movement.

EXAMPLE.   The manager of a large bank trust department holds bonds which will mature in three months. Funds received at maturity of the bonds will be available for reinvestment at that time. The manager could go long in financial futures contracts for Treasury bonds today, thus locking in the bond replacement price and yield. This strategy would provide protection against a possible decline in interest rates and higher bond prices. The manager is reluctant, however, to forgo the opportunity to benefit from lower bond prices if interest rates should rise.

In this example, a useful strategy may be to buy call options on Treasury bond futures. If interest rates decline, the bond futures price can be expected to move above the option strike price, and the option to purchase Treasury bond futures will be exercised. If interest rates increase, the option will be allowed to expire and the trust department manager will simply purchase the bonds at the (lower) market price.

SUMMARY

Financial market volatility of the past two decades has resulted in the development of new financial instruments and techniques designed to respond to this volatility. The days when prudent investment and portfolio management almost entirely involved assessing the characteristics of a particular security and the credentials of its issuer are gone. Today's financial institution manager must be aware of the risks and opportunities inherent in interest rate levels that can move quickly and unexpectedly. Indeed, the very survival of many financial institutions will depend upon the ability of institutional managers to respond quickly and correctly to these new challenges. An understanding, therefore, of financial futures and options markets is fundamental to successful management of financial institutions.

QUESTIONS

9-1.   Distinguish between a forward contract and a futures contract.

9-2.   Although exchange-traded financial futures have existed only since 1975, growth in their trading volume has been dramatic. Why has this been the case?

9-3.   Distinguish between a short hedge and a long hedge. If Nestles Company, a producer of food products, wishes to establish the price it pays for cocoa over the next several months, should the company take out a short position or a long position in cocoa futures? Explain.

9-4.   With reference to time value concepts, explain the inverse relationship between interest rates and security prices.

9-5.   Rather than make or accept delivery of financial instruments or commodities as specified in futures contracts, parties to the transaction frequently choose to offset their positions. Identify several likely reasons for this choice.

9-6.   An option for 100 shares of Citicorp with a striking price of $50 may be purchased by an investor. If the market price of Citicorp is $58 per share and the option price is $5, is the option a put or a call? Explain.

9-7.   In question 9-6, is the option in the money, out of the money, or at the money? Defend your conclusion.

9-8.   Explain how options on futures can allow a portfolio manager to hedge if future interest rate movements are unfavorable and at the same time benefit, if rate movements are favorable.

9-9.   If an investor buys a call option on a stock and the market price of the stock subsequently declines, what is likely to happen to the market price of the option?

PROBLEMS

9-1.   In May an Illinois farmer hopes to sell his wheat in August for $3.10 per bushel, thus ensuring a reasonable profit. September wheat futures are currently trading at $3.12 per bushel, and the farmer decides to hedge through the use of wheat futures contracts.
   a. Should the farmer buy wheat futures or sell wheat futures?
   b. Calculate the gain or loss per bushel as the result of offsetting futures contracts if the cash market price for wheat turns out to be $2.50, $3.00, and $3.50.

9-2.   In November a clothing manufacturer contracts to produce large quanitities of cotton dressses for delivery in one year. Approximately one million pounds of cotton will be required to produce the product, and delivery prices for the dresses are fixed in the contract. The company wishes to guard against the prospect that raw materials prices will increase when production commences next spring. The company notes that March cotton futures are currently trading at 73.8 ¢ per pound and that each contract calls for delivery of 50,000 pounds of cotton. The company decides to use the futures market to hedge their raw materials cost.
   a. Should the company go long or short in cotton futures?
   b. Calculate the gain or loss from offsetting the necessary quantity of cotton futures contracts if the cash price of cotton turns out to be 60 ¢ and 80 ¢.

9-3   The stock of Corporation X is selling for $50 a share, and six-month options with a striking price of $60 are selling for $5.25. Is the option a put or a call? Explain.

9-4.   For Corporation X above, compute the percentage change in the value of the option and the value of the stock if, on the day before the option's expiration, the stock is selling for
   a. $50 a share.
   b. $60 a share.
   c. $70 a share.

9-5.   On 23 October, 1987, the closing market price of Monsanto's stock was $70. Calls which would mature the following January with a strike price of $80 were traded at $4.
   a. Were the call options in the money, out of the money, or at the money?
   b. Compute the intrinsic value of the call.
   c. If the market price of Monsanto rises to $90 just prior to the January option expiration, what is the percentage return on investment for an investor who purchased a call on October 23?

9-6.   With reference to problem 9-5, put options with the same strike price and with a January maturity for Monsanto's stock were traded at $15 on 23 October 1987.

   a. Were the put options in the money, out of the money, or at the money?
   b. Compute the intrinsic value of the put.
   c. If the market price of Monsanto fell to $50 just prior to expiration of the put, what is the percentage return on investment for an investor who purchased a put on October 23?

9-7.   An investment portfolio contains a number of Treasury bonds with a par value of $100,000. The coupon interest rate per bond is $10\frac{3}{8}$ percent. Quarterly interest income for each bond is about $100,000 \times 10\frac{3}{8}\%/4 = \$2600$. Bonds of the type held in the portfolio are currently priced to yield 9.1 percent, and the futures price is 90-00. The premium for a three-months call on a bond of the type held within this portfolio and with a strike price of 92-00 is $1,000. Interest rates and bond prices are expected to be relatively stable for the forseeable future.

   a. Outline a call option-writing strategy whereby the portfolio return can be improved over the next three months.
   b. If calls were written for all of the Treasury bonds in the portfolio, calculate the percentage increase in portfolio return over the three month period assuming interest rates and bond prices are in fact stable.
   c. What are the potential risks inherent in the option-writing strategy developed in part a above?

9-8.   A portfolio manager with $50 million of 14 percent GNMA CDRs wants to be protected from interest rate risk over the next six months. Calculate the number of futures contracts required by the hedger.

9-9.   An insurance company has a corporate bond portfolio that it wants to hedge from interest rate risk over a one-year period. The bond portfolio has a face value of $100 million and a market value of $90 million. One-year, 8 percent Treasury bond futures contracts are selling at 85 percent of face value. An analyst has studied the relationship between movement of the corporate bond portfolio and Treasury bond futures and developed the following estimating equation:

$P_t = 0.04 + 0.9 P_c.$

Design an appropriate cross-hedge.

9-10.   Barry McCormack owns 100 shares of IBM. The market price of IBM in early November is $120, and IBM calls with a strike price of $145 are trading at $3.

   a. By writing one January IBM call option contract, how much will Barry receive before taxes and before brokerage commissions?
   b. What risk, if any, does Barry face in this decision?

CASE 7

Benneteil Life Insurance Company

Chief financial officer of Benneteil Life Insurance Company, Fred Lawrence had recently learned of the relaxation of regulations barring the insurance industry from the financial futures market. Consequently, he called a meeting of his associates to evaluate the implications of this new development for his company.

Treasurer Neil Rauch indicated during the meeting that he anticipated a sharp increase in interest rates within the next six months. He felt that he could prevent a major loss in the value of the company bond portfolio by selling government bond futures to be delivered in six months. This arrangement is called a short hedge, hedging a cash position with a short futures position. As a result, no matter what happens to interest rates, the losses in one market will be offset with gains in the other market.

Finance committee member David Bauer, who had been with the legal department for the last twenty-five years, raised some questions about the appropriateness of financial futures for an insurance company:

Bauer: The insurance industry enjoys the confidence and trust of the public because of a long history of cautious and conservative investment management. This reputation should not be lost to the dangerous practice of betting on future interest rates. Furthermore, there are some other hedging techniques that might be used to eliminate interest rate risk, such as repo financing. If the treasurer wants to ensure certain rates of return on a $1 million premium to be received three months from now, it is a simple matter to buy six-month T bills and immediately sell them to a buyer with an

This case was prepared by Shahriar Khaksari, Suffolk University.

agreement to buy them back three months later at a specific price which provides a fixed rate of return.

Laura Smyth, who recently finished her M.B.A. program and had just completed a three-day seminar about futures, was a strong advocate of financial futures:

Smyth: For us, financial futures are not a form of speculation. Failure to take advantage of the financial futures market to hedge would be a form of speculation because financial futures eliminate bets on future interest rates. We are talking about using the futures market to do things like reduce price fluctuation risk associated with bonds. Many of our trades will be with speculators. They will be assuming our risk. On the topic of repo financing, the repo market is simply no substitute for financial futures. The futures market, with its quarterly intervals, provides speculating and hedging opportunities for a period of up to two and a half years. This period is longer than repo financing. Moreover, the futures market provides convenience, flexibility, and liquidity along with readily available price quotations and lower transactions costs.

Noble: (an M.B.A. who had served on the investment committee for the last two years.) The reduction of risk through financial futures might be more valuable to insurance companies than to other financial institutions. First, the ability of insurance companies to fully diversify away the unsystematic risk in their portfolios is retarded by a very restrictive set of regulations. Second, their operation is very sensitive to systematic sources of risk such as inflation and interest rates that are viewed as a principal element behind most types of loss bearing by insurance companies (e.g., excessive claim losses, sales declines, losses in investment portfolio value, policy loans, and cancelations).

Lawrence thought that financial futures could be a useful tool. However, he was also aware of banks that had experienced considerable difficulties when traders got out of hand in the currency futures markets. He wanted to be sure that a sound policy and careful controls preceded an entry into the financial futures market. For purposes of further study, he asked Smyth to prepare examples of several possible hedging strategies for the next meeting.

After talking with Rauch and with the chief economist, Ms. Smyth concluded that interest rates would go up significantly during the next six months and then level off. On the basis of this prediction, she considered three major components of the company's portfolio.

GMNA Portfolio

Benneteil had $100 million face value of GMNA CDRs, half with 14 percent coupon rates and half with 12 percent coupon rates. The 12 percent certificates were selling at par, while the 14 percent certificates were selling at 111 percent of face value.

Corporate Bonds

Corporate bonds contained in the company's portfolio consisted of a well-diversified mixture of high-grade bonds with a face value of $4.2 billion and a book value of $4 billion. Since futures contracts in corporate bonds did not exist, a cross-hedge would be required. Smyth had estimated that the price sensitivity of six-month future delivery treasury bonds (as a percent of their face value) was 0.9 of that of corporate bonds.

Policy Loans

Historically, policy owners exercise their right to low-interest policy loans as interest rates rise, and pay off these loans as interest rates fall. In light of the predicted increase in interest rates, not only the market value of the present outstanding amount of loans would decline, but there also would be an increase in the total amount of policy loans. To meet increased policy loan demand, it would be necessary to sell securities earning a high rate of interest and then loan out these funds at the 5 percent loan interest rate specified in the policies.

On the basis of past experience, policy loans were expected to increase $108 million over the next six months. Since this increase would take place gradually, Smyth decided to sell the following Treasury bill contracts.

TIME	ESTIMATED CUMULATIVE INCREASE IN POLICY LOANS	FUTURES CONTRACTS TO BE PURCHASED TODAY
Next 3 months	$ 54 million	
3–6 months	108 million	108 3-month contracts
6–9 months	108 million	108 6-month contracts
9–12 months	54 million	54 9-month contracts

QUESTIONS

1. Design an appropriate hedge contract for the GNMA portfolio.
2. Design an appropriate cross hedge for the corporate bond portfolio.
3. Evaluate the proposed hedge contracts for policy loans. Would these contracts provide a good hedge? Can you suggest a better hedge?
4. If Benneteil enters the financial futures market, what policy guidelines would you recommend?
5. Would you recommend financial futures trading for Benneteil?

SELECTED REFERENCES

BLACK, F. AND SCHOLES, M.   "The Pricing of Options and Corporate Liabilities," *Journal of Political Economy* (May/June 1973): 637–54.

BREWER, ELIJAH.   "Bank Gap Management and the Use of Financial Futures," *Federal Reserve Bank of Chicago Economic Perspectives* (March/April 1985): 12–21.

CORNELL, BRADFORD, AND FRENCH, KENNETH.   "The Pricing of Stock Index Futures," *Journal of Futures Markets* (Spring 1983): 1–14.

FIGLEWSKI, STEPHEN. "Hedging with Stock Index Futures," *Journal of Futures Markets* (Summer 1985): 183–99.

KAUFMAN, GEORGE G. "Measuring and Managing Interest Rate Risk," *Federal Reserve Bank of Chicago Economic Perspectives* (January/February 1984): 16–29.

KOPPENHAUER, G. D. "Futures Options and Their Use by Financial Intermediaries," *Federal Reserve Bank of Chicago Economic Perspectives* (January/February 1986): 18–30.

RITCHKEN, PETER. *Options: Theory, Strategy, and Applications* (Glenview, Ill.: Scott, Foresman and Company, 1987).

SCHWARZ, EDWARD W., HILL, JOANNE M., AND SCHNEEWIS, THOMAS. *Financial Futures: Fundamentals, Strategies, and Applications* (Homewood, Ill.: Irwin Publishing Company, 1986).

Appendix 9-A
The Black-Scholes Option Pricing Model

The Black-Scholes option pricing model[1] (OPM) was developed in an attempt to understand the pricing of stock options. The model does, moreover, have fairly general use, since a number of other items, such as a call feature on a bond, are essentially options.

On the last day before expiration, the value of a call option is simply the difference between the market price of the stock and the striking price (or zero if the striking price exceeds the market price). The value of the option on earlier dates depends on the probability distribution of its value on the last date before expiration. While most options expire without being exercised because the stock price never reached the striking price, it is the possibility of the stock price passing the strike price that gives them value. A three-month option to buy a stock for $10 above the current market price would be of little value if the stock never changed in price by more than $5 in a three-month period. On the other hand, the option would have value if the stock regularly exhibited price fluctuations of $30 in a three-month period. Thus, the value of the option depends on the variability of price for the security on which the option is written.

The Black-Scholes model quantified this relationship between variability of the underlying stock's price and value of the option in the following formula:

$$\text{Value of option} = PN(d_1) - \frac{S}{e^{rt}} N(d_2)$$

where
P = current market price of the stock
S = striking price of the option
e = base of the common logarithm: 2.71828
r = short-term interest rate, continuously compounded
t = time in years (or fraction of a year) until expiration of the option
$N(d_1)$ = a value from the table of the normal probability distribution (table B-1) representing the probability of the Z value being less than d_1

[1]Fisher Black and Myron Scholes, "The Pricing of Options and Corporate Liabilities," *Journal of Political Economy* 81 (May/June, 1973): 637–654.

$$d_1 = [\ln(P/S) + (r + 0.5\sigma^2)t]/(\sigma\sqrt{t})$$
$$d_2 = [\ln(P/S) + (r - 0.5\sigma^2)t]/(\sigma\sqrt{t})$$

ln = natural logarithm

σ = standard deviation of the annual rate of return on the underlying stock, continuously compounded.

An Example

A call option will expire in six months (0.50 years). The stock on which the option is written is presently selling for $100 a share, and the striking price is $110. The continously compounded annual interest rate is 12 percent. The standard deviation of the annual rate of return on the underlying stock, continuously compounded, is 0.20. The value of this option is therefore estimated as follows:

$$d_1 = [\ln(100/110) + (0.12 + 0.5\,0.2^2)0.50]/(0.20\sqrt{0.50}) = -0.179$$
$$d_2 = [\ln(100/110) + (0.12 - 0.5\,0.2)0.50]/(0.20\sqrt{0.50}) = -0.321$$
$$N(d_1) = 0.50 - 0.0710 = 0.429$$
$$N(d_2) = 0.50 - 0.1259 = 0.374$$
$$\text{Value of option} = 100 \cdot 0.429 - (110/e^{0.12 \cdot 0.50})0.374 = \$4.16.$$

A Note on Continuously Compounded Returns

The concept of continuously compounded expected return and standard deviation is often a source of unnecessary confusion. Continuous compounding in general was explained in chapter 6. If a six-month Treasury bill is selling at 95 percent of face value (recall that Treasury bills sell at discount rather than pay interest), the continuously compounded annual interest rate (r) is found as follows

$$\$95e^{0.5r} = \$100.00$$
$$e^{0.5r} = 100/95$$
$$\ln(e^{0.5r}) = \ln(100/95)$$
$$0.5r = \ln(100/95) = 0.05129$$
$$r = 2 \cdot 0.05129 = 0.10258$$

As an example of continuously compounded standard deviation, consider a stock selling for $100. There are two possible prices a year from now, as shown below:

Probability	Price	Continuously Compounded Return
.4	100.00	$r = \ln(100/100) = 0$
.6	149.1825	$r = \ln(149.1825/100)$ $= 0.40$

Expected continuously compounded return = $.4(0) + .6(0.4) = 0.24$. Standard deviation of continuously compounded return = $\sqrt{.4(0 - 0.24)^2 + .6(0.40 - 0.24)^2} = 0.196$.

PROBLEMS

9A-1.   For the example used in the text, the value of the option was $4.16. Suppose the price of the stock was $110 when the option was three months from expiration. What would be the value of the option at that time?

9A-2.   On 1 May 1984, IBM stock was selling for $116\frac{3}{8}$ a share. A five-month option at a striking price of $120 was selling for $5\frac{3}{4}$. The continuously compounded annual interest rate was 10.5%. If you felt the continuously compounded standard deviation of annual return for IBM was 25 percent, would you consider the option to be overpriced or underpriced?

10

Overview of Asset and Liability Management

In the 1970s, regulators began to realize that a financial institution without an asset-libability policy was like a group of oarsmen without a captain. The institution could end up on the shoals even though each department worked hard and did its job well. If the institution is to be profitable and safe, the efforts of individuals must be coordinated in pursuit of a common goal. Asset-liability management is that coordinating effort.

Asset-liability management refers to the institution's overall policy with regard to the mix of assets and liabilities. Asset-liability management is generally the responsibility of an asset-liability committee (ALCO) including senior officers such as the senior loan officer, senior investment officer, treasurer, and chief financial officer. The success of this policy is measured in terms of the level and stability of profitability.

For a brief overview of the scope of decisions that must be made in the development of asset-liability policy, consider a sample set of asset decisions that must be made:

Amount of funds to hold for required reserves
Amount of funds to hold for secondary reserves
Amount of funds to use for needed physical assets
Amount of funds to use for loans
Amount of each type of loan: consumer, commercial, real estate, etc.
Amount of assets at each maturity level and amount of variable-rate loans
Amount of international asset exposure
Amount of investments

Maturity of investments
Tax-free versus taxable investments
International exposure.

On the liability side managers must decide on the amount of funds to be raised through deposits and the amount to be raised through borrowed funds. In addition, management must decide on the types of deposits and borrowed funds to use. Included in these decisions are the relative maturities and currencies. As an example, management must decide if it will raise interest rates on long-term deposits with the goal of attracting more fixed-cost funds.

Financial institution managers have increasingly come to realize that the institution is a system in which all forms of assets, liabilities, and equity interact in determining profitability. For example, an institution with a substantial amount of long-term loans will probably decrease its risk by securing long-term deposits, while an institution with short-term assets will increase its risk by seeking long-term sources of funds. Asset-liability management is the attempt to recognize these interactions.

Managers must also recognize that not all asset and liability accounts are under policy control. For example, cash requirements may be determined by regulators rather than policy. Likewise, there may be limited markets for certain deposit maturities so that it is extremely difficult if not impossible to attract more funds of that type. A life insurance company will have most of its liabilities in the form of policy reserves, and a pension fund has little control over the nature of its liabilities. Equity is also determined by regulatory requirements in many cases, and the amount of equity affects the required amount of liabilities. Asset-liability management sets the amounts of these assets and liabilities within policy control, given the amounts in accounts not under direct control.

We begin this chapter with a brief overview of the general types of assets and liabilities held by financial institutions. Then we look at the general objectives used in asset-liability management. Interest rate and liquidity risk—two important aspects of asset-liability management—are treated in more detail in chapter 11, while capital adequacy is considered in chapter 12. Loan management is also discussed in a separate chapter because of the importance of this particular aspect of asset-liability management.

TYPES OF ASSETS

Assets of financial institutions vary by maturity, ranging from overnight loans in the federal funds market to long-term securities and fixed assets. They also differ according to whether they are personal instruments, such as most loans, or impersonal debt instruments, such as Treasury obligations and corporate bonds (table 10-1).

Various classes of assets are of differing importance to different types of financial institutions. The data in table 10-2 came largely from reports to the government agencies overseeing the institutions. Since each agency consolidates information in a different manner, comparability among types of institutions is somewhat limited. However, some general observations are possible. Note, for example, that commercial banks hold substantial cash, deposits, and government securities, while savings and

Table 10-1

Categories of Financial Institution Assets

	SHORT-TERM	LONG-TERM

Impersonal	U.S. government
	    Treasury notes
	    Agency notes
	State and local notes
	Commercial paper
	Negotiable certificates
	    of deposit
	Federal funds
	Banker's acceptances
		U.S. government
		    Treasury bonds
		    Agency bonds
		State and local government
		    General obligation
		    Revenue
		Corporation bonds
		Corporation equity

Personal	Commercial loans Consumer loans	Commercial loans Consumer loans Mortgages
Other	Cash and deposits	Physical plant

loan companies have a substantially smaller percent of their assets in these categories. Traditionally, savings and loan companies have maintained a less liquid asset structure because their deposits were less volatile than the sources of funds to commercial banks. Note also that equity holdings are low for all depository institutions. The unstable nature of equity security values largely precludes their use as assets for depository financial institutions.

TYPES OF LIABILITIES

For depository institutions, liabilities consist primarily of deposits and borrowed funds. In addition, the institution must maintain some equity capital, and a minimum amount of equity is generally specified by regulators. Insurance companies have policy reserves

Table 10-2

Asset and Liability Structures of Major Types of Financial Institutions

	COMMERCIAL BANKS	SAVINGS AND LOAN COMPANIES	MUTUAL SAVINGS BANKS	CREDIT UNIONS	LIFE INSURANCE COMPANIES
Cash	8.1%		1.9%		
Securities	19.6	14.4%	13.7		60.4%
Loans	67.2	81.2	78.6	56.6	27.4
Other	5.1	4.4	5.7		12.2
Deposits	74.7	75.1	78.4	92.3	0.0
Other liabilities	18.6	21.0	13.4		93.1
Equity	6.7	3.9	8.2		6.9
Total	100.0	100.0	100.0	100.0	100.0

as a major liability. Policy reserves are amounts that have been paid by the insured and which the company can expect to eventually pay out in the form of benefits to the insured.

Liabilities for the major financial institutions are shown in table 10-2. Note that deposits are the major source of funds for all depository institutions, although banks rely on borrowing more than thrift institutions do. Life insurance companies, on the other hand, rely primarily on policy reserves as their liabilities.

CONSIDERATIONS IN ASSET-LIABILITY MANAGEMENT

There are five primary objectives or areas of consideration in asset-liability management. These include profitability, liquidity, risk, flexibility, and regulatory requirements. This same set of considerations guides all businesses, but with different degrees of emphasis.

Profitability

While financial institutions are important to the economy and society, this should not cloud the fact that individual institutions are normally profit-seeking businesses. With certain exceptions, they are owned by stockholders who have invested in the firm with the expectation of earning a rate of return commensurate with the risk involved.[1] If the institution is to attract equity capital, it must earn a competitive rate of return. Thus, the mix of assets and liabilities must be such that the income earned on the assets exceeds the interest paid on liabilities by an amount sufficient to cover costs and generate satisfactory profits.

Liquidity

Liquidity—the ability to meet all legitimate demands for cash—is more important for financial institutions than for other firms. The public confidence that institutions must have to attract funds is closely related to their ability to meet legitimate demands for cash, such as deposit withdrawals and insurance claims. While liability sources, including lines of credit and the federal funds market, are frequently used to meet liquidity needs, the primary source continues to be assets that can be sold or converted to cash quickly. Institutions hold a certain amount of funds in cash or in short-term marketable assets to meet liquidity needs, and also maintain lines of credit to use when additional funds are needed.

---

[1] A frequently heard debate about the role of business in society can be avoided by differentiating between the goals and results of business activity. A financial institution can earn a profit only if it provides some service for which society is willing to pay. This service results from the financial institution's pursuit of its profitability objective. For example, the availability of credit to automobile buyers results from conclusions by banks and finance companies that they can profit from these loans.

Risk

Since most of a typical institution's obligations are fixed and the equity base is generally small, the institution must be concerned about the risk of shrinkage in the value of its assets. A level of asset value shrinkage that would cause little difficulty in another type of business can reduce the institution's capital to the point where further expansion must be curtailed. Thus the financial institution must pay very close attention to risk.

Flexibility

Flexibility is an important concept related to both risk and return. Flexibility is essentially the ability to respond to unexpected changes, either problems or opportunities for investment. Profitability can be enhanced and risk can be reduced by managing assets so as to provide flexibility.

Regulatory Requirements

Regulatory requirements are designed to encourage safety and liquidity, as well as to promote the accomplishment of public policy goals. Regulatory agencies accomplish these objectives in at least three ways:

1. By specifying the nature of the assets which may be held
2. By specifying certain general relationships among assets, liabilities, and equity capital
3. By encouraging investment in assets designed to promote goals of a public policy nature.

Regulatory requirements are part of the explanation for differences in asset and liability structure observed in table 10-2. If savings and loan companies are compared with mutual savings banks, the higher level of securities on the balance sheets of savings banks results from differences in regulations affecting the two types of institutions. Savings and loan companies were created for the purpose of making mortgage money available, while mutual savings banks were created as a service to savers. The differences in their balance sheets are much less substantive than in the past as a result of deregulation.

The regulatory environment has already been discussed in some detail in chapter 3. For the purpose of this chapter, regulatory considerations can be thought of as constraints that limit the institution's actions in pursuing its objectives.

PRINCIPLES OF ASSET AND LIABILITY STRUCTURE MANAGEMENT

Once the objectives to be pursued in asset-liability management are identified, the question of how to achieve these objectives must be faced. In this section, we will consider some methods of achieving specific objectives and methods of analyzing the asset and liability structure with regard to these objectives. In studying these methods, it must be kept in mind that pursuit of one objective almost always involves a trade-off in terms of some other objective. The appropriate trade-off is always a difficult policy problem for management.

Profitability

The profitability objective permeates asset-liability management. Management tools covered in chapters 4, 5, and 6 all have important use in the management of assets and liabilities so as to maximize profitability. In general, profitability is achieved by maximizing the spread between interest rate earned and interest rate paid. Of course, it is necessary to subtract from this spread operating costs and an allowance for bad debt losses.

Interest rate differences between assets available to a financial institution are affected by operating costs, risk, and maturity. In equilibrium, the interest rate differences would be just sufficient to compensate for these three factors, and there would be no opportunity to increase wealth through asset selection. Likewise, the differences between interest rates on various sources of funds would be accounted for by these same variables. For example, interest rates would be lower for deposits than for borrowed funds of the same maturity, but the difference would be accounted for entirely by the higher operating costs associated with deposits, so the effective cost would be the same in either case. In this perfect-market equilibrium, managers would not be able to improve profitability.

Fortunately for financial institution managers, the world is not perfect. In a dynamic marketplace, new asset and liability products are constantly being developed. Furthermore, some institutions develop specialties, allowing them to operate more efficiently than others in particular areas and giving them operating cost advantages. Consequently, there are opportunities to invest in assets and raise funds in ways that will increase shareholder wealth. Pension funds, which do not have stockholders, maximize wealth by efficiently assembling and investing large quantities of funds, primarily in securities.

If a life insurance company is to create wealth, it must design innovative policies and then sell and administer these policies efficiently. A life insurance company that minimizes its cost of funds in this way can profitably invest in securities which are traded in a highly efficient public market. (Insurance companies are increasingly seeking to further improve returns through direct lending as well.) Finance companies raise most of their money by selling securities in an efficient financial market; they must design innovative loan products and deliver these products efficiently. Depository institutions must raise deposit funds at favorable costs and make profitable direct loans if they are to create wealth.

EXAMPLE. Colonial Bank is considering a new consumer loan product. The loans will carry an interest rate of 15 percent, but the rate earned by Colonial Bank, after deducting operating expenses and allowance for bad debts, will be 11 percent. Colonial Bank can raise additional deposit funds at an interest rate of 9.5 percent, but operating costs associated with these deposits will bring the effective interest rate to 10.5 percent. Colonial is required to maintain equal to 5 percent of total assets, pays a tax rate of 34 percent, and must earn 15 percent return on equity to satisfy investors. The profitability analysis of the new loan follows. In studying this profitability analysis, note that Colonial will raise deposits of only $95 for each $100 of loans because it must have equity capital of $5 for each $100 of assets.

Income per $100 of loans, net of operating expense and allowance for bad debts	$11.00
Interest expense per $100 of loans, including operating costs to serve deposits (0.105×$95)	9.98
Earnings before tax	1.02
Tax	.35
Net income	$0.67
Return on equity (0.67 ÷ 5.00)	13.4%

The loan product does not meet Colonial's profitability requirements and will therefore decrease shareholder wealth.

Riding the yield curve is often an important part of profitability management for financial institutions. Assume that the loans in the previous Colonial Bank example have average maturities of five years and that the 10.5 percent effective interest cost to Colonial is for five-year certificates of deposit. The yield curve is upward-sloping at this time, and Colonial can sell six-month certificates at a cost 1 percent less than the cost of five-year deposits. As shown below, funding with six-month certificates nearly doubles the profitability of the loans.

Income per $100 of loans, net of operating expense and allowance for bad debts	$11.00
Interest expense per $100 of loans, including operating costs to serve deposits (0.095×$95)	9.03
Earnings before tax	1.97
Tax	.67
Net income	$1.30
Return on equity (1.30 ÷ 5.00)	26%

Taking advantage of the yield curve can dramatically improve profitability, as illustrated in the Colonial Bank example. Most depository financial institutions will take advantage of yield curve shapes, typically maintaining a shorter average maturity for liabilities than for assets. However, this strategy is not without risk. If the short-term interest rate later rises above 11 percent, including operating costs, Colonial will suffer a loss on these loans. Losses of this type drove many savings and loans into bankruptcy in the 1970s and 1980s. Management of interest rate risk exposure is a major part of asset-liability management and will be discussed in detail later.

In considering the profitability of this loan product, with the company riding the yield curve, it is important to note that most of the benefits of riding the yield curve can be had without investing in the particular loan product; the institution can borrow short-term and invest the proceeds in long-term securities. Asset-liability management involves an overall decision about the difference between asset and liability maturity the institution is willing to accept, and then a decision about which particular assets and liabilities to acquire within that overall policy. Loan profitability analysis is of particular importance and is therefore a major part of chapter 13.

Liquidity

Although profitability is the major objective, liquidity is an absolute requirement. A financial institution must stand ready to meet all legitimate demands for funds, such as withdrawal demands. Failure to meet these demands immediately would destroy confidence in the institution, and confidence is essential for the survival of a financial institution.

Assets are the traditional source of liquidity for financial institutions. In addition to loans and longer-term investments, financial institutions hold primary reserve assets and secondary reserve assets. Primary reserve assets are those necessary to meet regulatory requirements. For example, a typical depository institution is presently required to hold primary reserves equal to 12 percent of net transaction accounts and 3 percent of nonpersonal time deposits with maturities of less than 18 months. Primary reserves are held in cash and in Federal Reserve deposits. These reserves are not available for use by the institution because a reduction in primary reserves would place the institution in violation of regulations.

Secondary reserves are short-term interest-bearing assets that can be sold quickly. They include such items as Treasury bills, banker's acceptances, and federal funds. A traditional approach was to develop a specific ratio of secondary reserves to total assets as a policy of the institution. This was basically a *stock* approach in that the focus was on balance sheet ratios and a belief that past experience or judgment allowed managers to determine a ratio that would provide liquidity in the future.

In the 1970s, many financial institutions turned their attention from assets to liabilities as a source of liquidity. They increasingly used the federal funds market to arrange overnight loans for the amounts needed to satisfy reserve requirements and therefore reduced the amount of secondary reserves held. A problem with this approach was that when one institution is experiencing outflow pressures, it is likely that other institutions are feeling these same pressures, and it may be difficult or impossible to borrow the funds needed.

The current approach to liquidity management emphasizes *flows* more than stocks, and the institution is viewed as an integrated system. Assets and liabilities are categorized according to maturity, and guidelines are developed with regard to acceptable gaps in each maturity range. For example, an institution may decide that liabilities maturing in one month cannot be more than 120 percent of assets maturing within that same time frame. Similar rules are developed for other maturities, with the exact standard depending on a study of the past stability of various asset and liability categories, and their interactions.

Liquidity management techniques are treated in detail in chapter 11.

Risk

Because of the small proportion of equity in their capital structures, financial institutions are particularly sensitive to the possibility of asset value shrinkage. Both prudent management and regulatory requirements dictate that risk be held to a relatively low level. The recognition, management, and control of risk are important roles of management in all financial institutions: interest rate risk and credit or business risk.

Interest Rate Risk

Interest rate risk refers to the fact that fluctuating interest rates change both the revenue and expenses of financial institutions. As pointed out in the Colonial Bank example, rising interest rates can rapidly turn a profit into a loss. As another example of interest rate risk, the value of a perpetuity of $100 a year would be $2,000 at a required return of 5 percent but would decline to $1,000 if the required return rose to 10 percent. Thirty-year U.S. government bonds were issued in November 1972 with a coupon interest rate of approximately 5.4 percent. In January 1981, the market interest rate on such bonds was approximately 12 percent, and the market value of those bonds had declined to less than 50 percent of their original value. While the original or face value could still be realized by holding the bonds until maturity, anyone wishing to sell one in 1981 would receive less than half the original investment.

With increased inflation and the accompanying instability of interest rates, interest rate risk has become an increasingly serious problem for financial institutions. The problem is aggravated by the fact that the assets of a financial institution frequently have longer maturities than the sources of the institution's funds. Savings and loan companies that made twenty-five-year loans at 5 percent in the early 1960s found themselves paying over 5 percent on most of their deposits before these loans matured.

Interest rate risk is difficult to eliminate for many financial institutions. An important service of depository financial institutions has traditionally been the provision of immediate liquidity to savers, while ensuring borrowers of a longer-term source of credit (asset transmutation was the name given to this activity in chapter 1). Depository institutions have tried to deal with the problem by seeking longer-term deposits in recent years and have succeeded in increasing the average maturity of deposit funds. They have also worked to reduce the average maturities of their assets. For example, a savings and loan may decide to increase its efforts to market second mortgage loans and take advantage of the 1980 legislation to enter other shorter-term lending such as automobile loans. Another approach to minimizing interest rate risk is the variable-rate loan, a loan with an interest rate tied to some general indicators of interest rates. Tools for management of liquidity and interest rate risk are the major focus of chapter 11.

Credit or Business Risk

Credit or business risk is associated with potential variability of the stream of cash flows from the asset itself. For a debt instrument, credit risk is the risk that the borrower will not meet his obligations under the debt contract. For equity investments such as common stock, the holder faces the risk that the company may suffer from reduced profitability, resulting in a decline in the value of the investment.

Credit or business risk can be controlled by investing in less risky securities, such as U.S. government obligations. Unfortunately, risk-free securities may pay lower returns, and a complete portfolio of these would require that the institution essentially forgo its profit objective. Risk can be controlled while still allowing reasonable profits through the use of portfolio analysis.

Portfolio Analysis   The central theme of the portfolio concept is that the assets of the institution should be thought of as part of a unified whole, not as the sum of a group of individual entities. By proper management of the asset mix, it is possible to create a group of assets with a total risk less than the sum of the risks of the individual assets. While this concept has long been recognized, it has received particular attention in recent years.

An example serves to highlight both the potential and limitations of portfolio analysis in controlling risk. While 5 percent of the loans made by Friendly Finance Company are expected to default under normal conditions, the portfolio of loans is riskless with regard to these losses. The defaults on 5 percent of the loans are simply costs and are reflected in the interest rates charged. What first appears to be a group of risky loans can be combined in such a way that the particular risk is virtually eliminated. However, the portfolio is riskless only with regard to this normal level of losses. The company still faces the risk of the loss rate being higher than the anticipated 5 percent. This can occur because of a recession or other economic problem resulting in higher unemployment among the borrowers. Thus although the risk related to individual securities can be eliminated through construction of a portfolio, certain overall risks remain. We refer to the risk that can be overcome through the use of portfolio approaches as *diversifiable* risk, and that which cannot be eliminated in this manner as *nondiversifiable* risk.

To further illustrate the essential nondiversifiability of certain risks, consider Friendly Finance Company again. While it is possible for Friendly to invest in assets other than consumer loans, many of the same nondiversifiable risks remain. High default rates occur during periods of economic downturn. At the same time, stock prices normally decline and other types of investments are subject to increased defaults. Consequently, further diversification is likely to be unsuccessful in eliminating all risk. Nondiversifiable risk can be eliminated only by movement to low-return, risk-free securities.

The recognition of diversifiable and nondiversifiable risk can be formal or informal. With the informal approach, we begin by identifying the types of risk involved and determining which are and are not diversifiable. The diversifiable risks must be estimated as carefully as possible so that they can be accurately treated as a cost factor. The degree of nondiversifiable risk can be measured by studying past patterns, if historical data are available, or by estimating the impacts of various conditions.

EXAMPLE.   A consumer finance company makes two general types of loans: loans secured by the item being purchased, such as installment loans for appliance purchases, and unsecured loans for purposes such as medical expenses and bill consolidation. The company has one-half of its funds in each category. Under normal conditions, default rates for secured loans average 4 percent, while default rates for unsecured loans average 6 percent. Normal conditions include a 5 percent unemployment rate. As the primary nondiversifiable risk is associated with unemployment, the default

Table 10-3

Default Rates of Various Levels of Unemployment

Unemployment Rate	DEFAULT RATE		
	Secured	Unsecured	Average
5%	4.00%	6.00%	5.00%
6	4.50	6.60	5.55
7	5.00	7.30	6.15
8	5.60	8.10	6.85
9	6.30	8.90	7.60

rates experienced for each type of loan during past unemployment periods are shown in table 10-3.

The company is considering a change in its mix of loan types. Obviously, average default rates at each unemployment rate depend on the mix of loans. For example, with 30 percent of the funds in secured loans and 70 percent in unsecured loans, the default rate at an 8 percent unemployment rate would be

$$0.30(5.6\%) + 0.70(8.1\%) = 7.35\%.$$

Expected average default rates for a range of unemployment rates and various loan portfolios are shown in table 10-4.

The information contained in table 10-4 does not tell the finance company what mixture of secured and unsecured loans would be optimal. However, it does provide a concise summary of the risks associated with each combination. Using the informal approach, the risks for each combination are judgmentally compared to the expected returns in choosing a preferred loan portfolio mix. Loan and security portfolios can be considered in unison using the same approach. Adjustment of the required return for nondiversifiable risk is covered in chapter 12.

Table 10-4

Average Default Rates for Alternative Loan Portfolio Mixes

Unemployment Rate	PROPORTION OF FUNDS IN SECURED LOANS				
	0.3	0.4	0.5	0.6	0.7
5%	5.40%	5.20%	5.00%	4.80%	4.60%
6	5.97	5.76	5.55	5.34	5.13
7	6.61	6.38	6.15	5.92	5.69
8	7.35	7.10	6.85	6.60	6.35
9	8.12	7.86	7.60	7.34	7.08

FLEXIBILITY

Flexibility is the ability to respond to changing conditions. Because of the inherent unpredictability of events, the ability to respond to unanticipated changes in business and economic conditions is an important ingredient of good asset management. A change in a tax law that makes second mortgages attractive is an example of a situation in which planning for flexibility would be rewarded. Such a situation presents the institution with the opportunity to make highly profitable loans and to gain new customers if funds are available to lend. A necessary level of flexibility can be attained through proper management of assets and liabilities. In general, flexibility in asset management is achieved through management of the maturity structure of securities and loans and through the holding of marketable assets.

In general, shorter security and loan maturities result in greater flexibility because the institution can make new investment decisions at more frequent intervals. However, this flexibility does not come without cost. Shorter-term loans and securities frequently carry lower interest rates. Furthermore, some institutions face only a limited demand for short-term credit. A savings and loan company, for example, has traditionally had little choice other than to hold a substantial portion of its assets in the form of long-term mortgages.

Having a portfolio with staggered maturities—one with certain proportions of loans and other securities maturing each period on a planned basis—is one method of gaining flexibility without forgoing longer-term, higher-yielding assets. Properly distributed maturities ensure a continued flow of cash to be used in making new loans or investments.

Finally, the existence of marketable securities and loans within the total portfolio increases flexibility while allowing investment in longer-term assets. Long-term securities can be sold in the open market if the institution faces a need for funds or if a particularly attractive opportunity for investment becomes available. The existence of interest rate risk and the associated risk of loss in the market value of securities, however, frequently precludes the conversion of this type of asset to cash.

BEYOND ASSET-LIABILITY MANAGEMENT

Making and financing loans has been the traditional work of financial institutions. However, lending is not a single activity but a series of activities, as outlined below.

> *Loan origination:* solicitation, evaluation of applications, completion of the various loan documents required, and provision of money to the customer.
>
> *Loan warehousing:* holding (owning) the loan during its life and receiving payments. The warehouser is the actual provider of money for most of the life of the loan.
>
> *Loan servicing:* processing payments as they are made and providing a collection effort when loan customers become delinquent.

With deregulation, financial institution managers are forced to focus on what they do best. For example, one financial institution, possibly a savings and loan, solicits mortgage loan applications, completes the necessary paperwork so that the mortgages qualify for government guarantees, and grants the loan, thereby furnishing money to the borrower. Qualification for government guarantees standardizes the loans and removes default risk. The originator then combines this loan with other loans in a package, along with a contract to provide servicing for a specified fee, and sells them to other investors such as insurance companies and pension funds. The originator may keep the servicing contract or sell it to someone else. The originator makes money from the origination and application fees, as well as from servicing fees or sale of the servicing contract. The buyer (who is the "warehouser" in the jargon of the trade) holds an asset that will generate a stream of principal and interest payments without any servicing efforts.

Depository financial institutions are particularly well suited for loan origination, and some have specialized in loan servicing. However, depository institutions have a disadvantage in warehousing unless they can fund the loans with long-term deposits. This is because depository institutions must satisfy capital adequacy requirements which can raise their effective cost of funds above those of nondepository competitors. In particular, it is argued that foreign banks have costs of funds below those of U.S. banks because many foreign banks are subject to less strict reserve and capital requirements.

Specialization within the lending process is not a new idea. Credit agencies have focused only on the collection of information about the applicant, and collection agencies have focused only on the collection effort for substantially delinquent customers. Mortgage bankers have focused on origination and/or servicing of mortgage loans. The recent change is in the volume of such activity. More institutions are involved, and the range of loans involved has increased substantially. Commercial loans, automobile paper, and credit card balances have all been *securitized,* which is the term used by financial institutions to describe the packaging of loans in a portfolio and the selling of securities which are shares in that portfolio.

Securitization gives the institution a broader range of choices than would otherwise be the case with asset-liability management. For example, an institution that rejects additional fixed-rate mortgages because of the interest rate risk involved may still profit by originating and servicing these mortgages while selling the mortgages themselves to institutions such as pension funds that are capable of accepting long-term fixed interest rate obligations.

As another example of how securitization has developed, large banks often securitize parts of their commercial loan portfolios, thereby selling them to foreign banks and smaller commercial banks. The foreign banks have lower costs of funds, while the smaller banks benefit from diversification. Many small banks in farming communities have gone bankrupt because a high percent of their loans were made to farms in a particular geographic area. Participation in commercial loans to major national companies diversifies the portfolios of these small banks, reduces their risks, and ensures continuation of banking services in their service areas.

SUMMARY

In this chapter we identified the primary types of assets and liabilities held by financial institutions. The assets consist primarily of financial obligations of others. They can be classified according to whether they are personal or impersonal and whether they are short-term or long-term. We also noted that the mixture of assets varies by type of institution, depending on institutional objectives, liability structure, and regulatory requirements. The primary types of liabilities are deposits and borrowed funds. The primary considerations in asset-liability management are

> *Profitability:* Most financial institutions are private, profit-seeking enterprises.
>
> *Liquidity:* The ability to meet all obligations on schedule and to meet withdrawal requests immediately is very important for financial institutions. Both regulatory requirements and the need to maintain public confidence make adequate liquidity imperative.
>
> *Risk:* Loss in income or asset value is particularly damaging to financial institutions because of their low ratio of equity to total assets. Risk can be recognized through informal methods or through statistical portfolio analysis techniques.
>
> *Flexibility:* Flexibility is the ability to respond to unanticipated changes in the form of either problems or opportunities. It is achieved primarily through management of maturity structure, marketability of assets, and maturity structure of liabilities.
>
> *Regulatory Requirements:* Regulatory requirements are designed to control risk and ensure that the institution provides the service for which it was created.

In recent years, financial institutions have increasingly moved beyond asset-liability management to concentrate on the area in which they have a competitive advantage: origination, warehousing, or servicing.

QUESTIONS

10-1.   Why is the percentage of commercial bank assets held in the form of cash items substantially higher than the percentage of thrift institution assets held in this form?

10-2.   The Financial Institution Deregulation and Monetary Control Act of 1980 instructed the regulatory authorities to move toward equal cash reserve requirements for commercial banks and thrift institutions. Why would it be deemed appropriate for banks and thrift institutions to move toward similar liquid asset percentages?

10-3.   Do required reserves provide a source of liquidity to a financial institution? Why?

10-4.   Why is it so difficult for thrift institutions to eliminate interest rate risk?

10-5.   For a life insurance company, list as many types of risk as you can think of. Categorize these risks as to whether they are diversifiable or nondiversifiable.

10-6.   By studying the current news, find an example of a financial institution that has profited from maintaining flexibility or has suffered losses as a result of the absence of flexibility.

PROBLEMS

10-1.   A new consumer loan product will generate interest income of 18 percent before deducting operating costs of 6 percent of loan balances. The finance company offering this product cannot accept deposits and raises money by selling intermediate-term bonds. The interest rate on these bonds is currently 10 percent. The company must maintain equity equal to 10 percent of total assets in order to maintain its credit rating. If the company faces a 34 percent tax rate and the required return on equity is 20 percent, is this loan product profitable?

10-2.   For the consumer finance company in problem 10-1, commercial paper is currently yielding 9 percent and the company could finance its assets with commercial paper rather than intermediate-term loans. Would the loan product be profitable if financed with commercial paper?

10-3.   Suppose the consumer finance company in problems 10-1 and 10-2 simply got out of the loan business and sold commercial paper for the purpose of investing in intermediate-term bonds. This would be a less risky business, and the company would need equity equal to only 3 percent of assets. Would this be a more profitable business than making loans? Given this analysis, what course of action do you recommend for the company?

10-4.   Old Fidelity Savings can sell six-month certificates of deposit with an interest rate of 7 percent and operating costs of 0.7 percent of deposits. The company can sell three-year certificates of deposit with an interest rate of 8 percent and operating costs of 0.3 percent. A loan product with a three-year life carries an interest rate of 14 percent, and operating costs are 4.5 percent of loan balances each year. Old Fidelity has a tax rate of 34 percent and a required return on equity of 15 percent. Old Fidelity maintains equity equal to 6 percent of assets. Is this loan product profitable?

10-5.   Suppose Old Fidelity (problem 10-4) uses six-month certificates as its source of financing. Assume that the interest rate on these certificates then rises from 7 percent to 8.5 percent because of a general increase in interest rates. What is the return on equity after the increase in interest rates?

10-6.   New Idea Credit Corporation can sell thirty-day commercial paper at 8 percent or intermediate-term bonds at 10 percent. Loans will provide a return of 11 percent after deducting operating costs. New Idea faces a 34 percent tax rate and maintains equity equal to 8 percent of total assets. Management recognizes that interest rates could rise and wants to finance assets in such a way that it will earn at least a 5 percent return on equity even if short-term rates rise to 12 percent. What mix of long- and short-term debt will achieve this result? What is the return on equity with this mix? (This problem can be solved with algebra or with a Lotus 1-2-3 sensitivity table.)

10-7.   A thirty-year zero coupon U.S. government bond carries an annual compound interest rate of about 10 percent in the current market. Suppose the required interest rate for this type of security rises to 12 percent. What is the percentage decline in the value of one of these bonds?

10-8. Thirty-year mortgages with equal monthly payments carry an interest rate of 10 percent. Suppose interest rates rise to 12 percent. What is the percentage decrease in the value of one of these mortgages?

10-9. Erstwhile Corporation has equity equal to 5 percent of assets. One-half of the company's assets are unaffected by changes in interest rates. The remaining assets are the mortgages described in problem 10-8. Starting from an interest rate of 10 percent, what increase in interest rates would cause the value of the assets to decline enough to wipe out Erstwhile's equity?

10-10. West End Savings and Loan has equity equal to 6 percent of total assets. One-half of the institution's deposits are short-term, with an average interest rate $\frac{1}{2}$ percent below the Treasury bill rate. The other half of the deposits are long-term and have an average interest rate of 8 percent. The institution has no other liabilities. Fixed-rate mortgages carry an interest rate of 10 percent at present, while variable-rate mortgages carry an interest rate 2 percent above the Treasury bill rate; West End has no other assets. West End has operating costs and bad debt losses totaling 2.5 percent of total assets. The Treasury bill rate is presently 6 percent, and West End wants to be sure of breaking even if the Treasury bill rate goes as high as 12 percent. What is the highest proportion of fixed-rate mortgage loans West End can have, given this restriction? With a 34 percent tax rate, what is the return on equity with this mix?

10-11. Metro Financial can make secured and unsecured loans. The secured loans carry an interest rate of 11 percent after all operating expenses except bad debt loss. The unsecured loans carry an interest rate of 13 percent after all operating expenses except bad debt loss. Bad debt losses depend on the unemployment rate, as shown below. Metro has equity equal to 8 percent of capital and can borrow funds at 9 percent. The expected unemployment rate is 6 percent. What mix of assets would ensure a return on equity no worse than -1 percent even if unemployment went to 10 percent?

Unemployment rate	4%	5%	6%	7%	8%	9%	10%
Secured loss rate	0.003	0.004	0.005	0.007	0.009	0.011	0.014
Unsecured loss rate	0.010	0.014	0.019	0.025	0.032	0.040	0.050

10-12. Citicorp's annual returns on assets in domestic and foreign markets are shown below. Do you see evidence of diversification benefits from foreign investment?

YEAR	1986	1985	1984
North America	0.56%	0.54%	0.52%
Caribbean and Latin America	1.35	1.28	0.94
Europe, Middle East, and Africa	0.24	0.56	0.67
Asia/Pacific	0.59	0.45	0.62
Total	0.57	0.62	0.62

SELECTED REFERENCES

BINDER, BARRETT F., AND THOMAS W. F. LINDQUIST. *Asset/ Liability and Funds Management at U.S. Commercial Banks* (Rolling Meadows; Ill.: Bank Administration Institute, 1982).

BOOTH, G. GEOFFREY, AND PETER E. KOVEOS. "A Programming Model for Bank Hedging Decisions," *Journal of Financial Research* 9 (Fall 1986): 271–279.

EISENBEIS, ROBERT A., HARRIS, ROBERT S., AND LAKONI-SHOK, JOSEF. "Benefits of Bank Diversification: The Evidence from Shareholder Returns," *Journal of Finance* 39 (July 1984): 881–894.

"Everything You Ever Wanted to Know about A/L Management. . .and Weren't Afraid to Ask," *ABA Banking Journal* (October 1986): 68–70.

GUREL, EITAN, AND PYLE, DAVID. "Bank Income Taxes and Interest Rate Risk Management," *Journal of Finance* 39 (September 1984): 1199–1206.

HASLAM, JOHN A. *Bank Fund Management* (Englewood Cliffs, N.J.: Prentice-Hall, 1984).

HERRING, RICHARD J., AND VANKUDRE, PRASHANT. "Growth Opportunities and Risk-Taking by Financial Intermediaries," *Journal of Finance* 42 (July 1987): 583–599.

KAUFMAN, GEORGE G. "Measuring and Managing Interest Rate Risk: A Primer," *Economic Perspectives* 8 (January/February 1984): 16–29.

MCCORMICK, JAMES M. "The Role of Securitization in Transforming Banks Into More Efficient Financial Intermediaries," *Midland Corporate Finance Journal* 5 (Fall 1987): 50–61.

ROSE, STANFORD. "Rethinking Securitization," *Midland Corporate Finance Journal* 5 (Fall 1987): 62–63.

ROSE, STANFORD. "Extending the Loan-Sales Revolution," *Midland Corporate Finance Journal* 5 (Fall 1987): 64–66.

STIGUM, MARCIA L., AND BRANCH, RENE O. JR. *Managing Bank Assets and Liabilities* (Homewood, Ill.: Dow Jones-Irwin, 1983).

Appendix 10-A
The Mean-Variance Portfolio Model

The mean-variance portfolio model is a formal method of recognizing risk in the construction of asset portfolios. It is discussed briefly here but is presented in more detail in many investments texts.[1]

The mean-variance approach is based on the assumption that investors will choose an investment portfolio with the objective of maximizing expected return and minimizing risk, measured as the variance of the probability distribution of expected returns.[2] The particular combination of risk and expected return chosen depends on the individual's attitude toward risk. However, everyone will be expected to choose a portfolio that provides the lowest variance for its level of expected return. Thus the

---

[1] See, for example, Jack Clark Francis, *Investment Analysis and Management*, 3d ed. (New York: McGraw-Hill, 1980).

[2] The variance (σ^2) is a measure of dispersion. Thus a greater variance indicates a greater range of possible outcomes. Specifically, the variance is computed as follows:

$$\sigma_p^2 = \sum_{i=1}^{m} X_i (R_{pi} - E_p)^2$$

where
σ_p^2 = variance of the portfolio
X_i = probability of condition i occurring
R_{pi} = return for the portfolio if condition i occurs
E_p = expected return for the portfolio
m = number of possible outcomes.

objective of mean-variance portfolio analysis is the identification of the lowest variance portfolio for each possible expected return.

The expected return for a portfolio can be stated as a weighted average of the expected returns for individual assets:

$$E_p = \sum_{i=1}^{n} P_i E_i$$

(10A-1)

where E_p = expected return for the portfolio
P_j = proportion of funds invested in asset j
E_j = expected return for asset j
n = number of assets in the portfolio.

The computation of the variance for the portfolio is complex. It depends on the covariance, a measure of the degree to which the returns for two assets move together. The covariance between two securities is a measure of the tendency for their returns to be similarly affected by changes in the environment. The formula for the covariance is

$$\sigma_{jk} = \sum_{h=1}^{m} X_h (R_{jh} - E_j)(R_{kh} - E_h)$$

(10A-2)

where m = number of different conditions that may occur in the environment
X_h = probability of condition h occurring
R_{jh} = expected return on security j if condition h occurs
R_{kh} = expected return on security k if condition h occurs.

The variance for a portfolio is a function of these covariance terms:

$$\sigma_p^2 = \sum_{j=1}^{n} \sum_{k=1}^{n} P_j P_k \sigma_{jk}.$$

(10A-3)

Equations 10A-1 and 10A-3 are then the two key equations used in the mean-variance portfolio model. For each possible expected return, we wish to identify the portfolio that minimizes variance. The set of such portfolios is what we identified as the *efficient frontier* in appendix 8-A. The institution can then choose from among these combinations of risk and return to select the trade-off between risk and return it feels is most desirable.[3]

We need not concern ourselves with the question of how to actually find the various combinations of expected return and risk that are on the efficient frontier.

[3]A significant body of finance theory would argue that the optimum portfolio is one that maximizes the ratio:

$$(E_p - r_f) \div \sigma_p$$

where r_f = risk-free interest rate, such as that available on Treasury bills
σ_p = standard deviation, the square root of the variance.

Computer programs are readily available for this purpose, given the set of expected returns and covariances for the assets.

The main problem in using this method is the set of inputs required. For each asset, the variance and the covariance with each other asset must be computed. For 5 assets, there are 15 covariance terms required, and for 20 assets, 210 covariance terms are required. To consider 1,000 assets we would require 500,500 covariance terms! Thus the number of covariance terms that must be estimated becomes quite large if more than a few assets are being used.

One way to overcome the large number of covariance terms needed is to use beta as a risk measure. In doing this, we assume that diversifiable risk will be eliminated by a large number of assets without any attention required. If this assumption is valid, the variance of a portfolio can be computed as follows:

$$\sigma_p^2 = \sigma_m^2 \left[\sum_{j=1}^{m} P_j B_j \right]^2$$

(10A-4)

where σ_m^2 = variance of probability distribution of expected returns for a portfolio consisting of all available securities; variance of returns for an index of stock market returns is normally used as this measure

B_j = beta for investment j.

Using this approach, the large number of covariance terms can be replaced with one beta for each asset. This approach is applicable when a large number of assets is being considered, such as in a portfolio of bonds and common stock. Again, computer programs are readily available for the purpose of identifying the set of efficient frontier portfolios if the expected return and beta for each asset have been computed.

11

Liquidity and Interest Rate Risk Management

Liquidity, the ability to meet all legitimate demands for funds, is absolutely essential to the survival of a financial institution. A savings bank that cannot meet withdrawal demands, for example, will lose the trust of its customers, and a financial institution cannot survive without trust. Most financial institutions give a high enough priority to liquidity management and manage their liquidity well enough so that actual liquidity failures are rare. Financial institutions have been less successful in managing interest rate risk though. Rising interest rates and bad loans are leading causes of financial institution failure.

We treat liquidity, interest rate risk, and loan decisions in some detail because of their importance to financial institutions. Loan decisions are treated as a separate chapter, but liquidity and interest rate risk are treated in one chapter because they are intertwined. Changes that affect liquidity risk often affect interest rate risk, and vice versa.

LIQUIDITY MANAGEMENT

To begin, it is helpful to expand on our simple definition of liquidity. Liquidity was defined as the ability to meet all legitimate demands for funds, but what is a legitimate demand, how fast must a legitimate demand be met, and what is a reasonable cost for meeting liquidity demands? In the case of a customer demanding a cash withdrawal, instantaneous availability in virtually all instances is the standard. Beyond withdrawal demand, loan demand is viewed as a legitimate demand for funds. Many institutions develop long-term relationships with their customers by meeting these customers' credit needs. A credit union that cannot grant a creditworthy member an automobile loan because it has no money available will most likely lose that member. The consequences of failure to meet loan demand are not as serious as the consequences of failure to meet withdrawal demand, but the long-term damage is still significant.

Liquidity is not an absolute concept, but a concept of time and cost. Almost all of a financial institution's assets eventually mature and are converted to cash. This conversion to cash can be speeded up by selling assets, and virtually all assets can be sold at some price. The loss on a sale depends on which asset was being sold and how quickly it is necessary to complete the sale. Alternately, an institution can usually borrow funds temporarily to meet liquidity demands, but the interest rate may be extremely high at times when other institutions are also experiencing strong liquidity demands. Thus, time and cost are intertwined in liquidity planning.

The cost of too little liquidity is the cost of borrowing, the loss experienced when selling assets quickly, or the damage done by failure to meet a legitimate demand for funds. The cost of excess liquidity is lost profitability. Assets held in highly liquid form typically earn low rates of interest, or no interest at all. Financial institution managers attempt to balance the cost of excess liquidity against the costs and damage associated with failure to provide for adequate liquidity.

Reserve Requirements and Liquidity Management

In order to evaluate liquidity requirements, it is necessary to differentiate between primary and secondary reserve assets. All depository and some nondepository financial institutions are required to maintain some minimum amount of liquid reserves. These reserves, called primary reserves, are generally held in the form of vault cash or deposits with Federal Reserve banks. For example, vault cash plus Federal Reserve deposits must be at least 12 percent of most transactions account balances.

Required primary reserves are the minimum level that must be maintained. The use of any of these reserves to meet demands for funds would take the institution below minimum levels and would bring a quick response from the regulatory authorities. However, primary reserve requirements are met through the maintenance of an average daily level of reserves over a two-week period. Therefore, primary reserves serve only as a very temporary means of meeting liquidity needs. Any use of these reserves must be offset by a higher level of reserves on other days. Primary reserves are more important as a liquidity cushion for the banking system than for an individual financial institution.

Liquidity needs can be met by the sale of certain assets, referred to as *secondary reserves*. Secondary reserve assets, which include Treasury bills, banker's acceptances, and federal funds, can be converted back to cash quickly with little or no loss in value. Financial institutions buy and sell these securities on a daily basis to meet their liquidity needs and primary reserve requirements.

Ways to Meet Liquidity Needs

A financial institution has a number of sources available for meeting its liquidity needs. *New deposits* are an ongoing source of liquidity. Withdrawals may be largely offset by new deposits, and new deposits can fund a part of new loan demand at a growing institution. *Maturing assets* are another important source. Loans are continually being paid off, and securities are continually maturing. These funds are available to reinvest or meet withdrawal demand. *Sale of assets* can become part of the plan when new deposits and maturing assets are not sufficient to meet liquidity demands. As previously discussed, secondary reserve assets are held specifically for this purpose, and almost any asset can be sold if the institution is willing to accept a large enough loss.

Borrowed funds have taken on increased importance in liquidity management, particularly for larger financial institutions. The federal funds market is the primary playing field for this activity; Federal Reserve bank deposits are borrowed on an overnight basis to increase average deposits for the two-week reporting period. Items considered primary reserves can then be used to actually meet daily demands for funds. Over the week, the institution borrows sufficient overnight deposits in the federal funds market to replenish its primary reserves and generate the necessary average balance of primary reserves for the two-week reporting period. Larger institutions usually borrow from smaller institutions. These smaller institutions often have less loan demand and therefore have excess liquid funds on which they are eager to earn interest.

A problem with reliance on borrowing is that liquidity pressures can grow throughout the financial system, particularly if the Federal Reserve acts to decrease the money supply. Overnight loans can become extremely scarce, and the rate can become extremely high. Institutions accept increased risk when they place excessive reliance on borrowed funds as a source of liquidity.

A final source of liquidity is borrowing from the Federal Reserve System, commonly referred to as using the *discount window*. It is understood that the discount window is not to be used as a regular source of funds but only as a source to be used infrequently to meet unanticipated liquidity demands. Excess use of this source will bring pressure from regulators.

Comprehensive Liquidity Management   Liquidity management is an integrated activity. It begins with maintenance of a sound capital position so that the financial institution can borrow money if necessary. The next step is management of the maturity structure of assets and liabilities so that the anticipated inflows correspond with anticipated outflows. Thus, management of the loan portfolio is intertwined with liquidity management. On a week-to-week basis, liquidity management is a response to the fact that cash flows cannot be predicted with complete certainty. Secondary reserve assets are bought or sold on a daily basis, and the institution borrows or lends in the federal funds market on a daily basis to meet its primary reserve requirements for the reporting period without holding excess idle funds. Liquidity measures are critical in planning these liquidity management activities.

Liquidity Measurement

Liquidity can be viewed from either a *stock* or a *flow* perspective. Stock views of liquidity focus on certain key ratios, such as

Loans ÷ total assets
Loans ÷ total deposits
Purchased liabilities ÷ total assets
Investment securities maturing in one year or less ÷ total assets

$$\frac{\text{Cash} - \text{required reserves} + \text{U.S. government securities}}{\text{Total assets}}$$

High levels of loans and high levels of purchased (borrowed) liabilities are viewed as indicators of an illiquid position, while high levels of cash, U.S. government securities, and securities maturing in one year or less are viewed as signs of a liquid position.

The problem with these stock ratios is that they do not really get at the dynamic nature of liquidity management. Cash inflows and outflows over a period are the actual determinants of liquidity. Stock ratios are only indicators of possible flows or resources for dealing with unexpected flows. A flow approach requires more effort but provides better insights.

Flow Approaches to Liquidity Measurement

A flow approach involves looking at liquidity reserves as a reservoir. The inflow may not equal the outflow on any particular day, and the reservoir serves to offset temporary differences between inflow and outflow. As with a water reservoir, the liquidity reserve cannot offset a permanent imbalance. It can only offset temporary imbalances.

If the flow approach is used, the variabilities of inflow and outflow are studied to determine the amount of liquid reserves that may be needed. The flow approach is similar to approaches used in inventory management, and inventory models have been applied successfully to liquid reserve problems. An approach to the problem has been illustrated in figure 11-1 which shows the cumulative value of net cash flows (cash

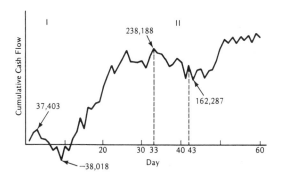

Figure 11-1: Cumulative cash flows.

inflows minus outflows) over time for a particular savings and loan. There are some periods of time during which cumulative net cash flows decline. These are periods of net cash outflows. Liquid reserves must be held or credit sources must be arranged to meet demands for funds during these periods of negative cash flow, or the institution must have some liability source it can call on at such times. For this institution, we see that the largest decline occurred between Day 33 and Day 43, when cumulative cash flows declined by $76,000. Thus a secondary reserve of $76,000 would have been sufficient to meet demand during the period examined. While the study of data for only two months would not be sufficient for determination of liquidity needs, the method can serve as a useful guide if flows are examined over a sufficiently long time period.

A further refinement is to break down the outflow during the negative flow periods into voluntary and involuntary outflows. An involuntary demand is something like a deposit withdrawal which must be met. A voluntary demand, such as a request for a loan, is one that can be avoided if funds are not available. Cumulative net cash flows, including new loans, are contrasted with cumulative net cash flows excluding new loans for the two periods of greatest cash outflow in figure 11-2. During Period 1 increased loan demand was being met from excess liquid funds. This time period contained no threat to liquidity (figure 11-2). However, Period 2 was a period of decreasing deposits. It represented the major test of the institution's liquidity over this time period. Secondary reserves of $53,000 would have been required to meet this demand.

Liquidity Gap Analysis

Liquidity gap analysis is a useful tool that captures some of the benefits of both stock and flow concepts of measurement. Liquidity gaps are reasonably easy to measure and serve as effective tools for management as well as measurement of liquidity. The gap at any particular level of maturity is the difference between maturing assets and maturing liabilities. This is illustrated for Reliable Financial Corporation in table 11-1.

A positive gap indicates that maturing assets exceed maturing liabilities, and vice versa. We note, then, that maturing overnight liabilities exceed maturing overnight assets by $10 million. This means that at least $10 million of new overnight liabilities

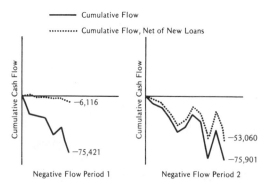

Figure 11-2: Cumulative flow for major negative cash flow periods.

Table 11-1

Liquidity Gap Illustration for Reliable Financial Corporation
(in $ millions)

MATURITY	ASSETS	LIABILITIES	GAP	CUMULATIVE GAP
Overnight	10	20	(10)	(10)
1–30 days	15	20	(5)	(15)
31–90 days	20	25	(5)	(20)
90–180 days	20	15	5	(15)
180–365 days	10	10	0	(15)
1–5 years	15	5	10	(5)
Over 5 years*	10	5	5	0

*Including equity.

must be arranged tomorrow to meet liquidity demands. From the cumulative gap, we note that liabilities maturing over the next 90 days exceed maturing assets by $20 million. Out of $65 million of liabilities maturing over that period, $20 million must be replaced with new liabilities unless the institution is to meet its liquidity needs in some other way, such as through the sale of assets. The cumulative gap will always end at $0, because assets equal liabilities and equity.

Financial institutions do not attempt to maintain $0 gaps in all maturities. After all, provision of liquidity is an important part of their function, and they earn profits by providing that liquidity. The objective is to determine acceptable gaps. An acceptable gap depends on the institutions's ability to sell assets, on the necessity for replacing maturing assets, and on anticipated ability to replace maturing liabilities. Since deposits are a major source of liabilities, the flow analysis methods previously discussed can be used to develop an acceptable gap and cumulative gap level for each maturity. There is, unfortunately, not an absolute formula for the correct gap, as this involves trade-offs between risk and return. Nevertheless, gap analysis has proved to be an extremely useful tool for developing, implementing, and monitoring liquidity policies.

INTEREST RATE RISK MANAGEMENT

Financial institutions almost always accept some interest rate risk. This is unavoidable because part of their function is to make loans for periods which exceed the average maturities of their liabilities. Therefore, most financial institutions suffer losses in profits or asset values when the general level of interest rates rises. The goal is to control interest rate risk to an acceptable level.

Savings and loans provide an example of what happens when financial institutions accept excessive interest rate risk. At a time when the cost of short-term funds was about 3 percent and the cost of long-term funds was about 5 percent, savings and loans committed the bulk of their assets to twenty-year fixed-rate mortgage loans with interest rates in the neighborhood of 6 percent. The savings and loans financed these loans with short-term funds, and a 3 percent spread between the interest rate received and the interest rate paid provided for a very comfortable profit margin. Then interest rates rose so that the savings and loans had to pay an average interest rate well above the rates they were earning on their loans. The institutions lost such large amounts of money that many of them went bankrupt. Banks also suffered losses, but the problems were not as severe because long-term loans were a smaller proportion of their total assets.

To deal with interest rate risk, it is first necessary to measure the extent of exposure. We begin with a discussion of how to measure interest rate risk and then look at ways to decrease it.

Measuring Interest Rate Risk

The three most common ways to measure interest rate risk exposure are interest rate gap analysis, duration analysis, and simulation. These techniques are discussed in the following sections.

Interest Rate Gap Analysis.   Interest rate gap analysis is similar to liquidity gap analysis, except that we are interested in time until maturity or repricing, whichever comes first, instead of time until maturity. Take Reliable Financial Corporation (table 11-1), for example; $4 million of assets in the one-to-five-years category and $4 million of the assets in the over-five-years category are variable-rate mortgages. One-fourth of these loans will be repriced at the end of each ninety-day period throughout the year. Therefore, the interest rate gap analysis is as shown in table 11-2.

As shown in table 11-2, the negative gap is all in the under-ninety-days category. In all categories beyond ninety days, the gap is positive; assets subject to repricing exceed liabilities subject to repricing. This does not, unfortunately, mean that the institution is free from interest rate risk. Cumulative gap analysis tells us that it will take over five years for the amount of repriced assets to equal the amount of repriced liabilities. Therefore, an increase in interest rates could lead to substantial losses. We will address ways to estimate the extent of possible losses after dealing with a couple of details of interest rate gap analysis.

Table 11-2

Interest Rate Gap Analysis for Reliable Financial Corporation
(in $ millions)

MATURITY/REPRICING	ASSETS	LIABILITIES	GAP	CUMULATIVE GAP
Overnight	10	20	(10)	(10)
1–30 days	15	20	(5)	(15)
31–90 days	22	25	(3)	(18)
90–180 days	22	15	7	(11)
180–365 days	14	10	4	(7)
1–5 years	11	5	6	(1)
Over 5 years	6	5	1	0

Measurement of repricing/maturity gaps is fairly straightforward, but it is not quite as simple as it might seem. One complication is in determining the exact maturity date. For a mortgage loan, for example, the amount of principal payment due each period is part of the maturity for that period. Thus, a thirty-year mortgage loan actually provides some maturing assets each month for thirty years. The problem is further complicated by the fact that very few thirty-year mortgage loans actually remain outstanding for thirty years. Some are repaid because the borrower sells the house, but refinancing is a more difficult problem to deal with. If we grant a 14 percent mortgage loan to a customer and mortgage interest rates subsequently fall to 10 percent, that customer will refinance, either with our institution or someone else. If we financed the loan with a long-term deposit paying 12 percent, we will face profit difficulties when we reinvest the funds at 10 percent. Thus, the institution may have interest rate risk even if it has no interest rate gap.

Limited repricing creates additional complications. Variable-rate loans generally have caps on how high the interest rate can go. A loan may, for example, have an interest rate 2 percent over the prime rate, with a cap so that the interest cannot exceed 14 percent. Thus, the loan can be repriced each year within limits. If the prime rate goes above 12 percent, there are no additional opportunities to reprice. Again, this leaves the institution exposed to interest rate risk.

Despite limitations, gap analysis has proved to be an extremely useful tool, both as a measure of exposure and as a tool for establishing policy. Top management can dictate overall policies with regard to interest rate gaps and can then monitor performance in relation to these policies. Deciding on the acceptable gaps is a difficult policy problem, and simulation can be helpful in setting policy.

Simulation.   Simulation can give fairly accurate answers with regard to the impacts of various interest rate scenarios, given a particular interest gap situation. Simulation consists of computing interest income and expense that would result from some specified asset and liability structure for several possible interest rate scenarios in the future. Both gap and simulation analysis are based on the reasonable premise that managers are not perfect forecasters of interest rates.

Simulation analysis is best explained with an example, and we use Basic Financial Corporation for this purpose. Managers at Basic are concerned about the possibility of rising interest rates. They want to make sure that they have an asset and liability structure that will allow them to survive a crunch. Basic is an extremely simple financial institution (to avoid a long, tedious example). The assets and liabilities of Basic are summarized as follows:

ITEM	DESCRIPTION	INTEREST RATE
Overnight assets	Prime rate loans	30-day T bill + 1%
Overnight liabilities	Passbook deposits	30-day T bill − 1%
30-day assets	Treasury bills near maturity	30-day T bill
1-year liabilities	Certificates of deposit	1-year Treasury − 1%
10-year assets	Fixed-rate balloon mortgages	10%

Table 11-3

Basic Financial Corporation Quarterly Profitability Simulation
(in $ millions)

| | Assets Liability | | *INCOME AND EXPENSES* | | | | | | | |
| | | | Year 1 | | | | Year 2 | | | |
			1	2	3	4	1	2	3	4
30-day rate			6%	8%	10%	12%	14%	16%	12%	8%
1-year rate			7%	8%	9%	10%	11%	12%	10%	8%
Overnight	20	55	−0.34	−0.51	−0.69	−0.86	−1.04	−1.21	−0.86	−0.51
30 days	20		0.30	0.40	0.50	0.60	0.70	0.80	0.60	0.40
1 year		40	−0.60	−0.60	−0.60	−0.60	−1.00	−1.00	−1.00	−1.00
10 years	60		1.50	1.50	1.50	1.50	1.50	1.50	1.50	1.50
Capital		5								
Net interest income			0.86	0.79	0.71	0.64	0.16	0.09	0.24	0.39
Operating expense			0.60	0.60	0.60	0.60	0.60	0.60	0.06	0.60
Net income			0.26	0.19	0.11	0.04	−0.44	−0.51	−0.36	−0.21
Annual income				$0.60				$−1.53		

A simulation analysis for Basic appears in table 11-3. Because of Basic's structure, the rate on T bills 30 days from maturity and the rate on one-year Treasury securities are the two relevant measures of general interest rates. Table 11-3 is a quarter-by-quarter profitability projection for one interest rate scenario. If the model is set up in a computer, it is a simple matter to change the interest rate scenario and generate a new set of quarterly profit projections.

Table 11-3 shows net interest income in each maturity category for each quarter. Note, for example, that it is assumed that the one-year Treasury securities are replaced with new one-year Treasury securities at the beginning of the second year. After net interest income is determined, operating expenses are then deducted to arrive at net income.

Given the interest rate assumptions and profitability simulation contained in table 11-3, Basic would have an annualized net income for the first quarter of $1.04 million (4 × $0.26 million), which would provide a return on equity capital of 20.8 percent (1.04 ÷ .05). However, the rising interest rate scenario results in a $1.53 million loss in Year 2, given Basic's asset and liability structure. Basic could survive over the two-year period but would lose some 30 percent of its equity in the second year. Although we have not carried out the analysis for additional years, it appears that Basic would have difficulty surviving an extended period of high interest rates.

Simulation analysis gives a financial institution an opportunity to plan for a financial structure that limits its interest rate risk to acceptable levels. Table 11-4 shows the simulation with Basic's asset-liability structure changed in two ways. First, the amount of overnight liabilities has been decreased by increasing one-year liabilities.

Table 11-4

Basic Financial Corporation Quarterly Profitability Simulation with a Modified Financial Structure (in $ millions)

	Assets	Liability	INCOME AND EXPENSES							
			Year 1				Year 2			
			1	2	3	4	1	2	3	4
30-day rate			6%	8%	10%	12%	14%	16%	12%	8%
1-year rate			7%	8%	9%	10%	11%	12%	10%	8%
Overnight	20	45	−0.21	−0.34	−0.46	−0.59	−0.71	−0.84	−0.59	−0.34
30 days	20		0.30	0.40	0.50	0.60	0.70	0.80	0.60	0.40
1 year		50	−0.75	−0.75	−0.75	−0.75	−1.25	−1.25	−1.25	−1.25
10 years	60		1.44	1.52	1.59	1.67	1.74	1.82	1.67	1.52
Capital		5								
Net interest income			0.78	0.83	0.88	0.93	0.48	0.53	0.43	0.33
Operating expense			0.60	0.60	0.60	0.60	0.60	0.60	0.60	0.60
Net income			0.18	0.23	0.28	0.33	−0.12	−0.07	−0.17	−0.27
Annual income				$1.03				−$0.62		

Second, the mortgage portfolio is split evenly between 10 percent fixed-rate mortgages and variable-rate mortgages carrying an interest rate 2.25 percent over the rate on one-year U.S. Treasury securities.

Note that the new asset-liability structure decreases profitability during the first quarter, which is the current interest rate situation, but losses in the second year are cut by 60 percent. Total profit for the two-year period is positive. Basic could survive a much more sustained high-interest period with this structure.

We should note that a change in asset-liability structure of this type cannot be achieved overnight. Movement from the structure in table 11-3 to that in table 11-4 may take years. Nevertheless, simulation analysis does allow management to assess interest rate risk and determine the type of asset-liability structure that will generate an acceptable level of risk. Short-term corrective actions such as hedging with financial futures will be discussed later in this chapter.

Duration

Duration has become an increasingly popular tool for measurement of interest rate risk. Duration is a measure of the sensitivity of an asset's value to changes in interest rates. The advantage of duration is that it allows us to summarize the sensitivity of an entire portfolio of assets or liabilities in a single number. Recall from chapter 5 that the formula for duration is

$$D = \frac{1P_1/(1+r)^1 + 2P_2/(1+r)^2 + \ldots + nP_n/(1+r)^n}{P_1/(1+r)^1 + P_2/(1+r)^2 + \ldots + P_n/(1+r)^n}$$

where P_1 is the cash flow in Year 1, P_2 is the cash flow in Year 2, etc., with no distinction made between principal and interest payments, and r is the required return. The denominator in this equation is the present value of all future cash flows, discounted at the required return, and is therefore the current value of the asset. The duration of an asset is the percent decrease in value of the asset in relation to the percent increase in $1 + r$ when the change in $1 + r$ is extremely small[1].

To illustrate the meaning of duration and its use in interest rate risk management, Colonial Savings grants a five-year, 10 percent, $1,000 mortgage. This mortgage is to be repaid with year-end payments of $263.80 to cover both principal and interest. Colonial finances the mortgage by selling a five-year, 10 percent, $1,000 certificate of deposit calling for payment of principal and all interest at maturity. The payment at maturity will therefore be $1,610.50 ($1000×1.10^5). The maturities of the mortgage and the certificate of deposit are the same, but the durations are substantially different:

$$D_M = \frac{1 \times 263.8/1.1 + 2 \times 263.8/1.1^2 + 3 \times 263.8/1.1^3 + 4 \times 263.8/1.1^4 + 5 \times 263.8/1.1^5}{1,000} = \underline{2.81}$$

$$D_{CD} = [5 \times \$1,610.5 \div (1.10)^5] \div 1,000 = \underline{5.00}$$

where D_M is the duration of the mortgage, and D_{CD} is the duration of the certificate of deposit.

The certificate of deposit has a longer duration because all of the payments are due at maturity, and it will therefore fluctuate in value more than the mortgage when interest rates change. Suppose, for example, market interest rates fall to 9 percent. The value of the mortgage will increase to $1,026.09, and the value of the certificate of deposit will increase to $1,046.72. Because the liabilities increase in value more rapidly than the assets, Colonial's value decreases with a decrease in interest rates in this example.

Duration management can be used to protect Colonial from at least some interest rate risk. Suppose passbook savings accounts, which have a duration of 0, also have interest rates of 10 percent. Colonial finances the $1,000 mortgage with $562 of certificates of deposit and $438 of passbook accounts. The duration of the liabilities is then

$$D = (562 \times 5 + 438 \times 0) \div 1,000 = 2.81.$$

With this financing, the durations of assets and liabilities are now equal. Suppose interest rates now increase to 11 percent. The values change as follows:

[1]Technically, the duration is

$$D = \frac{dV/V}{d(1 + r)/(1 + r)}$$

where V is the value of the asset.

	OLD	NEW
Value of mortgages	$1,000.00	$974.98
Value of five-year certificates of deposit	562.00	537.14
Passbook accounts	438.00	438.00
Value of liabilities	$1,000.00	$975.14
Assets minus liabilities	0	−0.16

By matching the maturities of assets and liabilities, the company is able to immunize net value (assets − liabilities) from interest rate movements. The small loss of $0.16 occurred because duration measures the change in value for only a very small change in interest rates. To hedge perfectly, it would have been necessary to continually adjust the mix of liabilities as the interest rate moved from 10 percent to 11 percent so that the durations remained matched at all time. This can be done if interest rates move continually rather than in sudden jumps.

While duration is a useful concept, it is not a panacea for all interest rate risk problems. To illustrate a limitation of duration, assume that Colonial cannot sell the mortgages and that the certificates of deposit will remain outstanding. Interest rates shift up to 11 percent at the beginning of the first year and remain at that level. The only interest revenue or expense that is affected is the interest rate on passbook accounts, because the interest on mortgages and certificates of deposit was contractually set at 10 percent. Interest income and expense for the year are as follows:

Interest on mortgages[2]	$100.00
− Interest paid on certificates of deposit	56.20
− Interest on passbook accounts (11%)	48.18
= Net interest income	−$ 4.38

Colonial is forced to show an income of −$4.38. This loss is shown despite the fact that there is almost no loss in market value. Book and market values of assets at the end of the year are as follows:

VALUE AT THE END OF YEAR ONE	MARKET	BOOK
Loan payment received	$ 263.80	$ 263.80
− Interest payment on passbook accounts	48.18	48.18
= Cash balance	215.62	215.62
+ Value of mortgage[3]	818.43	836.20
= Total assets	$1,034.05	$1,051.82

---

[2]The interest on the mortgage is the balance at the beginning of the year, times the contract interest rate. The rest of the payment is principal payment. Likewise, accrued interest equal to 10 percent of the certificate of deposit as of the beginning of the year is an accrued expense even though it is not actually paid out until later.

[3]The market value of the mortgage is the present value of the remaining payments discounted at 11 percent. The book value of the mortgage is the original balance of $1,000, less the principal payment. The principal payment is the $263.80 total payment, minus the $100 interest portion.

Passbook accounts	$ 438.00	$ 438.00
Certificates of deposit[4]	596.22	618.20
Total liabilities	$1,034.22	$1,056.20
Increase in net worth	−$0.17	−$4.38

Matching durations of assets and liabilities protected Colonial from changes in market value (except for 17¢), but the company was forced to report a loss of $4.38 and show a corresponding decrease in net worth of 4.38. It can be argued that this is because accounting rules are inappropriate, but that does not change the fact that Colonial will be required to report a loss in this instance.

The reported loss could be avoided if Colonial could sell the mortgages and retire the certificates of deposit for their market values. The gains from these transactions would be as follows:

ITEM	MORTGAGE	CERTIFICATE OF DEPOSIT	NET GAIN
Market value	$818.43	$596.22	
Book value	836.20	618.20	
Gain on settlement	−$ 17.77	$ 21.98	$4.21

The net gain of $4.21 would nearly offset the negative interest income of $4.38, leaving a loss of only 17¢ (which could have been avoided as well if the asset-liability structure were adjusted continually to match durations). However, Colonial would still have negative net interest income offset by these other gains. Investors tend to look at these gains with suspicion because they are subject to manipulation. An example of manipulation would be settlement of the certificates of deposit for a $21.98 gain while holding the mortgages to avoid reporting the $17.77 loss.

Because the institution does not have complete liquidity in all asset and liability accounts, and because the form in which income is reported matters, duration does not paint a complete picture of interest rate risk. Financial institution managers also express concern about the impacts of changes in yield curve slope which may not be fully captured in duration analysis. Many institutions use interest gap analysis and simulation instead of or in addition to duration analysis in measuring and managing interest rate risk.

Tools for Managing Interest Rate Risk

Management of interest rate risk begins with policy decisions about the amount of interest rate risk the institution is willing to accept, and philosophy in this regard varies widely. Some insitutions are willing to make substantial bets on their interest rate forecasts, while others stay much closer to a hedged position. In a recent conversation, the treasury department of one major bank described a competitor as having "bet the

---

[4]The market value of the certificate of deposit is the balloon principal and interest payment discounted at 11 percent. The book value is the original $562, plus one year's accumulated interest.

bank" on their interest forecast; the competitor was exposed to so much interest rate risk that its survival would have been in question if its interest rate forecasts had been wrong. The problem with bets of this type is that the institution effectively makes a new bet every few months. Being right nine out of ten times can still leave the institution insolvent.

Interest gap analysis and duration analysis are useful tools for implementing policy. Policy can be specified in terms of either acceptable gaps in each maturity/repricing range or in terms of acceptable gaps between asset duration and liability duration. Policy stated in this way is easy to interpret, and it is easy to monitor performance in relation to the standard. Simulation analysis is often used in deciding what interest gap or duration standards leave the company with an acceptable risk level. Because most institutions provide loans or acquire other assets with longer maturities than their liabilities, losses come when interest rates rise. Most institutions want an asset-liability structure that will allow them to survive a period of sharply rising interest rates. Some will go beyond this to accept only limited levels of income fluctuation.

Once an institution has developed an asset-liability management policy, implementation is the next problem. Implementation is made difficult by the fact that borrowing short and lending long is the business of a financial institution. Nevertheless, institutions have worked innovatively to develop ways to limit their risk to acceptable levels.

Because customers seldom want overnight loans, lengthening of liabilities has been an important area of focus. Finance companies that rely on public sale of securities rather than acceptance of deposits have been most successful in this area. They have decreased their reliance on commercial paper as a source of funds, while increasing their reliance on intermediate-term bonds. Depository institutions face a more difficult problem though. A desire for liquidity is one of the reasons depositors leave their money at financial institutions. Nevertheless, financial institutions have worked to develop an increased market for longer-term certificates of deposit, convincing some passbook account holders to move their money into certificates of deposit and attracting some funds that might otherwise go to the bond market. Negotiable certificates of deposit are an innovation that gives an institution funds for a specific period of time, while giving liquidity to the certificate holder through a secondary market in which certificates can be sold. In addition, depository institutions have raised some money by selling bonds.

Financial institutions have looked agressively to the asset side of the balance sheet as well. Savings and loans, for example, have broadened the mix of assets, including some credit card balances, automobile loans, home equity loans, etc. These loans have shorter maturities than traditional mortgage loans, and some of them are variable-rate contracts with interest rates tied to an index of general interest rates. A ten-year loan may be subject to repricing every quarter, for example, and therefore exposes the institutions to very little interest rate risk. Variable-rate mortgages have been another important innovation. Although it has been necessary to include interest rate caps to make variable-rate mortgages marketable, the borrower does carry part of the interest rate risk that was previously carried by the lender.

Several innovative financial instruments have given financial institutions new tools with which to manage interest rate risk. Financial futures, discussed in detail in chapter 9, are particularly useful. A futures contract to sell Treasury bonds, for example, will increase in price if interest rates rise. This will offset losses in the financial institution's asset portfolio caused by an increase in interest rates. Options are another alternative. An option to sell financial instruments will move up in value when interest rates rise, while an option to buy will move in the opposite direction. Writing options to buy or purchasing options to sell can again offset interest rate risk inherent in the institution's asset portfolio.

Interest rate swaps are another important innovation. With an interest rate swap, two institutions simply agree to swap interest income for two different assets. Suppose, for example, Chemical Bank has an average balance of $20 million in federal funds liabilities. These rates vary from day to day, and Chemical prefers a fixed interest cost. Chemical Bank may, for example, agree to pay First Boston the interest on $20 million of 1-year Treasury notes. In exchange, First Boston agress to pay Chemical the interest rate on $20 million of federal funds. Chemical effectively locks in a fixed cost on $20 million without changing its balance sheet. The interest Chemical receives from First Boston can be used to cover the interest rate paid for federal funds or other short-term sources of funds. Financial institutions often prefer swaps to futures or options because swaps are easy to arrange.

Securitization also plays an important role in the management of interest rate risk. As discussed in chapter 10, many loans are packaged and sold with the financial institution handling application, credit granting, and serving. Securitization has been popular with fixed-rate mortgage loans. Mortgage-backed securities increased from 5 percent of home mortgages in 1975 to 23 percent in 1985. Interest rate risk is a problem that will never go away, but financial institutions do have an increased array of tools available for dealing with it. In addition, they have an increased awareness of the importance of interest rate risk after the experiences of the 1970s and 1980s.

SUMMARY

Liquidity, the ability to meet all legitimate demands for funds, is absolutely essential to the survival of a financial institution. Liquidity planning must recognize not only withdrawal demands but also the importance of meeting loan requests if customer relations are to be maintained. Liquidity is a matter of time and cost in that almost any asset can be converted to cash at some cost and with the passage of some amount of time. In dealing with liquidity, it must be recognized that primary reserves, necessary to satisfy regulators, are not a source of liquidity for meeting loan and withdrawal demand. New deposits, maturing assets, sale of assets, and borrowing are sources of funds for meeting liquidity demand. Secondary reserve assets are assets that can be sold quickly to meet liquidity demands.

Liquidity is sometimes measured with balance sheet ratios, but it is a dynamic concept and is better measured by focusing on the flow of funds into and out of the institution. Studies of past flows and maturity gap analysis are two popular ways to measure and manage liquidity.

Interest rate risk is a problem for most financial institutions because one of their services is to accept short-term funds and make long-term commitments. Financial institutions are therefore hurt by rising interest rates. While some interest rate risk is probably unavoidable, institutions that want to survive must measure and control their interest rate risk exposure. Interest rate risk exposure is measured with interest rate gap analysis, simulation, and duration. Asset-liability management policies are often specified in terms of acceptable interest rate gaps or duration.

Institutions have available to them several tools for limiting interest rate risk. First, they can work to lengthen the maturity of their liabilities through such methods as selling bonds and vigorously marketing certificates of deposit. On the asset side, institutions can increase the mix of assets to include more short-term items and can use variable-rate loans to share interest rate risk with the borrower. Financial futures, options, and interest rate swaps provide additional tools for reducing interest rate risk.

QUESTIONS

11-1.   Define the term *liquidity*.

11-2.   What is meant by the statement that liquidity is a concept of time and cost. Give an example.

11-3.   Explain the difference between primary and secondary reserves.

11-4.   How is liquidity measured?

11-5.   What are the sources of liquidity available to a financial institution?

11-6.   Why do most financial institutions face at least some interest rate risk?

11-7.   What tools are available for measuring interest rate risk?

11-8.   What can financial institutions do to reduce interest rate risk?

PROBLEMS

The balance sheet of Provident Financial Corporation appears below and is used in problems 11-1 through 11-3. All dollar numbers are in $ millions.

ASSETS		LIABILITIES	
Cash	$128	Demand deposits	$345
Securities due within 30 days	92	Deposits due within 30 days	282
Overnight loans	115	Overnight borrowing	134
Securities due 30 days–1 year	147	Deposits 30 days–1 year	298
Loans due 30 days–1 year	348	Borrowed funds 30 days–1 year	115
Loans over 1 year	413	Borrowed funds over 1 year	83
Securities over 1 year	65	Deposits over 1 year	42
Fixed assets	49	Net worth	58
Total assets	$1,357	Total liabilities and net worth	$1,357

11-1.   Compute liquidity ratios and comment on the trends in liquidity. Liquidity ratios last year were as follows: Provident has $120 million of U.S. government securities and required reserves of $80 million.
Loans ÷ total assets = 0.662;
loans ÷ total deposits = 0.874;
purchased liabilities ÷ total assets = 0.260;
securities maturing in one year or less ÷ total assets = 0.36;
(cash − req. res. + U.S. gov. sec.) ÷ total assets = 0.15.

11-2.   Prepare a liquidity gap analysis for Provident.

11-3.   Prepare a rate gap analysis. In doing this, note that 40 percent of the loans with maturities longer than one year are variable-rate loans that are repriced at the beginning of each year.

11-4.   Shown below are the cash flows reported by Employee's Federal Credit Union over a twenty-six-week period. Analyze these flows and determine the maximum amount of liquid reserves that would have been needed over this period.

Cash Flows Experienced by the Employee's Federal Credit Union

WEEK	DEPOSITS	WITHDRAWALS	LOAN REPAYMENTS	NEW LOANS
1	10,000	7,000	3,000	7,000
2	10,600	7,400	3,000	6,000
3	10,900	7,600	3,100	7,000
4	11,800	7,400	3,100	8,000
5	11,600	7,800	3,150	7,000
6	12,000	8,200	3,150	7,000
7	13,000	8,500	3,150	8,000
8	12,500	8,700	3,170	7,000
9	10,000	9,200	3,175	5,000
10	9,600	9,800	3,180	5,000
11	9,400	10,200	3,180	4,000
12	9,200	10,500	3,185	4,000
13	8,400	11,300	3,190	3,000
14	6,400	11,800	3,190	1,000
15	5,200	14,200	3,195	500
16	4,000	15,800	3,195	500
17	4,200	16,200	3,200	300
18	4,400	15,300	3,200	200
19	5,000	12,800	3,200	200
20	5,000	11,700	3,205	0
21	5,200	11,000	3,210	0
22	5,400	10,300	3,210	200
23	5,600	9,000	3,210	200
24	6,000	7,900	3,210	500
25	5,800	6,400	3,210	1,000
26	6,400	6,400	3,215	2,000

11-5.   A balance sheet summary for First National Bank appears below. Compute the average durations of assets and liabilities. Suggest ways First National can decrease its interest rate risk.

AMOUNTS DUE	VALUE	AVERAGE DURATION
Assets		
Within 30 days	$3,000	0.05 years
31–180 days	2,000	0.30
181–365 days	2,000	0.75
366 days–5 years	5,000	2.00
Over 5 years	3,000	8.00
Liabilities and Equity		
Within 30 days	$4,000	0.04 years
31–180 days	3,000	0.30
181–365 days	1,000	0.75
366 days–5 years	4,000	2.50
Over 5 years	3,000	9.00

11-6. A four-year, 10 percent mortgage calls for equal year-end payments to cover both principal and interest. Compute the duration.

11-7. A four-year, 10 percent certificate of deposit calls for interest payments at the end of each year and a principal payment at the end. Compute the duration.

11-8. Suppose your bank grants a $100,000 loan, as described in problem 11-6, and finances the loan with the certificate of deposit described in problem 11-7. Immediately after this, interest rates on these instruments increase to 11 percent. What is the increase or decrease in income? What is the increase or decrease in market net worth (market value of assets minus market value of liabilities)?

11-9. What is the duration of a ten-year, 10 percent mortgage calling for equal payments at the end of each month to cover principal and interest? (Note: Lotus 1-2-3 or some other computational aid will be needed to avoid an extremely tedious computation.)

11-10. Bond A has a duration of ten years, and Bond B has a duration of six years. Each bond has a value of $1,000. The required interest rate is currently 8 percent. If the required interest rate changes to 8.01 percent, by how much will each bond change in value?

SELECTED REFERENCES

ANDERSON, GARY, AND CHIANG, RAYMOND. "Interest Rate Risk Hedging for Due-on-Sale Mortgages With Early Termination," *Journal of Financial Research* 10 (Summer 1987): 133–142.

BENESH, GARY A., AND CELEC, STEPHEN E. "A Simplified Approach for Calculating Bond Duration," *Financial Review* 19 (November 1984): 394–396.

BICKSLER, JAMES, AND CHEN, ANDREW H. "An Economic Analysis of Interest Rate Swaps," *Journal of Finance* 41 (July 1986): 645–655.

BIERWAG, G. O., KAUFMAN, GEORGE G., AND LATTA, CYNTHIA M. "Bond Portfolio Immunization: Tests of Maturity, One- and Two-Factor Duration Matching Strategies," *Financial Review* 22 (May 1987): 203–219.

CAKS, JOHN, ET AL. "A Simple Formula for Duration," *Journal of Financial Research* 8 (Fall 1985): 245–249.

FONG, H. GIFFORD, AND VASICEK, OLDRICH A. "A Risk Minimizing Strategy for Portfolio Immunization,"

Journal of Finance 39 (December 1984): 1541–1546.

HOWARD, CHARLES T., AND D'ANTONIO, LOUIS J.   "A Risk-Return Measure of Hedging Effectiveness," *Journal of Financial and Quantitative Analysis* 19 (March 1984): 101–112.

HOWARD, CHARLES T., AND D'ANTONIO, LOUIS J.   "Treasury Bill Futures as a Hedging Tool: A Risk-Return Approach," *Journal of Financial Research* 9 (Spring 1986): 25–39.

KOPPENHAVER, G. D.   "Selective Hedging of Bank Assets With Treasury Bill Futures Contracts," *Journal of Financial Research* 7 (Summer 1984): 105–119.

LITTLE, PATRICIA KNAIN.   "Financial Futures and Immunization," *Journal of Financial Research* 9 (Spring 1986): 1–12.

OGDEN, JOSEPH P.   "An Analysis of Yield Curve Notes," *Journal of Finance* 42 (March 1987): 99–110.

OTT, ROBERT A., JR.   "The Duration of an Adjustable-Rate Mortgage and the Impact of the Index," *Journal of Finance* 41 (September 1986): 923–933.

SCOTT, WILLIAM L., AND PETERSON, RICHARD L.   "Interest Rate Risk and Equity Values of Hedged and Unhedged Financial Intermediaries," *Journal of Financial Research* 9 (Winter 1986): 325–329.

STANHOUSE, BRYAN.   "Commercial Bank Portfolio Behavior and Endogenous Uncertainty," *Journal of Finance* 41 (December 1986): 1103–1114.

CASE 8

MARITIME FINANCIAL

The asset-liability committee at Maritime Financial was concerned about the possibilities of rising interest rates and wanted to be sure that they were adequately protected. The balance sheet appears in table 1, and information about the individual accounts on the balance sheet appears below.

Cash and Federal Reserve deposits were the primary reserves of the institution. Maritime was required to keep primary reserves equal to 12 percent of demand deposits.

U.S. Treasury bills were of various maturities, up to one year in length. These were held as secondary reserves.

U.S. Treasury notes had maturities of up to five years, with maturities spread fairly evenly over the period. These were held as an outlet for funds not needed to meet loan demand. These notes also provided some liquidity and flexibility, as they could be sold.

Consumer loans included automobile loans, remodeling loans, and unsecured personal loans. This was a new area for Maritime, and these loans were made only to existing customers. Thus, there was no market for a significant increase in these loans.

Mortgage-backed securities were securities such as GNMA certificates, which were backed by a portfolio of fixed-rate mortgages. These certificates could be sold, but the price would depend on the general level of interest rates, and these securities had durations averaging 7.46 years. If interest rates rose sharply, the runoff rate (repayment rate) could fall by 25 percent.

Fixed-rate mortgages were conventional thirty-year mortgage loans with a fixed interest rate. While runoff would not change the average interest rates for

Table 1

Runoff Analysis for Maritime Financial
(in $ thousands)

RUNOFF	AMOUNT	AVERAGE INTEREST RATE	DURATION	RUNOFF BY QUARTER							
				I	II	III	IV	V	VI	VII	VIII
Assets											
Cash and Federal Reserve deposits	$19,589		0	19,589							
U.S. Treasury bills	57,323	6.28%	0.66	14,692	13,286	14,387	14,958	1,456	1,254	1,343	1,585
U.S. Treasury notes	24,486	7.72	2.43	1,534	1,864	1,150	1,086				
Consumer loans	73,458	14.88	2.13	8,236	8,145	8,098	8,054	7,928	7,862	7,801	7,721
Mortgages											
Mortgage-backed securities	48,972	8.52	7.46	1,531	1,531	1,531	1,531	1,531	1,531	1,531	1,531
Fixed-rate	97,945	9.12	5.15	4,829	4,829	4,829	4,829	4,829	4,829	4,829	4,829
Variable-rate	146,916	8.48	0.25	3,673	3,673	3,673	3,673	3,673	3,673	3,673	3,673
Fixed assets	18,632			NA	NA	NA	NA	NA	NA	NA	NA
Total assets	$487,321			34,495	33,328	33,668	34,131	19,417	19,149	19,177	19,339
Demand deposits	$142,543	4.08	0	142,543	NA	NA	NA	NA	NA	NA	NA
Time deposits	296,664	5.88	1.12	85,826	53,227	36,413	17,465	14,633	11,987	11,826	8,884
Deferred tax	14,614			NA	NA	NA	NA	NA	NA	NA	NA
Net worth	33,500			NA	NA	NA	NA	NA	NA	NA	NA
Total liability and net worth	$487,321			228,369	53,227	36,413	17,465	14,633	11,987	11,826	8,884

other assets and liabilities, it was estimated that the average interest rate for the fixed-rate portfolio would increase approximately two basis points each quarter as a result of retirement of older, low-interest mortgages. If interest rates rose sharply, the runoff rate could fall by 30 percent, and the increase in average interest rate would slow to one basis point a quarter.

Variable-rate mortgages allowed adjustment at the start of each quarter to an interest rate 2 percent above the rate on one-year U.S. Treasury bills. Half of these had a 12 percent cap.

Demand deposits were funds that could be withdrawn on demand. For purpose of analysis, these included checking account balances, passbook account balances, and money market fund balances. The bulk of the interest went to money market accounts which paid a rate tied by a formula to money market rates. The effect was that the average interest cost for these accounts totaled approximately two-thirds of the ninety-day Treasury bill rate.

Time deposits were primarily certificates of deposit. Maturities and rates varied, but average interest rates on new certificates of deposit averaged 0.5 percent below the prevailing one-year Treasury bill rate. Balances in these accounts depended on the interest rate paid, with customers moving money freely in search of the institution currently paying the highest interest rate on certificates of deposit. A strong stock market would also draw money away from certificates of deposit.

Current market interest rates were as follows:

90-day U.S. Treasury bills (bond equivalent yield)	6.09%
1-year U.S. Treasury bills (bond equivalent yield)	6.48
5-year U.S. Treasury notes	7.78
20-year U.S. Treasury bonds	8.44
GNMA certificates	9.02
Fixed-rate conventional mortgages	9.82

Inflation rates had picked up a bit in recent quarters, and there was concern about rising interest rates. An economic service used by Maritime said that if the Fed responded vigorously, there would be a quick peaking of interest rates over the second and third quarters, with ninety-day Treasury bills going to 14 percent and twenty-year U.S. Treasury bonds going to 10 percent. In this scenario, short-term rates would then fall quickly, with long-term rates drifting downward. If the Fed did not respond vigorously, all rates would drift up over the two-year period, increasing by as much as 2 percent for all maturities.

Maritime had annual operating expenses equal to approximately 2.75 percent of total assets and had a 34 percent income tax rate. Maritime was a mature company and was experiencing little growth in total assets. Regulators required Maritime to maintain equity equal to at least 4 percent of total assets.

1. Prepare a liquidity gap analysis. Does Maritime have adequate liquidity?
2. Prepare a rate gap analysis.
3. Compute the average duration of assets and of liabilities.
4. Do a 1-year simulation analysis for rapidly rising interest rates. Ignore loan runoff.
5. Is Maritime subject to excessive interest rate risk? If so, how can interest rate risk be reduced.

12

Capital Adequacy and Required Returns

Even a well-run financial institution cannot eliminate all risks, and capital is the cushion against unanticipated losses. Capital amounts are set by managerial policy and by regulation. Capital requirements affect not only the risk, but also the required return on the company's assets. In the first part of this chapter, we look at how the appropriate amount of capital is determined. In the second part of the chapter, we look at the relationship between capital levels and required returns.

CAPITAL ADEQUACY

Capital consists of stockholder's equity and certain other sources of funds that have lower priorities than depositors' claims in the event of bankruptcy. If capital is 10 percent of total assets, for example, assets can suffer a 10 percent shrinkage in value without hurting the depositors (or deposit-insurance agencies). We will look at the function and types of capital before looking at ways the amount of capital is chosen.

Function of Capital

The basic function of capital in a financial institution is to serve as a cushion against unanticipated losses. The three primary risks are as follows:

1. Interest rate risk, which was discussed in chapter 11.
2. Credit risk, which is the risk of borrowers defaulting on loans. The risk of default on securities is also included in this category.

3. Theft, with the major theft risk being from fraud rather than from loss at gunpoint.

As discussed in chapter 11, interest rate risk affects the reported income stream as well as the values of assets and liabilities. Capital serves as a cushion against both income loss and loss in the value of assets. Loss of income is the interest rate risk that can force a financial institution into insolvency. A loss (negative income) reduces capital, and the institution is insolvent when capital becomes negative. The greater the capital, the longer the institution can survive during periods when interest expense rises faster than interest income.

Loss of asset value due to rising interest rates does not lead to default because financial institutions report asset values based on cost, not estimated market values. An institution whose assets have estimated market values less than the estimated market values of its liabilities can therefore continue to operate. Capital does, however, provide a cushion for market value loss in the event of forced liquidation. If regulators should declare the institution insolvent and decide to liquidate, capital provides a cushion so that creditors can be paid off even if assets are worth less than liabilities.

Financial institutions routinely establish reserves for credit losses. If losses remain at or below the expected level, no additional equity is needed. If, on the other hand, credit losses exceed expectations, the effect is the same as if interest expense exceeds interest income. The institution experiences a net loss instead of net income, and that loss reduces capital. Capital again provides a cushion for the unexpected. Theft is similar to credit loss in that it results in a loss which reduces net income, and capital provides a cushion.

In considering the function of capital, it is important to note what capital cannot do. *Capital cannot provide permanent protection against long-term losses.* A financial institution with operating costs running out of control, for example, will eventually use up its capital, and a higher level of capital will simply delay the inevitable. Capital can protect creditors in liquidation and can provide a cushion for a *temporary* imbalance between income and expenses.

Types of Capital

Capital is not a single item but a variety of different items that serve in one way or another as a cushion against income or asset value loss. Bank capital can be broken down as follows, based on categories currently used by regulators.

	Common stock
+	Paid-in capital in excess of par
+	Retained earnings
=	Common equity
+	Perpetual preferred stock[1]
=	Equity capital

[1]Perpetual preferred stock, plus qualified debt instruments cannot exceed one-third of primary capital. Qualified debt instruments cannot exceed 20 percent of primary capital.

+   Loan loss reserves
+   Qualified debt instruments[1,2]
+   Minority interest in consolidated subsidiaries

=   Total primary capital

+   Secondary capital (additional qualified debt[3] +
    redeemable preferred stock)

=   Total capital

To provide a perspective on the current status of capital, table 12-1 contains a summary of the capital of a sample of banks. One interesting aspect of these data is in primary capital, which shows a fairly small variance around the 7 percent average ratio of primary capital to total assets for all money center and major regional banks. This was, of course, heavily influenced by regulatory requirements. Ways of achieving this primary capital level varied widely though. Bank of America had a low common equity ratio because of prior losses, while Citicorp had a low common equity ratio as a matter of policy. J. P. Morgan and Banc One both maintain relatively high common equity ratios as a matter of policy. Substantial variance of policies with regard to total capital is also observed. These differences in capital structure could reflect differences in risk, but it seems more likely that they reflect differences in willingness to accept risk.

Measurement of Capital Adequacy

In determining the amount of capital needed, we are determining the amount of cushion needed to protect against unexpected losses. What is needed, then, is a way to estimate an adequate amount of cushion. The desired cushion may be viewed from the perspective of the managers, the shareholders, or the general public, represented by the regulators. Capital adequacy is measured in terms of simple ratios, risk asset analysis, and portfolio analysis, and in the context of a general examination of management soundness.

Ratio Approaches to Capital Adequacy

Ratio approaches are among the oldest methods of capital adequacy analysis and are still widely used by both managers and regulators. Ratio standards are generally expressed in terms of the ratio of capital to total assets. Ratio standards may be developed for equity capital, primary capital, or total capital.

A traditional approach to developing ratio standards is to use judgment to set a

---

[1]Perpetual preferred stock, plus qualified debt instruments cannot exceed one-third of primary capital. Qualified debt instruments cannot exceed 20 percent of primary capital.

[2]Includes perpetual debt and mandatory convertible notes.

[3]Includes perpetual debt and mandatory convertible notes beyond the amount that can be included as primary reserves without violating the one-third or 20 percent rules. Also includes nonmandatory convertible notes and subordinated long-term debt with an original average life of at least seven years.

Table 12-1

Capital as a Percentage of Total Assets for Selected U.S. Banks December 31, 1986

	MONEY CENTER BANKS			REGIONAL BANKS		
	Citicorp	Irving Bank	J. P. Morgan	Banc One Corp.	Barnett Bank	Bank of America
Common equity	3.89%	4.00%	6.34%	7.14%	4.84%	3.13%
+ Perpetual preferred	0.69	0.31	0.32	0.00	0.12	0.67
= Equity capital	4.58	4.30	6.67	7.14	4.96	3.80
+ Loan loss reserves	0.86	0.91	1.18	0.90	0.76	2.04
+ Qualified debt	1.34	1.04	0.48	0.00	0.72	1.07
+ Minority interest	0.04	0.09	0.00	0.00	0.00	0.01
= Primary capital	6.82	6.34	8.33	8.03	6.44	6.92
+ Add. qualified debt	4.04	1.34	1.72	0.37	0.12	1.17
+ Redeemable preferred	0.02	0.00	0.00	0.28	0.00	0.00
= Total capital	10.88%	7.68%	10.04%	8.68%	6.56%	8.09%

Source: Salamon Brothers.

level of capital that is believed to provide a reasonable cushion in light of past experience. Judgment may be supplemented by studies of past failures. For example, we might look at the failure percentages over a number of five-year periods and study the relationship between failure during each five-year period and capital ratios at the beginning of that five-year period.

When regulators are developing ratio standards, they are more interested in the solvency of the banking system than in single financial institutions. Furthermore, they want rules that are simple to explain and that provide a usable standard for monitoring performance. Regulators may study past failure experience of banks to determine capital ratios that will keep failures at an acceptable level. While there may be various ideas of an acceptable level of failure, one important characteristic of an acceptable level is that deposit insurance agencies such as the FDIC will be able to make good on their deposit guarantees. To make the system manageable, regulators want to set ratio standards that can be used for all institutions, or at least an entire class of institutions.

Risk-Based Capital Asset Approaches

Proposals for risk-based capital standards have been around for years and are getting increased attention. Regulators in the United States and Great Britain worked jointly to develop a standard in 1987. As an example of how a risk-based approach works, risk weights proposed for some specific asset categories follow.

RISK WEIGHT	ITEM
0%	Cash and claims on federal reserve banks
10%	Short-term claims on the U.S. government
25%	Short-term claims on depository institutions and long-term claims on the U.S. government
50%	Claims on agencies sponsored by the U.S. government and general obligation claims on state and local governments
100%	Claims on private entities and individuals.

Under the proposal being developed, off-balance sheet claims such as credit guarantees would also be given a weight and added to actual assets. A risk-weighted asset base would be developed in this way, and capital requirements would then be a percentage of that risk-weighted asset base.

The appeal of the risk-based approach is that it is a step forward from simply looking at total assets to looking at assets in terms of riskiness. The risk-based approach also has the advantage of requiring capital to support off-balance sheet sources of risk such as loan guarantees.

Critics, including many leading banks, object to risk-based approaches because each asset is effectively treated in isolation. To see the limitations of this approach, consider the risks of primary concern—interest rate risk and credit risk. Interest rate risk does not depend just on the maturity structure of the assets; it depends on the relationship between asset and liability maturity. To take one example of this problem, long-term claims on the U.S. government are given a weight of 25 percent in the proposed system. The potential riskiness of these assets can be demonstrated by the fact that a $1,000, twenty-year U.S. government bond purchase in 1975 would have declined to a market value of $680 in 1980. However, the risk to a financial institution holding this bond would have depended on how it was financed. If the institution funded the bond with twenty-year liabilities, it would have suffered no net loss.

Another complaint is that the risk-based approach ignores portfolio effects. It is true that common stocks lost an average of 20 percent of their value in one day on 19 October 1987. However, combining common stocks with a portfolio of other assets may actually reduce portfolio risk because common stock prices are not highly correlated with certain other activities.

Portfolio Approaches to Capital Adequacy

Portfolio approaches to capital adequacy are based on recognition of the complex set of interactions involved in a financial institution. These approaches specifically recognize the fact that two independent risky actions may be combined to create a position that is less risky than either of the independent positions. A bank that has matched the maturities or repricing dates of its assets and liabilities is less risky than an institution with the same asset base and a large interest rate gap. As another example, suppose one institution specializes in commercial loans while the other specializes in consumer loans. If these two institutions merge, total risk goes down, particularly from the viewpoint of insurance agencies such as the FDIC. The profitabilities of consumer and commercial loans are not perfectly correlated, so profitability in one area may be used to offset low profits in the other area. Likewise, international lending provides diversification. The mean-variance portfolio model discussed in appendix 10-A provides one way to apply portfolio concepts. However, an approach similar to the simulation approach used in chapter 11 is frequently more applicable.

EXAMPLE.   In table 11-3, we estimated income each quarter for an interest rate scenario involving rising interest rates. The loss anticipated in the second year would eliminate 31 percent of the institution's capital. In table 11-4, the sensitivity analysis was repeated using the same interest rate scenario but a modified asset and liability structure. The loss in the second year was reduced to 12 percent of capital. The cost of reduced risk was lower profitability. If interest rates did not rise, return on equity would be 21 percent with the original asset-liability structure and only 14 percent with the lower-risk structure.

Changes in the capital ratio provide additional opportunities in terms of risk-return trade-offs. The analysis in tables 11-3 and 11-4 was repeated using the same interest rate scenario but different levels of capital. Capital was used to replace overnight liabilities. The results for capital ratios from 2 percent to 10 percent of total assets are shown in table 12-2. The current return on capital is the return if interest rates do not change. The percentage loss in Year 2 is the loss that is anticipated if the rising interest rate scenario occurs.

There are two important lessons from table 12-2. First, the level of capital needed depends not just on the total amount of assets, but also on the types of assets and on interactions between assets and liabilities. Suppose, for example, regulators or managers consider a loss of 12 percent of capital in one year the maximum acceptable risk. To maintain this level of risk, 9 percent capital would be required with the higher-risk structure, and 5 percent equity would be required with the lower-risk structure. The second lesson is that management, to the extent that it has a choice, can trade off between increased capital and other methods of reducing risk in its efforts to maximize profitability. In this particular example, higher return is achieved at each level of risk by using the less risky asset-liability structure than by relying solely on increases in capital to reduce risk. The example focuses only on interest rate risk but could easily be expanded to include scenarios involving other risks such as increased loan losses.

Management Soundness. A broader view of capital adequacy takes into consideration the soundness of the institution's management in determining capital needs. Management soundness includes the skill and experience of the management team and also a number of indicators of the quality of management. These indicators include types of policies that are in place, various performance ratios such as operating costs ratios, earnings history, internal equity generation (annual retained earnings divided by total assets), and the loan portfolio quality measures discussed in chapter 13. While

Table 12-2

Interactions Between Capital Adjustments and Interest Rate Risk
(all numbers are percentages)

CAPITAL RATIO	2%	3%	4%	5%	6%	7%	8%	9%	10%
Table 11-3 structure									
Expected return on capital	45	32	25	21	18	16	15	14	13
Year 2 loss ÷ capital	94	59	41	31	24	19	15	12	10
Table 11-4 structure									
Expected return on capital	29	21	17	15	13	12	11	10	10
Year 2 loss ÷ capital	48	28	18	12	8	6	3	2	0

examiners look at management soundness, it is difficult to develop precise, easily interpreted measures.

Current and Future Regulation of Capital

For historical reasons, capital regulations for financial institutions are the responsibility of a diverse group of agencies. Pension funds to not have capital requirements, and insurance companies are regulated primarily by state agencies. Depending on the nature of their charters, depository institutions are regulated by one or more of the following agencies:

Federal Reserve Bank
Office of the Comptroller of the Currency
Federal Deposit Insurance Corporation
Federal Home Loan Bank Board
National Credit Union Administration
State Regulatory Authority

Present regulations are primarily based on ratios of total assets. As an example, Federal Reserve–FDIC standards for banks are as follows. For total capital, the lower of the two numbers may be considered adequate capitalization, depending on other aspects of the institution's condition.

TYPE OF BANK	COMMUNITY	REGIONAL	MULTINATIONAL
Primary capital	6.0%	5.0%	5.5%
Total capital	7.0%/6.0%	6.5%/5.5%	7.0%/6.0%

Several trends in the regulation of capital can be observed at the present time. First, capital requirements have been increasing in recent years. In the early 1980s, major banks were operating with primary capital ratios in the neighborhood of 4 percent. Second, there has been a movement toward leveling the playing field by creating similar regulations for various types of depository institutions. Third, there is an ongoing search for more precise ways to measure capital adequacy. The risk-based asset proposal is an example of these efforts.

Capital Regulation and Shareholder Wealth

Finance theory suggests that there is an optimal mix of debt and equity which minimizes the required return and maximizes the wealth of the shareholders. The optimal mix is based on considerations of taxes, risk, agency costs, and information assymetry.

Many bankers are of the view that they should operate with lower levels of equity than are commonly the practice and would do so if the regulators did not interfere. This conclusion comes partly from the fact that a lower equity ratio provides a higher return on equity for a profitable business. However, the benefits of a higher return on equity are at least partially offset by the increased risk involved. In a recent study, Shome, Smith, and Heggestad attempted to empirically test the relationship between value and equity capital ratios for large banks. They found that most large banks were undercapitalized from the shareholders' perspective and could increase the wealth of the shareholders by carrying more equity than the minimum required to satisfy regulators[4].

REQUIRED RETURNS FOR DEPOSITORY INSTITUTIONS

The capital policy of a financial institution has important implications for the required return that must be earned on assets if the institution is to satisfy its stockholders. Required returns are affected by the nature of the assets, by the institution's operating costs, and by the form of liabilities as well. An understanding of required returns is vital for pricing decisions such as loan and deposit interest rates, as well as for evaluation of potential new product offerings. An understanding of required returns is also vital for the development of capital policy and liability structure.

Several important factors affect the institution's required return. Required return is an opportunity cost, or the return that investors and depositors could expect from alternative opportunities of equal risk. One factor in the cost of funds is the general level of opportunities, which influences the overall level of competitive interest rates. Second, investors must expect a higher rate of return if they are to be persuaded to invest in assets subject to risk. The more risk associated with the asset and liability structure of the firm, the higher will be the return necessary to attract funds.

Deposit funds, to the extent insured, are essentially risk-free. However, financial institutions derive funds through issuance of securities and creation of liabilities, many of which are not covered or are covered only partially by insurance. Examples of these are large certificates of deposit, commercial paper, capital notes and debentures, federal funds borrowed, Eurodollars, preferred stock, and common stock. The required return for such funds will increase as perceived risk in the asset and liability structure increases.

Operating costs are a third factor affecting required return. In addition to covering opportunity costs and compensation for risk, the required return must cover the institution's operating expenses. In this section, the costs of the individual sources of funds are computed, and required returns are developed.

Cost of Equity

The cost of equity is the return required by holders of the common stock. This cost is a function of investment opportunities elsewhere and the perceived risk associated with a particular institution's common stock. Unfortunately, it is seldom possible to

[4]Dilip K. Shome, Stephen D. Smith, and Arnold A. Heggestad. "Capital Adequacy and the Valuation of Large Commercial Banking Organization," *Journal of Financial Research* 9 (Winter 1986): 331–341.

directly observe the required return for equity investors. Some method for using available information to estimate required return must be developed.

One widely used method of computing the cost of equity is the dividend growth model:

$$K_e = D/P + g$$

where K_e = required return on equity
D = dividends expected over the next year
P = current market price of the stock
g = constant annual growth rate of dividends (expected to continue indefinitely).

Suppose, for example, that Southwest Bank's common stock is presently selling for $50 per share. Dividends are expected to be $4 per share next year and are expected to grow 4 percent a year thereafter. The cost of equity for Southwest is

$$K_e = 4/50 + 0.04 = 0.12 \text{ or } 12\%.$$

If dividends grow as expected, an investor purchasing Southwest stock today for $50 will enjoy a 12 percent return on the investment. The required return on equity is a return that must be earned after income taxes have been paid. The required return before tax is $K_e \div (1 - T)$, where T is the tax rate. Thus, if the income tax rate is 46 percent and the required return on equity is 12 percent, the before-tax required return is $0.12 \div (1 - 0.46) = 22.22\%$.

Another approach to measuring the cost of equity is the risk-adjusted required return approach developed in appendix 8-A:

$$K_e = R_f + B(E_m - R_f)$$

where R_f = rate available on risk-free investments such as Treasury securities
B = beta, a measure of sensitivity of returns for the particular security and of conditions affecting common stock returns in general
E_m = expected return for securities in general.

The application of the dividend growth model requires stable dividend growth, and the risk-adjusted return method requires historical market price data for the stock. Lacking these, an institution may consider returns available on comparable securities for which there is an active market to estimate the returns available to investors in opportunities of equal risk. For mutual institutions there is no possibility of a market price for equity. The reserves of such institutions can be thought of as a form of equity, and the required return as a rate that could be earned on equal risk investments elsewhere if the institution did not exist. The returns available on common stocks of comparable risk would be a reasonable basis for an estimate.

Suppose, for example, the expected return for the market in general is 13 percent and the risk-free rate is 6.6 percent. Citizens Mutual Savings and Loan has no equity but has reserves which serve that purpose. Equity securities of similar companies have betas of approximately 0.844. The required return for Citizens is estimated to be

Table 12-3

Return on Equity for Financial Institutions

YEAR	1980	1981	1982	1983	1984	1985	1986
Return on equity							
Commercial banks	13.7%	13.1%	12.1%	11.2%	10.6%	11.3%	10.2%
Savings and loans	2.5	−16.6	−17.0	6.1	3.0	8.1	
Earnings yield for							
35 leading banks	21.4	18.4	21.2	16.2	16.1	12.8	10.1

$$K_e = 0.066 + 0.844 (0.13 - 0.066) = 12.0\%.$$

Table 12-3 provides some information on the returns on equity that have been realized by financial institutions in recent years. Also shown is the average earnings yield for leading banks, which gives some indication of investors' valuation of earnings.

Cost of Capital Notes and Debentures

The cost of capital notes and debentures (K_b) is the yield to maturity of existing notes or debentures (yield to maturity computation is covered in chapter 6) or the interest rate that would be required to sell new securities of this type. Southwest Bank has a debt series outstanding with a 9 percent yield to maturity. The cost of debt is therefore 9 percent.

Financial institutions frequently have other negotiated cost funds such as Eurodollar borrowings and federal funds. The cost of each such source is computed in the same way as was done for capital notes and debentures.

Cost of Time and Savings Deposits

The direct cost of interest-bearing deposit funds is the annual interest paid divided by the amount of interest-bearing deposit funds. Southwest Bank had average interest-bearing deposits of $100 million during its most recent fiscal year and paid total interest of $5.5 million. The direct cost of deposit funds is

$$K_{sd} = 5.5/100 = 5.5\%.$$

This direct cost actually underestimates the cost of deposit funds substantially. First, the cost of attracting and servicing funds should be added to direct interest payments. In addition, reserve requirements limit the amount that is available for investment. To adjust for this, the required reserves should be deducted from the $100 million and any return earned on reserves should be deducted from the cost. For Southwest Bank, the required reserves were $4 million, interest earned on reserves was $40,000, and the cost of serving these deposits was $1.5 million. The cost of interest-bearing deposit funds was therefore

$$K_{sd} = (5.5 + 1.5 - 0.04)/(100 - 4) = 7.25\%.$$

The cost of interest-bearing deposit funds can therefore be summarized in one formula:

$$K_{sd} = \frac{I_e + E - I_r}{S_d - R}$$

where
I_e = dollar annual interest paid on interest-bearing deposits
E = annual cost of attracting and servicing accounts
I_r = annual interest received on reserves, if any
S_d = average value of interest-bearing deposits
R = amount of required reserves for these deposits.

Cost of Non-Interest-Bearing Deposits

The direct cost of noninterest demand deposits is zero since no interest is paid, but indirect costs of attracting and servicing accounts are real. The cost of non-interest-bearing deposits (K_d) is computed in the same manner as the cost of interest-bearing deposits with the exception that the direct interest expense is zero. Southwest Bank has demand deposits of $60 million. Costs of attracting and servicing these deposits are estimated to be $3 million, and required reserves for these deposits are $7 million. No interest is earned on the required reserves. The cost of demand deposits for Southwest is

$$K_d = 3/(60 - 7) = 5.66\%.$$

Required Return on Assets

The next step is the computation of a required return on assets. This requires the combining of individual sources of funds in some manner. Since funds invested are a combination of funds raised from various sources, the required return is the total cost of those funds, divided by the total assets made available. The funds sources and costs for Southwest Bank are summarized in table 12-4. The required return on *net assets*—total assets minus required reserves—is as follows.

$$(53 \times 0.0566 + 96 \times 0.0725 + 10 \times 0.09 + 14 \times 0.2222) \div 173 = 8.08\%.$$

This is referred to as a *weighted average* required return because the computation weights each source of funds in terms of its total importance in the financial structure.

A loan, for example, must provide an 8.08 percent yield if it is to provide a 12 percent after-tax return on equity. If administrative costs associated with the loan are 3 percent of the average balance outstanding, then it will be necessary for the loan to carry an 11.08 percent APR to provide the 8.08 percent yield to the lender.

Occasionally, one will wish to deal with depreciable assets, municipal bonds, or other items with special tax implications. For these items, the after-tax benefit is

Table 12-4

Summary of Funds Sources and Costs for Southwest Bank
(in $ millions)

SOURCE OF FUNDS	AMOUNT OF FUNDS		INTEREST		OPERATING EXPENSE	COST OF NET FUNDS
	Gross	Net	Gross	Net		
Demand deposit	$ 60	$ 53	$ 0	$ 0	$3.00	5.66%
Time and savings deposits	100	96	5.50	5.46	1.50	7.25
Debentures	10	10	0.90	0.90	0	9.00
Common equity	14	14	NA	NA	0	22.22
Total	$184	$173	$6.40	$6.36	$4.50	

evaluated using the after-tax cost of funds, which equals the before-tax cost multiplied by 1 − T. If Southwest Bank with an 8.08 percent required return on funds and a 46 percent tax rate is considering a municipal bond, the bond must yield at least

$$8.08\% \times (1 - 0.46) = 4.36\%.$$

Spread Management and Required Returns

Many financial institutions rely on *spread management,* which uses the profitability model from chapter 6 to apply the required return concepts. For Southwest Bank, for example, the necessary APR on the loan portfolio can be determined as follows:

1. Before-tax required return on equity is 22.22 percent, so the required before-tax ROTA is $(0.2222 \times \$14$ million) $\div \$184 = 1.691\%$.
2. Assume all assets not used for primary reserves are invested in loans that have 3 percent operating costs. Total operating costs are therefore

Operating costs related to deposits	$4.50 million
Operating costs related to loans $(0.03 \times \$173)$	5.19 million
Total	$9.69 million

   Operating costs are therefore $\$9.69 \div \$184 = 5.266\%$ of total assets.
3. The spread, or difference between interest income and interest expense, must therefore be $1.691\% + 5.266\% = 6.957\%$ of total assets.
4. Interest expense is $\$6.40 \div \$184 = 3.478\%$ of total assets. Interest income must then be $6.957\% + 3.478\% = 10.435\%$ of total assets.
5. Interest on reserves is $0.04 million, so interest on the loans must be $0.10435 \times \$184$ million $- \$.04 = \$19.160$, which results in a required APR of $\$19.160 \div \$173 = 11.08\%$.

Note that this spread-focused approach results in the same required APR for the loan as that generated using a weighted-average required return approach. The difference is only in form.

Risk and Required Returns

Required returns for particular assets are often complicated by risk consider-ations. Suppose short-term funds cost 6 percent and long-term funds cost 10 percent. The yield on short-term assets is 8 percent, and the yield on long-term assets is 11 percent. Using a common cost of funds for all assets would result in choosing the long-term assets, while attempts to minimize the cost of funds would lead us to select the short-term source of funds. But this would leave us exposed to high levels of interest rate risk. To avoid illogical decisions that decrease value, risk must be factored into the analysis somehow.

One approach to handling interest rate risk is to assume the use of matched-maturity funding. Suppose, for example, the loan previously being considered by South-west Bank has a maturity similar to time and savings deposits and has no provision for repricing. We might then compute a required return as follows:

Required return = (0.08 × 22.22%) + (0.92 × 7.25%) = 8.45%.

The above approach is simple to use and frequently works. However, there may be cases where matched-maturity funding is expensive or impossible. Going back to the type of sensitivity analysis illustrated in table 12-2, we might ask about the marginal increase in liabilities and equity needed because of the type of asset being added. Suppose, for example, Southwest Bank wants to consider the alternative of increasing equity capital rather than using long-term liabilities to control risk. The company can raise new short-term funds costing 5.66 percent, but equity equal to 16 percent of the amount of new loans must be used to avoid increasing risk. With this technique, the required return for the loan would be

Required return = (0.16 × 22.22%) + (0.84 × 5.66%) = 8.31%.

In this case, Southwest can generate a lower required return by using more equity than it can achieve by relying on maturity matching to control risk.

REQUIRED RETURNS FOR NONDEPOSITORY INSTITUTIONS

For many nondepository financial institutions, the problem of required return is altered by the fact that the most important sources of funds fall into neither the equity nor the fixed-obligation category. This does not imply that the funds are costless.

While the payouts from many pension funds depend on the rate earned on the fund's investment portfolio, the beneficiaries still have the right to expect a return as high as that available from alternative investments of equal risk. Thus the required return also depends on the opportunities available elsewhere.

Take, for example, an employee pension fund at Alrite Products Corporation. Contributions to the employee pension fund are divided between mortgages insured by agencies of the U.S. government and common stocks, with half of the funds being invested in each category. If individuals did not contribute to the pension fund, they could invest directly in assets of similar risk. Thus the required return for the pension fund is the return investors could earn by dividing their funds between insured mortgages and a common stock portfolio with risk equal to that of the common stock portfolio held by the pension fund. The evaluation of pension fund performance is covered in more detail in chapter 18.

Insurance companies collect a pool of premiums from which they expect to pay claims. Policy reserves—funds held to meet claims—are the primary source of funds to an insurance company. As an example of the required return for such an institution, we look at a life insurance company writing whole life policies. The whole life policy is generally in force from the time of purchase until the death of the policyholder and pays its face value at the time of death. While the timing of the individual claim is unknown, its eventual payment is certain. Thus the company must build up reserves over the life of the policyholder. As the insured is aware of his eventual death, a policy of this type can be thought of as a combination of a savings plan to provide funds to heirs and insurance against the possibility of death before the savings plan has been completed.

Alternately, the insured can purchase temporary life insurance at a lower cost and invest the difference directly. The premiums charged and the dividends paid to policyholders depend on the return earned on the reserves. Thus, the ability to compete in the sale of policies depends on these returns. The reserves must earn a return similar to those available for other long-term savings instruments if the company is to be competitive.

While determination of the required return is somewhat different for a nondepository financial institution, the general principles are still the same. Each type of funds must earn a return that is at least equal to what the furnishers of these funds could have earned from alternative investments.

Since debt funds tend to have a lower cost than equity funds, we would expect that the required return could be decreased by increasing the ratio of debt to equity. Indeed, this will happen over some range. However, as the ratio of debt to total assets continues to increase, the institution's debt becomes an increasingly risky investment and the return required to attract such funds rises.[5] Furthermore, continual addition of debt increases the risk to equity investors, driving up the required return on equity. Thus there are limits beyond which the addition of fixed obligations increases, rather than decreases, the average cost of funds.

While the general relationship between capital structure and cost of funds is fairly well understood, identification of the exact combination which will minimize the average cost of funds for any given firm is elusive. Numerous studies of financial and nonfinancial corporations have failed to identify such a point.[6] However, what such studies have done is to give us a feel for the shape of the relationship between financial

---

[5]Of course, many deposits are insured; they do not become more risky. But financial institutions do borrow in the money markets, and these loans are not insured.

[6]See, for example, S. D. Magen, *The Cost of Funds to Commercial Banks* (New York: Dunellen, 1971).

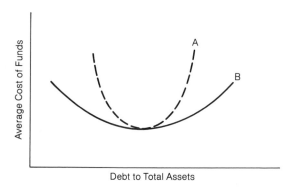

Figure 12-1:   Illustrative cost-of-funds curves.

structure and the cost of funds. Figure 12-1 shows two possible relationships between capital structure and the cost of funds. The actual relationship appears to be more like Curve B than Curve A. The cost-of-funds curve appears to be fairly flat over a broad range, indicating that within this range modest changes in the financial structure will not have a major impact on the cost of funds.

While the relatively flat cost-of-capital curve makes it difficult to locate the precise optimum cost of funds, it does indicate that within fairly broad ranges the institution is free to consider other factors in selecting a financial structure. The considerations of liquidity, insolvency risk, and flexibility can be given proper consideration without unduly impairing profitability.

SUMMARY

Capital is necessary as a cushion for loss because financial institution managers cannot predict the future with perfect accuracy. Capital provides a cushion for the three major types of risk: interest rate risk, credit risk, and theft. Capital also serves as a tool through which the regulators can implement policy. Capital can provide a cushion for temporary problems, but no amount of capital can provide permanent protection for long-term unprofitable activities.

Capital is not a single item. Primary capital includes common equity, perpetual preferred stock, loan loss reserves, and certain debt instruments. Total capital includes primary capital plus some other debt instruments and redeemable preferred stock. Regulatory capital standards are based primarily on ratios of capital to total assets. Other methods of measuring adequacy include risk-based capital measures, portfolio approaches, and management soundness analysis.

The required return is the return necessary to provide a satisfactory return to all providers of funds and maintain the value of the shareholders' investment. The required return for a financial institution is a function of the returns required by stockholders, depositors, and other lenders. In addition, the required return is affected by operating costs and reserve requirements. The required return is a key tool in product pricing and profitability planning.

QUESTIONS

12-1.   What is the main function of capital for a financial institution?

12-2.   From what types of risks does capital give protection?

12-3.   Why can a financial institution continue to operate when the market value of its liabilities exceeds the market value of its assets?

12-4.   Industrial corporations are free to use whatever financial structure they prefer, subject only to the willingness of lenders to furnish funds. On the other hand, the financial structure of a financial institution is closely regulated by government regulatory bodies. Why are the financial structures of financial institutions regulated while the structures of industrial corporations are not?

12-5.   Financial institutions typically have much higher proportions of their total funds furnished by depositors and other lender groups. Such large volumes of fixed obligations are normally considered risky, yet financial institutions typically have lower failure rates than industrial corporations. Why?

12-6.   Why are the capital ratios of savings and loans substantially lower than those of commercial banks?

12-7.   The cost-of-funds curve appears to be relatively flat over a broad range. What are the implications of this for managerial decision making?

PROBLEMS

12-1.   First City Bank has 300,000 shares of common stock outstanding. The stock is traded in the over-the-counter market (there is a market for the stock through local brokerage firms, but it is not traded on a stock exchange) where the present price is $40 per share. Dividends per share for the next year are expected to be $3 and have been growing at the same rate as earnings, 4 percent a year. The interest rate on Treasury securities is 6 percent, and the expected future return for stocks in general is approximately 12 percent. First City Bank's stock has a beta of 0.9. Compute the after-tax cost of equity using both the dividend growth model and the risk-adjusted required return approach. Based on a 34 percent rate, convert each of these to a before-tax required return on equity.

12-2.   Community Federal plans to raise additional funds through the sale of one-year certificates of deposit. The certificates will carry 9 percent interest, with annual compounding, and the estimated average cost of attracting one $1,000 certificate is $20. The reserve requirement is 10 percent, and reserves will earn 4 percent. Compute the cost of this source of funds.

12-3.   Old Reliable Life Insurance Company's financial structure consists of $1 billion in policy reserves and $100 million in equity. The before-tax required return on equity is estimated to be 18 percent. It is felt that policy reserves must earn a return at least as high as that currently available on high-grade bonds—8 percent. Compute the average cost of funds for Old Reliable.

12-4.   Old Reliable (problem 12-3) has office facilities, which earn no direct return, of $6 million. In addition, $50 million is put in liquid reserves that earn a return of 6 percent. The remainder of its funds are available for investment. What return must be earned on the remainder of the portfolio if the overall cost of funds is to be met?

12-5.   Neighborhood Bank has total assets of $110 million, with $100 million coming from deposits and $10 million coming from equity. The interest paid on deposit funds is 6 percent, and the cost of attracting and administering these accounts equals 1 percent of the average balance of deposits. The before-tax cost of equity is 20 percent. The bank is required to maintain non-interest-bearing liquid assets equal to 10 percent of deposits.
   a. Compute the cost of deposits.
   b. Compute the required return on funds available for investment (funds other than those held as required liquid reserves).

12-6.   Neighborhood Bank (problem 12-5) has the following asset structure.

Required reserves	$10,000,000
Investment securities	30,000,000
Loans	65,000,000
Physical assets	5,000,000
Total assets	$110,000,000

The required reserves earn nothing, the investment securities earn 7 percent, and the physical assets generate fee income, net of related expenses, of $200,000. What return must the bank earn on the loan portfolio?

12-7.   For Neighborhood Bank (problem 12-6), the annual cost of attracting and administering loans is 1.5 percent of the value of the loan portfolio. To achieve the necessary return on the loan portfolio, the average loan must carry what APR? What is the spread between the average APR required on a loan and the interest rate paid on deposits?

12-8.   For Southwest Bank, in table 12-4, suppose equity is decreased $4 million and demand deposits are increased $4 million. If the APR on the loans is 11.08 percent, what is the return on equity? Is this an increase or a decrease?

12-9.   Suppose the change suggested in problem 12-8 increases the cost of debentures to 10 percent and increases the cost of equity to 25 percent. Will the change increase the wealth of the shareholders?

12-10.   Delta Financial has total assets of $100 million, and $40 million of these assets are invested in short-term funds paying the Treasury bill rate, currently 5 percent. The remainder is invested in thirty-year fixed-rate mortgages paying interest rates of 11 percent. The company has operating costs equal to 3 percent of total assets. The financial structure is as follows. Ignore taxes and maturing portions of long-term assets and liabilities.

SOURCE	AMOUNT	COST
Short-term liabilities	$60 million	Treasury bill rate − 1%
Long-term liabilities	$30 million	8%
Equity	$10 million	

    a. What is the return on equity?

    b. Suppose equity were reduced to $5 million and short-term liabilities were increased to $65 million. What would the return on equity be?

12-11.   For Delta Financial in problem 12-10, suppose the interest rate on Treasury bills jumps to 10 percent and stays there. How long can Delta survive if it starts with $10 million of equity? If it starts with $5 million of equity?

12-12.   For Delta Financial in problem 12-11, you want to ensure that the company will not lose over 15 percent of its equity in any one year. You also want the highest possible return on equity. The asset structure cannot be changed, so you can change only liabilities and equity. Choose the combination of liabilities and equity that provides the maximum return on equity at current interest rate levels subject to these constraints.

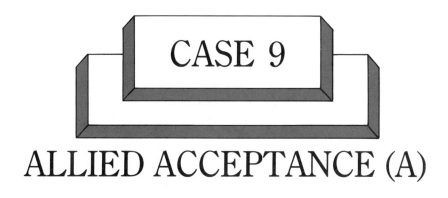

CASE 9

ALLIED ACCEPTANCE (A)

Allied Acceptance was a provider of automobile loans through dealers. As was typical in the business, the automobile dealer took the loan application and transferred it electronically to Allied. Allied then ran a credit check, primarily electronically, and made the credit decision. Allied never saw the customer unless the customer became delinquent. Because of the nature of the auto loan business, fixed assets were minimal, and operating costs, other than collection expenses, were minimal.

The business was highly competitive. Loan customers wanted low interest rates, while dealers wanted fast decisions and high approval rates. Operating efficiency and careful management of the cost of funds were the secrets of success in this business. The December 31 balance sheet of Allied appears in table 12-5.

The average interest rate on Allied's existing loans was 12.25 percent, but interest rates had declined somewhat and competition had driven the rate on new loans down to 12.00 percent. The average interest rate on Allied's existing bonds was 9.12 percent, and Allied could sell new bonds with an interest cost of 9.02 percent. The interest rate on existing and new commercial paper was 6.39 percent. Repayment of existing loans was such that the average balance for the upcoming year would be 80 percent of the December 31 balance. The volume of new loans would approximately match replacement. The repayment schedule on the bonds was such that the average balance for the upcoming year would be 85 percent of the December 31 balance.

Bad debt expense for Allied was 0.50 percent of total assets each year, and operating expenses other than bad debt expense were 2.96 percent of assets. Allied faced a 34 percent income tax rate and would be able to take advantage of loss carryback provisions of the tax code to obtain a refund equal to 34 percent of any loss.

Table 12-5

Allied Acceptance Balance Sheet for December 31

Cash	$ 6,791	Commercial paper	$399,413
Loans	606,633	Intermediate-term bonds	157,288
Fixed assets	4,011	Equity	60,734
Total assets	$617,435	Total liab. and net worth	$617,435

The stock of Allied was listed on the New York Stock Exchange, and the most recent trade was at a price of $23\frac{7}{8}$ a share. Dividends for the past year were $2.13, and dividends had been growing at a fairly constant rate of 4.5 percent a year, so dividends for the next year were expected to be $2.23.

QUESTIONS

1.   Estimate the before-tax cost of equity.
2.   Estimate the average cost of funds.
3.   What is the required APR for a new automobile loan to meet the required return?

ALLIED ACCEPTANCE (B)

The treasurer at Allied knew that minimizing the cost of funds was a critical part of the profitability picture. However, interest rate risk was also a problem. While interest rates had declined in the past two years, some economists were concerned about a rise in interest rates. After discussions with the executive committee, the treasurer decided to plan based on a particular high-rate and inverted yield curve scenario:

Interest rate on new loans	15%
Interest rate on new bonds	11%
Interest rate on new commercial paper	13%

For purposes of having a simple planning model, it was to be assumed that this shift occurred at the beginning of the year and continued throughout the year. Management was willing to accept a loss if this scenario occurred, but did not want the loss to exceed 10 percent of equity. With this type of cushion, the company could survive a wide variety of interest rate scenarios. It was assumed that a change in interest rates would not affect loan volume significantly. The financial structure could be adjusted by issuing more bonds at 9.02 percent, by selling more common stock, or by a combination of the two.

QUESTIONS

1. Select a combination of commercial paper, bonds, and equity that will maximize profitability at existing interest rates while meeting the safety objectives of management.

2. Assume the before-tax cost of equity is 20 percent with this new capital structure. Compute the new average cost of funds.

3. What is the new required APR for new automobile loans?

4. Given the competitive pricing situation, how should Allied price new automobile loans?

SELECTED REFERENCES

BENSTON, GEORGE J. "Why Continue to Regulate Banks?: An Historical Assessment of Federal Banking Regulations," *Midland Corporate Finance Journal* 5 (Fall 1987): 67–82.

BRAUER, GREGORY A. "The Value Impacts of Capital Adequacy Regulation and Stochastic Deposits," *Journal of Financial Research* 7 (Summer 1984): 95–103.

MAISEL, SHERMAN J., ED. *Risk and Capital Adequacy in Commercial Banks* (Chicago: University of Chicago Press, 1981).

MORGAN, GEORGE EMIR, III. "On the Adequacy of Bank Capital Regulation," *Journal of Financial and Quantitative Analysis* 19 (June 1984): 141–162.

MORGAN, GEORGE EMIR, III, AND SMITH, STEPHEN D. "The Role of Capital Adequacy Regulation in the Hedging Decisions of Financial Intermediaries," *Journal of Financial Research* 10 (Spring 1987): 33–46.

SHONE, DILIP K., SMITH, STEPHEN D., AND HEGGESTAD, ARNOLD A. "Capital Adequacy and the Valuation of Large Commercial Banking Organizations," *Journal of Financial Research* 9 (Winter 1986): 331–341.

SILVERBERG, STANLEY C. "Regulation of Bank Capital," *Issues in Bank Regulation* (Spring 1986): 7–10.

YOUNG, HARRISON. "Bank Capital Adequacy in the United States," *Issues in Bank Regulation* (Spring 1986): 3–5.

13

Loan Management

The loan portfolio is critical to the profitability of most financial institutions. Investing funds in securities does little for depositors that they could not do on their own and therefore does not add value. Lending, on the other hand, provides a service to society. If this service is carried out skillfully, the institution creates wealth for its shareholders and for society in general. But the loan portfolio is a two-edged sword. Loan management is also a primary determinant of default risk and interest rate risk, the two primary sources of financial institution failure.

THE CREDIT CYCLE

The process of loan management involves seven steps:

1. Loan product design
2. Marketing
3. The credit decision
4. Loan processing
5. Account maintenance
6. Collection
7. Monitoring.

PRODUCT DESIGN.   A traditional financial institution, with the regulators protecting it from competition, offered one or a few loan products and offered these same loan products without modification for decades. Profit was ensured by following the old banker's adage: "Don't make risky loans and don't pay the help too much."

In the deregulation era, product design has become the province of specialized marketing staffs who are constantly in search of features that customers will prefer and are willing to pay for. The process involves strategic analysis, creative design, market research, and profitability analysis. We will leave the marketing aspects of design to the marketers, but we will spend some time on the profitability analysis of loan products.

MARKETING.   Deregulation has intensified the marketing efforts of financial institutions. New loan officers are sometimes surprised to find that a major part of their effort is not the passing of judgment on applicants but the attraction of loan customers. While the actual marketing effort is carried out after product design, the choice of a marketing form is an integral part of product design. It is impossible to complete a profitability analysis without estimates of the cost of marketing a new loan. Marketing forms vary from direct contact by commercial loan officers to billboard advertising. Again, we will leave the development of marketing plans to the marketers.

CREDIT DECISION.   The fundamental fact of lending is that the safest customers seldom want loans. The job of credit analysis is to identify those customers for whom the risk of default is low enough to make a loan profitable. Credit analysis is a major field of study, and many universities offer one or more courses in this subject. While not providing in-depth coverage, we will cover the general principles of commercial and consumer credit analysis in this chapter.

LOAN PROCESSING.   Loan processing begins with completion of the application and ends with disbursement of the money to the customer, or rejection. The credit decision is part of loan processing. The design of a new loan product requires the design of a system for handling the processing, and the quality of processing is often an important part of the quality of the product itself. Some lenders have succeeded by concentrating on fast processing so that they can go from application receipt to loan disbursement in less time than their competitors. Many customers are willing to pay a premium for rapid, efficient processing. Many loan products have been delayed for months because of the time required to develop staff and design a system for processing and account maintenance.

ACCOUNT MAINTENANCE.   Account maintenance is the process of receiving payments and maintaining records. Efficient account maintenance can greatly affect the profitability of loans. Operations management is the professional field that deals with these issues.

COLLECTION.   A carefully designed loan policy will involve the acceptance of some credit risk, and therefore some failures to make required loan payments.[1] The collections function occurs when borrowers do not repay as promised. The first step in the collection effort is to turn a delinquent customer back into a current customer who will be

---

[1]A near exception is a country bank president of our acquaintance. At his retirement dinner, he lamented his one loan loss, a $200 loan to a young man who left town after losing his job in the 1930s. Until his retirement, the banker always hoped the young man would repay the principal and remove this one blemish. The minds of the financial analysts in the audience drifted to the thousands of profitable loans that must have been passed up in the failed pursuit of a perfect record.

a profitable customer in the future. When these efforts fail, the next effort is to recover what can be cost-effectively recovered. As with other activities, the objective is to carry out this function as efficiently and cost-effectively as possible. Cost-effectiveness must be viewed in a larger context than a single loan though. An institution that moves too aggressively on a minor delinquency may, for example, drive away someone who would have been a profitable customer for decades because the payment envelope fell behind the customer's radiator one month. In some instances, a collection effort is carried out simply to make a public statement that the institution is willing to push for collection.

MONITORING.   Monitoring helps ensure achievement of profitability objectives. Risk management is a particularly important aspect of monitoring. Financial institutions that do not keep a constant eye on the quality of their loan portfolio can get into serious difficulty quickly.

Our focus in this chapter will be on management policy rather than individual loan decisions. After surveying types of loans, we will focus on three policy-related areas: product profitability analysis, credit decisions, and monitoring.

TYPES OF LOANS

A financial institution chooses its loan portfolio structure in light of its liability sources and customer needs. Most institutions specialize, to at least some degree, in order to concentrate their lending activities in areas in which they have a competitive advantage. Loans can be classified according to type of borrower, use of loan proceeds, type of security, and maturity. The following overview of types of loans is organized according to type of borrower: people or businesses. Nonprofit organizations have needs similar to businesses and arrange similar types of loans.

Loans to People

The major categories of loans to people are mortgage loans, automobile loans, and the revolving credit represented by the plastic cards that swell our wallets. Other types of credit include loans for large expenditures such as boats, household furnishings, and college tuition. Types of loans and sources of loans are summarized in table 13-1. As is made clear in this table, mortgage debt is the chief debt of Americans, followed by automobile and credit card debt.

Mortgage debt accounts for three-fourths of the total debt of people in the United States, amounting to over $7,600 per person. Mortgage debt is used for the purchase of homes, although it is being increasingly used for other purposes because it is treated favorably by current tax law. Traditional mortgages carried fixed interest rates and were paid off over maturities of twenty or thirty years while being held by the original lending institution. Now, many mortgages carry interest rates which change regularly with some overall indicator of interest rates. In addition, mortgages are often combined in mortgage pools and sold rather than being held by the original lender. The value of mortgage pools nearly doubled from 1984 to 1987.

Table 13-1

Types and Sources of Loans Outstanding to People, 1987
(in $ millions)

Lender	TYPE OF LOAN					
	Total	Mortgages	Automobile	Revolving Credit	Mobile Home	Other
Commercial banks	$534,114	$264,983	$104,593	$ 91,401	$ 8,450	$ 64,687
Finance companies	180,976	38,328	97,900		8,580	36,168
Credit unions*	83,084		41,649	2,271		39,164
Retailers	40,482			36,087		4,395
Savings institutions	643,258	580,065	13,113	8,398	8,569	33,113
Gasoline companies	3,703			3,703		
Federal agencies	122,116	122,116				
Mortgage pools	635,224	635,224				
Other	199,053	199,053				
Total	$2,442,010	$1,839,769	$257,255	$141,860	$25,599	$177,527

Source: *Federal Reserve Bulletin.*

*Neither mortgages nor mobile home loans are broken out separately; they are included in "other."

A traditional automobile loan was for three years and carried a fixed interest rate. Now, automobile loans are often for maturities of four or five years, and some automobile loans carry rates that vary with the overall level of interest rates. Automobile loans are generally secured by a lien on the automobile. Leasing is often used as a direct substitute for lending, and the statistics on loans include some lease contracts.

Revolving credit includes credit card balances, retail store account balances, and balances on accounts such as automatic overdraft privilege checking accounts. These loans are generally unsecured, although some have been secured by mortgages to make the interest tax-deductible. Revolving credit has increased, replacing items like personal loans from finance companies and loans secured by home appliances. It is more efficient and economical to charge a television on your VISA card than to arrange for a separate loan.

Business Loans

Business loans can be classified according to purpose, maturity, and collateral. Businesses borrow money to acquire working capital (necessary cash and liquid reserve balances, inventory, accounts receivable, and prepaid expenses), equipment, and real estate. A summary of business loan types and sources appears in table 13-2. Working capital loans and equipment loans are lumped together in the commercial loan category.

Working capital loans are often short-term and are used for purposes such as a seasonal inventory buildup. Working capital loans are frequently made as *demand* loans, which technically means that the lender can demand repayment at any time.

Table 13-2

Types and Sources of Loans to Businesses
(in $ millions)

	Total	Commercial Loans	MORTGAGES		
			Commercial	Multifamily	Farm
Commercial banks	$770,470	$471,900	$253,261	$30,995	$14,314
Savings institutions	259,646		151,213	107,629	804
Life insurance co.	191,707		159,811	21,683	10,213
Finance companies	188,700	188,700	0	0	0
U.S. gov. agencies	36,635		6,592	19,606	10,437
Other	161,750		62,166	76,961	22,623
Total	$1,608,908	$660,600	$633,043	$256,874	$58,391

However, there is an agreement, either unsigned or in an accompanying letter, indicating the repayment plan. If a working capital need is longer in term, it may be financed with an intermediate-term loan having a specified maturity of several years or more. Working capital loans are provided by commercial banks and finance companies.

Working capital loans may be secured or unsecured. If a loan is secured, it is usually secured by a pledge of securities, inventory, or accounts receivable. Securities can be held by the lender and are therefore excellent collateral. Pledging of accounts receivable gives the lender the right to collect those receivables and keep the money in the event the borrower should default. The quality of this security is limited because the accounts receivable change on a daily basis, making monitoring difficult for the lender. An alternative is *factoring*, in which receivables are sold to a bank or other lender acting as a factor.

When inventory is used as collateral, several forms are possible. A *blanket lien* simply gives the lender a general claim against the inventory of the borrower. Because monitoring is difficult and partially finished goods would be of little value, the loan-to-value ratio is generally low. *Trust receipt lending*, also called floor planning, gives the lender claims on specified inventory items with specified serial numbers. Floor planning is used to finance automobile dealers and others selling large-ticket items with serial numbers. The control is better than with a blanket lien, but considerable monitoring is still necessary. One of the activities loan officer trainees get involved in is dropping in on auto dealers to help verify the existence of automobiles pledged for loans.

Field warehousing improves the collateral quality of a non-serial-number inventory by creating a separate area on the customer's premises in which pledged inventory is stored under the supervision of a bonded person. Field warehousing is an improvement over a blanket lien but has been the vehicle for some monumental frauds. A *terminal (public) warehouse receipt* is a much stronger form of security. The inventory is actually held in a public warehouse, and a receipt is necessary to reclaim the inventory. The receipt is then held by the lender. This type of collateral is used with various commodity items that can be sold easily and will not deteriorate in storage.

Interest rates on short-term bank loans are often tied to the bank's published *prime rate*. The safest loans were traditionally at the prime rate, while other short-term loans were a specified amount above the prime rate. The interest rates on existing loans were therefore changed whenever the bank announced a change in its prime rate. The prime rate is a little more difficult to interpret now because banks quote a prime rate and then discount from that prime rate for some of their best customers.

Purchase of equipment, such as machinery, trucks, and computers, is often financed by intermediate-term (more than one year and not more than ten years) loans, with the equipment pledged as collateral. Providers of these loans include captive finance companies owned by the manufacturer, independent commercial finance companies, insurance companies, and commercial banks.

Financial leases are often used as direct substitutes for loans. A financial lease calls for a fixed series of payments, like a loan, but title technically remains with the financial institution which acts as lessor. The lease often has tax advantages, and the lessor may be able to regain the asset more easily in the case of default. Leases are provided by equipment sellers, captive finance companies owned by equipment sellers, commercial finance companies such as General Electric Credit, and commercial banks. Leases are often used to finance the acquisition of buildings as well as equipment.

Real estate loans, which are used for the purchase of land and buildings, are typically long-term in nature and are usually secured by a lien on the asset involved. Commercial banks, seeking to avoid longer term real estate loans, often prefer construction loans and intermediate-term real estate loans. Life insurance companies, pension funds, and savings and loans all participate in the commerical real estate loan market.

LOAN PROFITABILITY ANALYSIS

Loan profitability analysis involves two primary efforts. First, it is necessary to identify the cash flows involved and determine the effective return that can be earned from the loan. Then the expected return is compared to the required return, which was determined using the methods discussed in chapter 12. A loan will increase shareholder wealth if the expected return exceeds the required return.

Among investments meeting this criterion, the highest possible return is desired, all else being equal. The return on an asset is not just the directly computed rate of return. It must be adjusted for the cost of acquiring and servicing the asset. While the administrative costs of acquiring and holding U.S. government bonds are quite small, a loan involves a processing cost, a credit examination cost, and general office overhead costs in addition to the cost of funds.

EXAMPLE.   Friendly Neighborhood Savings and Loan is experiencing insufficient demand for first-mortgage loans. Alternate investments, including second-mortgage lending to existing customers, are being considered. While Friendly has not previously been involved in this type of lending, other institutions in the area have, and data on their experience are available. The average second-mortgage loan carries an interest yield of 12 percent, net of bad debt losses, while U.S. government bonds are currently yielding 9 percent. Second-mortgage loans appear on the surface to be more attractive, however, the cost of servicing such loans must be considered.

The loan would be promoted through "stuffers" included with statements sent to regular customers. The cost would be relatively low, an estimated $5 per $1,000 of second-mortgage loans made. Credit investigation and other administrative costs associated with granting a loan would average $120 per loan. Ongoing administrative costs would average $0.50 per month per loan. Although managers anticipate that the original maturity of a typical second-mortgage loan will be seven years, the experience of others has shown that the average loan is repaid after three years. No penalty will be charged to people who repay early.

The profitability analysis is summarized in table 13-3. The monthly payment of $141.22 was found using table A-8. The outlay by the savings and loan equals the $8,000 loan amount plus the solicitation and processing costs, for a total of $8,160. The amount still owed (and therefore repaid) at the end of three years is determined using table A-8. It is the present value of $141.22 per month for four years, discounted at 12 percent per year.

The rate earned on these loans is found by taking the present value of the net monthly payments and final payments—using tables A-6 and A-8—at various interest rates to find the rate that generates a present value as close as possible to $8,160. This rate (yield) turns out to be about 11 percent (table 13-3). In other words, after taking into account the additional expenses associated with second-mortgage loans, a return of 11 percent is expected. The second-mortgage are more profitable than U.S. government bonds.

Table 13-3

Second Mortgage Profitability Analysis

Monthly payment (7 year, 12%, $8,000 loan)	$141.22
Processing cost	0.50
Net monthly payment received	$140.72
Loan amount	$8,000.00
Solicitation cost (8×$5)	40.00
Processing cost	120.00
Net outlay	$8,160.00
Amount received at the end of three years ($141.22×37.975)	$5,362.83

		10%		11%		12%	
Period	Payment	Present Value Factor	Present Value	Present Value Factor	Present Value	Present Value Factor	Present Value
1–36	$ 140.72	30.991	$4,361.05	30.545	$4,298.29	30.108	$4,236.80
36	5,362.83	0.7308	3,919.16	0.7200	3,861.24	0.6989	3,748.08
			$8,280.21		$8,159.53		$7,984.88

Timing and Profitability

In the previous example, an 11 percent return was estimated for a portfolio of second-mortgage loans. In many cases, however, the profit from a new venture will be delayed by start-up costs, and these start-up costs must then be recognized. Suppose the managers believe they can generate a $5 million portfolio of second-mortgage loans earning an average annual income of $0.11 \times \$5,000,000 = \$550,000$. However, initial start-up costs will be $300,000 after taxes.

Assume that the company must maintain equity equal to 5 percent of assets. The total initial cash inflow required from the stockholders is therefore $\$300,000 + 0.05 \times \$5,000,000 = \$550.000$. This may require the sale of additional stock to investors or the retention of funds that could otherwise be paid out to the shareholders.

Assume that the interest rate on deposits and other liabilities averages 9 percent (after adjusting for required reserves). The monthly cash flows to the stockholders, assuming a 34 percent tax rate, are

$$\text{Monthly cash flow} = (0.11 \times 5,000,000 - 0.95 \times 0.09 \times 5,000,000)(1 - 0.34)/12$$
$$= \underline{\$6,737.50}.$$

Assuming this loan product has an unlimited life, the return on equity is $6,737.50/ $550,000 = 1.225$ percent a month, or 14.7 percent a year. Investment in this loan product is attractive if the after-tax required return on equity is less than 14.7 percent.

Suppose, though, the loan product is expected to have a seven-year product life, after which $250,000 of equity needed to support the assets will be freed up. The return on equity over the product life is then found as follows:

$$\$550,000 = \$6,737.50 \times \text{present value factor from table A-8} + \$250,000 \times \text{present value factor from table A-6.}$$

By trial and error, the effective return to the shareholders is found to be 9 percent a year after taxes. This is below the return on equity generally earned by financial institutions.

Assignment of Joint Costs

One difficult problem in profitability analysis is the assignment of joint costs. Should part of the cost of maintaining a savings and loan building be assigned to second-mortgage loans since the existence of the building and other services makes second-mortgage lending possible? Or should these costs be ignored because they will continue whether or not the institution enters the second-mortgage market?

The traditional argument, and probably the appropriate one in this example, is that only the costs that will change—the marginal costs—should be considered. However, a typical financial institution offers a range of services supported by an organization and structure that will not change significantly with the addition or deletion of one service. Although certain costs are fixed, they must still be seen as a cost of the total package of services and must be met through charges for that package of services. Furthermore, certain services are offered below cost as a means of attracting more profitable business. The marginal cost approach must be applied with a strong dose of judgment, as the institution must price its services competitively and still cover its fixed costs.

CREDIT DECISIONS

The credit decision process depends on whether the loan is to an individual or to a business. Credit decisions for the two types of loans are substantially different, but there are important similarities. For both types of lending, the credit decision involves both risk and profitability. The object is not to minimize credit loss but to create the most value, which involves trade-offs between risk and profitability. Credit decisions for both individuals and businesses are based on the "three Cs" of credit—character, capacity, and collateral.

Character is of the highest order in lending decisions. Character refers to the borrower's desire to repay the loan as promised. If the loan applicant is not of good character, then other factors are of little importance; the loan will not be made. Analysis of character is generally based on past experiences of those who have dealt with the loan applicant.

Capacity refers to the customer's ability to repay the loan. Capacity is viewed in terms of the amount of cash flow in relation to loan payments, and the stability of cash flow. For an individual, cash flow is generally in the form of paychecks. Some people add another C of credit: *conditions*. Conditions refers to the overall economy or the particular economic changes that may affect the applicant. Analysis of these conditions is part of the analysis of the applicant's capacity to repay.

Collateral refers to assets that can be sold if the customer defaults and collection efforts fail. Collateral is important, but it serves only to limit the loss. Lenders make money by being repaid on schedule, and strong collateral would generally not overcome significant deficiencies in either character or capacity.[2] Some analysts use *capital* as a separate category, with capital representing the total amount of assets in relation to debt and collateral limited specifically to assets pledged to the particular lender.[3]

While the general principles of credit decisions are the same for loans to individuals and to businesses, the applications of these principles vary significantly. We begin by looking at the evaluation of credit applications from individuals and then turn to credit applications from businesses.

---

[2]An exception is the reverse mortgage loan sometimes used by retirees to supplement their income. The retiree receives a payment each month, which includes the mortgage loan balance outstanding. The loan in this case is based primarily on the value of the collateral, not the repayment ability of the borrower.

[3]Discriminate analysis, discussed in Chapter 16, is used to combine these various types of information.

Individual Credit Decisions

To begin, it must be understood that speed and efficiency are critical issues in granting credit to individuals. The person collecting credit information on a potential customer costs well over $10 an hour. For an automobile loan, the total difference between interest received and interest paid may be less that $500. Out of this $500, it is necessary to meet product design costs, marketing costs, processing costs, account maintenance costs, and collection costs. Given competitive pricing pressures, a few extra hours spent by a credit analyst can eliminate all profits. Furthermore, a delay in decision making can mean the loss of a customer. Despite these limitations, a credit analysis must be performed.

Character analysis is based primarily on past experience of the current lender or other lenders. A good deal of the information about past credit experience comes from local credit bureaus which specialize in maintaining files on the financial status and credit experience of individuals. Credit bureau files can often be accessed electronically be member financial institutions, so information can be assembled quickly and inexpensively. Checks on honesty in filling out the application are another important source of information about character. In some cases, lenders buy lists of people with good credit experience and then contact these people with direct mail advertisements. Direct contacts with lenders are more likely for larger loans, such as mortgage loans.

Capacity is measured using information related to income level and stability in relation to loan payments and other monthly payments required. Financial institutions often use rules of thumb such as limiting mortgage loan payments to 25 percent of income and total loan payments to 30 percent of income. These rules are, however, highly arbitrary. More refined approaches also consider numerous stability factors, such as home ownership versus rental, number of years at same address, number of years with same employer, level of education, etc. Economic conditions in the person's area of employment are also important. Other factors such as age, sex, and marital status were weighed in the past, but use of this information has been curtailed by antidiscrimination laws.

In consumer lending, the *collateral* of primary interest is the asset that is pledged as security for the loan. Nonpledged assets are difficult to control and may not be there in the event of default. A ratio of loan to value low enough to ensure recovery of the loan amount reduces the loss in case of default and increases the probability that the borrower will work through any difficulties encountered.

Unfortunately, it is not always possible to gain sufficient protection from the asset. Figure 13-1 illustrates typical loan balances for an automobile loan along with typical values for a car over its life. The result is that a window of potential loss opens up. If default occurs during the loss window, sale of the asset will not cover the loan. Furthermore, the borrower is not motivated to maintain and protect the value of the asset if seizure by the lender seems likely.

Other types of collateral have also proved to be surprisingly disappointing. Mobile home loans in the oil patch suffered from high default rates when unemployed owners forfeited their homes to the lenders and moved on. Most had market values

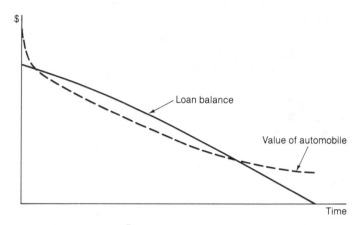

Figure 13-1:   Automobile value and loan principle over a typical loan life.

substantially less than the amount owed. Even mortgage loans have not been immune from asset value shrinkage. Declining local economies and the end of rapid inflation have caused home prices to decline sharply in areas such as Houston. Potential problems with collateral reinforce the importance of ability and willingness to repay the loan.

Once information about the loan applicant is completed, a credit decision must be reached. Judgment is the traditional approach. When judgment is used, an individual or credit committee reviews the application and passes judgment. Judgment is often aided by specific ratio standards such as payment-to-income and loan-to-value ratios. Many credit unions, for example, still rely on a credit committee for all loan decisions.

There is a growing movement toward the use of *credit scoring* instead of judgment. Credit scoring consists of assigning points according to characteristics and then granting credit if the borrower meets the lender's minimum point standards. A sample of the process appears in table 13-4.

Credit scoring systems create an economy-of-scale advantage. Expenses are involved in designing the credit scoring system, but benefits accrue once the system is designed. First, credit scoring systems allow quick decisions, which creates a competitive advantage. Second, credit scoring reduces costs by allowing quick decisions by people without extensive training or experience. Third, credit scoring systems bring objectivity to the process and therefore have a potential for improving the accuracy of credit decisions. Another advantage of objectivity is that the probability of discrimination against those who look or sound different than the decision maker is decreased. Finally, objective credit scoring creates a basis for monitoring the quality of loan portfolios.

Numerous consulting firms develop credit scoring systems for their clients, and some financial institutions develop their own systems internally. In either case, the scoring systems are developed from past data on similar types of loans. Essentially, the project is one of developing a scoring system that differentiates well between successful and problem loan customers and then setting a score that results in a profitability-maximizing level of lending.

Table 13-4

Sample Credit Scores

	CHARACTERISTIC	POINTS
Residence:	Rent, at same address more than 1–3 years	1
	Rent, at same address more than 3 years	3
	Own	3
	Own, at same address more than 5 years	5
Education:	High school graduate	1
	Some college	2
	Bachelor's degree	3
	Advanced degree	4
Employment:	1–2 years at present job	1
	2–5 years at present job	3
	Over 5 years at present job	5
etc.		

EXAMPLE.   Fidelity Financial has developed a credit scoring system for its new ready-access loan product. Interest on the loans will be 15 percent, annual operating costs are 3 percent of loan balances, and the required return is 10 percent. Management's objective is to earn as much income in excess of required return as possible. Credit loss expenses and total loan balances for various possible credit cutoff scores are in table 13-5, with the resulting profitability analysis. As an example of the computations, the income for the credit score shutoff of forty-four is as follows:

Income before required return = $36,000(0.15 − 0.03) − $208.8 = $4,111.2
Income in excess of required return = $4,111.2 − $36,000 × 0.10 = $511.2.

Table 13-5

Credit Score Profitability Analysis
(in $ thousands)

Credit score cutoff	Total loan balances	Annual credit loss expense	INCOME Before required return	In excess of required return
40	$25,000	$ 62,5	$2,937.5	$437.5
42	30,000	108.0	3,492.0	492.0
44	36,000	208.8	4,111.2	511.2
46	42,000	361.2	4,678.8	478.8
48	49,000	548.8	5,331.2	431.2

Credit Decisions for Commercial Loans

Business loans tend to be both larger and more individual in nature. Therefore, judgment is relied upon with much greater frequency. The three Cs of credit are again a useful framework for analysis.

Character is evaluated in a way similar to that for individuals. The lender's own experience and the experience of other lenders is important. Promptness in payment and honesty are key issues. Legal problems could also be a sign of lack of character. Information is often collected by direct contact with other creditors. However, reporting agencies such as Dun and Bradstreet are used to efficiently collect information about smaller loan accounts.

Capacity analysis tends to be more complicated for commercial loans than for individual loans. For short-term loans, the focus is frequently on liquidity. Borrowers often plan to sell inventory and collect receivables in order to repay short-term loans. The likelihood of this conversion to cash is a major objective of capacity analysis in these cases. Proforma analysis and ratio analysis are key tools. Ratio analysis involves comparing ratios, such as the ratio of current assets to current liabilities, to others in the industry and to ratios for the loan applicant company in the past.

For longer-term loans, capacity depends on the long-term profitability of the business. Financial ratios like the ratios of net income to sales and sales to total assets are given attention. Once again, comparison to other companies is used. Comparative statistics come from sources such as the annual *Financial Statement Studies* by Robert Morris Associates. There are numerous good texts on financial statement analysis available to guide the loan officer in this analysis.

While financial analysis of the loan applicant is important in capacity analysis, other factors also come into play. The quality of management is one of these factors. Experience in the field and understanding of the business are key factors considered in the evaluation. One reason banks sometimes specialize in lending to certain industries is that they have developed the necessary expertise to evaluate the quality of management in these industries.

A key question in all lending is, "How will the borrower repay? In commercial lending, the loan applicant's business plan is a big part of the answer to this question. The business plan covers both the use of the loan proceeds and the plans for repayment. The business plan also provides evidence of how well management understands the business.

Conditions in the industry, community, and general business environment are also an important part of the capacity evaluation process. Not only did business loans tied to oil go bad in droves, but the disease spread to unrelated business in areas dependent on the oil business. A similar pattern has developed with regard to farm and farm-related loans. Even a carefully laid business plan may not be sufficient in this type of environment.

Collateral analysis focuses on both the specific asset pledged and the other assets of the company. Lenders will again turn to the financial statements of the loan applicant, this time in search of value in the event of default. A cushion for loan repayment through asset sales can greatly decrease risk. Obviously, assets pledged as specific security for the loan give greater protection than assets in general, but all assets not specifically pledged to someone else provide some protection. Ratio standards such as the debt-to-total assets ratio are often used.

Once the analysis of a commercial loan applicant is completed, the decision process can take one of two forms. Individual officers of the lender often have authority to make loans up to specified sizes, with the limit being raised as an officer gains in experience. For loans above an individual officer's credit limit, a loan committee is used. The loan committee typically includes other loan officers, and it reviews the loan application, which is presented by the loan officer, and makes the decision. Certain very large or unusual loans must be approved by the chief executive officer or board of directors.

MONITORING THE LOAN PORTFOLIO

Continual monitoring of the quality of the loan portfolio is important to ensure profitability and, even more importantly, to control risk. Monitoring begins with an assessment of the distribution of the loan portfolio to be certain that distribution both geographically and across industries meets policy standards. Undue concentration in one area or industry leaves the lender exposed to wholesale defaults if economic difficulties develop. Interest rate risk analysis is another aspect of this portfolio-level analysis.

Beyond adherence to policy, managers are interested in trends in loan portfolio performance, including both profitability and safety. Profitability is measured using some of the measurement tools discussed at various places in this book. The quality of the loan portfolio can be monitored by following trends in several statistics. These include

1. Delinquency rate. This is the percentage of loans for which payments are past due. These can be broken down into categories such as over thirty days, over sixty days, and over ninety days.
2. Nonperforming assets as a percent of total assets. Nonperforming assets are assets repossessed through default and loans on which interest income is no longer being accrued.
3. Charge-offs as a percentage of loans. This is the percentage of loan balances that was deemed uncollectable and charged off during the period.
4. Recoveries as a percentage of the prior year's charge-offs. Recoveries are collections of previously charged-off loans. A high ratio of recoveries to charge-offs indicates a conservative policy with regard to charge-offs.
5. Loan loss coverage (income before loan losses ÷ loan loss provision). This ratio provides a measure of the institution's ability to absorb loan loss expenses from current income.
6. Loan loss reserves as a percentage of loans. This ratio provides another measure of the cushion established for loan losses.

Trends in each of these measures can be followed for a sign of deterioration in the quality of the loan portfolio or of deterioration in the cushion for losses. This monitoring makes it possible to take corrective action before the institution finds itself in severe difficulty.

SUMMARY

Loans are a primary source of profitability for most financial institutions, particularly depository institutions. Unfortunately, the loan portfolio is also a major source of risk. Careful management and monitoring of the credit cycle generates profitability while maintaining risk at acceptable levels.

Profitability management of loans begins with the product design stage in which the institution attempts to develop a competitive advantage by designing loan products that will provide increased satisfaction to customers. Profitability analysis is based on cash flows required for and generated by the product. A loan product that generates a rate of return above the required return is attractive, other things being equal.

Credit decisions are based on the three Cs: character, capacity, and collateral. Character refers to the willingness of the customer to repay. Capacity refers to the ability to repay, which depends on the strength of the borrower and economic conditions that will affect the borrower. Collateral refers to the assets, pledged or otherwise, that could be claimed and sold by the lender as a way to recover the loan in the case of default. With different guidelines, these basic principles are applied to both loans to people and loans to businesses.

Monitoring of loan performance on a continual basis is important if the institution is to remain safe and profitable. Monitoring can be carried out using a number of ratios that focus on loan quality and the cushion with which unexpected losses can be absorbed.

QUESTIONS

13-1. List and explain each of the steps of the credit cycle.

13-2. What are the major types of debt of individuals in the United States?

13-3. Discuss the advantages and disadvantages of the various types of security available for working capital loans.

13-4. Why is a financial lease considered a close substitute for a loan?

13-5. Give an example of a joint cost that might arise in loan profitability analysis.

13-6. List and define the three Cs of credit.

13-7. How does the application of the three Cs of credit differ in lending to people and lending to businesses?

13-8. Why is credit scoring more widely used for loans to people than loans to businesses?

13-9. What is the objective in monitoring the performance of the loan portfolio?

PROBLEMS

13-1.   The Financial Institution Deregulation and Monetary Control Act of 1980 allowed savings and loans to invest up to 20 percent of their funds in assets other than liquidity reserves and real estate mortgage loans. Community Federal Savings and Loan is considering automobile loans. The average automobile loan is for thirty-six months and carries an interest rate of 14 percent, compared to 12 percent for first-mortgage loan. It costs approximately $50 for promotion and $50 for processing for each loan granted. In addition, it costs Community Federal approximately $0.40 to process each monthly payment. To allow for unexpected bad debts, Community assumes that actual payments received will be 99 percent of contractual payment amounts. The average automobile loan is expected to be $6,000, and Community's required return is 9 percent. Will these loans be profitable?

13-2.   For the automobile loans discussed in problem 13-1, start-up costs will be $20,000 after taxes. The tax rate is 34 percent, and the required return on equity is 24 percent before taxes. The average cost of deposits and liabilities is 10 percent, and Community must maintain equity equal to 5 percent of assets. Community expects to generate a $1 million automobile loan portfolio and expects the auto loan product to last indefinitely. Will the loan product be profitable?

13-3.   Suppose the automobile loan described in problems 13-1 and 13-2 has a product life of only five years. Is the loan product profitable? Are there any intangible benefits associated with loans of this type by a savings and loan company? Do you anticipate any problems for savings and loans entering into lending of this type?

13-4.   Giant National Bank (GNB) is considering the purchase of an existing company as a way to enter the automobile lending market in the Southeast. The company being considered has a $100 million loan portfolio. As a buyer of dealer paper, its other assets are negligible. Income after operating expenses but before taxes and the cost of funds is 12 percent on the loan portfolio each year. To acquire the company, GNB must pay a premium of 5 percent over the book value of the loans. In addition, conversion during the first year of GNB's ownership will cost about $1 million. GNB's required return on funds is 11 percent. Should GNB acquire the automobile lender?

13-5.   Durban Financial's sources of funds are deposits (95 percent) and equity (5 percent). The required interest rate on deposits is 6 percent, and the before-tax required return on equity is 24 percent. Required reserves, which earn no interest, are 10 percent of deposits. Bad debt losses are 0.25 percent of assets each year, and other operating expenses are 2 percent of assets. Non-interest-bearing required reserve assets are 10 percent of deposits, and all other money is available for loans. What interest rate must Durban charge to earn its required return?

13-6.   Suppose Durban (problem 13-5) decided to use a 20 percent compensating balance requirement for its loans. The compensating balances would be held as non-interest-bearing deposits. What would the required interest rate for loans be?

13-7.   Shown below are data from the 1985 and 1986 annual reports from a bank division concentrating on loans to people. Analyze any changes in the quality of the portfolio.

YEAR	1986	1985	1984
Income before taxes and credit loss provision	$1,717	$1,141	
Provision for credit losses	1,017	646	
Income before taxes	700	495	
Net income	462	327	
Total assets	68,243	55,518	
Gross write-offs	1,172	719	386
Recoveries	214	134	100

13-8.   Lafayette Finance uses a credit scoring system and wants to set the required return so as to maximize income in excess of required return. Lafayette has an 8 percent required return. The interest earned on the loans is 12 percent, and operating costs are 2 percent of total assets. Total loan balances and bad debt expenses by cutoff score follow. Select the optimal cutoff score.

CUTOFF SCORE	TOTAL LOAN BALANCE (IN $ MILLIONS)	BAD DEBT EXPENSE (IN $ MILLIONS)
75	$384	$ 1.92
80	438	2.71
85	501	3.82
90	577	5.38
95	669	7.59
100	776	10.70

SELECTED REFERENCES

ALM, JAMES, AND FOLLAIN, JAMES R., JR. "Alternative Mortgage Instruments, the Tilt Problem, and Consumer Welfare," *Journal of Financial and Quantitative Analysis* 19 (March 1984): 113–126.

BOSMA, ROGER A. "Determining Quality in the Loan Portfolio," *The Bankers Magazine* (March–April 1987): 81–84.

HAYES, DOUGLAS A. *Bank Lending Policies: Domestic and International,* 2nd ed. (Ann Arbor, Mich.: Division of Research of the Graduate School of Business Administration, 1977).

LAMY, ROBERT E., AND THOMPSON, G. RODNEY. "Penn Square, Problem Loans, and Insolvency Risk," *Journal of Financial Research* 9 (Summer 1986): 103–111.

STEPHENS, RAY G. *Uses of Financial Information in Bank Lending Decisions* (Ann Arbor, Mich.: UMI Research Center, 1980).

TAYLOR, JEREMY F. "Credit Risk and the Logic of Lending," *Bankers Monthly Magazine* (May 15, 1986): 22–23+.

WOLFARTH, JOHN H. "Loan Profitability Analysis for Banks," *The Bankers Magazine* (March/April 1987).

CASE 10

SOUTHEAST IMPORTED AUTO LOANS (A)

By 1984, opportunities that provided both rapid growth and good profits were becoming increasingly hard to find. Managers at Universal Bank were therefore excited about auto-lending opportunities presented by the imported auto market as it existed in the southeastern United States. This market was consistent with Universal's strategy of national expansion in consumer lending. In addition, Universal's experience in the automotive credit market would minimize the cost of entry into this market.

The overall automobile market had shown little growth in recent years. However, sales of foreign cars continued to grow. Furthermore, automotive lending competition in the foreign car market was not so severe as in the domestic car market because the automobile manufacturers' captive finance companies had emphasized domestic auto financing. Thus they had not moved aggressively in the market for foreign car finance receivables. Universal's managers were convinced that they could sign up a large number of imported car dealers in the Southeast. They based their projections on the success they had enjoyed in the western and midwestern markets. It was estimated that average customer net finance receivables[1] would grow from $38 million in the first year to $500 million in the seventh year. Beyond this, little or no growth was anticipated.

The market could be served from a single branch in Atlanta. The foreign car dealers would handle the customer contact: Universal would approve the credit and buy the sales finance receivables from the dealers. It was also believed that Universal's other experience in automobile lending could be used to project branch costs. The typical size of a branch for automobile lending could be used to project branch costs.

---

[1]Net of unearned finance charges.

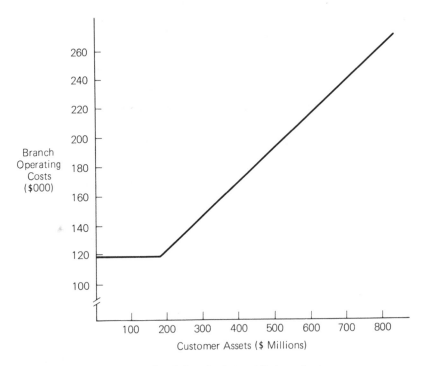

Exhibit 1:   Branch Operating Costs and Customer Assets

The typical size of a branch for automobile lending was $188 million in customer assets, and the operating cost for a typical branch was $119,000. It was estimated that branch operating cost would not be less than $119,000 a year even if customer assets were less than $188 million. However, experience with larger branches indicated that the so-called fixed costs varied with branch size: A $750 million branch had operating costs of $250,000. Exhibit 1 is a graphical representation of the apparent relationship between branch operating costs and customer assets.

The Atlanta branch would require a capital asset investment of $200,000, and personnel expenditures for start-up would be $100,000. From recent studies, the company had determined that the variable costs for attracting and processing a new loan were $83.31. These costs were in addition to the branch operating costs and the fees (dealer reserves) paid to dealers for originating loans. Moreover, bad debt expense was expected to average 0.40 percent of net finance receivables. It would cost $4.64 to process a payment.

A typical automobile sales finance transaction would require disbursement of $8,000 in loan proceeds and would carry a four-year maturity, with monthly payments. Very few loans would be repaid early, as foreign cars were not traded in quickly. These loans were expected to carry a 14.53 percent interest rate, and dealers would be paid a $56 fee (dealer reserve) at the time the sales finance contract was acquired. At steady state, the average customer net receivable would be $4,466.18. Thus, there would be an average of 111,952 ($500 million/$4,466.18) loans outstanding and 27,988 (111,952/4) loans made each year.

The cost of borrowed funds was estimated to be 11 percent, and equity would be 4 percent of total assets. The tax rate would be 46 percent.

QUESTIONS

1. Estimate the operating cost of a branch once the $500 million customer net receivable level is achieved.
2. The required steady-state accounting return on equity is 20 percent. Will the imported auto business achieve this 20 percent return?
3. Compute the accounting return on equity with equity equal to 5 percent of total assets.

SOUTHEAST IMPORTED AUTO (B)

Questions were raised about the realized return (internal rate of return) on equity in light of the fact that the steady state would not be reached until the seventh year. The cost of attracting and processing new customer finance receivables (loans) was almost certain to be higher during the start-up phase. It was estimated that the cost of attracting and processing a new loan would be $120 in the first year of operations and $100 in the second year. The cost of processing a payment would be $4.64 from the beginning.

To address the concerns about realized return, projections for each of the first six years were prepared (exhibit 2). To avoid tedious projections and complex calculations that do little to improve accuracy, the projections are based on the assumption that equity equal to 4 percent of average total assets for the year must be committed at the beginning of the year.[2] In general, it is assumed that all income and expenses for the year occur at the end of the year. The one exception to this generalization is that one-twelfth of the costs of acquiring loans, including processing costs and fees paid to dealers, occur at the beginning of the year (end of the previous year). This adjustment is used because the costs of making loans begin one month before payments begin.

[2]An exact realized return computation would require a month-by-month cash flow analysis. The use of annualized data in this example results in an error of approximately 1 percent.

Exhibit 2

Pro Forma Financial Statements

YEAR	0	1	2	3	4	5	6
Avg. net loan balance		38,038,985	135,657,786	275,767,815	400,481,797	469,507,020	496,072,521
Ending equity	1,529,559	5,434,311	11,038,713	16,027,272	18,788,281	19,850,901	20,008,000
Change in equity	1,529,559	3,904,752	5,604,401	4,988,559	2,761,009	1,062,620	157,099
No. loans made		9,324	18,648	27,988	27,988	27,988	27,988
Cost per loan		176	156	139.31	139.31	139.31	139.31
Pmts rec'd		60,606	233,100	517,586	853,442	1,138,016	1,310,702
Interest income		5,527,065	19,711,076	40,069,064	58,190,005	68,219,370	72,079,337
Interest expense		4,038,037	14,346,582	29,142,201	42,311,998	49,601,061	52,406,378
Bad debt		152,156	542,631	1,103,071	1,601,927	1,878,028	1,984,290
Operating costs							
Making loans	136,752	1,746,696	2,991,581	3,899,008	3,899,008	3,899,008	3,899,008
Collect pmts		281,212	1,081,584	2,401,599	3,959,971	5,280,394	6,081,657
Branch oper.	100,000	119,000	119,000	139,450	168,508	184,590	190,780
Total operations	236,752	2,146,908	4,192,165	6,440,057	8,027,487	9,363,993	10,171,446
Earnings before taxes	−236,752	−810,036	629,698	3,383,734	6,248,593	7,376,288	7,517,223
Tax	−108,906	−372,617	289,661	1,556,517	2,874,353	3,393,093	3,457,923
NI	−127,846	−437,419	340,037	1,827,216	3,374,240	3,983,196	4,059,301

QUESTIONS

1. Find the cash flow to the owners (net income minus increases in equity) each year for Years 0 through 7.

2. Cash flow each year after Year 7 will be the same as for Year 7. If projects are required to produce a 20 percent realized return on equity, would the Southeast imported auto business be attractive?

3. If the company were to start in the Southeast at the beginning of this year and in one new region (with the same patterns of income and expense growth) each year thereafter, what would be the accounting return on equity for imported automobiles six years from this year, assuming 4 percent equity?

4. What adjustments would you make in your program to move toward a 20 percent realized return on equity?

14

Bank Management

Like industrial corporations, commercial banks are private businesses operated for the benefit of their owners. The process of establishing management policies in pursuit of this objective is different and, in many ways, more complex than that of a nonfinancial corporation. Along with responsibilities to owners, management must consider the unique responsibility of a commercial bank to its community and the constraints imposed by the regulatory environment. It is thus necessary to consider the special objectives and constraints of commercial banks in developing management principles.

BANK OBJECTIVES AND CONSTRAINTS

Banks as Private Enterprises

Banks, like other private enterprises, establish policy aimed at achieving their primary objective: profitability. Profitability is more than simple profit; it is the level of profits relative to the assets committed. A satisfactory level of profitability is necessary to ensure proper returns to creditors and owners.

Like all business firms, banks generate liabilities and assets. Those who provide funds to banks do so by purchasing debt or equity securities issued by the bank or by placing funds on deposit. They provide funds for the purpose of receiving benefits in the form of services or expected future income. Thus banks are liable, as are other private businesses, to those from whom funds have been provided. They are liable to pay interest and ultimately return funds in the case of deposits and debt instruments issued. In addition, they are expected to meet dividend payments on equity as investor expectations dictate. Accordingly, management obligations to those who have provided funds are essentially comparable for commercial banks and private nonfinancial firms.

It stands to reason then, that bank funds must be invested in those assets that, when taken as a group, generate returns sufficient in amount to satisfy the legal requirements and expectations of depositors, creditors, and owners. A well-managed bank will generate a return on assets which not only covers minimum legal requirements and expectations but also provides retained earnings for support of future growth.

As is true in a nonfinancial private enterprise, proper management of assets and liabilities is critical to success and growth of commercial banks.

Competition

In a free enterprise system, external constraints are placed on private firms through the mechanism of competition. In competitive markets, firms bid for land, labor, capital and management talent. The interaction of supply and demand determines market prices for these resources. Similarly, prices for products and services are set by the forces of supply and demand. Thus, banks are not immune from competitive pressures. If wage levels are set below those offered in comparable employment circumstances, a bank will not be able to attract and retain competent personnel. Similarly, if compensating balance requirements and loan interest rates consistently exceed those charged by competing institutions, qualified loan customers can be expected to seek accommodations elsewhere. Thus, bank policy must reflect competitive forces in ways which are frequently similar to responses of nonbank firms.

Regulation

As discussed in chapters 2 and 3, the need to protect the safety of the public's funds has led to financial institutions' being more heavily regulated than most other types of business. Although the 1980s have witnessed a continued trend toward deregulation of the financial sector, no serious student of the financial system would argue that commercial banking regulations should be completely eliminated.

The need for banking regulations has long been justified on the grounds that unbridled competition would lead to massive bank failure and ultimate economic chaos. Consequently, the number of different banks and banking offices in the marketplace has been restricted. A new bank or branch will not be permitted by the regulatory authority if its existence would threaten the solvency of other banks in the market area. Similarly, to help maintain the solvency of the financial system, bank costs were held to artificially low levels. Prior to the Monetary Control Act of 1980, banks were largely prohibited from paying interest on transaction accounts, and competing financial institutions were largely prohibited from offering transaction accounts. This condition, together with Regulation Q restrictions on interest payments for time and savings deposits amounted to a government-imposed cost subsidy that favored commercial banks and that favored borrowers at the expense of savers.

Although the Monetary Control Act of 1980, together with the Garn–St. Germain Act, signaled a shift toward greater reliance on competition in allocating financial resources, the commercial banking industry is still subject to a huge network of regulations. Many of these regulations deal with questions of equity and social justice in credit allocation decisions. Such regulation, in addition to competitive forces and community responsibility, forms the complex of external constraints within which bank assets and liabilities must be managed.

Community Responsibility

In a nonregulated industry, competition is relied upon to ensure that needs of society are met. The acceptance of a charter to operate a bank carries with it certain community responsibilities which management must recognize and respond to. Economic growth and stability of an area may depend on the willingness of banks to make necessary credit available. But neither competition nor regulation will ensure that community needs are met. One of the most challenging problems for bank managers is the achievement of a proper balance between responsibility to owners and responsibility to the community.

CHOICE OF CHARTER

A group seeking to form a bank must first decide whether to seek a charter from the state or federal government. While most businesses can receive a corporate charter only from the state government, banks and certain other depository institutions may choose to apply for either a state or a national charter. This decision was traditionally made in light of the regulatory environment of the particular state versus regulations by the federal government. If all else were equal, the bank would prefer the charter giving it the greatest freedom.

The second question faced by a bank has been whether or not to be a member of the Federal Reserve System. A national bank was required to be a member, while a state bank had a choice. Prior to the Monetary Control Act of 1980, the primary advantage of membership was that the member bank could use the Federal Reserve System's services, such as borrowing at the discount window, wire transfer service, and check clearing. The primary disadvantage was that reserve requirements set by the Federal Reserve System applied only to member banks. Nonmember banks had their reserve requirements set by state banking authorities, with state requirements frequently being more lenient than those established by the federal government.

Increasingly, a number of smaller banks and some relatively large ones found that services provided by the Federal Reserve System did not justify the opportunity cost of required reserves. Indeed, the percentage of all commercial banks that were members fell from 49 percent in 1947 to 37 percent by 1980. The proportion of deposits held by member banks declined from 85 to 71 percent. By 1980, it was believed that this decline in membership, together with the growth in funds held by nonbank financial institutions, was impairing the ability of the Federal Reserve System to effectively implement monetary policy.

The Monetary Control Act of 1980 changed this picture by creating uniform reserve requirements for all depository institutions and by requiring that the Federal Reserve System establish prices for its services as well as make those prices available to all depository institutions. Thus the advantages of one chartering system over the other have diminished. By the late 1980s the proportion of banks which were Federal Reserve members had increased to 42 percent, and the share of deposits held by member banks was comparable to the 1980 level.

ASSET MANAGEMENT

Asset management in commercial banks is subject first and foremost to the constraint that assets must be highly liquid. Unlike a nonbank business which might forestall or delay payment without serious consequence, commercial banks must constantly be prepared to meet expected and unexpected demands for cash by depositors. Inability or even suspicion of inability on the part of banks to meet the demand for funds by depositors could lead to general distrust of commercial banks and ultimately to economic chaos. Hence, it is thus necessary that a large proportion of bank assets must be held in cash or in assets easily convertible to cash.

This results in a dilemma of some magnitude for the bank manager. On the one hand, there is the need to keep large sums in cash and low-yielding "near cash" assets. On the other hand, there is the need to meet community credit needs and to generate the levels of earnings necessary to meet costs. Such earnings provide a return to owners and constitute a source of funds which may be retained in order to sustain future growth. This liquidity-profitability trade-off is the central focus of bank asset and liability management.

Asset Structure of Commercial Banks

The first level of asset management policy deals with the allocation of funds among the major categories of assets: cash, investments, and loans. Other assets, including physical facilities, amount to a small proportion of total assets for the typical commercial bank.[1] Cash assets, which earn little or no return, are required to meet withdrawal demand from depositors. Investments, primarily in the form of short- and intermediate-term U.S. government and municipal securities, provide some income and can be quickly sold to provide additional cash. Loans, which are much less liquid assets, serve the credit needs of the community and provide the greatest source of profit. Shifts in the relative distribution of these asset categories have occurred in recent decades (figure 14-1).

Over the total period covered in figure 14-1, cash assets declined from 23.9 percent of all assets to 7.8 percent. Moreover, investments declined in relative importance from 44.0 percent of total assets to 18.1 percent. Loans, which in aggregate

---

[1]For large banks, however, the proportion of "other assets" has grown rapidly in recent years. Such growth reflects investment in foreign affiliates and other activities associated with the growth of international banking.

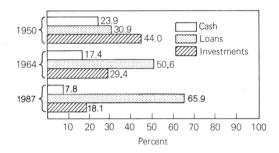

Figure 14-1: Asset structure for all commercial banks, 1950–1987 Graph excludes "other assets." Loans include federal funds sold and securities purchased under agreements to resell.
Source: *Federal Reserve Bulletin,* October 1987, and Board of Governors of the Federal Reserve System, *Banking and Monetary* Statistics, 1941–1970.)

traditionally yield a higher return but are less liquid, became increasingly important in relative terms. The data suggest that commercial banks, as a group, expanded their loan portfolio and, in the process, reduced liquidity over this time period. These changes reflect more aggressive management. As will be seen later, they also reflect an increase in the proportion of funds obtained from time and savings deposits, which are less volatile than demand deposits.

Cash Management

The most liquid of assets held by banks or any firm or institution is cash. But while cash is unsurpassed as a form of liquidity, the cost of holding cash is equivalent to the income which could have been earned through investment in alternative assets. Cash is held primarily for reserve requirements, day-to-day transactions, and as compensating balances with other banks in exchange for services. Unexpected cash needs are normally met through sale of certain liquid assets or through other methods rather than through the use of reserves. Since minimum reserve levels are generally fixed by law to ensure the solvency of the banking system and to accommodate monetary policy, they are not available for routine liquidity needs.

Effective cash management involves minimizing cash balances over and above minimum required reserves without compromising liquidity. This necessitates management procedures designed to minimize cash balances held for transaction needs and for compensating balance agreements.

Components of Cash   The total cash on the balance sheets of commercial banks is divided into four main categories:

1. Coin and currency inside the bank
2. Funds on deposit with Federal Reserve banks
3. Funds on deposit with other banks and depository institutions
4. Cash items (principally checks) which are in the process of being collected

As shown in table 14-1, cash represented 7.8 percent of all assets by June 1987. Currency and coin maintained on the premises represented 11.4 percent of those assets classified as cash. In other words, banks as a group found it necessary to maintain less than 1 percent of total assets in the form of currency and coin on the premises to

Table 14-1 Cash Assets of Commercial Banking Institutions, June 1987
(in $ billions)

CASH ASSETS HELD	AMOUNT	PERCENTAGE
Total cash assets	$213.2	100.0
Currency and coin	24.2	11.4
Reserves with Federal Reserve banks	33.8	15.9
Balances with other banks and institutions	80.8	37.9
Cash items in process of collection	74.4	34.9
Memo: All assets and proportion held in cash	$2,729.9	7.8

Source: *Federal Reserve Bulletin,* October 1987.

accommodate day-to-day transactions. Typically, coin and currency deposited in a given day is sufficient to accommodate cash disbursements, although local community needs and seasonal factors may result in temporary departure from such a generalization. Funds on deposit with Federal Reserve banks, funds on deposit with other banks and depository institutions, and cash items in the process of collection constituted a far larger component of total cash than did currency and coin on hand.

Reserve Requirements Prior to the passage and implementation of the Monetary Control Act, the question of membership in the Federal Reserve System was a significant influencing factor in bank profitability. Advantages of membership were weighed against requirements placed on member banks, chief among which was the stipulation that certain minimum cash balances (required reserves) be maintained. These required balances were usually stricter than those imposed by the states on nonmember banks.

The Monetary Control Act addressed these differences. An important provision of the act concerned reserve requirements and virtually eliminated the impact of the Federal Reserve System membership decision on bank profitability. Effective November 1980, sterile reserves were required of all banks, members and nonmembers alike. Sterile reserves are those which earn no interest. They must be held as cash in the vault or as direct or indirect[2] deposits with the Federal Reserve.

The quantity of required reserves for individual banks depends on the types and amounts of deposit liabilities maintained. These include transaction accounts, nonpersonal time deposits, and Eurocurrency liabilities. Transaction accounts include demand deposits, negotiable order of withdrawal (NOW) accounts, automatic transfer service (ATS) accounts, share draft accounts, and accounts permitting telephone or similar transfers for payments to third parties. Nonpersonal time deposits are defined as time deposits which are transferable *or* as time deposits held by corporations or by other institutions. Percentage reserve requirements before and after November 1980 are summarized in table 14-2.

[2]Indirect deposits are those which are "passed through" the correspondent network; e.g., Bank A maintains its required reserve balances in the form of deposits with Bank B. Bank B, however, "passes through" these balances by depositing them with the Federal Reserve System.

Table 14-2

Depository Institutions Reserve Requirements
(Percentage of Deposits)

Type of Deposit and Deposit Interval (in $ millions)	MEMBER BANK REQUIREMENTS BEFORE IMPLEMENTATION OF THE MONETARY CONTROL ACT		Type of Deposit and Deposit Interval	DEPOSITORY INSTITUTION REQUIREMENTS AFTER IMPLEMENTATION OF THE MONETARY CONTROL ACT	
	Percentage	*Effective Date*		*Percentage*	*Effective Date*
Net demand			*Net transaction accounts*		
0–2	7	12/30/76	$0–36.7 million	3	12/30/86
2–10	$9\frac{1}{2}$	12/30/76	Over 36.7 million	12	12/30/86
10–100	$11\frac{3}{4}$	12/30/76			
100–400	$12\frac{3}{4}$	12/30/76	*Nonpersonal time deposits*		
Over 400	$16\frac{1}{4}$	12/30/76	By original maturity		
			Less than $1\frac{1}{2}$ years	3	10/6/86
Time and savings			$1\frac{1}{2}$ years or more	0	10/6/83
Savings	3	3/16/67			
			Eurocurrency liabilities		
Time			All types	3	11/13/80
0–5, by maturity					
30–179 days	3	3/16/67			
180 days to 4 years	$2\frac{1}{2}$	1/8/76			
4 years or more	1	10/30/75			
Over 5, by maturity					
30–179 days	6	12/12/74			
180 days to 4 years	$2\frac{1}{2}$	1/8/76			
4 years or more	1	10/30/75			

Note: The Monetary Control Act of 1980 requires that the amount of transaction accounts against which the 3 percent reserve requirement applies be modified annually in accordance with an index established by the act. The original base in 1980 was $0–$25 million.

Source: *Federal Reserve Bulletin.*

The purpose of uniform reserve requirements for all depository institutions was to increase Federal Reserve control over the monetary system. The effect was to reduce reserve requirements for member banks and to impose sterile reserve requirements on nonmember institutions. In order to provide for an orderly transition, the new reserve requirements were to be phased in over a period of several years, ending in September 1987.

Deposits with Other Banks   Virtually all banks own funds left on deposit with other commercial banks. Generally, such funds are held in the form of demand deposits. If Bank A deposits funds with Bank B, Bank A does so in return for services which

Bank B is expected to provide. Bank B may act as a clearing point for checks drawn on Bank A; Bank B may provide other services such as advice and assistance in purchase, evaluation, or sale of securities. In fact, Bank A may hold deposits with a large number of other banks (called correspondent banks) in return for a variety of services offered by these correspondents. These deposits are referred to as compensating balances,[3] and the size of such balances, theoretically, is a function of the value of compensatory services performed.

Prior to November 1980, nonmember banks could generally include compensatory balances held with other banks when computing reserves. For this reason, balances held with other banks constituted a far larger proportion of cash assets for nonmember banks as compared to members. One consequence of the Monetary Control Act was the fact that compensating balances may no longer be counted for reserve purposes by nonmember state banks. Analysis of the value of services provided in relation to the opportunity cost associated with noninterest earning compensating balances is a particularly important component of cash management.

Methods of determining the cost of funds were developed in chapter 12. If management determines that the cost of balances held in return for services provided is greater than the value of the service, either the size of such balances should be renegotiated or the services should be acquired on a direct payment basis. Evaluation of compensating balances should be an ongoing process, and appropriate management policies and procedures providing for their analysis must be developed within the overall framework of cash management.

Evaluating Transaction Needs   Just as bankers expect their customers to plan for future cash needs through development of pro forma financial statements and cash budgets, banks should also plan for their own future cash needs. The volume of cash required for transactions is frequently predictable on the basis of past experience and future expectations. Too much idle cash results in income forgone: too little cash may result in forced sale of securities or in expensive borrowing in the money market. In both instances, the impact of poor planning for transaction needs can have a significant impact on profitability. The importance of good forecasts cannot be overemphasized. Good forecasting permits management to determine not only the appropriate size of the secondary reserve, but of the maturity distribution of securities included therein. Since longer-term securities normally carry higher yields, knowledge of cash requirements for anticipated future transactions permits management the opportunity to maximize income through investment of excess funds.

Techniques used in projecting transaction needs vary from a simple analysis of seasonal fluctuations based on the experience of prior years to highly sophisticated methods such as construction of econometric models. The appropriate forecasting technique for any given bank depends primarily on the institution's size and on the nature and magnitude of variables which influence changes in the composition of its assets and liabilities.

[3]Compensating balances refer to demand account balances which are required as a condition in many commercial loan transactions. The balances are to remain idle in the demand account.

Loan and Investment Management

The amount of total funds allocated to loans and investments is basically total assets less fixed assets and cash items. By the late 1980s, four-fifths or more of all bank assets were in the form of loans and investments.

The liquidity-profitability trade-off is most evident in these areas of asset management. Loans provide the primary source of bank earnings and community support. However, loans cannot be converted to cash quickly and economically; and we have seen that required cash reserves are not available to meet expected or unexpected deposit withdrawals. Thus, investments, which normally provide lower returns than loans, must be relied on as the main source of liquidity. Loan and investment policies must therefore be established in light of both profitability and liquidity needs.

Although no two banks are identical in the relative distribution of loan and investment portfolios, all banks must formulate loan and investment policies in relation to liquidity considerations. Liquidity is defined as the ability to meet demands by depositors and to satisfy reasonable loan demands without the necessity of incurring losses or undue expense in the conversion of assets. Variables influencing liquidity requirements for individual banks include the following:

1. Seasonal fluctuation of loans and deposits
2. Quality and structure of bank assets
3. Proportion of large borrowers and depositors
4. Trend and distribution of liabilities
5. Market area competition for the available money supply
6. Trend and distribution of earnings
7. Capital adequacy
8. Local and national economic conditions
9. Monetary policies of the Federal Reserve Board
10. Long-range economic trends of the market area.

Close examination of the above factors indicates that liquidity policy and hence investment and loan policies cannot be formulated in a vacuum. Investment and loan strategies depend not only upon one another but also upon variables which are influenced both internally and externally. The influence of certain factors may be predicted with reasonable certainty, e.g., seasonal fluctuations. Others require careful study and analysis of conditions based on data generated both internally and externally. It is sufficient to say at this point that variables influencing liquidity policy are constantly changing, and that the well-managed bank is one which is not only informed of such changes, but one which adapts loan and investment policies accordingly. Thus careful analysis of variables which influence liquidity will provide management with the basis for decisions leading to the appropriate mix of loans and securities.

Investment Management   Commercial banks maintain investments represented almost entirely by obligations of federal and other governmental units. Reasons for holding these investments include income, liquidity, diversification of assets, and flexibility.

Under normal economic conditions, returns available through investment in securities of comparable quality vary directly with maturity schedules. Thus, investment in Treasury bills maturing in less than one year frequently promises a return lower than that available in Treasury securities maturing several years hence. The primary purpose of investing in short-term securities is to provide for liquidity while earning at least some minimal return. Short-term securities of high quality may be sold quickly in the secondary market without serious risk of capital loss and serve as a backup measure in the event that cash is suddenly needed.

On the other hand, the well-managed bank should also maintain a portfolio of longer-term investment securities. Securities which mature over a period of several years, in addition to providing higher returns relative to short-term investments, provide for asset diversification and offer an outlet for funds still remaining after anticipated loan demand and secondary reserve requirements have been met. Long-term securities may be thought of also as an additional line of defense in the event that a totally unexpected need for cash develops and if such a need cannot reasonably be met through other alternatives. In this unlikely situation, long-term securities could be converted to cash quickly through sale in the secondary market. Typically, however, longer-term investments should be purchased for the purpose of providing asset diversification and reasonably high yields. Forced sale of long-term securities purchased during a period of generally rising interest rates will likely result in capital losses detrimentally affecting bank earnings.

Included in table 14-3 is a summary of asset structure for a sample of commer-

Table 14-3:

Percentage Distribution of Assets and Liabilities for a Sample of Commercial Banks

ASSETS	154 BANKS, DEPOSITS UP TO $50M	262 BANKS, DEPOSITS $50M–$200M	74 BANKS, DEPOSITS OVER $200M
Cash	5.0%	5.0%	6.3%
Treasury securities	20.0	18.3	12.3
Other investments	21.1	20.9	21.9
Loans	49.5	51.5	53.8
Other assets	4.4	4.4	5.8
Total assets	100.0%	100.0%	100.00%
LIABILITIES AND CAPITAL			
Demand deposits	26.3%	24.2%	23.3%
Time and savings deposits	63.0	62.5	59.3
Borrowings	0.8	1.3	4.8
Other liabilities	1.0	3.4	4.8
Capital accounts	8.9	8.6	7.8
Total liabilities and capital	100.0%	100.0%	100.00%

Note: Totals may not add to 100 because of rounding.

Source: Board of Governors of the Federal Reserve System, *Functional Cost Analysis: 1986 Average Banks*, p. 3.

cial banks as reported by the Federal Reserve for 1986. For the institutions represented in table 14-3, investments amounted to about 40 percent of assets for small banks and about one-third of assets for the largest bank category. For all banks, non-Treasury investments consisted almost entirely of obligations issued by federal, state, and other governmental units.

Notable in table 14-3 is the tendency for smaller banks to rely heavily on Treasury securities in calculating their investment strategy. Larger banks, on the other hand, having access to greater investment expertise in evaluating investment alternatives, rely to a proportionally greater extent on investment in security issues of state and local governmental units. Noteworthy also in table 14-3 is the fact that large banks calculated an investment portfolio proportionally smaller than that calculated by smaller and intermediate-sized banks. This tendency is explained by three considerations. First, large banks have a larger proportion of their deposits subject to the higher range of reserve requirements. Thus, a smaller proportion of assets are available for investment in other alternatives. In addition, as bank size increases, the capability to facilitate credit needs for loan customers, particularly those of large and prime corporate borrowers, is improved. Finally, the largest banks have the capability to invest in certain assets, such as domestic and foreign affiliates. Thus, a greater opportunity exists on the part of large banks to acquire higher-yielding loans and other assets instead of investing in securities.

Because commercial banks restrict their investment portfolios to high-grade debt securities issued primarily by governmental authorities, the risk of loss due to default of interest and principal payments is small. For this reason, and because most such securities may readily be converted to cash through sale in secondary markets, potential returns on these securities are less than returns available on loans of comparable maturity. Thus the primary source of earnings for commercial banks, and a primary reason for their existence, is to provide funds to borrowers in the form of loans. It is this important component of asset management, bank lending, to which we now turn.

Loan Management   The central focus of commercial banking concerns the acquisition and servicing of loans. Indeed, commercial banks are the primary, if not the only, source of loans for most small and medium-sized business firms. But while commercial banks provide a vital service to business organizations and to the community as a source of loans, they are not charitable organizations and cannot be expected to provide loans which may have widespread social merits but which may or may not be repaid. Indeed, banks have primary responsibility to those depositors who have entrusted their funds for safekeeping. Banks also have a responsibility to those who have provided debt and equity capital; thus banks are expected to operate profitably. It is through returns to equity holders in the form of dividends and through retained earnings that banks are able to continue in operation and to grow along with the communities they serve. Accordingly, the well-managed bank must institute loan policies designed to ensure that adequate control exists in the approval and disbursement of loans and that outstanding loans are monitored so as to ensure compliance with terms of the loan and ultimate repayment of principal and interest.

Table 14-3 contains information concerning the distribution of loans for 1986.

Table 14-4

Yields on Selected Loan Categories for a Sample of Commercial Banks, 1986

Loan Category	BANK SIZE Total Deposits for Reporting Banks		
	Under $50M	*$50M–$200M*	*Over $200M*
Real estate mortgage loans			
Gross yield	11.50%	11.76%	10.78%
Less: Expense	1.46	1.40	1.40
Loan losses	0.65	0.34	0.63
Net yield	9.38	10.03	8.74
Installment loans			
Gross yield	13.63	13.20	12.52
Less: Expense	3.94	3.26	2.78
Loan losses	1.20	0.68	0.62
Net yield	8.49	9.26	9.11
Credit card *			
Gross yield	NA	24.39	23.05
Less: Expense		12.66	10.69
Loan losses		1.64	2.41
Net yield		10.09	9.94
Commercial and other loans			
Gross yield	11.35	10.51	9.79
Less: Expense	2.48	1.91	1.48
Loan losses	2.17	1.86	0.74
Net yield	6.69	6.73	7.58
Money cost**	6.92	6.79	6.58

*Credit card yield data apply to "card banks." A bank is classified as a card bank if it administers its own credit card plan or is the primary regional agent of a national credit card plan. Unlike noncard banks, card banks fully fund the credit card outstandings. Credit card yield data above based on a sample of 39 banks with deposits from $50M to $200M and 37 banks with deposits over $200M. It is further noted that the money cost for the sample of card banks differed from that reported for the aggregate sample. The money cost for the sample of card banks was 6.80 percent and 6.66 percent respectively.

** Money cost is defined as the cost of processing demand deposits, time deposits (including interest expense), and nondeposit funds less any service charge or fee income. It is calculated as a percentage of available funds. Net yield shown above is before money cost.

Source: Board of Governors of the Federal Reserve System, *Functional Cost Analysis: 1986 Average Banks,* pp. 3, 38.

Notable in table 14-3 is the recognition that loans represent the largest single category of assets for commercial banks and amount to about half of the total.

Table 14-4 contains a summary of yields realized on selected categories of loans by banks grouped according to deposit size for 1986. While variations in realized yields occur over time, the data presented in table 14-4 are helpful in the interpretation of bank lending practices and the relative profitability of different categories of bank lending.

Real Estate Mortgage Loans   Real estate mortgage lending has long been an important component of commercial bank lending. At mid-1987, commercial banks held about 20 percent of all real estate mortgages outstanding and about one-third of those held by all financial institutions.

The largest banks, which tend to be located in major money market areas, invest most heavily in loans for commercial and industrial purposes, while smaller banks, many of which are located in rural and agriculturally oriented communities, invest heavily in non-real estate loans to farmers in support of agriculture.

For 1986, real estate loans provided gross yields that were somewhat lower than those for installment and credit card loans (table 14-4). Note, however, that bank expenses associated with making and administering real estate loans in relation to loans outstanding was substantially lower than that associated with installment and credit card loans. In consequence, because of the low expense of administration per dollar invested, real estate lending provided net yields that more closely approximated those associated with installment and credit card receivables.

While real estate lending can provide acceptable sources of revenue for commercial banks, the long-term nature of such lending contains inherent risk. Since the cost of generating and servicing such loans is relatively low per dollar outstanding, money cost and possible future increases thereof play a dominant role in the continued profitability of mortgage loans generated in previous years. In 1986, money cost as reflected in table 14-4 was under 7 percent. Should money cost increase dramatically in any given period, the net yield after money cost associated with fixed-rate real estate loans would obviously decline. The experience of recent years has served to illustrate this point. It is, of course, in the best interest of the bank manager to guard against such risk through the introduction of variable-rate mortgages (where mortgage interest rates automatically move up or down with the cost of money), through the use of contractual mortgage agreements (where interest rates are renegotiated at fixed time intervals, e.g., every three to five years), or by undertaking a policy whereby fixed-rate mortgage loans are packaged and sold in financial markets. Indeed, with the interest rate volatility of recent years, large numbers of depository financial institutions have developed a practice whereby all fixed-rate mortgages are packaged and sold. In this case, the lender retains all or some portion of the loan origination fees and may retain the loan servicing rights, thus ensuring at least some fee income. In the past several years, there has been a marked increase in this trend. Federal Reserve data show that mortgage-backed securities were one-third the value of all outstanding residential mortgages by mid-1987, up from about 5 percent in the mid-1970s.

Installment Loans   Over the years, installment lending by commercial banks has become an attractive source of revenue for commercial banks. Traditionally, and prior to World War II, commercial banks did not seek significant amounts of installment receivables and displayed little interest in consumer lending.[4] Following World War II, however, it became evident that yields available on consumer installment receivables were attractive in comparison with those available on commercial and other bank loans. Percentage rates quoted on installment loans were almost always quoted in terms of "add-on" or "discount" as opposed to simple interest. For example, a loan of $1,000 for a one-year period with interest and principal payable in equal monthly

---

[4]While installment loans may be made to business firms, most installment lending represents loans to consumers.

installments, and with a rate of 10 percent applied to the initial amount loaned ($1,000), produced a return of $100. But since the lender's original investment of $1,000 declines steadily over the time period, the true annual yield is substantially greater than 10 percent and approaches 18 percent (as explained in chapter 4). In addition, because of the short-term nature of installment loans, typically maturing within a few years or less, the size of the monthly payments are not materially affected by changes in the interest rate. The evidence suggests that consumers are not particularly sensitive to changes in installment loan interest rates and that such rates do not move freely with money market and mortgage interest rates. At mid-1987, commercial banks held 45 percent of the market for consumer installment receivables. This compares with 30 percent in 1960 and 13 percent at the beginning of the post-World War II era.

Interestingly, both gross yields and net yields for installment loans were higher than those associated with commercial and other loans, banks' traditional source of revenue (table 14-4). In addition, the previous discussion suggests that gross yields for fixed-rate installment loan portfolios could be adjusted as necessary by increasing rates for new installment loans to compensate for increased money cost. Thus the interest rate risk associated with installment loans is not nearly so significant as that associated with fixed-rate real estate lending.

Credit Card Loans: Credit card loans are among the most recent innovations in bank lending practices. Bank credit cards provide the holder with a preauthorized line of credit in some specified amount. Such cards may be used to acquire cash directly from a bank or to acquire merchandise from participating merchants. Gross yields available through credit card loans far outstrip those available through alternative lending categories (table 14-4). The high expense associated with bank credit cards reflects mainly the fact that average loan balances are small and administrative costs high per dollar outstanding. Also, credit card loss charge-offs are higher than charge-offs for other forms of bank lending. But while administrative costs are high in bank credit card lending, significant potential exists for reduction of such costs over the long term. It is in lending programs such as credit card operations, characterized by large volumes of routine transactions, that technological economies may prove to be significant. As technological improvements in this area continue, credit card lending may generate increased contributions to commercial bank profitability.

Commercial and Industrial Loans.   Loans for commercial and industrial purposes have always been the principal domain of commercial banks. While banks have sought to increase market shares for consumer installment receivables and have expanded operations to include credit card loans, commercial lending continues to represent the largest single component of bank lending practices. At mid-1987, commercial and industrial loans constituted about 31 percent of all loans outstanding for the industry.

Traditionally, commercial banks have preferred short-term business loans designed to meet seasonal needs for working capital purposes. Rates are tied to the prime lending rate, with large and established customers borrowing at the prime or best available rate. Loans to less established firms are typically made at interest rates that exceed prime by a margin judged sufficient to compensate for the increased credit risk.[5]

Commercial and industrial loans are essentially of two types. The first and traditional type represents those made for working capital purposes as discussed above. Risk associated with fluctuating interest rates is minimized for this type of loan because maturities are relatively short, averaging a few months at most and with rates adjusted in the event of loan renewal. The second major type of commercial and industrial loan is the *business term loan*. Term loans are those with original maturities of more than one year and are frequently made for the purpose of financing the acquisition of fixed assets. While data describing the extent of term lending in the banking industry are sketchy, available data suggest that the volume of term lending included in commercial and industrial loans increased in the postwar era. Traditionally, term loans have been made at fixed rates somewhat higher than those charged for short-term working capital loans. Higher rates are justified on the grounds that longer-term maturities represent increased exposure to the risk of fluctuating money cost.

Beginning with the experience of the early 1970s, when bank money costs increased dramatically as the result of severe fluctuations in money market rates, many banks turned to the practice of allowing term loan rates to vary with money market conditions. Thus many term loans are made with original maturities of several years but with interest rates tied to the prime rate or to some other index with rate adjustments frequently occurring several times per year. Indeed, with the continuing erratic behavior of interest rates in the late 1970s and early 1980s, an increasing proportion of all business loans were made with floating rates. Results of a Federal Reserve survey conducted in one recent year indicated that about 37 percent of all short-term commercial and industrial loans were made with floating rates, even though maturities averaged less than three months. Almost three-fourths of the long-term loans had floating rates.

LIABILITY MANAGEMENT

In recent years, commercial banks have devoted increased attention to the concept of liability management. As money costs climbed, and as the demand for bank loans increased, commercial bank managers became increasingly aware of the need to acquire funds to support asset expansion. Thus there developed a general awareness of the fact that desired levels of expansion could be met only through new means of attracting funds. Consequently, the management of commercial bank liabilities took on an importance comparable to that of asset management.

The nature of liabilities and liability management by commercial banks shifted markedly over the decades of the 1960s, 1970s, and into the 1980s. Over that period, in response to rising market interest rates and continued loan demand, bankers shifted

[5]With the volatility of interest rates prevailing in recent years, some banks began the practice of charging less than prime for some short-term loans to certain large business customers. The extent of such lending was unknown.

from a passive role as money gatherers to a role involving active competition for funds in the marketplace. In 1950, almost three-fourths of liabilities for all commercial banks were represented by non-interest-bearing demand deposits. The ratio of demand to time deposits was almost 3:1, and rates paid on time and savings accounts were low by today's standards. Loan demand during the previous decade was largely supported by available liabilities and by converting investment securities accumulated during the war and during the postwar period. Thus the efforts of bank managers were devoted primarily to asset management with little attention paid to the availability and structure of liabilities.

THE CHANGING NATURE OF BANK LIABILITIES

Aggregate liabilities of commercial banks for 31 December 1950, 31 December 1964, and June 1987 have been summarized (figure 14-2). While non-interest-bearing demand deposits dominated the liability structure in 1950, *time and savings deposits* became increasingly important with the passage of time. By 1987 time and savings deposits were clearly the most important source of funds for commercial banks. At the same time, the proportion of funds represented by demand deposits had declined from 73.8 percent in 1950 to 22.7 percent by 1987. Commercial bank borrowings, virtually nonexistent in 1950 had risen to 24.6 percent of total liabilities. Factors influencing this

Figure 14-2: Liability structure for all commercial banks, 1950–1987. (Source: same as figure 14-1.)
Note: Approximately three-fourths of 1987 transaction accounts are non-interest-bearing demand deposits. All transaction balances for 1950 and 1964 were non-interest-bearing demand deposits.

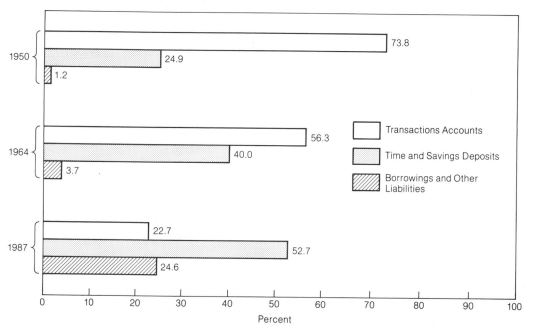

condition included a number of innovations in liability management which occurred. Included among these were the following:

1. Development of a secondary market for large-denomination certificates of deposit (CDs)
2. Issuance of consumer-type CDs
3. Expansion of the federal funds market
4. Eurodollar borrowings
5. Repurchase agreements

Development of a Secondary Market for CDs   A certificate of deposit (CD) issued by a bank is a receipt for funds placed on deposit. The funds must be left on deposit for the time specified on the certificate and bear interest at a rate established at the time of issuance. Prior to 1961, CDs were issued by a few banks. Total CD outstandings prior to 1961, however, constituted little more than 1 percent of total liabilities and less than 4 percent of total time and savings deposits.

While commercial banks had authority to issue CDs prior to 1961, many felt that to do so would encourage corporations and other large depositors, who were precluded by law from holding passbook savings accounts, to transfer funds from non-interest-bearing demand deposits to interest-bearing CDs. But beginning in early 1961, several large banks began to issue large CDs in negotiable form. At the same time, major securities dealers agreed to make a market for them. Thus the availability of negotiable CDs in large denominations and the liquidity provided by the ready availability of a secondary market provided corporations and other large investors with an alternative and highly liquid means for investment of temporary excess funds. Individual banks found that by varying rates for new issues slightly in relation to current market yields, the volume of new time deposits attracted could be substantially increased or decreased in accordance with current or projected needs for funds. Hence the ability of commercial banks to manage liabilities was improved dramatically with this turn of events.

Issuance of Consumer-Type CDs   While large negotiable CDs played an important role in bank liability management during the 1960s and 1970s, consumer-type CDs (savings certificates, nonnegotiable CDs, and negotiable CDs in denominations of less than $100,000) took on increasing importance following a change in Regulation Q in late 1965. In December of that year, ceiling rates under Regulation Q were increased for time deposits, while rates for passbook savings accounts were held at 4 percent. Subsequent changes in Regulation Q during the 1960s and 1970s maintained and in some cases expanded the rate differential between consumer savings and time deposits. Finally, because of disintermediation caused by increasingly higher yields on open market securities beginning in 1977, the federal regulatory agencies authorized the sale of certain new consumer-type certificates effective 1 June 1978. The most important of these was the six-month money market certificate, available in minimum denominations of $10,000 and with interest yield tied to the Treasury bill rate. Thus banks were in a position to provide a variety of time certificates in various denominations and maturities. Finally, the Monetary

Control Act of 1980 provided for a gradual phase-out of Regulation Q ceilings. Effective 1 October 1983, restrictions on maximum rate ceilings for all categories of time deposit accounts maturing in more than thirty-one days were removed. All remaining regulation Q ceilings were phased out by 31 March 1986.

Expansion of the Federal Funds Market   Previous discussion has emphasized the need for commercial bank managers to maintain an appropriate balance between liquid investments and higher-yielding loans. It has also been suggested that profitability objectives require that a minimum of excess cash over and above required reserves be held. Cash in the vault and deposits with Federal Reserve banks that exceed necessary requirements may represent evidence of inefficient management. So are balances held with correspondents in excess of that expected or required in return for services provided. On the other hand, it is not realistic to expect loan demand and investment requirements to precisely match the quantity of funds available for the purpose of meeting such demand or requirements. While the volume of deposit liabilities may be managed through variation in interest rates and in the maturity range of offerings, and while lending and investment policies and activities may be adjusted to affect the level and composition of assets, it is likely that too much or too little cash will be available for desired purposes at any given point in time. Further, it may be expected that divergences from the optimal level and composition of assets and liabilities would be an occurrence expected almost daily.

Throughout the 1960s and 1970s and into the 1980s, as interest rates rose and competitive conditions intensified, commercial banks responded to the need for finer adjustment in asset and liability management. A significant mechanism to provide for such adjustment was the *federal funds market.*

Federal funds are deposits held by commercial banks with the Federal Reserve System. The federal funds market refers to the exchange of claims between banks against such balances. Such exchange takes place through the loan of deposit balances by one bank to another. The bank which has borrowed federal funds is said to have "purchased" such funds, and the bank which has loaned federal funds is said to have "sold" such funds. From the point of view of the "selling" bank, federal funds constitute an asset, and from the point of view of the "buying" bank, a liability.

While federal funds and the federal funds market have existed for a considerable number of years, growth and development of the market began in earnest during the 1960s and was spearheaded, as were many major banking innovations, by major money market banks located principally in New York City. Federal funds transactions are commonly ones which represent loans for a period of only one day, although the length of time may be expanded if desired by the participating parties. Whether or not a bank is a member of the Federal Reserve System is not material insofar as market participation is concerned, since transactions may be handled through a correspondent.

Traditionally, federal funds were looked upon as an alternative to direct borrowing from the Federal Reserve System for the purpose of meeting reserve requirements. Thus banks needing reserves would borrow from other banks only if such funds were available at lower cost.

Beginning in the mid-1960s, in the face of strong loan demand and tight money, the federal funds rate began to exceed the discount rate (rate of interest charged by Federal Reserve banks to member banks). As more and more banks became aware of the convenience and potential of the federal funds market, participation in the market and the volume of transactions increased dramatically.

Available data suggest that small banks tend to be net sellers of federal funds (lenders), while large banks are net buyers (borrowers). In one recent year, for example, banks with total assets of less than $50 million, while important sources for federal funds did little borrowing in the market. On the other hand, the largest banks, particularly those with assets exceeding $1 billion, were heavy borrowers of federal funds. In effect, the federal funds market was functioning as a conduit whereby excess funds of small banks were utilized to support cash needs of large banks. Thus, from the viewpoint of bank managers, the federal funds market affords a convenient and flexible means to improve asset and liability management in promoting the goal of profit maximization.

Eurodollar Borrowings   Another highly significant development within the framework of liability management occurred within the spectacular growth in Eurodollar borrowings.

Eurodollars are deposits denominated in U.S. dollars and held by any bank located outside the United States—including foreign branches of U.S. banks. Dollars may be on deposit with foreign banks for a variety of reasons. They may exist for the purpose of facilitating trade, or they may have been deposited outside the United States so as to earn a higher rate of return. Most Eurodollar deposits are held in the form of short-term time deposits and thus earn interest.

Growth in this market became significant in the latter half of the 1960s. Impetus to this growth was provided by tight money conditions that prevailed at times and by Regulation Q ceilings which restricted the ability of banks to acquire desired levels of funds domestically. Hence large banks turned to foreign markets in search of additional funds.

Since Eurodollars represent borrowings rather than deposits, domestic banks were not restricted by interest rate ceilings. Thus a supply of funds from this source was virtually ensured for large banks when funds were needed.

Initially, Eurodollar borrowings were not subject to reserve requirements, thus adding to the desirability of this source from the viewpoint of individual banks. However, reserve requirements were imposed on certain Eurodollar borrowings in 1969, and the percentage requirement has changed from time to time in accordance with Federal Reserve System objectives.

Given the continued internationalization of business affairs and the expansion and growing importance of U.S. banks in foreign lands, as well as growth in the presence of foreign-owned banks in the U.S., it may be expected that Eurodollars will continue as an important nondeposit source of funds for commercial banks.

Repurchase Agreements   A "repurchase agreement" (RP or "repo") is a financing method by which a bank can acquire relatively large amounts of cash for short-term periods, frequently from its corporate customers. A repurchase agreement occurs when a bank sells securities, such as Treasury bills, to a securities dealer or to a corporation with an agreement to repurchase them at a stated price and a specified time. The sale is usually over a period of a few days. A bank manager may adjust his banks's reserve position by selling securities to a corporation on Friday with an agreement to repurchase these securities on Monday. The transaction, in this example, would have the effect of increasing the bank's average cash balance for the reserve period. A repurchase agreement is frequently preferable to sale of the securities in the open market with the intent to buy the same securities a few days later, because the risk of price fluctuation and brokerage commissions are both avoided.

The use of RPs as a source of funds for commercial banks increased with the surge in short-term interest rates in the late 1970s and early 1980s. The value of security repurchase agreements approximated 100 billion by 1987.

BANK PROFITABILITY

Analysis of income and expense data for a sample of commercial banks shows that the largest single source of revenue is loan interest and discount. The data further show that investment income tends to decline in proportion to total income as bank size increases (table 14-5). The income distribution reflects the previously noted fact that small banks tend to maintain a larger investment portfolio and a smaller loan portfolio compared to larger banks. Other income, reflecting revenue derived from trust services, computer service fees, fees derived through letters of credit, safe deposit box rentals, and other activities was proportionately greater for medium-sized and large banks. Medium-

Table 14-5

Percentage Distribution of Revenue and Expense Items for a Sample of Commercial Banks

REVENUE	154 BANKS, DEPOSITS UP TO $50M	260 BANKS, DEPOSITS $50M–$200M	81 BANKS, DEPOSITS OVER $200M
Loan interest and discount	53.5%	51.9%	55.8%
Investment income	38.8	36.1	33.3
Service and handling charge	1.7	2.1	2.3
Other income	5.9	9.8	8.6
Total revenue	100.0%	100.0%	100.00%
EXPENSE			
Salaries and fringes	15.1%	14.0%	14.8%
Other operating expenses	23.2	19.2	19.9
Interest expense	48.9	47.4	49.9
Total expense:	87.2%	80.7%	84.6
Net current earnings (before tax)	12.8%	19.3%	15.4%

Source: Board of Governors of the Federal Reserve System, *Functional Cost Analysis: 1986 Average Banks*, p. 3.

sized and large banks of course, have a greater capability to offer many such services. We note here that other income has become an increasingly important source of revenue for banks in the 1980s. In 1982, for example, other income ranged from 1.9 percent of total income for small banks to 3.9 percent of the total for large banks. As deregulation of the financial services industry progressed during the 1980s, competitive forces drove down net interest margins, forcing bank managers to look for other revenue sources.

Analysis of expense data for the sample group reveals that interest expense is clearly the dominant expense item for commercial banks. While total expense in relation to revenue, and therefore profitability, may vary from year to year by bank size, the 1986 data clearly show that midsized banks generated greater net current earnings compared to the other two groups (table 14-5). Among other factors, the data reflect economic realities of the time. Many small banks were experiencing pressures associated with a depressed agricultural sector. Many large banks were experiencing problems associated with loan portfolios that included large numbers of nonperforming loans, many of which had been made to Third-World countries. Profitability data for all commercial banks show that the banking industry, unlike thrifts, maintained profitability as deregulation commenced (table 14-6). The data suggest, however, that profitability declined generally over much of the period shown in the table.

We have noted the growth and changing composition of bank assets and liabilities that has occurred throughout recent decades. Many trends noted thus far suggest that the general composition of bank assets has become less liquid. And with the substitution of a greater volume of loans for cash balances and liquid investments, some would argue that asset structure is characterized by a greater degree of risk as the result of this process.

In addition, increased reliance on CDs, Eurodollars, and other forms of "pur-

TABLE 14-6

Profitability of Insured Commercial Banks

	NET INCOME AS PERCENTAGE OF	
Year	Total Assets	Total Net Worth
1978	0.76	12.9
1979	0.80	13.9
1980	0.79	13.7
1981	0.76	13.1
1982	0.71	12.1
1983	0.67	11.2
1984	0.64	10.6
1985	0.70	11.3
1986	0.64	10.2

Source: Data through 1980 from *Federal Reserve Bulletin* (July 1983), p. 498. Data after 1980 from *Federal Reserve Bulletin*, July 1987, p. 539.

Table 14-7.

Number of Banks Closed Because of Financial Difficulties
1934–1987

1934	61	1952	4	1970	8
1935	32	1953	5	1971	6
1936	72	1954	4	1972	3
1937	84	1955	5	1973	6
1938	81	1956	3	1974	4
1939	72	1957	3	1975	14
1940	48	1958	9	1976	17
1941	17	1959	3	1977	6
1942	23	1960	2	1978	7
1943	5	1961	9	1979	10
1944	2	1962	3	1980	10
1945	1	1963	2	1981	10
1946	2	1964	8	1982	42
1947	6	1965	9	1983	48
1948	3	1966	8	1984	78
1950	5	1967	4	1985	118
1951	5	1968	3	1986	138
		1969	9	1987	184

Source: *Annual Report,* Federal Deposit Insurance Corporation.

chased" funds, together with the removal of interest rate ceilings and a general reduction in the proportion of funds acquired through interest-free deposits, has contributed to upward pressure on the cost of bank funds. Indeed, with increased volatility of financial markets and with deregulation of the financial services industry, the number of banks closed because of financial difficulties began to grow dramatically. By the late 1980s, annual bank failures were in the three-digit range and growing—in sharp contrast to previous decades where failures had been all but nonexistent (table 14-7).

WINDS OF CHANGE

While legislative changes commencing in the 1980s have given banks some new powers, many argue that regulatory constraints imposed on the industry are preventing them from adjusting to the changing demands of the market. As a result, customers are increasingly turning to nonbank firms for financial products and services. Indeed, the American Bankers Association has noted that the market share of financial assets held by financial institutions declined by nearly 20 percent between 1975 and 1985.[6]

Regulatory constraints imposed on the industry are derived primarily through two of the nation's principal banking laws: the Glass–Steagall Act of 1933 and the Bank Holding Company Act of 1956 (chapter 3). The former separates securities underwriting

[6]American Bankers Association, *Statistical Information on the Financial Services Industry,* 4th ed., 1987, p. 1.

and commercial banking, and the latter limits the activities of bank holding companies to those which are "closely related to banking." Bank holding companies have thus far been denied permission to engage in financial services which relate to certain activities in areas such as insurance and real estate. These restrictions, together with restrictions imposed by other laws that hamper interstate banking, have served to keep American banks from becoming fully competitive in the world economy. Thirty years ago the United States had fifteen of the world's largest banking institutions, but global dominance by American banks has slipped dramatically. Only two U.S. banking companies, Citicorp and BankAmerica are now ranked in the world's twenty-five largest. Japan has fourteen, including the world's four largest. Two German, three British, and four French banks complete the list.[7] At this writing, national debate was in progress as to the appropriateness of repealing the Glass–Steagall Act and of further liberalizing the list of activities in which banks can engage.

SUMMARY

The objective of commercial bank managers continues to be one in which the welfare of the bank and hence the bank's stockholders is maximized. But because of the nature of commercial banking, managers must respond to a number of constraints to which their nonbank counterparts are not subject. A major implication to be drawn in any analysis of bank asset and liability management is the fact that no aspect of such management can stand alone. Asset management policies depend upon the nature and structure of liabilities and capital. In turn, decisions affecting liabilities and capital depend not only upon asset distribution but also upon their relationship to one another.

Discussion contained in this chapter illustrates the changing nature of commercial banking and the need for continued advancement of sound management policies and practices. Successful managers of commercial banks may no longer merely gather funds from inexpensive sources and invest in assets which may be conveniently available. To the contrary, the changing nature of commercial banking implies the need for more and greater expertise in the traditional functions of planning, organizing and control.

QUESTIONS

14-1.   In what way is asset management for commercial banks similar to that for industrial firms? In what way does it differ?

14-2.   What are the three main categories of assets for commercial banks? To what extent have these categories shifted over the past decades? How do you account for this shift?

14-3.   What are sterile reserves? How did the Monetary Control Act of 1980 influence the quantity of sterile reserves required of member banks? Of nonmember banks?

---

[7]"Treasury Now Favors Creation of Huge Banks," *The New York Times,* June 7, 1987, p. 1.

14-4.   What are some differences in *investment* management policies for small banks versus large banks? How do you account for these differences?

14-5.   What are some differences in *loan* management policies for small banks versus large banks? How do you account for these differences?

14-6.   Comment on the use of fixed versus variable interest rates for commercial and industrial loans by commercial banks. Why has the use of variable rates increased in recent years?

14-7.   What were the major innovations in banks' liability management which occurred in recent decades. In general, why did liability management take on such increased importance?

14-8.   Should the Glass–Steagall Act of 1933 be repealed? Develop a list of pro and con arguments in this regard.

14-9.   The number of bank failures has grown dramatically in the 1980s. Is this entirely the result of financial services industry deregulation or would the number of failures have grown even without deregulation of the industry?

PROBLEMS

14-1.   County Bank had the following income statement and balance sheet at 31 December 1986

INCOME STATEMENT (IN $ THOUSANDS)

Revenue

Loan interest and discount	$18,400
Investment income	15,500
Service and handling charges	700
Other income	1,400
Total revenue	$36,000

Expense

Salaries and fringes	$ 5,000
Other operating expenses	6,150
Interest expense	21,600
Total expense	32,750
Net current earnings before taxes	$3,250

BALANCE SHEET (IN $ MILLIONS)

Assets		Liabilities	
Cash	$ 50	Demand	$105
Treasury		deposits	
securities	70	Time and savings deposits	281
Other investments	124	Borrowings	18
Loans	220	Other liabilities	50
Other assets	36	Capital accounts	46
Total assets	$500	Total liabilities and capital	$500

a. With reference to tables 14-3, 14-5, and 14-6 analyze County Bank's financial performance. The tax rate is 50 percent.

b. Formulate a set of policy recommendations that might improve County's financial performance.

14-2.   Assuming that one half of County Bank's time and savings deposits (problem 14-1) are subject to reserve requirements, calculate County Bank's reserves for all of County's deposits using reserve requirements imposed by the Monetary Control Act and contained in table 14-2.

14-3.   Mercantile Bancorporation, a large bank holding company with deposits over $200 million had a 1986 loan portfolio as follows (in $ millions).

Real estate mortgage loans	$20
Installment loans	45
Credit card oustandings	35
Commercial and other	100
Total	$200

Using data contained in table 14-4, calculate the net interest spread (net yield less money cost) for the loan portfolio.

14-4.   A medium size bank has the opportunity to acquire a portfolio of automobile installment loans at the portfolio's par value of $10,000,000. The bank expects that interest rate yield and loan losses will be consistent with the average for medium size banks as reported in Table 14-4. Operating and servicing expenses associated with the portfolio would be $200,000 per year. If the bank purchases the portfolio however, it will forgo an alternate investment in a new credit reporting service which is expected to net $1.2 million per year before money costs and taxes. Which alternative should the bank choose?

14-5.   Commerce Bancshares is a medium size "Card Bank" with $2 million in credit card receivables and 5,000 credit card holders. Of the credit card holders, 75% are active. On the assumption that Commerce Bankshares' credit card yield and cost data are equal to that of banks of its size as reported in table 14-4, calculate the annual earnings, net of money cost, generated by the credit card portfolio.

14-6.   With reference to problem 14-5 above, calculate:

a. Annual earnings generated per active account.

b. Average outstanding balance per active account.

14-7.   John Kim, a newly appointed bank officer in the credit card division of Commerce Bancshares (problems 14-5 and 14-6) believes that a marketing campaign would increase usage rates and would also increase the total number of credit card holders to 6000, and that 85% of those would be active. Average outstanding balances per active account would remain the same (approximately $533). Unfortunately, the marketing program would require a decline in credit standards and average credit losses for the portfolio would likely increase from the 1.64% shown in Table 14-4 to 2.64%.

a. Calculate the expected annual earnings net of money cost generated from the credit card portfolio if the marketing program is undertaken.

b. Should Commerce Bancshares undertake the marketing program?

14-8. First Midwest, a large bank, has 10,000 safe deposit boxes available. Of these, 7,800 are rented and the average rental income is $21.50. Salaries and other expenses associated with the lock box department are $157,000 and occupancy expenses are $49,000. Is the lock box department profitable?

14-9. If the space occupied by the lock box department (problem 14-9) is not suitable for alternative uses, would the bank improve overall profitability if the lock box department were closed and the $157,000 in nonoccupancy expenses eliminated?

SELECTED REFERENCES

EISENBEIS, R., HARRIS, R., AND LAKONISHOK, J. "Benefits of Bank Diversification: The Evidence from Shareholder Returns," *The Journal of Finance* (July 1984): 881–892.

FELGRAN, STEVEN D. "Banks as Insurance Agencies: Legal Constraints and Competitive Advances," *Federal Reserve Bank of Boston New England Economic Review* (September/October 1985): 34–49.

HENDERSON, YOLANDA K. "The Taxation of Banks: Particular Privileges or Objectionable Burdens?" *Federal Reserve Bank of Boston New England Economic Review* (May/June 1987): 3–18.

KILBRIDE, B., MCDONALD, B., AND MILLER, R. "A Reex-

amination of Economies of Scale in Banking Using a Generalized Functional Form," *Journal of Money, Credit and Banking* (November 1986): 519–526.

PAVEL, CHRISTINE, AND ROSENBLUM, HARVEY. "Banks and Nonbanks: The Horse Race Continues," *Federal Reserve Bank of Chicago Economic Perspectives* (May/June 1985): 3–17.

SMITH, HILARY H. "Agricultural Lending: Bank Closures and Branch Banking," *Federal Reserve Bank of Dallas Economic Review* (September 1987): 27–38.

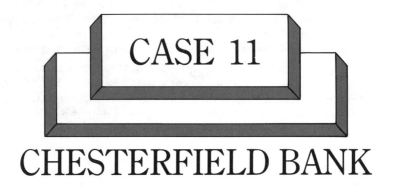

CASE 11

CHESTERFIELD BANK

As he hung up the phone, Frank Carney wondered whether the time had arrived. Carney, an executive vice-president of a bank located in St. Louis County was aware that recent consolidations within the Missouri banking community had created a surplus of experienced bank executives. Bank holding companys had acquired independent unit banks in the local community long ago and now seemed to be in the process of acquiring one another. Decisions which Carney formerly made himself, such as customer loan interest rates and certain employment policies, were now being made downtown at the holding company level. Although second in command at the bank, Carney felt more and more like a clerk—taking orders from holding company employees with considerably less banking experience than he.

The phone conversation had been with a long-time friend and business loan customer who thought, as did Carney, that a new, independent, bank could be successfully chartered and opened in the Chesterfield area. Carney's friend had just told him that a small group of investors stood ready to commit $1 million in equity capital if Carney would agree to run the new bank.

Chesterfield was a fast-growing unincorporated community located in west St. Louis County. Growth in the Chesterfield area had been quite strong, and an organized group was currently engaged in a drive that would likely result in the community's incorporation. Should incorporation occur, governmental units of the new municipality would be a potential source of deposits and would require banking services. Also, the rapidly growing number of businesses and relatively young households in the area appeared to be an excellent source for deposits and loan relationships.

Carney had recently received a copy of the Comparative Statement of Condition for State and National Banks in Missouri (Exhibit 1). In an accompanying letter prepared by Mr. Thomas B. Fitzsimmons, commissioner of banking for the state of Missouri, it was noted that state-chartered banks were granted new powers in March 1987. State-chartered banks could now (1) own and operate a collection agency, (2) own and operate a credit bureau, (3) provide consumer and business tax preparation services, and (4) provide mutual fund investment services. For starters, Carney decided to convert the data contained in Exhibit 1 to percentages so as to facilitate analysis. He decided to use ratios applicable to Missouri State Banks where possible and he believed that a new bank in Chesterfield could at least reach the industry averages after operating for a few years or so. For planning purposes, Carney assumed that the tax rate applied to net current earnings before tax would be about 26 percent. He wondered whether $1 million would be enough of an equity investment to support a deposit base sufficient in amount to generate an adequate loan volume and other income sources. His first step therefore was to construct pro forma financial statements so as to estimate the quantity of funds that might be generated in order to meet expenses and provide a source of profit to the owners.

QUESTIONS

1. Using the data contained in Exhibit 1 together with the ratios and other data contained in chapter 14, particularly table 14-5, construct pro-forma financial statements for the proposed new bank.
2. Would you expect actual ratios for a new bank, particularly for the first year of operations, to deviate from those projected for question 1. Develop examples of expected deviations.
3. Is $1 million a sufficiently large equity commitment to reasonably insure the success of the new bank?
4. Should the investors seek a state or a federal charter? What factors would likely determine the answer to this question?
5. Assuming that the new bank is eventually chartered, outline a method for promoting the bank's services.

Exhibit 1

Comparative Statement of Condition of State and National Banks in Missouri as of 31 December, 1986
and 31 December, 1985
($ millions)

	12/31/86			12/31/85	
	507 State Banks	*103 National Banks*	*610 All Banks*	*674 All Banks*	*Percentage Change*
Assets					
Cash and due from banks	$2,203	$4,270	$6,473	$5,699	13.6
Investment securities	6,992	4,793	11,785	11,108	6.1
Total loans and leases	13,011	15,677	28,688	25,919	10.7
Less: reserves	(186)	(224)	(410)	(356)	15.2
Federal funds sold	1,479	3,026	4,505	4,374	3.0
Fixed assets	337	528	865	801	8.0
Other real estate	93	52	145	157	−7.6
Other assets	440	659	1,099	1,107	−0.7
Total assets	$24,369	$28,781	$53,150	$48,809	8.9
Liabilities					
Total deposits	$21,770	$22,093	$43,863	$40,020	9.6
Deposits over $100M	2,356	3,288	5,644	5,638	0.1
Brokered deposits	73	201	274	272	0.7
Federal funds purchased	407	3,865	4,272	3,922	8.9
Other liabilities	340	949	1,289	1,358	−5.1
Total equity capital	1,852	1,874	3,726	3,509	6.2
Total liabilities	$24,369	$28,781	$53,150	$48,809	8.9
Earnings					
Interest income	$2,054	$2,033	$4,087	$4,372	−6.5
Interest expense	1,202	1,145	2,347	2,605	−9.9
Net interest income	852	888	1,740	1,767	−1.5
Provision for loan losses	155	157	312	287	8.7
Net income	194	224	418	384	8.9
Cash dividends	98	127	225	187	20.3
Net loan losses	135	126	261	250	4.4

Source: Commissioner of Finance, State of Missouri.

Exhibit 2

Comparative Statement of Condition of State and National Banks in Missouri as of 31 December, 1986,
and 31 December, 1985
(Percent of Total Assets Except Where Noted)

	12/31/86			12/31/85
	507 State Banks	103 National Banks	610 All Banks	674 All Banks
Assets				
Cash and due from banks	9.0%	14.8%	12.2%	11.7%
Investment securities	28.7	16.7	22.2	22.8
Total loans and leases	53.4	54.5	54.0	53.1
Less: reserves	−0.8	−0.8	−0.8	−0.7
Federal funds sold	6.1	10.5	8.5	9.0
Fixed assets	1.4	1.8	1.6	1.6
Other real estate	0.4	0.2	0.3	0.3
Other assets	1.8	2.3	2.1	2.3
Total assets	100.0%	100.0%	100.0%	100.0%
Liabilities				
Total deposits	89.3	76.8	82.5	82.0
Deposits over $100M[1]	10.8	14.9	12.9	14.1
Brokered deposits[1]	0.3	0.9	0.6	0.7
Federal funds purchased	1.7	13.4	8.0	8.0
Other liabilities	1.4	3.3	2.4	2.8
Total equity capital	7.6	6.5	7.0	7.2
Total liabilities	100.0%	100.0%	100.0%	100.0%
Earnings	100.0%	100.0%	100.0%	100.0%
Interest income				
Interest expense	58.5	56.3	57.4	59.6
Net interest income	41.5	43.7	42.6	40.4
Provision for loan losses	6.5	5.7	6.1	6.8
Net income (as % of assets)	0.8	0.8	0.8	0.8
Net income (as % of equity)	10.5	12.0	11.2	10.9
Dividend payout ratio	50.5	56.7	53.8	48.7
Loan loss ratio[2]	1.2%	1.0%	1.1%	1.1%

[1] As a percentage of total deposits.
[2] Provision for loan losses/total loans and Leases.

15

Consumer Financial Services and Finance Company Management

While consumer financial services are offered by a broad array of institutions, finance companies have long served as an important source of credit for American households. Traditionally, finance companies have differed sharply from commercial banks and other deposit-type financial intermediaries. On the one hand, finance companies had far greater flexibility in the acquisition of assets and liabilities. Yet, generally they did not have access to lower-cost deposit funds and their funds cost were subject to prevailing rates in money and capital markets.

The events of recent years, however, have blurred traditional distinctions between finance companies and depository financial institutions. The phase-out of Regulation Q ceilings has narrowed the cost of funds advantage historically enjoyed by depository financial institutions. This and other regulatory developments and technological innovations have encouraged competition by finance companies in mortgage lending and in other markets, markets traditionally reserved for depository financial institutions. Indeed, terms such as *consumer banking, nonbank banks, loophole banks,* and similar terms—virtually unheard of a few years ago, fill the pages of financial newspapers and journals today. This new terminology is indicative of turmoil in the financial services industry, turmoil unleashed with deregulation of the industry in the 1980s.

We begin our discussion with a review of the traditional structure of the consumer finance industry. Following this review, we consider the events of recent years where finance companies have played a major role in the evolutionary expansion of consumer financial services.

TYPES OF FINANCE COMPANIES

Although all finance companies are similar in that their principal function is to make loans, they differ in terms of the loans they specialize in. Some are predominantly *consumer loan companies,* with their principal activity the granting of direct cash loans to individuals or households. Other finance companies are referred to as *commercial loan companies,* with all or a major proportion of their loans being made to business units. Still others are *sales finance companies* whose principal function is to purchase retail time sales contracts from nonfinancial businesses. Although most finance companies began by focusing entirely on one of the activities described above, many individual finance companies today offer a broad range of financial services to businesses and consumers alike.

Finance companies are *stock* companies in the sense that they are privately owned entities with ultimate control vested in their owners. The nature of ownership differs, however. Some are operated as units of bank holding companies or as subsidiaries of conglomerates, and others are *dependent* or *captive* finance companies formed by parent firms to finance the sale of goods manufactured by the parent. Perhaps one of the more familiar dependent or captive finance companies is General Motors Acceptance Corporation. Still other sales finance companies are *independent,* ranging in size from a single office to multiple offices located throughout the nation.

The asset and liability data for domestic finance companies for 1987 show that loan receivables accounted for about 87 percent of gross assets (figure 15-1). The data also show that finance companies are highly leveraged, with debt representing about 88.9 percent of the capital structure. Clearly, finance company profitability is highly dependent upon the difference (spread) between the cost of borrowed funds and interest revenue earned from loan receivables.

Figure 15-1: Selected financial data for domestic finance companies. (Source: *Federal Reserve Bulletin,* June 1987, p. A37).

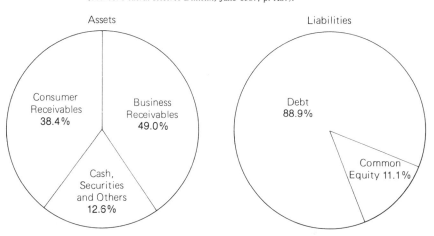

GROWTH AND DEVELOPMENT OF FINANCE COMPANIES

Unlike commercial banks and thrift institutions, finance companies are not dependent on deposits as a source of funds and have had far greater flexibility in choosing the types of loans and investments to be acquired. In addition, banks and thrift institutions are generally precluded from branching across state lines, while many finance companies operate nationwide. Also, although most states severely restrict the number of branches which may be maintained by depository institutions within the state, states do not restrict the number of finance company offices. In contrast to depository financial institutions, finance companies have been relatively free to innovate and to seek out various types of loan and other investment portfolios.

In some cases, finance companies have paved the way in developing profitable lending innovations and in establishing the relative safety of many types of lending operations. Examples of lending activities of this type include direct consumer lending and the development of retail time sales lending activities. However, once the industry developed successful lending programs such as the financing of retail automobile time sales contracts, it experienced severe competitive pressures from other financial institutions such as banks and credit unions. In many cases, other lending institutions entered and eventually overtook certain traditional finance company lending markets once the finance companies had established the relative safety and profitability of those markets.

Following World War II, households expanded their debt obligations not only in an absolute sense but also in relation to their incomes (table 15-1a). Installment debt obligations, which totaled $2.5 billion and represented less than 2 percent of disposable income in 1945, grew dramatically over the next several decades (figure 15-2). By 1987, consumer installment credit represented 19 percent of consumer disposable personal income.

Although finance companies participated in this postwar growth of consumer credit receivables, the industry's share of total market receivables began to decline (table 15-1b). This decline began to appear by the mid-1950s as commercial banks and

Table 15-1a

Consumer Installment Credit by Holder
(in $ millions)

YEAR	TOTAL	COMM. BANKS	FINANCE COMPANIES	CREDIT UNIONS	MISC. LENDERS, RETAILERS & OTHERS
1945	$ 2,462	$ 745	$ 910	$ 102	$ 705
1950	14,703	5,798	5,315	590	3,000
1955	28,906	10,601	11,838	1,678	4,798
1960	42,968	16,672	15,435	3,923	6,938
1965	71,324	28,962	24,282	7,324	10,756
1970	101,161	41,895	31,123	12,500	15,643
1975	162,237	78,703	36,695	25,354	21,485
1980	313,472	147,013	76,756	44,041	45,662
1987	591,276	264,946	138,745	81,682	105,854

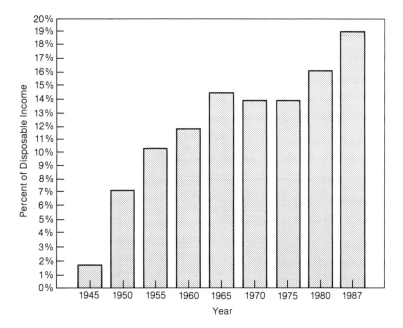

Figure 15-2:   Consumer installment credit outstanding as a percentage of disposable income. (Source: 1987 *Economic Report of the President* and *Federal Reserve Bulletin.*)

Table 15-1b

Consumer Installment Credit by Holder
(Share of the Market)

YEAR END	TOTAL	COMM. BANKS	FINANCE COMPANIES	CREDIT UNIONS	MISC. LENDERS, RETAILERS, AND OTHERS
1945	100.0%	30.3%	37.0%	4.1%	28.6%
1950	100.0	39.4	36.1	4.0	20.4
1955	100.0	36.7	41.0	5.8	16.6
1960	100.0	38.8	35.9	9.1	16.1
1965	100.0	40.6	34.0	10.3	15.1
1970	100.0	41.4	30.8	12.4	15.5
1975	100.0	48.5	22.6	15.6	13.2
1980	100.0	46.9	24.5	14.0	14.6
1987	100.0	45.3	23.4	13.6	17.8

Note: 1987 data are for July. All other data are for December 31.

Source: *Federal Reserve Bulletin,* various issues.

Table 15-2

Consumer Installment Credit by major type of credit
outstanding
(in $ millions)

TYPE OF CREDIT	AMOUNT	PERCENT
Automobile	$251,081	42.5
Revolving	138,704	23.5
Mobile home	25,858	4.4
Other	175,633	29.7
Total	$591,276	100.0

Source: *Federal Reserve Bulletin,* November 1987, p. A40. Data
are for July 1987.

credit unions experienced ever-increasing market domination. Beginning in the 1950s, commercial banks and credit unions became more aggressive in consumer credit markets. This, combined with their ability to attract lower-cost (deposit-type) funds and therefore offer consumer financing at lower rates, resulted in a strong competitive advantage for commercial banks and thrift institutions. Table 15-2 provides an overview of consumer credit, by major type of credit outstanding.

ASSET MANAGEMENT

A review and discussion of the major categories of consumer and business receivables held by finance companies is useful in the development of an understanding of consumer financial services and finance company operations (table 15-3). Each of these will be discussed in turn.

Table 15-3

Major Types of Credit Outstanding Held by Finance Companies

CONSUMER RECEIVABLES	BUSINESS RECEIVABLES
Retail passenger automobile paper	Wholesale paper
Mobile homes	Automobiles
Revolving consumer installment credit	Other consumer goods
Personal cash loans	Equipment and industrial
Second mortgage loans	Retail paper
Other consumer installment loans	Commercial vehicles
	Business, industrial, and farm equipment
	Lease paper
	Automobile paper
	Business, industrial, and farm equipment
	Other business credit
	Loans on commercial accounts receivable
	Factored accounts receivable

Consumer Receivables

Retail Passenger Automobile Paper   Retail passenger automobile paper refers to receivables generated through the sale of new or used automobiles under terms of a conditional sales (or similar) contract. Receivable such as these are originated through automobile dealers and are subsequently sold or assigned to a financial institution. A typical procedure is as follows:

1. The automobile dealer negotiates the selling price and trade-in allowance for a new or used car with the purchaser.
2. Following agreement on these cash sales terms, the dealer may offer to finance the automobile with the customer to pay monthly payments over time. Given an extended payment arrangement, the sale would be termed a "time sale" as opposed to a "cash sale."
3. The customer at this point may choose to (a) pay the cash price from his own funds, (b) arrange financing directly through a lender of his choice, or (c) accept the dealer's offer to finance the automobile.
4. If the dealer's financing offer is accepted, the customer will complete a credit application.
5. Information concerning the transaction—e.g., price and description of the automobile, down payment, requested contract maturity, and credit information—is telephoned or otherwise transmitted to the lending institution.
6. On the basis of information submitted, the lending institution will (verbally) approve, reject, or suggest modification of contract terms (required down payment, maturity, comaker, etc.).
7. If the contract is approved by the lending institution, the sale is consummated. The contract is endorsed by the dealer and sold or assigned to the lender, who in turn issues the dealer a check for the principal balance financed.

Certain features of the time-sales contract and its subsequent sale or assignment to the lender are noteworthy and influence the potential risk and profitability of the transaction.

First, the nature of the dealer's endorsement influences the level of risk inherent in the transaction. The contract may be endorsed "without recourse," with "full recourse," or in some other way so as to partially protect the lender in the event of customer default. If the endorsement is "without recourse," the dealer has no responsibility in the event of customer default and any collection or collateral repossession expense must be borne by the lender. If a "full recourse" endorsement is used, credit risk for the lender is substantially reduced or eliminated, and the dealer is committed to absorb the losses in event of customer default. Under terms of a "partial repurchase" or other limited recourse agreement, the dealer is obligated to absorb losses up to some fixed sum or is perhaps obligated only until a given number of payments have been paid by the customer.

Hence, the nature of contract endorsement is important from a managerial aspect. Obviously, if all else is equal, the financial institution would prefer to have all contracts endorsed on a full recourse basis. Even in the case of full recourse endorsements, however, the financial institution faces certain risks. Full recourse endorsement by financially unsound dealerships may provide little protection to the lender. Even in the case of financially sound dealerships, risk exposure may be substantial if the institution relies excessively on dealer endorsements and relaxes credit standards or regularly accepts contracts with cash advancements in excess of the "quick" or wholesale value of the collateral. The extent to which recourse endorsements may be required by financial institutions varies over time as well as with the nature of the collateral and the geographic location. In larger urban areas where lenders compete vigorously in the retail automobile paper market, a lender who wishes to participate in this market may have little choice other than to purchase the paper on a nonrecourse basis, particularly with regard to contracts secured by new automobiles. On the other hand, dealers in rural areas tend to have fewer financing outlets and must frequently endorse time sales contracts on a recourse basis.

A second feature associated with time sales financing and one with considerable influence on potential profitability associated with the financing of retail paper involves the tradition of dealer participation in finance charges. Because competition among financial institutions for retail auto receivables is intense, most financial institutions which seek these receivables offer some program whereby a portion of finance charges from times sales contracts is shared with the dealer. For example, a particular lender might establish a (retail) rate to the public of, say, 7 percent add-on. If the amount financed were $5,000 over thirty-six months, total finance charges would be $1,050 ($5,000 × 7% × 3 years). Suppose the same institution established a net rate of 6 percent add-on (net rate is the rate retained by the lender). The financial institution would seek to net $900 ($5,000 × 6% ×3 years) and the difference of $150 ($1,050 − $900) would be paid to the dealer as an incentive for offering the contract to the lender. This dealer participation in finance charges is frequently referred to as "dealer reserve." Also, the proportion of total finance charges received by the dealer is influenced by the type of collateral, contract maturity, competition, and other factors.

When the contract is sold or assigned to the lender, the lender may issue an additional check to the dealer in the amount of the finance charge participation. More

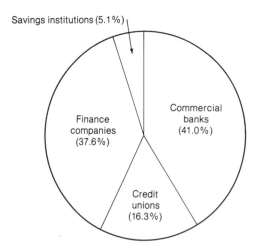

Savings institutions (5.1%)

Finance companies (37.6%)

Commercial banks (41.0%)

Credit unions (16.3%)

Figure 15-3: Share of the market for consumer automobile finance receivables, by major type of holder.
(Source: *Federal Reserve Bulletin*, November 1987, p. A40.)

commonly, however, the dealer reserve is entered as a liability on the lender's books and paid at periodic intervals. Frequently, the reserve account is established in such a way that the account may be charged to cover losses arising through defaults on contracts that had been partially or fully guaranteed by the dealer.

From a managerial point of view, competitive conditions frequently dictate dealer participation in finance charges. The amount of participation and the terms under which reserves are available to offset credit losses should be carefully monitored. Changes in competitive conditions and analysis of the profitability of retail paper should influence policy decisions regarding relationships between the lender and dealers.

Of the $251 billion in retail automobile receivables that were outstanding in mid-1987, finance companies held 37.6 percent of the total (figure 15-3).

Mobile Home Financing   Although mobile homes may be financed through mortgage instruments in ways that are similar to the financing of residential real estate, finance companies and many commercial banks have traditionally financed mobile homes in a manner similar to that for automobiles: through use of conditional sales (or similar) contracts.

Several aspects of the financing of mobile homes by finance companies differ from those of new automobile financing (table 15-4). Principal differences include

Table 15-4

Finance Rates and Other Terms for Selected Types of Consumer Credit

AVERAGE FINANCE RATES	1980	1985	1987
Commercial banks:			
New automobiles (48 months)*	14.3%	12.9%	10.2%
Personal loans (24 months)	15.5	15.9	14.0
Mobile homes (120 months)*	15.0	15.0	13.2
Credit card	17.3	18.7	17.9
Auto finance companies:			
New automobiles	14.8	12.0	10.7
Used automobiles	19.1	17.6	14.5
OTHER TERMS			
Maturity (months)			
New car	45.0	51.5	53.5
Used car	34.8	41.4	45.2
Loan-to-value ratio (percent)			
New car	87.6	91.0	93.0
Used car	94.2	94.0	98.0
Amount financed			
New car	$6,322	$9,915	$11,176
Used car	3,810	6,089	7,527

*For 1980, loan maturities for new cars and mobile homes were 36 and 84 months, respectively.

Source: *Federal Reserve Bulletin,* November 1983 and November 1987, p. A41. 1987 data are for May.

MOBILE HOME FINANCE RECEIVABLES

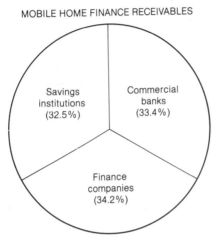

Figure 15-4: Share of the market for consumer mobile home finance receivables, by major type of holder.
(Source: *Federal Reserve Bulletin*, November 1987, p. A40.)

higher finance rates and larger average amounts financed. Maturities for mobile home loans have averaged about thirteen years in recent times (*not* shown in table 15-4). This compares to average maturities of about four and one-half years for new cars and about forty-five months for used cars by 1987. By 1987, consumer mobile home installment credit receivables held by all lenders were about $26 billion (table 15-2). Of this total, commercial banks, savings institutions, and finance companies each held about one-third (figure 15-4).

Like automobile financing, conditional sales contracts for mobile homes may be subject to full or partial dealer recourse arrangements. Dealer participation in finance charges is common within the industry. Because mobile homes (unlike residential real property) have traditionally been subject to rapid depreciation, and because of the greater complexity and potential loss in the sale of mobile homes in the event of customer default, management should exercise considerable care in establishing relationships with individual dealers, evaluating credit applications, and selecting terms.

Revolving Consumer Installment Credit

During the 1970s and 1980s, revolving credit was the fastest growing single segment of the consumer credit market. Revolving credit is accessed mainly with credit cards and is extended by banks, retailers, and gasoline companies, among others (figure 15-5). While the annual compound growth rate for total consumer installment credit from 1970 through the latter half of the 1980s was about 11 percent, annual growth in revolving credit receivables was about 23 percent over that same period. On average, about 62 percent of U.S. households have at least one credit card, and the proportion of households holding credit cards tends to increase as family income rises.

Personal Cash Loans   Personal or direct cash loans constitute a large but declining portion of finance company consumer receivables. According to sample data gathered by the American Financial Services Association, loans of this type represented

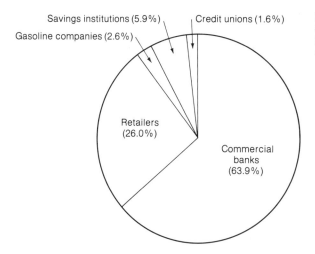

Savings institutions (5.9%)

Gasoline companies (2.6%)

Credit unions (1.6%)

Retailers
(26.0%)

Commercial
banks
(63.9%)

Figure 15-5: Share of the market for revolving credit receivables, by major type of holder. (Source: *Federal Reserve Bulletin,* November 1987, p. A40.)

one-third of all finance company receivables in 1977. By 1987 however, personal loans were less than 10 percent of all finance company consumer receivables.

Unlike other types of loan receivables such as those secured by automobiles or mobile homes, direct cash loans are typically small in size. They may be secured by household goods and other miscellaneous assets, or may be unsecured. Finance rates for personal loans in excess of 20 percent are common within the industry. Although these rates have traditionally been high compared to the finance rates associated with automobile or mobile home loans, finance company personal loans tend to be relatively small in size and are costly to administer. Also, because of competitive pressures, increasing funds costs, and state-mandated interest rate ceilings, the relative profitability of personal loans by finance companies has fallen over the years.

A particular problem area for finance company management with regard to small personal loans is the fact that finance companies must compete for funds in money and capital markets where interest rates are not regulated. At the same time, maximum rates for personal loans are fixed by the various states. In a 1978 study of the consumer finance industry in Missouri, the authors found that the combination of high funds costs and fixed state interest rate ceilings had resulted in a decline of the industry in Missouri.

From a management perspective, the future attractiveness of the market for relatively small personal loans is questionable at best. Indeed, the proliferation of bank credit cards that carry cash advance privileges has likely contributed to a declining need for small personal cash loans.

EXAMPLE   Telcom Finance Company has developed cost and revenue data concerning personal cash loan operations for all company activities within a particular state (table 15-5). The maximum APR under the state usury statute for direct cash loans is 15 percent, and Telcom's cost of funds is currently 10 percent. Is Telcom's personal cash loan business profitable?

Analysis of data contained in table 15-5 reveals that Telcom's interest rate

Table 15-5

Personal Cash Loan Profitability Analyses

ANNUAL OPERATING EXPENSE	$ TOTAL	$ PER ACCOUNT
Advertising	170,091	$3.62
Bad debts (net)	1,537,121	32.70
Legal	153,898	3.27
Postage and printing	109,346	2.33
Rent and utilities	366,850	7.80
Salaries	1,539,618	32.75
Administration	1,028,948	21.89
Telephone	195,756	4.16
Other	292,500	6.22
	$5,394,128	$114.74
Average number of accounts		47,005
Average outstanding balance		$2,000
Maximum permissible APR		15%
Annual cost of funds		10%
Interest rate spread		5%

spread is insufficient to cover operating expense and produce a profit. The average spread provides revenue of $100 (0.05 × $2,000) per account, thus failing to cover operating costs by $14.74 ($100 − $114.74). The company is losing $692,854 (47,005 × $14.74) per year on operations within the state. Management strategies to improve performance and restore profitability within the state include the following:

Reduce annual operating costs to a point below $100 per account

Increase average loan balances (perhaps through a second mortgage or auto loan program)

Improve the mix of funds sources in an effort to reduce funds cost

Undertake activities, perhaps in conjunction with industry trade associations to increase permissable APRs for direct cash loans

Given the existing average outstanding cash loan balance of $2,000, the existing operating cost structure and current funds cost of 10%, an APR of 15.737% [$2,000 × (APR − 10%) = $114.74] would represent the breakeven APR.

Second-Mortgage Loans

A second-mortgage loan (sometimes called a "home equity loan") is one secured by real estate but where the real estate collateral is subject to some prior lien. The prior lienholder has priority in the event of foreclosure and liquidation of the real estate collateral.

Information concerning the total volume of second-mortgage lending is rela-

Table 15-6

Percentage of Banks Offering or Planning to Offer a Home
Equity Line of Credit Secured by a Second Mortgage,
1985

	BY SIZE OF ASSETS	
Asset Size ($M)	*Currently Offers*	*Plans to Implement in 1986*
Under $50	5.5%	6.8%
$50–100	19.0	20.2
$100–500	35.3	25.4
$500–1,000	61.2	20.4
$1,000 and over	75.4	16.9

Source: American Bankers Association, *1986 Retail Bank Credit Report.*

tively sketchy and frequently inconsistent. There is, however, general agreement that lending of this type has been among the fastest growing forms of credit to consumers. On the basis of estimates provided by the American Financial Services Association and by the Federal Reserve, second-mortgage loan receivables grew rapidly during the 1970s and 1980s. According to survey data provided by the Federal Reserve and by the American Financial Services Association, second-mortgage real estate receivables held by finance companies were $1.9 billion in 1975, $13.1 billion in 1981, and about $15.9 billion in 1986. Moreover, the popularity of second-mortgage loans was enhanced by certain changes in federal tax laws that were enacted in 1986. The Tax Simplification Act of 1986, among other things, provided for the gradual phase-out of tax deductions for consumer loan interest expense. Interest expense associated with home mortgages, however (with certain exceptions), continued to hold. As a consequence, banks, thrifts, and other lenders began to promote the use of home equity loans to refinance short-term consumer debt, to support large expenditures such as those required for a college education, and to finance the purchase of automobiles and other consumer goods. By 1986, large numbers of financial institutions were offering home equity credit lines secured by a second-mortgage. Table 15-6 provides data concerning the number of commercial banks that were offering or planned to offer home equity loans by 1986. The 1980s therefore began to witness a certain amount of substitution between mortgage and consumer debt.[1]

From a managerial perspective, home equity loans provide substantial flexibility. Such loans when properly made and documented would be expected to carry little risk. Exceptions may occur of course. A prolonged recession in the local economy, for example, could impact negatively on employment opportunities and depress property values. Maximum second-mortgage loan rates and collection procedures are generally

[1]For an analysis of such substitution, see "Changes in Consumer Installment Debt: Evidence from the 1983 and 1986 Surveys of Consumer Finances," *Federal Reserve Bulletin,* (October 1987): 767.

specified in the laws of the various states. Typically though, such loans may be made at fixed interest rates or at floating rates tied to some index, such as the prime lending rate posted by some specified large bank. They may call for principal and interest payments over some fixed interval or they may call for interest-only payments for some specified time period, e.g., ten years, with the principal due at maturity. Some lending institutions make home equity loans with the customer borrowing the entire equity in his home. Most however, require that some minimum equity, e.g., 20 percent, remain in the home after home equity loan proceeds are disbursed. Many home equity lending programs provide the customer with a line of credit where the customer has the option of drawing against the line until the maximum credit is reached.

EXAMPLE   TransHome Financial is a finance company subsidiary of a large bank holding company. The subsidiary specializes in second-mortgage loans where the customer's home serves as loan collateral. The company's lending policy provides that home equity loan customers may borrow up to 85 percent of the "quick" sale value of the real estate collateral, less the existing first-mortgage loan. The quick value is assumed to be 95 percent of appraised value. As an example, suppose a customer's property appraises at $80,000 and the existing first-mortgage balance is $40,000. The quick value would be $80,000 × 0.95 = $76,000, and the customer could borrow 76,000 × 0.85 − $40,000 = $24,600. Of course, TransHome requires that the customer have an acceptable prior credit payment history and that the company verify statements contained on the loan application such as income and length of employment.

In addition to the aforementioned lending policy which concerns loan collateral and customer character, the company has developed certain guidelines as a measure of loan repayment capacity and which are applied to home equity loan applications. On average, for example, TransHome has found that the typical consumer home equity loan applicant has 62 percent of gross salary income remaining after taxes, social security, and certain other required expenditures which are common for most households. On average then, this 62 percent of gross salary is available to meet mortgage, auto, revolving charge, and certain other expenses typically incurred by consumers. TransHome's statistical analysis of its customer base has also shown that consumer applicants require a minimum of $150 per month per household member in remaining income after mortgage and other debt obligations so as to cover items such as food, personal, and other miscellaneous expenditures.

Mike and Rachel McKillip have applied for a home equity loan with TransHome. Their combined salaries total $5,000 per month and they have two dependent children. Over the years, their home has appreciated in value and was recently appraised at $175,000. The McKillips' existing first-mortgage payment is $1150 per month and their current first-mortgage loan balance is $100,000. Auto loan payments total $250 each month, and minimum monthly payments on bank credit card and other revolving charge agreements amount to $200 per month. The McKillips would like a fixed-rate home equity loan with monthly payments spanning 15 years in the maximum amount possible for educational purposes. The current APR quoted by TransHome is 12 percent. Collateral and repayment capacity analysis is summarized in table 15-7. Maximum property loan value is 85 percent of the quick sale value or $141,313. After deducting the existing

Table 15-7

Home Equity Loan Analysis

Maximum property collateral value	$141,313
($175,000 × 0.95 × 0.85)	
Maximum home equity loan	41,313
($141,312.50 − 100,000)	
Required monthly payment	496
(15 year, 12%, $41,313 loan)	
Maximum capacity payment	900
($5,000 × 0.62 − $1,150 − $450 − ($150 × 4)	

Note: All values rounded to the nearest dollar.

mortgage loan of $100,000 the maximum home equity loan is therefore $41,313. The required mortgage loan payment of $495.82 (rounded in the table to $496) is determined using table A-8 ($41,313/83.322 = $496) or by using a financial calculator. It is the payment associated with a present value of $41,313, with payment occurring monthly over fifteen years and where the annual interest rate is 12 percent. The highest home equity monthly payment that the McKillips could afford, given TransHomes policy guidelines, is $900. Consequently, the McKillips qualify for the home equity loan and TransHome Financial would approve the loan.

Other Consumer Installment Loans Other consumer installment loans include finance receivables secured by personal property such as refrigerators or television sets. Goods such as this are sold and financed in a manner similar to that described in the financing of retail passenger automobile paper.

Evaluating Consumer Credit Applications

The analysis of consumer credit applications is similar to business credit evaluation in some respects and different in others. In both cases, the three Cs of credit (character, capacity, and collateral) must by considered.

Character refers to the reputation of the potential borrower in terms of his perceived reliability in repaying the loan. Finance companies, as do other consumer lenders, contact prior or existing creditors, the names of which are typically disclosed by the applicant in his credit applications. These credit references are asked to furnish information concerning the applicant's record with them. In addition to direct contact with creditors, the lender might communicate by telephone or teletype with the local credit bureau or lenders' exchange, where a file containing the applicant's credit repayment history is maintained. This file frequently contains employment history and residence information in addition to an evaluation of loans and other credit repayment history. The credit evaluation agency will have accumulated this credit information as the result of the applicant's prior requests for credit and subsequent inquiries from other lenders.

Capacity refers to the applicant's potential ability to repay the loan from current income or existing resources. The credit manager must evaluate the applicant's ability to repay the loan, in view of the borrower's existing financial obligations and income limitations.

Finally, *collateral* represents the security to which the lender may turn in the event of loan default. Collateral repossession in order to liquidate a loan is viewed as a last resort by finance company lenders.

Business Receivables

Wholesale Paper   Wholesale paper refers to trust agreements or similar legal documents which arise during the course of inventory financing. To induce sellers of "large-ticket items" such as automobiles, heavy duty trucks, farm equipment, and other items which are frequently sold on time sales contracts to offer these contracts to a particular lender, a finance company (or other lender) may offer to finance the whole-sale value of the dealer's inventory. Such financing—also referred to as "*floor planning*"—is typically provided as an accommodation to the dealer.

Suppose that a franchise for a new car or truck dealership is awarded to a businessman in the local area. The dealership will be expected to develop a certain amount of retail time sales finance paper, and it is likely that a number of financial institutions will have an interest in purchasing this retail paper. The dealer, on the other hand, will likely carry large inventories of the product, and these inventories must generally be financed. Typically, one or more lenders would approach the dealer and offer to finance the inventory in exchange for the opportunity to finance the retail contracts. The lender may agree to establish a *floor plan line of credit* whereby the dealer maintains inventory financed by the lender up to the amount of the established credit line. Once the floor plan arrangement has been negotiated, the manufacturer will be authorized to draft on or bill the lender for subsequent shipments of inventory items to the dealer. As the dealer sells the floor planned units, he is expected to remit payment for sold items promptly to the lender.

Because of competitive conditions, wholesale dealer paper is typically financed at break-even interest rates, with the interest rate tied to the prime lending rate plus, say, 1 percent. Because of the small interest rate spread and the inventory monitoring cost, floor planning in and of itself is not a particularly profitable operation. Wholesale financing accommodations are generally provided to the dealer with the expectation that the dealer will offer "compensating retail paper" to the lender. On the basis of experience, the lender knows that a considerable portion of "big-ticket items" such as new cars, trucks, etc., are financed. Since the dealer is in a position to control the placement of a certain proportion of the retail time sales paper, the dealer is expected to offer this paper to the lender who has provided the floor plan accommodation. Of course, if the floor planning lender rejects a particular financing transaction, the dealer may well seek to sell the time sales contract to some other lender.

Floor planning can involve considerable risk to the lender, and considerable management attention should be given to its control. Even relatively small dealers may require floor plan lines amounting to several hundred thousand dollars. For large dealerships, the value of floor planned inventory can amount to a millon dollars or more, amounts which may be far in excess of the dealer's equity investment.

The risk of potential loss through wholesale financing is perhaps greatest during depressed economic periods when dealer sales volume may be low. Indeed, examples abound where particular dealers, faced with high fixed costs and working capital requirements, have defaulted on inventory trust agreements. The default may go undetected by the lender for a considerable period of time because the dealer simply defers payment on sold inventory items and enters into a floor plan "float." The float may at first involve a delay in payment of sold inventory items for a few days with the proceeds from current sales used to pay the lender for floor planned units sold in the prior time period. If depressed economic conditions continue, the float may build gradually over time, reaching the point where the lender suffers considerable losses.

Although the nature of wholesale financing is such that the risk of a dealer being "out of trust" is always present, controls can be instituted to minimize potential losses. Frequent unannounced floor plan inventory checks by the lender are a critical component of such controls. Insistence on the timely preparation and submission of dealer financial statements, followed by analysis of such statements on an ongoing basis, is another means of control.

Finally, management should systematically evaluate the quantity and profitability of the compensating retail paper purchased from individual dealers. If the quantity and quality of the retail paper is insufficient to justify the investment and risk associated with the dealers' wholesale receivables, and if this condition cannot be improved, the floor plan line should be terminated.

Retail Business Receivables In addition to time sales contracts secured by consumer durables, finance companies also purchase time sales contracts secured by commercial assets such as heavy-duty trucks, farm equipment, and other industrial products. Frequently, commercial time sales contracts secured by assets such as these are purchased from dealers in ways that are similar to the procedure described for retail passenger automobile paper.

On the one hand, the financing of commercial equipment carries with it the prospect for enhanced profitability. The amount financed under individual contracts tends to be substantial when compared with consumer durables such as automobiles or household products. On the other hand, collateral such as heavy-duty trucks and other types of industrial products is difficult to dispose of in the event of foreclosure. Because of the large balances financed and the lack of a readily available secondary market for most types of industrial equipment, there exists considerable risk of loss on individual time sales contracts.

Large finance companies with branches located throughout the nation have competitive advantages in the financing of certain types of industrial equipment. First, it is possible to diversify portfolio holdings of this paper on a geographic basis, reducing the impact of credit losses caused by regional economic slowdowns. Second, commercial banks are reluctant to purchase contracts secured by "on-the-road" commercial vehicles such as tractor-trailers financed for "owner-operators," because the equipment may be far away and physically difficult to repossess in the event of default. From a practical point of view, the lender must have the capability to enforce terms of the time sales contract, and as a last resort, to take physical possession of the collateral when it appears that the purchaser is unable or unwilling to meet his contractual obligations. Large finance companies with a national network of branches have this capability.

LIABILITY MANAGEMENT

On average, finance companies carry seven to eight dollars in debt for each dollar of equity capital. Lacking deposit funds as a major source of debt, they must bid for funds in a competitive marketplace. With the cost of these funds being a major part of their total costs, finance companies depend on skillful liability management to minimize interest expense and achieve a satisfactory level of profitability.

However, minimizing the cost of funds is only one consideration in liability management. A second major factor is interest rate risk. The average finance company loan has a maturity of several years. A shorter liability maturity exposes the finance company to the risk of having to refinance maturing liabilities at interest rates higher than the net rates being earned on loans. In a period of falling interest rates, liability maturities longer than loan maturities can leave the institution in the position of being committed to high-cost sources of funds while competition is driving down the rates charged on loans. Thus interest rate risk is a major consideration in liability management.

Finally, availability of funds is a major consideration for finance company management. Money and capital markets are quite impersonal; they make no commitment to provide funds. Past experience such as collapse of the commercial paper market following the Penn Central default confirms the importance of ensuring that some source of funds will always be available to finance existing loans.

A summary of the liability structure of finance companies for 1987 can be found in figure 15-6. Each of the major sources of funds covered there is discussed in the following paragraphs.

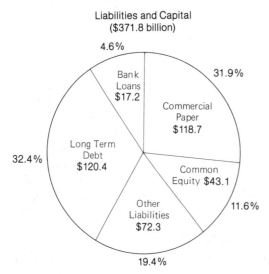

Figure 15-6: Liability structure for domestic finance companies, mid-1987 ($ billions).
(Source: *Federal Reserve Bulletin*, November 1987, p. A37.)

Bank Loans

Finance companies have traditionally relied on commercial banks as key sources of funds and frequently borrowed against revolving credit lines. Such reliance is particularly true for the smaller finance companies which lack access to national credit markets.

For the industry as a whole, bank loans were about 4.6 percent of total liabilities and capital by mid-1987, down from twice that proportion as recently as 1983. The aggregated data (contained in figure 15-6), however, obscure the fact that liability structure differs markedly for finance companies depending on firm size.

In fact, of about 2,800 finance companies surveyed by the Federal Reserve System in one recent year, less than 2 percent were responsible for about 80 percent of total industry liabilities. Further evidence of finance company concentration was contained in a report developed by the American Financial Services Association, where about 82 percent of finance company consumer receivables were held by their sample survey group of 29 finance companies.[2] These larger firms tend to rely proportionately less on commercial bank loans and proportionately more on commercial paper. Regional and small firms, however, draw heavily on bank credit lines in financing their operations.

Bank borrowing is frequently accomplished by drawing down on a prenegotiated revolving line of credit. This source of borrowing has the important advantage of ensuring availability. However, interest rates on such lines are frequently tied to the prime rate; the cost of bank credit varies from the prime rate for the soundest companies to three or four percentage points over prime for the smaller firms. Thus the interest rate may vary, and the benefit of ensured availability is offset by exposure to interest rate risk. Normally, credit arrangements of this type require a compensating balance and/or a fee of about 0.5 percent of the credit line. Charges or balances are frequently required regardless of whether or not the line is used. Therefore, a price is paid for availability which makes bank credit a sometimes expensive source of funds.

Finance company managers using bank credit should seek to minimize the cost of these funds. It may be possible, for example, to negotiate a reduced commitment fee—or a lower compensating balance—in return for the firm's payroll account. Alternatively, the finance company might suggest a smaller compensating balance, but one which would be kept in the form of a non-interest-bearing time deposit (one on which the bank would be required to hold proportionately smaller reserves). In short, the cost of bank credit is an important component of finance company cost, and new innovative financing techniques can have important implications for company profitability.

Commercial Paper

The commercial paper market is a major source of funds for large finance companies. According to data contained in figure 15-6, financing of this type represented almost a third of the industry's financial structure in 1987. In fact, finance company commercial

[2]Finance Companies, 1977–1986," *American Financial Services Association Research Report* and *Second Mortgage Lending Report Supplement*, p. 2.

paper outstandings contained in figure 15-6 represented 34 percent of all the then outstanding domestic commercial paper.

The use of short-term bank loans and commercial paper in financing such a large part of operations is consistent with the principle of matching the maturity of assets and liabilities. Finance companies, as our previous discussion indicated, hold large volumes of short-term self-liquidating retail and wholesale receivables. The commercial paper and bank loans, combined with long-term debt, provide a liability structure with an average maturity similar to that of the assets.

Financing of this type also provides flexibility. The volume of financing requirements can be adjusted on a daily basis, principally by varying the rate of interest that the issuing company is willing to pay.

Of course, a principal reason for the popularity of commercial paper among finance companies is the fact that interest rates for the paper are consistently below the bank prime rate. It should be noted, however, that the rate of interest applicable to commercial paper does not represent the entire cost. Smaller issuers generally place their paper through dealers who charge a fee. Larger firms place commercial paper directly with investors; thus large firms are faced with the expense associated with the maintenance of commercial paper managers and staff.

In addition to selling costs, commercial paper issuers face the cost of maintaining backup, unused lines of bank credit, as expected by the investment community. Under normal circumstances, maturing commercial paper is redeemed through issuance of new paper. However, there may exist market conditions under which the issuer would find it difficult to "roll over" maturing paper and would be forced to rely on bank credit to redeem it. Since these lines of credit are paid for with non-interest-compensating balances or by direct payment of fees, part of the cost savings of commercial paper is offset by the cost of ensuring availability of funds through banks.[3]

Bonds and Other Long-Term Debt Financing

Like industrial corporations, finance companies rely on bonds and other long-term debt as sources of financing. Long-term sources have the advantage of ensuring the availability of funds at a fixed interest rate for a specific period of time. Thus they provide a solution to the availability problem.

One major disadvantage of long-term debt is that it has historically been more expensive than short-term funds. However, this disadvantage is somewhat offset by the fact that most bonds are callable; they can be retired early, at the option of the issuer, typically with the payment of a call premium. If interest rates rise after a bond has been issued, the issuer continues to pay interest at the prior low rate. On the other hand, if market interest rates fall, the bonds can be called and replaced with a new, lower interest rate issue. Thus the higher average cost of long-term debt is at least partially

[3]Recall from chapter 7 that discount interest rates must be converted to the bond equivalent yield (annual percentage rate) before the rate can be compared to bank loan interest rates. The methodology for this conversion is developed in chapter 7.

offset by inclusion of the call feature or by other features that provide flexibility in adjusting to changes in interest rates.

Given the advantage of ensuring availability of funds, and with the cost and interest rate risk problems mitigated by callability, bonds have been an important source of funds for financing companies. Bonds and other long-term debt totalled 32 percent of finance company sources of funds (figure 15-6).

Equity Capital

Finance companies differ from most other financial institutions in that regulators do not impose a minimum equity level requirement on them. They are free to choose a debt-to-equity ratio in keeping with market forces and their own objectives.

Finance companies face two major considerations when choosing a financial structure. First, like any company, they recognize that the value of the owner's investment is affected by financial leverage. A higher debt-to-equity ratio can lead to a higher return on equity if funds are invested in assets which earn a rate of return greater than the cost of debt. However, beyond some point, further increases in debt increase the risk of insolvency, which drives up both the interest rate on debt and the required return on equity. Finance companies with less risky and better diversified asset portfolios can use proportionately less equity. Survey data from the early 1980s indicated that larger finance companies with total assets over $25 million had equity equal to 14 percent of total assets in 1980. At the same time, finance companies with total assets under $5 million had equity of about 46 percent of total assets. These smaller companies normally concentrate in limited types of lending in narrow geographic areas and are not nearly so diversified as the larger firms.

In addition to the threat of insolvency, finance companies must consider the effect of their equity ratios on their access to the debt markets. Finance companies that allow the equity cushion to fall too low may find it difficult or impossible to market commercial paper. Similarly, a low equity ratio may impair the firm's ability to acquire other short- or long-term debt funds at reasonable cost.

FINANCIAL SERVICES IN TRANSITION: MANAGERIAL IMPLICATIONS

The foregoing discussion emphasized the traditional role and structure of the consumer finance industry. Data presented early in this chapter, and specifically market share data contained in table 15-1, suggest that finance companies reached their peak in the 1950s and that their share of consumer finance receivables declined over the next two decades. This trend appeared to bottom out in the mid-1970s and 1980s. While it is too early to draw conclusions as to the ultimate structure of the market for financial services in general, and consumer financial services in particular, this section will analyze developments in consumer financial markets which have occurred over time and which appear to have accelerated dramatically in the 1980s.

Consumer Banking, Nonbank Banks, and Loophole Banking

In 1970, Congress, in amending the Bank Holding Company Act, defined a *commercial bank* as a company that *accepts demand deposits and makes commercial loans.* Also, the Bank Holding Company Act, as amended, required companies that owned one or more banks to register with the Federal Reserve. These *registered bank holding companies* were then subject to rules and supervision by the Federal Reserve. Activities in which they could engage were restricted.

A key restriction faced by banks and by bank holding companies concerned their ability to expand across state lines. The principal statutory restrictions on geographic activities of banks are contained in the *McFadden Act of 1927* and the *Douglas Amendment to the Bank Holding Company Act.* The McFadden Act prohibits interstate branching and permits each state to set branching restrictions within the state for national as well as for state banks within its borders. The Douglas Amendment prohibits bank holding companies from acquiring banks in other states unless the state in which the acquired bank is located has specifically provided for such out-of-state entry.

Although bank holding companies were prohibited from owning and operating commercial banks across state lines, they were not prohibited from owning and operating certain other businesses, including finance companies, which may expand across state lines.[4] Beginning in the 1970s, some large bank holding companies (including Bank of America, Citicorp, Manufacturers Hanover, Security Pacific Corporation, and others) acquired finance companies. In some cases, the finance companies so acquired began to appear more "banklike." Market research conducted by one major bank holding company showed that people liked banks because they had a full product array, low rates, and were reputable and stable, but disliked banks because of their impersonal atmosphere, inconvenient hours, and the belief that it was difficult to get money from them. Finance companies were viewed by these same consumers as easy places to borrow money, as convenient, and as more personal. But finance companies were also viewed as not reputable and as high-rate lenders. A number of such finance companies began to emphasize home equity (second-mortgage) loans and simultaneously deemphasized small cash loans and other traditional finance company markets. Also, as inflation mounted and as deregulation of the financial sector proceeded in the 1980s, some large savings and loan associations failed and were acquired, in some cases, by finance company subsidiaries of bank holding companies.[5] Finally, by 1984, a major "loophole" surfaced which appeared to open the door to substantial interstate banking activity. In March of that year, the Federal Reserve approved the

[4]A 1970 amendment to the Bank Holding Company Act restricted bank holding companies activities to those "closely related to banking or managing or controlling banks as to be a proper incident thereto. . . ." See table 3-1 for a list of permissable bank holding company activities.

[5]In 1982, acting under emergency conditions, the Federal Reserve Board and the Federal Home Loan Bank Board authorized both interstate and interindustry mergers. The most notable (and controversial) of these involved Citicorp's (a New York based bank holding company) acquisition of Fidelity Federal Savings and Loan Association of Oakland, California. The Garn–St. Germain Depository Institutions Act of October 1982 specifically authorized such acquisitions under certain specified conditions.

application of United States Trust Corporation of New York to convert its Florida trust subsidiary to an institution that could accept consumer deposits and make consumer loans—a consumer bank. Within weeks, a large number of major bank holding companies applied for permission to conduct similar operations across state lines. Clearly, the floodgates had been opened. Dramatic changes in traditional methods of providing consumer financial services were anticipated.[6]

True to expectations, over the next few years, the number of consumer banks grew dramatically. Sears-Roebuck for example, acquired a sleepy community bank in Delaware called Greenwood Trust. Greenwood Trust had one drive-in teller and one desk for a lending officer in January 1985. Greenwood Trust's nine employees made loans to local chicken farmers and merchants. After Sears acquired Greenwood and after selling off the bank's commercial loan portfolio to change its status to a nonbank bank, Sears decided to make it the issuer of its new Discover credit card. In little more than a year, Greenwood's assets grew from $12 million to $2 billion.[7] Retailers such as J. C. Penney and financial giants including American Express, Merrill Lynch, Beneficial Finance, and Dreyfus Corporation, among many others, have taken advantage of the loophole and operate limited-service banks. The growth of such consumer banks invited the wrath of many critics, not the least of which were small community banks and their trade organizations.

Finally, by late 1987, Congress addressed the issue of nonbank, loophole banks. Included within the *Competitive Equality Banking Act of 1987* was a provision which amended the Bank Holding Company Act of 1956 in such a way as to redefine the term "bank." The new definition included any FDIC-insured institution, as well as non-FDIC institutions that accept deposits and write commercial loans. The 1987 act, while "grandfathering" limited-service banks acquired on or before 5 March 1987 (thus permitting companies that acquired such banks to retain the bank without being regulated as a bank holding company), placed severe restrictions on future growth. Specifically, existing consumer banks were limited to future asset growth by an amount equal to 7 percent per year. Clearly, this new law would place severe restrictions on the planned growth anticipated by those who had set up limited-service banks as a means of expanding financial services.

SUMMARY

Traditionally finance companies have differed sharply from their major competitors—banks and thrifts. Events of recent years, however, have sharply reduced these traditional distinctions. The advantages that finance companies have traditionally enjoyed—the ability to expand without geographic restriction, the ability to open or close

---

[6]The loophole concerned the definition of a bank which was contained within the Bank Holding Company Act (a company that accepts demand deposits and makes commercial loans). It was argued that if an institution engaged in all banking activities *except* commercial lending *or* acceptance of demand deposits, then the institution was not by definition a bank.

[7]"Limited Banks Giant Hurdle," *The New York Times*, July 2, 1987.

branches virtually at will, the reduced level of regulatory supervision (compared with banks and thrifts)—have served to identify finance companies as a major catalyst by which the regulatory geographic constraints imposed on depository institutions can be circumvented. It seems certain that the market for consumer financial services will become increasingly competitive and that new products and innovations will be introduced by the market leaders. Successful managers within the consumer financial services industry will successfully identify the conditions which surround them and formulate policy decisions based on this environment.

QUESTIONS

15-1.   Beginning in the late 1950s, the market share of installment credit held by finance companies declined. How do you account for this decline?

15-2.   Should consumers finance large purchases, such as a new or used car, directly through the dealer? Why might this be to the customer's advantage or disadvantage?

15-3.   Distinguish between the various ways in which a time sales finance contract may be endorsed before being sold to a financial institution by a dealer.

15-4.   What is meant by the term "dealer reserve"?

15-5.   Why have finance companies emphasized second-mortgage lending in recent years?

15-6.   Define the term "floor planning" and comment on the inherent riskiness of this type of financing from the lender's point of view.

15-7.   Certain types of equipment, such as heavy trucks and trailers, are financed by finance companies. Why might finance companies pursue this type of lending while depository and thrift institutions do not?

15-8.   In addition to interest charges, there may be certain additional costs implied when finance companies borrow from banks. Comment on these.

15-9.   Why are finance companies such heavy issuers of commercial paper? Are there significant costs associated with the issuance of commercial paper above and beyond interest paid to purchasers of the paper?

15-10.   Suppose that the balance sheets of a large bank were contrasted with that of a large finance company. Would the proportion of assets financed by equity capital tend to be greater for the finance company as compared to the bank? Why or why not?

15-11.   What is meant by "loophole banking" or "nonbank banks"?

15-12.   Identify the major legislative restrictions on the geographic expansion of banks and bank holding companies.

15-13.   What were some of the significant developments of recent years that may ultimately lead to interstate banking?

PROBLEMS

15-1.   General Finance Company is subject to a state usury ceiling. The present ceiling is 18 percent APR. The company has operating costs per account of $125 per annum. In addition, General's cost of funds before tax is 12 percent and average loan balances are $2200.
        a. Is General Finance Company's cash loan portfolio profitable?
        b. If General's cost of funds increased to 13 percent, would cash loan operations be profitable?

15-2.   National finance, a large sales finance company requires a before-tax return of 10 percent on its portfolio of retail auto finance receivables. Given average loan advances (proceeds) of $8,000, administrative costs of $10 per auto loan per month, a typical dealer reserve of $180 per transaction (which is paid to the dealer "up front" together with the loan proceeds), and average loan maturity of thirty-six months, calculate:
        a. The minimum average monthly payment necessary to earn the required rate of return.
        b. The retail rate (APR) charged to the public which corresponds to your answer to part a.
        c. If the dealer reserve were eliminated, what would the monthly payment and APR be?

15-3.   Padberg Financial Services, Inc., a large, diversified financial services company, has a capital structure comparable to that of the industry (figure 15-6). Padberg's long-term bonds carry a yield to maturity of 13 percent; bank borrowing is at the prime rate (currently 11 percent), and the commercial paper rate is 10 percent. The company calculates a required rate of return on equity capital of 20 percent. Other liabilities include items such as deferred taxes and accounts payable. These other liabilities, from a practical point of view, are seen by the company as "costless."
        a. Calculate the weighted average (before tax) cost of capital for Padberg.
        b. Is Padberg correct in assuming the other liabilities to be costless?

15-4.   Jamestown Finance Company offers a home equity lending program similar to that used by TransHome Financial (table 15-6). The company calculates the maximum property collateral value in the same way as does TransHome (appraised value × 95 percent ×85 percent) and computes the maximum capacity payment in the same manner as does TransHome. As a matter of company policy however, maximum maturities for fixed-rate loans are ten years rather than the fifteen-year maximum quoted by TransHome and the current annual interest rate quoted by Jamestown is ten percent. For a household consisting of four persons, a home appraised at $150,000, an existing first mortgage of $80,000, annual household income of $48,000, and total monthly mortgage and other debt payments of $1300, calculate:

a. Maximum property collateral value
b. Maximum home equity loan
c. Required monthly payment for maximum loan
d. Maximum customer capacity payment
e. Assuming acceptable employment and credit history, should the maximum loan be granted?

15-5. If conditions identical to those in problem 15-4 existed except that household income was $38,000 rather than $48,000, what would be the maximum capacity payment and hence the maximum loan granted?

15-6. Answer problem 15-5 on the assumption that part of the home equity loan proceeds were to be used to retire an existing obligation and thus reduce the monthly debt payments by $300 (from $1300 to $1000). Should this have any bearing on the loan decision? If so, what would then be the maximum capacity payment and hence the maximum loan granted?

15-7. Midwest Finance, a large sales finance company has $50 million in outstanding commercial paper which will soon mature. The firm must decide whether to roll over the commercial paper by selling new (ninety-one day) paper or to take out a ninety-one day bank loan. The current discount rate for ninety-one day commercial paper when sold through dealers by firms the size of Midwest is 7.125 percent, and the current prime rate (APR) is 8.25 percent. If Midwest borrows at the prime rate, there is no compensating balance requirement and no other loan fees. If Midwest sells commercial paper, investors require that the firm have a standby bank commitment for $50 million in the event Midwest is unable to roll over the paper in the commercial paper market ninety-one days hence. Banks are currently charging a fee of $\frac{1}{4}$ percent of the amount of the commitment per each ninety-one day period. What should Midwest do?

15-8. First Heritage Bank wishes to expand its portfolio of consumer automobile finance receivables and is considering floor planning automobiles at several dealerships in its local lending market. Such floor planning would involve a commitment of $10 million to finance the dealers' inventories. If First Heritage commits the $10 million, it would be necessary to employ one person on a part-time basis at a cost of about $12,000 per year to administer the associated floor plan paperwork, filing, etc. Another, more experienced person would be needed on a full-time basis at an annual cost of $30,000. Ongoing expenses associated with the floor plan arrangement such as filing fees, telephone, travel, and related items would amount to about $10,000 per year. Just to break even on the floor plan arrangement, First Heritage believes it must quote an interest rate sufficient to earn the prime rate and to recover the associated floor plan costs. Calculate the break-even floor plan interest rate.

15-9. Community Credit Union wishes to sell its portfolio of 2,500 automobile loans and claims that the portfolio is worth $12 million. First Heritage Bank would like to acquire the portfolio if it could earn at least 10 percent after operating expense but before taxes on its investment. The average auto loan was originally made for $9,000 at an APR fixed at 10 percent and with an original maturity of forty-eight months. The average remaining loan contained within the portfolio has a maturity of twenty-four months. Acquisition of the portfolio would require up-front costs of about $1 million, and servicing expenses incurred each month are expected to be $5,000. Also, in recognition of bad debt expense, Heritage calculates that about 99 percent of the portfolio loan payments will actually be received each month. Calculate the maximum bid that First Heritage should make for the portfolio.

15-10. Margie Yeager, a recent college graduate plans to purchase a new car priced at $11,000. Regardless of the purchase price, Margie plans to make a down payment of $1,000. The dealer will finance the new car for forty-eight months at a cutrate APR of 4 percent with GMAC or will immediately discount $900 off the purchase price if Margie pays cash or finances the car elsewhere. Margie cannot pay cash for the car but could borrow from her local bank where the APR associated with forty-eight-month car loans is 11 percent. Which alternative should Margie select?

SELECTED REFERENCES

AVERY, ROBERT B., ELLIEHAUSEN, GREGORY E., AND KENNICKELL, ARTHUR B. "Changes in Consumer Installment Debt: Evidence from the 1983 and 1986 Surveys of Consumer Finances, *Federal Reserve Bulletin* (October 1987): 761–778.

DURKIN, THOMAS A. *Finance Facts Yearbook* (Washington, D.C.: American Financial Services Association) (published annually).

GOODMAN, JOHN L., AND LUCKETT, CHARLES A. "Adjustable-Rate Financing in Mortgage and Consumer Credit Markets," *Federal Reserve Bulletin* (November 1985): 818–835.

MCALEER, YSABEL B. "Industrial Banks as Thrift Institutions, 1983" (Washington, D.C.: American Financial Services Association, 1984).

MCALEER, YSABEL B. *Finance Companies 1977–1985: American Financial Services Association Research Report and Second Lending Report Supplement* (Washington, D.C.: American Financial Services Association, 1986).

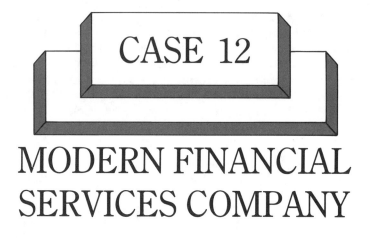

CASE 12

MODERN FINANCIAL
SERVICES COMPANY

It was mid September 1975, and the problem was a troublesome one for Bill Teal, regional vice-president of Modern Financial Services Company, a consumer finance company headquartered in Missouri. An interesting interpretation of Missouri usury law had come to his attention only two weeks ago—a business opportunity had become apparent. If this interpretation was legally correct, then large-balance, direct cash loans secured by real estate (second-mortgage loans) could be made to Missouri consumers. The vitality and profitability of company lending operations in Missouri could be restored. On the other hand, what if this interpretation was incorrect? What were the risks of entering this potentially profitable home equity lending market in Missouri? As Teal weighed these potential benefits and consequences, he reviewed certain events of recent months and years and considered the current status of his industry.

THE CONSUMER FINANCE INDUSTRY

The traditional business of consumer finance companies—the making of direct cash loans to young, typically working-class households—was on the decline. Bank credit cards with cash advance privileges and competitive gains by credit unions were eroding the market share of finance companies for consumer loans. While the market for consumer installment receivables had more than doubled in the last ten years, finance companies had not kept pace with that growth (exhibit 1). Within Missouri, one of the states over which Teal exercised management authority, the problem was particularly

Exhibit 1:

Consumer Installment Credit by Holder
(in $ millions)

YEAR END	TOTAL	COMM. BANKS	FINANCE COMPANIES	CREDIT UNIONS	MISC. LENDERS, RETAILERS, AND OTHERS
1945	$ 2,462	$ 745	$ 910	$ 102	$ 705
1950	14,703	5,798	5,315	590	3,000
1955	28,906	10,601	11,838	1,678	4,798
1960	42,968	16,672	15,435	3,923	6,938
1965	71,324	28,962	24,282	7,324	10,756
1970	101,161	41,895	31,123	12,500	15,643
1974	155,384	75,846	36,208	22,116	21,214

Consumer Installment Credit by Holder
(Share of the Market)

YEAR END	TOTAL	COMM. BANKS	FINANCE COMPANIES	CREDIT UNIONS	MISC. LENDERS, RETAILERS AND OTHERS
1945	100.0%	30.3%	37.0%	4.1%	28.6%
1950	100.0	39.4	36.1	4.0	20.4
1955	100.0	36.7	41.0	5.8	16.6
1960	100.0	38.8	35.9	9.1	16.1
1965	100.0	40.6	34.0	10.3	15.1
1970	100.0	41.4	30.8	12.4	15.5
1974	100.0	48.8	23.3	14.2	13.7

Source: *Federal Reserve Bulletin,* various issues.

acute. The impact of restrictive state usury laws[1] together with steady increases in the cost of funds for the industry had triggered an exodus of the industry from the state (exhibits 2 and 3). Large numbers of finance company offices had been closed within Missouri and some firms had simply sold their Missouri portfolios and departed the state.

A recent internal analysis of sixty-eight Modern branch offices had resulted in identification of the ten best, the middle forty-eight, and the ten worst performing offices in terms of profitability (exhibit 4). Four of the five offices in Missouri ranked with the lower portion of the middle forty-eight and one was included with the ten worst. This profitability study confirmed what Teal's nineteen years of experience with Modern had already told him. Profitable branches

[1]Effective 9 January 1975, the maximum annual interest rate applicable to direct personal cash loans in Missouri was 26.6 percent for the first $500 outstanding principal and 10 percent for principal balances beyond $500. This consumer finance law is an exception to the statutes governing general interest rates. Prior to 1975, the maximum allowable rate on balances beyond $500 was 8 percent.

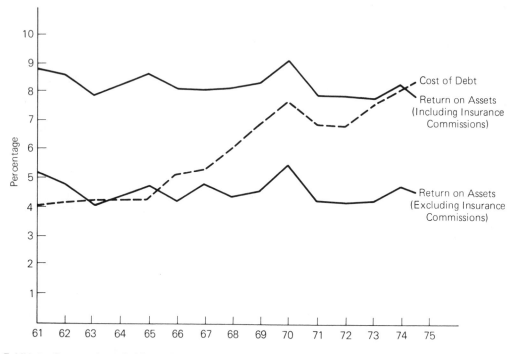

Exhibit 2:   Return on Assets for Missouri Finance Companies
Source: Return on assets calculated from data contained in consolidated annual reports of Missouri finance companies, which are submitted to the Division of Finance, State of Missouri. Cost of finance company debt estimates based on finance company commercial paper and high grade corporate bond rates weighted to reflect aggregate industry debt structure.

Operate within a favorable legal environment
Do well in business development
Are more leveraged in terms of accounts and dollar revenue per employee
Have cleaner portfolios
Have more effective managers.

In reviewing the results of this profitability analysis, Teal noted the small average loan sizes for Missouri offices. He knew that operating expenses of 9.2 percent and accounts per branch employee of 181 would be difficult to further leverage. New customers tended to be in their early twenties and were attracted to and accepted by banks once their credit history was established. Given the legal limitations of a 10 percent APR on Missouri loan balances beyond $500, attempts to increase loan sizes would reduce portfolio yield. Offices were small, and the traditional consumer finance business was dying. Industry lobbyists had been unsuccessful in getting rate relief through the Missouri legislature. But higher rates for small loans, thought Teal, were not really the answer. The answer was in repositioning; the production and marketing of a wide variety of consumer financial services at reasonable rates; a new image, a new kind of financial institution. It had been two years now since Modern was acquired by World Bancshares, a large bank holding company—two years since the repositioning

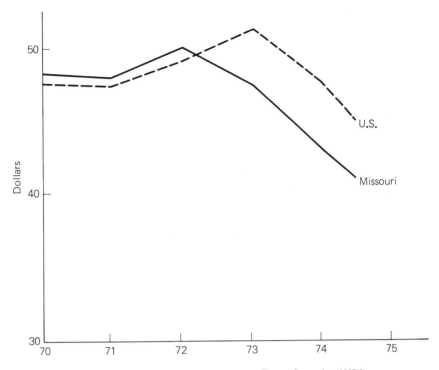

Exhibit 3:   Per Capital Loans by Consumer Finance Companies (1967 $)
Source: Research Department, Household Finance Corporation.

Exhibit 4:

Modern Financial Services Corporation Office Profitability Analysis
(in $ thousands, 1974)

	BEST 10	MIDDLE 48	WORST 10	MISSOURI
Average ANR[1]	$647	$542	$340	$493
Average loan size				
Direct	$1.581	$1.531	$1.219	$1.049
Sales finance	0.356	0.346	0.422	0.417
Operating expenses/ANR	8.0%	9.2%	13.2%	9.2%
Accounts per employee	240	200	154	181
Portfolio yield	19.5%	21.3%	21.4%	19.3%
Charge-offs/ANR	1.0%	2.3%	6.1%	1.9%
Branch-controllable contr.[2]	10.1%	5.6%	1.5%	4.0%

[1]Annual net receivables.
[2]Branch-controllable contribution represented branch profit before home office overhead (2 percent) and before taxes (50 percent × branch net profit after home office overhead was deducted). The minimum acceptable branch-controllable contribution was 4.4 percent if World's requirement of 1.2 percent RORA (return on risk assets) was to be achieved.
Note: World's 1974 equity was 6 percent of total capital. A controllable contribution of 4.4 percent less 2.0 percent equals 2.4 percent before taxes and 1.2 percent after taxes. 1.2%/6% = 20%.

of Modern had commenced in earnest. Modern was on its way as a new kind of financial institution. But until now, Missouri did not fit the mold; the legal environment had not been right. Core new products, particularly second-mortgage loans, could not profitably be marketed in Missouri.

THE MODERN FINANCIAL SERVICES CONCEPT

That the traditional business of consumer finance companies—small personal loans to working class families—was declining, was apparent to the new owners of Modern. Early research showed that people liked banks because they had a full product array, offered low rates, and were reputable and stable; people disliked banks for their impersonal atmosphere, for their inconvenient hours, and for their alleged reluctance to give out loans. Finance companies, on the other hand, were viewed by these same consumers as friendly, convenient places willing to lend money, though somewhat disreputable and expensive lending places.[2] The repositioning strategy then, was one where the best features of banks and the best features of the finance companies could be combined. This repositioning strategy, or Modern Financial Services concept, was to rely heavily on the strongly consumer-oriented package goods concept of product management. Consumer financial services were to be thought of in terms of products designed to meet a particular consumer need. Home equity loans, closed-end loans, revolving credit lines, pattern pay plans, balloon notes, sales financing, mobile home loans, sheltered financing, bridge loans, insurance services, travelers checks, financial planning seminars, and other "products" would be immediate or eventual components of the repositioning. Rather than simply offering these new products at existing Modern offices, the repositioning was to be "tested" in four states.

By July 1974, Modern financial centers had been opened in four western cities. The new offices were highly visible, attractive, and expensively refurbished. Unlike the traditional finance company office with closetlike cubicles designed to connote privacy but which, according to company research, contributed to customer anxiety—Modern financial centers contained round tables, designed to create a sense of equality and to reduce customer anxiety. The core product offered by the Modern financial centers was the second-mortgage loan.[3] By June 1975, it was clear that the test was successful. These financial centers had attracted high-quality customers in sufficiently large numbers, in accordance with profit models previously developed for the various financial products. The decision was made to convert all Modern offices to financial centers.

The Modern financial concept, particularly second-mortgage lending, had

---

[2]See exhibit 5 for rate data—banks versus finance companies.

[3]As housing prices climbed in the early 1970s, homeowners found that they had increased equity in their homes—equity which could be used as collateral for relatively large loans. Real estate (home equity) borrowers tended to demonstrate considerable income, employment, and residential stability. Average loan sizes were $10,000 or more, and delinquency rates were low. Because of reduced administration expenses per dollar loaned, combined with low delinquency rates, the Modern financial centers were able to offer such loans at rates considerably less than those associated with small personal loans.

Exhibit 5:

Finance Rates for Selected Types of Consumer Installment Credit
(Average Rates in Effect for December 1974)

AVERAGE FINANCE RATES	COMMERCIAL BANKS	FINANCE COMPANIES
Personal loans	13.6%	20.7%
Credit card plans	17.21	NA
Automobiles		
New	11.62	13.1
Used	NA	17.9
Mobile homes	11.7	13.6
Other consumer goods	13.3	19.5

Source: *Federal Reserve Bulletin.*

caught on. But the company operated in states that did not permit the tested products (particularly home equity loans) to be offered at all. In Missouri, the products could not be offered at competitive rates given the original interpretation of Missouri law. It was against this background when, on 2 September 1975, an excited young marketing manager, Terry Means, burst into Teal's office and announced that Enterprise Loan Company was marketing home equity loans in Missouri. "I heard their commercial on the car radio on my way to work," he said.

THE DECISION

The same day, after receiving Means's message, Teal conferred with Tom Harris of Modern's legal department. Harris contacted the legal department of Enterprise to learn the basis of its second-mortgage program. Tom then reviewed chapter 10 of the revised Missouri statutes—the chapter concerning interest rates. Section 10.02, defining "residential real estate," and "residential real estate loan," and Section 10.01, concerning real estate loans exempted from any interest rate ceiling, were of particular significance (exhibit 6). It was the interpretation of these statutory provisions by Enterprise that consumer loans could be secured by real estate without rate restrictions, so long as the loans were not made for the "acquisition, construction, repair, improvement, or refinancing" of residential real estate.

    Over the next few days, the statute was evaluated within Modern's legal department. A review of Missouri law did not reveal any previous decisions which defined "real estate loan." There was a federal statute that defined a real estate loan to be a loan secured by real estate, but this was not necessarily a precedent to be followed by Missouri courts. Although the state banking department was contacted, it had not yet taken a position on the matter. Contact was made with several legislators to see if any of them could shed light on the legislative intent. Some were sure that it was not

Exhibit 6:

Chapter 10 Interest Rates

___

Section 10.00 Contract Rate

After 9 January 1975, parties may agree, in writing, for the payment of interest, not exceeding ten percent per annum, on money due or to become due upon any contract.

Section 10.01 Unlimited interest, when allowed

Notwithstanding the provisions of Section 10.00, it is lawful for the parties to agree in writing to any rate of interest in connection with any
1. Loan to a corporation;
2. Business loan of five thousand dollars or more, but excluding loans for any agricultural activity;
3. Real estate loan, other than residential real estate loans and loans secured by real estate used for an agricultural activity.

Section 10.02 Definitions
1. "Business Loan" shall mean a loan to an individual or a group of individuals, the proceeds of which are to be used in a business or for the purpose of acquiring an interest in a business. The term shall also include a loan to a trust, estate, cooperative, association, or limited or general partnership.
2. "Corporation" shall mean any corporation, whether for profit or not for profit, and including any urban redevelopment corporation.
3. "Lender" shall include any bank, savings and loan association, credit union, corporation, partnership, or any other person or entity who makes loans or extends credit.
4. "Residential real estate: shall mean any real estate used or intended to be used as a residence by not more than four families.
5. "Residential real estate loan" shall mean a loan made for the acquisition, construction, repair, or improvement of real estate used or intended to be used as a residence by not more than four families. The term shall also include any loan made to refinance such a loan. No loan secured by residential real estate shall be considered to be a business loan.

Section 10.03 Penalties for Usury

If a rate of interest greater than permitted by law is paid, the person paying the same or his legal representative may recover twice the amount of the interest thus paid, provided that the action is brought within five years from the time when said interest should have been paid. The person so adjudged to have received a greater rate of interest shall also be liable for the costs of the suit, including a reasonable attorney's fee to be determined by the court.

___

intended to open the door to unlimited rates on second mortgages, while others thought that a loophole existed for such loans.

Was Enterprise's interpretation correct? Was there legal authority to make Missouri home equity loans for certain purposes (e.g., college tuition or short-term debt consolidation) with no legal interest ceiling? On the one hand, Harris argued that the company should not venture into this business (Missouri home equity loans) because, from a practical standpoint, the use of the loan proceeds cannot be controlled. On the other hand, Harris believed there were significant reasons that could support a legal argument that there was a loophole in the law. He thought the statute had been ill-drafted. But given that, on its face it appeared to permit the activity; though there was no apparent legislative history to support a contention that the Missouri legislature intended to allow such loans to be made at rates exceeding 10 percent. However, no one could judge how a Missouri court would decide if the same question was put to it.

Although Russ Pluta, Modern's CEO was the ultimate decision maker, Teal knew that Pluta would follow his recommendation. He knew also that he must decide soon. Competitive pressures were mounting. Other finance companies were beginning to enter the market. If Modern were to enter the Missouri home equity market, then newspaper and radio advertisements must be prepared. It was either "join" or "get out of the business in Missouri."

QUESTIONS

1. Identify the key issue or issues represented by this case.
2. Should Modern begin making second-mortgage loans in Missouri? If so, identify any apparent risks and develop a management strategy to minimize or eliminate these risks.

16

Thrift Institution Management

The thrift institutions—savings and loan companies, savings banks, and credit unions—rank second only to commercial banks in total assets held by a financial institution category. With assets of well over $1 trillion in 1988, they provide an outlet for savings of individuals as well as an important source of real estate and consumer credit.

The cumulative balance sheets of these institutions provide a quick overview of their characteristics (table 16-1). All three types of thrift institutions have liability structures composed primarily of savings deposits. Both savings and loan companies and savings banks hold the bulk of their assets in the form of mortgage loans. Their combined mortgage loan holdings are greater than those of commercial banks and account for about half of all mortgage debt not held by government agencies. In contrast, credit unions invest most of their funds in consumer loans, with mortgage loans making up only a small proportion of total assets.

As depository financial intermediaries, the thrift institutions have many characteristics in common with commercial banks. In fact, as a consequence of the monetary control act of 1980 and the Garn–St. Germain Act of 1982, the similarity is increasing as their services have expanded to include transaction accounts and a wider variety of lending. However, they are more vulnerable to interest rate changes than are commercial banks. With an average asset maturity substantially longer than average deposit maturity, the thrift institutions, and particularly savings and loans, suffered from the effects of rising, unstable interest rates. Thus they have a unique set of management problems.

Table 16-1

Total Assets and Liabilities of All Thrift Institutions, June 1987 (in $ billions)

	SAVINGS AND LOAN ASSOC.	FSLIC-INSURED FEDERAL SAVINGS BANKS	STATE-CHARTERED AND OTHER SAVINGS BANKS	CREDIT UNIONS
Cash			$5	
U.S. government securities	$138		14	
Other securities			21	
Mortgage loans	525	191	156	
Other loans	286	18	35	91
Other assets			14	
Total Assets	$947	$264	$245	$161
Savings deposits	$716	$190	$188	
Other liabilities	195	59		
Capital	39	15	57	
Total liabilities and net worth	$949	$264	$245	$161

Note: Missing data are a result of differences in reporting requirements, and certain data are preliminary.

Source: *Federal Reserve Bulletin.*

CHARACTERISTICS OF THRIFT INSTITUTIONS

Savings and Loan Associations

Little more than a decade ago, a savings and loan could be characterized as an institution that accepted passbook savings deposits, paying a maximum rate set by federal regulation, and then used these funds to make mortgage loans for the purchase of homes. As late as 1970, mortgage loans represented 85 percent of S&L assets, while passbook savings represented 60 percent of total sources of funds to these institutions. Sheltered by regulation and serving a vital need for housing credit, S&L's saw their assets grow from one-tenth those of commercial banks in 1950 to 45 percent of commercial bank assets in 1980.

By 1980, however, pressures for change were inescapable. Rising, unstable interest rates had led savers to remove their money elsewhere in search of interest rates higher than the low, regulated rates paid by depository institutions. To make matters worse, the S&Ls held many old mortgages that were paying interest rates below the current cost of funds. In response to these problems and a general demand for decreased regulatory protection of business, the Depository Institution Deregulation and Monetary Control Act of 1980, the Garn–St. Germain Act of 1982, and subsequent regulatory changes have given S&Ls the authority to offer a broad range of services while both requiring and allowing them to compete for funds by paying market rates.

A typical S&L at present has a liability structure consisting of checkable deposits (accounts on which checks can be drawn), passbook savings, a series of certificates of deposits paying competitive market interest rates, and borrowed funds. The typical S&L's asset structure now consists of 60 percent mortgages, or mortgage-backed securities, down from 85 percent mortgages in 1970. The S&L offers an entire market basket of mortgage products rather than the one or two alternatives that were offered to the borrower a decade ago. It has taken advantage of increased investment authority to increase its security holdings, particulaly corporate securities. It has also increased investment in commercial mortgages and has begun offering consumer loans. Also, S&L's may now make non-mortgage commercial loans.

These changes in asset and liability structure have led to important changes in industry structure. Because larger S&L's have an advantage in offering a broad range of service, and because of failures and mergers within the industry, the number of S&L's has decreased dramatically. Between 1970 and 1987, the number of S&L's declined from about 5,700 to about 2,900. Despite the decrease in the number of S&L's, the total assets of these institutions have continued to grow, although the growth rate has been somewhat erratic in recent years. In addition to consolidation, there have been important changes in the ownership of savings and loans. The Garn–St. Germain Act of 1982 established a procedure subject to regulatory approval whereby commercial banks and S&Ls could cross state lines and acquire S&Ls in imminent danger of insolvency. As a result, major bank holding companies, especially Citicorp, have moved aggressively to acquire a national network of S&Ls, hence they have entered markets they were not previously allowed to enter. Savings and loans provide an excellent case study of an industry in transition.

Savings and loan companies are chartered by either the federal government (through the Federal Home Loan Bank Board) or the state in which the institution wishes to set up business. Over half of the savings and loans are presently federally chartered.

A savings and loan may have the more common mutual form or the stock form of ownership. The depositors and borrowers of a mutual savings and loan elect a board of directors who oversee the company as would any other corporate board of directors. With the stock form of ownership, stockholders own the company, select the directors, and face returns and risk as do stockholders in other firms. Some existing savings and loans have switched from mutual ownership to stock ownership in recent years, primarily to raise capital by selling more stock. It has also been argued that the existence of a group of stockholders interested in profitability leads to greater efficiency.

The primary regulatory body for savings and loans is the Federal Home Loan Bank Board. It examines all federally chartered savings and loans and all state-chartered savings and loans that have joined the federally chartered institutions in having their depositors' funds insured by the Federal Savings and Loan Insurance Corporation (FSLIC). Over 98 percent of savings and loans assets are held by institutions insured by the FSLIC. Deposits are presently insured up to $100,000.

A somewhat confused regulatory structure exists with this dual chartering system. Federal regulations may apply to only federally chartered savings and loans or to all federally insured savings and loans. State regulations may apply to all state-chartered savings and loans or only to those not insured by the FSLIC. For example, variable-rate mortgages began in California with state-chartered savings and loans being allowed to grant variable-rate mortgages. The Federal Home Loan Bank Board did not try to stop insured state-chartered institutions from extending variable-rate mortgages, but federally chartered institutions were not given authority to enter the market until six years later.

In addition to acting as a regulatory agency, the Federal Home Loan Bank System acts as an important source of credit for savings and loans. The Federal Home Loan Bank System was formed in 1932 and organized into twelve regional banks. These banks, which are public corporations similar to the Federal Reserve banks, grant savings and loan companies direct loans with maturities from a few months to ten years.

Federal Home Loan banks have three sources of funds to loan to member savings and loans. Capital is supplied by member savings and loans, which must purchase capital stock equal to 2 percent of their mortgage loan balances. In addition to capital stock, members are encouraged to make deposits of excess funds. Federal Home Loan bank capital stock and deposits totalled about 3 percent of savings and loan assets in recent years. Supplementing these funds, the system sells consolidated debentures which are the joint obligations of the twelve banks.

Federal Home Loan bank lending is supplemented by Federal Home Loan Mortgage Corporation purchases of mortgages from savings and loans and mutual savings banks. The Federal Home Loan Mortgage Corporation finances these purchases by selling public bond issues secured by packages of mortgages purchased from savings and loans. Federal Home Loan bank debentures and mortgage-backed securities outstanding exceeded $200 billion by 1987. Thrift institutions also gained the right to borrow from the Federal Reserve System under provisions of the deregulation act.

Savings Banks

Savings banks were traditionally chartered by states as mutual institutions, i.e., owned and operated, at least in theory, by the depositors and not by stockholders. These mutual savings banks were designed to serve purposes similar to those of savings and loans but had some differences resulting from their historical development. Savings and loans were formed by people who wanted to purchase homes. In some cases, the savers even drew lots to determine when each one would be allowed to borrow. Mutual savings banks were formed originally by European immigrants on the East Coast of the United States and were started to provide a place to serve small savers and encourage thrift.

These traditional savings banks operate in only seventeen states, with 90 percent of their deposits being in five northeastern states: New York, Massachusetts, Connecticut, Pennsylvania, and New Jersey. Prior to 1978, federal chartering of savings banks was not available, and all savings banks operated under state charter. Their total asset size—25 percent of that of savings and loans—indicates that they are an important factor in the few states in which they do have substantial operations.

In contrast with savings and loans and most other corporations, the traditional (mutual) savings bank board of directors is not elected by the owners. It is a self-perpetuating organization with existing members of the board electing a new board member if a former member resigns. While this situation may seem unusual, new board members of other businesses are frequently selected by the management of the existing board, with the vote of the shareholders being little more than a rubber stamp. In any case, the board of a savings bank is held accountable under the standards of fiduciary responsibility.

The liabilities of traditional savings banks are similar to those of savings and loans. They offer passbook savings accounts as well as various time deposit accounts. They were the first institutions to offer NOW accounts.[1] Like other insured thrift institutions, their deposits are insured to $100,000.

Traditional savings banks have had broader lending and investment powers, as determined by the states in which they were chartered. While heavy in mortgage loans, they have always had the power to invest in corporate securities, both debt instruments and stock. The typical mutual savings bank therefore, tended to be more diversified than an S&L. Such differences, as the ensuing discussion will suggest, are likely to decrease as the effect of legislation enacted in recent years begins to be felt.

The Federal Home Loan Act of 1932 provided bank system membership for three types of mortgage-making financial intermediaries. Included among these were *savings and loan associations,* to accept deposits from savers and lend money for home mortgages, and *savings banks,* to accept deposits, make residential mortgages, and lend money for other types of real estate development, including commercial projects. Savings banks could also invest in high-quality corporate and government bonds and in stocks. Although insurance companies could join the Federal Home Loan Bank System, few did.

Until 1933, the states chartered all S&L's and savings banks. The Homeowners' Loan Act of 1933 gave the Federal Home Loan Bank Board the power to grant federal charters to savings and loan associations, but federal charters could not be given to savings banks. In 1978, however, the legislation was amended and the bank board was authorized to grant federal charters to savings banks. Finally, the Garn–St. Germain Act of 1982 permitted new thrift institutions to receive federal charters and organize as stock corporations. This 1982 law also made it easier for federally chartered mutual institutions to convert to stock ownership (or vice versa) and to therefore raise equity capital through the sale of capital stock. Another important feature of the Garn–St. Germain Act was the fact that it eliminated differences in the kinds of business in which federal savings and loan associations and federal savings banks could engage. Since a number of states did not permit state-chartered S&L's and/or savings banks to organize as stock corporations, many such institutions proceeded to switch from a state charter to a federal charter and to organize as stock corporations. An interesting effect of these recent legislative developments is the fact that there exist, as a practical matter, no

---

[1]Negotiable order of withdrawal accounts; these essentially serve as checking accounts and are now included under the general heading "transaction accounts."

remaining differences between a federally chartered savings and loan and a federally chartered savings bank.[2]

At least partly as a result of this 1982 law, and over the next several years, the number of state-chartered savings banks and S&L's declined and the number of such federally chartered institutions increased. And between 1982 and early 1987, while the number of stockholder-owned S&L's and savings banks grew, the number of mutuals declined. Indeed, by early 1987, of the 366 traditional savings banks, about 112 had switched from mutual to stock organizations. Of this 112, 31 had federal charters and were now called federal savings banks. Also, by early 1987, about 430 institutions which were formerly savings and loans had converted to federal savings banks.[3] In addition, between 1982 and 1987, the proportion of S&L's that were stockholder owned grew from 20 percent to 40 percent.

Credit Unions

Credit unions have been the fastest growing type of depository financial institution in recent decades, with assets in 1988 of well over 100 times their 1950 level. However, in total assets, credit unions are still only 6 percent of the size of commercial banks and considerably smaller than S&L's and savings banks (table 16-1).

The key requirement for a credit union is *commonality*. All members of the credit union must have some common bond, with the most frequent bond being place or means of employment. A physical location is frequently provided by the employer, and much of the work is contributed by the employee members. It is also common practice for loans to be repaid through withholding from the borrower's pay, thereby minimizing collection problems. Another major advantage traditionally enjoyed by credit unions has been their tax-exempt status. With minimal operating costs, no taxes, and limited collection problems, credit unions have been able to offer competitive interest rates on deposits yet still provide loans at rates below those available from other lenders. With these advantages, it is little wonder that their growth has been rapid.

While the type of credit union described above still exists, another type has also evolved. This other type serves interest groups with many thousands of members, such as all people who are employed by educational institutions in a major city. In at least one case, residence in a particular state senatorial district has been used as the common bond. Credit unions of this type have offices resembling those of other depository

---

[2]Because of widespread public knowledge of the financial difficulties faced by many S&L's in the 1980s, and because of heavy drains on the industry's federal insurance fund, some savers began to lose confidence in the savings and loan industry. At least partly in response to this perception, some S&L's proceeded to convert their charter to that of a federal savings bank under the assumption that this name change—which now allowed use of the word "bank" in their title—would improve their public image. See, for example, "Insolvent S&L's Stay Open, Losing Billions, Despite Disposal Plan," *Wall Street Journal*, November 16, 1987.

[3]National Council of Savings Institutions, *National Fact Book of Savings Institutions*, Washington, D.C. 1987.

institutions and rely on professional managers. Their cost structures are also more closely aligned with those of the other depository institutions.

Of the 18,000 domestic credit unions, about ⅔ have federal charters and ⅓ have state charters. Charters, supervision, examination, and deposit insurance are provided by the National Credit Union Administration. Depositors are protected by deposit insurance provided by the National Credit Union Association for up to $100,000 per account. Credit unions can borrow from the Federal Intermediate-Term Credit Bank.

As with other thrift institutions, credit unions take deposits from their members and make loans to them, investing liquid reserves and excess funds in other securities, primarily U.S. government obligations. Credit unions offer time and passbook savings accounts like the other thrift institutions. They also offer share draft accounts, which serve as checking accounts for members.

The credit unions differ sharply on the asset side. While they have authority to make mortgage loans, only about 3 percent of their assets are presently invested in mortgages, primarily because they generally lack the capital to make such loans. They concentrate on consumer loans, with automobile loans being the most common.

MANAGEMENT PRINCIPLES FOR THRIFT INSTITUTIONS

As with any other business, the financial management of a thrift institution involves a profitability/risk trade-off. Profitability is the primary motive for most business ventures, and additional risk is frequently the cost of added profit. Like other businesses, the thrift institution faces various alternatives, each with different risk and return characteristics. The appropriate risk/return combination is both a management decision and a matter for regulatory control.

At first glance, there may be some question about the appropriateness of the profitability objective as there are frequently no stockholders to benefit from such profitability. However, as economists have long pointed out, competition forces all business in the direction of profitability maximization. In perfect competition, each business will operate in such a way as to minimize its cost per unit of output, and market competition will force the price to a level just sufficient to meet these lowest possible production costs plus a profit sufficient to attract the necessary capital. In perfect competition, individual firms cannot affect selling price. They can affect profitability only by minimizing unit production cost. In such an environment, only firms that maximize profitability will earn enough to continue producing.

Recent experience of thrift institutions has underscored the effectiveness of market forces in requiring profitability maximization. When general interest rates rose rapidly and the interest rates that financial institutions were allowed to pay on passbook deposits were not increased correspondingly, savers removed their funds from thrift institutions and invested them directly with purchases such as Treasury bills. When Treasury bills in denominations of less than $10,000 were eliminated to discourage disintermediation, money market mutual funds arose to serve the needs of small savers by offering each investor an interest in a large portfolio of money market instruments. Institutions then found themselves bidding in relatively free markets for funds held by the money market funds. Regulation was not very successful in protecting the thrift institutions from competitive forces.

Even the limited protection from competition provided by past legislation was virtually eliminated with deregulation in the 1980s. In addition to broadening lending authority, deregulation has phased out most limitations on interest rates paid and some limitations on interest rates charged by institutions, leaving the setting of these rates to market forces. With interest income and expense now being set by market forces, the profitability objective will become increasingly dominant for financial institutions.

Risk for the thrift institution arises from three sources. *Default risk* refers to the failure of borrowers to repay loans. Default losses on first-mortgage loans must be held to very low levels because of the small margins traditionally existing between the cost of funds to thrift institutions and the interest rates on these loans. *Interest rate* risk arises from the fact that thrift institution loans are frequently for longer maturities than are their liabilities. Rising interest rates have forced thrift institutions to pay more for some deposits than is being earned on many of the older loans that are still on the institutions' books. With rising and fluctuating interest rates in recent years, interest rate risk has been greater than default risk. It permeates almost every aspect of thrift institution management. *Liquidity risk* also arises from the short-term nature of liabilities. While an industrial corporation may be a few days late with its payments and experience no substantial difficulties, a thrift institution would be seriously damaged if it were unable to meet withdrawal demands. The risk of being unable to meet withdrawal demand must be kept in mind when developing the asset structure.

Finally, the *service obligation* of a thrift institution creates another problem and set of trade-offs for management. Charters are not granted for the benefit of institution stockholders or managers. They are issued for the benefit of the community the institution is expected to serve. The supposed purpose of deposit interest rate regulations was not to ensure a happy level of profitability, but to ensure the safety of depositors' funds and a steady supply of money to the housing industry. Laws such as the Community Reinvestment Act are aimed at ensuring that thrift institutions meet their social responsibility as defined by legislators. Should a thrift institution pursue its own profitability within the constraints created by such laws? Or should it go beyond this and make its own judgments about the social objectives it should be striving for? These issues have been frequently debated but never settled. However, growing competition decreases the ability of institutions to make decisions on other than profitability grounds.

In pursuing its objectives, the thrift institution must answer five primary asset and liability management questions:

1. Which loans should be made?
2. What quantity and specific type of liquid reserves should be held?
3. What investment outlet(s) should be used for funds not committed to loans or liquid reserves?
4. What mix of liabilities should be used?
5. How much equity capital is needed?

While these various questions represent separate areas of management within the institution, the policy decisions are not made in isolation. For example, interest rate risk depends on the relative maturities of assets and liabilities. The investments chosen as outlets for idle funds should be considered in light of the asset/liability mix to decrease overall risk. These and other interrelationships must be considered in developing policy so that the sum of the management decisions in the various areas results in a harmonious whole. These interrelationships are stressed in the following discussion.

Loan Management

As indicated earlier, thrift institution lending is dominated by mortgage loans. Thrift institutions continue to hold more mortgages than all other private financial institutions combined and are an important factor in mortgage lending overall (table 16-2). Consumer loans, the second important category, are considered in detail in chapter 15 and are discussed in this chapter only in terms of their contribution to the risk-returns characteristics of the overall loan portfolio.

Mortgage Loan Markets   While table 16-2 confirms that savings institutions (savings and loans together with savings banks) held some $823 billion in mortgage loans in 1987, perhaps even more revealing is the shifting nature of the mortgage loan market since deregulation commenced in 1980. Data contained in the table show that total mortgage outstandings grew by about 86.5 percent over the time period. Of particular significance, however, is the growth of mortgage instruments secured by mortgages but

Table 16-2

The Mortgage Loan Market, mid-1987 (in $ billions)

	DOLLARS	*MARKET SHARE*	*PERCENTAGE CHANGE SINCE 1980*
Commercial banks	$542.6	19.8%	106.3%
Savings institutions*	823.2	30.0	36.5
Life insurance companies	198.1	7.2	51.1
Finance companies	36.9	1.3	212.7
Federal agencies**	196.5	7.2	71.9
Mortgage pools or trusts[†]	612.4	22.3	330.4
Individuals and others[‡]	335.2	12.2	62.5
Total	$2,744.9	100.0%	86.5%

*Includes holdings of all savings banks and all savings and loan associations.
**Held directly by Government National Mortgage Association, Farmers Home Administration, Federal Housing Administration, Veterans Administration, Federal National Mortgage Association, Federal Land Banks, and Federal Home Loan Mortgage Corporation.
[†]Outstanding principal balances of mortgage pools backing securities insured or guaranteed by certain agencies included in the previous note.
[‡]Includes mortgage companies, real estate investment trusts, state and local credit agencies, state and local retirement funds, noninsured pension funds, credit unions, and other U.S. agencies.

Source: *Federal Reserve Bulletin.*

traded in the secondary markets. Note that mortgage pools or trusts grew proportionally more rapidly than did mortgage loans made and held by institutions represented in the table.

This important and relatively recent development in mortgage lending markets reflects the growing trend toward securitization. Depository financial institutions have traditionally collected funds in the form of deposits and then loaned these deposits to direct borrowers. However, the risk associated with holding long-term, fixed-rate assets, financed with shorter-term liabilities, together with advances in information technology, has contributed to this rapid growth in mortgage-backed securities. As recently as 1975, mortgage-backed securities as a percentage of all mortgage securities stood at about 5 percent.[4] By 1987 these "packaged and sold" mortgages represented 22.3 percent of the total market. Many bank and thrift managers are today seeking to reduce the average maturity of their assets by temporarily warehousing mortgage loans which they have originated, but the long-term funding is accomplished through the use of various types of mortgage securities. In some cases, the originating financial institutions retains the servicing rights, collecting and forwarding the monthly mortgage payments as a service to the permanent owner in return for a fee charged for this service. In many cases, securities based on mortgages are bought for investment purposes by depository institutions. About one-third of the $612 billion in mortgage-backed securities shown in table 16-2 was held by savings institutions. This amount was in addition to the $823.2 billion in mortgage loan receivables, that was directly held by savings institutions.

Types of Mortgage Loans   The most common mortgage loan made by a thrift institution is the *conventional mortgage*. Conventional mortgages involve no guarantee by a third party such as a public or private insurance agency. The institution relies on the creditworthiness of the borrower and on the value of the property. A 20 percent down payment is normally required, but loans for up to 95 percent of the value of the property are permitted by regulators if the amount over 80 percent is insured by a separate agency or is covered by a special reserve account. Loans for over 80 percent of property value frequently carry higher interest rates.

A typical conventional loan has traditionally involved a fixed-interest rate and equal monthly payments for a maturity of up to forty years. However, there have been some recent changes—the so-called alternate mortgage instruments—aimed at dealing with current market conditions. The *graduated payment loan* is one such adaption, designed to help house buyers deal with the higher house payments associated with inflation and higher interest rates. With the graduated payment loan, the payments are smaller during the early years. Typically, interest only is paid during the early years, up to five years. Payments necessary to amortize the mortgage begin after this initial period.

The *adjustable rate mortgage* loan (ARM) is a type of conventional loan designed to protect the lender from problems caused by fluctuating interest rates. The lender can adjust the interest rate as frequently as once each month, with the rate tied to

[4]American Bankers Association, *Statistical Information on the Financial Services Industry,* 4th ed., 1987.

an agreed-upon index of market interest rates. The interest rate must be decreased if the index falls and the interest rate change can be accommodated by extending loan maturity, changing the payment, adjusting the principal loan balance through negative amortization, or some combination of these.

Variable-rate mortgage arrangements do not eliminate interest rate risk; they simply pass it on to the borrowers. Even a two percentage point increase in the interest rate can result in a 20 percent increase in monthly payments. As long as short-term deposits are used as a source of funds for long-term loans, someone must bear the interest rate risk.

While indexing the mortgage rate has been widely heralded as the solution to the thrift institutions' interest rate risk problem, its future is still in doubt. In California, where state-chartered institutions have been allowed to offer variable-rate mortgages, the precursor of the adjustable-rate mortgages, for some years, results have been mixed. A study of the California experience showed that variable-rate mortgages peaked in 1976, with only 17 percent of California savings and loans offering variable-rate mortgages and 46 percent of the mortgages granted by these institutions being variable-rate. The use of variable-rate mortgages in California declined from 1976 to 1978, when the study ended. One reason for the decline was that institutions were only willing to offer beginning interest rates approximately 0.25 percent lower for variable-rate mortgages. Because this was not enough to encourage voluntary selection of a variable-rate mortgage, variable-rate mortgage borrowers tended to be lower-income, lower-down-payment borrowers who had no alternative in a tight market. If variable-rate mortgages were to be issued to people other than poorer credit risks, and be issued when money was readily available, it was necessary that they be made attractive somehow.

Many institutions have responded to this challenge by offering adjustable-rate mortgages at interest rates tied to an index of short-term interest rates. This might mean an initial interest rate of 2 percent or more below the fixed mortgage rates available in certain market conditions. Other institutions have offered adjustable-rate loans with the initial rate 5 percent or more below rates on fixed-rate loans, with the rate being raised each year until it parallels some index of market interest rates. This latter type of loan is designed to encourage first-time home buyers by keeping the initial payment low, as well as to encourage the use of variable-rate mortgages. The low interest rate in the first few years is offset by a subisdy by the home seller or by a high enough interest rate later to cover the early losses. These various incentives have achieved the desired result: More than half of new mortgages in some recent years have been adjustable rate. An unfortunate side effect is an unmeasured increase in default risk as borrowers face sharply increased monthly payments. This potential problem is particularly severe with the mortgages that carry initial interest rates deeply discounted from prevailing interest rates.

In addition to conventional first-mortgage loans, the thrift institutions also make second-mortgage loans. Second-mortgage loans are covered in chapter 15 and are based on a claim to the property which is subordinate to a first-mortgage loan against that same property. These loans are used for purposes such as remodeling, short-term debt consolidation, educational expenses, and investment. They are normally of shorter maturity than first-mortgage loans, thereby reducing interest rate risk.

Besides conventional mortgages, thrift institutions also make Federal Housing Administration (FHA) and Veterans Administration (VA) insured loans. These loans are granted by private lenders, but are insured by the U.S. government so that the lenders are protected in the event of default. The primary objective of these insurance programs was the provision of mortgage credit to those without sufficient funds to make the down payments required for traditional mortgage loans. These insurance programs made it possible to buy a house with a down payment of a few percent or less.

It turned out that the FHA and VA programs served two purposes in addition to direct aid to borrowers. Because these mortgages are insured with regard to default risk and are otherwise standardized, they are readily marketable. Thus, these insurance programs aided in the development of a secondary market for mortgages. These insurance programs also demonstrated that even people who made very small down payments were unlikely to default. As a result, private insurance plans also developed and lenders began making loans with down payments of 5 percent and 10 percent without FHA or VA insurance.

Credit Analysis   Mortgage loans differ from other consumer lending in their long-term nature and in the narrow margins between interest rates paid on deposits and interest rates charged. Credit analysis is based on the standard three Cs of credit: character, capacity, and collateral. But the application of these factors is different primarily in that the focus must be long-term and losses must be held to a very low rate.

Character analysis is little different than that for other loans. Past character is the best evidence concerning future character. The lender checks with the local credit bureau and other financial institutions with which the applicant has dealt to determine if other financial obligations have been treated seriously and honestly. It has been frequently argued that the mortgage payment is the last payment people will default on, while medical bills are about the first category to suffer. Whether these differences result from different senses of obligation or from the importance of protecting the home from foreclosure is not certain, but it is a factor to consider in character analysis. Therefore, special emphasis is placed on any past mortgage loan experience. Of course, it is illegal to consider matters such as sex, marital status, or race in any aspect of the loan analysis. Lenders may not extend their character analysis to pass moral judgment on such things as living arrangements. The character analysis must focus on the handling of financial responsibilities.

Capacity deals with the ability to meet loan payments. Standard policy for an institution may be that mortgage loan payments cannot exceed 25 percent of income, for example, or that total loan payments cannot exceed 35 percent of income. These policies are based on past experience with regard to default rates. In addition to present income, the stability of income in the future must also be considered. A past record of employment instability or employment in a profession suffering from frequent periods of high unemployment would be a negative factor even if present income were satisfactory. The equal credit opportunity act requires that sex not be considered in evaluating the stability of income and that alimony be considered as income. Questions about childbearing plans are not allowed in evaluating income stability.

Collateral takes on special importance with mortgage loans because it is difficult to forecast an individual's income over the long time periods involved. The loan decision involves both the appraised value (discussed below) and the loan-to-value ratio. Collateral provides protection if an individual's income declines, but the depression of the 1930s and more recent experiences in the Farm Belt and oil-producing states showed that it is of little help if everyone's income declines sharply. Experience with VA and FHA loans in the last 30 years has convinced lenders that, under normal circumstances, they can safely lend 90 percent and even 95 percent of the face value. These loan-to-value ratios have not been tested in a depression, but 50 percent loan-to-value ratios provided no protection for the financial system in the 1930s.

The Credit Decision   The loan decision is technically made by a loan committee made up of officers of the institution. However, efficiency and regulatory requirements make relatively standardized policy necessary. The loan committee does not have the time or expertise about individual cases to provide carefully considered judgments in each case. In addition, legislation such as the Community Reinvestment Act and the Equal Credit Opportunity Act require the credit policy be consistent and fair, not arbitrarily considering factors such as race, sex, or property location. In addition, institutions are required to give an answer if an individual inquires as to why his or her application was turned down. A general statement such as "our loan committee voted against it" is usually not adequate. If the institution has specific policy, it can make loan decisions efficiently and without illegal bias.

Institutions do not normally vary the interest rate by risk class, with the exception of variation by down payment size. This is a matter of tradition as well as a matter of regulation. Regulators discourage risk taking by quickly downgrading delinquent loans and requiring extra capital to support them, thereby decreasing the ability to make further loans. In addition, it is illegal to quote different rates or terms based on race, sex, marital status, or property location. The institution can protect itself from inadvertently developing an illegal policy by quoting the same terms for all first-mortgage loans.

Market forces also discourage the offering of different rates for different risk classes. Because more than 90 percent of applicants are typically approved, higher-rate, high-risk loans would have to come from this additional 10 percent. Many of these would not be acceptable credit risks at any additional rate they could possibly afford to pay. In addition, credit analysis is not so precise an art as to make risk classification precise, opening up problems of bias charges and general ill will. In competitive markets, these are costly problems.

Setting credit standards that are expected to result in low default rates has traditionally been a matter of judgment based on senior management's experience (and bias) as to what characteristics lead to default. Recently, this approach has been supplemented by statistical studies aimed at increasing the objectivity and accuracy of policy determination. The most widely used statistical approach is *discriminant analysis*. The analysis begins with loans that have been made in the past and classifies them as good or bad based on payment experience. For each of these loans, information is collected on a number of factors that are believed to be important in determining failure rates. Based on a statistical procedure beyond the scope of this discussion, but readily available on most computers, a *discriminant function* is developed. Rakes[5] developed the following discriminant function for a group of mortgage loans:

$$Z = 1.647 - 0.442I - 0.0398C + 0.218A$$
$$- 0.136E + 0.066W$$

where
I = loan-to-income ratio
C = number of unsatisfactory credit indications from previous creditors
A = 0 if the wife is as old as or older than the husband; 1 if the husband is older than the wife
E = 0 if a borrower is classified as having stable employment; 1 if a borrower is classified as having unstable employment
W = wife's age.

If the Z score is above 0.5, the loan is expected to be good, and if the score is below 0.5, the loan is likely to be bad. This particular model was developed by testing a large number of variables, most of which did not turn out to be good predictors. The model should be taken as illustrative only, since it was based on data from one city and is based only on applications from families. In addition, the two age variables might be considered unfair discrimination under present laws.

Statistical methods have the benefit of potential increases in accuracy and increased objectivity which increase the fairness and profitability of credit decisions. The fact that losses continue to occur is an indication of the limits of precision. Nobody can predict exactly who will lose their job, suffer ill health, etc. It is only possible to predict these things in terms of probabilities.

Appraisal Because collateral is important, and because houses are not standard units like stocks or bonds, an accurate estimate of property value is necessary. As loan-to-value ratios have risen, the accuracy of the appraisal has become increasingly important. The fact that most defaults occur early in the life of the mortgage increases the importance of accurate value estimation. The appraisal is normally performed by a professional appraiser who either works for the institution or works independently, performing appraisals for various institutions. There are various approaches to appraisal, depending on the situation.

Replacement cost is an approach that can be used with newer properties. If similar structures are being built, the replacement cost is both easily determined and relevant. The appraiser examines construction costs and land costs in the area, making adjustments for any particular features of the individual property. The replacement cost can also be adjusted for depreciation, if any. The approach is of little use in evaluating older homes, many of which are selling at fractions of their replacement costs.

Present value of benefits is an approach used primarily for income properties. Essentially, the appraiser estimates the useful life of the property, the rental income over that life, and the expenses that will be incurred. The value of the property then equals the present value of the benefits minus the present value of expenses.

Market value is the ultimate objective of all lender appraisals, since the lender

[5]Ganas K. Rakes, "A Numerical Credit Evaluation Model for Residential Mortgages," *Quarterly Review of Economics and Business* (Autumn 1973): 73–84.

wants to estimate what the property could be sold for if the borrower were to default. With an older house, a direct market value appraisal is often the only method that can be used. The property is not expected to generate income and may be selling below its replacement cost because houses of its type are not being built any more. The appraiser begins by studying recent transactions in the area to determine the prices other properties have sold for. Adjustments are then made for differences between the particular property and others in the area. Price per square foot is an important part of this approach, with adjustments then being made for location and other features of the property. Needless to say, the skill and experience of the appraiser is very important in going from prices other properties have sold for to an estimate of the likely market value of the property under consideration.

Appraisers have frequently been accused of contributing to the decline of older neighborhoods by appraising property at less than a potential buyer is willing to pay, making it impossible to obtain a loan. Appraisers do consider the present condition of the neighborhood and apparent trends in property condition in preparing their estimates. Therefore, it is likely that a previously deteriorating neighborhood will find appraisals lagging behind redevelopment efforts. Critics of appraisal practices argue that property is worth what someone will pay for it and therefore cannot be appraised at less than the currently agreed-to sale price. However, the lender is interested in the price the property could be sold for if the buyer should default.

Interest Charges Interest charges on mortgage loans are set in light of the institution's profitability objective. The limit on how much the institution can charge is set by competitive market forces. If the institution sets its interest charges on mortgage loans above those for competing institutions, it is likely to attract only those high default risk borrowers who do not qualify for a loan at another institution. The lowest rate that could possibly be charged is determined by the cost of funds to the institution plus costs of processing, administering, and collecting loans. Again, competition causes these charges to be quite similar for institutions. The average cost of funds and interest rate charged by savings and loans illustrate the relatively stable relationship between the cost of funds and the interest rate charged (figure 16-1).

In addition to direct interest charges, points are a common requirement with mortgage loans, conventional or otherwise. Points are a form of initial service charge for granting a loan. Each point is 1 percent of the loan amount. Points raise the effective interest rate, especially if the loan is repaid early.[6] Thus they provide a means of ensuring recovery of fixed costs when a loan is repaid soon after being granted. They also provide a means of raising the effective interest rate if there is some reason it cannot be raised directly. Points and service charges fluctuate from year to year. They presently average 2 percent, which, in effect, raises interest rates by about 35 basis points for a typical mortgage loan. Points and service charges are included in the loan interest rates in figure 16-1. Prepayment penalties of six months or more of interest may also be required if the loan is prepaid.[7]

---

[6]See chapter 4 for a detailed discussion of this relationship.

[7]Federal Home Loan Bank Board regulations prohibit prepayment penalties for adjustable mortgage loans (AMIs) made by member institutions.

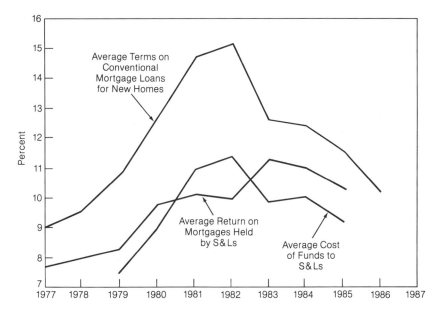

Figure 16-1:   Average mortgage interest rates and S&L cost of funds.
(Source: *National Fact Book of Savings Institutions,* 1987, and *Statistical Abstract of the United States.*)

Escrow payments provide both decreased risk and a bit of extra return. In addition to loan repayment, the borrower pays an amount each month equal to one-twelfth of the estimated annual tax and insurance expense for the property. Escrow payments decrease risk by ensuring that borrowers are saving money to pay insurance and taxes. Since interest is not normally paid on these funds, they provide interest-free deposits.

Mortgage Loan Risk   An analysis of mortgage loan risk requires that a distinction be drawn between diversifiable and nondiversifiable risk. Because a life insurance company can accurately predict the number of deaths among a group of insured each year, benefit payments are an expense rather than a risk. The same thing could be said for mortgage loans if the loss rate were steady from year to year. The risk of default for an individual loan would simply be an expense for the portfolio of loans. Unfortunately, the charge-off rate may be three times as high during a recession as during periods of economic expansion. The loss rates during normal times are a diversifiable risk and can be treated as an expense, but the fact that default rates vary with economic conditions cannot be diversified away within the conventional loan portfolio.

Other risks may be related to specific lending areas. In the 1950s, some thrift institutions that were heavily committed to lending in the older parts of cities suffered large losses as those neighborhoods declined with migration to the suburbs. At other times, lenders have suffered losses because a factory or industry in their area suffered a decline. This happened in Cape Canaveral with one phasing down of the space program. In recent times, savings and loans located mainly in the Southwest suffered huge losses as the result of depression in the real estate, agricultural, and oil industries. In

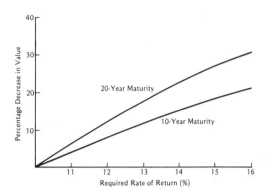

Figure 16-2: Percentage decrease in the value of a 10 percent mortgage loan with various required rates of return.

1986, 80 percent of all S&L's were profitable and earned $9 billion—a respectable return on assets and equity. The 20 percent that were unprofitable, however, managed to lose more than the profitable institutions earned.[8] The potential risk associated with regional depressions can be at least partially diversified away by investing some funds in nonmortgage loans and by investing in mortgages over a broader lending area.

As indicated earlier, interest rate risk is another type of risk that is of particular importance to thrift institutions. In the 1950s and early 1960s, thrift institutions received most of their funds in the form of short-term passbook deposits and loaned an increasing proportion of these deposits in the form of long-term mortgage loans. During this period, the yield curve generally had a "normal" shape: Short-term rates were below long-term rates. The institutions earned steady profits by taking deposits at the short-term rates and making loans at the higher long-term rates. Beginning in the mid-1960s, a period of rising and volatile interest rates developed and the nation experienced many periods in which short-term rates were higher than long-term rates. To keep deposits, the institutions found it necessary to pay interest rates which were, at times, more than double the interest rates on older loans. If the older loans were sold to meet withdrawal demand, they could only be sold at substantial discounts from their face values. The value of an outstanding mortgage loan can easily decline by 30 percent or more if the general level of interest rates rises (figure 16-2).

This type of risk had profound unfavorable effects on the profitability of savings banks and savings and loans in the early 1980s (table 16-3) and cannot be eliminated through diversification. This type of risk is nondiversifiable in that a rising interest rate affects all outstanding fixed interest rate loans in the same general manner. However, it can be evaluated using gap analysis and controlled through adjustable-rate loans, diversifying into other types of loans (with shorter maturities), bidding for deposits with longer maturities, and the use of financial futures contracts.

While wishing to maximize profitability, the thrift institution also desires to minimize risk. This can be partially achieved by eliminating diversifiable risk through diversification. However, interest rate risk and nondiversifiable default risk remain problems that are dealt with at least partially through a profitability/risk trade-off.

[8]*National Fact Book of Savings Associations,* 1987, and "Bailout Welcomed in Texas," *The New York Times,* November 21, 1987, p. 17.

Table 16-3

Retained Earnings as a Percentage of Total Assets Held by Selected
Types of Financial Institutions, 1977–1986

YEAR	SAVINGS BANKS	COMMERCIAL BANKS	SAVINGS AND LOANS
1977	0.55	0.45	0.71
1978	0.58	0.50	0.77
1979	0.46	0.53	0.64
1980	−0.12	0.51	0.13
1981	−0.82	0.46	−0.71
1982	−0.73	0.40	−0.62
1983	0.15	0.34	0.24
1984	0.01	0.39	0.15
1985	0.60	0.37	0.27
1986	0.99	0.36	−0.03

Note: Data represent retained earnings after all expenses, taxes, and dividends paid depositors as a percentage of average assets. Data for commercial banks are for FDIC-insured institutions.
Source: National Council of Savings Institutions, *National Fact Book of Savings Institutions*, 1987, p. 28.

Mortgage Loan Documents   Once it has been decided that the risk and costs associated with a mortgage loan are low enough to make the loan profitable at the interest rate that can be charged, the necessary documents must be prepared.

The lender is first concerned with the title to the property, wishing to be sure that the borrower has a clear title. This is normally provided by a title company which searches the records at the county recorder's office for liens or other claims and provides a certificate of insurance against any undiscovered claims. Of course, the new mortgage must also be filed in the recorder's office if the lender's claim is to be protected.

The borrower's debt is represented by a simple promissory note indicating the amount owed, interest, and repayment schedule. The note also makes reference to the mortgage. The mortgage is essentially a transfer of title to the lender with the provision that the transfer is voided if the borrower repays the loan and interest as called for in the note. Court decisions have interpreted the mortgage as only giving the lender the right to satisfy his claim through sale of the property. Any excess over the debt and reasonable expenses must be returned to the borrower.

Consumer Loans   Except for credit unions, thrift institutions have had little experience with consumer loans. However, deregulation has given expanded authority to all thrifts. The authority to make consumer loans makes the profitability/risk aspects of these loans of interest.

There seems to be a general misperception that consumer loans are much more profitable than mortgage loans because their face interest rates have been higher. However, analysis of the profitability of consumer finance companies does not bear this out. The higher interest rates charged are offset by higher loan origination and servicing costs plus higher default rates. Profits end up being similar to those of other financial institutions.

However, consumer loans have an attraction other than high profitability. If they provide profits as high as those of mortgage loans, they can be useful as a source of risk reduction. First, they may provide some limited diversification with regard to default risk. Though mortgage and consumer loans both suffer default rates during economic downturns, consumer loans provide some diversification from risk associated with the value of real property in a specific lending area. This diversification is, however, likely to be limited by the fact that many consumer loans are made to existing mortgage customers. Consumer loans may also provide some diversification in times when demand for real estate loans is limited. However, consumer loan and mortgage loan demand tend to be correlated, again limiting the diversification advantage.

The major contribution of consumer loans to risk reduction is not from diversification, but from reducing the interest rate gap. The average maturities of consumer loans are a fraction of those of mortgage loans. These shorter maturities can reduce the average maturity of the loan portfolio, matching it more closely to the maturity of the institution's liabilities. Consumer loans may prove to be an important source of interest rate risk reduction.

Investment Portfolio Management

A depository institution faces the expenses associated with having an office facility readily accessible to the public. One way of recovering these expenses is by making direct loans at rates above what could be earned by investing in securities. A depository institution simply could not earn enough to survive by taking deposits and investing only in securities. However, depository institutions do place part of their funds in securities for a number of reasons. First, institutions hold securities as a source of liquidity because they can be sold quickly if cash is needed to meet withdrawal demand. Institutions may also hold securities as a means of decreasing interest rate risk or default risk. Finally, institutions invest in securities when they do not have sufficient loan demand for all their funds. The excess is invested in securities until needed.

Recent changes in authorization to hold securities other than U.S. government securities have increased the usefulness of the investment portfolio as a source of diversification. Unfortunately, the fact that all credit losses vary with the business cycle tends to limit diversification to specific risks associated with real estate values in limited geographic areas. Like consumer loans, securities make their greatest contribution to risk reduction by reducing the average maturity of the institution's assets, thereby decreasing interest rate risk. Since interest rates on short-term assets are lower than those for longer maturities during most time periods, the shorter maturities and associated decreases in interest risk come at the expense of lower returns. The thrift institution that does not recognize this when short-term rates are low will find these securities of no help in dealing with interest rate risk.

Liquidity Reserves

The liquidity needs of thrift institutions have traditionally been less than those of commercial banks because their deposit levels have been more stable. However, that situation will bear close watching in the years ahead. Transaction account services, into which thrift institutions are expanding, normally represent unstable account balances. In addition, depositors are showing increasing willingness to move their funds in response to a small change in interest rates.

The thrift institutions have constant inflows from loan repayments and interest payments. Likewise, they have constant, predictable outflows in the form of expenses and interest on deposits. They also have less predictable cash flows in the form of loan demand and net deposit flows (deposits less withdrawals). Since the institution can reject all loan applications if it lacks funds, these may not seem like a source of unexpected liquidity demand. However, institutions prefer to meet loan demand in their area when possible. Failure to meet loan demand will detract from their present ability to attract deposits and their future ability to attract loan applications. A net outflow of deposits represents a higher-priority liquidity demand. Failure to respond instantly to any withdrawal demand would seriously jeopardize the institution's ability to attract funds.

Liquidity needs can be set by ratio standards, such as a certain percentage of total deposits or certain percentages of each type of deposit. However, this type of approach does not really capture the cash flows experienced by an institution. A cumulative cash flow chart, as illustrated in Chapter 11, figure 11-1 is a more useful approach. Past experience as illustrated in the chart can be modified by adjusting for changes in the asset and liability structure. For example, daily cash inflow will be greater if the institution has changed its loan mix to reduce the average maturity.

Likewise, outflow can be reduced through a change in the mix of deposits, with increases in long-term deposits leading to decreased outflows and increases in transaction accounts to increased potential outflows. Increased liquidity reserves invested at low interest rates are one of the costs of short-term deposits. Net deposit flows of savings and loans (figure 16-3) give an illustration of the cash flow effects of various economic conditions. With their asset and liability mix undergoing rapid change, the thrift institutions will need to reexamine their cash flow assumptions carefully in the years ahead.

When the thrift institution faces a demand for liquidity, it can sell securities. The first act would normally be to sell short-term securities, as these can be sold at or near their face value. Longer-term securities can also be sold, but they will be sold at a loss if interest rates have risen since they were purchased. The institution can also bid for extra funds by raising the interest rates on deposits. The institutions can also borrow money from their respective federal credit sources—e.g., the Federal Home Loan Bank System—and from the Federal Reserve System.

To maintain liquidity, thrift institutions can also sell loans. FHA and VA loans have traditionally been the most salable because they are guaranteed and standardized.

However, as the movement toward packaging and securitization of mortgage loans continues, mortgage pool packagers such as the Federal Home Loan Mortgage

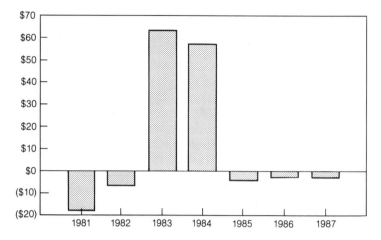

Figure 16-3: Net deposit flows for savings and loans.
Source: *National Fact Book of Savings Associations.*

Corporation and others engaged in similar activities are increasingly moving into the purchase of conventional loans. As an example of increased securitization of conventional mortgage loans, the Federal National Mortgage Association (Fannie Mae), in early 1988, announced plans to purchase biweekly conventional mortgages. These were mortgage loans which some institutions had begun making where payments are made every two weeks, for a total of twenty-six payments a year. Each payment is equal to half of the monthly payment on say, a thirty-year, fixed-rate loan, but where the extra payments each year shorten the maturity to about twenty years.[9]

Regulatory liquidity requirements are probably of more importance for monetary policy and system liquidity than for the liquidity of the individual institution. They are based on relatively simplistic ratio approaches.

Liability Management

In the last three decades, liability management at thrift institutions has undergone two revolutions and is in the midst of the third. In the 1950s and early 1960s, interest rates remained relatively steady and rate ceilings on deposits were not significantly below market rates, if at all. Thrift institutions profited from the yield curve by paying the market rate for passbook savings accounts and loaning these funds to purchasers of residential real estate at the higher long-term rates.

Beginning in the mid-1960s, the environment changed in five important ways:

1. Interest rates began an upward trend.
2. Because interest rate ceilings were not increased correspondingly, the rate paid on deposits became fixed by regulation rather than determined by market forces.

[9]Biweekly Loans Seen Helped by Fannie Mae," *The Wall Street Journal*, January 18, 1988, p. 13.

3. Free market interest rates fluctuated substantially from year to year.
4. In the absence of ability to compete for funds, the thrift institutions experienced erratic deposit flows.
5. There were many periods in which short-term interest rates rose above long-term rates.

These changes caused frequent periods of sharp savings outflows and sometimes pushed the cost of funds above the interest rates on loans still outstanding. It was a major change in the liability management environment from a stable, free market to an administered, erratic market.

Following the change in market stability, a revolution in liability maturity developed. The thrift institutions and commercial banks asked for and received authorization to offer large-denomination and long-term certificates of deposit at higher-interest rates to allow them to compete for funds. While rate ceilings for these accounts existed, these ceilings reached levels almost triple those for passbook accounts. Certificates of deposit for more than $100,000 carried no interest rate ceilings at all. The differences in interest rate ceilings resulted in major changes in the liability structure of thrift institutions. For example, passbook accounts, which accounted for 90 percent of savings and loan deposits until the mid-1960s, accounted for less than 20 percent in 1980. Savers moved their funds to the longer-term deposits or to money market funds which can pool funds and purchase the $100,000 certificates of deposit without interest rate restrictions.

With the phasing in of the Financial Institution Deregulation and Monetary Control Act of 1980 together with the Garn–St. Germain Act of 1982, a third revolution in liability management was set into motion. With the removal of interest rate restrictions, thrift institutions were free to bid for funds over the full yield curve. This presented major new challenges and opportunities in the area of liability management.

The new laws gave thrifts the opportunity to integrate asset and liability management to a greater extent. With a complete yield curve available, the thrift institution can bid for funds of any maturity and price loans of each maturity in relation to the cost of funds of that maturity. The thrift institution can act as a financial intermediary, offering the borrower the full range of maturities and rates available in the financial markets. For example, savings and loans are increasingly offering fixed-rate mortgages at the cost of long-term money, and variable-rate mortgages at the rate presently charged for short-term funds. The borrower can decide whether to pay the long-term rate or pay the short-term rate and take the risk of rates rising later.

Active liability management, use of adjustable-rate mortgages, diversification of loan portfolios, and the use of financial futures have allowed thrift institutions to combine asset and liability management to control risk. However, two problems remain. First of all, many institutions are still saddled with old mortgages made at lower interest rates. These loans will continue to be a burden for some years. Second, accommodations of the maturity needs of both borrowers and savers is one of the important services provided by financial institutions. If the thrift institutions do not provide this service, they will face great difficulty in attracting customers. Therefore, management of interest rate risk rather than the total elimination of risk is the challenge facing thrift institution managers.

SUMMARY

Historically, thrift institutions have specialized in taking passbook deposits and making loans: real estate loans for savings banks and savings and loans; consumer loans for credit unions. In recent years, however, the financial system has been deregulated and the deposit and loan mix has changed. Deposits now include transaction accounts and a greater proportion of time deposits relative to passbook savings. For savings and loans and savings banks, the loan mix is beginning to include larger proportions of consumer and business loans relative to mortgage loans. And while S&L's and savings banks still rely heavily on mortgage assets, a large proportion of direct mortgage loans are today made at variable interest rates. Also, many mortgage assets made and held by S&L's and savings banks are mortgage-backed securities rather than direct mortgage loans originated and held by the institution.

Other significant changes occurring in the 1980s have included the conversion of large numbers of mutual institutions into stock institutions, resulting in the ability of these institutions to raise capital in private equity markets. Partly for this reason, hundreds of savings and loans have converted to federal savings banks, institutions which were virtually nonexistent prior to the 1980s.

Like all financial institutions, thrifts are regulated. The principal regulatory agencies are as follows:

1. Savings and loans: Federal Home Loan Bank Board
2. Federal savings banks: Federal Home Loan Board
3. State-chartered savings banks: state authorities.

It is noted, however, that more than one regulatory agency may have authority over any given financial institution, depending on the nature of specific activities. Many traditional savings banks, including those which have joined the Federal Home Loan Bank System for the purpose of acquiring a federal savings bank charter, continue to be insured by the FDIC rather than the FSLIC. Also, the Federal Reserve System now sets reserve requirements for *all* depository financial institutions.

Like all businesses, thrift institutions seek to maximize profitability. This can be achieved by minimizing the cost of funds, maximizing return on assets, and maximizing operating efficiency. Unfortunately, increased asset return frequently results in increased default risk. Increasing the spread between asset return and funds cost frequently requires the acceptance of interest rate risk and liquidity risk. These risk-return trade-offs are a major factor in thrift institution management.

QUESTIONS

16-1.   The growth of secondary mortgage markets has been quite dramatic in the 1980s. What caused this rapid growth?

16-2.   What factors contributed to the development and growth in the number of federal savings banks in the 1980s?

16-3. Comment on the central differences between savings and loans and credit unions. Why do these differences exist?

16-4. Certain risks faced by thrift institutions are diversifiable and others are not. Identify examples of diversifiable versus undiversifiable risk.

16-5. Why did the government want to regulate the interest rate paid on deposits, and why has the effort to regulate these rates been abandoned?

16-6. It was once believed that a down payment of up to 50 percent was needed for a mortgage loan. Many thrift institutions today make mortgage loans of up to 95 percent of appraised value. How do you account for this change in attitude?

16-7. During 1984, about two-thirds of all home loans made by savings and loans were made with adjustable rates. Two years later, during 1986, only about 38 percent of all such loans were made with adjustable rates. What are some possible explanation of this difference?

16-8. Explain the difference between an adjustable-rate and a graduated payment loan.

16-9. Explain the three methods of appraisal. Which method is most important for existing single-family housing?

16-10. What courses of action are avilable to a thrift institution manager wishing to reduce interest rate risk?

PROBLEMS

16-1. A 9 percent, twenty-year loan with annual payments carries a service charge of three points. If the loan is repaid after the second annual payment, what is the effective interest rate? [Hint: the effective interest rate is the rate that causes the present value of the cash flows (payments) to equal the loan, net of points.]

16-2. A 7 percent, thirty-year loan for $50,000 was made ten years ago. The loan called for equal monthly payments. How much is still owed today?

16-3. If the current interest rate for the loan described in problem 16-2 is 12 percent, what could the loan be sold for? What is the percentage decrease from face value?

16-4. Bridgeton Savings Bank has been requested to commit $10 million in fixed-rate thirty-year mortgages to a local single-family home builder at current interest rates (10 percent). The commitment would expire at the end of six months. In return for the commitment, Bridgeton would receive a commitment fee of one-fourth of one percent of the commitment. If Bridgeton makes the commitment, the savings bank will earn net interest revenue sufficient in amount to cover expenses associated with making and administering the loans over the six-month period. Bridgeton plans to sell the loans at the end of six months, thus recovering the $10 million and retaining the commitment fee as before-tax profit associated with the transaction.

    a. If at the end of six months market interest rates have increased to 11 percent for thirty-year loans, what would Bridgeton's profit or loss from the transaction then be?

    b. Calculate Bridgeton's profit or loss under the assumption that market interest rates drop to 9 percent.

    c. How can Bridgeton reduce or eliminate exposure to the interest rate risk illustrated by your answers to parts a and b?

SELECTED REFERENCES

CASE, KARL E., AND SHILLER, ROBERT J. "Prices of Single-Family Homes Since 1970: New Indexes for Four Cities," *Federal Reserve Bank of Boston New England Economic Review* (September/October 1987): 45–56.

DUNHAM, CONSTANCE R. "Mutual to Stock Conversion by Thrifts: Implications for Soundness," *Federal Reserve Bank of Boston New England Economic Review* (January/February 1985): 31–45.

EPLEY, DONALD R., AND MILLAR, JAMES A. *Basic Real Estate Finance and Investments* (New York: John Wiley and Sons, 1984).

FEDERAL HHOME LOAN BANK BOARD. *A Guide to the Federal Home Loan Bank System,* Washington, D.C., 1987.

KAUFMAN, GEORGE G. "The Federal Safety Net: Not for Banks Only," *Federal Reserve Bank of Chicago Economic Perspectives* (November/December 1987): 19–28.

MACHONEY, PATRICK I., AND WHITE, ALICE P. "The Thrift Industry in Transition," *Federal Reserve Bulletin* (March 1985): 137–156.

NATIONAL COUNCIL OF SAVINGS INSTITUTIONS. *National Fact Book of Savings Institutions,* Washington, D.C. (published annually).

UNITED STATES LEAGUE OF SAVINGS INSTITUTIONS, *Savings Institutions Sourcebook,* Chicago, Ill. (published annually).

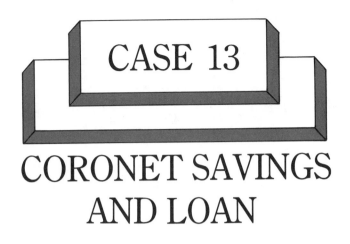

CASE 13

CORONET SAVINGS AND LOAN

The monthly management review at Coronet Savings and Loan was of special interest to John Burke. It was his first monthly review meeting, as he had joined Coronet as treasurer less than a week earlier. In addition, the results for the previous year had just become available and were to be discussed. He anticipated that this meeting would be extremely helpful to him in developing his plans. Furthermore, Susan Wingate, the president, had indicated her desire to get his assessment of things while he still had the fresh perspective of an outsider.

The meeting opened with a presentation of the annual financial results (exhibit 1) by the controller, Ronald Schmitz. Schmitz noted that Coronet's profits had recovered nicely from the previous year, when high interest rates combined with an inverted yield curve had resulted in a large loss. Schmitz had assembled some preliminary industry average ratios (exhibit 2) by using the financial results of a dozen competitors that had released their results earlier. Again, he noted good news. Coronet's return on equity was well above the industry average, while it had been well below the industry average in the previous year. Schmitz finished an otherwise rosy analysis with a note of concern: He was worried about interest rate risk resulting from reliance on fixed-rate loans and short-term deposits. "Coronet has been burned by this strategy before," he concluded.

Robert Parrish, the chief loan officer, took strong exception to Schmitz's comments on fixed-rate loans. "Interest rate risk is part of this business," he said. "We've beaten our competitors in new loan growth, asset growth, deposit growth, and profitability. The primary reason is our firm commitment to the fixed-rate mortgage while others are trying to push variable rates. We are a market-oriented business, and the product the customer wants is the fixed-rate mortgage."

Exhibit 1

Coronet Savings and Loan
Balance Sheet and Annual
Income Statement
(in $ millions)

Interest income	$211
Interest expense	144
Operating expense	36
Other income	−3
Earnings before tax	28
Income tax	11
Net income	$ 17

Cash	$ 23	Passbook deposits	$ 290
Investments	197	Time deposits	1,186
Loans		Borrowed funds	351
Real estate	1,590	Deferred income tax	32
Other loans	82	Other liabilities	58
Other assets	119	Net worth	94
Total assets	$2,011	Total liab. and net worth	$2,011

Burke had been asked to give a brief presentation of financial market conditions. As part of his presentation, he displayed the current yield curve (exhibit 3).

There were general statements of pleasure that for most of the past year the yield curve had had a "normal" upward slope. "As long as this shape holds," said Parrish, "we're in great shape."

"If it doesn't," replied Schmitz, "we'll be the Laclede Avenue branch of BankAmerica."

"Accountants are all the same," exclaimed Parrish. "If we listened to them, we'd be the Laclede Avenue phone booth!"

Wingate interrupted the conversation: "We've gone over this strategic issue a

Exhibit 2

Industry-Average Ratios

Return on net worth	0.137
Ratios to total assets:	
Loans	0.820
Investments	0.104
Deposits	0.812
Borrowed funds	0.091
Net worth	0.051
Interest and fee income	0.106
Operating expense	0.015
Other income	0.001

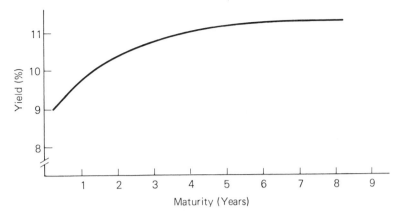

Exhibit 3: Current Yield Curve

dozen times, and we're not going to resolve it with mutual unpleasantries. We need to take a hard look at this whole issue, and it's a top priority of mine. Burke has a fresh perspective here, but he's been around this business a while. Burke, I want you to give top priority to a thorough study of this issue of matching or not matching asset and liability maturities."

After discussion of a few noncontroversial points, the meeting broke up.

Later in the day, Parrish stopped into Burke's office. "I want to be sure you don't start with false notions about our position," he said. The mortgage market is very competitive in this town. We've managed to keep the interest rate on our fixed-rate loans about half a percent below the average rate for the city and still maintain a profit by not pushing adjustable rates. Our competitors are charging as much as 2.5 percent less for adjustable-rate loans, compared to our 1.75 percent difference. And they're not getting rid of any risk. Many of those loans have such steep interest buy-downs from the builders that monthly payments will double in a couple of years. Default rates will skyrocket when that happens. Our approach creates no more risk and greatly improves our competitive position. We owe our growth and profit to this strategy."

Burke heard Parrish out while trying to be both courteous and noncommital. It was clear to Burke that any suggestions involving a change in loan policy would net him a powerful enemy. The next day, Burke received a memo from Schmitz (exhibit 4) reiterating his concern about the risk of current policy.

QUESTIONS

1.   Use ratio analysis to compare Coronet to the industry. Identify Coronet's strengths and weaknesses.
2.   Prepare a gap analysis.
3.   Recommend policy.

Exhibit 4:   Memo

TO: John Burke, Treasurer

FROM: Robert Schmitz, Controller

TOPIC: Asset and Liability Maturity

After yesterday's meeting, I am certain you will be needing information about the maturity structure of our assets and liabilities. I have been keeping track of that situation, as the summary below illustrates.

MATURITY SCHEDULE
(IN $ MILLIONS)

MATURITY[a]	INVESTMENTS	LOANS	DEPOSITS	BORROWED FUNDS
Less than 6 months	78	53	602[b]	236
6 months–1 year	53	53	503	62
1 year–2 years	48	100	166	
2 years–3 years	16	105	89	32
3 years–4 years	2	112	53	21
Over 4 years		1,249	63	
Total	197	1,672[c]	1,476	351

[a] Maturity time for each dollar of principal is the date on which that dollar must be repaid or the rate must be readjusted to market rates.
[b] Including $290 million of passbook deposits and NOW accounts.
[c] Duration equals 8.5 years.

It is obvious that we have a serious mismatch between asset maturity and liability maturity. In my opinion, this spells excessive risk.

As you need additional information, just let me know.

17

Insurance Company Management

The primary business of insurance companies is the elimination of certain financial risks for individuals. Most events insured against occur to a stable, predictable percentage of a certain population group on a regular basis. The events may represent risk for individuals, but they are a predictable expense for the population as a whole. The insurance company serves by converting the individual's risk to an individual expense. The premiums it charges those who choose to be insured are sufficient to pay benefits to that proportion of the insured group that suffers the loss insured against.

In addition to the insurance function, many insurance companies also serve a financial intermediary function. A whole life insurance policy is an important example of this function. Since the whole life policy normally remains in force until death and pays a benefit at death, the eventual payment for each insured person is a certainty. The only real insurance provided is against the financial loss associated with premature death. Thus the policy serves as both an insurance against premature death and a savings program. In this provision of a savings program, the insurance company acts as a financial intermediary, accepting and reinvesting savings.

Because of these dual roles, there are two distinct management areas in an insurance company. The insurance function is typically the most visible and employs the greatest number of persons. It involves the retail sale of insurance as well as the determination of the probabilities of certain events, payment of claims, and the recording of the millions of transactions involved. The other aspect of management deals with equally large sums of money but is less visible and requires fewer employees. This is the management of the nearly $1.3 trillion in assets, which place insurance companies above savings and loans in total asset size.

Like all financial institutions, insurance companies are dealing with deregulation and changing markets. In response, they have expanded services to compete with other institutions, innovated the design of insurance products, and changed their marketing methods. Thus, they are full participants in the financial services revolution.

SCOPE OF THE INSURANCE BUSINESS

Insurance Concepts

Diversifiability is the essential concept underlying most insurance activity. Death may result in financial hardship to a family. Since no one knows if he or she will die in the next year, the family faces financial risk. This risk can be eliminated through a type of group diversification. For example, one could get together with a group of other people of the same age and agree that each will contribute to a pool with the funds being divided among the dependents of those who do die during the year. Under normal conditions, the percentage of a particular age group that dies during a year remains quite stable (unless, for example, the cooperating group were all serving on the same battleship in wartime). Therefore, one could predict the amount his or her dependents would receive in the event of death, and the individual risk would be converted to an expense.

In earlier times, associations such as burial societies did collect funds from their members and redistribute the funds like an insurance company. However, this service is now provided primarily by insurance companies who estimate the percentage of the population that will suffer some particular financial loss. They then sell policies to individuals. An appropriate price is set that will ensure benefits to those who suffer the loss, cover operating expenses, and provide a reasonable profit.

While diversification is the key to most insurance, we should note that there are insurance policies written in cases where the risk is not really diversifiable. Lloyds of London frequently provides insurance in cases in which there may not be enough people facing the risk to provide diversification. Wealthy individuals simply place large amounts of capital at risk, betting on such things as the possibility of rain in Sikeston on the day of the Bootheel rodeo. However, this is a relatively small part of the total insurance picture. Even Lloyds does most of its business in the more mundane field of marine insurance. Earthquakes and floods represent more important areas in which diversification is difficult to achieve. Frequently the participation of government has been necessary in order to provide insurance in such cases.

As do all companies, the insurance companies wish to maximize return and minimize risk. Income comes from premiums and from return on the investment portfolio. The insurance company's risk is not that of an individual claim; this is a programmed expense. The primary risks arise from possible loss in investment portfolio value and the possibility that the company's estimates of total claim payments for the population insured are too low. If their estimates of the dollar claims paid out are wrong, the insurance companies can suffer large losses. For example, a particularly severe winter combined with a rapid inflation of health costs can cause a health insurance company to experience more claims than predicted and a higher dollar cost per claim. Since rising interest rates have caused the value of some outstanding stock and bond issues to decline in value 50 percent or more, the risk of portfolio value loss is also great.

Types of Insurance Companies

Insurance companies can be classified according to the type of insurance provided. Some insurance companies specialize, while others are willing to insure life, health, home, automobile, and business. Multiple offerings are frequently handled through wholly owned subsidiaries. For example, Prudential Insurance Company sells life insurance; its subsidiary, Prudential Property and Casualty Company, sells property and liability insurance.

Insurance companies can also be classified according to how they market their services. Some companies serve only a special group and promote their services only to members of that group. Teachers' Insurance and Annuity Association is one such example of this. Other companies have a group of agents that sell only insurance offered by them. Still other companies market their insurance through general agencies that sell their insurance plus that offered by other companies. This latter approach is particularly common for companies that do not offer a full range of insurance. A growing amount of insurance is sold through group sales, particularly to groups of employees. Some group sales are handled by agents, and some are handled by employees of the insurance company involved. Group sales lower the sales cost per insurance dollar and create the opportunity to price insurance according to the characteristics of a particular group rather than the general population.

Insurance companies can also be classified according to type of ownership. A *stock insurance company* is formed like most other corporations. Common stock is sold to investors who risk the loss of all or part of their investment if the insurance company does not profit, and enjoy the benefits of higher returns if the company does profit.

Mutual insurance companies have no stockholders and are owned by the policyholders. They typically charge a higher premium than a stock company to provide a cushion for larger than expected losses, but then pay a dividend each year based on the actual loss experience for that year. Since the policyholders accept the risk of greater than expected loss experience in this manner, they enjoy lower insurance costs when loss experiences are favorable. In the life insurance field, where mutual insurance companies are most important, 94 percent of the companies are stock companies, but 41 percent of the face value of policies and 53 percent of the assets are held by mutual companies.

Types of Insurance

Insurance business can be divided into three broad categories: life insurance, property and liability insurance, and health and disability insurance.

A comparison of the relative importance of these types of insurance can be made in terms of assets held or premiums received (figure 17-1). Life insurance domi-

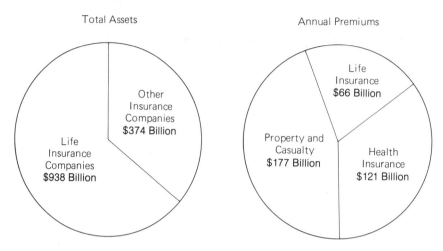

Figure 17-1: Selected financial data for life and nonlife insurance companies.
(Source: *Life Insurance Fact Book,* 1987–88, and *Statistical Abstract of the United States.* Health premium data are for 1984; all other data are for 1986.)

nates in terms of assets held because life insurance business involves receipt of premiums during one year with payments from those premiums to occur many years in the future. Many other types of insurance involve collection of premiums during a year and payment of claims from those premiums during the same year.[1] A look at premiums received yields a different picture. Life insurance premiums are far less than those for property and liability insurance.

Life Insurance   Life insurance policies can be broken down according to the method by which they were sold. The categories are

> *Ordinary:* Life insurance sold to an individual by an agent or employee of the life insurance company, with premiums normally being paid by mail monthly, quarterly, semiannually, or annually.

> *Group:* Life insurance sold to cover all members of some group. The most common group would be all employees of a firm, who receive the insurance as a fringe benefit. The group policy may still give some options to individual members of the group.

> *Credit:* Life insurance sold in connection with a loan. The policy is normally for the amount of the loan and is normally marketed to borrowers by lenders. The lender may or may not own a captive insurance company for the purpose of selling these policies.

> *Industrial:* Insurance sold in small amounts to relatively low-income buyers. Collection of premiums is normally on a weekly basis with the agent calling on the insured rather than relying on them to mail in premiums.

[1]Assets of health insurance companies are not reported separately because health insurance is written by life insurance companies and property and liability companies as well as by separate companies.

Table 17-1

Growth of Life Insurance in Force
(in $ billions)

	WHOLE LIFE		ENDOW-MENT		TERM		TOTAL		
	1974	1985	1974	1985	1974	1985	1974	1985	1986
Ordinary	$654.0	$1,995.9	$43.0	$49.5	$312.0	$1,201.9	$1,009.0	$3,247.3	$3,658.2
Group	6.6	8.4	0.1	0.5	820.9	2,552.7	$827.6	$2,561.6	2,801.0
Industrial	33.1	23.7	2.9	1.3	3.4	3.2	$39.4	$28.2	27.2
Credit	—	—	—	—	109.6	216.0	$109.6	$216.0	233.9
Total	$693.7	$2,028.0	$46.0	$51.3	$1,245.9	$3,973.8	$1,985.6	$6,053.1	$6,720.3

Source: *Life Insurance Fact Book.*

As shown in the last column of table 17-1, ordinary and group sales together accounted for 96 percent of all life insurance in force in 1986. Industrial insurance sales declined over the time period considered in table 17-1.

Probably more important than method of sale, life insurance differs in type of coverage and pattern of payment. *Whole life* insurance is expected to remain in force for the life of the insured and pay the contracted-for benefit upon death. *Straight life,* which represents over 80 percent of the whole life insurance in force, requires payment each period (year, quarter, and so on) until death.

Limited pay life requires payment for a certain number of years and then continues to provide coverage until the insured dies and benefits are paid. Of course, premiums are higher for limited pay life than for straight life.

Since benefits are paid at eventual death, the payment of benefits from these policies is a certainty unless the policy is canceled. In the early years of the policy, when very few people in the age group are dying, most of the premiums must be invested to provide funds to pay claims as the insured people get older and the death rate for that group increases. Total lifetime premiums are frequently less than death benefits because the life insurance company has the premiums to invest for most of a century. Most of these policies have cash values based on these savings that are being built up. The insured member can normally either cancel the policy and receive the cash value or borrow against the cash value and keep the insurance in force, with any amount borrowed being deducted from the benefit in the event the insured person dies while the loan is outstanding. Many people who purchase such policies keep them in force until retirement, when their dependents no longer need protection from the financial loss of their death, and then cash them in. Thus these policies serve as both insurance programs and savings programs. From the other side, these policies put the insurance company in the position of acting as a financial intermediary, accepting funds that it must return to the insured persons at some later date and investing these funds to earn a profit in the meantime.

Endowment policies also put the insurance company in the position of acting as a financial intermediary. An endowment policy pays the insured a specific amount at a specified future date. If the insured dies before this date, the same amount is still paid.

These policies are frequently sold as a combined savings program to help sons and daughters with their education and insurance programs to guarantee that funds for education will be there in the event the parent dies before the children reach college age.

Term policies are pure insurance. If the premium is paid on a term policy and the insured does not die during the year, there is no cash value, although the policy may frequently be extended simply through payment of another premium. In brief, term insurance is similar to automobile, health, and home insurance in that the only benefit received is insurance against certain risks over the period covered by the premium.

From the buyer's point of view, term and whole life insurance can be compared by subtracting the cost of term insurance from the cost of whole life insurance to determine the amount effectively being placed in a savings plan. The cash value at the time the policy will likely be cashed in can be compared to the effective savings plan contributions embedded in the whole life premium and the rate of return earned on the savings plan can be measured. One insurance company, for example, quotes the following first-year premiums for a $100,000 life policy, for a twenty-two-year-old person.

INSURANCE TYPE	FIRST-YEAR PREMIUM
Whole	$532
5-year renewable level term	134
20-year decreasing term	83

If an individual buys the whole life policy and dies after ten years, the person's dependents receive $100,000. If the same individual buys term insurance and invests the difference between the whole life and term premium each year, the insured's beneficiaries may then be entitled to receive both the insurance and the value of the investment. Therefore, the insurance portion of whole life may be viewed as decreasing term insurance covering the difference between $100,000 and the acccumulated cash (savings) value of the policy. For this reason, whole life can be compared to decreasing term; of the $532 premium for whole life insurance, $449 ($532–$83) is actually a contribution to a savings plan. Using table A-3, one notes, for example, that $449 invested each year for thirty years at 10 percent would grow to $73,856 (449 × 164.49). This can be compared to the cash value of the whole life policy after thirty years to determine whether the whole life policy pays an effective interest rate of more or less than 10 percent.

The move toward term insurance meant that life insurance companies were losing one of their products; instead of selling insurance and savings programs, they were selling only insurance. Furthermore, the growth of group sales meant a declining market share for companies geared toward individual sales, which require a more expensive marketing effort. The insurance industry has responded to these problems by developing two new products: variable life and universal life.

Variable Life Insurance   Variable life insurance, introduced in the United States in 1971, addresses one of the competitive disadvantages of whole life insurance. The life insurance company needs to guarantee certain cash values to the insured and cannot count on interest rates remaining high. Therefore, the life insurance company must assume a low return on invested funds in designing its policies. This means that in periods of high-interest rates the implied return on a whole life policy is well below that available on other investments. The variable life insurance policy is a variation on whole life insurance that addresses this problem by allowing the insured to participate in both risk and return. Like whole life insurance, the variable life insurance policy has premiums based on a conservative return assumption such as 4 or 5 percent. As with whole life, the insured's annual premium, after the cost of administration and the mortality cost (approximately equal to the cost of one-year term insurance) is invested. At the end of each year, any excess return over the low assumed return is used to purchase additional paid-up whole life insurance. Consequently, the amount of insurance depends on the return earned by the company on invested funds.

From the buyer's point of view, the problem with variable life is that it seldom fits insurance needs. The returns earned by the insurance company's investments are primarily dependent upon the general level of interest rates. For most individuals, the amount of life insurance needed is not determined by the general level of interest rates. While variable life insurance has grown rapidly in recent years, it still represents only about 1 percent of whole life insurance in force.

Universal Life Insurance   Universal life insurance is an attempt to allow policyholders to participate in higher returns when they are earned, while packaging the form of participation to better fit the insured's needs. The universal life policy is like a straight life policy, except that returns earned in excess of the low assumed return accrue to the benefit of the insured through adjustment to the cash value of the policy. In addition, the insured may vary both the amount of insurance and the amount of premiums from time to time. This type of policy has certain tax advantages in that the return earned accumulates tax-free to the insured unless the policy is canceled. This type of policy allows the insured to participate in market interest rates while also having the ability to alter insurance and cash payments to fit changing needs. Universal life is a much newer type of policy than variable life, having been introduced in 1979. However, universal life in force grew dramatically in the 1980s and by 1986 represented almost 20 percent of all ordinary life insurance in force (figure 17-2).

Life insurance companies also offer *annuity plans*. The purchaser of an annuity makes a single payment or a series of payments for which the life insurance company then agrees to make monthly payments for the rest of the insured's life. Annuities are used primarily as a means of providing retirement income. They are purchased by individuals who want more retirement income than that provided by their employers or by small employers as a means of providing a pension plan. In addition to providing a regular savings program, the annuity may allow greater monthly income than the individual could achieve by investing funds elsewhere. For a sixty-five-year-old retiree, a conservative (from the annuity payer's viewpoint) life expectancy is twenty years. If the interest rate on Aaa-rated bonds is 10 percent, a retiree with $100,000 could invest in high-grade bonds and receive $10,000 a year without reducing the principal. As shown in table A-7, $100,000 at 10 percent would provide $11,746 a year with the principal being gone by the end of the twenty years. An individual, not knowing when he will die,

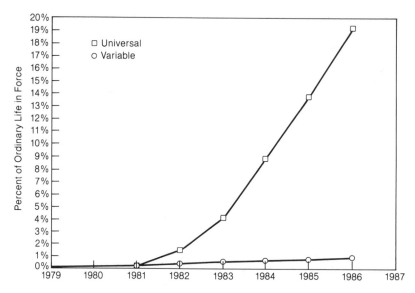

Figure 17-2: Universal and variable life insurance as a percentage of ordinary life insurance in force. (Source: *Life Insurance Fact Book*, 1987.)

cannot really afford to consume the principal of his funds if he wishes to be sure of the income for his entire life. However, the insurance company can make payments based on average life expectancy, with losses from those who live longer being offset by gains from those who die sooner. Even after subtracting its operating expenses, the insurance company may be able to offer a greater payment than could be earned by private investment. With whole life policies, it is generally possible to exchange the cash value for an annuity at age sixty-five. Annuity plan premiums received by life insurance companies grew dramatically in relation to insurance premiums following passage of pension fund legislation in the 1970s.[2] By 1986, annuity premium receipts were $84 billion and, for the first time, exceeded life insurance premiums (which were $66 billion in 1986). Much of this annuity premium increase was associated with pension plan funding for small companies.

Property and Liability Insurance   The property and liability insurance field provides protection against financial losses to property and against lawsuits. Most things insured against in this category would be considered accidental, though theft is certainly not an accident to the thief, and negligence of some type is normally argued in liability cases.

As previously noted, premiums for property and liability insurance exceeded those for life insurance. A detailed listing of types of property, liability, and allied insurance and annual premiums appears in table 17-2.

Automobile insurance is the single largest category, accounting for a large

[2]Pension funds and associated legislation will be discussed in chapter 18.

Table 17-2

Premiums for Selected Property, Liability,
and Allied Insurance, 1986
(in $ millions)

TYPE OF COVERAGE	PREMIUMS
Automobile	$73,386.4
Liability other than automobile	22,856.6
Fire	6,933.2
Homeowners multiple peril	15,222.0
Commercial multiple peril	16,190.3
Workers' compensation	20,431.2
Inland Marine	3,898.6
Other	17,633.8

Source: Insurance Information Institute, *Property/Casualty Fact Book*, 1987–88.

portion of total property and liability insurance. Included is protection against damage to the policyholders and their own automobiles in an accident, as well as insurance against lawsuits arising from an accident.

Multiple peril and fire and allied lines make up a group of insurance programs protecting property owners from financial loss from fire, theft, storm damage, etc. The trend among these policies is for writing single policies providing combined coverage for storm, theft, and certain other risks, as well as fire.

Workers' compensation is insurance by the employer against claims for injuries by workers. Benefits provided are determined by state law, and employers are required to carry this insurance in most cases.

Liability, including malpractice but excluding worker's compensation and automobile, is an important source of premium income. This includes personal liability insurance carried by many professionals.

Marine insurance covers the risks its name implies. Protection against financial loss from theft, storm damage, and other types of risk is provided for ships and their cargoes. Insurance against political loss is covered separately (see chapter 19).

Surety and fidelity insurance generally provides a guarantee that a certain course of action will be carried out. This may be required when late or inadequate completion of work would cause serious financial losses to one party to a contract. In such a case, insurance may be required to protect one party to a contract from loss if the other party should fail to complete work as agreed to.

Health Insurance   Health insurance covers medical expenses and income loss associated with accident and illness. Insurance premiums in this field have increased rapidly in recent years, with increases in the number of people insured and increases in medical expenses.

Blue Cross and Blue Shield organizations presently account for a large but declining proportion of total health insurance premiums. Blue Cross was started by hospitals as a means of decreasing their collection problems, and Blue Shield was started by doctors for the same purpose. The plans are incorporated separately in each state, with premiums and benefits varying by state. The point is sometimes made that these programs are not technically insurance, but are prepayment programs started by hospitals and doctors with payments to them rather than the insured. However, this is an irrelevant technicality from the point of view of the insured who receive protection from unexpected medical expenses. Life insurance companies are the dominant factor in health insurance not written by Blue Cross and Blue Shield.

Property and liability insurance companies provide the remainder. Approximately 10 percent of health insurance benefits paid by life insurance companies are to replace lost income. Blue Cross and Blue Shield provide no loss-of-income protection.

General health insurance is primarily sold in the form of group policies. Group sales account for 80 percent of private health insurance and a higher percentage for Blue Cross and Blue Shield. "Special" policies such as cancer insurance are more frequently sold as individual policies.

REGULATION OF INSURANCE COMPANIES

Most regulation of insurance companies is carried out by the individual states. Each state creates its own laws and regulates insurance companies selling insurance within its boundaries, as well as those with headquarters there, causing national insurance companies to face fifty different sets of regulations. While specific rules vary from state to state, the same general areas—finance and investment policy, premium rates, contract provisions, and sales practices—are regulated in all states.

Finance and investment policies are regulated to ensure that funds will be available to honor claims. Minimum amounts of capital and surplus are needed to start selling insurance, and certain ratios of capital, surplus, and reserves must be maintained for all additional insurance written. In addition, the types of investments the insurance company can make are regulated. Life insurance companies are generally required to invest in bonds and mortgages, with only a limited investment in equity securities. Property and liability insurers, on the other hand, are normally allowed to invest in equity securities in amounts up to the value of the company's capital and surplus.

Premium rate regulations require that rates be adequate but not excessive. In addition, rate structures must not discriminate unfairly. In some states, all rates must be approved by the insurance commissioner in advance. In other states, rate increases do not need to be approved in advance, but the insurance commissioner can reduce premiums retroactively if they are found to be unjustified.

Rate regulation does not ensure that each company will offer the same rate for the same insurance; each company may adjust its rates for its loss experience. In light of these rate differences, there has been some movement toward letting market forces play a bigger role in the rate-setting process.

Contract provision regulation has resulted in a good deal of standardization across states. Regulation in this area followed complaints from people who filed claims and found out too late that the "fine print" excluded many things they thought were covered. Comparison shopping for policies is much easier when standard language is used.

A new aspect of the regulation of premium rates and contract provisions is the unisex requirement. Important federal court rulings in recent years have held insurance and benefit plans with different costs or benefits for men and women to be discriminatory, even if based on sound actuarial evidence about differences in life expectancy between the sexes. The result has been a movement toward unisex rate tables, which means that women experience reduced pension costs (or increased benefits) and increased life insurance costs. The reverse is true for men.[3]

The U.S. Congress has considered legislation to clarify this issue and set standards. One aspect of this legislation is that it moves the federal government more deeply into the regulation of insurance companies. The federal government's intervention has traditionally been limited to issues such as antitrust and fraud.

Sales practices are also regulated, although it is not always clear whether the purpose of regulation is to protect consumers or those in the insurance business. Laws banning deceptive advertising are clearly for the purpose of protecting consumers. However, the benefit from laws that forbid agents from returning part of their commission to the policyholder as a means of price competition is not so clear. Laws requiring testing and licensing of those who would sell insurance are supposed to ensure that insurance agents are knowledgeable, but the tests in some states are so easy as to be of little value.

MANAGEMENT CONSIDERATIONS

Management of an insurance company involves the actuarial job of accurately determining the risks involved, the marketing job of selling insurance to groups or the public, the operations management job of processing premiums and claims as efficiently as possible, and the financial management job of investing funds and maintaining an appropriate capital base.

Operations Management

The insurance company essentially acts as an intermediary by accepting premiums, deducting its expenses and a reasonable profit, and returning the remaining funds in the form of benefits. While the exact amount to be paid in benefits is not known in advance, premiums are set in light of anticipated operating expenses and benefit expenses. Operating and marketing expenses can be a substantial portion of total premiums. Holding these costs to a minimum is an essential part of successful insurance

---

[3]Many companies are already using new unisex tables that average the mortality projections for men and women. Since the proportion of men to women in a particular group is not equal, a simple way to prepare a unisex table is, for example, to take a weighted average of the deaths per thousand in a particular age group, with the weights being based on the proportion of men and women in the group.

company management. Insurance companies have dealt with these costs by being leaders in the use of such things as computerized data processing and lockbox collections[4] to operate at maximum efficiency.

Marketing Management

Successful marketing involves packaging the insurance in forms that are attractive to customers and reaching the customers in the most cost-efficient way possible. A major portion of total operating costs can relate to the marketing effort. For example, 40 percent of life insurance company operating costs are for commissions to agents, who may receive 100 percent or more of the first year's premium as the commission for selling a whole life policy. Agent commissions are only part of the marketing expense, as they do not include advertising or the expense of the marketing staff that helps to design policies, supervise and train agents, and so on.

As insurance buyers have become sophisticated and price conscious, the emphasis has switched from developing attractive packaging methods to the development of efficient marketing methods. Group insurance has shown substantial increases in market share because of the economies of scale involved. A group life insurance program can be sold to 2,000 employees of a company in a small portion of the time required to sell a policy to each individual. Physical examination costs are eliminated for health and life insurance policies since a large group is involved and the group's health characteristics can be estimated without individual physicals.

Group life insurance increased from 20 percent of life insurance in force in 1950 to 42 percent in 1986. Group health insurance has also grown dramatically, and group automobile insurance is being promoted.

The role of other financial institutions in the sale of insurance remains an unanswered question. Many financial intermediaries have recently made important steps toward becoming financial supermarkets, with banks having gained, for example, the right to offer stock brokerage services.

Since lenders have traditionally sold credit life insurance and credit disability insurance in connection with their credit granting activities, it would be a short step for them to begin selling other types of insurance. Furthermore, a lender would have a marketing cost advantage in selling a homeowner's policy or automobile insurance to a person arranging financing for a house or an automobile. The lender would also offer the convenience of one-stop shopping for financial services.

One reason financial intermediaries have been restricted from expanded insurance sales rests with the argument that they would have an unfair competitive advantage; borrowers would feel intimidated in making their insurance decisions and would not shop for the best price. With companies like Sears offering checkable money market funds, stock brokerage services, and insurance, pressure is beginning to build from financial intermediaries for the right to expand their insurance offerings. Consequently,

---

[4]A lockbox collection plan involves establishment of a post office lockbox where customer payment is received. The firm's bank picks up the checks, notifies the firm, and begins the check-clearing process, thereby reducing check collection time and speeding cash flow.

Table 17-3

Mortality Tables

| | COMMISSIONERS 1980 STANDARD | | | | 1983 INDIVID- UAL ANNUITY EXPECTA- TION OF LIFE *(years)* | | UNITED STATES TOTAL POPULATION *(1979–1981)* | |
| | *Male* | | *Female* | | | | | |
Age	Deaths per 1,000	Expectation of Life (years)	Deaths per 1,000	Expectation of Life (years)	Male	Female	Deaths per 1,000	Expectation of Life (years)
0	4.18	70.83	2.89	75.83	—	—	12.60	73.38
5	0.90	66.40	0.76	71.28	74.10	79.36	0.37	70.00
10	0.73	61.66	0.68	66.53	69.22	74.42	0.20	65.10
15	1.33	56.93	0.85	61.76	64.36	69.47	0.69	60.19
20	1.90	52.37	1.05	57.04	59.50	64.55	1.20	55.46
25	1.77	47.84	1.16	52.34	54.66	59.64	1.32	50.81
30	1.73	43.24	1.35	47.65	49.83	54.75	1.33	46.12
35	2.11	38.61	1.65	42.98	45.03	49.87	1.59	41.43
40	3.02	34.05	2.42	38.36	40.25	45.02	2.32	36.79
45	4.55	29.62	3.56	33.88	35.57	40.20	3.66	32.27
50	6.71	25.36	4.96	29.53	31.07	35.46	5.89	27.94
55	10.47	21.29	7.09	25.31	26.77	30.83	9.02	23.85
60	16.08	17.51	9.47	21.25	22.62	26.32	13.68	20.02
65	25.42	14.04	14.59	17.32	18.63	21.98	20.59	16.51
70	39.51	10.96	22.11	13.67	14.96	17.87	30.52	13.32
75	64.19	8.31	38.24	10.32	11.72	14.02	45.07	10.48
80	98.84	6.18	65.99	7.48	8.96	10.61	68.82	7.98

Source: *Life Insurance Fact Book.*

we may be on the verge of another revolution in the marketing of insurance and even in the structure of the insurance industry.[5]

Actuarial Science

The work of the actuary is key to the profitable operation of an insurance company. The actuary is primarily a statistician, working with past loss experience and other factors to predict future losses for a particular group. For example, table 17-3 contains widely used projections of life expectancy and annual death rates for the population as a whole. The life insurance company can use this information to set rates for life insurance.

If actuaries worked only with experience for the total population (such as that in table 17-3), there would be little need for the thousands of people presently employed as actuaries. The actuaries must deal with several subgroups of the population and use

[5]See, for example, Steven D. Felgran, "Banks as Insurance Agencies: Legal Constraints and Competitive Advances," *Federal Reserve Bank of Boston New England Economic Review,* Sept/Oct, 1985, pp. 34–39.

this information to construct policies that will be cost-competitive in the marketplace and profitable to the company. For example, it is recognized that college professors have lower mortality rates than the population as a whole (despite the wish of an occasional student). A separate mortality table for this particular profession makes it possible to market a policy specifically to this profession at a premium cost below what would have to be charged to the general population and still make a profit. The growing importance of group sales has heightened the importance of separate actuarial computations for each group. Likewise, the sale of insurance to special low-risk groups means that the general population not included in some low-risk group has a higher incidence of loss than the total population, including these various low-risk groups. Thus the expected loss rate for the general population changes continually and must be watched carefully.

Variations in loss ratios are not limited to life insurance. For example, automobile insurance rates incorporate a number of factors that result in higher or lower loss experience. Classifying people as lower accident risks than they actually are will result in losses for the company. Classifying them as higher risks than they actually are will result in the policy being overpriced and business being lost to competing companies.

In addition to predicting the incidence of unfortunate events, the actuary must also predict their costs. The amount to be paid is fixed for most life insurance policies, but must be estimated for health insurance and property and liability insurance. The importance of the actuary in these areas has been particularly important during periods of rapid inflation.

In addition to predicting costs, it is also necessary to predict security returns. Because many life insurance policies and annuity plans involve a period of many years between premium receipt and benefit payment, premiums are based on assumptions about the rate at which funds can be invested. One-thousand dollars invested for forty years at 10 percent per year will grow to $45,259, while the same amount invested for the same time period at 15 percent would grow to $267,864. A company's profits and losses can be dramatically affected by failures in these projections.

Example   To illustrate using a basic example, suppose Amerisure Life Insurance Company wished to calculate a one-year term life insurance premium for a large group of 25 year old persons. The group is assumed to be representative of the total population and a mortality rate of 1.32 per thousand (table 17-3) is assumed. Suppose further that all premiums are collected on day one of the policy year and all benefits are paid on the last day of the year. Amerisure currently earns eight percent on its investment portfolio. The pure insurance premium (P) per dollar of policy face value and net of administrative and other costs is the discounted present value of expected future claims. It is calculated as follows

$$P = \frac{\dfrac{\$1 \times 1.32}{1,000}}{(1+.08)}$$

Thus, the one year pure insurance premium that would be charged for, say, a $100,000 face value policy, given the above illustration, would be $122.22 ($100,000 × 0.0012222)

The foregoing example of course, is quite basic and a discussion of the skills necessary to perform competently as an actuary is well beyond the scope of this book. Many universities have degree programs in actuarial science, and there are a number of professional associations devoted to maintaining high standards of actuarial practice:

American Academy of Actuaries
1720 I St., N.W., 7th floor
Washington, D.C. 20006

Casualty Actuarial Society
One Penn Plaza
New York, N.Y. 10119

Crop-Hale Insurance Actuarial Association
209 W. Jackson Blvd.
Chicago, Ill. 60606

ASSET AND LIABILITY MANAGEMENT

Liabilities and Capital

An understanding of the liabilities of insurance companies is necessary to develop an appropriate approach to management of assets. The dominant liabilities for both life and nonlife insurance companies are reserves based on the fact that premiums are collected as much as a year ahead for nonlife insurance companies and most of a lifetime ahead for life insurance policies. The amounts expected to be paid out over the period covered by the premium are carried as a reserve when that premium is first received. As claims are paid, both cash and reserves are reduced. If claims exceed reserves, capital and surplus are decreased, and vice versa. The long lives of many life insurance policies versus those of nonlife insurance companies result in much larger policy reserves for life insurance companies.

In addition to the higher absolute amount of reserves, life insurance companies have a much higher ratio of reserves to equity. The lower capital levels for life insurance companies result from both management decisions and regulatory requirements. They are based on recognition of the fact that life insurance obligations are easier to predict than the obligations of most other insurance companies. In addition, the accumulation of funds for certain death benefits means that the dollar value of liabilities per face value of insurance is higher for life insurance than for other insurance. Therefore, a higher ratio of liabilities to equity does not necessarily mean a higher ratio of insurance face value to equity. Accident rates and the amount of settlement per accident have varied. This has been particularly true with high inflation.

The size of the equity base has important implications for asset management. With a limited equity base, the life insurance companies can endure less asset value shrinkage than can nonlife companies.

Assets

The primary assets of insurance companies are investment portfolios in the form of government and corporate securities (table 17-4). Investment portfolios are held for two reasons. Because the insurance companies collect premiums with insurance cover-

Table 17-4

Asset Structure of Life Insurance Companies, 1986
(in $ billions)

ASSETS	AMOUNT	PERCENTAGE
Government securities	$144.6	15.4
Corporate securities		
Bonds	342.0	36.5
Stock	90.9	9.7
Mortgages	193.8	20.7
Real estate	31.6	3.4
Policy loans	54.1	5.8
Other assets	80.6	8.6
Total	$937.6	100.0

Source: *1987 Life Insurance Fact Book.*

age provided for some time after collection, they have these funds to invest until they are paid out as benefits. On the liability side, this shows up as reserves. The second category of funds are held as protection against losses due to factors such as excessive benefit expense or shrinkage in the value of assets. On the liability side of the balance sheet, these funds are represented by surplus and equity accounts. The investment policy is determined by the two purposes the portfolio serves.

The liquidity needs from the investment portfolio are minimal. Most insurance companies are continually expanding in size, with premiums received during any month being more than sufficient to meet all cash outflows for that month. Actual sale of securities would be necessary only if premium revenue declined. The company will add to its portfolio and reserve accounts from month to month unless its volume declines or disintermediation occurs. The allocation of the life insurance dollar for U.S. life insurance companies for 1986 is shown in table 17-5.

This is not to say that day-to-day cash management is not an important function in an insurance company. A large insurance company will have cash flows of several million dollars a day. A company may be able to improve profit by half a million dollars a year or more by reducing idle cash equal to one day's cash flow. Therefore, the companies follow cash flow over the week and month very closely to keep as much cash as possible invested. If premiums for a particular company tend to come in around the first of the month, with claims paid at an even rate over the month, the company will have idle cash during the early part of the month. These funds will be invested in money market instruments, with adjustments being made on a daily basis. Because these day-to-day cash flows vary with such things as mail delivery and are not totally predictable, there may be short-term liquidity demand that requires the sale of money market instruments. This short-term money management problem is linked to management of the investment portfolio only to the extent that the company must decide how much to invest in money market instruments for liquidity reserve purposes.

Liquidity demands of a more serious nature arise from disintermediation. Whole life and endowment policies normally give the holder the right to borrow a large portion of the reserve attributed to the policy at an interest rate stated in the contract. With rising

Table 17-5

Life Insurance Company Dollar 1986:
U.S. Life Insurance Companies

INCOME	
Premiums	71.5¢
Net investment earnings and other income	28.5
	100.0
HOW USED	
Benefit payments and additions to funds for policy holders and beneficiaries	
Benefit payments in year	50.6¢
Additions to policy reserve funds	32.0
Additions to special reserves and surplus funds	1.3
	83.9
Operating expenses	
Commissions to agents	5.2
Home and field office expenses	7.8
	13.0
Taxes	1.7
Dividends to stockholders of stock life insurance companies	1.4*
	100.0

*For stock companies only, this ratio would be 2.4¢ per dollar.

Source: *1987 Life Insurance Fact Book.*

interest rates, people have found these *policy loans* to be a low-cost source of funds and have borrowed heavily, either to meet credit needs or to invest at higher interest rates. In addition, if a whole life or endowment policy is canceled, the insured is paid most of the reserve associated with that policy. This is the *cash value* spelled out in such policies. Cancelation of whole life policies, to be replaced with term policies, has also occurred during periods of high interest rates. The relative stabilities of cash flow demands for death benefits and loan and cash surrender payments are shown in figure 17-3. Downturns in loan and cash surrender demand are in periods when interest rates are falling, while rapid increases in this demand are during periods of rising interest rates. Outflows have not been sufficient to cause net outflows for all insurance companies, but they have been sufficient to lead to substantial net outflows for individual companies.

The pressures to earn returns on portfolios come from two sources. First, insurance companies are clearly profit-seeking ventures, and portfolio return is an important source of revenue, equaling 28.5 percent of the life insurance dollar in 1986. Unlike mutual thrift institutions, even mutual insurance companies pay profit-based dividends to members who also elect directors. Thus, virtually all insurance companies are overseen by directors elected by people who share in the profits. In addition to direct profitability to the owners, investment portfolio return indirectly affects profitability through the ability of the company to price policies competitively. For all insurance companies, and particularly for a life insurance company, the premiums depend on an assumption about rates of return on the firm's investments and on an assessment of risks. For a $10,000 benefit payment fifty years in the future, the annual investment

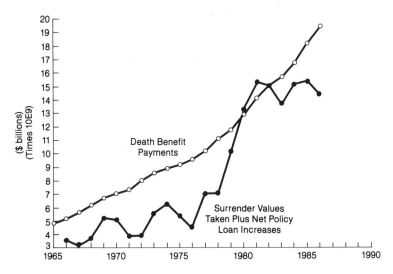

Figure 17-3:   Cash outflow demands on life insurance companies.
(Source: Based on data in *1987 Life Insurance Fact Book.*)

necessary to accumulate this amount is $8.59 if the interest at which funds can be invested is 10 percent, and $1.39 if the interest rate is raised to 15 percent. If a 20 percent rate of return could be assumed, the payment would fall to $0.22. Premiums required for some life insurance policies are therefore quite sensitive to the return that can be earned on the investment portfolio. The assumption of a low long-term investment return at a time when interest rates were high was one factor leading to the increased portion of the life insurance premium dollar going to term insurance.

For life and nonlife insurance companies, the amount of new insurance which a particular company can write is limited by the amount of equity and surplus. Return on the investment portfolio increases the amount of surplus.

Tax considerations have traditionally differed by type of insurance company and lead to different policies with regard to the investment portfolio. The two main forms of tax paid are state premium taxes—a percentage of all premiums collected in a particular state—and income tax. Income tax is the most important of the taxes for both life and nonlife companies. All insurance companies are taxed at standard corporate income tax rates (formerly 46 percent and presently 34 percent). However, prior to certain changes which were contained in federal tax laws enacted in 1984 and 1986, the tax base income to which the tax rate applied varied according to the type of insurance being sold.

Under prior tax laws, life insurance companies could allocate half their underwriting profits[6] for each year to a policyholders' surplus, with the balance being allocated to a shareholders' surplus. The amount allocated to the policyholders' account was recognized as taxable income only if it was transferred to the shareholders' account. Since it would be transferred to the shareholders' account only if it were to be

---

[6]Underwriting profits (or losses) are premiums earned less losses and expenses. They do not reflect investment earnings.

used to pay dividends, the life insurance company could effectively retain half of its underwriting earnings without paying income tax on them. Other insurance companies paid tax on all their profits, whether or not they were retained. In effect then, the marginal federal income tax for a life insurance company under prior tax laws could be half that for a nonlife company or industrial corporation.

Because of this difference in tax treatment, nonlife companies held a substantial proportion (almost half) of their assets in the form of state and local government obligations, while life insurance companies held less than 2 percent of their assets in this form. State and local government securities pay lower returns than other securities do, but returns associated with these municipal securities were not subject to federal income tax. The yield spreads between municipals and other securities prior to tax law changes enacted in 1986 were such that they were attractive only to investors with an effective income tax in the neighborhood of 40 percent or higher. Thus they were attractive to nonlife companies but not to life insurance companies. Tax law changes enacted in 1984 and particularly in 1986 are likely to impact on portfolio investment decisions with regard to taxable versus municipal (tax-exempt) securities. The preferential treatment afforded to life insurance companies as discussed above has been eliminated, and certain provisions in the 1986 tax law, in effect, increase the taxable income base for a property and casualty insurance company by an amount equal to 15 percent of tax-favored income. Thus insurance company portfolio managers will likely adjust the distribution of taxable and municipal securities in the light of these new tax laws.

Regulation of portfolio policy by state authorities is aimed at protecting the insured by protecting the portfolio from shrinkage in value. Life insurance companies are severely restricted with regard to investment in equity securities, to direct investment in real estate, and to other investments perceived to be risky. Nonlife companies are usually allowed to invest in equity securities up to the amount of their own equity and surplus. However, the attractiveness of equity securities is decreased by procedures the regulators use in computing the insurance company's equity and surplus. Equity securities are carried at their current market values; bonds can be carried at their face value or original cost. If rising interest rates cause both stock and bond values to decline, the company holding only bonds will not suffer a decline in portfolio value from the regulators' viewpoint, but losses will be recorded for the company with equity investments. The consequent reduction in recognized capital can impair the company's ability to sell additional insurance, since certain ratios of capital to insurance face value are required. Nonlife insurance companies hold 21 percent of their assets in equity securities, while life insurance companies hold about 10 percent of their assets in this form.

Risk   As with any other company, the insurance company cannot think of the riskiness of a single security in isolation from the investment portfolio, nor can the investment portfolio be viewed in isolation from the other aspects of the company's business. An insurance company faces four major types of risks.

Excessive benefit costs are the first type of risk. They can occur because of a natural disaster, because inflation drives average claim amounts to higher than anticipated levels, or simply because the company's original estimates of losses were wrong.

Sales declines represent the second type of risk. They can occur because a severe economic downturn eliminates either the ability to pay for premiums or the need for certain types of insurance. Business insurance would be the most obvious example, as the need for it decreases during a recession when business activity declines or businesses close. Demand for life insurance, particularly whole life, may also decline in inflationary periods as people look for investments that will provide some protection from inflation.

Portfolio value loss is a risk that results from a similar set of factors. As inflation rates rise, the general level of interest rates rises as well. A rise in the general level of interest rates results in a decline in the market value of existing fixed-income securities. In addition, common stock returns have been negatively correlated with the inflation rate in recent years. An economic downturn can also have a negative impact on portfolio value through defaults on bonds and mortgages, and through a reduction in common stock values as profits decline. Default rates on the types of securities that insurance companies hold have remained low even in economic downturns, but losses in market value have been substantial. For example, a bond with an 8 percent coupon rate and twenty years to maturity would be selling at 70 percent of its face value if the general level of interest rates for this risk class were to increase to 12 percent. Likewise, but less surprisingly, we have seen the average value of a share of common stock decline 40 percent or more. With their low ratios of equity capital to total assets, the insurance companies cannot absorb large losses of this type.

Cancelation and policy loan risks are primarily problems faced by companies offering whole life or endowment policies. These withdrawals generally occur during periods of high interest rates but could also occur in severe economic downturns. Of course, high interest rate periods and economic downturns are both periods when the values of securities may be low. For fixed-income securities, the maturity value is not affected by a decline in current market value. The decline in market price is significant because: (1) it reflects an opportunity loss in that higher-yielding securities are currently available, and (2) if the company should need cash, the bonds would have to be sold at a loss. As indicated earlier, a loss in the value of equity can have an immediate negative impact on equity and surplus ratios, even in the absence of a need to sell the securities at depressed prices.

The conditions which might lead to each of the various types of losses are summarized as follows:

PROBLEM	CAUSES
Excessive claim losses	Inflation, natural disasters
Sales declines	Inflation, economic downturn
Losses in investment portfolio	Inflation, economic downturn
Policy loans and cancelations	Inflation, economic downturn

Since inflation and economic downturn are factors influencing most types of losses, particularly for life insurance companies, the investment portfolio does not provide significant opportunity to diversify away risks from other aspects of the business.

Portfolio Strategy   Because of this limited opportunity for diversification, insurance companies pursue a conservative portfolio strategy. Long-term fixed-income securities are the primary investment for both life insurance and nonlife companies. Because of previously discussed tax differences, life insurance companies traditionally held large quantities of corporate bonds and mortgages, while nonlife insurance companies traditionally held larger quantities of state and local government securities. There has been a switch in emphasis in mortgage holdings away from FHA and VA mortgages and toward commercial mortgages. In addition to higher return, commercial mortgages create the opportunity for "equity participations" through which the insurance company can participate in profits if the venture is successful.

Within the investment portfolio, the normal principle of eliminating diversifiable risk is followed to the extent possible. Unfortunately, legislation designed to ensure safety may actually increase the difficulty of achieving proper diversification. Regulations are based on the view that high-grade fixed-income securities are nearly risk-free. Restricting insurance companies to heavy investment in these securities and restricting them from such areas as direct investment in real estate have left them exposed to the full effect of interest rate risk associated with inflation. Portfolio managers have sought to diversify within these regulatory limits. The movement to commercial mortgages with equity participations is one such example, giving some of the diversification benefits of real estate ownership without violating restriction of direct real estate ownership or direct common stock purchase. Convertible bonds are another investment medium providing similar opportunities.

To deal with interest rate risk, it must be remembered that the life insurance companies base their premiums on expected investment return. If management knew the policy would not be canceled or borrowed against, investment maturity could be based on expected eventual payment date, thereby insuring a rate of return. This would not be entirely possible for payments expected to be made sixty years in the future, but forty-year maturities are available and would be sufficient to cover most commitments. Unfortunately, the picture is complicated by a number of uncertainties, including the fact that bonds can be called and policies can be canceled or borrowed against. The problem of high-yield bonds and mortgages being repaid when interest rates fall could be dealt with through increased holdings of U.S. government securities, which are generally not callable. However, with the experience of more than two decades of rising interest rates and almost no bonds being called, the insurance industry seems content to accept call risk. Convertible bonds and equity participation in real estate loans provide at least some diversification in this regard.

Portfolio strategy to deal with the possibility of excessive withdrawals through loans and cancelations is primarily dealt with through a balancing of the maturity structure so that any demand can be met through maturing securities rather than by selling securities at a discount. This has been combined with some movement toward raising the policy loan interest rate in new contracts or making it a floating rate tied to some money market indicator.

An insurance company that temporarily finds itself with an insufficient supply of shorter-term securities can hedge in the financial futures markets. By entering into forward contracts to sell, it can effectively convert some long-term U.S. government securities or mortgages to short-term securities.

In summary, insurance companies face significant risks tied to the inflation rate and economic conditions. These risks cannot be very effectively diversified away, but they are problems of the short and intermediate term in which securities might have to be sold below cost. If a company has its maturity structure designed evenly so that it can avoid the necessity of selling securities before maturity, the risks are manageable. A poorly designed maturity structure could quickly result in insolvency in the face of withdrawal demand.

SUMMARY

Insurance companies act as intermediaries for risk. They do so by collecting funds from all members of a large group in order to pay benefits to certain members of the group who suffer some consequence. This consequence is diversifiable from the point of view of individuals. The three main types of insurance and annual representative premiums are

Life insurance	$66 billion
Property and liability insurance	177 billion
Health insurance	121 billion

The life insurance companies are a larger factor than these premium levels indicate. Life insurance companies receive almost half the health insurance premiums and billions more in payments toward annuity plans. In addition, life insurance company assets are much greater than those of all nonlife insurance companies.

Insurance companies also act as financial intermediaries in collecting savings from individuals and reinvesting them. Their investments of about $1 trillion make them an important source of investment capital.

Regulation is left almost entirely to state governments. Regulations vary by state, with insurance companies required to meet regulations of states in which they sell insurance. Regulations cover investment and finance policies, premium rates charged, contract provisions, and sales practices.

Like most companies, insurance companies are guided by the profitability objective in the four main areas of management: operations management, actuarial science, marketing management, and financial management. Operations management consists of efficiently and economically handling the millions of transactions involved. Actuarial science consists of accurately estimating the percent of the population that will suffer a particular insurable event. Marketing management involves designing policies that fit buyers' demands, but increasingly involves the development of cost-efficient methods of sales. Financial management consists of determining and maintaining the proper amount of equity and managing the investment portfolio.

The portfolio manager attempts to maximize profitability while dealing with four types of risk: (1) excessive benefit costs; (2) sales declines; (3) portfolio value loss; (4) cancelation and policy loan demands. These risks must be met within the constraints of regulations which affect investment policy. Such regulations tend to restrict equity investments, and tax laws prior to 1987 had the effect of favoring state and local government securities for nonlife insurance companies but not life insurance companies. The fact that most types of potential losses tend to occur in periods of high inflation or economic downturn make them difficult to eliminate through any portfolio strategy, especially in the face of regulatory restrictions. Balancing maturities to avoid the necessity of selling securities at a loss and purchasing fixed-income securities with equity participation options are important strategies.

QUESTIONS

17-1.   What pressures would cause a mutual insurance company to pursue a profitability objective? How do these pressures differ from those on a mutual savings and loan company?

17-2.   Why do life insurance companies dominate in asset size even though they receive less than half of total insurance premiums?

17-3.   For regulatory purposes, bonds can be counted at their face value even if their current market price has declined. If bonds were revalued to current market price, some insurance companies would be insolvent.

        a. Which type of company—life or nonlife—would be more likely to be pushed into insolvency by a revaluation of fixed-income securities to current market value?

        b. What is the effect of this situation on the protection offered to policyholders?

17-4.   As a regulator, what portfolio management rules would you suggest to improve diversification by insurance companies?

17-5.   Why is it difficult to purchase insurance for damage due to acts of war?

17-6.   For an insurance buyer, which type of insurance company—stock or mutual—would be expected to provide lower total costs if claims expense is lower than anticipated? Higher than anticipated?

17-7.   Why can a life insurance company operate with a higher liability-to-equity ratio than a nonlife insurance company?

17-8.   Under what conditions would a property and liability insurance company find it necessary to sell assets from its portfolio? What is the appropriate maturity structure for property and liability insurance company assets?

17-9.   Why has universal life insurance grown so rapidly in recent years?

PROBLEMS

17-1.   Amerisure Life Insurance Company plans to promote a $50,000 face-value term life insurance policy to a large group of persons aged twenty. In order to sign up as many candidates as possible and thus develop a base for sales of additional insurance products, the company plans to calculate a first-year premium that will allow the firm to simply recover expected death benefit payments. Amerisure calculates a mortality rate for the United States total population of 1.20 per 1,000 (table 17-3). The company further assumes that all premiums will be collected on the first day of the policy period and will be invested to earn 9 percent per annum. Finally, all claims are assumed to be paid on the last day of the policy period. Calculate the first-year premium.

17-2.   Tom Joseph, an Amerisure executive argues that the plan outlined in problem 17-1 would be too costly. Joseph points out that the plan would seek to solicit one million potential customers at a cost of $6 per solicitation but that only about 5 percent of this group would be expected to purchase the insurance. The cost of servicing those that do sign up is expected to average 10 percent of premiums collected. Joseph argues that for planning purposes, solicitation and servicing costs should be assumed to be incurred on Day 1 of the policy period and that the premium should be sufficient to cover all costs. If the company accepts Joseph's argument, what would the first-year premium for the $50,000 face value policy be?

17-3.   Dan Fitzhenry, a twenty-two-year-old major league baseball player has been offered a $1.3 million package for the forthcoming season. The package includes $300,000 payable immediately, and the remaining $1 million is to be paid monthly over a twenty-year period beginning next month. Fitzhenry's contract further specifies that the ball club will purchase an annuity on his behalf through Michigan Mutual, a major insurance company, so that Fitzhenry can be certain that the $1 million will ultimately be paid. Assuming that Michigan Mutual currently offers annuities with an implied interest return equal to 9 percent per annum compounded monthly, calculate the equivalent present value of Fitzhenry's compensation package.

17-4.   Suppose Fitzhenry (problem 17-3) wished to receive the entire compensation package in the form of equal monthly payments for the rest of his life. Assuming the package's present value and the implied interest return of 9 percent remains the same, what would be Fitzhenry's (undiscounted) total lifetime compensation in return for his services in the forthcoming season? (Note: Actuarial remaining life expectancy for a twenty-two-year-old male is about fifty years.)

17-5.   New Horizons Life Insurance company has equity equal to 8 percent of total assets. The company's assets are as follows:

ITEM	MATURITY	COUPON OR FACE RATE	YIELD TO MATURITY*	FACE VALUE
Bonds	30 years	8.0%	10.0%	$2,000,000
Bonds	10 years	9.0	10.0	3,000,000
Bonds	5 years	9.0	9.0	3,000,000
T bills	90 days	8.0	8.0	5,000,000
Mortgages**	20 years	8.0	10.0	5,000,000

*Based on market price: assume annual interest payments for bonds.

**These involve monthly payments over the twenty-year period.

a. If these assets were revalued to market value, would the company be solvent?

b. If yields to maturity on all securities rose one more percentage point, would the company still be solvent?

c. If requirements were changed to require that fixed-income securities be carried at market value, what would be likely to happen to the average maturities of insurance company assets?

17-6.   Your insurance company can invest funds at 4 percent, 90 percent of the first year's premium is paid as a sales commission, and operating expenses are 10 percent of premiums. For someone who lives for thirty years (and pays thirty-one premiums, with the first being paid today):

    a. What would be the annual premium necessary for a straight life insurance policy for $20,000?

    b. What would be the annual premium necessary for a twenty-year limited payment life insurance policy for $20,000?

    c. Rework parts a and b on the assumption of a 7 percent return on invested funds.

17-7.   Following are financial statements for Old Reliable Life Insurance Company. The board of directors has noted that the profitability of the company is below average. Compare the financial statements of Old Reliable to those for life insurance companies in general and suggest methods for improving profitability.

Old Reliable Life Insurance
Income Statement
Year Ending 31 December 1986
(000,000 omitted)

Premium revenue	$146
Investment portfolio income	44
	190
Benefit payments and reserve additions	145
Operating expenses	41
Taxes	1
Net income	$ 3

Balance Sheet
31 December 1986
(000,000 omitted)

Demand deposits and currency	$ 8
Corporate equity	70
Treasury bills	12
U.S. government bonds	40
State and local government bonds	21
Corporate bonds	281
FHA and VA mortgages	190
Commercial mortgages	20
Policy loans	60
Other assets	40
Total assets	$742
Policy reserves	$550
Other liabilities	50
Equity and surplus	142
Total liabilities and net worth	$742

CASE 14

UNIVERSAL LIFE INSURANCE

Ann Howard was impressed by the sales presentation. The twenty-two-year-old bank management trainee had only recently graduated from college and had not previously considered an insurance policy as a form of investment. Insurance, she recalled from discussions in some of her college classes, should be purchased for protection but was generally viewed as a poor savings vehicle in that returns on invested capital earned by the industry were quite low. This meant that dividends paid on some policies were low, and savings that accrued on whole life and certain other policies seemed artificially low. Some of the points made by the insurance salesman seemed quite valid though. Life insurance companies, she knew, invested heavily in long-term, fixed-income securities which were normally held to maturity. In the later 1970s and early 1980s, as the sales representative had pointed out, current market interest rates had been high relative to the insurance industry's portfolio yields. By the late 1980's, however, the situation had reversed itself. The addition of higher-yielding securities to the insurance industry's investment base over the past decade meant that the industry's net rate of investment income was high relative to current market yields (table 1). Ann was particularly interested in the salesman's suggestion that she consider the purchase of a universal life policy. She thought that this option might serve her well both with her insurance needs and as a savings program.

UNIVERSAL LIFE INSURANCE

During the 1970s and 1980s, because of high inflation and higher-yielding alternative investments, the life insurance industry experienced a declining share of

Table 1

Rate of Return on Selected Items

YEAR	NET RATE OF INVEST- MENT IN- COME, LIFE INS. COS.	PRIME RATE CHARGED BY BANKS	MONEY MARKET DEPOSIT ACCTS	ONE-YEAR TREASURY BILLS	CORP AAA BONDS
1970	6.36%	7.91%		6.48%	8.04%
1975	6.36	7.86		6.28	8.83
1977	6.89	6.82		5.71	8.02
1978	7.31	9.06		7.74	8.73
1979	7.73	12.67		9.75	9.63
1980	8.02	15.26		10.89	11.94
1981	8.57	18.87		13.14	14.17
1982	8.91	14.86		11.07	13.79
1983	8.96	10.79	8.36%	8.80	12.04
1984	9.45	12.04	8.10	9.92	12.71
1985	9.63	9.93	6.71	7.81	11.37
1986	9.35	7.50	6.46	6.08	9.02

consumers' financial assets (figure 1). To combat this trend, the industry developed a number of innovative forms of life insurance products. The most successful of these was introduced in 1979 and was termed universal life insurance. Unlike the more traditional forms of life insurance where premiums were fixed and payable at specific times, universal policies were flexible premium policies that allowed the policyholder to change the death benefit from time to time and to vary the amount or timing of premium payments. Premiums are credited under the policy; mortality charges and expense charges are deducted, and interest is credited at rates which may change from time to time. Universal had proven to be an extremely popular product for consumers and by the late 1980s accounted for at least 20 percent of all ordinary life insurance in force (see figure 17-2).

TERM LIFE INSURANCE

Another alternative Ann had considered was the purchase of a term policy that would accommodate her insurance needs and simply invest directly in money market funds or in some other type of savings program. Ann had previously decided that $50,000 in life insurance would accommodate her needs and had received information by mail concerning a term life insurance policy. The term policy contained no savings feature, and the premium payable might vary dramatically over the life of the policy, depending on whether the company continued to enjoy investment returns sufficient to pay high dividends as had been the case in recent years.

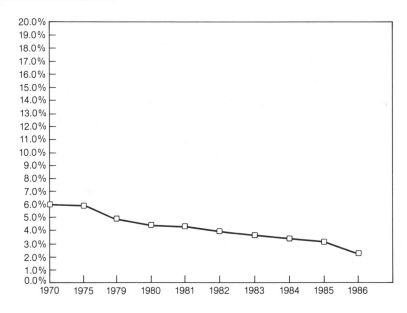

Figure 1   Life insurance reserves as a percentage of consumers' financial assets.

THE ANALYSIS

The salesman who had proposed a universal life policy had left Ann with a computer printout which outlined the policy's premium and cash values to age sixty-five, given a number of assumptions. The proposal was for a $50,000 face value policy, and the salesman had suggested a premium of $204 annually, with the first premium payable when the policy was issued. After deducting mortality and expense charges, the remaining funds in Ann's account would earn interest at whatever the company's current investment rate of return happened to be, except that the rate was guaranteed to be at least 4.5 percent at all times. The computer printout had generated policy cash value data under two assumptions. The first assumption was that the universal cash value would grow by an amount equal to the company's current earnings rate (9 percent). The second assumption was that the cash value would grow at the minimum guaranteed rate of 4.5 percent. Ann decided to compare cash flow data for the first twenty years both for the universal life policy (as contained in the insurance company's printout) and for an alternative where $204 would be set aside annually to purchase term insurance and invest the rest. She decided to compare the alternatives under a favorable scenario where universal cash values would grow at the high current rate of 9 percent and where the term premiums would benefit by virtue of a continuation of the current high dividend rate (table 2). The unfavorable scenario (table 3) assumes that universal cash values would grow at the guaranteed rate of 4.5 percent and that no dividends would accrue with respect to the term policy. Ann decided to analyze the two alternatives and to generate accumulated savings (column 8 of tables 2 and 3), assuming rates of 5, 7, and 9 percent on currently available plus accumulated savings. While interest rates had

Table 2

Universal Life versus Term Under Favorable Assumptions

YEAR (1)	AGE (2)	UNIVERSAL LIFE PREMIUM (3)	UNIVERSAL CASH VALUE[1] (4)	DEATH BENEFIT (5)	TERM LIFE PREMIUM[2] (6)	SAVINGS AVAILABLE (3)−(6) (7)	ACCUMULATED YEAR-END SAVINGS[3] (8)
0	22	$204	$ 0	$50,000	$83	$121	$127
1	23	204	117	50,000	76	128	268
2	24	204	245	50,000	76	128	416
3	25	204	384	50,000	76	128	571
4	26	204	537	50,000	76	128	735
5	27	204	703	50,000	77	128	905
6	28	204	885	50,000	77	128	1,084
7	29	204	1,077	50,000	77	128	1,272
8	30	204	1,287	50,000	77	128	1,470
9	31	204	1,517	50,000	77	128	1,677
10	32	204	1,767	50,000	83	121	1,888
11	33	204	2,034	50,000	83	121	2,109
12	34	204	2,327	50,000	83	121	2,341
13	35	204	2,640	50,000	83	121	2,585
14	36	204	2,982	50,000	83	121	2,841
15	37	204	3,344	50,000	107	98	3,086
16	38	204	3,739	50,000	107	98	3,342
17	39	204	4,160	50,000	107	98	3,612
18	40	204	4,614	50,000	107	98	3,895
19	41	204	5,099	50,000	107	98	4,192

[1]Assumes 9 percent return on invested capital.
[2]Current high dividend rate assumed.
[3]Assumes 5 percent tax-free return on currently available plus accumulated savings.

increased somewhat over the last year (table 4), Ann knew that current rates on pass-book savings were about 5 percent and that rates in general were low relative to the late 1970s and early 1980s. She made a mental note also that cash values generated under the universal life policy were not taxable. Interest earnings on personal savings, she knew, might be subject to taxes under current tax laws.

QUESTIONS

1. Develop accumulated savings data (column 8 in tables 1 and 2) assuming tax-free returns of 7 percent and 9 percent.

2. Are there any inherent advantages or disadvantages of the universal option as compared to the term and personal investment option?

3. Which alternative should Ann Howard select?

Table 3

Universal Life versus Term Under Unfavorable Assumptions

YEAR (1)	AGE (2)	UNIVERSAL LIFE PREMIUM (3)	UNIVERSAL CASH VALUE[1] (4)	DEATH BENEFIT (5)	TERM LIFE PREMIUM[2] (6)	SAVINGS AVAILABLE (3)−(6) (7)	ACCUMULATED YEAR-END SAVINGS[3] (8)
0	22	$204	$0	$50,000	$83	$121	$127
1	23	204	$104	50,000	151	53	189
2	24	204	214	50,000	151	53	254
3	25	204	328	50,000	151	53	323
4	26	204	448	50,000	151	53	395
5	27	204	573	50,000	149	56	473
6	28	204	698	50,000	149	56	555
7	29	204	830	50,000	149	56	641
8	30	204	961	50,000	149	56	731
9	31	204	1,099	50,000	149	56	826
10	32	204	1,237	50,000	179	26	894
11	33	204	1,381	50,000	179	26	966
12	34	204	1,527	50,000	179	26	1,041
13	35	204	1,679	50,000	179	26	1,120
14	36	204	1,833	40,000	179	26	1,202
15	37	204	1,982	50,000	252	(48)	1,212
16	38	204	2,133	50,000	252	(48)	1,222
17	39	204	2,279	50,000	252	(48)	1,233
18	40	204	2,421	50,000	252	(48)	1,244
19	41	204	2,552	50,000	252	(48)	1,256

[1]Assumes 4.5 percent return on invested capital.
[2]No dividends assumed.
[3]Assumes 5 percent tax-free return on currently available plus accumulated savings.

Table 4

Key Interest Rates, January 12, 1988

KEY RATES (in percent)	YESTERDAY	PREVIOUS DAY	YEAR AGO
Prime rate	8.75	8.75	7.50
Discount rate	6.00	6.00	5.50
Federal funds	6.71	6.89	6.19
3-Month Treasury bills	5.62	5.70	5.36
6-Month Treasury bills	6.29	6.34	5.42
7-Year Treasury notes	8.73	8.75	6.93
30-Year Treasury bonds	9.10	9.11	7.37
Telephone bonds	10.00	9.98	8.61
Municipal bonds	8.40	8.40	7.08

SELECTED REFERENCES

AMERICAN COUNCIL OF LIFE INSURANCE. *Life Insurance Fact Book,* Washington, D.C. (published annually).

BORCH, KARL. "Additive Insurance Premiums: A Note." *The Journal of Finance* (December 1982): 1295–1298.

FELGRAN, STEVEN D. "Banks as Insurance Agencies: Legal Constraints and Competitive Advances," *Federal Reserve Bank of Boston New England Economic Review* (September/October 1985): 34–49.

INSURANCE INFORMATION INSTITUTE. *Property/Casualty Fact Book,* New York: Insurance Information Institute (published annually).

KRAUS, ALAN, AND ROSS, STEPHEN A. "The Determination of Fair Profits for the Property-Liability Insurance Firm," *The Journal of Finance* (September 1982): 1016–1028.

URRUTIA, JORGE L. "Market Feasibility of Retroactive Liability Insurance," *Journal of the Midwest Finance Association* (1986): 13–22.

VAUGHAN, EMMETT J. *Fundamentals of Risk and Insurance* (New York: John Wiley Publishing Company, 1986).

18

Pension Fund Management

"If 'socialism' is defined as 'ownership of the means of production by the workers'—and this is both the orthodox and the only rigorous definition—then the United States is the first truly 'Socialist country.' . . . Indeed, aside from farming, a larger sector of the American economy is owned today by the American worker through his investment agent, the pension fund, than Allende in Chile had brought under government ownership to make Chile a 'Socialist country,' than Castro's Cuba has actually nationalized, or than had been nationalized in Hungary or Poland at the height of Stalinism." Peter Drucker[1]

Private pension plans have assets of $1⅓ trillion, while combined assets of public and private pension plans exceed $2 trillion. Among financial institutions, only commercial banks have more assets than pension funds.

The growth in importance of pension funds has been a recent phenomenon. In the 1930s pension fund assets amounted to only about $2.5 billion, and as late as 1950 private pension fund assets amounted to only $12 billion. However, these assets had grown to $151 billion by 1970, making pension funds major financial institutions. From this level, the growth rate increased sharply following Labor Day 1974 when ERISA—the Employee Retirement Income Security Act—was signed into law, increasing required pension fund reserves and leading to projections of a continued high rate of growth in pension fund assets.

As Drucker points out, even these growth numbers may understate the importance of pension funds to the United States economy and society. In combination, the

[1]Peter Drucker. *The Unseen Revolution* (New York: Harper and Row, 1976).

pension funds hold controlling interest in the common stock of most large American corporations.[2] Their continued growth and potential use of that control could lead to major changes in the economic structure of the country. Proper management of pension funds is a matter of concern for the welfare of the country, not to mention the welfare of the individuals covered by the plans and the companies contributing to them.

TYPES OF PENSION FUNDS

Pension plans are operated by private companies, private associations, insurance companies, state and local governments, and the federal government. Government-sponsored funds are normally controlled by legislation of the sponsoring government unit, while private funds are regulated through ERISA. Regardless of the sponsor or guiding legislation, certain common principles underlie the management of the assets of any pension fund. Following an overview of the types of funds and types of regulation, the principles of fund management will be developed.

As a prelude to examining the various types of funds and sponsors, it is necessary to understand the difference between a funded and an unfunded pension plan. A funded plan maintains assets sufficient to meet its remaining obligations over the lives of the persons covered by the plan. The plan's obligations rise from payments already received, and it would be in a position to meet those obligations if no further contributions to the fund occurred. All private pension plans and some government sponsored plans are now of the funded variety. An unfunded plan counts on current payments to meet current obligations and maintains assets sufficient to meet obligations for only a short time. Because it can guarantee payment through its taxing ability, the U.S. government can sponsor unfunded pension plans. However, private firms and most state and local governments have no way other than funding to guarantee that commitments will be honored.

Social Security

Social Security (Old Age, Survivors, and Disability Insurance Program) is, of course, the broadest pension program, presently paying benefits averaging $537 a month to 38 million people. It was started as a program to provide a floor level of retirement income to contributing workers; it has been expanded to serve a number of other needs including disability and survivors' dependent benefits. Many private pension plans are designed to mesh with social security, providing a supplement to fill the gap between Social Security and some desired level of retirement income. Social Security payments are adjusted for inflation each year. Such adjustment is an important consideration and a source of security in periods of high inflation. Because portfolio value may not increase with inflation, few private plans are in a position to promise payments adjusted for inflation. Social Security obligations are primarily unfunded, with total assets of the Social Security trust fund presently being equal to only a few months of benefit payments.

[2]Ibid., p. 20.

Civil Service Retirement System

Federal civilian employees are covered by the United States Civil Service Retirement System, which presently has approximately 2.1 million retired recipients. Civil service employees do not participate in the Social Security system. The civil service retirement system is one of the few plans with benefits completely adjusted for inflation.

The Civil Service Retirement System is designed to be a fully funded system, with contributions by both the U.S. government and its employees. Unfunded liabilities are to be made up from appropriations over a thirty-year period. At the present time the fund has approximately 3.5 million beneficiaries and assets of close to $200 billion.

Those retiring from the Armed Services are not covered by the Civil Service Retirement System but are covered by a separate plan.

State and Local Government Pension Funds

Pension plans of state and local governments have increased in importance with the increase in the number of persons employed by state and local government. These plans presently have approximately 3 million beneficiaries and over $500 billion in assets. Legislation in 1950 and 1954 made state and local government employees eligible to participate in social security, and most have done so. State and local governments have been slow to integrate their pension plans with Social Security, thus some government employees can actually increase their income by retiring. State and local government pension plans are not covered by all the federal laws that govern the management of private pension funds. They are controlled primarily by state and local legislation. For private plans, the idea of investing corporate pension funds in the company involved has been largely rejected because of the risk to the employee if both the company and the pension fund fail. However, state and local employees do not seem to have similar protection. Their assets have sometimes been used to underwrite unsound fiscal policies by purchasing the debt instruments of the local government when other lenders were unwilling to hold the debt.

Private Pension Funds

Private funds represent the bulk of pension fund assets to be managed, though they do not provide coverage to as many people as does the Social Security System. Private plans can be further divided into the following categories:

Insurance company-sponsored plans
Noninsurance company plans
Single company plans
Multicompany plans

Life insurance-related plans are normally used by small firms, as these firms have found the costs of managing their own plans to be excessive. The plan sponsored by a life insurance company has the advantage, particularly for the small fund, of being guaranteed by the life insurance company itself and not merely by the assets of the particular fund. The most common life insurance arrangement is the "group deferred annuity." With this plan a paid-up annuity[3] is purchased for each employee each month, and the policies are held by a trustee (usually a bank or trust company). The employee is protected by the pension plan, and the plan requires minimal management time on the part of the company. Assets of life insurance-related funds are approximately one-third of all private pension plan assets. Approximately 17 million people are covered by such plans.

The nonlife insurance funds represent $1 trillion of assets, including both single-company and multicompany funds. Contributions to private plans are made by employers (or employers and employees), with the contribution typically being made to a fund administered by a bank or trust company. Because these plans are designed to be fully funded, their assets are quite extensive. The trustee invests the funds and makes payments to the retirees in accordance with the provisions of the plan. Some large companies have their own investment staffs that handle the investment of the fund directly. The amount of contribution and the investment policy are directed by legislation as well as company policy and possible agreements between employer and union. Because funds are invested in relatively safe assets, employees can expect to receive their pensions even if the company should fail. Like life insurance-sponsored plans, these plans cannot make commitments unless they can be justified by actuarial experience and the value of the assets on hand.

Multicompany plans normally arise from union contracts, although there are exceptions such as the Teacher's Insurance and Annuity Association started by the Carnegie Foundation to provide a multiemployer pension plan for teachers. Multicompany plans are particularly popular in industries where employees tend to continue in the industry for long periods of time but change employers frequently. The multicompany plan provides job mobility—a desirable feature from an economic efficiency viewpoint—without jeopardizing pension protection. Industries with multiemployer plans include construction, motor transportation, trade (wholesale and retail), and some service industries. With a multiemployer plan, contributions are made to a pension fund managed by a board of trustees. The board may be made up of representatives of both management and labor.

Unfortunately, several major multicompany pension funds have been racked with scandal resulting from misappropriation of funds to the benefit of trustees. A number of prison sentences have been imposed for improper use of funds. Despite some problems and the necessity for continuous supervision, these funds provide needed pension protection in mobile professions.

Keogh plans are a special arrangement allowed to individuals who are self-employed or are not covered by a pension plan at their place of employment. An individual is allowed to deduct from his or her taxable income contributions to a private

---

[3]An annuity is a simple promise to pay a specific amount per month for life, beginning at a particular age. A paid-up annuity requires no further payments on the part of the recipient. As an example, suppose a company buys a $1 paid-up annuity for each employee each month. An employee who works forty years before retirement will receive $480 per month at retirement.

pension plan in amounts up to 15 percent of earned income (up to a limit of $1,500 for an employee and $7,500 for a self-employed person). Funds may be placed with a bank or thrift institution, a life insurance company, a mutual fund, or in certain government bonds.

REGULATION OF PENSION FUNDS

Most pension fund regulation now in effect traces from the 1974 Employee Retirement Income Security Act (ERISA), which was strengthened by the Retirement Equity Act of 1984. The objectives of the act were the encouragement of increased pension benefits and protection of benefits. The act does not require employers to have pension plans, but sets standards for plans that do exist. The act covers seven major areas:

1. Who must be covered by pension plans
2. Status of accrued benefits when an employee leaves an employer (vesting)
3. The pension rights of an employee's spouse
4. The amount of assets that must be accumulated to vest projected pension benefits (funding)
5. Standards of conduct and responsibility for pension fund managers (fiduciary responsibility)
6. Plan termination insurance to protect employees in the event a canceled plan has insufficient assets to meet its commitments
7. Reporting and disclosure requirements

Who Must Be Covered   A very important feature of the coverage aspect of the legislation is that it does not require employers to have pension plans. It also does not require that existing plans be continued. It only requires that any plan that does exist meet certain standards. Basically, a plan must cover any full-time employee who has worked for the company one year and is twenty-one or older. While issues such as the definition of "full time" are sufficient to keep a battery of attorneys employed, they need not concern the reader interested in the general principles guiding pension fund management.

Vesting   An employee is vested on the day his or her right to pension benefits becomes certain. Before ERISA, there were cases of companies discharging employees in their early sixties to negate forty years of accumulated pension benefits. Under present legislation, there are two allowed vesting plans. The simplest is complete vesting of all employees no later than five years after beginning employment with the particular employer. The other allowed schedule provides 20 percent vesting after three years service, with the vested benefit then increasing 20 percent a year until the employee is 100 percent vested.

Vesting does not guarantee benefits at retirement equal to what would have been earned if the employee had stayed with the company. Most pension plans base benefits on years of employment and income. The vested employee receives benefits based on the amount of service up to departure from the employer. For the employee who receives vested rights in the form of a cash settlement when leaving the employer, the law allows the employee to defer tax on the payment if it is reinvested in an individual retirement annuity or invested in the new employer's plan.

Spouse Rights   The pension plan must pay benefits to the employee's surviving spouse after the employee's death unless the spouse waives that right. Of course, the surviving spouse benefits decrease the size of the pension payment; the amount of adjustment is determined by the relative ages of the two people and other actuarial factors.

Funding   Private pension funds are required to maintain assets equal to the present value of future benefits. This requirement is designed to ensure that benefits will be paid as provided. Unfunded plans simply pay current benefits from current operating revenues. If the company sponsoring an unfunded plan ceased operation, employees and retirees would simply lose their benefits. Thus ERISA required that all plans be funded. Pension plans are given thirty years to amortize obligations for past services and become fully funded. Because determining the amount of funds needed and the best method for achieving funding are major management problems, these topics will be considered in a separate section.

Fiduciary Responsibility   This refers to the standards that must be followed in managing pension funds assets. A fiduciary is a trustee, investment adviser, or other person who has the authority to make decisions with regard to investment of the fund's assets. First, fiduciary responsibility standards prohibit transactions that would involve a conflict of interest. A fiduciary cannot invest the funds for any purpose other than the benefit of those covered by the plan. Specifically, transactions from which the trustee may personally gain are prohibited.

The second aspect of fiduciary responsibility is the "prudent man" rule. The fiduciary is required by the law to act "with care, skill, prudence, and diligence under the circumstances then prevailing that a prudent man acting in a like capacity and familiar with such matters would use. . . ." Managing the investment portfolio in consideration of this rule and other objectives is another major aspect of pension fund management and will be discussed as a separate section.

Plan Cancelation Insurance   ERISA called for the creation of the Pension Benefit Guarantee Corporation (PBGC) to protect pension fund beneficiaries in the event a plan was terminated and its assets were not sufficient to meet its future obligations. The PBGC was modeled after the Federal Deposit Insurance Corporation which guarantees bank deposits. The employer is responsible for unfunded liabilities at plan termination time up to a limit of 30 percent of net worth, with the PBGC making up the difference.

Like the FDIC, the PBGC charges insurance premiums that are sufficient to cover isolated failures. Because the PBGC has had to pay a number of claims, it has not been able to accumulate enough capital to handle a really major pension fund failure. The failure of LTV Corporation was a particularly damaging blow, and the PBGC's net worth was projected to be −$3 billion at the end of 1987. It is assumed that the federal government will provide additional financial backing to supplement increases in insurance rates if necessary. A really large failure would require the federal government to step in if commitments were to be honored.

Reporting and Disclosure Requirements   Disclosure regulations, like other aspects of ERISA, arose from prior abuses. Employees were often surprised to find that after thirty years of employment, they had no vested interest when a plan was terminated or they were dismissed; they had built their retirement security upon a false assumption about their pension coverage. Additionally, the lack of oversight to ensure that fiduciary standards were being met resulted in millions of dollars in benefits being lost. The present reporting requirements set standards for reports to both the government and covered employees. Plans must now submit to the Secretary of Labor each year an audited financial report similar in detail to the reports companies issue to their shareholders. Employees must be given a description of the plan written in language that the average person can understand. The employee must be given a new copy of the description every ten years if no changes have occurred and every five years if changes have occurred.[4]

The reporting requirements have been frequently criticized. The cost and time required for an annual audit has been blamed for the cancelation of many plans. In response, plans with fewer than 100 participants have been exempted from a large portion of the reporting requirements; plans with individual benefits fully guaranteed by an insurance company have been exempted from the auditing requirement. Reporting requirements continue to be an area of debate; several changes have occurred, and more are likely to occur.

MANAGEMENT POLICY

Pension fund assets have become large relative to total corporate assets; pension fund expenses have become a substantial portion of total labor expense. Additionally, many people depend on pension plans as an important employee benefit and source of retirement security. From the points of view of both employees and the company, proper management decisions are important. In this section, we discuss the four major areas of management policy:

1. Benefits to be received
2. Vesting procedures
3. Funding of liabilities
4. Investment policy for the fund portfolio

---

[4]Of course, participants must also be notified of any changes as they occur.

Benefits

Interestingly, government regulation has much less to say about the benefit formula than other aspects of the pension plan. This is partly explained in terms of the types of problems prompting ERISA. Failure to receive expected benefits was the major problem addressed. In addition, full disclosure and assurance of ability to meet commitments has been the thrust of most financial regulation.

The government's main interest in benefit formulas relates to discrimination. Benefit payments in some plans were adjusted for life expectancy; a woman retiree would receive a smaller monthly pension check than a man with the same employment experience because her life expectancy was greater and she could expect to receive more checks. This practice has been ruled discriminatory. The government is also interested in discrimination against lower-income employees. The Internal Revenue Service compares benefits to key employees with benefits to other employees and disallows tax deductability of pension plan contributions if certain standards are not met.

Since there is considerable freedom in establishing a benefit formula, this provides a rich area for gains through proper decision making by management. Most pension plans are tied to years of service, and there is an increasing trend toward tying the plan to income levels as well. The exceptions to income relationship normally occur in plans negotiated with unions where income levels do not vary greatly. Where benefits are tied to income, there is the additional question of whether it should be tied to average income for all years of employment or only the few years immediately preceding retirement. Additional problems involve integrating with social security and dealing with inflation.

To begin, there is the basic question of what amount of income a retiree needs. Many experts feel that a retired person needs income, including Social Security, of 60 percent to 70 percent of preretirement income to maintain the preretirement standard of living. Savings come from decreased taxes and elimination of the expenses associated with going to work. Higher-income employees need a lower replacement ratio as they consume a smaller portion of their take-home pay and will recognize greater tax savings in retirement.

While needs do not necessarily depend on years of employment, most benefit programs are based on income and length of service. After all, wages themselves are based on service rather than need. Programs are normally designed to provide a "satisfactory" level of retirement income to an employee who has spent a large number of years with the employer or covered by the multiemployer plan.

A major problem in benefit plan development is the question of how to integrate the plan with Social Security. A company sponsoring a plan will reasonably view its contributions to the pension fund and to Social Security as a package of retirement benefits. Companies that started pension plans years ago with no effort to integrate them with Social Security have found their total pension costs rising sharply as Social Security benefits and taxes have increased. In some cases, the situation has reached the point where employees can increase their after-tax income by retiring. Thus the need to integrate pension benefits with Social Security is widely recognized. There are three approaches to integration: the excess approach, the offset approach, and the cap approach.

The excess approach ties pension benefits to the Social Security contributions made by the employer. Social Security taxes are based on income up to a certain level, referred to as the base. A typical excess formula for annual pension income is

$$P = 0.01 I_1 + 0.02 I_2$$
where P = annual pension benefit
   I_1 = total income earned during employment to which Social Security tax was applied
   I_2 = total income during employment to which Social Security tax did not apply (income above the base)

The formula might be modified to consider average income for the last few years of employment multiplied by years of employment instead of actual total income. When the pension is based on income for the last few years, it is also common practice to redefine I_1 and I_2 in terms of income above and below the base during the last few years of employment. Regardless of the precise formula used, the objective of the excess approach is to integrate employer pension fund and Social Security expenses.

The offset approach is designed to integrate employee Social Security income and pension income. A typical offset formula would be

$$P = 0.04 I - S$$
where I = total income during employment
   S = annual Social Security benefits

Modifications would involve using average income for recent years or only subtracting some percentage of Social Security benefits.

On first glance, an offset approach might seem more fair to the employee in that it focuses on achieving a total employee income goal rather than a total company expense goal. However, an offset approach results in serious distortions during a period of rapid inflation. Social Security benefits are tied to the cost of living, thereby providing at least some protection from inflation. The offset approach eliminates this protection by decreasing the company pension by an amount equal to any increase in Social Security cost of living adjustment. At recent inflation rates, the offset approach would move a pension plan participant from a comfortable level of income to poverty within a normal postretirement life span. Thus the offset method appears to be unsuccessful in either ensuring retirement income or integrating company costs.[5]

The cap approach is a modification of the offset approach. A typical cap formula would be

$$P = 0.02 I \text{ or } (0.8 I/n) - S, \text{ whichever is less}$$
where n = number of years of employment

Again, income for recent years might be used in place of total income. This approach effectively establishes a cap on total benefits, becoming an offset approach

---

[5]For an argument in favor of the offset method, see Lloyd S. Kay, "The Pension Benefit Formula: An Element in Financial Planning," *Financial Executive* (July 1978): 24–30.

when combined benefits would otherwise exceed some percentage of preretirement income.

As with the regular offset approach, the cap approach leads to serious distortions during inflationary periods. If the cap is at 80 percent of preretirement income and the consumer price index triples during a participant's retirement years, the total benefit ceiling, in real dollars, would fall to approximately *one-fourth* of preretirement income. Under present Social Security practices, this would mean a complete halt in pension income. Like the offset approach, the cap approach fails to integrate company expenses or provide retirement income security.

Inflation is, of course, the problem that makes the development of a sound benefit formula so difficult. Failure to include an inflation adjustment provision in the benefit formula leaves the employee exposed to the risk of having retirement income eroded by inflation. However, it is very difficult for a pension plan to provide inflation protection. If a company knew that the plan would continue indefinitely and the ratio of workers to retirees would remain stable, pension benefits could be tied to salary and paid on an on-going basis, as is done with Social Security. However, pension plans must be funded on the assumption there will be no new employees and existing commitments must be paid from an investment portfolio. There is no sound actuarial basis for determining the amount of expected inflation to use in computing future benefits and present fund contribution needs. In addition, there is a dearth of investments whose value will grow at the inflation rate. Therefore, adequate inflation protection is very difficult to provide.

A number of approaches have been used to attempt to offset the effect of inflation. One of these is the variable annuity approach under which pension income depends on returns earned on the pension plan investment portfolio. Unfortunately, portfolio returns have tended to be low during periods of high inflation, compounding the retiree's problems. The use of an excess rather than an offset approach helps to decrease the bite of inflation somewhat and still produces a predictable cost structure. Basing retirement income on income the last few years before retirement rather than overall years of employment serves to provide protection against inflation occurring before retirement. Finally, some pension plans simply promise to adjust pension benefits for inflation. However, it is not clear what resources they would have with which to meet such promises in the face of high rates of inflation, low investment porfolio returns, and a declining ratio of working participants to retired participants.

Development of a benefit formula is much more than a question of how much should be spent on pension benefits. It involves questions of who should receive the greatest share, how other sources of retirement income should be considered, and how to deal with inflation. The development of a rational benefit plan—one that is equitable and safe for both the company and the employee—is the first, and possibly the most important, decision facing the pension fund manager.

Choice of Vesting Plans

The choice of a vesting plan involves the desire to control costs, the desire to retain qualified employees, and the desire to provide an equitable program. The cost of a pension plan and the benefits that the employer can afford to provide are affected by the vesting arrangement chosen. Within a given dollar cost constraint, the employer can choose between more generous benefits or more generous vesting. ERISA sets the minimum standards that must be met, with some plans providing vesting in excess of the minimum. The plan must meet one of two minimum standards:

1. Total vesting after five years on the job.
2. 20 percent vesting after three years' service, with the vested benefit then increasing 20 percent a year until the employee is 100 percent vested

Choice of vesting plan has an effect on the rate at which vesting is achieved (table 18-1). An employer wishing to minimize cost should choose the plan that would produce the lowest level of vesting for his particular group of employees.

The relative costs of the five year and phased-vesting plans would depend on turnover patterns within the particular company or industry, though phased vesting would seem to be more equitable.

We can see (table 18-1) that the choice of minimum vesting standard does not matter for the employee who leaves before the third or after the sixth year. The benefit impacts of the various vesting choices are illustrated below for a worker beginning employment at age twenty. The law allows pension funds to exclude income earned before age twenty-one and during the first year of employment in computing benefits, though time for vesting of benefits begins with the date of actual employment. The company's formula for annual pension benefits is

$P = V \times 0.02 \times I$
where $P=$ annual pension benefit, beginning at age 65
   $V=$ vesting percentage from table 18-1
   $I=$ total income earned after twenty-first birthday

If the employee leaves at age twenty-four, after four years of employment at a salary of $1,000 per month, cumulative eligible income (I) is $36,000, because income for the year before the employee is twenty-one is excluded. We see that the vested percentage is 40% after four years, using phased-in vesting, and 0 otherwise (table 18-1). Thus, with phased-in vesting, the employee who starts at age twenty, earns $1,000 per month, and leaves after four years, will be eligible for an annual pension at age sixty-five of

$P = 0.40 \times 0.02 \times \$36,000 = \$288.$

Table 18-1

Percentage Vesting Under Alternate Formulas

YEARS OF EMPLOYMENT	3	4	5	6	7
5-year full vesting	0	0	100	100	100
Phased-in vesting	20	40	60	80	100

Table 18-2

Illustrative Vested Annual Benefit Payments Under Alternate Formulas (in $)

YEARS OF EMPLOYMENT	3	4	5	6	7
5-year full vesting			960	1,200	1,440
Phased-in vesting	96	288	576	960	1,440

Vested pension entitlements for this employee under various minimum vesting standards are summarized in table 18-2.

Since funding must equal the present value of vested benefits, the cost of the employee's service is clearly affected by the benefit vesting plan chosen. Suppose the company were to choose a more generous program such as complete immediate vesting. At the end of four years, the vested annual benefit for the employee used in the previous example would be

$$P = 1.0 \times 0.02 \times \$48{,}000 = \$960$$

Thus the vested annual benefit for the employee could be between $0 and $960 using the same basic benefit computation but varying eligibility and vesting rules. Cost differences could be increased manyfold by changing vesting provisions for a plan with high turnover in the early years.

Choosing the right combination of benefits, eligibility, and vesting is indeed difficult. First, it is necessary to ascertain the preferences of employees; within a total pension benefit budget, what combination of benefits, eligibility, and vesting would they prefer? Second, it is necessary to carefully estimate cost impacts of all alternatives, based on estimates of employee income and turnover. Third, it is necessary to consider questions of equity. Fourth, it is necessary to consider risk; a plan involving high benefits offset by slow vesting could be disastrous if turnover declined sharply. Finally, it is necessary to develop the plan within the constraints of the requirements of ERISA.

Types of vesting continue to vary substantially from plan to plan, with some plans offering complete vesting after three years. However, complete immediate vesting is rare, and the trend appears to be toward five-year vesting, a method that delays vesting about as long as is allowed. Five-year vesting also has the advantage of being easy for employees to understand.

Funding of Liabilities

A problem of more concern to pension fund sponsors than managers, but worthy of a brief discussion, is the funding of pension obligations. Basically, ERISA requires that pension funds work toward becoming *fully funded*. A pension fund is fully funded if it holds assets equal in value to the present value of all future benefits earned to date. Contributions must be sufficient to meet current obligations and amortize past obligations over a thirty-year period for a single-employer plan and forty years for a multiemployer plan. In theory, most plans would gradually become fully funded.

Several problems have arisen in the funding area. First, contractual changes in benefit formulas and actuarial assumptions have created new unfunded liabilities. Second, fluctuations in the prices of securities have changed the level of funding. Third, there are various questions as to the definition of an unfunded liability. While ERISA provides for insurance to protect beneficiaries from losses due to insufficient funding, companies are at least partially liable for the unfunded liabilities in the case of plan termination and must make contributions sufficient to amortize the unfunded liabilities as discussed above. Among other problems, credit ratings are adversely affected by unfunded liabilities.[6]

The assets needed to meet funding requirements depend on actuarial assumptions about employee turnover and beneficiary life span. Fortunately, actuaries have excellent life span data and reasonably good turnover data to work with. Unfortunately, the same cannot be said for salary growth and investment return assumptions. A recent survey revealed that the median salary growth assumption was 5 percent and the median investment return assumption was 6 percent.[7] With salary growth being substantially greater than investment return in those years, contribution formulas proved inadequate, creating a stream of new unfunded liabilities.

Without getting into complex details, we should take a brief look at the problem of defining unfunded liabilities. If we hire an employee and ignore, for simplicity of illustration, the possibility of his leaving employment before retirement, we can compute the present value of eventual benefits using appropriate actuarial assumptions. At any given time, some of the amount needed will be on hand, with the rest to be accumulated from future contributions. Thus, the present value of projected benefits is divided between assets on hand and the present value of future contributions. Most of, a small percentage of, or none, of the present value of future contributions may appear as an unfunded liability,[8] depending on the accounting method selected. While we are certain, given our actuarial assumptions, what the present value of future needed contributions is, the accounting conventions give wide latitude in choosing what portion of this present value should be assigned to unfunded liabilities and what portion should be considered "present value of future normal pension costs." While it is generally agreed that not all of the present value of future benefits should be considered a present liability—since much of it is dependent on assumed future employee income—there is substantial room for disagreement.

Underfunding has been a problem. The negative net worth of the PBGC and the increased insurance rates arise from unfunded liabilities. At the same time, other companies found themselves in excess funding positions after the stock market rise of the first half of the 1980s. While some plans were failing, and dropping their problems at the door of the PBGC, other plans were being liquidated so the sponsoring company could remove money in excess of that required for full funding.

[6]Patrick J. Regan, "Credit Ratings and Pension Costs," *Financial Analysts Journal* (March/April, 1979): 6–7.

[7]*Pension and Investments*, January 2, 1978.

[8]Paul A. Gerwitz and Robert C. Phillips, "Unfunded Pension Liabilities . . . The New Myth." *Financial Executive* (August 1978): 18–24.

Managing the Pension Fund Portfolio

The classic risk-return trade-offs of finance are most clearly seen in the area of portfolio management. A high return on the portfolio can serve to lower pension fund expense to the company and/or increase employee pension benefits. Unfortunately, increased expected return is normally achieved only by accepting increased risk (chapter 7). The importance of risk exposure is illustrated by the events of 19 October 1987, a day on which private, noninsured pension funds lost approximately $100 billion of asset value in one hectic day of stock trading. If risks are taken and the fund suffers losses, increased contributions are required or pensions are jeopardized. The fund must be guided by a portfolio management policy that gives adequate operational guidelines with regard to risk and return.

In establishing policy, the first thing that must be decided is who will have primary management responsibility. Where the pension plan is negotiated with a union, there is frequently a board of trustees consisting of members from both management and labor. In the case of some large funds, the sponsoring company decides to manage the funds directly, paying investment advisers to provide recommendations and banks to provide custodial services. However, most companies assign funds to a trustee, either providing general policy statements or leaving the trustees to develop their own policies. The division of funds among several trustees is common practice; funds are periodically reallocated among trustees according to their past performance. When several trustees are used, each may be given different guidelines. For example, an insurance company may be given funds to invest in real estate; and a brokerage firm funds to invest in common stock.

Parties serving as trustees include banks, insurance companies, brokerage firms, and investment counselors such as those who manage mutual funds. Banks, the institutions that traditionally dominated this area, have experienced increasing competition from these other groups. Services are heavily marketed, and competition to achieve the best performance is intense, sometimes leading to concerns about unsound investment policy.

Factors to consider in the choice of trustees include:

Investment skill
Costs
Administrative skill
Size and financial strength[9]

In addition to the obvious need to invest profitably and prudently for a reasonable fee, the trustee has complex record-keeping responsibilities. Failure to keep proper records and maintain proper administrative controls led to multimillion dollar losses of securities in the later 1960s and early 1970s.[10] Finally, the standards of fiduciary responsibility

[9]Patrick J. Davey, *Financial Management of Pension Plans* (New York: The Conference Board): 46.
[10]For an interesting discussion of these problems, see John Brooks, *The Go-Go Years* (New York: Weybright and Talley, 1973): 182–205.

cannot be effectively enforced unless the trustee has the size and financial strength to provide at least some backing for commitments made.

Regardless of who accepts responsibility for managing the portfolio, a management policy must be developed. The policy typically specifies, among othe things:

Types of investments
Risk levels
Performance objectives
Restrictions on investment in sponsoring company's securities

Modern mean-variance portfolio theory provides a logical starting point for the development of management policy. For these purposes, there are two primary lessons from portfolio theory:

1. Risk should be viewed in the context of a portfolio rather than for each security separately.
2. Higher expected return is normally associated with greater risk.

The portfolio approach to risk is based on the observation that some risks can be diversified away—effectively eliminated—when risky securities are combined in portfolios. For example, the risk that one automobile design will be favored over others can be diversified away by owning stocks in all automobile companies. However, even a well-diversified portfolio will move up and down in value with market conditions in general. Thus, risk associated with market conditions in general cannot be eliminated through diversification. Portfolio theory argues that rational people will eliminate diversifiable risk by constructing portfolios consisting of a number of different investments. Opinion varies on the number of securities necessary to construct a well-diversified portfolio, but most writers agree that no more than thirty securities are required.

A closely related body of literature argues that markets are *efficient*, meaning that no investor has superior information or superior ability to evaluate information. Thus the *efficient market hypothesis* argues that the investor cannot expect higher returns except through the acceptance of greater risk.

The implications of the above analysis for pension fund portfolio management are quite significant. First, the portfolio should not contain diversifiable risk, since there is no reward for such risk. Thirty is probably a sufficient number of securities to achieve this objective unless the thirty are concentrated in certain industries.

We might also consider the point of view in determining risk. To the extent benefits are not insured, risk should be examined from the point of view of the beneficiary. For example, a concentration in real estate would not provide reasonable diversification if most beneficiaries had real estate investments in the form of their homes and did not own other assets. Heavy investment in the sponsoring company would not be wise, as income risk to the employees is already tied to the well-being of the company.

Finally, plans and objectives must consider the risk-return trade-off and should not be based on the assumption that the fund manager can regularly achieve superior results without accepting greater than average risk. Stating return objectives without reference to risk may simply lead to greater risk being accepted in keeping with the risk-return trade-off.

This problem has sometimes been handled in the pension fund area by specifying a weighted average beta[11] level and specifying that the portfolio be well diversified, then attempting to maximize return within these constraints.

ERISA creates a set of standards that must be considered in applying the principles of portfolio theory. Of particular interest are ERISA's standards of fiduciary responsibility:

1. The fiduciary must act only for the purpose of providing benefits to the fund's participants and defraying reasonable costs.
2. The fiduciary must act "with care, skill, prudence, and diligence under the circumstances then prevailing that a prudent man acting in a like capacity and familiar with such matters would use in the conduct of an enterprise of a like character with like aims."
3. The fiduciary must diversify the portfolio to minimize the risk of large losses.
4. The fiduciary must comply with the plan's documents if they are consistent with ERISA.

The prohibition on conflict of interest, the requirement that plan documents be followed, and the instruction to diversify cause little difficulty. In fact, portfolio theory tells us something about how to achieve diversification. Unfortunately, the prudent man rule, as presently interpreted, causes some confusion. In its earlier history in common law, the prudent man rule was interpreted as prohibiting equity investments of any type. However, the application has changed over the years and the concept of investment versus speculative securities has developed. A frequent interpretation is that only the stocks of very safe, well-established companies can be included in a portfolio.

Under ERISA, there has been an attempt to reinterpret the prudent man rule in light of portfolio theory. Unfortunately, it takes years for an adequate base of case law to be built, and portfolio managers cannot wait to act.[12] As a practical matter, they frequently limit equity investments to a narrow list of well-established companies held by numerous other institutional portfolios. The equities of some companies were "institutional favorites" in September 1987 (table 18-3). Investing in such "favorites" provides excellent protection from liability under the prudent man rule. However, the practice results in a two-tier market consisting of a small group of stocks favored by the institutions and the rest of the market being largely ignored by institutions.

One problem with limiting all investment to a list of older, stable companies is that it may not provide complete diversification. Diversification does not come entirely from large numbers of securities. Holding stock of all steel companies would clearly leave the portfolio undiversified with regard to factors affecting the steel business. Likewise, the holding of only old, stable companies and the complete exclusion of

---

[11]Recall that beta measures the sensitivity of returns for a security of portfolio to returns for securities in general.

[12]For an excellent discussion of this problem, see Roger D. Blair, "ERISA and the Prudent Man Rule: Avoiding Perverse Results." *Sloan Management Review* (Winter 1979): 15–23.

Table 18-3

Stocks Currently Favored by Institutional Portfolios

COMPANY NAME	NUMBER OF INSTITUTIONS HOLDING
Abbott Laboratories	728
American Express	877
American Home Products	782
American Telephone and Telegraph	793
Amoco Corporation	808
Atlantic Richfield	855
Bell South Corporation	783
Bristol Meyers	892
Chevron Corporation	779
Coca Cola	726
Digital Equipment	900
Dow Chemical	788
duPont (El) deNemours	787
Eastman Kodak	957
Emerson Electric	643
Exxon Corporation	1,029
General Electric	1,284
General Motors	941
GTE Corporation	795
Hewlett Packard	802
International Business Machines	1,734
Johnson and Johnson	841
McDonald's Corporation	721
Merck and Company	920
Minnesota Mining and Manufacturing	843
Mobil Corporation	865
NYNEX Corporation	729
Pacific Telesis Group	733
Pfizer, Inc.	814
Philip Morris Co.	991
Schlumberger Ltd.	854
Sears Roebuck	786

*Standard and Poors Stock Guide, October 1987. While the data are based on a survey of 2,700 institutions, excluding pension funds, it is believed that pension funds do not differ from other institutions with regard to which particular stocks are favored at a given time.

innovative newer companies leaves portfolios exposed to risks unique to established companies and may limit returns by excluding highly profitable opportunities.

From society's viewpoint, the use of a list of institutional favorites has important implications for resource allocation. With the growing importance of pension funds and other institutional portfolios, the favored companies have ready access to new capital while other companies are virtually shut off from the capital markets. Specifically, the innovative new companies that traditionally provide a major source of economic growth have had their access to the capital markets severely restricted.

As the above discussion shows, the prudent man rule sets requirements that would be considered unnecessary and even harmful from the perspective of portfolio theory. Because case law is an evolutionary type of law, we can expect that portfolio risk will come to be fully recognized.

In addition to portfolio theory and fiduciary responsibility, the pension fund manager can also expect certain standards to be set by the sponsoring company. The following is a typical example of a performance objective.

> The portfolio should earn an average return over a five-year period of at least 20 percent greater than the S & P 500 stock index and at least 10 percent per annum.

A beta range may also be specified, though this is less common.

Performance standards of the type illustrated are particularly difficult to meet in light of what we know about portfolio theory, efficient market theory, and fiduciary responsibility. If everyone is to purchase securities from the same restricted list, everyone has the same information. Nobody has superior ability to analyze available data and earning a superior return is going to be a most difficult project. In fact, the theory tells us that a higher return can be earned only through the acceptance of a higher risk. There is no evidence that objectives of the type illustrated are attainable. Moving funds from portfolio manager to portfolio manager in search of "superior" performance is likely to be unproductive.

The considerations discussed above have led to some degree of consensus as to what should be included in a pension fund portfolio. The mix of pension fund portfolio assets has developed over the years (figure 18-1). From a time when equity was almost entirely excluded from trusteed portfolios, thought on the subject evolved to the point that by the end of the 1960s—a decade in which stock prices rose sharply—common stock became the dominant asset, accounting for almost three-fourths of pension fund assets. The poor stock market returns of the 1970s caused a further rethinking, with a growing interest in the asset that performed well in the 1970s: real estate.[13] There has also been a limited move to internationally diversified portfolios designed to decrease risk and increase return. The consensus as to what a "prudent man" would invest in continues to evolve with changing market conditions.

Portfolio Performance Measurement   Both for purposes of analyzing past performance and for projecting future returns, performance measures must be developed. First it is necessary to compute an annualized rate of return. This problem is made a bit difficult by the fact that funds are added and deducted periodically. It is necessary to separate performance of the portfolio from the impact of additions and withdrawals of funds. The problem is illustrated below for two pension funds over a two-year period.

---

[13]Elbert Bressie, "When Will Pension Funds Enter the Real Estate Market?" *Financial Executive* (April 1979): 26–29.

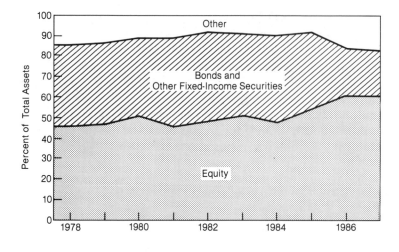

	Fund A	Fund B
Starting market value	$1,000	$1,000
Cash contributed at the start of the first year	1,000	0
First-year return	80%	80%
Cash contributed at the start of the second year	0	1,000
Second-year return	10%	10%
Ending value	$3,960	$3,080

Each fund started with $1,000 and received $1,000 in additional contributions over the two-year period. Can we conclude that Fund A was better managed because the terminal value was higher? More careful examination shows that return earned by each fund was identical for each year. The higher ending value for Fund A was a result of the timing of contributions from sponsors, not differences in performance by portfolio managers.

The *geometric mean return* (time-weighted rate of return)[14] is a method used to put returns on a comparable basis. The geometric mean return for a portfolio is computed using the following formula:

$$G = \sqrt[n]{(1 + r_1)(1 + r_2) \ldots (1 + r_n)} - 1 \qquad (18\text{-}1)$$

where G = geometric mean or time-weighted rate of return
   r_i = return (price appreciation and dividends) during period i
   n = total number of periods over which evaluation is to occur

For the portfolios illustrated above, the geometric mean return is

$$G = \sqrt[2]{(1 + 0.8)(1 + 0.1)} - 1 = 40.7\%$$

[14]In financial analysis, the geometric mean of a series of annual returns over time is viewed as the annual compound rate of growth inherent in the series of returns.

The geometric mean return, not being affected by the timing of contributions, is the same for each portfolio. Thus, it measures the performance of the portfolio manager, not the effects of contribution and withdrawal timing.

While the geometric mean return is a useful method of evaluating returns, it does not include any method of recognizing differences in risk accepted. Based on portfolio theory, a widely used risk adjustment measure is the reward to variability ratio:

$$\frac{R_p - R_f}{\sigma_p} \tag{18-2}$$

where R_p = average return for the portfolio over the periods for which performance is being evaluated
   R_f = average return on risk-free investments over the same period
   σ_p = standard deviation of returns for the portfolio over this period

For one portfolio to outperform another, it should have a higher ratio [equation (18-2)].

SUMMARY

Pension fund management involves three sets of trade-offs and one set of contradictions. The first trade-off involves the desire to provide maximum benefits at a minimum cost. The second trade-off involves the desire to provide maximum benefits to individuals and the desire to provide coverage to as many people as possible. Within a particular total cost limit, various combinations of vesting, participation rights, and benefit formulas are possible. The choice involves legal constraints of ERISA, employee desires, union labor contract provisions, and management judgment. The third trade-off is the classic risk-return trade-off faced in virtually all portfolio management problems. Higher returns reduce cost and allow improved benefits, but involve greater risk of loss. Most pension funds are managed quite conservatively with regard to risk. Finally, there is a conflict between portfolio risk as recognized by modern portfolio theory and individual security risk as defined through the prudent man rule. Pension fund management consists of developing both benefit and portfolio management policy in line with these offsetting and contradictory considerations.

QUESTIONS

18-1.   Why have pension fund assets grown so rapidly since the passage of ERISA?

18-2.   Do you feel it is appropriate for the federal government to sponsor unfunded pension plans? Why? Do you feel it is appropriate for state and local governments to sponsor unfunded pension plans? Why?

18-3.   While pension funds together own enough stock to exercise effective voting control over many major U.S. corporations, they have not done so. What reasons can you think of for their failure to attempt to exercise control?

18-4.   What groups of people are *not* protected by ERISA?

18-5.   What factors should be considered in developing a vesting formula?

18-6.   Should a pension fund sponsor give the fiduciary standards such as "outperform the stock market average by at least 2 percent"? Why?

18-7.   It has been claimed that the prudent man rule "discourages true diversification." Comment on this claim.

18-8.   In light of efficient market theory, can international diversification of the pension fund portfolio be considered "prudent"?

PROBLEMS

18-1.   An employee retires after working twenty years and earning total wages of $500,000 and an annual income of $40,000 in the year before retirement. The pension benefit formula calls for an annual pension equal to 4 percent of total income earned. What will be the annual pension for this employee? If the employee also receives Social Security payments of $500 a month, will the combined Social Security and pension payments provide adequate retirement income?

18-2.   For the retiree in problem 18-1, assume that inflation is 5 percent a year. Social Security payments will increase with inflation (with the first increase occurring at the start of the second year of retirement), but pension payments will not increase. In terms of retirement-date purchasing power, how much income will the retiree have in the tenth year of retirement?

18-3.   For the retiree in problems 18-1 and 18-2, assume the company uses an excess approach, with the annual pension benefit being 5 percent of income on which Social Security was not paid and 2 percent of income on which Social Security was paid. Social Security was paid on half of the person's income. What is the pension benefit?

18-4.   For the retiree in problem 18-1, assume the company uses the offset approach, with annual pension benefits equal to 6 percent of total income, minus Social Security benefits. How much will the employee receive per year in combined pension and Social Security payments at the start of retirement? If inflation is 5 percent a year, how much will the employee receive ten years later, expressed in retirement-date buying power?

18-5.   For the retiree in problem 18-1, suppose the company uses the cap approach, with annual benefits equal to the lesser of 4 percent of total income or

(Total income/number of years employed) − social security benefits

How much will the retiree receive in combined annual pension benefits and Social Security payments immediately after retirement? If the inflation rate is

5 percent, how much will the employee receive ten years after retirement in retirement-date buying power?

18-6. You begin to work for a company at age twenty-one. Thereafter, you change jobs every five years, just prior to completing your fifth year of employment. Finally, you retire just before your sixty-sixth birthday. Assuming your income did not change, you would be vested for what percentage of total benefits from all employees using

  a. Five-year full vesting?
  b. Phased-in vesting?

18-7. Turnover of employees for Ellsworth Corporation is high, 65 percent leaving as shown below. Exit rates are as follows:

Year after being hired	1	2	3	4	5
Percent leaving	20	20	10	10	5

If Ellsworth wants to minimize its pensions costs, should the company use five-year full vesting or phased-in vesting?

18-8. A pension fund portfolio received $100,000 from the sponsor at the beginning of the first year. Through investment return, this amount grew to $120,000 by the end of the first year. The fund then received an additional contribution of $30,000 from the sponsor, bringing the total value up to $150,000. Through investment return, the value grew to $160,000 by the end of the second year. What was the geometric mean return for the two-year period?

18-9. Pension fund Portfolio X earned an average return of 20 percent a year with a standard deviation of 20 percent. Pension fund Portfolio Y earned an average return of 24 percent with a standard deviation of 25 percent. If the risk-free interest rate was 8 percent, which fund was the superior performer?

18-10. Annual rates of return earned by two pension fund portfolios follow. Which portfolio had the better performance?

Year	1	2	3	4	5	6	7	8
Realized return								
Portfolio A	0.20	−0.15	0.00	0.30	−0.20	0.40	0.30	−0.20
Portfolio B	0.15	−0.10	0.00	0.20	−0.10	0.30	0.20	−0.10

CASE 15

THE COMPUTECH PENSION PLAN

In May 1988, Alecia Snyder was having lunch with Bryan Kemp, president of Computech, the computer software company with which she had been employed since completing her bachelor's degree in mathematics and computer systems four years before. Kemp asked Snyder how she was doing in the evening M.B.A. program at Springfield State, and she mentioned that they were presently studying pension funds in the financial institutions course. Kemp asked her what she thought of Computech's pension plan. She replied that she had not really given it a lot of thought but intended to look at the plan over the weekend. She thought this would be good reinforcement for her classroom exercises.

Kemp had been meaning to sit down and give some thought to the pension plan himself but did not feel very knowledgeable in this area. He asked Snyder to prepare a written analysis of the plan with any recommendations for changes. He told her he would instruct his secretary to allow her access to all of the files relating to the pension plan. While this was outside Snyder's normal area of responsibility as a systems programmer, she was pleased with the opportunity to use her newly acquired knowledge and to make a favorable impression on Kemp.

THE COMPANY

Computech was one of the many small software companies spawned by the rapid growth in computer usage. Much of this growth was stimulated by a key antitrust ruling

This case was prepared by Neil E. Seitz with assistance from Fred C. Yeager and William B. Gillespie. Dept. of Finance, Saint Louis University.

requiring large manufacturers such as IBM to price their software services separately from their computer hardware. This allowed companies such as Computech to enter the business of designing information systems and writing computer programs to meet the needs of individual computer users. This was entirely a service industry, with the software companies offering little more than skilled systems analysts and programmers.

Computech had been organized in 1970, when Kemp and three other employees of a large computer manufacturer resigned to form their own software company. They believed that a small software firm with reduced overhead could serve smaller businesses more effectively. Therefore, Computech specialized in providing programs and systems designs for small- to medium-sized businesses.

Because Computech's overhead costs were minimal, and because its concentration on the Springfield market virtually eliminated travel expense, Computech was able to offer its services at lower prices than those offered by the large manufacturers. However, Computech was not alone in this. There were approximately fifteen independent software firms operating in the Springfield area and competing directly with Computech. To succeed in this environment, it was necessary to attract high-quality programmers and analysts, and to offer programming and systems analysis services at the lowest possible prices.

Computech had indeed been able to compete successfully in this environment. From the original group of four people, Computech had grown to a total of twenty-four employees in eight years. Mr. Kemp attributed his success to three factors. First, all four of the original organizers had outstanding "human skills" as well as experience and ability in software creation. Thus, they were able to interact effectively with employees and customers. Computech had continued this pattern by always giving consideration to human skills as well as computer skills when hiring employees. Second, Computech had always offered its employees a good working environment and employee benefit package. This was believed to be important for attracting employees and for developing loyalty in an industry known for high employee turnover. Third, Kemp used the same services he sold to his customers. Very soon after the company began operations, Mr. Kemp implemented a management information system which provided excellent cost accounting data. This system contributed to appropriate pricing policies and provided excellent controls so that costs were kept in line. Thus Computech was competitive in price while providing excellent employee benefits.

Kemp felt that the company was now at a point where greater attention to long-term planning was required. In addition, he felt that there were areas in which increased efficiency could be achieved if he only had the time to do the analysis. If Snyder's study of the pension plan worked out, he hoped to assign her several other studies relating to financial planning.

THE PENSION PLAN

Shortly after the company was formed, Kemp realized the importance of developing inducements to attract and keep employees. A company needed to be cost-effective with employee benefits if it was to attract high-quality employees. While most software firms offered almost no fringe benefits at that time, Kemp believed that the addition of fringe benefits would increase the likelihood of attracting and retaining competent personnel. The first benefit which Computech provided was a term life insurance program. This benefit was obtainable at a low cost, since most of the employees were relatively young. This benefit seemed to be helpful in recruiting, and more benefits were soon added. These included medical insurance and a pension program.

The pension program, which was begun in 1972, was serviced by an insurance company. Like most smaller companies, Computech could not afford to provide portfolio and administrative management for a pension fund covering a relatively small number of people. Each month, Computech forwarded to the insurance company a sum equal to 10 percent of the gross income of each eligible employee. Half of this was contributed by Computech and the other half was deducted from the employee's salary. While no employee was required to participate, all eligible employees had elected to participate.

Pension fund contributions were used to purchase "units" in the insurance company's portfolio: a bond portfolio and a common stock portfolio. When the employee reached retirement age, the accumulated value of his units could be taken as a lump sum payment or could be used to purchase a fixed or variable annuity, at the employee's option. The variable annuity would provide fluctuating pension payments dependent on financial market returns, while the fixed annuity would simply pay a fixed return based on the number of units owned, the value of these units, and certain actuarial assumptions.

Computech had chosen to have half of the funds used to purchase stock portfolio units and half used to purchase bond portfolio units. The bond portfolio units remained at a constant price of $10. Each year, the beneficiary's bond account was credited with an amount equal to the yield on the pension fund bond portfolio times the value of his account at the beginning of the year, minus an administrative charge of 0.5 percent of asset value. The value of a unit in the stock portfolio changed each month with the values of the stocks in the portfolio. Dividend or interest income was reinvested on behalf of the beneficiary in additional units. Holding period return (HPR) earned on the stock portfolio each year was computed as

$$HPR = \frac{P_t - P_{t-1} + D_t}{P_{t-1}}$$

where P_t = price of a unit at the end of the year
        P_{t-1} = price of a unit at the beginning of the year, and
        D_t = dividends per unit during the year

Annual return on the stock portfolio, as well as average yield on the bond portfolio and relevant market information covering a twenty-year period, appears in exhibit 1. Both sets of returns are before the 0.5 percent per year service charge.

While Computech did not have enough employees to consider managing its own pension fund portfolio, certain options to the existing arrangements were available:

1. Change the bond and stock portfolio mix.
2. Change to a different insurance company.
3. Cancel the pension fund and give each employee a 5 percent pay raise. Employees who wanted pension protection could make private arrangements to pur-

chase mutual fund shares or make other investments with tax treatments similar to those for the pension fund contributions.

4. Replace the pension program with a profit-sharing program in which employees would be given shares of Computech with a book value equal to some fraction of net profit for the year. For the last three years, this would have resulted in an average cost approximately the same as the pension plan, but it would not have represented as great a drain on cash flows. The four founders presently held all of Computech's stock.

In addition to a possible change in the plan format, Kemp wondered if certain plan participant eligibility requirements should be changed. Under present rules, an employee became eligible for participation after three years of full-time employment. One-fourth of total wages paid by Computech were paid to employees who worked twenty hours a week or less, and one-third of the full-time employees left Computech during their first three years of employment. A recent study of the software industry, conducted by an industry trade association, concluded that half of the employees of a typical software firm changed employers before completing three years of service and only one-fifth of the employees tended to stay with the same company ten years or more. Kemp wondered whether the present eligibility rules were optimal with regard to cost and with the objective of attracting and maintaining a stable, talented work force.

Kemp did not give Snyder the impression that he was considering any particular change in policy with regard to the pension plan. As near as she could determine, his only interest was in a complete review to determine if the pension plan was the best available for achieving the objectives desired in a cost-efficient manner. Snyder collected information on the performance of the insurance company's fund in the years since Computech had been involved and for earlier years. She also collected the information on general stock market performance and interest rates that appears in table 1. She took this material home with her for the weekend to begin examining the problem.

QUESTIONS

1. Analyze the performance of the pension plan as compared to overall market performance. Has the insurance company fund outperformed the general market with regard to equity? Debt?

2. In what ways would a stock distribution plan as an alternative to the pension plan for Computech be more desirable? Be less desirable?

3. What changes, if any, should Snyder recommend to Kemp?

SELECTED REFERENCES

ARNOTT, ROBERT D. "The Pension Sponsor's View of Asset Allocation," *Financial Analysts Journal* 41 (September/October 1985): 17–23.

BERNSTEIN, P. L. "Asset Allocation: Things Are Not What They Seem," *Financial Analysts Journal* 43 (March/April 1987): 6–8.

Table 1

Computech Pension Fund Performance

Year	Equity Portfolio HPR	BOND PORTFOLIO		S&P 500 HPR	10-Year U.S. Govt. Bond Rate	6-Month T-Bill Rate	Inflation Rate
		Average Int. Rate	Market Price[1]				
1968	6.14%	5.62%	96.48%	10.84%	5.65%	5.47%	4.70%
1969	−5.49	6.06	95.42	−8.32	6.67	6.85	6.10
1970	−3.14	6.69	93.81	3.51	7.35	6.56	5.50
1971	20.10	7.15	96.34	14.12	6.16	4.51	3.40
1972	17.14	7.47	98.19	18.72	6.21	4.47	3.40
1973	−18.09	7.75	98.71	−14.50	6.84	7.18	8.80
1974	−30.94	8.20	96.66	−26.03	7.56	7.93	12.20
1975	31.98	8.76	95.36	36.92	7.99	6.12	7.00
1976	21.14	9.06	98.24	23.64	7.61	5.27	4.80
1977	−6.37	9.15	100.47	−7.16	7.42	5.51	6.80
1978	8.57	9.28	99.46	6.39	8.41	7.57	9.00
1979	15.91	9.58	97.22	18.19	9.44	10.02	13.30
1980	26.59	10.38	92.17	31.48	11.46	11.37	12.40
1981	−1.54	11.52	89.67	−4.85	13.91	13.78	8.90
1982	21.94	12.54	91.81	20.37	13.00	11.08	3.90
1983	25.04	12.94	98.54	22.31	11.10	8.75	3.80
1984	4.72	13.37	98.05	5.97	12.44	9.80	4.00
1985	32.65	13.45	101.79	31.06	10.62	7.66	3.80
1986	21.83	13.06	106.87	18.54	7.68	6.03	1.10

[1]As a percentage of cost.

BODIE, ZVI, ET AL. "Corporation Pension Policy: An Empirical Investigation," *Financial Analysts Journal* 41 (September/October 1985): 10–16.

EZRA, D. DON, AND AMBACHTSHEER, KEITH P. "Pension Funds: Rich or Poor?" *Financial Analysts Journal* 41 (March/April 1985): 43–56.

FELDSTEIN, MARTIN, AND SELIGMAN, STEPHANIE. "Pension Funding, Share Prices and National Savings," *The Journal of Finance* 36 (September 1981): 801–824.

HAWTHORN, F. "The Dawning of Performance Fees," *Institutional Investor* 20 (September 1986): 139–140+.

KOTLIKOFF, L. J., AND SMITH, D. E. *Pensions in the American Economy* (Chicago: University of Chicago Press, 1983).

LIEBOWITZ, M. L. "Pension Asset Allocation Through Surplus Management," *Financial Analysts Journal* 43 (March/April 1987): 29–40.

LYNN, ROBERT J. *The Pension Crisis* (Lexington, Mass.: Lexington Books, 1983).

MCKENNA, FRED W., AND KIM, YONG H. "Managerial Risk Preferences, Real Pension Costs, and Long-Run Corporate Pension Fund Investment Policy," *Journal of Risk and Insurance* 53 (March 1986): 29–48.

MICHAS, NICHOLAS A. "The Performance Measurement and Evaluation of a Corporate Retirement Plan: A Case Study," *The Financial Review* 21 (November 1986): 537–550.

PAUSTIAN, C., AND COHEN, S. "FASB 87 Impact Puts Pension Executives in Quandry Over Strategy," *Pension and Investment Age* 15 (June 1, 1987): 3+.

ROSEN, KENNETH. "The Role of Pension Funds in Housing Finance," *Housing Finance Review* 1 (April 1982): 147–177.

"Shifting the Asset Mix," *Institutional Investor* 21 (May 1987): 147–148.

"What's Ahead for Actual Assumptions?" *Institutional Investor* 20 (June 1986): 135–136.

19

International Aspects of Financial Institution Management

The topic of international finance is extremely broad, including the problems of exchange rate and balance of payments policy, the myriad international financial institutions, and the international aspects of financial management. In keeping with the purpose of this text, we concentrate on the international aspects of financial institution management and the role of financial institutions in facilitating international business. We concentrate on the primary financial problems and needs encountered by business and financial institutions dealing in the international sphere, and discuss the institutions, instruments, and conventions that have been developed to meet these needs.

DEVELOPMENT OF INTERNATIONAL BUSINESS

Economic history is characterized by growing interdependence. The industrial revolution led to interdependence between people and business units, and the growth of international business has led to growing interdependence between nations. The result has been a rising standard of living and a growing challenge to financial managers and policymakers.

Reasons for International Business

When asked why international business has expanded so rapidly, economists are quick to cite the *theory of comparative advantage*. Just as income within countries has been increased through specialization by individuals, world income can be increased through specialization by countries. For example, a country with a limited population and substantial potential for hydroelectric energy might concentrate on manufacturing processes requiring high-energy inputs and purchase products requiring extensive manual labor from a country with a large, low-skill population. Both countries would gain from the exchange.

The theory of comparative advantage certainly accounts for a substantial amount of export and import activity in a world in which raw materials, energy, capital, labor, and technology are so unevenly distributed. The advanced economies have primarily sold goods requiring highly skilled labor and capital-intensive production. Their imports, by comparison, have been raw materials and products requiring a substantial input of low-skill labor.

Technological advantage is a type of comparative advantage which deserves special attention. A country may have a technological advantage because of a sudden breakthrough, a highly educated population, or heavy investment in a particular technology. It could be argued that United States' domination of the international computer market for a number of years depended on some important conceptual breakthroughs, as well as on a heavy investment in engineering development and on a highly educated population. By comparison, the development of a new class of airplane, such as the Anglo-French Concorde, depends primarily on an engineering application of known technology. The fixed cost of converting this known technology to a tested airplane is measured in billions of dollars. The country that takes the initial risk in making this investment has a decided cost advantage over other countries considering their own production. Had the Concorde proved commercially feasible, the United States and Russia are the only other countries that could have been expected to make the investment necessary to develop a competitive airplane. Other countries wishing to own such airplanes would have purchased them from one of these countries, selling other goods to obtain the necessary funds.

Moving from import-export to internationalization of production, technological advantage again comes to play. A company with developed technology may take advantage of that technology by producing at home or in other countries. The production of foreign-designed automobiles in the United States is one such example. The construction of United States-designed calculators in developing countries for sale in the United States is an even more striking example of companies roaming the globe in search of comparative advantage in any one phase of their operation.

Differences in capital accumulation rates and in investment opportunities represent other reasons for foreign business. Other things being equal, investors will place their funds where the highest return can be earned. If a country has a mature economy, a nongrowing population, and a high savings rate, domestic investment opportunities are likely to be limited and businesses will look overseas for opportunities paying higher returns. Frequently, these may be found in countries with growing populations and limited savings. The overseas investments of oil-producing countries can also be explained in terms of an inability to find domestic investments paying a high rate of return. Their economies cannot absorb such huge amounts of capital efficiently.

Diversification and risk control are other motivations for foreign business. Investments or business operations in numerous countries help to diversify away risks unique to a particular country. Both business cycle risks and risks associated with government instability can be at least partially diversified away through international expansion.

Finally, much international business activity is motivated by the desire to avoid taxes or government regulation. For example, production may be moved to a country with minimal pollution laws. By operating in several countries, it is frequently possible, through altering methods of cost allocation, to shift at least some profits to the country with the most favorable tax structure.

Growth of International Business

International business is of growing importance to the United States (table 19-1). Particularly in the period since World War II, the United States has grown to be a major power in the international marketplace. Concurrently, the international marketplace has grown to be a major factor in the U.S. economy.

While the growth in international business is itself impressive, the changing nature of international business is of even greater significance. The trend has been away from the traditional import-export form of business toward truly multinational business, characterized by capital, technology, materials, and people moving across national boundaries with increased freedom. The dollar value of foreign investment by the U.S. in foreign countries and by foreign countries in the U.S. is shown in table 19-1.

Since World War II, exports and imports have grown at a more rapid rate than has the Gross National Product; inflows and outflows of capital have grown at an even faster rate.

Analyses of these international accounts and their rates of growth tend to underestimate the internationalization of business; they do not capture foreign control of

Table 19-1

Exports, Imports, and Capital Flows of the United States
(in $ billions)

YEAR	EXPORTS	IMPORTS	CAPITAL OUTFLOW	CAPITAL INFLOW
1946	12	5	1.6	2.1
1950	10	12	1.4	1.9
1955	14	12	1.5	1.5
1960	20	15	4	2.3
1965	26	22	6	0.7
1970	42	40	9	6
1975	107	98	40	16
1980	224	250	86	54
1985	214	339	32	127
1986*	220	367	98	223

*Estimated

Source: Department of Commerce, Bureau of Economic Analysis, and summarized in *Economic Report of the President.*

Table 19-2

Exports as a Percentage
of Gross National
Product, 1985

Belgium	68
Netherlands	55
Denmark	31
Sweden	31
West Germany	29
Austria	26
Canada	26
United Kingdom	22
France	19
Japan	14
Australia	13
United States	5

Source: *Statistical Abstract of
the United States.*

capital raised and invested within a country. For example, the building of a Volkswagen plant in the United States financed with borrowing in the United States, shows up as neither import nor capital flow. Thus, the growth of international business has been much more rapid than the growth of the domestic economy.

Banking provides yet another example of the growth of international business. In 1960, eight U.S. banks had overseas branches, and assets in these branches totaled $3.5 billion. By 1985, 164 U.S. banks had overseas branches with assets totaling $294 billion.

Before leaving this overview, we should note that for all this growth, international business remains much less important to the United States than to most other developed countries. The international business of some other countries can be compared to that of the United States (table 19-2). Because of its internal resources and diversity, the United States depends on foreign trade much less than any other developed capitalistic country.

SPECIAL PROBLEMS ENCOUNTERED IN INTERNATIONAL BUSINESS

The company involved in international business faces a number of problems not faced by the domestic company. First, there is the problem of managing exchange rate risk arising from the fact that different currencies are involved and the relative values of these currencies are subject to unexpected change. Second, the exporter or importer faces noncompliance risk arising from distance and lack of familiarity with the customer or supplier. Third, those involved in international business face country or sovereign risks—risks related to the economy, political, and social factors in a given country.

Finally, the truly international business faces the problem of raising and investing money in the international money and capital markets. Financial institutions aid nonfinancial businesses with each of these problems and use the international markets to make investments and raise funds for themselves. Each of the main problem areas of international business is discussed in the following sections.

EXCHANGE RATE RISK

One of the major problems in international finance results from the fact that the value of one currency relative to another is continually changing. Any international contract involving future payment requires that one side agree to transact in a currency other than that of his native country and accept the risk that the amount involved will, when converted to his own currency, be different than anticipated.

While we usually expect risk to decline as we gain experience in a particular area, foreign exchange risk has increased concurrent with the increased volume of international business. From the end of World War II until the late 1960s, exchange rates were held nearly constant by international agreement. The cornerstone of the agreement was the U.S. commitment to buy or sell any amount of gold at $35 an ounce. Imbalances between exports and imports were cleared through purchase and sale of U.S. dollars or gold. The lack of gold stock growth in relation to business growth led to problems in the 1960s; the first major break in stability was the devaluation of the British pound in 1967. What has happened since then is illustrated in figure 19-1, using the British pound and the German mark as examples. While the dollar has generally strengthened against the pound and weakened against the mark, it has become more volatile against both currencies. International business continues to grow in the face of this instability, because methods of dealing with these risks have been developed.

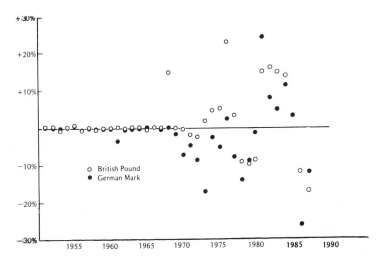

Figure 19-1 Percentage change in value of the dollar with respect to other currencies.

Managing Exchange Rate Risk

The possibility of a change in the relative values of currencies creates two primary types of risk: *translation risk* and *transaction risk*. These risks and methods of dealing with them are discussed in the following paragraphs.

Translation risk arises primarily from accounting conventions. A U.S. firm with interests in several countries must somehow convert all of its assets to dollar values for the purpose of preparing annual reports. The current rules on translation are spelled out in *Financial Accounting Standards Board Statement 52 (FASB 52)*.

As a very simple example of what happens under current accounting rules, consider a U.S. firm that owns securities denominated in deutsch marks (DM) and also owes money payable in DM. The securities are valued at 2,000 DM and the debt is for 1,200 DM; the company's DM monetary assets exceed its DM monetary liabilities by 800 DM. If the DM is worth $0.60 at the beginning of the year and $0.50 at the end of the year, the company will be required to report a loss of $80 (0.60 × 800 − 0.50 × 800) for the year, even though it did not sell the securities or pay the debt. The risk of having to report a loss because of the rules used in translating foreign assets, liabilities, and income to U.S. dollars is referred to as *translation risk*. Translation problems can also arise in areas like depreciation computation and inventory/cost of goods sold calculations when business is conducted in more than one country.

The situation becomes more complex when the U.S. firm has subsidiaries operating in various countries. Current rules may require the company to report an exchange rate loss even if one subsidiary has DM monetary assets and another subsidiary has DM monetary liabilities of exactly the same amount. Under FASB #52 these DM asset and liability positions are not necessarily netted against each other in consolidation when they are housed in different subsidiaries. Thus, there is the potential for the company to be exposed to translation risk if any subsidiary has a mismatch between financial assets and liabilities denominated in other currencies.

Transaction risk represents a more immediate and more real risk. Transaction risk occurs when there are outstanding contracts calling for payment or receipt in a currency other than that of the home country. They occur because of purchase or sale on credit as well as from contracts for future delivery with the price agreed upon today. Suppose a U.S. firm agrees to purchase German goods for one million DM at a time when the exchange rate is $0.6075 per DM. The goods are to be delivered and paid for in ninety days and the importer has contracted to resell them for $620,000 in the United States. At the present exchange rate, the goods would cost $607,500 (1,000,000 × 0.6075). Thus the importer expects to sell the goods for $12,500 above cost. However, if the exchange rate should rise to above 0.62 by the end of the ninety-day period, the products will be sold at a loss instead of a gain. Clearly, some method of eliminating these risks is desirable.

Balance sheet hedging (also referred to as money market hedging) provides an effective method of controlling exchange rate risk. It is most widely used to control translation risk, although it can be used to control transaction risk. Essentially, a company (or each subsidiary of a company) strives to have net financial assets in each currency exactly equal to financial liabilities in that currency. We started this example with a company that had DM assets 800 DM in excess of its DM liabilities. A balance sheet hedge would consist of arranging an 800 DM loan and using the proceeds to make investments denominated in dollars. The company that contracted to pay for German goods in ninety days could hedge by buying marks today and investing them in German bank certificates of deposit or other DM-denominated investments. This would, however, have the disadvantage of tying up funds for ninety days.

Currency futures provide another widely used method of hedging against exchange rate risks. Currency futures, or forward exchange contracts, are handled in a manner similar to forward contracts for commodities. Two parties enter into a contract, agreeing to exchange a certain amount of one currency for a certain amount of another currency at a specified future date. If we enter into a futures contract for French francs, we ensure ourselves a certain number of francs at a specified price while the other party is ensured a certain amount of dollars at a fixed price in francs.

The use of a forward exchange contract can be illustrated with the German goods example from above. The forward exchange quotes from the *Wall Street Journal* appear in table 19-3. Our purchaser of German goods sees that he can purchase ninety-day forward exchange contracts for marks at 0.6136. In other words, he can contract to purchase marks at $0.6136 each. This ensures him a total cost of $613,600 and secures a profit on the purchase and resale of goods.

The forward exchange market operates in a manner similar to the over-the-counter securities market. There is no central meeting place.[1] The market consists of a few large banks and a handful of foreign exchange dealers and brokers who make a market among each other. The banks then transact with customers either directly or through their correspondent banks. Participants in the market include industrial corporations as well as financial institutions covering their own positions and speculators hoping to make a profit by correctly predicting the direction of forward exchange rates.

The forward exchange market is quite limited. There are only a few major currencies involved, and the longest contract normally available is for 180 days.

Currency swaps are another useful tool for managing exchange rate risk. A currency swap is a spot transaction in one direction offset by a futures contract in the opposite direction. For example, we exchange dollars for yen today, agreeing to reverse the transaction at a specified future date. The exchange rate at the future date is agreed to now but may not be the same as the spot rate. Swaps may be used when futures contracts are not available. Swaps are sometimes offered by governments wishing to stabilize their currency.

Currency options provide yet another—and rapidly growing—approach to controlling exchange rate risks. Like other option contracts, the currency option gives its holder the right, but not the obligation, to purchase a stated amount of a particular currency at a fixed price prior to a specified expiration date. A U.S. company with a DM liability could eliminate its exchange rate risk by purchasing an option to acquire DM at a fixed price. The option contract is particularly popular when the future obligation is

---

[1]An exception is the Chicago Board of Options Exchange, which maintains a physical location for dealing in currency futures.

Table 19-3

Foreign Exchange

Friday, January 8, 1988
The New York foreign exchange selling rates below apply to trading among banks in amounts of $1 million and more, as
quoted at 3 p.m. Eastern time by Bankers Trust Co. Retail transactions provide fewer units of foreign currency per dollar.

Country	U.S. Fri.	$ equiv. Thrs.	CURRENCY PER U.S. $ Fri.	CURRENCY PER U.S. $ Thrs.
Argentina (Austral)	.2646	.2857	3.78	3.50
Australia (Dollar)	.7060	.7075	1.4164	1.4134
Austria (Schilling)	.08606	.08658	11.62	11.55
Belgium (Franc)				
Commercial rate	.02895	.02914	34.54	34.32
Financial rate	.02886	.02907	34.64	34.40
Brazil (Cruzado)	.01343	.01364	74.44	73.34
Britain (Pound)	1.8125	1.8060	.5517	.5537
30-Day Forward	1.8100	1.8037	.5525	.5544
90-Day Forward	1.8051	1.7993	.5540	.5558
180-Day Forward	1.7972	1.7929	.5564	.5578
Canada (Dollar)	.7781	.7770	1.2852	1.2870
30-Day Forward	.7771	.7762	1.2868	1.2884
90-Day Forward	.7756	.7747	1.2893	1.2909
180-Day Forward	.7735	.7725	1.2929	1.2945
Chile (Official rate)	.004099	.004302	243.97	232.43
China (Yuan)	.2687	.2687	3.7220	3.7220
Colombia (Peso)	.003786	.003815	264.10	262.14
Denmark (Krone)	.1575	.1587	6.3480	6.3025
Ecuador (Sucre)				
Official rate	.003953	.0040486	253.00	247.00
Floating rate	.004454	.004728	224.50	211.50
Finland (Markka)	.2480	.2491	4.0320	4.0140
France (Franc)	.1800	.1795	5.5545	5.5725
30-Day Forward	.1799	.1793	5.5595	5.5780
90-Day Forward	.1794	.1788	5.5735	5.5925
180-Day Forward	.1788	.1781	5.5925	5.6140
Greece (Drachma)	.007619	.007675	131.25	130.30
Hong Kong (Dollar)	.1286	.1285	7.7770	7.7800
India (Rupee)	.07628	.07639	13.11	13.09
Indonesia (Rupiah)	.0006039	.0006061	1656.00	1650.00
Ireland (Punt)	1.6100	1.6200	.6211	.6173
Israel (Shekel)	.6452	.6441	1.5500	1.5525
Italy (Lira)	.0008264	.0008278	1210.00	1208.00
Japan (Yen)	.007773	.007728	128.65	129.40
30-Day Forward	.007795	.007750	128.29	129.03
90-Day Forward	.007836	.007789	127.62	128.38
180-Day Forward	.007902	.007852	126.55	127.35
Jordan (Dinar)	2.9762	2.9155	0.336	0.343
Kuwait (Dinar)	3.7106	3.6590	.2695	.2733
Lebanon (Pound)	.002030	.002146	492.50	466.00
Malaysia (Ringgit)	.3945	.3948	2.5350	2.5330

Malta (Lira)	3.1496	3.1447	.3175	.3180
Mexico (Peso)				
Floating rate	.0004545	.0004545	2200.00	2200.00
Netherland (Guilder)	.5405	.5422	1.8500	1.8460
New Zealand (Dollar)	.6465	.6475	1.5468	1.5444
Norway (Krone)	.1579	.1579	6.3325	6.3320
Pakistan (Rupee)	.05731	.05714	17.45	17.50
Peru (Inti)	.03030	.03030	33.00	33.00
Philippines (Peso)	.04824	.04824	20.73	20.73
Portugal (Escudo)	.007366	.007380	135.75	135.50
Saudi Arabia (Riyal)	.2666	.2666	3.7505	3.7505
Singapore (Dollar)	.4909	.4921	2.0370	2.0320
South Africa (Rand)				
Commercial rate	.5090	.5105	1.9646	1.9589
Financial rate	.3187	.3200	3.1377	3.1250
South Korea (Won)	.001263	.001258	791.70	795.10
Spain (Peseta)	.008893	.008956	112.45	111.65
Sweden (Krona)	.1677	.1685	5.9620	5.9350
Switzerland (Franc)	.7429	.7438	1.3460	1.3445
30-Day Forward	.7460	.7469	1.3404	1.3389
90-Day Forward	.7515	.7520	1.3306	1.3297
180-Day Forward	.7596	.7601	1.3165	1.3157
Taiwan (Dollar)	.03511	.03511	28.48	28.48
Thailand (Baht)	.03970	.03969	25.19	25.19
Turkey (Lira)	.0009679	.001012	1033.13	987.82
United Arab (Dirham)	.2723	.2723	3.673	3.673
Uruguay (New Peso)				
Financial	.003552	.003660	281.50	273.25
Venezuela (Bolivar)				
Official rate	.1333	.1333	7.50	7.50
Floating rate	.06897	.03396	14.50	29.45
W. Germany (Mark)	.6075	.6064	1.6460	1.6490
30-Day Forward	.6095	.6084	1.6407	1.6436
90-Day Forward	.6136	.6125	1.6297	1.6327
180-Day Forward	.6198	.6185	1.6135	1.6167
SDR	z	1.37814	z	0.724998
ECU	1.24774	1.25844	......	....

Special Drawing Rights are based on exchange rates for the U.S., West German, British, French and Japanese currencies. Source: International Monetary Fund.

ECU is based on a basket of community currencies.

Source: European Community Commission.

z-Not quoted.

Source: Reprinted by permission of the *Wall Street Journal* © Dow Jones & Company, Inc., January 11, 1988. All rights reserved.

uncertain; an offer to purchase something with payment in DM has been made, for example, and there is still a question about whether the offer will be accepted. Unlike stock options which are heavily traded by individual investors, most currency options are written by large banks and purchased by corporations.

The European currency unit (ECU) is another vehicle for decreasing exchange rate risk. The ECU is a package of currency consisting of stated amounts of the currency of each of the countries in the European Economic Community. If a loan or other contract calling for future payment is stated in ECUs, the portfolio effect reduces the exchange risk associated with any single currency.

Interest Rates and Exchange Rates

The relationship between exchange rates and interest rates is an excellent example of how the opportunity for arbitrage serves to remove market differentials. The "spot" or current U.S. dollar equivalent for French francs is 0.1800, while the 180-day future rate is 0.1788 (table 19-3). This reflects an expectation that the value of the franc will fall relative to the dollar. International finance theory would suggest that changes in exchange rates are strongly affected by differences in inflation rates between countries. A future rate for the franc below the spot rate is evidence that investors expect the French inflation rate to be higher than the U.S. inflation rate over the next 180 days.

Since interest rates normally increase when expected inflation increases, we would expect interest rates to be higher in France than in the United States. However, the forward exchange rate sets a limit on how much higher or lower this rate will be. Suppose, for example, that 180-day U.S. Treasury bills are presently selling at a discount sufficient to provide a 4.0 percent return over the 180-day period (an equivalent yield of 8 percent on an annual basis). If 180-day French government obligations were selling to yield 4.5 percent per 180-day period, a French investor or financial institution could improve return with no increase in risk by purchasing a U.S. Treasury bill and selling U.S. dollars on a 180-day forward contract. The return on a 5,341,880 French franc investment would be as follows:

Purchase dollars at current spot rate (5,341,880 × 0.1800)	$961,538
Purchase U.S. Treasury bills with a face value of $1,000,000, discounted to yield 4 percent over a 180-day period	$961,538
Simultaneously purchase a forward contract for $1 million worth of French francs in 180 days at 0.1788 per franc: $1,000,000/0.1788	5,592,841 F
Hold Treasury bills until maturity and receive face value	$1,000,000
Complete forward contract to purchase francs	5,592,841 F
Return earned 5,592,841 ÷ 5,341,880 − 1	4.70%

If French government 180-day obligations are selling to yield less than 4.7 percent per 180-day period, the French investor can improve his position by investing in U.S. Treasury obligations and using a forward exchange contract to protect himself from exchange rate risk. The reverse is also true. If the rate in France were over 4.7 percent, an American investor could improve his position by purchasing French government obligations and hedging against exchange rate risk by contracting to sell francs in 180 days.

The calculation of the interest rate that would prevent investors from either country gaining by investment in the other country can be found using a simple formula instead of the extensive calculation above:

$$R_f = \frac{S}{F}(1 + R_d) - 1$$

(19-1)

where R_f = interest rate for the period on risk-free obligations in the foreign country
S = spot value of a unit of the foreign country's currency
F = forward value of a unit of the foreign country's currency
R_d = domestic risk-free interest rate for the period

Applying the formula to the previous example, we confirm the previous solution and the correctness of the formula:

$$R_f = \frac{0.1800}{0.1788} (1 + 0.04) - 1 = 4.70\%.$$

Of course, the fact that everyone could take advantage of this risk-free opportunity to increase return is likely to decrease or eliminate such opportunities. A flow of capital from France to the United States and the offsetting demand for future contracts to buy francs would drive the French interest rates up, the U.S. interest rates down, and the forward value of francs up until the potential profit disappeared. Thus we would expect to find the relationship between interest rates and exchange rates shown in equation 19-1 to hold in general.

FINANCING EXPORTS AND IMPORTS

The purchase and sale of goods across international borders involves several problems that do not exist or are much less difficult to handle for domestic sales. First, a contract calling for future payment requires that payment be specified in some currency. If the contract calls for payment in the importer's currency, the exporter must accept the risk that an unfavorable movement in the exchange rate between the two currencies will result in his receiving less than anticipated, and vice versa. Second, the problem of dealing with noncompliance—failure to deliver goods according to contract or failure to make payment according to contract—is more difficult to deal with because of distance, unfamiliarity, and different legal systems. Third, credit is needed for longer periods of time because of distances and shipping times involved. Exchange rate risk was treated as a separate topic. The second two problems are treated in this section.

Assuring Compliance (Banker's Acceptances)

Every domestic seller of goods on credit must make the sale decision based on knowledge of the creditworthiness of the potential buyer. The decision is normally based on substantial personal knowledge of the buyer or readily available credit information sources. In the international marketplace, information on creditworthiness is limited by distance, language barriers, infrequency of trade, and other factors. Furthermore, a domestic firm's credit manager is likely to be quite knowledgeable with regard to the status of a claim in the courts in the event of a payment default. In the international marketplace, the status of a claim in the courts, and even the proper jurisdiction, is likely to be subject to question. Thus, legal remedy is uncertain and expensive. Finally, the distances involved in shipment frequently make longer credit periods necessary, again increasing risk exposure.

From the buyer's point of view, there are also increased risks. A failure to ship goods per contract specifications on a domestic order can be remedied by returning goods or turning to a familiar court system. Again, great distances and unfamiliar court systems decrease the buyer's confidence in his ability to achieve adequate remedies in the case of default. The problem is again complicated by lack of direct knowledge about the seller. The problems cited above must be overcome if international trade is to flourish. The procedures that have evolved for dealing with these problems are outlined in the following paragraphs.

Transaction procedures must deal with the uncertainties suffered by both exporter and importer. Essentially, the procedures that have evolved recognize two facts:

1. Trust, not the availability of legal remedies, is the foundation for most transactions.
2. A promise to pay by a major international bank will be accepted with little or no question.

The process involved in substituting the bank's credit for the individual importer's credit is outlined in figure 19-2.

First, of course, importer and exporter must come to an agreement on product, price, shipping method, etc. Second, the importer applies to the bank for a letter of credit. The letter of credit authorizes the seller to write a draft on the buyer's bank for a specified amount upon shipment of the goods. Upon receipt of the letter of credit, the seller ships the goods. The seller then forwards the draft and the bill of lading (proof of shipment) to the seller's bank. The seller's bank forwards this material to the buyer's bank, possibly going through a correspondent if the two banks do not have a correspondent relationship. The buyer's bank examines the documents to ensure that the shipment was consistent with the letter of credit. If the draft is a sight draft, the buyer's bank then pays the seller's bank by crediting its account. More typically though, the letter of credit authorizes a draft payable on a specified date up to 180 days after shipment. If this is the case, the buyer's bank marks the draft "ACCEPTED" or "I ACCEPT" and returns it to the seller's bank. The draft is now referred to as a *banker's acceptance* because it has been accepted and is virtually certain to be paid upon maturity.

Upon receipt of the accepted draft, the seller's bank will ask the seller for instructions. The seller may want to hold the draft until maturity and receive the full face value. Or instead, the seller may instruct the bank that it wants to receive its money right away. In this case, the amount the seller will receive is the discounted value, an amount enough below the face value to provide a competitive return to whoever holds the banker's acceptance until maturity. The seller's bank may hold the draft until maturity and then receive the face value, earning the difference between the face value and what it paid the seller.

If neither the seller nor the seller's bank wants to hold the draft, two alternatives remain. The buyer's bank may simply pay the discounted value immediately; thus, it will pay out less than it will collect from the buyer and will earn a return similar to what it

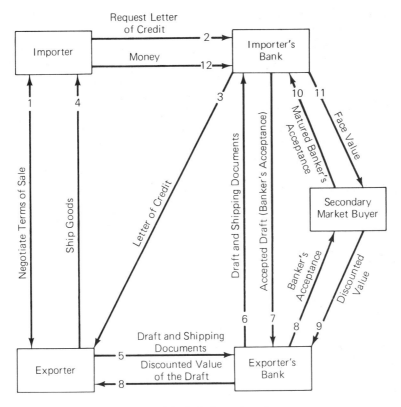

Figure 19-2   Banker's acceptance flow.

could have earned elsewhere. Most banker's acceptances are held by either the buyer's bank or the seller's bank. However, if neither of these banks has funds available to invest, the draft can be sold in a limited second market. In a sale in the second market (figure 19-2), the seller's bank will receive the discounted value immediately, and the second market buyer will receive the face value at maturity. This secondary market sale would be handled by the seller's bank, which would contract one of the several government securities dealers who also make markets in banker's acceptances. Of course, the banker's acceptance could, like any money market instrument, be sold again before maturity if the original borrower needed funds. Many banker's acceptances sold in the secondary market are held by commercial banks as secondary reserves.

In addition to handling the problem of assuring compliance, banker's acceptances have become an important method of financing imports and exports. One reason they are popular as a financing method is that they allow the buyer's bank to provide credit to a customer even when it is fully loaned up. The letter of credit and the marketable banker's acceptance provide a way to finance a purchase without the seller, the buyer, or the buyer's bank being required to tie up funds. Banker's acceptances outstanding in the United States totaled $68 billion late in 1987.

Export Credit Insurance

Export credit insurance provides a method of dealing with both country risk and risk associated with a particular customer. In the United States, export credit insurance is provided primarily through the Foreign Credit Insurance Association (FCIA), an association of insurance companies working in conjunction with the Export-Import Bank of the United States. FCIA provides insurance against both commercial risk and political risk on American products sold abroad for credit. Commercial risks involve delayed payment or failure to pay for reasons covering the gamut of factors leading to failure to pay in domestic trade. FCIA has paid off in cases of failure running from competitive difficulties to theft, fire, and earthquake. Political risk covers war, expropriation, cancelation of import and export licenses, and so on. Insurance can be provided for short periods of time or for credit terms up to seven years in certain cases. Policies are normally sold for all shipments over a period of time rather than for just one shipment. The percent of loss covered by the policy varies from 90 percent to 98 percent. Premiums depend on length of time involved, category of country, and the riskiness of the credit involved.

Special Sources of Import-Export Credit

While the banker's acceptance has proved to be a very useful method of handling transactions and a satisfactory source of short-term credit, it does not meet all the needs of exporters for extended credit terms. Most developed countries have some government agency which provides credit to encourage exports. In the United States that organization is the *Export-Import Bank.* The Export-Import Bank was started in 1934 to aid companies in importing and exporting. Actually, it was started to encourage the development of trade with Russia.

The Export-Import Bank is a quasi-public agency with a president and vice-president appointed by the President of the United States. The bank is financed through the purchase of equity, all of which is owned by the U.S. Treasury.

The Export-Import Bank's primary mode of activity involves support of commercial banks. The Export-Import Bank guarantees intermediate-term export obligations with maturities of six months to five years. Additionally, the Export-Import Bank purchases debt obligations of foreign borrowers from United States banks. Both short- and intermediate-term obligations are purchased in this manner. Through these two routes the Export-Import Bank provides funds or support to banks lending money to exporters.

In addition to the support of banks, the Export-Import Bank also makes direct loans to foreign purchasers of U.S. goods. These direct loans are primarily participation loans with other financial institutions. Finally, the Export-Import Bank makes loans to foreign financial institutions that in turn loan money to small businesses purchasing U.S. goods.

As the above brief outline shows, the Export-Import Bank acts primarily in conjunction with other financial institutions. It serves to increase the ability of financial institutions to serve the needs of their customers rather than as a source of competition to financial institutions. The private financial institution can frequently provide greater credit service at lower risk by using the services of the Export-Import Bank.

The Private Export Funding Corporation (PEFCO) can reasonably be thought of as another extension of the services of the Export-Import Bank. The PEFCO was formed in 1970 through the efforts of the Bankers' Association for Foreign Trade. It makes loans to foreign purchasers of U.S. goods. All of its loans are guaranteed by the Export-Import Bank. Because it is privately owned—primarily by a group of large banks— PEFCO provides another source of credit, drawing on the Export-Import Bank guarantee to increase the supply of export credit available. PEFCO borrows in the long-term security markets, issuing secured notes.

INTERNATIONAL CAPITAL MARKETS

Along with the change from concentration on export-import operations to multinational production has come an increased tendency to turn to international capital markets for funds. Companies are motivated to use the international capital markets by considerations of balance sheet hedging, cost, and tax considerations. Funds are raised through Eurobonds, foreign bonds, and financial institutions specializing in international lending.

A *foreign bond* is issued primarily in one country, is denominated in the currency of that country, and is the obligation of a corporation headquartered in another country. For example, a foreign automobile producer such as Toyota or Volkswagen might issue dollar-denominated bonds in the United States for the purpose of building a plant in the United States. These would be foreign bonds because they are denominated and sold in the United States but are an obligation of the foreign manufacturer. Such a bond issue might be motivated by cost of capital considerations or a desire for exchange rate hedging.

Foreign bond issues are sold through the services of financial institutions normally handling bond underwritings in the country in which the issue is being sold. In the United States, this would be an investment banking firm. In most other countries, commercial banks are allowed to provide this service and are the institutions primarily involved.

A *Eurobond* is in a sense a more truly "international" issue. The Eurobond is sold principally in countries other than the country of the currency in which it is denominated. It is usually underwritten by an international syndicate of underwriters: major European banks, European branches of United States banks, and banks from other major financial centers. For tax and other reasons, the issue is usually sold to people who are not citizens or residents of the country of denomination. These bonds are usually sold on general reputation rather than financial analysis or bond ratings. Thus, only the best known international firms are able to use this source of funds. Approximately two-thirds of the amount of Eurobonds outstanding is denominated in U.S. dollars. Not infrequently, companies headquartered outside the United States use the Eurobond market to raise funds in other non-U.S. countries, denominated in U.S. dollars.

U.S. companies selling bonds overseas were hampered by a U.S. withholding tax requirement and are still hampered by a requirement that they identify foreign purchasers of their bonds. These rulings have been circumvented through the use of an offshore finance subsidiary. The finance subsidiary is incorporated in a tax haven country such as Switzerland, the Bahamas, or the Netherland Antilles. The subsidiary is wholly owned by the United States company, and its sole purpose is to borrow money through the sale of bonds and relend it to the parent company, thereby paying interest from a foreign country and avoiding the U.S. regulations.

In addition to the above-mentioned bond markets, there are a number of financial institutions that specialize in providing capital on an international basis. Most of these specialize in loans to countries, but some also participate in purchases of private debt and equity. Foremost among these is the World Bank Group. The primary institution of the World Bank Group is the International Bank for Reconstruction and Development, also called the World Bank. The World Bank makes loans only to countries. The International Finance Corporation, another member of the World Bank Group, specializes in direct investments in businesses in developing countries. It specializes in participation equity investments in basic industries such as steel and cement. Finally, there are a number of national development banks and private development banks that specialize in private loans. The Atlantic Development Group for Latin America (ADELA) is a good example. It is owned by more than 200 large corporations and invests in participations in private business enterprises in Latin American countries.

Country Risk

Country risk has always been a problem faced by international businesses. It has become a problem of growing concern in recent years as banks and other private companies have become more involved in loans or joint investment projects with foreign governments. Country risk, at its most obvious level, deals with the political and social stability of the country. Revolutions or social upheavals occur with sufficient frequency to be considered real risks to international businesses.

Other country risks relate more to the economic position of the country. For example, direct loans and joint investments with a foreign government become risky if that government is so heavily in debt that its ability to make payments is in question. Problems of this type have arisen with regard to bank loans to foreign governments. Some governments borrowed heavily in the late 1970s and early 1980s in anticipation of increased exports or of higher oil prices. These did not occur, and the governments were left with no way to repay their foreign debts without applying such stringent internal economic policies that they would risk revolution.

Latin America has been a particularly troublesome area with regard to problem loans over the past several years. Latin American countries have developed large debt burdens and have suffered declines in per-capita income in recent years. Brazil, for example, had foreign debt service obligations of 5.8 percent of gross domestic product in 1987. A near crisis was triggered in early 1987 when Brazil declared a moratorium on $12 billion of interest to foreign lenders while demanding more loans and restructuring of existing debt to bring its debt service to $2\frac{1}{2}$ percent of gross domestic product. Brazil's threat was a general default if it did not get what it wanted.

Loans by major U.S. banks to large developing country borrowers are summa-

Table 19-4

Developing Country Loans by Nine Leading U.S. Money Center Banks as of September 30, 1986 (in $ millions)

COUNTRY	LOANS OUTSTANDING	PERCENTAGE OF TOTAL CAPITAL
Brazil	$15,000	33.2%
Mexico	13,428	29.7
Venezuela	6,744	14.9
Argentina	5,914	13.1
Chile	4,136	9.2
South Korea	3,758	8.3
Philippines	3,567	7.9

Source: Thomas H. Hanley, et al. *A Review of Bank Performance.* New York: Salomon Brothers, Inc. 1987.

rized in table 19-4. These nine banks account for approximately 60 percent of total U.S. bank loans to these countries.

Export credit insurance is one response to country risk. By acquiring export credit insurance, a company can eliminate or sharply decrease both credit and country risk.

Another response to both credit and country risk is the rise of the international banker as a provider of information. A U.S. company considering a sale to a Brazilian company can use the services of Citibank or another of the international banks. Citibank's local office in Brazil will be able to provide information about the specific company involved that would not be readily available to the exporter from other sources. In addition, Citibank can provide important information about political and economic conditions so that the exporter can better guage both near-term risk and the likelihood of the business relationship's becoming permanent. A major part of the activity of international bankers is the provision of information of this type to their customers.

INTERNATIONAL BANKING AND INTERNATIONAL CREDIT MARKETS

In the previous parts of this chapter, international banks have been mentioned in relation to various aspects of the solution of international business problems. In this section, we focus directly on the development and operation of these international banks.

European banks became active in the international markets during the period of colonization and have therefore had several centuries of experience. U.S. banks, on the other hand, were largely restricted from international activities until the Federal Reserve Act of 1913. However, this authorization did not lead to a rush toward international banking; by 1919, only one bank had established an overseas branch. The Edge Act of 1919 further expanded the authority of banks to engage in international activity.

This act did not lead to a rush either. As late as 1960, only eight banks had overseas branches, and these branches had assets totaling $3.5 billion.

Growth of U.S. international banking remained modest through 1965 but then accelerated rapidly. By 1970, there were seventy-nine banks with foreign branches, and assets held by these branches totaled $46.5 billion. By 1985, there were 164 banks with overseas branches. Overseas branches totaled 1,001; assets held by these branches totaled $294 billion. Since 1960, the number of banks involved has increased twenty fold, and assets involved have increased a hundredfold.

This rapid growth occurred for two reasons. First, growth of international business was rapid during this period (table 19-1). U.S. businesses expanding their international activities needed new services, and U.S. banks moved to provide these services. Second, various capital flow constraints were introduced by the U.S. and other governments when they experienced balance of payments deficits. Thus, it became quite difficult for a bank to serve its customers' needs from a domestic base. Overseas branches made it possible to raise money in other markets, thereby avoiding capital flow restrictions.

International Banking Offices

Banks wishing to enter into international activities have a number of choices with regard to the types of arrangements they can use. These range from simply establishing correspondent relationships with foreign banks to operation of full-service facilities.

Correspondent Relationships   Correspondent relationships with other banks are an important part of banking in the United States. Similar correspondent relationships are maintained with foreign banks. Because banks maintain deposits with their correspondents, the correspondent relationship can be used to clear checks or drafts and transfer funds by adding to or subtracting from each other's account balances. Correspondent banks can also be used for foreign exchange needs and to provide information about local conditions. As will be seen later in this chapter, the correspondent relationship is a key factor in the operation of the Eurodollar market.

Representative Offices   Representative offices provide a low-level method for a bank to have a direct presence in another country. The representative office has no assets other than furniture. However, it provides an important contact point to gain the information necessary to keep customers informed about the country where the office is located. The representative office also provides a facility for soliciting business and maintaining contact with correspondent banks.

Shell Branches   Shell branches are used to enter into foreign transactions such as Eurodollar transactions, currency transactions, and participations in syndicated loans that would be more heavily regulated in the home country or would be taxed if carried out in the home country. Nassau and the Cayman Islands are popular locations for shell branches. Actions carried out through these branches normally reflect decisions made at the home office and are simply executed by wire from the branch location. Over half of the banks with overseas operations have only shell branches. In addition, banks with more extensive overseas operations also have shell branches to avoid taxes or regulation.

Foreign Branches   Foreign branches operate as branches of the domestic parent bank and are located in foreign countries. Because the foreign branch is a legal part of the parent bank, it is subject to reserve requirements and other regulations that apply to the parent. In addition, these branches are subject to the banking laws of the country in which they operate. Because of their status as a legal part of the parent, foreign branches are viewed as very safe by depositors because they have the full credit of the parent behind them. Foreign branches are an extremely important vehicle for provision of international banking services. They make loans, take deposits, handle funds transfers and foreign exchange, and provide information to businesses wishing to do business overseas.

Edge Act Corporations   Edge corporations were first allowed under the Edge Act of 1919. They are established as subsidiaries of banks and are allowed to engage in international financing activities prohibited to the parent corporation. Edge Act corporations may own foreign banking subsidiaries (banks can only have foreign branches) and are also allowed to make equity investments. Edge Act corporations are used to finance long-term industrial projects by providing long-term debt and equity capital.

Consortiums and Syndicates   Many loans are too big for any single bank to handle. A standard method of handling larger business has been the syndicate. This is simply an agreement among a number of banks for each bank to grant a business or a country a specified amount of the total loan for which it has applied. Syndicated loans are common in both domestic and international lending. A consortium bank, on the other hand, is a separately incorporated bank owned by a number of other banks and used as a vehicle. Nordicbank, for example, is a consortium bank organized by a number of banks located in Scandinavian countries to carry out international banking activities.

INTERNATIONAL PAYMENTS SYSTEM

Like a domestic payment system, the international payment system depends on instructions to banks to transfer ownership of deposits rather than on the physical transfer of currency or metal. The process can be illustrated with a draft created through import of goods to the United States. Let us say that German goods were purchased with a letter of credit authorizing the German firm to write a draft of $1 million on Morgan Guaranty Trust, the United States purchaser's bank. The German exporting company deposits the draft with its bank, Deutsche Bank, acquiring a $1 million deposit denominated in dollars. Deutsche Bank gains an asset of $1 million in the form of a deposit with Morgan and a $1 million liability in the form of a customer deposit. The German exporter may now use the dollar deposit to pay dollar obligations, convert it to marks, or hold it as a dollar investment.

Suppose the German firm owes $1 million to a British firm that wants payment in the form of a deposit at National Westminster Bank in London. The German firm instructs Deutsche Bank to transfer the $1 million to National Westminster in payment. Deutsche Bank carries out this instruction by wiring Morgan in New York to transfer ownership of a $1 million deposit to National Westminster. Morgan then notifies National Westminster by wire that the $1 million has been credited to its account and National Westminster notifies its customer, completing the transaction.

If the German business had no dollar debts, it could decide to convert the funds to deutsche marks. The German firm would instruct Deutsche Bank to convert the dollars to marks. As a major money market bank, Deutsche Bank will have an inventory of dollar deposits for trading purposes and will be able to immediately quote the German firm a rate. Assuming the conversion rate in table 19-3, the German firm will be able to exchange a $1 million deposit for 1,646,000 marks (minus the fee charged by the bank). Payment will be made by deducting $1 million from the German firm's dollar deposit balance and adding 1,646,000 to its mark balance. Because the bank made the exchange based on its own position, its dollar deposit assets have remained constant while its dollar liabilities have decreased. Deutsche Bank still has the $1 milion deposit with Morgan.

As a continual buyer and seller of deposits denominated in various currencies, Deutsche Bank may decide to simply hold the dollar deposit in its own inventory. If, on the other hand, Deutsche Bank now feels that it is holding excess dollars, its trading department will use its telephone networks to exchange some dollars for marks. Suppose Deutsche Bank feels that its dollar holdings are excessive and Credit Lyonnais in France—one of the money market banks with which Deutsche Bank is in constant contact—feels that its mark holdings are excessive and its dollar holdings are low. Credit Lyonnais' holdings of marks are in the form of a deposit with Dresdner Bank in Germany. Credit Lyonnais and Deutsche Bank agree to an exchange at the presently quoted rate of 1.6460 marks per dollar. Credit Lyonnais wires Dresdner Bank to transfer ownership of a 1,646,000 mark deposit to Deutsche Bank, and Deutsche Bank wires Morgan to transfer ownership of a $1 million deposit to Credit Lyonnais, which completes the transaction.

The number of banks acting in the foreign exchange market in this manner is quite limited. In the United States, only about two dozen banks maintain positions in the leading currencies. Other banks serve their customers' needs by dealing with one of these leading banks. The leading banks adjust their positions by buying and selling between one another, primarily through one of the six brokers that deal in foreign exchange. Normally, banks within a particular money center, such as New York, would contract most of their exchanges with other banks in the same area. However, traders in foreign exchange departments will constantly watch rates in other money market centers and be ready to buy or sell in one of those markets if the rate is different than that in the local market. Thus, while most trades occur within a local market, there is a parity between rates quoted at different locations around the world.

A third alternative is also possible. Either the German exporter or Deutsche Bank may decide to hold the dollar deposit and loan it out to earn interest. When this is done, a Eurodollar deposit is created. The Eurodollar market represents a special international money market worthy of additional attention.

Eurodollar Markets

The Eurodollar, as an investment or loan source, follows from the international payment system as described above. The German exporting company has received payment in the form of a demand deposit with Morgan Guaranty Trust, which has been credited to the account of Deutsche Bank. The German firm decides to convert the dollar demand deposit to a time deposit with its bank rather than to convert it to marks or to use it for payment purposes. Thus, Deutsche Bank, the German firm's bank in this example, continues to have a dollar-denominated liability and an offsetting dollar-denominated asset in the form of a deposit with Morgan Guaranty Trust. The relevant accounts for the three entities are summarized in the following T accounts.

GERMAN EXPORTER

Time deposit with Deutsche Bank	$1,000,000		

DEUTSCHE BANK

Demand deposit with Morgan	$1,000,000	Time deposit from German exporter	$1,000,000

MORGAN GUARANTY TRUST

	Demand deposit from Deutsche Bank	$1,000,000

At this point Eurodollars have been created. A Eurodollar is defined as a U.S. dollar-denominated deposit held by a bank outside the United States, including a foreign branch of a U.S. bank. Deutsche Bank is now paying interest on a time deposit and holding a non-interest-bearing demand deposit. One possible course of action is for Deutsche Bank to exchange the demand deposit for a certificate of deposit at the interest rate presently being quoted by Morgan. If this is done, the only change in the above T accounts is the change in the Deutsche Bank deposit with Morgan from demand to time. Deutsche Bank may decide to loan the Morgan demand deposit to another bank. This is the point where the funds enter the active Eurodollar market. The loan to another bank may be for as short as overnight or for as long as six months.

The center of the Eurodollar market is in London, with the London interbank offer rate (LIBOR) being the primary Eurodollar rate. Like the federal funds rate in the United States, the LIBOR represents the rate paid by banks on large ($500,000 or more) deposits from other banks. Besides London, there are active markets in Frankfurt, Paris, Amsterdam, Zürich, Geneva, Basle, Milan, Vienna, Toronto, Luxembourg, Montreal, and Singapore.

Suppose Deutsche Bank, lacking a direct dollar borrower, decides to deposit the funds with Barclays, a London bank, at the current LIBOR. Deutsche Bank will contact Barclays by wire to arrange for the desired maturity. Barclays, a major money market bank, stands ready to make Eurodollar loans or to accept Eurodollar deposits. After making arrangements with Barclays, Deutsche Bank wires instructions for the transfer to Morgan. These transactions have not caused any changes in the financial statement of the German exporter, which still holds a dollar-denominated time deposit with Deutsche Bank. However, the accounts of the other parties have changed as shown in the following T accounts.

DEUTSCHE BANK

Time deposit with Barclays Bank	$1,000,000	Time deposit from German exporter	$1,000,000

BARCLAYS BANK

Demand deposit with Morgan	$1,000,000	Time deposit from Deutsche Bank	$1,000,000

MORGAN GUARANTY TRUST

		Demand deposit from Barclays Bank	$1,000,000

Of course, Barclays will want to find a profitable use for the Morgan demand deposit as quickly as possible. Suppose Barclays loans the money to Brazil, an oil-importing country, by crediting Brazil's demand deposit. The only accounts that change are those of Barclay, which now appears as follows:

BARCLAYS BANK

Demand deposit with Morgan	$1,000,000	Time deposit from Deutsche Bank	$1,000,000
Loan to Brazil	$1,000,000	Demand deposit from Brazil	$1,000,000

How much time is required to complete this series of transactions? The funds can flow from the German exporter to Brazil in a few hours through the use of wire transfers.

Brazil will most likely use the funds to pay an oil-exporting country in dollars. Thus Brazil instructs Barclays to transfer ownership of the deposit to the oil exporter. After this transaction, the accounts of all parties appear as follows:

GERMAN EXPORTER

Time deposit with Deutsche Bank	$1,000,000	

DEUTSCHE BANK

Time deposit with Barclays	$1,000,000	Time deposit from German exporter	$1,000,000

BARCLAYS BANK

Demand deposit with		Demand deposit from	
Morgan	$1,000,000	oil exporter	$1,000,000
Loan to Brazil	$1,000,000	Time deposit from	
		Deutsche Bank	$1,000,000

BRAZIL

	Loan from Barclays	$1,000,000

OIL-EXPORTING COUNTRY

Demand deposit with	$1,000,000
Barclays	

MORGAN GUARANTY TRUST

	Demand deposit from	$1,000,000
	Barclays	

We should now observe several points about the Eurodollar market. First, its entire growth was based on an underlying dollar-denominated demand deposit at Morgan. Total credit granted never exceeded the amount of this deposit. All Eurodollar transactions involved transfer of ownership of deposits based on this Morgan account back to the United States.

Another point we should notice is that the banks were never exposed to exchange rate risk. Their dollar assets and liabilities were always equal. Exchange rate risks are borne by the exporters and importers. These parties could, of course, eliminate their risks through transactions in the foreign exchange futures market.

There is also the question of why Eurodollar transactions occur at all. The German firm could have held a Morgan time deposit itself, and Morgan could have made a loan to Brazil. This does not occur for reasons that include knowledge and convenience of transaction. It is more convenient for the German exporter to deal with its bank, for example. More important, the arrangement allows the banks to circumvent regulations aimed at limiting interest rates and money expansion. We showed Deutsche Bank lending the entire amount of its dollar deposits. In reality, the banks act on a fractional reserve basis, receiving many Eurodollar deposits and loaning out less than they receive in deposits, with the remainder held as reserve. However, reserve requirements are minimal compared to regulations in the United States.

We should also note that the phrase "Eurodollar market" is a misnomer in two senses. First, the market is not limited to Europe. A dollar deposit in a U.S. bank owned by anyone outside the United States meets the definition of a Eurodollar. There are active markets outside Europe, particularly in Asia. Additionally, market activity of this type is not limited to dollars. There are active markets in deposits of all major currencies outside their home countries. The market for all currencies is referred to as the *Eurocurrency market.*

Bank Use of the Eurodollar Market

Thus far, we have treated the Eurodollar market as a market in which banks serve the deposit and credit needs of their customers. The Eurodollar market also serves as an important money market in which banks can borrow funds to meet liquidity needs and invest idle funds at a profit.

An American bank facing a liquidity problem can attempt to adjust reserves by using the federal funds market or other sources within the United States. Alternatively, the bank can turn to the Eurodollar market for funds. This is done through an overseas branch of the American bank. Let us go back to the situation as it occurred immediately after Deutsche Bank received the time deposit from the German exporter. Instead of depositing funds in Barclays, Deutsche Bank could have deposited the funds with an overseas branch of an American bank. Suppose Citibank in the United States is presently in need of funds. The London branch of Citibank may accept the deposit from Deutsche Bank and gain, as an asset, the demand deposit with Morgan. The London branch of Citibank then notifies Morgan by wire that it wants the demand deposit transferred to Citibank. We should note that no increase in bank deposits occurred. Citibank simply used its overseas branch to bid for deposits presently with other U.S. banks. While the bidding for funds results in no direct increase in deposits in the United States, it may result in an indirect increase as interest rates are bid up and holders are encouraged to hold their Eurodollar deposits longer.

Instead of a shortage, suppose Citibank has an excess of funds. Suppose further that Eurodollar rates are presently more attractive than domestic money market rates. Citibank can loan funds to its London branch, showing a demand deposit as an asset and a loan as an offsetting libability. The London branch can then loan this demand deposit in the Eurodollar market, earning a favorable rate of return.

The aggressiveness of banks in using the Eurodollar market to invest idle funds can be illustrated by the example of a typical bank operating a branch in Luxembourg, one of the major international banking centers in Europe. From opening time until late in the afternoon, the branch stands ready to accept overnight deposits or lend on an overnight basis, charging slightly more on loans than the rate it pays on deposits. Late in the afternoon, the Luxembourg branch has overnight deposits in excess of overnight loans. The Luxembourg branch then transfers the idle funds to the bank's New York branch. It is six hours earlier in New York, so the New York branch has a good chance to find an outlet for the funds. As the banking day draws to a close in New York, the New York branch transfers idle funds to a branch located farther west to gain additional business hours. This process continues until the idle funds are finally transferred to the Singapore branch where a profitable overnight loan is found. The transfer of this deposit in a series of steps all the way from Luxembourg to Singapore was done to avoid the loss of one day's interest. Such actions are feasible because wire transfers are inexpensive and one day's interest on $1 million is frequently over $300. Over the course of a year, a bank could increase its profit $1 million by placing an average of $10 million each banking day in this manner.

SUMMARY

With the increased volume of international business, financial institutions have become increasingly involved in the international financial markets. They are involved in these markets both to serve the needs of their customers and to meet their own liquidity and profitability objectives.

Financial institutions help their customers complete international transactions through such approaches as the letter of credit, draft, and bill of lading, and through other specialized arrangements. Financial institutions help their customers exchange one currency for another and hedge against exchange rate risk through their foreign exchange departments. They also help customers in using international money markets to create balance sheet hedges. Additionally, financial institutions provide export credit insurance, and certain institutions specialize in providing export credit.

Financial institutions also aid their customers in tapping the international capital markets. While there is no truly international equity market, there are two types of international bonds. A foreign bond is issued primarily in one country, is denominated in the currency of that country, and is the obligation of a corporation headquartered in another country. A Eurobond is sold principally in countries other than the country of the currency where it is denominated. In addition to these international bond markets, certain firms specialize in long-term loans, particularly in developing countries.

The Eurocurrency markets represent the primary international money markets. The Eurodollar is defined as a dollar deposit in a United States bank owned by a person, business, or institution outside the United States. In addition to helping customers through this market, banks use it as a source of liquidity adjustment and temporary investment.

The history of financial system development on the international front is similar to that for the domestic financial system. Institutions and instruments have developed in response to specific needs and the profit opportunities they created. While the growth of international business was not caused by financial institutions, it probably would not have occurred without them.

QUESTIONS

19-1. Give an example of international business activity that can be explained through the theory of comparative advantage.

19-2. Capital flows *into* the United States have increased sharply in recent years (table 19-1). What factors have led to this increased inflow?

19-3. What are the main financial problems faced in international business that are not encountered in domestic enterprise?

19-4. International business is relatively less important for the United States than for other developed countries (table 19-2). What are the reasons for this?

19-5.   What is translation risk? How does a company normally protect itself from translation risk?

19-6.   Translation risk only involves accounting entries. Why would a company be concerned about translation risk?

19-7.   What factors have caused exchange rates to become less stable in recent years?

19-8.   Find the most recent spot and ninety-day rate for Japanese yen. Are people expecting the yen to increase or decrease in value relative to the dollar in the next ninety days?

19-9.   An American company will sell goods to a German company, agreeing to grant one-year credit terms and accept payment in marks. How can the company hedge against exchange rate risk?

19-10.   It is common practice for sales between businesses in the United States to be on an open account basis. Why is this not common practice in international trade?

19-11.   Explain the difference between a foreign bond and a Eurobond.

19-12.   Most domestic payments are made through paper order, in the form of checks. How are international payments normally made?

19-13.   How would a business go about raising funds in the foreign bond market?

19-14.   Explain how a bank uses the Eurodollar market to adjust its liquidity position. Can the banking *system* adjust its liquidity through the Eurodollar market?

PROBLEMS

19-1.   A Danish subsidiary of a U.S. company has Japanese yen monetary assets of 10 million yen and has no yen liabilities. A German subsidiary of the same U.S. parent has a 10 million yen liability and no yen assets.
   a. Is the consolidated company exposed to exchange rate risk?
   b. If the answer to part a is yes, specify the transactions that could be used to eliminate exchange rate risk.

19-2.   Find the present yield for ninety-day U.S. Treasury bills. Also find the spot and ninety-day exchange rate for the British pound. What would the equilibrium rate for ninety-day British government obligations be under these conditions?

19-3.   British government obligations with 180 days to maturity are selling to provide an 8 percent *annual* yield, while U.S. government obligations of similar maturity are selling to yield 8.5 percent. Is the relationship between these two interest rates in equilibrium (table 19-3)? If not, what type of transaction would take advantage of this disequilibrium?

19-4.   An Italian exporting company receives $1 million payment from a United States importer in the form of a deposit in the name of the Italian firm's Rome bank—in dollars at Citibank. The Italian firm converts its deposits to a time deposit with a London bank; the London bank in turn loans those deposits to a customer in the form of a dollar demand deposit with the London bank. Show the status of the relevant accounts of the Italian exporting company, the London bank, the London borrower, and Citibank.

19-5.   Commonwealth Bank, a U.S. money center bank, has a German subsidiary with 1,000 DM of German monetary assets and 600 DM of German monetary liabilities. The value of the mark is currently $0.60.

   a. Suppose the mark is valued at $0.70 by the end of the year. What will be the gain or loss?

   b. Suppose the mark is valued at $0.50 by the end of the year. What will be the gain or loss?

   c. How can Commonwealth eliminate this exchange rate risk?

19-6.   The spot and six-month forward rates for the deutsche mark are 0.60 and 0.61, respectively. The interest rate per six-month period is 5 percent in the United States and 3.28 percent in Germany. Are these relationships in equilibrium?

19-7.   Given the situation in problem 19-6, suppose the U.S. government wants to drive up the value of the dollar. The U.S. government tightens the money supply so that the interest rate in the United States rises to 7 percent per six-month period. If the futures rate and the German interest rate do not change, what is the new equilibrium spot price of the deutsche mark?

19-8.   One of your bank's customers has arranged to sell products in Japan. Your customer will incur total costs of $1 million and has contracted to sell the products in ninety days for 129 million yen. Based on rates shown in table 19-3, is the value of the yen expected to rise or fall over the next ninety days?

19-9.   For the customer in problem 19-8, suppose the exchange rate is 130 yen to the dollar in ninety days. What will be your customer's profit or loss?

19-10.   If the customer described in problem 19-8 takes advantage of the forward rates quoted in table 19-3 to lock in the exchange rate, what will be your customer's profit or loss?

19-11.   Purchasing power parity theory suggests that the exchange rate between U.S. dollars and another currency will be such that the number of U.S. dollars needed to purchase a particular good can be exchanged for enough units of the foreign currency to buy the good in the foreign country. Colonel Sanders recently opened a fried chicken outlet in Beijing, China. If a chicken dinner sells for $2.49 in the United States and the exchange rate is 3.722 yuan per dollar, what is the purchasing power equilibrium price of a chicken dinner in Beijing? Are there forces in place to ensure that this relationship will hold?

19-12.   Shown below are U.S. real interest rates and the exchange value of the U.S. dollar (this is a weighted-average exchange value weighted in proportion to trade done with each country). What relationship do you see between the inflation rates, interest rates, and exchange rates?

Year	1977	1978	1979	1980	1981	1982	1983	1984	1985	1986
Real int. rate	0.6%	−0.5%	−3.4%	−0.8%	4.6%	8.8%	7.0%	8.1%	6.6%	6.5%
Exchange rate	103	92	88	87	103	117	125	138	143	112

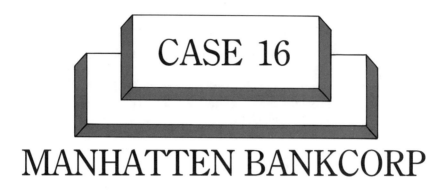

CASE 16

MANHATTEN BANKCORP

The May 1987 meeting of the board of directors at Manhatten Bankcorp was to be devoted to a review of Manhatten's international position and a detailed analysis of the Brazilian situation. This review was prompted by Brazil's demand for restructuring of its international debt.

Manhatten was one of the largest banks in the United States and was a member of the group of twelve leading banks regularly designated money center banks. Like all these banks, Manhatten was a major player in the international markets. Manhatten's international exposure is summarized in tables 1 through 3, and its performance relative to other banks is summarized in table 4.

Latin American loans had become a problem for many large banks, including Manhatten. Some Latin American countries, such as Mexico and Venezuela, had substantial oil reserves and had borrowed heavily with anticipation of paying off the debt with oil revenues. Instead, OPEC collapsed, oil prices fell, and these countries were left without sufficient income to service their debt. Governments were understandably reluctant to impose severe hardship on their citizens and risk revolution in order to pay foreign bankers.

Brazil was not a significant oil-producing country but had borrowed heavily in anticipation of a rising level of productivity. Brazil's foreign debt, relatively speaking, was among the largest in the world. Foreign debt service, including principal and interest, was 5 percent of the gross domestic product. A democratic election had returned the government to civilian control in 1985 after two decades of rule by the military. Needless to say, the new government was not eager to impose austerity mea-

Table 1

Foreign Exposure of Manhatten Bankcorp[1]

YEAR	1982	1983	1984	1985	1986
Foreign office loans/total assets	54.1%	50.4%	46.0%	42.6%	40.1%
Money center banks	41.9	41.4	38.5	35.4	32.5
Foreign office deposits/total assets	74.6	67.4	59.7	56.5	56.5
Money center banks	48.6	45.4	43.9	42.1	40.2
Difference	−20.5	−17.0	−13.7	−13.9	−16.4
Industry	−6.7	−4.0	−5.4	−6.7	−7.7
Int'l loan charge-offs/					
Total loan charge-offs	44.9	54.7	41.6	38.7	30.9
Money center banks	28.2	34.6	28.1	33.4	26.2
Int'l nonperforming loans/					
Total nonperforming loans	59.4	59.4	59.4	59.4	59.4
Money center banks	33.3	40.0	48.7	39.5	30.5
Int'l earnings/net income	70.3	54.4	61.5	54.6	49.3
Money center banks	49.7	39.0	35.3	24.6	35.4

[1]The banking statistics for this case are taken from Thomas H. Hanley, et al., *A Review of Bank Performance* (New York: Salomon Brothers, Inc., 1987).

Table 2

Geographic Distribution of Manhatten's Assets and Profitability in 1986

	INCOME	ASSETS	PERCENTAGE OF ASSETS	ROTA
North America	$568	$101,432	55	0.56%
Latin America and Caribbean	257	19,016	10	1.35
Europe, Mideast, Africa	99	40,678	22	0.24
Asia, Pacific	134	22,887	12	0.59

Table 3

Latin American Exposure, 1986

	EXPOSURE/ASSETS		EXPOSURE/CAPITAL	
	Manhatten	Compet-itors	Manhatten	Compet-itors
Mexico	1.4	1.7	20.8	29.7
Brazil	2.3	2.3	34.1	33.2
Argentina	0.7	0.9	10.4	13.1
Venezuela	0.5	0.8	7.4	14.9

Table 4

Performance Assesment of Manhatten

	MANHATTEN	MONEY CENTER BANKS		
		Lower Quartile	Average	Upper Quartile
CAPITAL ADEQUACY (% of assets)				
Common equity	3.89%	4.3%	4.6%	3.2%
Loan loss reserves	0.86	1.0	1.1	1.2
Primary capital	6.82	6.7	7.1	7.3
Total capital	10.88	8.5	9.9	10.6
PROFITABILITY				
Return on total assets	0.58%	0.63%	0.71%	0.82%
Return on equity	12.56	12.42	13.7	15.06
MARKET STATISTICS				
Market value/book value	0.95	0.74	0.90	1.19
Price-earnings ratio	8.4	6.6	7.3	8.3

sures at home. Manhatten had renegotiated substantial portions of Brazil's debt in 1986, both increasing the maturity and decreasing the interest rate.

The demands made by Brazil in 1987 were much more substantial than those leading to the renegotiations in 1986. Dilson Funaro, Brazil's finance minister, took an around-the-world trip to impress bankers with the seriousness of Brazil's position. Brazil wanted to renegotiate its debt to reduce debt service to 2.5 percent of the gross domestic product. Furthermore, he demanded an additional $3 billion of credit. Finally, he wanted to carry out the renegotiation without using the International Monetary Fund, thus avoiding the economic policy interference that would come with that aid. To make sure everyone understood his position, he declared a moratorium on the $12 billion in interest payments that were due in 1987.

Mr. Funaro had several reasons to hope that this ploy would win the terms he wanted. He was backed by the fact that Ecuador and Chile had both suspended interest payments. Mexico, which table 5 shows to be similar to Brazil in many ways, was in the process of renegotiating its foreign debt. There is an old saying that, If I can't pay a $1,000 loan, I'm in trouble, but if I can't pay a $1 million loan, the bank is in trouble. Brazil had $108 billion of foreign debt, with $23 billion of that amount owed to U.S. banks. This made Brazil one of the world's leading debtor nations. A suspension of interest by Brazil would be a serious blow to the foreign income of leading U.S. banks.

Brazil had become one of the leading industrial powers in Latin America and was moving away from underdeveloped country status. It had a land area approximately 91 percent of that of the United States and a population 60 percent of that of the United States. The country had a well-developed industrial base and a foreign trade surplus. Furthermore, it had the benefit of being able to maintain a very small military expenditure. However, Brazil suffered from an annual inflation rate of over 200 percent

Table 5

Economic and Demographic Characteristics

	USA	BRAZIL	MEXICO
Population (000) in 1986	240,856	143,277	81.709
Annual growth from 1980 to 1986	0.9%	2.5%	2.6%
Square miles (000)	3,615	3,286	762
Population per square mile	67	44	107
Life expectancy at birth	75	60	66
Infant mortality per 1,000 live births	11	80	53
Public education expenditure ÷ GNP	6.8%	3.2%	2.7%
Illiteracy rate among adults		22.3%	9.7%
Gross national product (in 1983 $ millions)	3,298	272	158
Per capita	13,492	1,987	1,997
Inflation rate, 1984–1985	3.6%	227.0%	57.7%
Trade balance, 1984 ($ millions)	−112,510	13,086	12,799
Debt service ratio[1]		26.6%	34.3%
Military expenses as a percent of GNP	6.6%	0.7%	0.6%

[1]Principal and interest payments on foreign debt ÷ exports.

and also suffered from uneven distribution of the wealth. Despite the fact that large numbers of Brazilians had improved their economic well-being with the growth of a modern industrial economy, substantial portions of the population were still left out. This was reflected in high rates of illiteracy, high rates of infant mortality, and short life expectancy.

The banks faced two basic alternatives. They could meet Brazil's demands only by accepting substantially lower interest rates or by deferring part of the interest. Alternately, the banks could decide to call Brazil's bluff and find out if it was prepared to convert the moratorium to a default or more permanent suspension. A default would have very undesirable consequences for Brazil, as well as for the major banks of the world. As shown in table 6, investors were already showing limited enthusiasm for banks with heavy foreign exposure. Manhatten Bankcorp was a major lender and had often been a leader in setting bank policy toward Latin America, so the decisions reached at the board meeting could have important national and international consequences.

QUESTIONS

1. Compare Manhatten's foreign exposure to that of other money center banks. Is Manhatten's exposure greater or less? Is Manhatten's exposure increasing or decreasing?

Table 6

Stock Market Response to Money Center Bank Performance

BANK	MARKET/BOOK[1]	PRICE-EARNINGS RATIO	FOREIGN INCOME/ TOTAL INCOME	LOAN LOSS RESERVE/ ASSETS	EQUITY CAPITAL/ ASSETS	ROTA
A	1.222	8.1	0.084	0.0107	0.0559	0.0085
B	1.167	7.5	0.224	0.0104	0.0495	0.0079
C	0.673	6.4	0.203	0.0111	0.0518	0.0065
D	0.753	6.9	0.262	0.0109	0.051	0.007
E	0.753	8.4	0.493	0.0086	0.0457	0.0058
F	0.949	7.2	0.375	0.0091	0.0469	0.006
G	0.607	5.4	0.304	0.0134	0.0481	0.0054
H	1.504	9.5	0.487	0.0118	0.0654	0.0119
I	0.728	7.0	NA	0.0197	0.0575	0.0065
J	1.733	13.8	0.272	0.0061	0.0602	0.0085
K	1.088	7.4	0.099	0.0112	0.0526	0.0078
L	0.776	6.4	NA	0.0147	0.0575	0.0071

[1]The market price of a share of stock, divided by the book value per share.

2.   Evaluate the profitability of Manhatten's Latin American business in relation to its other business.

3.   Compare Manhatten's exposure in Brazil and Mexico to that of other money center banks. Is Manhatten's exposure greater or less? Is Manhatten's exposure increasing or decreasing?

4.   Recommend a strategy for responding to Brazil's demands for additional restructuring. In developing this recommendation, some of the things that must be considered include
       a.   Manhatten's capital adequacy and loan loss provision
       b.   Manhatten's profitability position
       c.   The stock market's response
       d.   Manhatten's exposure internationally and in Brazil
       e.   Brazil's economic and demographic conditions
       f.   The political stability of Brazil
       g.   How a settlement with Brazil will affect negotiations with other debtor nations

SELECTED REFERENCES

ABUAF, NISO. "Foreign Exchange Options: The Leading Edge," *Midland Corporate Finance Journal* 5 (Summer 1987): 51–58.

ADLER, MICHAEL, AND DUMAS, BERNARD. "Exposure to Currency Risk: Definition and Measurement," *Financial Management* 13 (Summer 1984): 41–49.

BALDWIN, CARLISS Y. "Competing for Capital in a Global Environment," *Midland Corporate Finance Journal* 5 (Spring 1987): 43–63.

BOOTH, GEOFFREY G., DUGGAN, JAMES E., AND KOVEOS, PETER E. "Deviations from Purchasing Power Parity, Relative Inflation, and Exchange Rates: The Recent Experience," *Financial Review* 20 (May 1985): 195–218.

COTNER, JOHN S., AND SEITZ, NEIL E. "A Simplified Approach to Short-Term International Diversification," *Financial Review* 22 (May 1987): 249–266.

CRYSTAL, K. ALEC. "A Guide to Foreign Exchange Markets," *The Federal Reserve Bank of St. Louis Review* 66 (March 1984): 5–18.

EATON, JOHATHAN, GERSOVITZ, MARK, AND STIGLITZ, JOSEPH. "The Pure Theory of Country Risk," *European Economic Review* 30 (June 1986): 481–513.

GARLICKI, T. DESSA, FABOZZI, FRANK J., AND FONFEDER, ROBERT. "The Impact of Earnings Under FASB 52 on Equity Returns," *Financial Management* 16 (Autumn 1987): 36–44.

GRAMMATIKON, THEOHARRY, SAUNDERS, ANTHONY, AND SWARY, ITZHAK. "Returns and Risks of U.S. Bank Foreign Currency Activities," *Journal of Finance* 41 (July 1986): 671–683.

KIDWELL, DAVID S., WAYNE MARR, W., AND RODNEY THOMPSON, G. "Eurodollar Bonds, Alternate Financing of U.S. Companies," *Financial Management* 14 (Winter 1985): 18–27. Also see "Correction" in *Financial Management* 15 (Spring 1986): 78–79.

KRAYENBUEH, THOMAS E. *Country Risk* (Lexington, Mass.: Lexington Books, 1985).

LESSARD, DONALD R. "Recapitalizing Third-World Debt: Toward a New Vision of Commercial Financing for Less-Developed Countries." *Midland Corporate Finance Journal* 5 (Fall 1987): 6–21.

MCCLELLAN, JOEL, Ed. *The Global Financial Structure in Trasition* (Lexington, Mass: Lexington Books, D.C. Heath and Company, 1984).

ROEHL, TOM. "Data Sources for Research in Japanese Finance," *Journal of Financial and Quantitative Analysis* 20 (June 1985): 273–276.

SHAPIRO, ALAN C. "Currency Risk and Country Risk in International Banking," *Journal of Finance* 40 (July 1985): 881–893.

Appendix A—Tables

Table A-1

Compound Value of a Dollar (Annually Compounded)

YEAR	3%	4%	5%	6%	7%	8%	9%	10%	11%	12%	13%	14%	15%	18%	20%	25%
1	1.0300	1.0400	1.0500	1.0600	1.0700	1.0800	1.0900	1.1000	1.1100	1.1200	1.1300	1.1400	1.1500	1.1800	1.2000	1.2500
2	1.0609	1.0816	1.1025	1.1236	1.1449	1.1664	1.1881	1.2100	1.2321	1.2544	1.2769	1.2996	1.3225	1.3924	1.4400	1.5625
3	1.0927	1.1249	1.1576	1.1910	1.2250	1.2597	1.2950	1.3310	1.3676	1.4049	1.4429	1.4815	1.5209	1.6430	1.7280	1.9531
4	1.1255	1.1699	1.2155	1.2625	1.3108	1.3605	1.4116	1.4641	1.5181	1.5735	1.6305	1.6890	1.7490	1.9388	2.0736	2.4414
5	1.1593	1.2167	1.2763	1.3382	1.4026	1.4693	1.5386	1.6105	1.6851	1.7623	1.8424	1.9254	2.0114	2.2878	2.4883	3.0518
6	1.1941	1.2653	1.3401	1.4185	1.5007	1.5869	1.6771	1.7716	1.8704	1.9738	2.0820	2.1950	2.3131	2.6996	2.9860	3.8147
7	1.2299	1.3159	1.4071	1.5036	1.6058	1.7138	1.8280	1.9487	2.0762	2.2107	2.3526	2.5023	2.6600	3.1855	3.5832	4.7684
8	1.2668	1.3686	1.4775	1.5938	1.7182	1.8509	1.9926	2.1436	2.3045	2.4760	2.6584	2.8526	3.0590	3.7589	4.2998	5.9605
9	1.3048	1.4233	1.5513	1.6895	1.8385	1.9990	2.1719	2.3579	2.5580	2.7731	3.0040	3.2519	3.5179	4.4355	5.1598	7.4506
10	1.3439	1.4802	1.6289	1.7908	1.9672	2.1589	2.3674	2.5937	2.8394	3.1058	3.3946	3.7072	4.0456	5.2338	6.1917	9.3132
11	1.3842	1.5395	1.7103	1.8983	2.1049	2.3316	2.5804	2.8531	3.1518	3.4785	3.8359	4.2262	4.6524	6.1759	7.4301	11.642
12	1.4258	1.6010	1.7959	2.0122	2.2522	2.5182	2.8127	3.1384	3.4985	3.8960	4.3345	4.8179	5.3503	7.2876	8.9161	14.552
13	1.4685	1.6651	1.8856	2.1329	2.4098	2.7196	3.0658	3.4523	3.8833	4.3635	4.8980	5.4924	6.1528	8.5994	10.699	18.190
14	1.5126	1.7317	1.9799	2.2609	2.5785	2.9372	3.3417	3.7975	4.3104	4.8871	5.5348	6.2613	7.0757	10.147	12.839	22.737
15	1.5580	1.8009	2.0789	2.3966	2.7590	3.1722	3.6425	4.1772	4.7846	5.4736	6.2543	7.1379	8.1371	11.974	15.407	28.422
16	1.6047	1.8730	2.1829	2.5404	2.9522	3.4259	3.9703	4.5950	5.3109	6.1304	7.0673	8.1372	9.3576	14.129	18.488	35.527
17	1.6528	1.9479	2.2920	2.6928	3.1588	3.7000	4.3276	5.0545	5.8951	6.8660	7.9861	9.2765	10.761	16.672	22.186	44.409
18	1.7024	2.0258	2.4066	2.8543	3.3799	3.9960	4.7171	5.5599	6.5436	7.6900	9.0243	10.575	12.375	19.673	26.623	55.511
19	1.7535	2.1068	2.5270	3.0256	3.6165	4.3157	5.1417	6.1159	7.2633	8.6128	10.197	12.056	14.232	23.214	31.948	69.389
20	1.8061	2.1911	2.6533	3.2071	3.8697	4.6610	5.6044	6.7275	8.0623	9.6463	11.523	13.743	16.367	27.393	38.338	86.736
25	2.0938	2.6658	3.3864	4.2919	5.4274	6.8485	8.6231	10.835	13.585	17.000	21.231	26.462	32.919	62.669	95.396	264.70
30	2.4273	3.2434	4.3219	5.7435	7.6123	10.063	13.268	17.449	22.892	29.960	39.116	50.950	66.212	143.37	237.38	807.79
35	2.8139	3.9461	5.5160	7.6861	10.677	14.785	20.414	28.102	38.575	52.800	72.069	98.100	133.18	328.00	590.67	2465.2
40	3.2620	4.8010	7.0400	10.286	14.974	21.725	31.409	45.259	65.001	93.051	132.78	188.88	267.86	750.38	1469.8	7523.2
50	4.3839	7.1067	11.467	18.420	29.457	46.902	74.358	117.39	184.56	289.00	450.74	700.23	1083.7	3927.4	9100.4	70065

Table A-2

Compound Value of a Dollar (Monthly Compounding)

YEAR	3%	4%	5%	6%	7%	8%	9%	10%	11%	12%	13%	14%	15%	18%	20%	25%
1	1.0304	1.0407	1.0512	1.0617	1.0723	1.0830	1.0938	1.1047	1.1157	1.1268	1.1380	1.1493	1.1608	1.1956	1.2194	1.2807
2	1.0618	1.0831	1.1049	1.1272	1.1498	1.1729	1.1964	1.2204	1.2448	1.2697	1.2951	1.3210	1.3474	1.4295	1.4869	1.6403
3	1.0941	1.1273	1.1615	1.1967	1.2329	1.2702	1.3086	1.3482	1.3889	1.4308	1.4739	1.5183	1.5639	1.7091	1.8131	2.1007
4	1.1273	1.1732	1.2209	1.2705	1.3221	1.3757	1.4314	1.4894	1.5496	1.6122	1.6773	1.7450	1.8154	2.0435	2.2109	2.6905
5	1.1616	1.2210	1.2834	1.3489	1.4176	1.4898	1.5657	1.6453	1.7289	1.8167	1.9089	2.0056	2.1072	2.4432	2.6960	3.4458
6	1.1969	1.2707	1.3490	1.4320	1.5201	1.6135	1.7126	1.8176	1.9290	2.0471	2.1723	2.3051	2.4459	2.9212	3.2874	4.4131
7	1.2334	1.3225	1.4180	1.5204	1.6300	1.7474	1.8732	2.0079	2.1522	2.3067	2.4722	2.6494	2.8391	3.4926	4.0087	5.6521
8	1.2709	1.3764	1.4906	1.6141	1.7478	1.8925	2.0489	2.2182	2.4013	2.5993	2.8134	3.0450	3.2955	4.1758	4.8881	7.2388
9	1.3095	1.4325	1.5668	1.7137	1.8742	2.0495	2.2411	2.4504	2.6791	2.9289	3.2018	3.4998	3.8253	4.9927	5.9606	9.2709
10	1.3494	1.4908	1.6470	1.8194	2.0097	2.2196	2.4514	2.7070	2.9891	3.3004	3.6437	4.0225	4.4402	5.9693	7.2683	11.874
11	1.3904	1.5516	1.7313	1.9316	2.1549	2.4039	2.6813	2.9905	3.3351	3.7190	4.1467	4.6232	5.1540	7.1370	8.8628	15.207
12	1.4327	1.6148	1.8198	2.0508	2.3107	2.6034	2.9328	3.3036	3.7210	4.1906	4.7191	5.3136	5.9825	8.5332	10.807	19.476
13	1.4763	1.6806	1.9130	2.1772	2.4778	2.8195	3.2080	3.6496	4.1516	4.7221	5.3704	6.1072	6.9442	10.202	13.178	24.943
14	1.5212	1.7490	2.0108	2.3115	2.6569	3.0535	3.5089	4.0317	4.6320	5.3210	6.1117	7.0192	8.0606	12.198	16.069	31.946
15	1.5674	1.8203	2.1137	2.4541	2.8489	3.3069	3.8380	4.4539	5.1680	5.9958	6.9554	8.0675	9.3563	14.584	19.595	40.914
16	1.6151	1.8945	2.2218	2.6055	3.0549	3.5814	4.1981	4.9203	5.7660	6.7562	7.9154	9.2723	10.860	17.437	23.894	52.400
17	1.6642	1.9716	2.3355	2.7662	3.2757	3.8786	4.5919	5.4355	6.4333	7.6131	9.0080	10.657	12.606	20.848	29.136	67.110
18	1.7149	2.0520	2.4550	2.9368	3.5125	4.2006	5.0226	6.0047	7.1777	8.5786	10.251	12.249	14.633	24.927	35.528	85.950
19	1.7670	2.1356	2.5806	3.1179	3.7665	4.5492	5.4938	6.6335	8.0083	9.6666	11.666	14.078	16.985	29.803	43.323	110.08
20	1.8208	2.2226	2.7126	3.3102	4.0387	4.9268	6.0092	7.3281	8.9350	10.893	13.277	16.180	19.715	35.633	52.828	140.98
25	2.1150	2.7138	3.4813	4.4650	5.7254	7.3402	9.4084	12.057	15.448	19.788	25.343	32.451	41.544	87.059	142.42	485.79
30	2.4568	3.3135	4.4677	6.0226	8.1165	10.936	14.731	19.837	26.708	35.950	48.377	65.085	87.541	212.70	383.96	1674.0
35	2.8539	4.0458	5.7337	8.1236	11.506	16.293	23.063	32.639	46.176	65.310	92.345	130.53	184.46	519.68	1035.2	5768.1
40	3.3151	4.9399	7.3584	10.957	16.311	24.273	36.110	53.701	79.834	118.65	176.27	261.80	388.70	1269.7	2790.7	19876
50	4.4733	7.3645	12.119	19.936	32.780	53.878	88.518	145.37	238.64	391.58	642.29	1053.1	1725.9	7579.2	20284	235997

Table A-3

Compound Value of an Annuity of $1 (Annual Payment, Annual Compounding)

YEAR	3%	4%	5%	6%	7%	8%	9%	10%	11%	12%	13%	14%	15%	18%	20%	25%
1	1.0000	1.0000	1.0000	1.0000	1.0000	1.0000	1.0000	1.0000	1.0000	1.0000	1.0000	1.0000	1.0000	1.0000	1.0000	1.0000
2	2.0300	2.0400	2.0500	2.0600	2.0700	2.0800	2.0900	2.1000	2.1100	2.1200	2.1300	2.1400	2.1500	2.1800	2.2000	2.2500
3	3.0909	3.1216	3.1525	3.1836	3.2149	3.2464	3.2781	3.3100	3.3421	3.3744	3.4069	3.4396	3.4725	3.5724	3.6400	3.8125
4	4.1836	4.2465	4.3101	4.3746	4.4399	4.5061	4.5731	4.6410	4.7097	4.7793	4.8498	4.9211	4.9934	5.2154	5.3680	5.7656
5	5.3091	5.4163	5.5256	5.6371	5.7507	5.8666	5.9847	6.1051	6.2278	6.3528	6.4803	6.6101	6.7424	7.1542	7.4416	8.2070
6	6.4684	6.6330	6.8019	6.9753	7.1533	7.3359	7.5233	7.7156	7.9129	8.1152	8.3227	8.5355	8.7537	9.4420	9.9299	11.259
7	7.6625	7.8983	8.1420	8.3938	8.6540	8.9228	9.2004	9.4872	9.7833	10.089	10.405	10.730	11.067	12.142	12.916	15.073
8	8.8923	9.2142	9.5491	9.8975	10.260	10.637	11.028	11.436	11.859	12.300	12.757	13.233	13.727	15.327	16.499	19.842
9	10.159	10.583	11.027	11.491	11.978	12.488	13.021	13.579	14.164	14.776	15.416	16.085	16.786	19.086	20.799	25.802
10	11.464	12.006	12.578	13.181	13.816	14.487	15.193	15.937	16.722	17.549	18.420	19.337	20.304	23.521	25.959	33.253
11	12.808	13.486	14.207	14.972	15.784	16.645	17.560	18.531	19.561	20.655	21.814	23.045	24.349	28.755	32.150	42.566
12	14.192	15.026	15.917	16.870	17.888	18.977	20.141	21.384	22.713	24.133	25.650	27.271	29.002	34.931	39.581	54.208
13	15.618	16.627	17.713	18.882	20.141	21.495	22.953	24.523	26.212	28.029	29.985	32.089	34.352	42.219	48.497	68.760
14	17.086	18.292	19.599	21.015	22.550	24.215	26.019	27.975	30.095	32.393	34.883	37.581	40.505	50.818	59.196	86.949
15	18.599	20.024	21.579	23.276	25.129	27.152	29.361	31.772	34.405	37.280	40.417	43.842	47.580	60.965	72.035	109.69
16	20.157	21.825	23.657	25.673	27.888	30.324	33.003	35.950	39.190	42.753	46.672	50.980	55.717	72.939	87.442	138.11
17	21.762	23.698	25.840	28.213	30.840	33.750	36.974	40.545	44.501	48.884	53.739	59.118	65.075	87.068	105.93	173.64
18	23.414	25.645	28.132	30.906	33.999	37.450	41.301	45.599	50.396	55.750	61.725	68.394	75.836	103.74	128.12	218.04
19	25.117	27.671	30.539	33.760	37.379	41.446	46.018	51.159	56.939	63.440	70.749	78.969	88.212	123.41	154.74	273.56
20	26.870	29.778	33.066	36.786	40.995	45.762	51.160	57.275	64.203	72.052	80.947	91.025	102.44	146.63	186.69	342.94
25	36.459	41.646	47.727	54.865	63.249	73.106	84.701	98.347	114.41	133.33	155.62	181.87	212.79	342.60	471.98	1054.8
30	47.575	56.085	66.439	79.058	94.461	113.28	136.31	164.49	199.02	241.33	293.20	356.79	434.75	790.95	1181.9	3227.2
35	60.462	73.652	90.320	111.43	138.24	172.32	215.71	271.02	341.59	431.66	546.68	693.57	881.17	1816.7	2948.3	9856.8
40	75.401	95.026	120.80	154.76	199.64	259.06	337.88	442.59	581.83	767.09	1013.7	1342.0	1779.1	4163.2	7343.9	30089
50	112.80	152.67	209.35	290.34	406.53	573.77	815.08	1163.9	1668.8	2400.0	3459.5	4994.5	7217.7	21813	45497	280256

Table A-4

Compound Value of an Annuity of $1 (Monthly Payments, Monthly Compounding)

YEAR	3%	4%	5%	6%	7%	8%	9%	10%	11%	12%	13%	14%	15%	18%	20%	25%
1	12.166	12.222	12.279	12.336	12.393	12.450	12.508	12.566	12.624	12.683	12.741	12.801	12.860	13.041	13.163	13.475
2	24.703	24.943	25.186	25.432	25.681	25.933	26.188	26.447	26.709	26.973	27.242	27.513	27.788	28.634	29.215	30.733
3	37.621	38.182	38.753	39.336	39.930	40.536	41.153	41.782	42.423	43.077	43.743	44.423	45.116	47.276	48.788	52.836
4	50.931	51.960	53.015	54.098	55.209	56.350	57.521	58.722	59.956	61.223	62.523	63.858	65.228	69.565	72.655	81.144
5	64.647	66.299	68.006	69.770	71.593	73.477	75.424	77.437	79.518	81.670	83.894	86.195	88.575	96.215	101.76	117.40
6	78.779	81.223	83.764	86.409	89.161	92.025	95.007	98.111	101.34	104.71	108.22	111.87	115.67	128.08	137.25	163.83
7	93.342	96.754	100.33	104.07	108.00	112.11	116.43	120.95	125.69	130.67	135.89	141.38	147.13	166.17	180.52	223.30
8	108.35	112.92	117.74	122.83	128.20	133.87	139.86	146.18	152.86	159.93	167.39	175.29	183.64	211.72	233.29	299.46
9	123.81	129.74	136.04	142.74	149.86	157.43	165.48	174.05	183.18	192.89	203.24	214.27	226.02	266.18	297.63	397.00
10	139.74	147.25	155.28	163.88	173.08	182.95	193.51	204.84	217.00	230.04	244.04	259.07	275.22	331.29	376.10	521.93
11	156.16	165.47	175.51	186.32	197.99	210.58	224.17	238.86	254.73	271.90	290.46	310.56	332.32	409.14	471.77	681.93
12	173.07	184.44	196.76	210.15	224.69	240.51	257.71	276.44	296.83	319.06	343.30	369.74	398.60	502.21	588.44	886.84
13	190.50	204.17	219.11	235.45	253.33	272.92	294.39	317.95	343.81	372.21	403.43	437.76	475.54	613.49	730.70	1149.3
14	208.47	224.71	242.60	262.30	284.04	308.02	334.52	363.81	396.22	432.10	471.85	515.93	564.85	746.55	904.17	1485.4
15	226.97	246.09	267.29	290.82	316.96	346.04	378.41	414.47	454.69	499.58	549.73	605.79	668.51	905.62	1115.7	1915.9
16	246.04	268.34	293.24	321.09	352.27	387.21	426.41	470.44	519.93	575.62	638.35	709.06	788.83	1095.8	1373.6	2467.2
17	265.69	291.49	320.52	353.23	390.13	431.80	478.92	532.26	592.72	661.31	739.20	827.75	928.50	1323.2	1688.2	3173.3
18	285.94	315.59	349.20	387.35	430.72	480.09	536.35	600.56	673.93	757.86	853.98	964.17	1090.6	1595.1	2071.7	4077.6
19	306.80	340.67	379.35	423.58	474.25	532.38	599.17	676.02	764.54	866.66	984.59	1121.0	1278.8	1920.2	2539.4	5235.8
20	328.30	366.77	411.03	462.04	520.93	589.02	667.89	759.37	865.64	989.26	1133.2	1301.2	1497.2	2308.9	3109.7	6719.1
25	446.01	514.13	595.51	692.99	810.07	951.03	1121.1	1326.8	1576.1	1878.8	2247.1	2695.8	3243.5	5737.3	8485.3	23270
30	582.74	694.05	832.26	1004.5	1220.0	1490.4	1830.7	2260.5	2804.5	3495.0	4373.3	5493.0	6923.3	14114	22978	80302
35	741.56	913.73	1136.1	1424.7	1801.1	2293.9	2941.8	3796.6	4928.3	6431.0	8431.8	11103	14677	34579	62049	276822
40	926.06	1182.0	1526.0	1991.5	2624.8	3491.0	4681.3	6324.1	8600.1	11765	16179	22354	31016	84580	167385	953990
50	1389.3	1909.4	2668.7	3787.2	5448.1	7931.7	11669	17324	25924	39058	59196	90179	137993	505216		

Table A-5

Present Value of a Dollar (Annual Compounding)

YEAR	3%	4%	5%	6%	7%	8%	9%	10%	11%	12%	13%	14%	15%	18%	20%	25%
1	0.9709	0.9615	0.9524	0.9434	0.9346	0.9259	0.9174	0.9091	0.9009	0.8929	0.8850	0.8772	0.8696	0.8475	0.8333	0.8000
2	0.9426	0.9246	0.9070	0.8900	0.8734	0.8573	0.8417	0.8264	0.8116	0.7972	0.7831	0.7695	0.7561	0.7182	0.6944	0.6400
3	0.9151	0.8890	0.8638	0.8396	0.8163	0.7938	0.7722	0.7513	0.7312	0.7118	0.6931	0.6750	0.6575	0.6086	0.5787	0.5120
4	0.8885	0.8548	0.8227	0.7921	0.7629	0.7350	0.7084	0.6830	0.6587	0.6355	0.6133	0.5921	0.5718	0.5158	0.4823	0.4096
5	0.8626	0.8219	0.7835	0.7473	0.7130	0.6806	0.6499	0.6209	0.5935	0.5674	0.5428	0.5194	0.4972	0.4371	0.4019	0.3277
6	0.8375	0.7903	0.7462	0.7050	0.6663	0.6302	0.5963	0.5645	0.5346	0.5066	0.4803	0.4556	0.4323	0.3704	0.3349	0.2621
7	0.8131	0.7599	0.7107	0.6651	0.6227	0.5835	0.5470	0.5132	0.4817	0.4523	0.4251	0.3996	0.3759	0.3139	0.2791	0.2097
8	0.7894	0.7307	0.6768	0.6274	0.5820	0.5403	0.5019	0.4665	0.4339	0.4039	0.3762	0.3506	0.3269	0.2660	0.2326	0.1678
9	0.7664	0.7026	0.6446	0.5919	0.5439	0.5002	0.4604	0.4241	0.3909	0.3606	0.3329	0.3075	0.2843	0.2255	0.1938	0.1342
10	0.7441	0.6756	0.6139	0.5584	0.5083	0.4632	0.4224	0.3855	0.3522	0.3220	0.2946	0.2697	0.2472	0.1911	0.1615	0.1074
11	0.7224	0.6496	0.5847	0.5268	0.4751	0.4289	0.3875	0.3505	0.3173	0.2875	0.2607	0.2366	0.2149	0.1619	0.1346	0.0859
12	0.7014	0.6246	0.5568	0.4970	0.4440	0.3971	0.3555	0.3186	0.2858	0.2567	0.2307	0.2076	0.1869	0.1372	0.1122	0.0687
13	0.6810	0.6006	0.5303	0.4688	0.4150	0.3677	0.3262	0.2897	0.2575	0.2292	0.2042	0.1821	0.1625	0.1163	0.0935	0.0550
14	0.6611	0.5775	0.5051	0.4423	0.3878	0.3405	0.2992	0.2633	0.2320	0.2046	0.1807	0.1597	0.1413	0.0985	0.0779	0.0440
15	0.6419	0.5553	0.4810	0.4173	0.3624	0.3152	0.2745	0.2394	0.2090	0.1827	0.1599	0.1401	0.1229	0.0835	0.0649	0.0352
16	0.6232	0.5339	0.4581	0.3936	0.3387	0.2919	0.2519	0.2176	0.1883	0.1631	0.1415	0.1229	0.1069	0.0708	0.0541	0.0281
17	0.6050	0.5134	0.4363	0.3714	0.3166	0.2703	0.2311	0.1978	0.1696	0.1456	0.1252	0.1078	0.0929	0.0600	0.0451	0.0225
18	0.5874	0.4936	0.4155	0.3503	0.2959	0.2502	0.2120	0.1799	0.1528	0.1300	0.1108	0.0946	0.0808	0.0508	0.0376	0.0180
19	0.5703	0.4746	0.3957	0.3305	0.2765	0.2317	0.1945	0.1635	0.1377	0.1161	0.0981	0.0829	0.0703	0.0431	0.0313	0.0144
20	0.5537	0.4564	0.3769	0.3118	0.2584	0.2145	0.1784	0.1486	0.1240	0.1037	0.0868	0.0728	0.0611	0.0365	0.0261	0.0115
25	0.4776	0.3751	0.2953	0.2330	0.1842	0.1460	0.1160	0.0923	0.0736	0.0588	0.0471	0.0378	0.0304	0.0160	0.0105	0.0038
30	0.4120	0.3083	0.2314	0.1741	0.1314	0.0994	0.0754	0.0573	0.0437	0.0334	0.0256	0.0196	0.0151	0.0070	0.0042	0.0012
35	0.3554	0.2534	0.1813	0.1301	0.0937	0.0676	0.0490	0.0356	0.0259	0.0189	0.0139	0.0102	0.0075	0.0030	0.0017	0.0004
40	0.3066	0.2083	0.1420	0.0972	0.0668	0.0460	0.0318	0.0221	0.0154	0.0107	0.0075	0.0053	0.0037	0.0013	0.0007	0.0001
50	0.2281	0.1407	0.0872	0.0543	0.0339	0.0213	0.0134	0.0085	0.0054	0.0035	0.0022	0.0014	0.0009	0.0003	0.0001	0.0000

Table A-6

Present Value of a Dollar (Monthly Compounding)

YEAR	3%	4%	5%	6%	7%	8%	9%	10%	11%	12%	13%	14%	15%	18%	20%	25%
1	0.9705	0.9609	0.9513	0.9419	0.9326	0.9234	0.9142	0.9052	0.8963	0.8874	0.8787	0.8701	0.8615	0.8364	0.8201	0.7808
2	0.9418	0.9232	0.9050	0.8872	0.8697	0.8526	0.8358	0.8194	0.8033	0.7876	0.7721	0.7570	0.7422	0.6995	0.6725	0.6097
3	0.9140	0.8871	0.8610	0.8356	0.8111	0.7873	0.7641	0.7417	0.7200	0.6989	0.6785	0.6586	0.6394	0.5851	0.5515	0.4760
4	0.8871	0.8524	0.8191	0.7871	0.7564	0.7269	0.6986	0.6714	0.6453	0.6203	0.5962	0.5731	0.5509	0.4894	0.4523	0.3717
5	0.8609	0.8190	0.7792	0.7414	0.7054	0.6712	0.6387	0.6078	0.5784	0.5504	0.5239	0.4986	0.4746	0.4093	0.3709	0.2902
6	0.8355	0.7869	0.7413	0.6983	0.6578	0.6198	0.5839	0.5502	0.5184	0.4885	0.4603	0.4338	0.4088	0.3423	0.3042	0.2266
7	0.8108	0.7561	0.7052	0.6577	0.6135	0.5723	0.5338	0.4980	0.4646	0.4335	0.4045	0.3774	0.3522	0.2863	0.2495	0.1769
8	0.7869	0.7265	0.6709	0.6195	0.5721	0.5284	0.4881	0.4508	0.4164	0.3847	0.3554	0.3284	0.3034	0.2395	0.2046	0.1381
9	0.7636	0.6981	0.6382	0.5835	0.5336	0.4879	0.4462	0.4081	0.3733	0.3414	0.3123	0.2857	0.2614	0.2003	0.1678	0.1079
10	0.7411	0.6708	0.6072	0.5496	0.4976	0.4505	0.4079	0.3694	0.3345	0.3030	0.2744	0.2486	0.2252	0.1675	0.1376	0.0842
11	0.7192	0.6445	0.5776	0.5177	0.4641	0.4160	0.3730	0.3344	0.2998	0.2689	0.2412	0.2163	0.1940	0.1401	0.1128	0.0658
12	0.6980	0.6193	0.5495	0.4876	0.4328	0.3841	0.3410	0.3027	0.2687	0.2386	0.2119	0.1882	0.1672	0.1172	0.0925	0.0513
13	0.6774	0.5950	0.5228	0.4593	0.4036	0.3547	0.3117	0.2740	0.2409	0.2118	0.1862	0.1637	0.1440	0.0980	0.0759	0.0401
14	0.6574	0.5717	0.4973	0.4326	0.3764	0.3275	0.2850	0.2480	0.2159	0.1879	0.1636	0.1425	0.1241	0.0820	0.0622	0.0313
15	0.6380	0.5494	0.4731	0.4075	0.3510	0.3024	0.2605	0.2245	0.1935	0.1668	0.1438	0.1240	0.1069	0.0686	0.0510	0.0244
16	0.6192	0.5279	0.4501	0.3838	0.3273	0.2792	0.2382	0.2032	0.1734	0.1480	0.1263	0.1078	0.0921	0.0573	0.0419	0.0191
17	0.6009	0.5072	0.4282	0.3615	0.3053	0.2578	0.2178	0.1840	0.1554	0.1314	0.1110	0.0938	0.0793	0.0480	0.0343	0.0149
18	0.5831	0.4873	0.4073	0.3405	0.2847	0.2381	0.1991	0.1665	0.1393	0.1166	0.0975	0.0816	0.0683	0.0401	0.0281	0.0116
19	0.5659	0.4683	0.3875	0.3207	0.2655	0.2198	0.1820	0.1508	0.1249	0.1034	0.0857	0.0710	0.0589	0.0336	0.0231	0.0091
20	0.5492	0.4499	0.3686	0.3021	0.2476	0.2030	0.1664	0.1365	0.1119	0.0918	0.0753	0.0618	0.0507	0.0281	0.0189	0.0071
25	0.4728	0.3685	0.2872	0.2240	0.1747	0.1362	0.1063	0.0829	0.0647	0.0505	0.0395	0.0308	0.0241	0.0115	0.0070	0.0021
30	0.4070	0.3018	0.2238	0.1660	0.1232	0.0914	0.0679	0.0504	0.0374	0.0278	0.0207	0.0154	0.0114	0.0047	0.0026	0.0006
35	0.3504	0.2472	0.1744	0.1231	0.0869	0.0614	0.0434	0.0306	0.0217	0.0153	0.0108	0.0077	0.0054	0.0019	0.0010	0.0002
40	0.3016	0.2024	0.1359	0.0913	0.0613	0.0412	0.0277	0.0186	0.0125	0.0084	0.0057	0.0038	0.0026	0.0008	0.0004	0.0001
50	0.2235	0.1358	0.0825	0.0502	0.0305	0.0186	0.0113	0.0069	0.0042	0.0026	0.0016	0.0009	0.0006	0.0001	0.0000	0.0000

Table A-7

Present Value of an Annuity of $1 (Annual Payments, Annual Compounding)

YEAR	3%	4%	5%	6%	7%	8%	9%	10%	11%	12%	13%	14%	15%	18%	20%	25%
1	0.9709	0.9615	0.9524	0.9434	0.9346	0.9259	0.9174	0.9091	0.9009	0.8929	0.8850	0.8772	0.8696	0.8475	0.8333	0.8000
2	1.9135	1.8861	1.8594	1.8334	1.8080	1.7833	1.7591	1.7355	1.7125	1.6901	1.6681	1.6467	1.6257	1.5656	1.5278	1.4400
3	2.8286	2.7751	2.7232	2.6730	2.6243	2.5771	2.5313	2.4869	2.4437	2.4018	2.3612	2.3216	2.2832	2.1743	2.1065	1.9520
4	3.7171	3.6299	3.5460	3.4651	3.3872	3.3121	3.2397	3.1699	3.1024	3.0373	2.9745	2.9137	2.8850	2.6901	2.5887	2.3616
5	4.5797	4.4518	4.3295	4.2124	4.1002	3.9927	3.8897	3.7908	3.6959	3.6048	3.5172	3.4331	3.3522	3.1272	2.9906	2.6693
6	5.4172	5.2421	5.0757	4.9173	4.7665	4.6229	4.4859	4.3553	4.2305	4.1114	3.9975	3.8887	3.7845	3.4976	3.3255	2.9514
7	6.2303	6.0021	5.7864	5.5824	5.3893	5.2064	5.0330	4.8684	4.7122	4.5638	4.4226	4.2883	4.1604	3.8115	3.6046	3.1611
8	7.0197	6.7327	6.4632	6.2098	5.9713	5.7466	5.5348	5.3349	5.1461	4.9676	4.7988	4.6389	4.4873	4.0776	3.8372	3.3289
9	7.7861	7.4353	7.1078	6.8017	6.5152	6.2469	5.9952	5.7590	5.5370	5.3282	5.1317	4.9464	4.7716	4.3030	4.0310	3.4631
10	8.5302	8.1109	7.7217	7.3601	7.0236	6.7101	6.4177	6.1446	5.8892	5.6502	5.4262	5.2161	5.0188	4.4941	4.1925	3.5705
11	9.2526	8.7605	8.3064	7.8869	7.4987	7.1390	6.8052	6.4951	6.2065	5.9377	5.6869	5.4527	5.2337	4.6560	4.3271	3.6564
12	9.9540	9.3851	8.8633	8.3838	7.9427	7.5361	7.1607	6.8137	6.4924	6.1944	5.9176	5.6603	5.4206	4.7932	4.4392	3.7251
13	10.635	9.9856	9.3936	8.8527	8.3577	7.9038	7.4869	7.1034	6.7499	6.4235	6.1218	5.8424	5.5831	4.9095	4.5327	3.7801
14	11.296	10.563	9.8986	9.2950	8.7455	8.2442	7.7862	7.3667	6.9819	6.6282	6.3025	6.0021	5.7245	5.0081	4.6106	3.8241
15	11.938	11.118	10.380	9.7122	9.1079	8.5595	8.0607	7.6061	7.1909	6.8109	6.4624	6.1422	5.8474	5.0916	4.6755	3.8593
16	12.561	11.652	10.838	10.106	9.4466	8.8514	8.3126	7.8237	7.3792	6.9740	6.6039	6.2651	5.9542	5.1624	4.7296	3.8874
17	13.166	12.166	11.274	10.477	9.7632	9.1216	8.5436	8.0216	7.5488	7.1196	6.7291	6.3729	6.0472	5.2223	4.7746	3.9099
18	13.754	12.659	11.690	10.828	10.059	9.3719	8.7556	8.2014	7.7016	7.2497	6.8399	6.4674	6.1280	5.2732	4.8122	3.9279
19	14.324	13.134	12.085	11.158	10.336	9.6036	8.9501	8.3649	7.8393	7.3658	6.9380	6.5504	6.1982	5.3162	4.8435	3.9424
20	14.877	13.590	12.462	11.470	10.594	9.8181	9.1285	8.5136	7.9633	7.4694	7.0248	6.6231	6.2593	5.3527	4.8696	3.9539
25	17.413	15.622	14.094	12.783	11.654	10.675	9.8226	9.0770	8.4217	7.8431	7.3300	6.8729	6.4641	5.4669	4.9476	3.9849
30	19.600	17.292	15.372	13.765	12.409	11.258	10.274	9.4269	8.6938	8.0552	7.4957	7.0027	6.5660	5.5168	4.9789	3.9950
35	21.487	18.665	16.374	14.498	12.948	11.655	10.567	9.6442	8.8552	8.1755	7.5856	7.0700	6.6166	5.5386	4.9915	3.9984
40	23.115	19.793	17.159	15.046	13.332	11.925	10.757	9.7791	8.9511	8.2438	7.6344	7.1050	6.6418	5.5482	4.9966	3.9995
50	25.730	21.482	18.256	15.762	13.801	12.233	10.962	9.9148	9.0417	8.3045	7.6752	7.1327	6.6605	5.5541	4.9995	3.9999

Table A-8

Present Value of an Annuity of $1 (Monthly Payments, Monthly Compounding)

YEAR	3%	4%	5%	6%	7%	8%	9%	10%	11%	12%	13%	14%	15%	18%	20%	25%
1	11.807	11.744	11.681	11.619	11.557	11.496	11.435	11.375	11.315	11.255	11.196	11.137	11.079	10.908	10.795	10.521
2	23.266	23.028	22.794	22.563	22.335	22.111	21.889	21.671	21.456	21.243	21.034	20.828	20.264	20.030	19.648	18.737
3	34.386	33.871	33.366	32.871	32.386	31.912	31.447	30.991	30.545	30.108	29.679	29.259	28.847	27.661	26.908	25.151
4	45.179	44.289	43.423	42.580	41.760	40.962	40.185	39.428	38.691	37.974	37.275	36.595	35.931	34.043	32.862	30.159
5	55.652	54.299	52.991	51.726	50.502	49.318	48.173	47.065	45.993	44.955	43.950	42.977	42.035	39.380	37.745	34.070
6	65.817	63.917	62.093	60.340	58.654	57.035	55.477	53.979	52.537	51.150	49.815	48.530	47.292	43.845	41.749	37.123
7	75.681	73.159	70.752	68.453	66.257	64.159	62.154	60.237	58.403	56.648	54.969	53.362	51.822	47.579	45.032	39.508
8	85.255	82.039	78.989	76.095	73.348	70.738	68.258	65.901	63.660	61.528	59.498	57.566	55.725	50.702	47.725	41.369
9	94.545	90.572	86.826	83.293	79.960	76.812	73.839	71.029	68.372	65.858	63.478	61.223	59.087	53.314	49.934	42.823
10	103.56	98.770	94.281	90.073	86.126	82.421	78.942	75.671	72.595	69.701	66.974	64.405	61.983	55.498	51.745	43.957
11	112.31	106.65	101.37	96.460	91.877	87.601	83.606	79.873	76.380	73.111	70.047	67.174	64.478	57.326	53.230	44.844
12	120.80	114.22	108.12	102.47	97.240	92.383	87.871	83.677	79.773	76.137	72.747	69.583	66.628	58.854	54.448	45.535
13	129.05	121.49	114.54	108.14	102.24	96.798	91.770	87.120	82.814	78.823	75.120	71.679	68.480	60.132	55.447	46.076
14	137.04	128.48	120.65	113.48	106.91	100.88	95.335	90.236	85.539	81.206	77.204	73.503	70.075	61.201	56.266	46.497
15	144.81	135.19	126.46	118.50	111.26	104.64	98.593	93.057	87.982	83.322	79.036	75.090	71.450	62.096	56.938	46.827
16	152.34	141.64	131.98	123.24	115.31	108.12	101.57	95.611	90.171	85.199	80.646	76.470	72.634	62.843	57.489	47.084
17	159.65	147.84	137.24	127.70	119.10	111.33	104.30	97.923	92.134	86.865	82.060	77.671	73.654	63.469	57.941	47.285
18	166.74	153.80	142.24	131.90	122.62	114.29	106.79	100.02	93.892	88.343	83.303	78.716	74.533	63.992	58.311	47.442
19	173.63	159.52	147.00	135.85	125.91	117.03	109.06	101.91	95.469	89.655	84.395	79.626	75.290	64.430	58.615	47.564
20	180.31	165.02	151.53	139.58	128.98	119.55	111.14	103.62	96.882	90.819	85.355	80.417	75.942	64.796	58.864	47.660
25	210.88	189.45	171.06	155.21	141.49	129.56	119.16	110.05	102.03	94.947	88.665	83.073	78.074	65.901	59.579	47.901
30	237.19	209.46	186.28	166.79	150.31	136.28	124.28	113.95	105.01	97.218	90.400	84.397	79.086	66.353	59.844	47.971
35	259.84	225.85	198.14	175.38	156.53	140.79	127.55	116.32	106.73	98.469	91.308	85.058	79.566	66.538	59.942	47.992
40	279.34	239.27	207.38	181.75	160.92	143.82	129.64	117.77	107.72	99.157	91.784	85.387	79.794	66.614	59.979	47.998
50	310.58	259.26	220.20	189.97	166.20	147.22	131.83	119.17	108.63	99.745	92.164	85.633	79.954	66.658	59.997	48.000

Appendix B

The Standard Normal Distribution

Table B-1

The Standard Normal Distribution

z	.00	.01	.02	.03	.04	.05	.06	.07	.08	.09
0.0	.0000	.0040	.0080	.0120	.0160	.0199	.0239	.0279	.0319	.0359
0.1	.0398	.0438	.0478	.0517	.0557	.0596	.0636	.0675	.0714	.0753
0.2	.0793	.0832	.0871	.0910	.0948	.0987	.1026	.1064	.1103	.1141
0.3	.1179	.1217	.1255	.1293	.1331	.1368	.1406	.1443	.1480	.1517
0.4	.1554	.1591	.1628	.1664	.1700	.1736	.1772	.1808	.1844	.1879
0.5	.1915	.1950	.1985	.2019	.2054	.2088	.2123	.2157	.2190	.2224
0.6	.2257	.2291	.2324	.2357	.2389	.2422	.2454	.2486	.2517	.2549
0.7	.2580	.2611	.2642	.2673	.2704	.2734	.2764	.2794	.2823	.2852
0.8	.2881	.2910	.2939	.2967	.2995	.3023	.3051	.3078	.3106	.3133
0.9	.3159	.3186	.3212	.3238	.3264	.3289	.3315	.3340	.3365	.3389
1.0	.3413	.3438	.3461	.3485	.3508	.3531	.3554	.3577	.3599	.3621
1.1	.3643	.3665	.3686	.3708	.3729	.3749	.3770	.3790	.3810	.3830
1.2	.3849	.3869	.3888	.3907	.3925	.3944	.3962	.3980	.3997	.4015
1.3	.4032	.4049	.4066	.4082	.4099	.4115	.4131	.4147	.4162	.4177
1.4	.4192	.4207	.4222	.4236	.4251	.4265	.4279	.4292	.4306	.4319
1.5	.4332	.4345	.4357	.4370	.4382	.4394	.4406	.4418	.4429	.4441
1.6	.4452	.4463	.4474	.4484	.4495	.4505	.4515	.4525	.4535	.4545
1.7	.4454	.4564	.4573	.4582	.4591	.4599	.4608	.4616	.4625	.4633
1.8	.4641	.4649	.4656	.4664	.4671	.4678	.4686	.4693	.4699	.4706
1.9	.4713	.4719	.4726	.4732	.4738	.4744	.4750	.4756	.4761	.4767
2.0	.4772	.4778	.4783	.4788	.4793	.4798	.4803	.4808	.4812	.4817
2.1	.4821	.4826	.4830	.4834	.4838	.4842	.4846	.4850	.4854	.4857
2.2	.4861	.4864	.4868	.4871	.4875	.4878	.4881	.4884	.4887	.4890
2.3	.4893	.4896	.4898	.4901	.4904	.4906	.4909	.4911	.4913	.4916
2.4	.4918	.4920	.4922	.4925	.4927	.4929	.4931	.4932	.4934	.4936
2.5	.4938	.4940	.4941	.4943	.4945	.4946	.4948	.4949	.4951	.4952
2.6	.4953	.4955	.4956	.4957	.4959	.4960	.4961	.4962	.4963	.4964
2.7	.4965	.4966	.4967	.4968	.4969	.4970	.4971	.4972	.4973	.4974
2.8	.4974	.4975	.4976	.4977	.4977	.4978	.4979	.4979	.4980	.4981
2.9	.4981	.4982	.4982	.4983	.4984	.4984	.4985	.4985	.4986	.4986
3.0	.4987	.4987	.4987	.4988	.4988	.4989	.4989	.4989	.4990	.4990

Index